three in love

THREE

ménages à trois

IN LOVE

from ancient to

modern times

BARBARA FOSTER, MICHAEL FOSTER,
AND LETHA HADADY

HarperSanFrancisco
An Imprint of HarperCollins*Publishers*

HarperCollins Web Site: http://www.harpercollins.com

HarperCollins®, ☰ ®, and HarperSanFrancisco™ are trademarks of HarperCollins Publishers Inc.

FIRST EDITION

Designed by Laura Lindgren

Library of Congress Cataloging-in-Publication Data
Foster, Barbara M.
　　　Three in love : ménages à trois from ancient to modern times / Barbara Foster, Michael Foster, and Letha Hadady.
　　　　　p.　cm.
　　　Includes bibliographical references and index.
　　　ISBN 0–06–251295–1 (cloth). — ISBN 0–06–251296–X (pbk.)
　　　I. Group sex—History.　I. Foster, Michael. II. Hadady, Letha. III. Title.
　　　HQ23.F73　1997
　　　306.77—dc21　　　　　　　　　　　　　　　　　　　　　　　　　　　　97-6074

97 98 99 00 01 (RRDH) 10 9 8 7 6 5 4 3 2 1

This book is dedicated to lovers everywhere,
whether alone or by twos or threes——or more.

Contents

Preface: Three on Three

*T*HE AIR HINTED OF AUTUMN WHILE WE
hurried to the movies. We wanted to see ourselves. The three of us, one
man and two women, had been a New York–based menage a trois
through the eighties, a decade officially oblivious to our lifestyle. Now, in
1990, wondering if other threesomes were converging on the theater, we
headed to the downtown opening of Philip and Rose Kaufman's *Henry and
June.* Ironically, the title neglected the other woman, Anaïs Nin, on whose
diary the film was based. Nin was really the first person of this unholy
trinity.

On the ticket line we spoke in undertones about Henry Miller's novels of bohemian Paris. Ezra Pound, center of a lifelong triad, had called
them "dirty books worth reading." Miller, the gangster author, would
have loved the storm of publicity raised by the X rating initially assigned
the movie. We speculated about his shadowy wife June, a Brooklyn moll
who doted on Dostoyevsky. And could Nin have guessed that she would
become scribe to the most talked-about threesome since Jules, Jim, and
Catherine gamboled on the Left Bank?

We were seated for the intensely impersonal ritual, popcorn and all,
that is moviegoing. Amid a crowd of strangers, we linked moist palms in
the darkness. We were all voyeurs bending toward what the poet Hart
Crane called the "flickering panoramic sleights." Did we feel Henry, June,
and Anaïs anoint their successors? When the lights came up, we looked
round for additional acolytes. The audience walked out in pairs. No doubt
some found the movie tame compared with the videos they watched at home.

But outside, ahead of us, a menage walked the wind-nipped street: a
young woman and two guys. She placed her head on one's shoulder and
they kissed before she gave the other equal time. At the Café des Artistes

the mustachioed proprietor regarded us without favor. Courting couples occupied the tables for two; he refused to give us one for four, and there were no tables for three. There seldom are. Finally, wedged into an odd corner, feeling as conspiratorial as gays before Stonewall, we faced one another.

Barbara, a professor, is a biographer of adventurous women. Weaned on *Dick Clark's American Bandstand*, she knows it takes two to tango but three to do the dance of love—the one that's been happening since the Serpent peddled fruit to Adam and Eve. Michael, novelist and historian, comes from Brooklyn, but unlike Henry Miller he doesn't claim citizenship there. He and Barbara found Letha in Paris, where the famous semiologist Roland Barthes had dedicated a lecture to her, "The Singing Voice." The movie had brought up those good and bad times.

During the late seventies Letha and her husband were American students living hand to mouth in the Marais—chic now, poor then. Barbara and Michael were in Paris for a week to research the life of Alexandra David-Neel, the explorer, the continuation of a quest they'd begun in India. One day Michael wandered out of the Musée Guimet to notice an attractive blond woman sitting at an outdoor café reading David-Neel's *My Journey to Lhasa*. He stared so intently that she rushed to pack up the book and pay the check, and when he spoke to her in broken French she burst out laughing.

They spent some hours together before she left him, she thought forever, with a kiss and a refrain from a French love song. Meanwhile Letha's husband sat admiring Barbara's miniskirted legs in the museum library. When he asked for her telephone number, she told him to contact her in New York. When the two couples finally dined together in a Manhattan restaurant, they felt that the earlier meetings could not simply have been chance. In due course a recombination occurred, resulting in a divorce, a menage a trois, and a much-praised biography of David-Neel.

Since 1981, then, we three had, in a sense, been married to one another. Now we were about to embrace a story grander than our own, one that demanded a new name: triography, the study of threes in love. You won't find it among the subject headings in the Library of Congress catalog. Reference works ignore it, including an *Encyclopedia of Sex*, which claims to cover "all aspects of sexuality." Although Alexandre Dumas *père*, that musketeer of the boudoir, quipped long ago, "The chains of marriage are so heavy it takes two to bear them, sometimes three," the menage remains a smutty secret, the last taboo.

It's as though Moses had issued an eleventh commandment: Thou shalt love only one. But the Bible is rife with threes, from the seduction of

Lot by his two daughters to the aged King David who, to prolong his years, slept naked between two virgins. When Arno Karlen, a psychoanalyst who lives around the corner from us in Greenwich Village, decided to write *Threesomes*, a study of contemporary menages, he realized that sexologists had no idea what to make of the phenomenon. Talk-show audiences were quicker to decide: they reviled the long-standing triads whom Karlen brought along as guests.

We've had similar things happen. Even casual acquaintances may pose intimate and embarrassing questions, such as who sleeps with whom and who pays the bills. As is typical, a woman at a party who was obviously pursuing Michael insinuated to Letha that she should look elsewhere for love and that her role as third was immoral and unnatural. Meanwhile a guy hung around Barbara, figuring that she must be fair game. Everyone expects jealousy and violence among a threesome, and they are shocked to discover that our menage has lasted this long.

In fact, European thought from Kant on has recognized a third lurking in the shadow of the altar. Simone de Beauvoir casually remarked, "Marriage finds its natural fulfillment in adultery." Her lifetime partner, Jean-Paul Sartre, understood the compelling attraction of three and modeled his fictional trilogy *The Age of Reason* on their real-life liaisons. Perhaps the menage a trois is misunderstood because it builds an emotional structure that is inclusive. Jealousy, which we suppose natural, is the main stumbling block. Yet a jealous rage is foreign enough to human nature that we treat it as a compulsion; we speak of a jealous person as being in the clutches of "the green-eyed monster." A menage, on the contrary, demands choice and mutual consent.

At the café we talked about the Kaufmans' film, disappointed when it fell back on the clichés of the classic "love triangle." Still, Anaïs Nin's tempestuous affair with Henry and June, soaring toward the stars only to descend with the swiftness of a roller-coaster, is a good illustration of what can happen in a threesome, for whether jealousy or compassion prevails is the crux of the adventure in this erotic realm. Because the menage has a witness—the third or even a fourth persona—it magnifies the issue of trust that bedevils any relationship. The menage plays out in exaggerated form the repertoire of romance, from infatuation to quarrel.

That evening we realized that this genre of love story remained dim to many. The menage a trois is much more than a couple gone wrong. Glancing around the place, smoky as Miller's La Coupole or Beauvoir's Deux Magots, we spotted the young threesome that had just come in out of the chill. They were cozy, but if we hadn't seen them before, would we have tagged them for a menage? When the eye grazes over *trois* at a table, the mind makes an excuse: it must be a boy, girl, and her brother. Of course, discreet signals can be sent. But could we, who'd grown up on the barricades of the sexual revolution, come out?

We'd survived being single, married, and three. We'd made the scene, passed through existentialism to the nonexistence of "the void." We'd traveled to the East and written and lectured, and more books were on the way. Yet our lovestyle made us alien. Before we could convey our intimacies, our deepest feelings, we needed to trace the lineage of three in love. We sought a tradition.

By the time we left the Café des Artistes, with a wink to the neophyte menage on our way out, our quest was on.

part one

PARAMETERS

The Tao begot one.

One begot two.

Two begot three.

And three begot the ten thousand things.

Tao Te Ching

chapter 1

THE MEANING OF MENAGE A TROIS

From Plato to Sleaze

W HAT HAPPENS WHEN THREE PEOPLE become romantically entangled with one another, in a more or less positive way, and one, at least, leaves a record of the relationship and its outcome? Especially if the arrangement lasts, it's called a "menage a trois." The term is universal, and it has aged long enough in the American language to dispense with French accents. Although a Texas newspaper complains that many of us pronounce it "Men Age at Roy's," we all recognize the term and suppose, mistakenly, that we know its meaning. We don't. An otherwise sophisticated film producer told me that if you grew up in Brooklyn, you thought it always involved a dog.

The phrase in its country of origin literally means "household of three." The French *ménage* stems from the Latin *mensa*, meal or table, and menage a trois has a domestic ring. The vision of a trio breaking bread or seated round the hearthside fits into our plan more appropriately than the sort of hasty liaison dubbed "a quickie." A full-fledged threesome is a distinctive style of love demanding not only several persons but their interaction over time and space. Menages a trois have a deep and extensive history as the oldest alternative form of family. But this is not to neglect the role of the menage as a favorite sexual fantasy for both men and women.

The usually authoritative *Oxford English Dictionary* defines the term as "an arrangement or relationship in which three people live together, usu-

ally consisting of a husband, his wife, and the lover of one of these."
This description is stale and limited. It is true that a menage has tended to
be made up of two members of the same gender and one of the other,
and often enough it begins with a restless couple. The arrangement has at
times overridden a monogamous marriage and at others buttressed it.

The usages chosen by the *OED* include the following:

1891 G. B. Shaw *Quintessence of Ibsenism* 116. An elderly gallant
who quite understands how little she [Hedda Gabler] cares for
her husband, and proposes a *menage a trois* to her.

1933 *Times Lit. Suppl.* 19 Oct. He meets and marries a highly
sexed waitress, who inevitably tires of the mother's dominance
of the *menage a trois.*

1959 Norman Mailer *Advertisements for Myself* 285. A *menage-a-
trois* was completed—the bohemian and the juvenile delinquent
came face-to-face with the Negro, and the hipster was a fact in
American life.

1959 *Times* 28 Dec. This happy *menage-a-trois*—the errant
wife, the lover and the unsuspecting husband.

Sex is not the sole defining feature of these relationships. Typically,
the *OED* has chosen arrangements that aren't necessarily positive. In Ibsen's
drama, Hedda Gabler, despite her husband's connivance, chooses death
over a backdoor affair with a man she dislikes. Loveless sex would have
reinforced the hypocrisy she could no longer stand. In the final example,
the so-called menage is "happy" because the husband is ignorant of the
affair, so it is really an instance of cheating. This confusion of the menage
a trois with adultery is unfortunate but common.

Norman Mailer, on the other hand, uses the menage a trois as a
metaphor for the "three-way union" whose virtual offspring was the hipster. Actual menages do form with such ideal goals in mind, and they have
given birth to works of art, heroic deeds, and entire literary movements.
Either the triad has a multiplying effect on each person's talents, or it creates a dynamic all its own.

A curious old term overlooked by the *OED* is the "metaphysical
menage a trois," which indicates a spiritual or symbolic coming together.
Sigmund Freud thought of himself, the deceased Nietzsche, whom he
considered his mentor, and the alive and beautiful Lou Salomé along these
lines. The *New York Times* has referred to Sylvia Plath, Ted Hughes, and
Janet Malcolm—who wrote a biographical meditation on Plath and

Hughes—as a metaphysical threesome. Composers Robert and Clara Schumann had the younger Johannes Brahms as a longtime houseguest, and each influenced the others' music. An erotic current between Clara and Johannes may have sped Robert's nervous breakdown. Their music, played on the same program, is called a menage a trois. The metaphysical menage, like the sexual, is the linking of several energies into one to produce a remarkable result.

Nowadays, depiction of the intense magnetism that was supposed to draw lovers together, whether by twos or threes, has largely been replaced by books and articles on genetically determined sexual preferences. This type of evolutionary psychology generates heat over whether biology favors monogamous marriage or polygamy of some sort. Helen Fisher, in her often cited *Anatomy of Love*, makes a case for "natural patterns that prevail around the world." She sees forming into pairs, mating, and separating to repeat the cycle as the natural reproductive strategy of certain species, including humans.

Unfortunately, replies Robert Wright in a *Time* cover story titled "Infidelity: It May Be in Our Genes," research has discovered that humans are not a "pair-bonding species. Women are promiscuous by nature, desiring more than one mate, and men are even worse." Writes the neo-Darwinist Matt Ridley, "The best that men can hope for is a good-looking younger mistress and a devoted wife who is traded in every decade or so." This would lead to a proliferation not only of first- but of second- and third-wives clubs, providing the sequels to a very successful book and movie.

Can we humans learn anything from our fellow creatures? Percy Shelley claimed that the polygamy of the noble horse offered a model for humans. Animals can and do form menages a trois. According to a leading North American breeder, the ideal ostrich family is two females and one male. Gorillas, who are very sensitive, with a childlike, emotive intelligence, have been known to mate by threes, and sometimes cats, who are nothing if not willful, do it *à trois*. At Washington's National Zoo the female panda Ling-Ling and her selected mate, Hsing-Hsing, had trouble getting together. He preferred to chew bamboo shoots. A second male, Chia-Chia, was imported from London, but he turned out to be a wife beater. However, his presence awakened Hsing-Hsing, who now found Ling-Ling more to his liking. The offspring of the three was a bouncing baby bear.

Three in Love is about choice, not genes. Our approach echoes that of Simone de Beauvoir, who wrote, "Humanity is not an animal species, it is a historical reality." Humans love and breed by numerous arrangements, all of which have their defenders. Sir Richard Burton, nineteenth-century seeker of the forbidden and the exotic, traveled from the Nile to Utah to investigate "the Mormon menage a trois." He found church elders who praised male polygamy as the will of God. But he decided that the Mormon version, lacking the mystery of harems and veils, had all the monotony of monogamy, only multiplied.

The menage a trois is as venerable as the book of Genesis. In the U.S. Senate debate that led to the denial of federal benefits to the partners of single-sex marriages, Jesse Helms cracked, "God created Adam and Eve, not Adam and Steve." That same God also created a third, the Serpent, an androgynous symbol of both male and female. According to Genesis, the human race began when Adam and Eve, growing weary of Eden, became intimate with this Other.

In order to understand the menage a trois, to set its bounds, we need to borrow the logic of the philosopher who was born into the Golden Age of Greece and whose name has been given to a form of love. Plato spoke of four steps by which his pupils could know a subject: *name, definition, image,* and *knowledge* (that is, the facts). We have dealt with the evolution of our subject's *name* and the confusion surrounding its *definition.* To wrap our minds around the menage a trois, to understand what it means, we'll look at examples of three in love but also, because concepts are defined at their margins, we'll see where menage shades into something else.

First, the "trois" part. The number three has a magical and religious significance. There were three Magi, three Graces (brilliance, joy, and bloom), and three bears in the fairy tale. We give three cheers, hope for three wishes, and admire a triple threat. According to the *I Ching,* the mission of three is to turn darkness into light. The Romans worshiped using a tripod to hold the sacred flame, and they raced in three-wheeled chariots because this configuration provided an inherent stability. In Scandinavian mythology the tree of life that supports the universe has three roots.

Plato's mentor, the mathematician Pythagoras, described the sequence of numbers as follows: "The one [male] is the creator which produced the primal motion or dyad, the two [female], which in turn produced the first number, three, which is a symbol of the cosmos." Pythagoras held one and two to be in opposition, the finite versus the infinite, joined "in a triangle [when] the three was in action." Plato taught that three was the original number, animating the universe as fire, air, and water. These semimystical ideas underlie the nature of the couple versus the triad, indicating that the latter is a superior development of the former.

Traditionally, some native peoples regard three as the grouping required for conception. The anthropological pioneer Robert Briffault observed that the New Zealand Maori believed that "the moon is the permanent husband or true husband of all women." The moon was thought of as masculine. Though a Maori woman married a man, he couldn't impregnate her without the intercession of the moon spirit, the paternity of the child being shared. The belief in the need for a third party to fecundate the womb, to potentize the male sperm, also plays a crucial role in the Judeo-Christian nexus.

In midcentury Bishop Fulton J. Sheen, an influential spokesperson for the Catholic Church, wrote the homily *Three to Get Married*. In the chapter "Love Is Triune," Sheen criticized the duality—the essential aloneness—of coupledom. "If there is only the *mine* and *thine*," he declared, "there is impenetrability and separateness." Sheen, a man of the cloth, had heard in confession about the power plays, ego trips, and "mental torture" that characterize many marriages. "Love has a triune character and implies lover, beloved, and love [itself]," he concluded. Perhaps he'd observed that most ritual of courting poses—a man and a woman seated across a table—in which lie the seeds of opposition.

"It takes three to make love," asserted the bishop. His point of reference was the Trinity or its third person, the Holy Ghost. Yet he describes fairly the benign, mediating effect of a third when ego is put aside. While jealousy may lurk in the corners of the most successful triad, the dynamic attracts outsiders. A menage a trois tends to draw satellites, a fourth person. Freud wrote that "every sexual act [is] a process in which four individuals are involved." He referred to each person's double or bisexual identity. In our observation, the actual fourth is something of a voyeur, a witness to the drama who perhaps acts as scribe to record it. When the fourth does join in, he or she usually fails to deflect the feelings among the original three.

A menage may be only two. The cartoonist Jules Feiffer, in discussing the original Superman comic strip, termed its crucial love situation "a schizoid and chaste menage a trois." Lois Lane, a newswoman on the *Daily Planet*, loves Superman. Since he comes from Krypton, his molecules are too dense for the usual sort of lovemaking. Besides, he's busy saving Metropolis from various fiends. Meanwhile his alter ego, Clark Kent, has a crush on Lois, who thinks Clark is a drip. Throughout the millions of Superman comic books and four movies, as well as the television series, three personae who inhabit two characters act out their amorous cross-purposes, forever joined at the hip.

Superman is the epic American hero, no more or less mythical than Rome's Aeneas or England's King Arthur. The original movie, in which Christopher Reeve played the "man of steel," went through a variety of conceptual approaches from Greek tragedy to Broadway spoof, but finally the story captured the tension of "a love triangle in which two [of the] people are the same person." The sequels dropped the chaste element, and though Lois and Superman aren't seen in bed, they soar through the sky together, she on top of him, and Clark can only hear about it and remember.

The menage a trois can't be defined by number alone. It implies a plenitude not so much of crude sex as of the erotic. It intimates a more communal pleasure than church, state, or the new/old breed of loud-mouthed commentator can tolerate. But a menage is not equivalent to sleeping around, and it is inherently more stable than the serial monogamy famously practiced by a Liz Taylor or Zsa Zsa Gabor or the admitted infidelity of a Magic Johnson. Although menagers are not necessarily bisexual, the expectation that we must limit ourselves to one gender, spouse, or family creates a rickety platform, likely to sink under the torrent of our desires.

Even among the sophisticated, the paradigm of one for one lurks in the recesses of the ego. An amusing instance occurs in Bob Fosse's *All That Jazz*. The screen version of the director-choreographer's autobiography was filmed shortly before his heart gave out. Fosse (Roy Scheider), while conversing with a beautiful (female) Angel of Death, apologizes because he can't stick to one woman. He fondly recalls how he once lived harmoniously with two women. One morning he woke up to find one of them gone, her note on the bureau: "I can't share you anymore. I want you alone or not at all. Please try to understand."

The Angel inquires if he was upset at losing her. Fosse, a modern-day Casanova, replies no, he was flattered that she took him so seriously. Returns the Angel, "Sure the note was for you?"

A menage a trois can be not only a physical grouping but also a point of view. Lawrence Lipton, best known as chronicler of the Beat scene, recognized the ambiguous space the menage inhabits when he wrote, "We are here on the borderline between conventional marriage and extramarital varietism." To Lipton, host of an infamous crash pad in Venice Beach during the sixties, the menage appeared conservative. His most knowing observation was that a threesome happens first *in the mind*. It's a function of the erotic imagination that may apply to anyone.

"Fantasied superimposition," he wrote, is "the least mentioned and most heinous crime, and most widely practiced one, among the avowed adherents of the Judeo-Christian moral code. . . . It is *the* unmentionable." Lipton refers to fantasizing that your bed partner is somebody else—perhaps an actual person you know and want or have glimpsed or seen in the media, but usually someone younger or better looking. In a variant, you imagine your partner is making love to somebody else, again attractive. This may be taken for a homoerotic fantasy, but it is actually a fantasy of three in bed. The longer a monogamous relationship runs, the more likely it is that one or both partners will employ this device—or find that during sex their mind has been seized by the image of a third.

We all bring to the boudoir the image of the desired one, and often it doesn't match our actual lover. "Who is the third who walks always beside you?" asked T. S. Eliot. He should have asked how he or she got into your bed. While movies and TV inculcate the erotic images of the hunk and the sex symbol, however modified to suit current taste, a more sophisticated strain of advertising plays up threes.

You've seen the ads for Italian clothes: a pretty young model embraces two studs who, gazing at her raptly, are at her service. The designer happens to be a woman. In another ad, this one for jeans, one man has his head on a woman's breasts while he feels another woman's . . . closeness. A Calvin Klein threesome, androgynous in their underwear, peer at us from the side of a New York bus. They are suggestively blue. While the eye sees, the mind projects.

Lipton finds the enjoyment of such a fantasy while having sex "a sound and beneficial practice." It's a form of voyeurism that for some becomes the engine of their sexual desire. For example, when Simone de Beauvoir and Jean-Paul Sartre first coupled at the Sorbonne, they swore to tell each other everything about their so-called contingent affairs. And as their mutual sexual partner Bianca Bienenfeld observed, "Such a promise logically lends itself to a certain voyeurism: whatever one person reveals about his or her lovemaking is provocative and exciting for the other. . . . The promise to tell all intensifies feelings and emotions [that] become infectious."

In brief, the best *definition* of menage a trois can't be found in a dictionary, because it is a charged way of looking at love that demands sharing and imagination.

Preexistent *images* lodged in convinced minds pose a formidable hurdle to communicating seriously about the menage a trois. On television's afternoon soaps, the young and the restless are increasingly forming into "torrid trios," often with an incestuous wrinkle. "Three's a crowd pleaser!"

crows *Soap Opera Digest*. On a popular talk show, an average Joe confesses to a menage of convenience: his wife spends too much and is too demanding in bed, so he shares the burden with another man. On a late-night show, a Midwest housewife relates how her husband picks up men in the supermarket to have sex with her while he videotapes the event. Similar goings-on typify the $325 million-a-year amateur erotic video business, in which menages a trois are a staple.

These are junk-food versions of the real thing. Three sensationalist styles of sex, the feedstock of the tabloids, have become confounded in the popular mind with three in love: adultery, prostitution, and, for lack of a better word, perversion. Adultery usually leads to a classic love triangle, which mingles erotic excitement with the dread of exposure. Since such affairs involve lying and cheating, the extent to which they exist resists quantification. Adulterers aren't about to confess to pollsters who come into their own homes! This was the actual methodology used by the "Sex in America" survey ballyhooed by the media in the midnineties to prove that "Faithfulness in Marriage Thrives," as the *New York Times* headlined. Sex spiced with danger, the "fatal attraction," remains a potent lure. A *Chicago Tribune* feature begins:

> Somewhere in Manhattan lives a woman who is convinced her husband would kill her if he learned of the affair she has carried on for five of the eight years they've been married.
>
> "I think I'd be dead, I honestly do, but I can't stop," says the 33-year-old secretary, who meets her lover in a friend's apartment nearly every day after work.

Whether actual or a type, this unnamed woman, out of fear of her husband, has created a second family. Her affair has the routine of married life minus the boredom. It modifies the intriguing thesis of Denis de Rougement (borrowed by Camille Paglia) that the essence of adultery is an external compulsion, a victory of passion over happiness. At any rate, deceit and guilt remain the leitmotif of adultery. There is the challenge of getting away with it, of passing what Rougement ironically terms "the supreme test that one day or other awaits every true man or woman." Adultery and the menage a trois do share at their inception a desire to live to the full. But they quickly take diverging paths. Adultery thrives on suspicion, jealousy, and rage. A menage demands honesty and, at a minimum, the acquiescence of three. Their full cooperation would be better. Menages worth writing about depend on the compassion, leading toward love, of all persons in the relationship. Unlike the open marriage of the 1970s, which elevated the run-of-the-mill affair to the status of a learning experience, a true menage is purposeful. It will have an outcome in both the spiritual and the material worlds.

Prostitution and perversion together constitute what we'll dub "the sleaze factor." They may share with the menage a trois certain athletic feats. But the spirit of these things runs in a contrary direction. Power is an issue in prostitution, and a 1996 *Playboy* interview with Heidi Fleiss, the notorious madam, opens, "She was among the most powerful women in town. . . . She had a direct line to A-list stars and studio execs, running the most exclusive call-girl service in Los Angeles." One of these clients was reportedly fond of a $40,000 fantasy. Heidi talked to him while her "whore goddess" associate did what the client wanted. Heidi chatted about other men, the more the merrier, who'd had her goddess. In Nick Broomfield's clever documentary film, *Hollywood Madam*, Heidi recounts asking her goddess to "tell—about the time you went to Hawaii with those four Japanese men." She knows the location of a man's most erotic spot—between the ears.

Multiplicity can be a powerful sexual stimulant. The recent Michael Keaton movie of that name would have been still duller if it hadn't led up to his wife spending the night in bed with all four of his clones, each of whom was different enough to be a new guy. Of course, fantasy has its limits. As Heidi reminded *Playboy*, "you absolutely still need that warm body next to you." She has cheerfully confessed to being stoned and sharing anonymous guys with her buddy Victoria Sellers, calling herself a "total pervert." She's just adding to her Hollywood image; it's guilt and silence that make for perversion.

Alan Bloom, in *Love and Friendship*, diagnosed America as an emotional wasteland, devoid of eros and courtship. In contrast, those who form triads, whether entirely successful or not, encounter plenty of feeling. Psychoanalyst Arno Karlen, soon after he had begun his investigation into menages, realized that "*Threesomes* would be as much a study of communication styles as sexual gymnastics." Karlen observed his subjects' initial difficulty in expressing feelings such as jealousy or desire. However, "when a triangle gets acted out in bed . . . either the [participants] talk about those feelings, or the relationship explodes on them." One woman summed it up: "Our threesome was the emotional can opener of my life."

The reality of threes in Karlen's conservative university set would startle America's best-known sexologist, Dr. Ruth Westheimer. In 1995 in her syndicated column she printed a letter from an elderly man involved in a menage with his wife and the widow of their best friend (a man who had died recently). All three enjoy the menage, but there is a difficulty over oral sex: the widow likes it, the wife never has and resents it being done. "These kinds of situations are always fragile," warns the good doctor; therefore, drop the menage. On the contrary, we find the situation both normal and touching. The widow is seeking a family to make up for her loss. She wants to continue her sex life and has invigorated the sex life of the couple. Now the three will have to talk about what each has wanted, and feared, for the last forty years. Is that bad, Dr. Ruth?

Three in Love is neither a sociological treatise nor a how-to manual. Instead, this is an erotic history of all the good stuff they never told you in school. It is triography—the three lives of the rich and famous, the starving artist and tortured poet, the successful novelist, the proud conqueror, and the over-the-hill movie star. It weaves a tapestry from the fantasy of sexual abundance that runs through our collective subconscious. It is a book of manners and morals, past, present, and future.

The nuclear family has exploded, that's a fact, and new configurations are emerging from the debris. Patricia Ireland, on assuming the presidency of the National Organization for Women, came out not as a lesbian or bisexual but as a menager. For a long time she has shared her life with her husband, a painter who lives in Florida, and a woman lover in Washington, D.C., where she works. Ireland and her husband met during student days and married in the 1960s, and they are devoted to each other. This "commuter" menage, along with other flex-time domestic arrangements, is bound to grow more common.

Ireland told the *New York Times*, "What I have described is who my family is, not my sexuality. I don't see why I can't have my cake and eat it too."

Only in a menage a trois. The cavils of moralists, psychologists, and politicians aside, here's the record of those who have tried it and of the remarkable things they have done.

chapter 2

INTRODUCTION TO TRIOGRAPHY

A Historical Overview of Threes

The plural of spouse, it is spice.
ANONYMOUS

*I*N CLINT EASTWOOD'S OVERLOOKED *Bronco Billy*, released in 1980, he plays the sharpshooting Billy, ringmaster of a circus/rodeo that stumbles through the modern-day West. His dysfunctional crew is joined by a runaway heiress, Antoinette Lily, played by Sondra Locke. Billy has an equally hidden past as a shoe salesman in New Jersey. He explains that an unexpected incident changed his life: he caught his wife in bed with his best friend. Lily asks what he did about it:

> BILLY: I shot her.
> LILY: Why didn't you shoot *him?*
> BILLY: He was my best friend.

A long stay in prison mellowed Billy and gave him the courage to live his dream. But his sanguinary response to the love triangle, while extreme, has been supported, at least in theory, by Western society since the demise of medieval chivalry. The French diplomat Denis de Rougement wrote the most convincing statement on the inevitability of tragedy in eros; called *Love in the Western World*, it was composed on the eve of World War II, which partly accounts for his pessimism. "Happy love has no history," Rougement wrung his hands. "Romance only comes into existence where

13

love is fatal. . . . Passion means suffering. There we have the fundamental fact."

Bronco Billy may not have entirely understood, but he would have agreed. Rougement himself cowered before the facts of love. Jean-Paul Sartre, who knew the man in Paris before the war, remarked that because he had "extolled the mad virtue of fidelity, he was liable to all the temptations and seductions of the reigning queens of high society." Rougement, in fear and trembling of being seduced, refused to let his wife leave his side even to visit their son. He achieved fidelity by the tired method of employing a ball and chain.

If happy love has no history, it is because no one has perceived one major theme running through its entire length. Study of the menage a trois opens up a new geography, a landscape populated by threes but paradoxically unmapped. Its explorers have been content, ecstatic, or crestfallen, but they have all set out to reach one goal: bluntly stated, they wanted to free their erotic life. Plato's fourth criterion for knowing a subject—the criterion that he termed *knowledge*—demands that we examine the facts of three-way love stripped of moral blinders. We can't permit our judgment to be swayed by the mores of the moment, and though our personal experience helps us to evaluate a particular triad, it doesn't guarantee that we will find the truth.

Sexually speaking, historical periods seem to oscillate with some regularity between the open and free, even licentious, and the highly structured or puritanical. The moral view of the menage a trois has followed this pattern. But because this is a practice more done than talked about, we will look toward whichever class in a society is most imitated, for it thus formulates the rules of desire. There are going to be surprises.

In ancient times the Hebrew patriarchs or Greek solons, and later the Caesars, decreed morals. Standards of behavior, whether or not strictly followed, flowed from the top down. The lawgivers of biblical Israel didn't engrave monogamy on their tablets. Solomon, acclaimed for wisdom, maintained a thousand wives. Even a modest subject of this opulent king could increase his progeny by impregnating both his wife and her handmaid (body servant). Male polygamy was the rule among the ancients, and the menage a trois plays a key role in biblical genealogy. Nobel laureate Isaac Bashevis Singer posited "a desire for sexual community" that as a boy he first noticed in the Pentateuch: "All the peculiarities of modern man had their roots in the very dawn of civilization."

Polygamy is, after all, a gender-neutral term, and modern women are considering it an option, formally or informally. "Just like birds," claims a

March 1994 article in the *Washington Post,* "women may be having it both ways by conducting affairs with genetically more valuable men while not leaving their husbands." The situation is reversed in African-American communities in major cities. Because many of their young virile men are killed or incarcerated, "mate-sharing" has become a topic discussed by black women in forums and on talk radio. But plural relations must be open to both men and women. Psychologist Julie Mallory-Church quips, "I wouldn't mind having an extra wife myself." Indeed, a Mormon lawyer, one of several wives in one family, wrote the *New York Times* that polygamy was "attractive to the modern career woman."

In Plato's Athens, the crucible of Western civilization, the menage was typical but entirely to the benefit of males. The orator Demosthenes, in arguing a court action against a prostitute who'd passed herself off as a citizen, summed up classical sexual mores: "Mistresses we keep for pleasure, concubines [slaves] for daily attendance upon our persons, and wives to bear us legitimate children and be our housekeepers." The city was studded with statues sporting erect penises, and men casually showed their genitals in public. Yet the sense of propriety that prevailed and could be enforced legally demanded that each enact his (or more likely her) assigned sexual role and no other.

Athens had a class of respected prostitutes known as the *hetaera,* a sort of companion or mistress. (The refined Parisian courtesan of the nineteenth century is a close descendant. Dumas's Camille, not to mention Greta Garbo's, is a well-known fictional example.) The foreigner Aspasia became the most celebrated hetaera and a teacher of rhetoric. She is said to have ghost-written the speeches of Pericles, the uncrowned king of the Golden Age, who affronted Athenian society by divorcing his wife and moving Aspasia into his home. This exclusivity of Pericles' affection, his feeling of romantic love for a prostitute, gave his political opponents their most powerful weapon against him.

Under the Roman Empire we find a de facto turnabout in the position of the free-born woman, especially if she came from an aristocratic family. The wife, taking up the center of the menage, obtained the desirability the Greeks had once accorded to the hetaera. Adultery became the fashion among the rich, and in the first century C.E. Seneca, complaining about the high divorce rate, quipped that a wife with only two lovers was considered virtuous.

The wars and rapine of the Dark Ages and the damnation of sex by Christianity encouraged a low opinion of love and women. In contrast, the sixth-century king of Gaul, Lothar, married Ingund and, according to

Gregory of Tours, "loved her with all his heart." Ingund missed her sister Aregund, whom she praised highly to the king. Lothar, ostensibly to find Aregund a husband, traveled to her domain, fell in love at first sight, and married Aregund too. Ingund stipulated only that Lothar "let his hand-maid live in the enjoyment of his favor," and the three reigned happily ever after.

Of all the concepts of love in days of yore, the subtlest is the courtly love that began in the High Middle Ages. Although it returned to a married woman the Roman right to choose her bed partner, its roots lie more in knightly chivalry. Chivalry has been defined by diplomat-author Harold Nicolson as "a body of sentiment and practice, of law and custom, which prevailed among the dominant classes of a great part of Europe between the eleventh and sixteenth centuries." During all this time monogamy received mostly lip service. "Adultery was regarded as more commendable than marriage and the husband who objected was viewed as a boor," sums up Nicolson.

In France, a show of jealousy could be chastised by the courts of love, dominated by women. A well-known cautionary tale was that of Lord Raymond, who had killed young Guillem, his wife Soremunda's lover, and then served his roasted heart for dinner. The lady became so upset she threw herself out of the castle window and perished. When the king of Aragon learned of the outrage, he imprisoned Raymond, confiscated his estates, and ceremoniously buried the bodies of the two lovers in a single grave.

While the rules of courtly love dictated that a likely young man dedicate himself without thought of reward to the service of an older married woman, the outcome of these liaisons was more natural. Nicolson assures us "that [the ladies] often, and quite early in the proceedings, surrendered to the passion in their champion's eyes." Chivalry—in the story of Tristan, Isolde, and King Mark, for example—also made what appears to be a contrary demand: the knight must pledge undying loyalty to his lord, the lady's husband. The chivalric relationship was three-sided. Nicolson, by showing the woman's role as passive, underestimates her growing influence in the world of courtly intrigue. It's a surprising oversight when we recall that he was married to Vita Sackville-West, the formidable model for Virginia Woolf's *Orlando.*

In the four hundred years from the Italian Renaissance until the French Revolution, the nobles who gathered in klatches in the corridors of royal palaces (which often doubled as urinals) in hope of a nod from His Majesty as he proceeded by—and still more the writers, painters, and musicians who served this underwashed aristocracy—had the effective say on conduct. The church held sway over common folk, but courtiers and ladies-in-waiting and their artistic purveyors paid little mind to morality. Behind perfumed handkerchiefs they conducted their affairs with the cynicism of Machiavelli.

Choderlos de Laclos's *Dangerous Liaisons,* which has been adapted by Christopher Hampton for stage and screen, sums up the ancien régime at the depths of its conniving. This epistolary novel, written by a bored military officer, begins as a series of amorous coups plotted by Madame de Merteuil, who employs her lover the vicomte de Valmont as her proxy. Her lust for the young women he seduces at her instigation is barely concealed. At the same time, Merteuil, with the cunning of a black widow spider, gradually ensnares and immobilizes Valmont himself.

Laclos plotted triangles of seduction that when fitted together form rectangles; common to each is Merteuil. Each seducer deflects some of his or her sexual energy into letters, which act as a sort of mirror, multiplying the pleasure of each by writing and reading about the details of the conquests. This is a more refined version of the voyeurism we all practice when watching a love scene at the movies—a voyeurism essential to the creation and enjoyment of art. The relationship of Merteuil and Valmont breaks down only when he enters a love affair that is so overpowering he ceases to observe and begins to feel.

The menage that is about power has the makings of a deadly love triangle. Triangulators, those sexual teases who incite a rivalry for their favors, are usually unsure of their own worth. The MIT philosopher Irving Singer observes that we all wish to be loved by others "because we recognize that we then have greater *reason* to love ourselves." The triangulator takes the fillip of love from several at once but gives back little. He or she may be a narcissist and, like all narcissists, may need reassurance. By the end of *Dangerous Liaisons,* Merteuil, fond of admiring herself in the mirror, catches smallpox and becomes hideous to look at. Her appearance reflects the inner truth.

Despite being equally rooted in eighteenth-century French soil, where the finest strains of the modern menage originated, Jean-Jacques Rousseau's mother-mistress, Madame de Warens, was the opposite of Merteuil. She was a woman obsessed with giving of herself and claimed to receive no pleasure from sex. Nonetheless she bestowed her favors freely. For young Rousseau, a poverty-stricken wanderer, loving this woman in a menage with an older, wiser man whom he also came to love provided the sheltering family he'd never known. The experience shaped his philosophy of sharing and led to his writing the novel that shocked all Europe, *Julie.* Rousseau, as he grew older and suffered disappointments but continued to labor on his *Confessions,* became egomaniacal: "I have begun on a work which is without precedent," he boasted, "whose accomplishment will have no imitator."

In our day of telling all, we know Rousseau to be mistaken on this last count. In any case, cultural originators have long been attracted to menages a trois. A successful and self-involved threesome was formed by the marquis du Châtelet, his younger wife, Emilie, and the philosopher Voltaire. The two men shared not only one woman but their money and influence at court. Though a scientist, Emilie loved to gamble. But she risked everything when at forty-one she became pregnant by a young man-about-court. Mesdames de Warens and Châtelet were Romantics before their time.

It would be hard to invent a more romantic tale than that of Lady Emma Hamilton and Admiral Lord Nelson. Too often forgotten is her husband, Sir William, ambassador to Naples and art collector extraordinaire. This is the menage that helped sink the French fleet and defeat Napoleon. Both in fact and fiction, menages have gone to war with a will, and it was on purpose that the movie version of this threesome, *That Hamilton Woman,* was released in 1940 during the Battle of Britain. On the other hand, Lord Byron, the nineteenth century's most publicized lover, escaped from his menage, in which he played the sanctioned role of *cavaliere servente* to Count and Countess Guiccioli, by joining the revolution in Greece against Turkish rule. There he died a martyr to freedom, though dissipation also took its toll. In the twentieth century, Lord Louis and Lady Edwina Mountbatten and Pandit Nehru formed a triad that steered India through the tumultuous transition from colony to independent nation. A menage with a woman in the middle has often accomplished great things.

The Romantic rebels, especially the Pisan circle formed around Percy and Mary Shelley, extolled the transforming power of love. They sounded the death knell of the arranged marriage while extending the concept of family beyond the biological. Especially now, we need to remember Bertrand Russell's wise observation that "marriage is rooted in family rather than family in marriage." There is no single God-given definition of either, though the Bible makes clear that the Lord of Hosts approves of abundance and fecundity, which we have termed sexual plenitude.

From Victoria's pomp-filled coronation in 1837 until the storm clouds of world war threatened the European order, hypocrisy reigned supreme. The Victorian era, which extended into the twentieth century, featured manners that were at odds with practice. A successful bourgeois gentleman, who would in mixed company say piano "limb" rather than "leg," might well keep a mistress at a nearby *résidence secondaire;* his wife, relieved of childbearing, might well acquiesce. The Victorian credo was to avoid getting caught at the pleasurable—or, once caught, to deny having done it. Great Britain kept a conspiracy of silence about the suspected state secret: that Victoria had a lover, John Brown, an upper servant who had saved her life.

In France, Victor Hugo, the "great man" personified, never doubted that women found him irresistible. Victor grew up amid a triangle: his mother was cool to his supposed father, a Bonapartist officer, and she loved another general, going into deep mourning after the latter died. Victor had two father figures, as would Bernard Shaw and Orson Welles. Such a parental mix often produces a Don Juan. Victor married his childhood sweetheart, Adèle, but after the critic Sainte-Beuve became his wife's admirer, he found a young actress, Juliette Drouet, who gave up her career to become his mistress for life. This love triangle with an attached fourth mellowed into a lifelong menage a trois, and the women became as devoted to each other as to Victor, especially when he did battle against Napoleon III.

Émile Zola, another enemy to injustice, maintained two families, one with his wife, Alexandrine, and another with a former seamstress who bore his two children. They mixed rather well, but Zola kept up the facade of monogamy that was essential for his defense of Captain Dreyfus. Charles Parnell, on the other hand, in order to defend the reputation of his lover Katie O'Shea, refused to contest an action for divorce filed by her husband, a scheming politician who turned on the Irish champion. Parnell, by placing sentiment first, set back Irish independence by fifty years. The political menage has often provided cover, but only in return for discretion.

In contrast, the American menage has often been characterized by individual nonconformity. In 1870 Victoria Woodhull, the first woman to run for president, campaigned on a Free Love platform. Dubbed "Mrs. Satan" by the press, she blew the cover off the cozy menage of the country's leading preacher, Henry Ward Beecher, Beecher's protégé, Tilton, and Tilton's wife. Woodhull, a genuine free lover, also joined in a menage with her husband and Tilton, and she even went to bed with Beecher! An ensuing trial triggered the original media sex circus, an American perennial.

The Wild West gave rise to a loosening of the straitlaced Victorian character. Outlaws Butch Cassidy and the Sundance Kid shared their schoolteacher-lover, Etta Place. The liberated mores of the frontier carried over into the twentieth century, both in real-life characters such as bank robbers Bonnie and Clyde, who had a thing for thirds, and superb movie roles for the likes of Robert Redford, Paul Newman, Warren Beatty, Clint Eastwood, Faye Dunaway, Jean Seberg, and Farah Fawcett (in the excellent made-for-television feature *The Substitute Wife*).

In staid Amherst, Massachusetts, in the early 1900s, townsfolk still addressed Austin Dickinson as "squire." The poet Emily's older brother fell in love with vivacious Mabel Todd, whose astronomer husband, David, seduced her lady friends when he wasn't trying to communicate with Martians. He liked to watch his wife and Austin, who became his best friend, make love. Voyeurism and its twin, exhibitionism—both basic human drives—came more easily to the Amherst trio than making the obscure, voyeuristic poetry of Emily known to the world.

Yale scholar Peter Gay dates the end of Victorianism to the rise of Freudian doctrine in the early twentieth century. Our interest in Sigmund Freud lies not in his clinical work but his overlooked position as the last German Romantic. It was because Oedipus dared to live his fantasy that Freud regarded him as the primal hero. But there are certain circles and entire historical moments that encourage the repressed to surface. Since the nineteenth century, bohemian Paris has represented the artistic and the sensual. The sculptor Rodin filled his atelier with striking models, a pair of whom ignited his sensuality: "I can still see them," he reminisced, "two Italian girls, one dark, the other blond. They were sisters, and both were the perfection of absolutely opposite natures. One was superb in her savage strength. The other had that sovereign beauty of which all the poets have sung."

Rodin kept his dreams in the realm of art. But living with a pair of women under the same roof, making love to wife and model on a revolving basis, was the inspiration that brought artists such as Augustus John, Jacob Epstein, Alberto Giacometti, and Pablo Picasso to their easels. Salvador Dalí preferred watching his wife, Gala, take on a younger man. In a switch, the surrealist Leonore Fini had two lifelong male companions. The much-honored British artist Sir Stanley Spencer claimed he couldn't work at all unless he had two wives!

The classic statement of bohemianism is Henri-Pierre Roché's *Jules et Jim*. Based closely on Roché's own erotic experiences before and after World War I, the novel was made into a movie by François Truffaut, starring Jeanne Moreau, and it has influenced filmmakers and others more often than we can know. Roché, an art dealer in Paris just when modern art was being invented, was an inveterate menager who found himself in a trio with Marcel Duchamp and Beatrice Wood, who would later become a famous potter. He was a true Casanova, capable of loving both men and women, a civilized human being who lived and wrote a three-part *Romeo and Juliet*.

"For the Bloomsbury set," observed writer Penny Wark in the Sunday *Times* recently, "the menage a trois was virtually normal." In that stiff-upper-lipped Bohemia, the scene sometimes resembled musical chairs in an elegant country home. Lytton Strachey, the eminent biographer, presided over a threesome at Ham Spray, the other two being artist Dora Carrington and her husband, Ralph Partridge. This "Triangular Trinity of Happiness" had a fourth, young Gerald Brenan, the finest writer in English on Spain. Carrington was mad for gay Lytton, who when not enlightening the world on things intellectual, was keen for war hero Ralph. Gerald, Ralph's best friend, was mad for Carrington, while husband Ralph lived part time in town with Frances, whom he would marry after Lytton had died and an inconsolable Carrington had killed herself with a shotgun.

Brenan continued in his love for Carrington. Years later, while married and living in Spain with his American wife, Gamel, he tried to add Carrington's look-alike niece, Joanna, to his Andalusian menage. It wasn't Joanna but Carrington that Brenan wanted. This is the sort of threesome we have dubbed the ghost menage. Writers as distinct as Richard Wagner (in *The Flying Dutchman*) and Noël Coward (in *Blithe Spirit*) have understood the power of a third who is not corporeal, but they haven't recognized that this type of menage a trois is directly related to the fantasy third in sexual relations. In the case of a ghost, the third has become an obsession.

Those who write about menages a trois, even those who direct or act in such plays or films, are likely to have been involved in a triad, and this gives a special charge to their work. Warren Beatty saw himself in journalist John Reed, who mingled social and sexual revolution in his Bolshevik days in early-twentieth-century Greenwich Village. Beatty showed courage in making *Reds* in 1981, his version of the three-way romance among the radical Reed, radically chic Louise Bryant, and the young Eugene O'Neill. The episode caused O'Neill enough guilt to write *Strange Interlude*, his first Broadway success. This grueling five-hour experience is the classic dramatic exploration of multiple love, just as Noël Coward's *Design for Living* is the comic.

The period between the wars was a high time for erotic exploration. Beginning in the 1920s, Ezra Pound lived with his wife, Dorothy, and mistress, Olga, for several decades in Italy, weathering World War II. This menage had a male chauvinist spirit that is properly tagged fascist. Another famous macho, Ernest Hemingway, shared a cottage on the Riviera with his first wife, naïf Hadley Richardson, and voguish Pauline Pfeiffer, who would become his second. He delayed writing about the affair until the 1950s; his novel *Garden of Eden* was published posthumously.

In the early 1930s in back-alley Paris, Henry Miller and his wife, June, and Anaïs Nin engaged in their three-way tussle. A decade later in now-famous cafés along the boulevards, Jean-Paul Sartre and Simone de Beauvoir captivated disciples and shared the spoils, male and female. Beauvoir's lesbian romances and the voyeuristic edge to her relationship with Sartre surfaced after her death when a weighty stack of personal letters was found in a cabinet. Indeed, if *Three in Love* focuses on men and women in the arts, it is because they are driven to leave records of their passion. Even in the 1990s, there are threesomes we won't learn about until well into the next century.

The 1996 show of Beat artifacts at the Whitney Museum of American Art demonstrated that the public is once again fascinated by the lifestyle of these American Existentialists. The center of the Beat movement, as the New York museum seemed anxious to forget, was San Francisco, and the nexus of this plexus was the modest home Carolyn Cassady made for her husband, Neal, and her lover, Jack Kerouac, in the Russian Hill neighborhood. Neal and Jack, though buddies and look-alikes, were very different types—action and observation paired. Although Kerouac in his work remained as shy about the threesome as he'd been in bed, Carolyn told all in her memoir, *Off the Road.* "How lucky could a girl get?" she still sighs.

We now find ourselves in the realm of the celebrity. The menage a trois occupies a central place in the libido of the rich and famous. A number of fine American names surface: Harriman, Whitney, Pulitzer, Kennedy. As the story came out in divorce court in Palm Beach, when Roxanne Pulitzer asked her best friend, Jacqui Kimberly, to engage in a threesome with her husband, Herbert, as a favor, Jacqui replied, "Roxanne, I don't think there's a man alive who's never had that fantasy." Yes, but the rich get to act on it. As a class they have been shrewd enough to leave morals to the bourgeoisie. Pamela Harriman was termed "the greatest courtesan of the century" by William Paley. She parleyed a string of wealthy husbands—in tandem with well-placed lovers—to win prominence and respectability. In 1993 President Clinton appointed her ambassador to France. Nothing could be more fitting, as the French would say.

Having more than one lover has always been one of the privileges of power. Celebrities, however, may try to hide their involvement, or they may trumpet it. Political figures from Lenin to Eleanor and Franklin Roosevelt to François Mitterrand have successfully used the menage to camouflage their extramarital affairs. Prime Minister Harold Macmillan tolerated an uncomfortable menage of convenience with his wife and close confidant, who were lovers. Ironically, it was the kinky menage of call girls Christine Keeler and Mandy Rice-Davies with a high-society doctor, who acted more or less as their pimp, that was central to the spy scandal that brought down Macmillan's government in the 1960s.

There are stars who glitter all the brighter due to their unconventional love life. Josephine Baker, her husband-manager, Pepito, and novelist Georges Simenon were briefly a threesome. On the cusp of war, lounging on the Riviera, Marlene Dietrich, her husband, Rudi, and novelist Erich Maria Remarque lived à trois while Nazi tanks rolled across Eastern Europe. Marlene liked to take joint vacations accompanied by her daughter as well as Rudi and his mistress, Tamara, though she usually let Tamara look after the girl. Certainly Marlene would do her part to bolster the morale of Allied troops, lots of them.

Kenneth Tynan wrote of Dietrich, "She has sex, but no particular gender." The same could be said of that ultimate woman of mystery and allure, Greta Garbo. For years she managed a carefully concealed menage a trois with Valentina and George Schlee, who respectively designed her clothes and managed her finances. In the wings conspired a shadow menage of Garbo's former lovers, photographer Cecil Beaton and Hollywood's most desired lesbian, Mercedes de Acosta, who'd become allied by necessity. Acosta was an early feminist who married but refused to take her husband's name; Beaton is usually tagged as gay.

Marjorie Garber's recent Vice Versa, a learned and welcome study of bisexuality, lists a whole raft of celebrities who have practiced a bisexual life with even greater secrecy than they might have maintained had they been simply gay. Perhaps it's true, as Garber claims, that androgyny finds a natural outlet in the menage a trois. But few of the contemporary menages studied by Arno Karlen had a gay component, at least that he could find. Rather, the threesome mixed sexuality and camaraderie in a unique blend. A successful threesome becomes trisexual. Three in love is special, a thing apart, although not necessarily smooth sailing.

Roseanne, the opposite of Garbo, in 1993 purposely broadcast the news of her "three-way marriage," which included then-husband Tom Arnold and her much younger protégée, Kim Silva. According to Vanity

Fair, Roseanne showed the live audience of her TV sitcom Kim's eight-carat diamond ring, saying, "We got engaged to her, and all three of us are getting married. She deserves to be our little woman." For a time the three were inseparable, and Tom cracked about his wife and Kim, "These guys hang out so much together that they get PMS at the exact same time." Who was sleeping with whom never really surfaced. But if Roseanne and Kim had been transposed to biblical times, they would have been matriarch and handmaid. Roseanne, who liked Kim to dress in clothes identical to her own, had created an alter ego to accomplish what she supposed she could no longer do: have a child.

In a few weeks the menage gave way to claims that it had been a publicity stunt. Recriminations followed, and Roseanne divorced Tom. Then she remarried and conceived—and this is once again the story of Sarah and Hagar. The older woman, sexually inspired by the younger, becomes fertile and then banishes her rival.

Freudians might rationalize this incident by means of "an inverse Oedipus complex," a term we have seen applied to the story of Dracula, who also favored menages a trois. But Oedipus is the wrong Greek myth with which to explain threesomes, especially of the celebrity sort. Every star is a successful narcissist, creator of a mirror image that he or she admires and believes in. Archie Leach, who became Cary Grant, no doubt felt more at ease in his menage with longtime companion Randolph Scott and the young hustler who became the clothes designer Mr. Blackwell than in any of his numerous marriages to women, who tended to leave him fairly soon.

Narcissists enter into a relationship as both ego and alter ego, and they need two others, often diametrically opposed, in order for both these selves to be satisfied. For the likes of Laurence Olivier or Warren Beatty, one is not enough. Rock musicians are the most clear-cut narcissists and often sexually ambiguous, so it comes as no surprise that the Rolling Stones's Mick Jagger, Keith Richards, and Marianne Faithfull formed a menage. Jagger's androgynous image presented a sex symbol to millions of male and female fans.

Sex heroics aside, real heroes have often been menagers. Marguerite Duras, experimental writer and filmmaker, was a Resistance fighter during the German occupation of France, and her personal story might have been titled "The Lovers." And Oskar Schindler, the savior of the camps, was a steady wife-and-mistress man rather than a libertine.

Whether celebrated or obscure, menagers all drink at the same fountains of narcissism, voyeurism, and the irreducible need to be three. They are all tried in the fire of jealousy. The inner dialectic of passion versus compassion remains constant. The questions of who is mine and to whom do I belong are posed and answered ever anew. If selfishness prevails in even one breast, the relationship will degenerate into a classic love triangle, with its spying, quarrels, blaming, divorce, and violence. But if and when a menage coalesces, a special energy can and has made fascinating things happen—in the arts, movies, or life. In *our* life.

These stories we tell are love stories. A menage, like any family, relies on trust. In the story of the Russian trapeze act called the Flying Cranes we find a breathtaking example of this truism. Night after night, Lena, "a ballerina of the air," flies high above the ground to be caught by Vilen, her former husband. Then she is swung back, soars again, and is caught by Mikhail, her present lover. The beautiful young woman takes a leap of faith. A split second's delay caused by the slightest hesitation could let the thirty-year-old slip to her death below. If these three acrobats feel negative emotions, it had better be down on the ground.

Lena, a great favorite with audiences, compares her flying, her linking of the two men, with sex. "In performing," she says, "we are making love. The day when this inner light stops . . . I must stop performing."

Every menage a trois is a performance. Each participant is an acrobat who slips from the cords of possession to fly, hopeful of landing safe.

chapter 3

THE MYTH OF MENAGE

{Oedipus; Sigmund Freud; Genesis}

A threefold cord is not quickly broken.
ECCLESIASTES

THE BLOODY TRIANGLE

*T*HE MENAGE A TROIS AND THE TRIANGLE begin as flip sides of the same coin. Jealousy and love are opposite and equal seats on the emotional seesaw. What we need is a countermythology to break the spell exerted by the love or classic triangle, which has behind it the weight of a romantic (and tragic) tradition of literature and psychology. The transparent workings and predictable outcome of the bloody triangle appeal to detective, preacher, and hack writer alike. The motive of a jealous third has been too handy for too long in solving too many pulp-fiction and screen murders.

By the mid-1990s, the press caught onto the fascination aroused by three-way love. Faux triads abound, and every sort of thing from business mergers to cocktails has been termed a "menage a trois." Says Ian Schrager, impresario of the Delano, Miami's trendy new hotel, "There seems to be this menage-a-trois happening between New York, L.A., and this place." An even more favorable use of the term is found in a food column in the *Houston Post* quoting Patrick Esquerre, proprietor of bakeries and cafés, on his involvement with a public radio station in a program to feed the poor: "It is a menage a trois. There are three of us together. Everybody is happy. It is like a love affair." We know that the menage, when it is happy, can be ecstatic.

But the *Post*'s sister paper, the *Chronicle*, greeted with hostility a 1995 revival on television of *Summer Lovers*, a delicious 1980s film set in the Greek isles and starring Daryl Hannah, Peter Gallagher, and Valerie Quennessen as the loving trio. The catch phrase "it's a dead-end relationship" reveals the critic's bias. He goes on to complain that the threesome is implausible because "no one is injured." What is the origin of this certainty among the vendors of popular culture that three-way love must inevitably lead to dismemberment and death?

Even well-meaning attempts to right the balance flounder in ambiguity. In mid-1994 a *New York Times* article, headlined "Three Is the Loneliest Number," claimed as news the increasing number of movies, domestic and foreign, based on the "eternal triangle." Love stories have always involved a triangle in its simple sixteenth-century definition (cited by the *OED*): "nothing else to say, but a figure of three corners." The premise of boy and girl falling for each other while a third causes complications is hoary with age. Once upon a time the girl's father could stand in love's way, as in the Broadway hit *The Heiress*, based on Henry James's *Washington Square*. Today, the play's meddling father would amount to a minor annoyance. A current complicator would be the lover of the boy or girl—or both.

Unfortunately, the "Loneliest" article failed to make any clear distinction between a hostile, bloody triangle and a menage a trois. Its drift was that "American films have strict rules for romantic triangles, but the game changes when the French get into it." Instead of ending in a couple and an odd man or woman out, French films are "nuanced." This distinction is not as valid as it once was. American movies of the nineties such as *Wedding Banquet*, *Three of Hearts*, *Threesome*, and *Boys on the Side* are genuinely about three-way love; in them, you can't be sure who is going to wind up in bed with whom.

Ironically, the complicit triad also lies at the heart of the most classic American films. *Gone With the Wind*, *Casablanca*, and *Shane* all give the lie to the indefensible notion that a woman can love only one man at a time. Indeed, the menage in each case revolves around the female protagonist, played by Vivien Leigh, Ingrid Bergman, and Jean Arthur, respectively. The two men loved by the woman respect and admire each other and are so complementary that together they make one perfect man. In the great Civil War epic, Leslie Howard's Ashley represents the Old South, Clark Gable's Rhett Butler the New, and Scarlett, who identifies with the land, needs both men in order to flower. In the 1930s Margaret Mitchell had the fate of the poverty-stricken South in mind when she deliberately made this statement in her novel.

In 1941's *Casablanca*, a hokey tale of intrigue that is really an allegory set in a North African purgatory, the combined energies of Rick, the soldier of fortune, and Victor Lazlo, the idealist, are needed to defeat the Nazis and rescue Ilsa (Europe). This was a call to arms to a still-neutral America, one in which Humphrey Bogart risks his life for Paul Henreid as well as for Bergman, and Henreid, who carries on the good fight, helps to redeem the alcoholic Bogart. *Casablanca* features a well-defined fourth, Claude Rains as Captain Louis Renault, the cynical French prefect of police. Louis is content to admire Rick and his doings, though to Ilsa he makes the revealing remark: Rick "is the kind of man that, if I were a woman—and *I* were not around—I would be in love with." This has a homoerotic tinge but is more importantly an example of what I. B. Singer calls "coupling"—the natural desire of a man or woman to share a loved one with their best friend.

In *Shane*, the most mythical and stylized of Westerns, Marian Starrett loves both her constant, homesteading husband, Joe, and the mysterious gunfighter, Shane. Although the men share the affections of the woman and of the couple's son, Joey, played by Brandon de Wilde, there is also a deep understanding and appreciation between them. Alan Ladd must fight the equally heroic Van Heflin for the right to risk his life against the cattle baron's hired killers. I'm doing it "for you," he tells Jean Arthur, "and Joe—and little Joey." In crucial moments the menage acts like family.

True, by the end of each movie the woman can have only one of the men. Blame the censors. In any case the choice is hers. This is radically different from the love triangle, whose predictably unhappy outcome caused George Bernard Shaw to declare adultery "the dullest of subjects." Yet in September 1996 adultery became *Newsweek*'s cover story, in an article that views it as a form of revenge rather than lust. The writers quip that infidelity isn't about "whom you lie with. It's about whom you lie to."

Aside from cheating, the triangle is characterized by helplessness and a sense of doom. TV soap operas often toss a hint of incest into the mix, as in the case of a young buck who is sleeping with both a mother and her daughter.

But the love triangle can also be found at the heart of grand opera. In Puccini's turn-of-the-century masterpiece *Tosca*, based on the play made famous by Sarah Bernhardt, the love triangle of Tosca, a famous soprano; Mario, the artist whom she loves; and Baron Scarpia, the chief of police, leads to the annihilation of all three. The opera is set during the Napoleonic Wars in Rome, where Mario is hiding revolutionaries who plot to overthrow the monarchy and establish a republic. Tosca, beautiful and possessive, dotes on her handsome lover. Meanwhile Scarpia, always introduced by three menacing chords, sings of his plans to force Tosca to be his mistress.

Scarpia orders Mario tortured within Tosca's hearing. The Romantic idealist holds out while she, unable to bear her lover's pain, gives up the revolutionaries. The baron promises to spare Mario if Tosca will yield to him, and she agrees. But Scarpia has deceived her, and he orders Mario shot. "Tosca, mine at last!" boasts the villain, moments before Tosca plunges a knife into his heart.

In his cell Mario writes a last nostalgic letter to Tosca, singing the aria, "And the stars shone." The nobility of the lovers has raised their ill fate to a destiny. Tosca, who witnesses the execution of her beloved, leaps from a rampart to her death. As one critic noted, "in *Tosca*, eros conveys only a negative image . . . of exasperation, irresponsibility, cruelty, and finally death." Which is what the bourgeois audience wished to believe, and still does when viewing such Hollywood depictions of illicit love as Adrian Lyne's successful *Fatal Attraction*.

If nineteenth-century opera and drama celebrated the cruelty and misfortune of the triangle, it was up to that eminent Victorian Sigmund Freud to bring this unhappy worldview into the modern age, all in the name of science. It is Freudianism that declares the Oedipal version of the love triangle to be an essential stage of human development. The young Viennese student shared the obsession with the Greek myth of Oedipus that runs from Schiller through Nietzsche. Freud may or may not have been a scientist, but he was surely the last of the German Romantics.

Sigmund, when at the university in the 1870s, imagined his bust mounted among those of distinguished professors in the arcaded court. It would be inscribed with the following line from Sophocles' *Oedipus the King:* "Who knew the famous riddles and was a man most mighty." When on his fiftieth birthday Freud's disciples presented him with a medallion inscribed with these very words, he was struck dumb. However, it was not fate but his education in the broader sense that united Freud with Oedipus.

Nineteenth-century German writers were captivated by the story of Oedipus, whose "love of the mother and jealousy of the father" Freud would declare to be of "universal application." Friedrich Schiller, author of *Oedipus Tyrannus*, as a young man suffered from the tyranny of an authority figure, the duke of Württemberg, who drafted him into his army. He deserted and found refuge at the estate of a fellow soldier; there he fell in love with his comrade's mother and sister. In 1788 Schiller married another young woman although he was in love with his bride's sister as well; he nursed the hope that she would leave her husband so he could live in a menage with both women. Freud, who acted parts in Schiller's plays, may have acted on a similar fantasy toward the younger sister, Minna, of his wife, Martha.

In *Freud's Women* Lisa Appignanesi repeats Jung's allegation that Sigmund got Minna pregnant and arranged to have the fetus secretly aborted. Sigmund and the sisters formed a conspiratorial but chaste threesome before the marriage, and he felt he shared a "wild, passionate nature" with the younger one. Minna never married but became Freud's close confidante. They traveled together (without Martha and the six children) throughout Italy. Regardless of whether Freud committed an incestuous adultery, he had dreams about it. Yet he confided to Jung that love affairs detracted from theory; only when he had shed his libido would he dare to write a "Love Life of Mankind."

Freud's insistence on the tragic nature of the romantic triangle is largely based on the intellectual tradition in which he found himself immersed. The life and work of Heinrich von Kleist, for example, indirectly influenced Freud. At thirty-four Kleist shot his willing companion Henriette in the heart before shooting himself in the mouth. The dramatic double suicide marked the end of an intolerable triangle. In a farewell note to his cousin Marie, who loved him, Kleist wrote:

> Can it console you that I never would have exchanged you for this woman if she had wanted nothing more than to live with me? . . . The decision that she came to in her soul, to die with me, drew me. . . . A tumult of joyousness, never experienced before, gripped me, and I cannot conceal from you that her grave is more precious to me than the beds of all the empresses of this world.

Friedrich Nietzsche's passionate admiration of Kleist would be made known to Freud by Lou Andreas-Salomé, who was the living link between Romanticism and psychoanalysis, a cross between the femme fatale of the nineteenth century and a modern feminist—but that is a chapter to itself. Both Freud and Nietzsche regarded Oedipus as a hero, the man who had broken the spell of the past by acting out his fantasy. In *The Interpretation of Dreams* Freud wrote of Oedipus, "Here is one in whom these primaeval wishes of childhood have been fulfilled, and we shrink back from him with the whole force of repression by which those wishes have since that time been held down within us."

Since Freud's day the triangle that engendered such tragedy has become a commonplace of novels, plays, movies, and songs. Whether or not Oedipus's experience is universal, we all know how to speak of the bloody triangle. But when, on the other hand, three people intersect and are drawn toward a menage a trois and its creativity, we are capable of no more than a smirk.

In America we find that adultery, with its lies and cheating, grows ever more attractive and costly. As a recent *New York Times* article observed, "serial monogamy has become a luxury reserved for billionaires." So Americans marry later in life or not at all and have their children out of wedlock. We need a third way based on a mythology counter to Greek tragedy or artificial moral choice. Fortunately, we have the beginning of the remedy at hand in the Judeo-Christian Bible, which presents us with a fine crop of acceptable menages a trois.

EDEN

In the beginning were three: Adam, Eve, and the Serpent. And the Lord God was the fourth, the voyeur who looks on but doesn't participate—in this case he eavesdrops. Interpretations of Genesis go back to Saint Paul, who regarded it as allegory. In any case, as feminist Savina Teubal alleges, "biblical scholarship depends . . . on contemporaneous societal values." To the church fathers, Eve's indiscretion, the original sin, eliminated humanity's moral freedom. They held the temptations of the flesh to be inherent in the seed of Adam and irresistible; hence we were all damned without the intervention of Mary, for Mary, as Joseph Campbell has noted, is the "Ave" who, with her son Jesus, rights the sin of "Eva."

Thanks to Bill Moyers's television special, Genesis is hot. Everyone seems to be expressing his or her personal feelings about the creation myth. But if we keep to the *narrative* of the tale and avoid a moral spin, the man, woman, and serpent constitute the original threesome. In paradise, where not much happens, their coming together portends action.

Suppose we were to write the scenario of a low-budget movie, *The Eden Caper.* The story is simple if a bit contrived: newlyweds Adam and Eve have suffered the trauma of creation and are amnesia victims. They find themselves in a mysterious garden "eastward in Eden." A river waters the garden and flows out of it, but they remember nothing of the countryside beyond. It's pleasant, and all the plants and "swarms of living creatures" are at their disposal. The pair are "both naked, the man and his wife," but they feel no shame. No wonder, because recognizing or "uncovering" nakedness, in biblical terms, means to have sexual relations. This couple has forgotten how to do it! Eve, especially, is getting antsy.

Enter the third, the Serpent, whom Joseph Campbell terms "the subtle old master of the garden." A rival, a new sort of god, a big operator called by his initials, YHWH, has muscled in on the Serpent's territory. This God claims to be the exclusive proprietor of all this life. He's brought in Adam and Eve, because to be a landlord you need tenants, and to be God you need worshipers. To make sure the humans don't remember any past gods or figure out how he operates, YHWH forbids them to eat the fruit of two trees in the center of the garden: the tree of knowledge and the tree of immortality. This gives the Serpent, who understands human nature better than does YHWH, a chance for revenge.

YHWH has issued commands, warning Adam and Eve that if they fail to obey him they will die. But these first humans don't know from death. The Serpent begins by asking them a question: "Yea, hath God said, ye shall not eat of every tree of the garden?" This ambiguous query, which is meant to create doubt, triggers the action: cameras are rolling. The serpent is no mere phallic symbol, as the Freudians tell it, but androgynous, emblematic of either male or female sexuality, of knowledge and healing. True, the serpent, like the phallus, can rise and swell on its own. But the serpent is female in its sinuosity, vaginal in its coil. In ancient Semitic religions it was identified with fertility, both of the womb and earth. Michelangelo and Raphael each painted the Serpent as a beautiful woman, the object of Adam's and Eve's loving gaze. With the most compelling visuals and best lines, the Serpent is the star of our movie.

Milton's "subtlest beast" neither lies nor tells the truth. It assures Eve she won't die if she eats the fruit of the tree—at least, she won't die right away. She gives the fruit to Adam, who wastes no time in joining the conspiracy against YHWH. Then "the eyes of them both were opened and they knew that they were naked." Now they remember how to do it. The knowledge of that tree was carnal, the ability to procreate. Afterward, Adam and Eve sew fig leaves together and make themselves aprons. The fruit eaten was not an apple (there weren't any in the desert paradise!) but a fig, symbolic of the male scrotum and oral sex. Copulation, sodomy, and voyeurism make Genesis a sexy book.

YHWH, who has been listening to the goings-on as though he has the garden bugged, proceeds to lay a guilt trip on Adam and Eve. Adam blames her for seducing him, and she confesses, "The serpent beguiled me, and I did eat." Primitive people think of snakes, who mate in coils and lay hundreds of eggs, as lustful. But of this initial three only the Serpent shows character. Rather than hide behind the others, the Serpent takes his punishment like a man.

In the dénouement Adam and Eve are expelled from paradise and find a tough new world. He must work for a living, she gets pregnant and gives birth in pain, and the Serpent has to crawl on his belly in the dust. This is not a happy ending and won't do for our movie. Wouldn't it be nicer if Adam and Eve, all forgiven, move to California, start over, and build a nice house on the beach in Santa Monica? The Serpent uses his salesmanship to take over companies. Don't laugh; that's how the movie *Indecent Proposal* goes. This early nineties adaptation of the Eden myth grossed over $200 million worldwide and was the subject of intense controversy.

Indecent Proposal is the Californicated version of Jack Engelhard's novel of the same name, which was a hard-hitting cautionary tale set in unglamorous Atlantic City. Engelhard rather likes the movie, which he says retains the three essential factors of his novel: temptation, recrimination, and forgiveness. While it's amusing to think of Robert Redford playing the Serpent, the tempting fruit of our time is not knowledge, even carnal, but wealth. The selling of Demi Moore for a million dollars by husband Woody Harrelson may have been denounced by feminists, but a survey taken by Oprah, who did an entire show on the film, found that over half the women in her audience would sell *themselves* for a high enough price.

Engelhard's novel, written with the sparseness of Hemingway but the moral intensity of I. B. Singer, was overlooked until the movie hit. Philosophical in a street-smart way, it encompasses themes from the whole of Genesis. The male protagonist, Joshua Kane, is unassuming but a part-time Israeli commando. He lives in Philadelphia with his beautiful blond wife, Joan, who has left her wealthy mainline connections to share Joshua's meager life. Haunted by his parents' poverty (they were expelled from France by the Nazis), Josh takes Joan to the casinos of Atlantic City, hoping to get rich. Instead, they meet Ibrahim, the billionaire ruler of an oil-rich kingdom. A prince of the desert dressed in black, he is a more ruthless serpent than Redford's businessman, and he adds the polarity (and attraction) of Arab versus Jew to the class distinctions that separate (and unite) Josh and his shiksa.

Ibrahim, who boasts he can buy people, makes the infamous proposal to Josh and Joan. She, like her screen counterpart, accepts. The screenwriter, Amy Holden Jones, grasped one basis of menage when she defended her concept: "Demi Moore is given a chance to commit adultery with a very attractive man, and yet she can tell herself that she is doing it for her husband. That's every woman's fantasy." Jones supposes that unlike men, women must overcome a barrier of guilt in order to take what they want.

The novel's action is more three-way than Jones's script allows. Josh realizes that Ibrahim "wanted me, my capitulation, as much as he wanted Joan." Josh resists the deal, but Ibrahim plays on Joan's "forbidden yearnings and fantasies." Also on Josh's, who declares him "more than a man . . . a force that controlled lives." Both he and Joan get into the immorality of it. Josh, on the night of the deal, though drugged, wakes up in his hotel room to the realization that Joan and Ibrahim had "made love in my bed as I slumbered." He can still *smell* them. Afterward, Joan had removed his street clothes, and the pair had tucked him in before departing to continue their games in Ibrahim's suite.

This night isn't the end of their entanglement. Jew and Arab, the men are brothers (as were Cain and Abel) even when murderously jealous. The Gentile woman is between them, but neither can wholly have her. The outcome will be a rupture of the fragile tolerance that unites the three—a descent into the bloody triangle.

Although Joshua Kane searches for a precedent for the deal he has made, he can't find one. Yet there are indecent proposals in the Bible. Abraham, on journeying into Egypt, asked his young, beautiful wife, Sarah, to deny they were married and say she was his sister (she *was* his half-sister). Pharaoh took her as a concubine and exceeded Abraham's expectations by loading him with "sheep, oxen, asses, male and female slaves, she-asses and camels"—the equivalent of a million dollars.

When affliction struck the court, Pharaoh angrily sent away Sarah and Abraham, but they kept their ill-gotten gains. Abraham was rich in "cattle, silver, and gold," thanks to having rented out his wife. In the present controversy under way over Genesis, amid the attacks on and apologies for what is a mythical narrative, Rabbi Burton Visotzky has at least made clear that Abraham is "a pimp." This seems the main source of the patriarch's wealth. After leaving Egypt, Abraham again claimed Sarah was his sister and sold her to Abimelich, king of Gerar, who dreamed that Sarah was Abraham's wife and then confronted him. Abraham explained to the king that he feared for his life, then made the remarkable confession that he'd told Sarah, "At every place whither we shall come, say of me: he is my brother." A man who makes a habit of selling his wife is indeed a pimp. But what does this make Sarah?

With the pair as they traveled through the Negev desert was the young servant Hagar. Savina Teubal cites Arab folklore that Pharaoh insisted Sarah select one of his handmaids as a personal companion. She chose Hagar, "for whom she had conceived a liking," and Teubal believes their bond was so intimate that Hagar was almost her equal. Perceiving the pair as sisters offers a neglected insight into the joint conception of the Jewish and Arab peoples, both of which stem from this menage a trois of people as compromised as any others.

Although we have no knowledge of whether Sarah conceived with Pharaoh, she had borne Abraham no children. Because she had ceased to menstruate, she offered Hagar to her husband to "consort with." Substituting a maidservant as the bearer of children was customary, and a woman's maid often became her husband's secondary wife. The first wife would take credit for the servant's offspring, especially sons; indeed, she could claim them as her own by the magic inherent in naming them. These Semitic tribes, wandering the desert with their flocks, were serious about begetting children.

Hagar bore a son to Abraham in his eighty-sixth year, called Ishmael. But YHWH, along with two angels, visited Abraham to promise that he would have a son by Sarah. Hearing this, Sarah laughed, saying, "Now that I am withered, am I to have enjoyment—with my husband so old?" Clearly, the pair had grown rusty in that department. Nonetheless Sarah conceived and gave birth to Isaac. Assuming YHWH intervened, we can say that it takes three to conceive. Another explanation would be that Sarah was occasionally fertile, and Abraham, though one hundred years old, was sufficiently stimulated by intercourse with Hagar to get his sperm count up.

At any rate, the intimacy of Abraham, Sarah, and Hagar anticipates humanity's many later menages. A reference to this original triad occurs in I. B. Singer's *Enemies: A Love Story*. Herman Broder is Singer's alter ego, and his first wife, Tamara, after she has unexpectedly survived the Holocaust, adopts Yadwiga, his Polish second wife and their former servant who had sheltered Herman during the war. Together the two women raise Herman and Yadwiga's child, while he, on the run from various complications, sends them money. Singer, like YHWH, approves of a polygamous family unit.

However, Hagar wasn't as humble as Yadwiga, nor was Sarah as compassionate as Tamara. After each biblical woman had borne a son, they fell out over which boy would inherit the patriarch's goods and authority. Sarah demanded of Abraham, "Cast out this bondwoman and her son." Custom was on her side, and the Lord advised Abraham to do as she bid him. How a father felt about sending his consort and child into the wilderness where he supposed they would die (though the Lord preserved them), we aren't told. The family unit had deteriorated into a love triangle. But from the cohabitation of Abraham, Sarah, and Hagar were born those who would become the forefathers of the Arab and Jewish peoples. Isn't this a more positive model for humanity than Oedipus's helpless doom?

The menage a trois is a motif found throughout the Bible. Jacob married two sisters, Leah and Rachel, and though Leah was homely and Rachel beautiful, Leah bore Jacob three sons. "When Rachel saw that she bore Jacob no children, Rachel envied her sister." Thus she gave Jacob her maid, Bilhah, in order to "be built up" by a proxy child. Bilhah conceived and gave birth "upon her mistress's knees"; Rachel named the boy Naphtali, and he was regarded as hers. When finally the sisters made a deal over some aphrodisiacal herbs, they were both impregnated by Jacob in short order. Then their father, Laban, tried to prevent Jacob from removing to Canaan (the promised land), and the sisters united with their husband into a tight family of three in support of their rights.

In contrast to the severe penalties decreed for homosexuality and incest, even adultery, the God of the Old Testament approved of consensual polygamy. Saul, David, and Solomon all engaged in it. The Mormons, before the United States government made war on them, cited chapter and verse to prove that Jesus approved of polygamy. There is an assumption that multiple marriage has no place in the modern world, but this assumption is made by the same determinists who claim that jealousy will inevitably triumph in any three-way liaison. Interestingly, there exists in Israel a rural colony of polygamous Yemenis whose customs date from the biblical era. Flown to the promised land in 1950 under Operation Magic Carpet, the men have been permitted to keep two legal wives, though not to marry twice once in Israel. Says the leading rabbi of the Yemenite community in Tel Aviv, "It's perfectly legal according to the Torah, 100 percent permitted."

In 1992 Gloria Deutsch, a reporter for the *Jerusalem Post*, interviewed the family of Ovadia Mezember, which consists of his wives, Jamila and Rahel, and twenty-three sons and daughters. "In spite of the considered opinion of experts . . . that polygamy cannot work," wrote Deutsch, "they appear to live in perfect harmony." A Yemenite rabbi explained to her that in the old country a man took a second wife sometimes because his first was barren, at other times because he was rich and she was a status symbol. But the rabbi's most cogent explanation was that "[a man] can feast on ox meat, but sometimes he feels like a taste of lamb as well." Deutsch wondered about the women.

Ovadia, in his sixties, came from a family rich in sheep and goats, and when he was fifteen his father picked Jamila as his bride; she was twelve. Shortly before they left for Israel, he fell in love with Rahel and asked permission of Jamila to take her as his second wife. Jamila agreed, and as she now says, "I'm not sorry. We get on really well." There were never any quarrels about where Ovadia would spend his nights, and his eldest son referred to one of the bedrooms as his "father's workroom." Because it was rough in the early years, the women helped each other to deliver their children. The whole clan is friendly, open, and content. About his two wives, Ovadia boasts that it took strength. Then he reflects, "When the time comes, they'll bury us all together."

And with that we'll move on to the love stories and the conflicts of the threes who have made history: statesmen and poets, divas and daredevils, lords and ladies. Yet these humble, pastoral Yemeni should be celebrated along with their more famous brothers and sisters.

part two

THE
ARISTOCRACY
OF THREES

The Middle Ages can hardly be seen as propitious for any form of sophisticated love. Peter Lombard, a leading twelfth-century theologian, declared that the passionate love of a man's own wife was adultery. The term "courtly love" was unknown until in 1883 a French medievalist named Gaston Paris used it to describe a twelfth-century romance that related the story of King Arthur, Queen Guinevere, and her lover, Sir Launcelot. C. S. Lewis believed that courtly love sprang full blown in the south of France into a heretical poetry that glorified "humility, adultery, courtesy and the Religion of Love." The philosopher Irving Singer holds that courtly love was a reaction to a system that imposed marriage on the bride for the advantage of her parents and that it was "explicitly sexual much of the time."

Simone de Beauvoir put it plainly: "The feudal husband was guardian and tyrant, and the wife sought an extramarital love: knightly love was the compensation for the barbarism of official mores." But what did the lord of the manor, off hunting or deflowering the daughter of one of his vassals, as was his due, think of his wife's affair with a young knight or troubadour? We have two divergent answers: one points the way to the bloody triangle of the Romantic operas, today's tabloid murders, and Hollywood thrillers, and the other leads to the menages a trois of the Age of Reason and the antics of nineteenth-century bohemians, as well as of present-day celebrities.

The traditional "childe" ballads, the popular but unwritten songs of the folk, portray the adulterous passions of the nobles, but these songs don't end well. In one a knightly lover is advised to take hold of the shepherd's daughter "by the middle so small" and "lay her down on the plain" at once. A cuckolded lord can be expected to run through his wife's young swain before milord "cuts off her paps" and she bleeds to death. At least a certain Lord Barnard repented sufficiently of his wrath to bury his wife and her lover together.

However, during the High Middle Ages, courts of love dominated by noblewomen were handing down verdicts that rendered the husband powerless. One famous case concerned a knight who fell in love with a lady already pledged to another knight. She promised to bestow her favors on him if ever she was bereft of her champion. Soon afterward the lady and this champion were married. When the first knight demanded that the lady keep her promise, she refused, arguing that she retained her husband's affection. Queen Eleanor of Aquitaine, deciding an appeal on this decision made by the countess of Champagne, declared, "Real love cannot exist between married persons. We are therefore in favor of the lady granting the love that she had promised." The lady must sleep with the knight or be ostracized, and her husband had nothing to say about it.

By the fifteenth century the role of women was in decline, and courtly love was a poetic memory. Yet while the new learning of the Renaissance spread, at the court of François chivalry was revived and spread across the channel to England. Ladies again had their champions who jousted in their name at showy tournaments. No woman knew better how to manipulate this Disney version of chivalry than Diane de Poitiers, born into the provincial aristocracy at the turn of the sixteenth century. She would become the mistress of two kings, father and son, and the de facto ruler of France. Greater than a queen, Diane would reign over the courts of love.

chapter 4

THE COURTS OF LOVE

{Diane de Poitiers, Henry II, and Catherine de' Medici;
Molière, Armande Béjart, and Michel Baron;
Voltaire and the Marquis and Marquise du Châtelet}

The horseman became the cavalier. Swords changed from
weapons to ornaments. Women were omnipotent.
VOLTAIRE

GODDESS OF THE MOON

*D*IANE DE POITIERS RODE AND HUNTED
in the French countryside from the time she was a little girl. She had a
haughty air, long limbs, a cold, lunar beauty, and a legendary complexion
pampered by bathing in ass's milk. At fifteen her father married her to a
wealthy and powerful nobleman in his midfifties, an official of King
François I. Diane produced two daughters and managed the household at
Anet, her husband's Norman castle. In 1523 the king sentenced her father
to death for plotting against him. The devoted daughter not only saved
her father's life but became François's mistress. According to Pierre
Brantôme, a chronicler of court life, Diane's father, reprieved on the gal-
lows, burst out, "God preserve the fair cunt of my daughter, which has
served me so well."

Diane, after her husband's death in 1532, made tracks for Paris and
the most glamorous court in Europe. Here she spotted nine-year-old
Henry, an awkward prince who was ignored by François. The king, the
epitome of Renaissance elegance, insisted that all his courtiers acquire
mistresses, but his younger son's penis was malformed. Diane assured

41

François he needn't worry. When the dauphin died and Henry stood in line for the throne, she mentored him for his rulership. At fourteen Henry was married to dumpy Catherine de' Medici, also fourteen, the niece of Pope Clement VII, who performed the ceremony. Clement hung around to see that the marriage was consummated. When after several weeks the teenagers had failed to accomplish the task, he left in disgust and soon died. Diane's skills were sorely needed.

Her enemies attributed Diane's allure to sorcery, and she appears to have been skilled in the use of alchemical nostrums, especially gold taken in homeopathic doses. She had style, dressing in Donna Karan–like black and white, which highlighted her almond eyes and porcelain complexion. Diane and Henry made love for the first time in a so-called obscene château where the windows depicted erotic scenes. But while aphrodisiacs might seduce the prince, who became Henry II in 1547, other factors secured the king's lifelong devotion. Under Diane's tutelage he became a handsome, chivalric knight, jousting always as her champion. The court noticed and approved.

At the coronation of the king and queen, Diane wore a duplicate of Catherine's jewel-encrusted gown. To no one's surprise, the heavy crown was lifted from Catherine's head and placed at Diane's feet. Diane easily upstaged Catherine at tournaments or when all three traveled together. Yet each woman appreciated the other's prudential value. Joseph Barry pointed out that "Catherine intrigued with Diane to keep the King at least to the two of them as courtiers seeking advancement pushed their wives toward the royal bed." When Henry conceived a child with an Italian beauty, his wife and mistress conspired to oust the interloper.

Pressure mounted for a male heir to the throne. Diane feared that Catherine might be replaced by a less complaisant rival. While physicians claimed Catherine was barren, Diane gave her a pouch to wear round her neck containing amulets and the ashes of a frog. More to the point, she practiced coitus interruptus with Henry, then sent him to sleep with Catherine. The result was, over a period of years, the births of nine legitimate heirs to the throne. Henry gave Diane huge sums for services rendered. She chose the children's nurses, tutors, and governesses and had more influence on them than did their parents. It is no exaggeration to say that Diane was the de facto ruler of France.

Diane and Henry, true to the chivalric code, were decorous in public, but in private they devoured courtly romances. Contemporaries believed Diane had bewitched the king; after twenty-five years, in her fifties, she still kept his love. An Oedipal explanation, resorted to by Barry, cannot explain the conscious and considered role played by each of the three. Catherine was curious to know what Diane had that she didn't have. So, according to Brantôme, she had a hole drilled in the ceiling of Diane's bedroom and peered through at the couple while they were dallying. Catherine watched as the barely clad couple caressed each other "with a panoply of delicious follies . . . until they rolled from the bed to the floor . . . and pursued their love play on the thick carpet." Despite her haughty exterior, Diane in lovemaking was warm, free, and giving, which was the inimitable secret of her success.

In 1559 Henry, wearing Diane's black and white and jousting for the love of her, caught a lance in his eye at a tournament. Even before the king died, an anti-Diane faction at court demanded her nose be cut off. Instead, Catherine stripped the distressed goddess of all her possessions except for her original Norman estate, to which she retired. Brantôme, who saw her at sixty-five, wrote, "Her grace, her majesty, her fine appearance were all just as they had always been." Although Diane hadn't seemed to age, she died a few months later of a fall from a horse.

Catherine's actions had been motivated more by a political rivalry with Diane than by jealousy as it is usually understood. A true Medici, she was determined to rule by their trademark cunning and deceit. In August 1572 Catherine persuaded her son Charles IX to order the Saint Bartholomew's Day massacre of his Protestant subjects, nearly destroying the country and making her own name infamous. Perhaps while she was a member of the menage a trois that raised France to new heights of culture and chivalry, Catherine experienced a temporary reprieve from her own treacherous nature.

THE COURT OF THE SUN KING

The religious wars and dynastic upheavals that wracked sixteenth- and seventeenth-century Europe created an unfavorable environment for courtly dalliance. In Britain the Virgin Queen, Elizabeth I, tended to business. Puritanism gained influence over the popular mind and brought with it an epidemic of witch trials. England and New England seemed plagued by witches who fornicated with the devil, expert at taking on the form of a man, beast, or invisible incubus. Devils became popular thirds in alleged menages a trois.

For example, in 1618 at Lincoln Castle Margaret Flower confessed to "two familiar spirits sucking on her, one white, the other black-spotted, the white sucked under her left breast, and the black-spotted within the inward parts of her secrets." She was executed "to the terror of all beholders." As late as 1704 Eleanor Shaw and Mary Philips, after being threatened with death, admitted to a threesome with the devil, who "had carnal knowledge of them." The two women confessed to being witches and "cursing and raving were hanged."

Meanwhile, in France, His Christian Majesty Louis XIV, who reigned from 1643 to 1715, was constructing the magnificent palace and gardens of Versailles in order to house a paradise of decorum. The French court was a manicured world far from the bustle of Paris, and the conduct of its inmates was based on a precise code of manners. Harsh words, frowns, and mourning clothes were not permitted; clouds could not distract from the radiance of the Sun King. There were a thousand pitfalls of gaucherie into which the novice might fall. But with all this attention to form, the halls still reeked. Sanitary facilities were neglected. Counts and countesses peed anywhere, love affairs were carried on under staircases, and love itself became a smutty joke.

As a young man Louis had fallen in love with the niece of his minister Mazarin. Horrified, Mazarin explained to the royal lad that marriage was an affair of state and he must wed the homely infanta of Spain. An embittered Louis complied but thereafter kept a mistress and bedded many a chambermaid. Louis advised his dutiful Spanish consort to keep on good and intimate terms with his current favorite. In 1664 this was Louise de la Vallière, nineteen and silvery blond, for whom he threw a stupendous seven-day entertainment to celebrate the opening of the gardens of Versailles, envisioned as their "enchanted isle."

The fete was officially dedicated to the queen, whose plastered-on smile announced her approval. Elaborate theatricals were organized by the comedian in favor, one Molière. When the monarch transferred his affections from la Vallière to Madame de Montespan, he made the former mistress his confidante and obliged her to sit guard outside his bedroom door while he sported with the newly chosen one. The monarch had an affection for his own past affections.

"A mistress," declared Louis XIV, "is the most dangerous of favorites." Yet a desirable mistress was as essential to the courtier as was the wife he'd married for her fortune. The essential thing was to tame love with reason. This tenet of the neoclassical menage held not only for aristocrats by birth but for the aristocracy of talent, the artists and writers who served the former. The theater was central to the French court, and no playwright of the period has proved more lasting than Molière, who was born Jean-Baptiste Poquelin in 1622 into a merchant family. To ensure his future, the boy's father purchased him the office of upholsterer to the king. But desire for a theatrical career and for Madeleine Béjart, a beautiful actress of twenty-two, caused the young man to neglect his position and change his name. Impetuous Molière had traded security for a profession whose members (unless they repented) were damned by the church.

Madeleine had a protector, the count of Modène, by whom she'd had a daughter at twenty. The nobleman recognized the child as his, and she was given over to Madeleine's mother, Marie Herve Béjart. Conveniently, the count was exiled to the provinces. In June 1642 Madeleine, who'd taken Molière as her interim lover, joined the count, still her protector. Nine months later a daughter, Armande, was born. Madeleine claimed the child was her mother's and thus her sister; she may have wished to disguise the count's unwillingness to own the girl. Marie Herve, a widow in her forties, was unlikely to have borne a child. Besides, an actress getting on in years (by seventeenth-century standards) would prefer a younger sister to a growing daughter.

Now Molière renounced his place at court and formed the Illustre Théâtre with Madeleine and several other Béjarts, including little Armande! Contemporary gossip was certain that Madeleine was Armande's mother and Molière her father. He raised her with paternal affection. Twice the playwright's company failed and he was imprisoned for debt. Finally he took to the provinces and toured for a dozen years. The troupe shared a familial intimacy.

As compensation for his troubles, Molière, though homely, bedded the actresses, not caring if he was wounding the faithful Madeleine. He kept a careful eye on Armande, who by thirteen played the coquette onstage and off. Under the feudal laws of the ancien régime he might well feel proprietary about his ward. Armande was pleased to edge out more experienced players and to become the favorite of the troupe's director.

In 1658 Molière returned to Paris, where he became an instant hit with the king. The company performed at the Palais Royal, bored Louis XIV with tragedy but made him smile at farce. In 1661 the company presented Molière's first notable comedy. *The School for Husbands* concerns two mature gentlemen who raise their wards to be perfect wives—one strictly, the other with understanding. Barry tells us that for its time and place, the play "was the ideal public spectacle, but it was also, as so often, despite Molière's disclaimers, a private journal."

In *The School for Husbands* Molière played the middle-aged man of reason who refuses to take stern measures with his young wife. Instead, he believes he must win her heart in order to ensure her virtue. Warned that she will waste his money on finery and on parties where young men will cuckold him, Molière's character scoffs. Early the next year Molière the man married Armande, then nineteen. Marie Herve and Madeleine Béjart were witnesses. He was immediately accused by a rival theater manager, in a brief sent to the king, of "having married the daughter after having slept with the mother." Since Molière continued to amuse Louis, his majesty disregarded the manager's insinuation of incest, that Armande was "the daughter of her husband, wife of her father."

The probability is that Armande was not Molière's daughter in a biological sense. He had courted the young woman under her mother's nose, and Madeleine, in order to oust a rival leading lady, had connived in the marriage. She even provided a dowry. Madeleine continued to act under Molière's direction and to live close by the newlyweds. The count of Modène, who also married the daughter of his mistress, acted as godfather to Molière and Armande's child, a common custom for a grandparent. But Molière failed to realize that Armande regarded him more as a father than a lover.

Not a year after his marriage Molière's company presented *The School for Wives*, a study in disenchantment. "No sooner was Armande Mademoiselle de Molière than she thought she was a duchess," claimed H. C. Chatfield-Taylor, an early biographer of Molière. In *Wives* the bride-to-be (Armande) is raised by her benefactor (Molière) in a country convent in order to be kept in ignorance. But nature cannot be contravened. She is not attracted to the older man and runs off with a handsome young suitor. Molière's prescience is touching: his every fear would come true as Armande made the most of her position and took pains to be attractive to all men except her husband. Molière played the cuckold both onstage and in real life, growing resigned at last.

At Louis's grand fete of 1664 at Versailles, Armande glowed before the gallants of the court. The heady spring evenings and sensual atmosphere, the example of the king and his mistress, encouraged the seduction of a not unwilling young woman. From then on Armande openly gambled, received gifts, and went out with fashionable suitors. It is fortunate that Molière turned to his study and wrote his three masterpieces: *Tartuffe, Don Juan,* and *The Misanthrope.* Rather than blame his straying wife, the edge of his wit was honed on himself, the ridiculous husband.

Molière was growing older and ill with consumption. He was somber but denied Armande nothing. To a friend who suggested he have Armande shut up in a convent, he wrote, "When I think how difficult it is for me to overcome my passion for her, I tell myself that perhaps she has the same difficulty in vanquishing her penchant for being a coquette, and I find myself in a position of pitying her more than I blame her." Was Armande seeking revenge for his infidelity to *her* mother?

Into this tense situation came Michel Baron, a pretty orphaned boy of thirteen, already a strolling player. Molière saw his youth reincarnated before him and adopted the lad. They became inseparable, which caused Armande to hate this rival. One day at rehearsal, she slapped Michel across the face. He quit, which sank Molière deeper into illness. Several years later would come the supreme test of his civility.

At eighteen handsome Michel Baron returned to Molière's company and household; the former was beginning to lose popularity, the latter was cold as ice. Playing Amour opposite Armande's Psyche, Michel swept the audience and his leading lady off their feet. A passionate affair raged between the actor playing the god of love and Paris's favorite actress. Molière looked on with tolerance, patience, and even love. The young lovers took a two-month holiday. When the fires banked, they returned to the company. Michel became an outstanding leading man. Armande, nearing thirty, tried to make a caring wife to her husband.

If the affair continued, it gladdened Molière. Madeleine had died, and he was soon to join her. He groomed Michel to take his place onstage. In spite of losing favor with the king, he struggled to maintain his company. In February 1673 the ailing Molière took the lead in *The Imaginary Invalid*. Armande and Michel begged him to cancel the show, but the old trouper dragged himself to opening night. Shaken throughout the performance by violent coughing, he made it seem hypochondriacal, keeping the audience in stitches. After the curtain he collapsed and was carried home. His loved ones kept a vigil at his bedside. Because the priest arrived too late, Molière hadn't confessed before he died, and the archbishop of Paris ruled him ineligible for a religious funeral.

A determined Armande went to Versailles and threw herself in front of the king, begging him to intercede. Louis paused but continued down the Hall of Mirrors, trailed by a retinue of scornful courtiers. Next day the archbishop had a change of mind: there would be a discreet burial after sunset in church grounds. A great crowd, among them the weeping Michel and Armande, followed Molière's coffin to the cemetery by the glare of torches, as though at the theater.

THE AGE OF REASON

The easygoing morals of the French Enlightenment set the stage for menages a trois. Eighteenth-century France was the dominant world power, and the font of the country's social life, from which all fashion flowed, was Versailles. A Frenchwoman of any pretension, once she had married and produced an heir, was obliged to take lovers. Theodore Besterman, Voltaire's biographer, states, "The husbands ... claimed full freedom for themselves, and were civilized enough to grant it to their wives so long as appearances were respected."

However, the story of François-Marie Arouet, known to posterity as Voltaire; Florent Claude, the marquis du Châtelet; and his wife, Emilie de Breteuil, transcends attitudes of civility or complaisance and enters the realm of a fully cooperative menage a trois. The three lived for an extended period of time under the same expansive roof and formed a mutual attachment that should be called love. Whether the menage reached the final stage of cohesion, analogous to the "merging" that Irving Singer claims is the goal of a couple in love, is more debatable. We think they did—for a while.

Voltaire, witty, skeptical, urbane, personifies the so-called Age of Reason. In reality he lived in an age of irrational risk that ended in revolution. Born into a bourgeois family in 1694, Voltaire could never be certain of the identity of his biological father. Each time he sent off a play or verses to his publisher, he wondered if the manuscript would trigger his arrest, and in fact, in 1717 writing a satire on the aristocracy caused him to be imprisoned without trial in the Bastille for eleven months. From then on Voltaire wrote letters on sensitive matters in a kind of code, and he made nonsensical statements to placate the authorities. Speculating in commodities, he made lots of money in the hope of putting himself out of reach of church and state.

Nicolas Largillière paints a portrait of the bright-eyed man of letters at twenty-four:

> The nose is long and slightly bulbous; the mouth large, sensitive, smiling. The whole face is crowned by a very high forehead, and framed by a full unusually long, loose page boy wig; a red and buff waistcoat is elegantly unbuttoned at top and bottom to show the handsome shirt and lace jabot, the coat is of dark emerald velvet with large gold buttons.

Voltaire was a man about town. He became the lover of the marquise de Berniers; Nancy Mitford, author of *Voltaire in Love*, commented that he "was on very friendly terms with her husband and had rooms in their Paris house." However, among his mistresses was Adrienne Lecouvreur, the great dramatic actress. Her protector, the powerful chevalier de Rohan-

Chabot, had Voltaire beaten and thrown into the Bastille a second time, after which he was exiled to England. Here he became a disciple of Locke and empiricism. When he returned to France a rich speculator in 1726, he was prepared to subject his nation to a rapier wit and, worse to the French, praise of the English.

In 1733, when Voltaire met twenty-seven-year-old Emilie, the marquise du Châtelet, he was thirty-nine and used hair powder and essence of jasmine, and wore white gloves indoors; moreover, he swore he was "too ill to make love." The charmer who roused this hypochondriac was described by Madame du Deffand, the haughty salon hostess, as "a big and dried-up woman, with an overheated complexion, sharp face, pointed nose." These are the words of an embittered rival. Voltaire's niece, another rival, called Emilie "very pretty," and Mitford concludes she was "a handsome woman."

Born in 1706, the daughter of a high court official, Emilie was raised in Paris, where she became a prodigy among her sex. Her father ensured that she learn Latin along with her brothers, and she also acquired Italian and English. To study the stars, she mastered mathematics and physics. Yet her worship of knowledge never interfered with a fondness for fine clothes, jewelry, and primping. In 1725 Emilie married the marquis du Châtelet, who, although he came from a noble family, was a soldier of limited means. They quickly produced two children, then moved to Paris where Emilie began her amorous career. About Florent Claude, Theodore Besterman has written: "The marquis was not a man of mark, but he was gentle, understanding, and easy-going. His wife never failed in her respect and affection for him—and this was rare in a society in which happy and united married couples could be counted on one's fingers."

It may have been the duc de Richelieu who introduced Emilie to his friend Voltaire; he had been her lover and remained close. Richelieu was grandnephew to the famous cardinal and was reputed to be the Don Juan of the court. In 1734 Voltaire and the marquise acknowledged their liaison by jointly attending the wedding of Richelieu and the princesse de Guise. The two men left thereafter for a military camp in Germany, Voltaire in flight from arrest and Richelieu to fight a duel with a prince of Guise, who thought him too low to marry into the family. Voltaire tried to settle the quarrel, but Richelieu shot and killed his opponent.

In 1734 Voltaire, always under suspicion by the government, decided to live with Emilie at Cirey, the Châtelets' isolated château on the border of Champagne. He described his motivations:

I was weary of the idle and turbulent life of Paris, of the crowd of fops, of the bad books printed with official approval and royal privilege, of literary cabals, of the meanness and rascality of the wretches who dishonored literature. I found a young lady who felt more or less as I did, and who resolved to spend several years in the country to cultivate her mind. It was the woman who in all France had the greatest disposition for all the sciences.

Voltaire found the countryside plain, there were no amusements, and he was four days by coach from Paris. However, Cirey provided him with more than a quiet place to write. The marquis was usually in residence, and the three formed a family united around a hatred of hypocrisy and worship of the goddess Athena as reincarnated in Emilie. "I confess that she is tyrannical," Voltaire admitted. "To pay her court you must talk metaphysics, when you would like to talk love." His Cirey period was to last for fifteen years, during which time he embraced the faith of reason and science.

Initially, the triad had to thwart not only snide Parisian tongues but also the couple's parents on both sides, who considered themselves humiliated by Emilie's liaison with a commoner—and one given to pamphleteering! The marquis interceded for his wife and convinced his relations that "he regard[ed] Voltaire as a man of honor and his best friend." Emilie was a woman given to violent attachments. Earlier, she had attempted suicide when scorned by a lover. Voltaire, on the other hand, entered the arrangement believing it would be impermanent. The duc de Richelieu advised the pair "not to love each other too much [and] in that way, the love would last. Better to be friends for life than lovers for a few days."

The marquis adopted an amiable view of the menage thrust upon him. Joseph Barry pointed out that "Monsieur du Châtelet was proud of his wife's having elected, and been chosen by, so eminent an intellectual companion as Voltaire." There was something more to his complaisance: Voltaire, via a long-term loan, made possible the rehabilitation of the dilapidated château and estate. Emilie beautified the house and added extensive gardens, while Voltaire built a gallery and purchased an expensive collection of scientific instruments. The lovers engaged in leisurely dialogues while strolling along picturesque canals amid a one-hundred-fifty-acre park.

André Maurel, in *The Romance of Madame du Châtelet and Voltaire*, agreed that Emilie's husband had no difficulty living in a menage a trois. "He cannot even resist a certain regard for this man who spends so lavishly. This friendly feeling is to increase with the years, and we shall find him later championing Voltaire." Nor did the philosophic lover feel any anxiety, and the three often supped pleasantly together. Emilie confided to Richelieu that she'd had doubts about leaving Paris and the court, but Voltaire was "the enchantment and torment of [her] life."

The philosopher was likewise smitten but in a calmer way. "How fortunate that I can admire her whom I adore," he quipped. At Cirey the pair's labors became intertwined with their romance. From morn till night they generated an intellectual charge that startled visitors. In July 1744, Madame du Deffand wrote, "It is a rare sight. The two of them are there . . . plunged in gaiety. One writes verse in his corner, the other triangles in hers." Voltaire set off a wing for himself and Emilie, and the marquis took care not to impose. However, the influence of this gentle warrior who'd fought several campaigns was palpable. He employed a resident priest to conduct services and built an altar with an elaborate crucifix.

Voltaire believed in luxury and surrounded himself with fine paintings and porcelains. But Emilie, who'd arrived bearing two hundred packages, outdid him. Her bedroom was designed so that everything matched, even the dog baskets. It displayed paintings by Watteau and an amber desk set from the prince of Russia. Another visitor, Madame de Graffigny, commented on the improvement in Emilie's possessions, especially her jewel box: "It is finer than that of mme de Richelieu . . . when mme du Châtelet was at Craon she hadn't so much as a tortoise shell snuff-box. Now she has fifteen or twenty, in gold, in precious stones, in lacquer, in enamel."

Graffigny marveled at the paradoxical marquise, who in the midst of ostentation scribbled mathematical formulas on scraps of paper. Both Emilie and Voltaire had written essays on fire. Graffigny read them and preferred Emilie's, of whom she wrote, "Our sex should raise an altar to her." The writing was accomplished at night in just one week, during which Emilie hardly slept, plunging her arms into cold water to stay awake. When the essays were submitted to the Académie des Sciences neither won, but among all the entries only these two featured actual experiments.

Emilie, who corresponded with scientists all over Europe, saw no contradiction in also spending hours arranging the folds of a dress. Nevertheless, her influence on Voltaire's thought was profound. She criticized his dramas, led him to question his own beliefs, and interested him in science and in history as a science. Voltaire's histories and biographies are landmarks on the way to modern, objective scholarship. His play *Mahomet*, a cutting attack on religious fanaticism, was written at Cirey in 1740. It was a hit in Paris before being banned and became a favorite with Pope Benedict XIV.

Above all, Emilie encouraged Voltaire's interest in Sir Isaac Newton's physics, the most potent weapon in demolishing the medieval fortress of sanctioned orthodoxy. Voltaire came to believe that Newton was the greatest man who had ever lived. In 1736 he began a work that would make Newton's physics easily accessible, and after the French authorities refused permission, it was published in Amsterdam in 1738 as *Elements of the Philosophy of Newton*. Because the scientist was little known outside England, Voltaire's popularization made an immense impression on the Continent, comparable only to Darwin's *Origin of the Species* a century later. In an intellectual sense, Newton, via Voltaire, began the French Revolution.

The authorities continued to threaten Voltaire with prison, much to the distraction of Emilie. "I have to save him from himself at every turn," she wrote to a mutual friend. "I shall pass [my life] in fighting against him for his own sake . . . in trembling for him." Emilie kept Voltaire's papers under lock and key and argued against publishing his radical thoughts on the nature of God. Through her husband's connections at court, she interceded for Voltaire, yet he continued to be spied on by the police.

Cirey provided tranquillity and ease for studies. The lovers had to create their own culture and amusements. One hour might be devoted to philosophical readings, another to poetry recitations, yet another to a performance of a new play by Voltaire in the tiny theater he'd built. Dressed and powdered, the author dedicated his works to the critic who was harshest on them. "I cultivate them for you," he wrote to Emilie, "to merit spend[ing] the rest of my life at your side, in the heart of refuge, peace and perhaps truth."

What of monsieur le marquis? When he was in residence, Emilie's husband participated in the entertainments. Guests were drafted into acting in plays or operas. Monsieur gloried in the presence of Voltaire. In fact, the comrades doted on each other. Voltaire used his influence to gain an honorary appointment for Châtelet at the court of Lorraine; there the marquis lobbied the treasury for money owed to his guest. They quarreled only when he complained that Voltaire left to attend to other friends or to business.

Into paradise a serpent must creep. The crown prince of Prussia, soon to become Frederick II, waged a lengthy campaign to make Voltaire an ornament at his court. But the king's blandishments, including expensive gifts, were unequal to Emilie's insistence that Voltaire remain at her side. He had an additional incentive to stay in France: a budding affair with his niece Marie Louise Denis, married to an army contractor. By the time Monsieur Denis died in 1744, leaving a poor but extravagant widow, Voltaire and the young woman were already lovers. Worse for Emilie, he had ceased to sleep with her, although her love for him hadn't waned.

Marie Louise, aware of her uncle's genius, resented Emilie's keeping him away from Paris society. She claimed her rival was "a woman of wit and talent [who] makes use of every imaginable device to fascinate him— from cunning treatment of pompons to the citing of passages from the best philosophers." But after ten years of a happy and productive menage, Marie Louise cleverly won away her quarry.

Voltaire began to spend time away from the Châtelets, either at the Prussian court or in Paris. In 1745 the marquis wrote to thank him for legal advice, adding that "he absolutely relied on Voltaire never to leave Madame du Châtelet." Yet the philosopher's correspondence with his niece, unearthed in the 1960s, shows an erotic, two-timing side to his nature. While dissimulating a passion he no longer felt with Emilie, he complains to Louise that he is bound by the duties of friendship. He sends her in Italian "a thousand kisses. My soul kisses yours, my prick and my heart are in love with you. I kiss your pretty bottom and all your adorable person."

Emilie's extreme nature had withered Voltaire's passion, if not his admiration. She wasted enormous sums gambling. The more she lost, the deeper she plunged. In an autobiographical essay she justified her addiction: "The soul needs to be shaken up by hope and fear. Gambling brings it within range of these two passions and keeps it in a healthy state." Voltaire objected to Emilie's playing cards with cheats at court, although the speed and accuracy with which she mentally added up the score astounded him. He once watched her lose the equivalent of a hundred thousand dollars in an evening.

By 1747 Emilie was deeply into her major work, a translation of Newton's *Principia Mathematica* with commentary. But she knew Voltaire's heart was no longer hers alone. The pair traveled, spending weeks in a château that had been a gift from Henry II to Diane de Poitiers, then at Luneville Castle, where Stanislaus, the former king of Poland, and his ex-court resided. Here, in a spin-off menage, Emilie took a lover, the marquis de Saint-Lambert. Voltaire was fond of this congenial and talented young man, but he was startled to find Emilie and his rival naked in her boudoir. Afterward, she swore to Voltaire she still loved him. She supposed that he would be pleased she'd chosen his friend. He naturally agreed to the arrangement. While he lingered in Lorraine, he wrote Louise that he missed her "ravishing bottom . . . which has so often given me erections and plunged me in a flood of delight."

Jean-François de Saint-Lambert, who was thirty-two to Emilie's forty-one, was a courtier who could never be confused with a fop. Equally adept with pen or sword, he swept the neglected marquise off her feet. Voltaire never again showed jealousy and, at one point, finding himself in a room above the lovers, he wrote mock-heroic verses to celebrate the occasion. Saint-Lambert was a ladies' man generally disliked by other men, but he had the distinction to be the third in menages with both Voltaire and Rousseau; he won the former's regard and the latter's admiration.

In April 1748 Emilie gained Voltaire's permission for Saint-Lambert to join the household at Cirey. But the younger man played coy, which made Emilie want him more. While she and Voltaire dreamed of devoting themselves to their new loves, they became engrossed in their writing: in his case the tragedy of *Semiramis,* and in hers the translation of Newton. Unfortunately, she found herself pregnant at a time when her husband was absent. He would have gladly accepted Voltaire as the father, but due to his age and fragile health, that was unlikely. The marquis, who knew nothing of Saint-Lambert, would object if the old menage was disturbed.

Châtelet was sent for, and Emilie and Voltaire wined and dined him, she in a low-cut gown and glittering diamonds. Voltaire told racy stories and, at bedtime, exited. For the next three weeks the marquis and marquise acted like newlyweds, whereupon Emilie informed her proud husband he would again be a father. Here the three were inseparably involved not only in creating knowledge but a new human life. Shortly, the menage separated. Emilie and Voltaire went to Paris where she continued to work on Newton and he would see his niece.

Arrangements were made for Emilie to lie in at Luneville in the queen's own apartment. Saint-Lambert urged her to make the journey well before she was due. She begged him not to reproach her, that as a point of honor she must stay in Paris to finish the Newton. "It's a terrible task and I need an iron head and health to do it," she added. Through the seventh month of pregnancy she worked alongside Voltaire, continuing after he'd gone to bed until five in the morning. Finally, in her ninth month, in residence at the Polish court, the marquise du Châtelet sent off her *Commentary on the Mathematical Principles of Newton* to the Royal Library of Paris. It is a standard in French to this day.

In September 1749 Emilie gave birth. Voltaire reported that a little girl came into the world at her mother's writing desk, and for want of a cradle, she was placed on a large volume! Emilie appeared fine, but later she went into convulsions and died. On hearing the news, Voltaire stumbled out into the passage. Devastated, he reached the castle door without knowing what he'd done. He fell down an outside stairway, knocking his head on the flagstones at the bottom.

Everyone was grief stricken. Voltaire wrote, "I have not merely lost a mistress, I have lost the half of myself." To Frederick the Great he wrote of Emilie, "She was a great man whose only fault was in being a woman."

Before dying, the marquise had divided her personal papers into packets for her intimates. Those designated for her husband contained Voltaire's letters to her. The marquis complied with his wife's instructions, which were to read and burn them all. Thus the marquis added to the loss of his dear Emilie the destruction of the intimate records of a most civilized menage a trois. Voltaire remained on hand to give him moral support. "I am not abandoning M. du Châtelet in our mutual sadness," he explained to his niece, whom he called "the only hope of my life."

Voltaire spent a month at Cirey wandering around as though seeking his old love. For a time, he occupied the marquis's Paris townhouse. But he soon set up house with Madame Denis, whom Carlyle would term "gadding, flaunting, unreasonable." At fifty-five, the philosopher was convinced he would not long outlive Emilie. He actually lasted thirty years more, and after he died in 1778, famous and revered, his niece sold his papers to Catherine of Russia.

According to historian Ira Wade, "by 1749 Voltaire completed his education. Never thereafter did he enter new intellectual fields, and when in later years his views on certain particular subjects shifted somewhat, he still based them on the same material which he and Madame du Châtelet had assembled in the Cirey period." In his menage a trois with the Châtelets, the philosopher had found the best of all possible worlds.

chapter 5

THREE IN MIND

{Jean-Jacques Rousseau, the Baroness de Warens, and Claude Anet;
Rousseau, Sophie d'Houdetot, and the Marquis de Saint-Lambert}

*She showed me how much she loved him
in order that I might feel the same affection for him.*
JEAN-JACQUES ROUSSEAU

*I*N HIS PREFACE TO *French Lovers* JOSEPH
Barry remarks, "The *ménage à trois* is assumed, perhaps rightly, to be
another French contribution to that design for living among the varieties
of love's arrangements." Menages a trois date back, as we have seen, to the
Bible, while the foremost practitioner of threesomes, at least of the eighteenth century, was Casanova, an Italian. But the French have given the
menage its name and spirit. Barry violates this spirit when he adds, "My
preference goes to a *ménage à quatre:* a quartet is more equitable and fair.
The examples, alas, are rare." Because foursomes soon splinter, examples
are close to nonexistent. What does appear to be a French contribution to
the varieties of love, specifically that of Jean-Jacques Rousseau, is nearly as
elusive: the metaphysical menage—an imaginative rather than physical
relationship. This is a threesome united by fate—karma is a better
term—but purified of passion.

Rousseau's life is a skein of contradictions. He was born a bourgeois,
like Voltaire, but in Geneva in 1712 to a watchmaker of French Protestant
origin. Although his father married above his station and eventually
became a dancing master, and though Rousseau insisted on the status of a

gentleman, he would fail as a gallant both in the drawing room and the boudoir. Rousseau, in his lengthy, posthumous *Confessions*, recounted a series of sexual misadventures that stemmed, in part, from problems with his private anatomy and a chronic bladder ailment. His most lasting relationship was with a domestic servant whom he finally married and by whom he, or other men, fathered five children. These the pioneer theorist on the raising of children abandoned to an orphanage.

While Rousseau's name is associated with sentiment, we shall see that what really excited the first Romantic was a menage a trois centered on an aristocratic woman he could adore and completed by a man he admired. Later in life Rousseau preferred that these two be lovers while he practiced sexual renunciation. Was Rousseau a masochist? "I have possessed few women," he insists, "but I have not failed to get a great deal of satisfaction in my own way, that is to say imaginatively."

One week after birth Rousseau lost the mother who might have bolstered his self-confidence. His father, who blamed him for his mother's death, tormented him with guilt. When the father fled Geneva, Jean-Jacques was left an orphan. The boy was undisciplined, and this resulted in a series of beatings from his new caretaker. When a spinster of forty whipped his behind because he was slow to learn the Bible, the twelve-year-old experienced the pain as sensual, leaving him with a new sort of desire.

The spinster saw the boy grow hard—an old translation of the *Confessions* calls it "a forward instinct of sex"—and left off beating him. Later, Rousseau would write, "To fall on my knees before an imperious mistress, to obey her commands, to be forced to beg for her forgiveness, have been to me the most delicate of pleasures."

As an apprentice engraver, Rousseau's rebellion against abuse by his master led to his running away from Geneva. Starting in 1728 he vagabonded. Traveling in company with that segment of the proletariat Marx would term *lumpen*, sleeping in fields or caves and sharing the rough fare of peasants, Jean-Jacques experienced dangers and privations no other literary man of his century could draw on. He didn't merely get to know the common folk; he lived their life as "Nature's free son."

Early in his journeys, the sixteen-year-old stopped in Annecy, Savoy (now France) at the home of baroness de Warens, a Catholic convert who had fled a loveless marriage in Switzerland. Her religion aside, the baroness was well ahead of her time. She would have found herself at home in Venice—California. Rousseau describes himself when he first caught sight of her: "I was well set up, I had a pretty foot, fine leg, an easy manner, lively features, a pretty little mouth, black hair and eyebrows, small and deep-set eyes, which darted forth the fire with which my blood was kindled." A contemporary portrait shows a full-figured young man whose sensitive expression might well appeal to a woman of the baroness's caliber.

Her maiden name was Françoise-Louise de la Tour, and she had taken the rash step of abandoning home and husband to fling herself into the arms of the Catholic church. The king of Sardinia, who also ruled Savoy, paid her a pension to convert other wavering Protestants and to spy on the Swiss. Warens was twenty-nine when the shabbily dressed Rousseau first saw her "face radiant with charm, fine blue eyes filled with sweetness, a ravishing complexion, and the contours of an enchanting bosom." She was petite, quick to smile, and wore her ashen blond hair in a careless fashion. Maurice Cranston, the most precise biographer of Jean-Jacques, describes the moment: "Two extraordinary souls had met and recognized their kinship—the motherless child and the childless mother, the romantic youth and the sentimental woman, the adventurer and the adventuress."

Madame de Warens initiated Jean-Jacques's amorous education, and he claimed she formed his soul. She also provided him, at her lovely home and gardens, with books and the leisure to think. She influenced *Émile*, Rousseau's treatise on education. Émile (Rousseau) is chaste because he has an idealized image of his beloved. Never mind that the actual woman was a spendthrift bohemian who wasted her pension, borrowing ahead, barely scraping through at the last moment. Or that she entertained an itinerant throng of con men, political agents, and charlatans and was forever conjuring up outlandish moneymaking schemes that failed. Madame's favorite pursuit was alchemy, which taught her to prepare herbal elixirs and remedies. Jean-Jacques was certain she had wasted her great, unspecified talents.

In transports the youth kissed the chair Warens sat on and treasured by his bedside objects she'd touched. Once, when he saw a hair on her food, he snatched the morsel from her lips and gobbled it down. Warens in turn inflamed the young man by permitting him to watch a priest, one of a retinue of fawning males, lace her corset; she sang love songs to him and let him suck her jam-covered fingers. Shyness often made Rousseau tongue-tied, a defect that caused pedants to write him off as stupid. Warens, though, knew her jewel only needed polishing to sparkle brighter than those gifted with superficial wit.

Despite Rousseau's worship of "Mamma," who called him "little one," he was destined to be a revolutionary. He looks forward to Walt

Whitman, the Beats, and other "inebriates of air" (in Emily Dickinson's phrase) who have roamed the landscape finding in it intoxication. Rousseau's natural man, whom he preferred to the sophisticate, was savage but free and strong. But the essence of the bond between the poet Whitman and the French philosopher is that each was isolated from his peers by his sexual inclination, at odds with the contemporary norm—or at least with what was admitted as normal.

In 1730 Madame de Warens, after packing Jean-Jacques off on a fool's errand, disappeared from Annecy. The lad returned and hung about. Serving girls tried to distract him, but he had a distaste for their coarse hands and manners. One day he got into a little adventure with two French girls of a proper class. They chatted and flirted the whole day long. Both were pretty, and the lad had no wish to choose between them. At a château,

> we dined in the farmer's kitchen, the two friends seated on benches on either side of the long table, and their guest between them on a three-legged stool. . . . What an enchanting remembrance! . . . No supper at any of the *petites maisons* of Paris could be compared to this meal, not only for gaiety and cheerfulness but, I declare, for sensual enjoyment.

Afterward they went into the orchard to finish the meal with cherries. Jean-Jacques climbed a tree and threw down a bunch right in one girl's bosom. "If my lips were only cherries, how readily would I throw them into the same place," he thought. The idyll of the cherry orchard has been painted by any number of salon artists. Rousseau's savoring of this bucolic memory speaks volumes about how little pleasure he took in physical sex. When he was left alone with one of the girls, he froze in fright. The need to take refuge in a threesome, which helped to avoid the demands of one woman, is Rousseau's erotic leitmotif.

In autumn 1731 Jean-Jacques was reunited with Madame de Warens, this time in Chambéry, capital of Savoy, where she could better carry out her schemes. They lived in a grim apartment where he was thrown into close proximity with a fellow Swiss, Claude Anet, Warens's steward. A sober, loyal man slightly older than Jean-Jacques, he was a gifted herbalist and ran madame's business. One day after his mistress berated him, Anet, who showed little on the outside, downed a phial of laudanum (opium). Warens, terrified, confessed to Jean-Jacques that Anet was her lover. The pair forced Anet to regurgitate what he'd swallowed. Rousseau had to recognize that his "mamma" was a sexual being and that Anet was deeply in love with her.

On his side, young Jean-Jacques felt only increasing respect for the man who had much to teach him in the way of deportment. Anet responded in kind, and the men conceived a sincere friendship. Jealousy, Rousseau insists, dissolved in a perfect threesome. "One proof of the excellent character of this admirable woman, Mme de Warens, is that all those who loved her loved one other." The young man did feel emboldened to quit his minor government post and take up the teaching of music, which led coincidentally to his sexual initiation.

The happy Jean-Jacques built his adopted family a teahouse complete with decorations, rugs, and a bed in the midst of a garden in the suburbs. He taught music to charming young ladies, and though these were shy, their mothers flirted brazenly with the young maestro. Warens, becoming fretful, decided to put her stamp on her protégé. In "language full of feeling and good sense," according to Rousseau, she propositioned him, giving him a week to make up his mind. The poor virgin grew nearly hysterical as the days passed. He was young, vigorous, eager to assume the prerogative of manhood. Further, he loved his mamma, but she no longer aroused him; there was no heat. What was our hero to do?

Jean-Jacques rationalized that madame meant to rescue him from the snares of the world, interposing her body between him and other designing matrons. He salved his conscience and embraced Mamma, though with mixed feelings: "While pressing her in ecstasy in my arms, I wetted her bosom with my tears." Although Rousseau claimed that he felt as if he were committing incest, he was able to obviate the consequences by observing of his mamma, "as she was by no means sensual and had not looked for enjoyment, she felt no gratification, and never experienced remorse." The young man supposed Mamma's only joy resided in pleasing those whom she loved.

Rousseau was caught in the dichotomy of the mother and the whore, marvelously elucidated in the 1973 French film of that name, the culmination of the New Wave, which starred Jean-Pierre Léaud as the young wastrel who oscillates between the opposite female poles. But in the film, as in life, contrast turns into confusion, and Léaud ends by marrying the self-confessed whore who is carrying his child. Young Jean-Jacques, regardless of scruple, could perform his filial duty to Madame de Warens, especially since their rendezvous were held in the charming teahouse, but he never got used to seeing in bed the woman he'd intended for a pedestal. His problem wasn't that he worshiped Woman, especially the maternal;

rather, he worshiped class. For Rousseau, sex was something to engage in with the serving maid, and though he didn't value sensation highly, it had its place. Concerning Warens, he clearly states, "I had a tender mother, an adored friend; I needed a mistress." The distinction is traditional to any Romance culture, yet the Romantics widened the gulf between the good (wifely) woman and the bad (sexy) one. Happily, Rousseau's predicament was solved by the other man, Claude Anet, who kept Mamma happy and whom he came to esteem. The feeling between the two men, if not quite love, was of a great regard. Modern writers have not known what to make of this triad. Cranston assumes Anet was miserable enough to die of grief; the scholar Jean Hagstrum refers to it as "an Oedipal nest." True, the dignified Anet acted paternally toward both Rousseau and Warens, but within the bounds of his station. This was no jealous triangle. According to the *Confessions*, the menage, centered on Warens, had become a family of choice:

> How often did she move our hearts and make us embrace with tears, at the same time telling us that we were both necessary to her happiness in life! ... Thus a companionship was established between us, of which there is, perhaps, no other example upon earth. All our wishes, cares and inclinations were in common; none of them went beyond our little circle. The habit of living together, to the exclusion of the rest of the world, became so strong that if during the course of our meals, one of the three was absent, or a fourth came in, everything was upset, and in spite of our special bonds of attachment, our *tête-à-têtes* were not so sweet as our party of three.

The trio had merged as effectively as any loving couple, and it was cohesive to the point of disliking outsiders. Rousseau's error was to assume its uniqueness, but this was habitual from a man who supposed his *Confessions* would have no imitator.

Now that Jean-Jacques was her lover, Warens paid for dancing and fencing masters in a vain attempt to make him socially presentable. In spring 1734 Anet, on an expedition to the mountains to find a rare plant, contracted influenza and died. Rousseau's grief for his faithful friend equaled Warens's own. Yet he did something he would recall with shame: "The vile and unworthy thought came to my mind that I might inherit his used clothes, particularly a handsome black coat." When he spoke of it, Warens burst into bitter tears. But he would have to step into his older friend's shoes, not least of all sexually. No wonder Jean-Jacques desired, as a badge of seniority, a gentleman's black coat.

For the next four years Rousseau acted as Madame de Warens's exclusive manager and lover and failed on both counts. Lacking Anet's influence over madame, he couldn't keep her from running up debts. With her last sou, she bought him a little silver sword, fancy shoe buckles, and linen shirts. Rousseau, foreseeing the ruin of his home and happiness, left on several long walking tours that accomplished nothing but to vent the gypsy in his soul. In the spring of 1738, Rousseau returned from a trip to Geneva where he'd collected a small inheritance left by his mother, which he planned to give to his surrogate mamma. Thunderstruck, he found his idol had taken on a new steward and lover, Jean Winzenried.

He was a Swiss in his midtwenties, tall, flaxen-haired, strong, and boisterous, a former wigmaker who knew how to plow a field. In brief, the fellow was everything Rousseau disliked. "I saw all the happy future which I had depicted to myself vanish in a moment," he lamented in the *Confessions.* Warens informed him that things could go on as before, that he would lose none of his rights. But he would have to share her bed with another man.

Warens's attempt to reestablish her menage a trois, with Rousseau taking the part of instructor to the crude Winzenried, failed. Her debts were unmanageable, she was nearing forty and growing stout, and her choice of a rough-hewn hunk as lover showed even the idealizing Rousseau that she liked her sex brut. For two years he would retreat to an isolated cottage at Les Charmettes in order to bury his head in books, gaining for himself an education superior to that found in the academies, where the burning question was still "Is the world we inhabit a sphere?" Then the budding philosopher left for Paris, where his reputation would be made and his virtue endangered.

In Paris Rousseau again set up his dichotomy between the mother and the whore. In the capital women were dominant in cultural life through their salons. The patronage of a prominent lady was essential. Denis Diderot, the guiding spirit of the universal encyclopedia that young, passionate devotees of science and reason were compiling, made clear that both its ideas and style had been developed from conversing with the great ladies who were their patrons and lovers.

Rousseau had already written a play and an opera when in the spring of 1746 he started to frequent Madame Dupin's salon at the Hôtel Lambert. Although madame was faithful to Monsieur Dupin (a tax collector), their enormous wealth and intellectual pursuits compensated for this faux pas. In return for a meager salary and the Dupins' kind word to the director of the Paris Opera, Rousseau became ghostwriter on a pair of amateur tomes on economics and morals. The Dupins took credit for work that was Rousseau's, but they provided him with an indispensable place in society.

The "citizen of Geneva," as Rousseau began to sign writings that needed to be anonymous, remained a provincial, even a prig. He was appalled by the infidelities of the ladies whom he had to court. He wrote disapprovingly that "for most of the women, the lover was the trusted intimate attached to the house." Yet in 1744 he took for a mistress Thérèse Le Vasseur, a plain laundress, in an alliance that was to last the rest of his life. Twenty-three-year-old Thérèse, the most well-meaning of a gargantuan family, offered Rousseau a mirror image of the blind devotion he'd felt toward Madame de Warens. As he put it, "I wanted someone to live with her [Warens's] pupil, in whom I might find the simplicity and docility of heart she had found in me." Rousseau did finally marry Thérèse but only after surrendering each of their five newborns to the orphanage. As the philosopher grew older, his bladder stones worsened so that he was incapable sexually. George Sand heard from her grandmother, Madame Dupin's daughter-in-law, that Rousseau couldn't have children. Clearly, he was convinced that those birthed by Thérèse were fathered by other men.

Contemporaries were not abashed by an arrangement whereby Rousseau lived with and supported Thérèse's ravenous family but socialized with intellectuals and aristocrats. He admitted his mistress's shortcomings. "At first I tried to improve her mind," he wrote, "but my efforts were useless. Her mind is what Nature has made it; culture and teaching are without influence upon it." Rousseau noted she couldn't count or tell time, and he made her malapropisms famous by compiling them in a booklet for the amusement of his patrons. Rousseau's mistress kept house and cooked his meals. She provided him with a companion who was good-natured—in his terms, "natural."

Above all, his companion reminded him of the earth from which he had sprung. When one of the great ladies berated him for giving up the babies, he replied that he couldn't afford to keep them. In an accusing tone he continued, "Madame, nature wishes us to have children because the earth produces enough to feed everybody. It is the style of life of the rich, it is your style of life which robs my children of bread." This is the author who, in 1755, published *The Origin of the Inequality Among Mankind*, which is the first herald of the class struggle, and in 1762 *The Social Contract*, which denounced the divine right of monarchs and proclaimed the right of the people to overthrow a tyrannical government.

By the mid-1750s Rousseau had fought in pamphlet wars, listened to endless salon chatter, and known both triumph and despair. His opera had been a hit, and he had refused to attend an audience at court that would have meant a royal pension. As a member of the Five Bears—who included Baron Grimm (of fairy-tale renown) and the marquis de Saint-Lambert—he had danced attendance on Madame Louise d'Epinay, who held one of the most important salons and who would write a notable memoir. D'Epinay had married a rake, then taken as her official lover Francueil, Rousseau's patron. When she gave him the clap, acquired from her husband, Francueil left her. Grimm, for a time Rousseau's closest friend, fought a duel to defend d'Epinay's good name, and D'Epinay became Grimm's mistress. Rousseau assumed his favored role of confidant to d'Epinay. Flirty, artificial letters flew back and forth between them. When Rousseau, visiting d'Epinay's vast estate, admired a dilapidated lodge in the woods, she seized the opportunity to place in residence her own great man.

D'Epinay remodeled the hermitage into a charming cottage and in 1756 installed there her "dear bear," along with Thérèse and her backbiting mother, who had to be carried in by porters. As Rousseau summed up, "I have left behind me the world and its pomp." By now he was more like a middle-aged lion who though nursing his wounds, was dangerous enough for the state to consider deporting. In early spring, with the first buds on the trees, Rousseau underwent a rebirth. Long walks in the woods with his faithful dog, as well as gardening, revived his spirit sufficiently so that he denounced d'Epinay's lover, Grimm, and quarreled with Diderot about the rightness of withdrawing from society. Though he felt too old for love, he wished for a companion to whom he could open his heart.

Nearby in a modest house resided the Countess Sophie d'Houdetot, d'Epinay's sister-in-law. She too was unhappily married—to an unattractive Norman aristocrat. Her lover was the marquis de Saint-Lambert, the soldier-poet who had been the lover of Madame du Châtelet and with whom Rousseau had a strong mutual attraction. Saint-Lambert contributed to the Encyclopedia, and his pastoral poetry was highly regarded in his time. If his character lacked depth, his surface was exquisitely polished. The Seven Years' War (called the French and Indian in America) had commenced, and the colonel—Sophie got him the rank—joined his regiment on the German frontier. He wrote to her requesting that she visit Rousseau to cheer him and give him news.

Thérèse and her mother despised the country. So in midwinter 1757 Rousseau curled up alone with his cat to begin his famous novel of sentiment, *Julie, or The New Héloïse.* Sophie, whose carriage had stuck in the mud, arrived splattered but laughing, and she charmed the hermit. She was far from beautiful, as we can tell by Fragonard's portrait. Her complexion was lightly pitted by childhood smallpox. Her eyes were too round, and being short-sighted caused hesitation in her movements. But intelligence and refinement showed in her expression, neatly framed by long black tresses. She was witty and good. Rousseau found it praiseworthy that she sought him out to please Saint-Lambert. He was hopeful that "the friendship, which was beginning to be formed between us, would make this society agreeable to all three."

Sophie returned just as unexpectedly in April, mounted and dressed as a man. Rousseau, in the midst of a work that would inspire lovers for generations to come, was captivated. He soon paid back her visit, and they walked and botanized. Sophie spoke naively of her passion for Saint-Lambert, and Rousseau, trembling at the time, later wrote, "She inspired me with all those feelings for her which she had expressed for her lover." He thought himself absurd at forty-five to fall in love, especially with one whose heart was taken by another. But once more he gave in to the magnifying effect of a threesome, not least because the other man, polished and admirable, was everything he despaired of becoming.

Through the summer Rousseau left off writing about his ideal woman, Julie, for he had found her in human form. He saw Sophie as often as he dared, including, which was a grave error, at the château of Madame d'Epinay. With Grimm gone to war, d'Epinay expected Rousseau's attentions to fill the gap; instead, he mooned over her sister-in-law, of whom she was secretly jealous. Sophie, infatuated with Saint-Lambert, scarcely noticed the intrigue that was brewing. "She spoke of nothing with more pleasure than of the intimate and delicious society which could be formed of the three of us," recalled Rousseau.

Rousseau found no fault with Sophie's handling of his mad crush on her. She encouraged his transports without giving him hope of more, which in any case his aggravated bladder would have made difficult. Delighted to act like a schoolboy, he left love notes in romantic nooks. The pair were intimate, even passionate, holding hands, weeping together, embracing in the moonlight in Sophie's garden. But to the end Rousseau insisted, "She granted me nothing that could expose her to the charge of infidelity."

Scandal was another matter. D'Epinay spied on the soul mates and pumped Thérèse and her mother for information. Thérèse would never understand Rousseau's declaration that he loved Sophie too much to possess her. Thérèse, of an inferior social class, could not influence the main action. She nipped from the sidelines. D'Epinay wrote a poison-pen letter to Saint-Lambert, who soon arrived to evaluate the situation. He showed no anger toward the friend to whom he'd entrusted his mistress. He was a typical conquering man of the eighteenth century, cool and fastidious. Besides, he was in literary matters Rousseau's protégé. He was favorable to a menage of some sort, writing to his mentor, "I have a continual desire in my heart to gather together those whom I love and esteem most, and I have always made a charming picture to myself the way in which I would pass my life . . . together with her [Sophie] and you."

Saint-Lambert, ill from the camp, resigned from the army to live with his mistress. The three laid plans for an intimate companionship sufficient unto themselves and excluding outsiders. Yet these dreams of a utopian arrangement never materialized. According to Matthew Josephson, one of his biographers, Rousseau imagined himself "director of their souls; the triad would flourish; and the whole complex relationship would be perfectly calculated to stimulate him with all its nuances and mysteries of the human heart, which he could turn into literature." Sophie, frightened of losing Saint-Lambert, asked Rousseau for the return of her letters, admitting (to his horror) that she had burned his. Ever the gentleman, Saint-Lambert gently rebuffed the philosopher, who returned to the idealized world of fiction. Now, however, he had Sophie as a model for his heroine. He portrayed an angel.

The extreme emotion in which Rousseau had indulged, resulting in a disappointment entirely foreseeable, unhinged his suspicious mind. He abandoned the hermitage and broke definitively with his former friends: d'Epinay, Diderot, the entire Enlightenment. He turned to God, attacked Voltaire's deism, and even the theater. Everyone thought him mad. Living in a humble cottage outside Paris, in the years 1758 to 1762, Rousseau wrote his major works. None was more significant than *Julie*, which he finished in the winter of 1759. Even before publication, a buzz began among the literary set that swept the salons. *Julie* became the first international blockbuster. The originator of the Romantic novel, it is the story of a virtuous menage a trois, of young lovers who overcome temptation, and of a husband who conquers jealousy. Voltaire, who felt the novel was claptrap, quipped that they "live together all three . . . like good Swiss citizens."

Rousseau's pure menage could come to fruition only in fiction. Outwardly, at least, the citizen of Geneva had made peace with himself. Toward the end the philosopher returned to his Protestant faith. Driven into exile in Switzerland, he wrote the *Confessions,* the first true study of an inner life. In 1778 he died poor and ignored.

In both Rousseau's life and work the unit that looks to the new society, to a revolution in human nature, consists of three. That Rousseau was a visionary is undeniable. "Almost all the men, not only of the eighteenth century but of the beginning of the nineteenth were molded by Rousseau," writes André Maurois. "[He] taught Napoleon, perhaps Goethe, even Stendhal, how to love." His influence on women was no less profound. To quote a feminist scholar, Gita May, "some of the most independent-minded women who played a leading part in revolutionary politics and on the European literary stage—Mme de Staël . . . and George Sand come readily to mind—remained loyally steadfast disciples and admirers of Rousseau throughout their turbulent lives."

We have a coda courtesy of Chateaubriand, the writer who made popular the notion of "the noble savage." In 1800 he visited the home of Monsieur and Madame d'Houdetot, who had survived the revolution and the Terror. In the dining room between the old couple sat the former marquis de Saint-Lambert, eighty-three. After many adventures, the three had lived together amicably for the last ten years.

Saint-Lambert had achieved a measure of fame with his admired epic, *Two Friends: A Tale of the Iroquois,* which describes how two braves of the Six Nations, best friends, marry one young woman (Ermie) whom they both love. Of course she is a stand-in for Sophie, but was the author thinking of Rousseau and himself and the menage that never happened? The tale ends on a sentimental note: "The happy Ermie was always vigilant, sweet, attentive, laboriously a model of conjugal fidelity."

Although in 1775 Saint-Lambert was made an honorary citizen of New Haven, Connecticut, for his writings in favor of the cause of independence, he never visited America.

chapter 6

IN THE REALM
OF THE SENSES

{Casanova; The Marquis de Sade}

What is love if it is not a kind of curiosity?
CASANOVA

*C*ASANOVA AND THE MARQUIS DE SADE
—what contrasting images these two call up! However, each man was a product of the Age of Reason, and their lives curiously mirror each other's. The former specialized in menages of cooperation, the latter in compelling his victims. Casanova was born poor yet raised himself to be the envy of all men, making his name synonymous with "great lover." The other, scion of an aristocratic family, made of his name a byword for perversity. Yet both were realists who rejected mysticism in favor of the physical senses, amplified by imagination. Although their definitions of *Nature* diverged, each claimed to follow its tenets. Each, in need of an audience, expressed his sexuality in a threesome or in a larger group. Just as the exhibitionist depends on the voyeur and by definition pleasure can't exist without pain, so the chevalier and the marquis were linked by more than historical coincidence.

THE ORIGINAL CASANOVA
Giacomo Giovanni Casanova, better known as Jacques Casanova, the self-styled chevalier de Seingalt, entered the world stage at Venice in 1725. The

68

boy's mother (a cobbler's daughter turned actress), Zanetta Farussi, had married an actor, Gaetano Giacomo, who according to his son's fanciful genealogy was descended from an illustrious Spanish family. Probably, Gaetano was not his biological father. John Masters, one of several novelists attracted to Casanova, remarks that "at that time, 'stage' was almost synonymous with 'brothel.'" Jacques's mother, who didn't love him, "was barely distinguishable from a whore." His actual father was probably Michele Grimani, of a patrician family that owned the theater where the Casanovas played.

After Gaetano died in 1733, Zanetta's chances improved. She become the mistress of such theatrical figures as the playwright Goldoni, whose memoirs describe her as a pretty and talented widow. She had little time for mothering, and when her career took her to Germany, she left the boy with his grandmother. Once he began to study with a private tutor and later at the University of Padua, his intelligence became evident. The man would author, aside from his *Memoirs* (also know as *The History of My Life*), which run to twelve volumes, twenty-four works on everything from canon law to alchemy.

In the early nineteenth century, not long after Casanova's death, historians denied he had ever existed. This is because his autobiography, masterfully set against the background of the ancien régime, was first suppressed, then greeted with incredulity as a fairy tale. Written in French, the *Memoirs* appeared in German in 1822 in bowdlerized form; a subsequent French translation from the German added spurious episodes and altered the author's views. One moralist expressed his outrage that Casanova not only committed bad deeds but took pleasure in writing about them. Not until 1960 was an authentic version published in several languages. When we add to the censorship two hundred years of denigration by those with lesser abilities, literary or amorous, it is clear why Casanova's lifework remains undervalued.

The lad's first love was Venice, an aristocratic, decadent republic in which carnival lasted half the year. Rich and poor, monks and nuns, joined in. Wearing a mask permitted a bishop to couple with a fishmonger's daughter. It was out of this labyrinth of canals and intrigue that the youth grew to be a strapping six-footer with dramatic olive skin, a strong Roman nose, and bedroom eyes. He had long lashes, regular eyebrows, sensual lips, and a lively expression. Always on the prowl to discover what lay up the next skirt, he bragged, "To cultivate the pleasures of my senses was throughout my life my main preoccupation. I never had any more important objective." The Marquis de Sade could have made the same remark, except that his tastes were more bizarre and he failed in his attempts to satisfy them.

Scholars are divided on the amount of fabrication in Casanova's autobiography. Did he really make love to hundreds of women? Are the *Memoirs* a manual in seduction, the how-to of a rake's progress? Did he take to bed mothers and their daughters, including his own daughter? Arthur Symons, the nineteenth-century critic, anointed the *Memoirs* "the most valuable document which we possess of the society of the eighteenth century, more entertaining than *Gil Blas* or *Monte Cristo.*" The biographer Guy Endore added, "His remarkable tale is better than any picaresque novel ever written." Listen to what Casanova tells us: "Since I never aimed at a set goal, the only system I followed . . . was to let myself go wherever the wind which was blowing drove me." His wanderings were neither planned nor invented.

The *Memoirs* lack plot but abound in characters Casanova met and commented on: Voltaire, Rousseau, Benjamin Franklin, Catherine and Frederick the Greats, George III, two popes and several cardinals, and those two philosopher-charlatans Cagliostro and the Count of Saint-Germain. This is scarcely to mention innumerable men of some and no account and the most beautiful and sexy women of every country in Europe. But are the *Memoirs* a psychological narrative, the truthful presentation of a certain human type in its natural environment, as Havelock Ellis believed? In fact, Casanova's insight goes only so far, blocked by an avidity to excuse and deceive himself. "Go wherever your impulse leads you," he proclaimed. "Take whatever Fate offers, unless you feel a strong dislike for the gift." Sade, a hedonist of a different stamp, could have agreed to the word.

Casanova's early years passed unremarkably as he studied for the priesthood and fended off the advances of older girls. On returning to Venice in 1742, the youth of seventeen, although he had taken minor orders, surrendered his virginity—prophetically to two sisters. His superior, a priest who upbraided him for pomading his hair, had a niece, Angela. She made the young man's heart throb, not to mention a more sensitive part of his anatomy. One moment hot, the next cold, she led him on without yielding. Jacques wormed his way into the company of her two friends, orphaned sisters named Nanetta and Marta Savorgnan, who lived with a maiden aunt. One night, when Angela failed to show up at a rendezvous, the teenage sisters comforted the unhappy suitor. Jacques accepted their caresses, at first to punish Angela, but then, according to his account, he fell "invincibly in love with the two girls on the instant."

Casanova later denied he was an arch-seducer of women, claiming he must be himself seduced first. Falling in love so easily was vital to his success, for it enabled him to sincerely pursue the object of his desire. Though virgins, the sisters required few preliminaries. He fed them Cyprus wine to make them giddy, then convinced them to lie beside him naked in the dark. By his own recollection over fifty years later:

> I began with the one toward whom I was turned, not knowing whether it was Nanetta or Marta. I found her curled up and covered by her shift. I soon convinced her that her best course was to pretend to be asleep and let me go on. To crown my labors it was necessary that she should join in them openly and undeniably, and nature finally forced her to do so.

Casanova turned to perform the same service for the second sister. "I began by delighting her soul," he writes, "assuring myself that she was as untouched as her sister." His euphemism for cunnilingus is typical of the writer, as was his insistence that she frankly join in the lovemaking: "Throwing off the mask, she clasped me in her arms and pressed her mouth on mine." Afterward, the threesome swore eternal friendship before washing up, which so renewed their ardor that they "spent the rest of the night in ever varied skirmishes." Casanova boasted of his sexual readiness and endurance, which he liked to exhibit.

With Angela forgotten, the Savorgnan sisters awarded Jacques a key to their garret room. Undisturbed he visited his "angels" two nights a week. This success launched Casanova on a lifetime exploration of the female anatomy. Meanwhile, he transformed this spontaneous, innocent menage a trois into a guiding principle. Virgins and trollops fell for him. Sometimes he employed the domino theory on two friends, convinced that if one fell, the other would soon follow suit. Nor did he hesitate in his *Memoirs* to misrepresent the age of his conquests, who may have been mature women used to such romps. Initially Jacques was most successful when appealing to motherly instincts. But as he grew older and jaded, he needed younger women, girls really, often in tandem. François Roustang in his *Quadrille of Gender* decided, "If Casanova has neither a pair of sisters nor any doubt about gender, he cannot gain access to the woman." The great lover was an androgyne, able to exhibit masculine and feminine characteristics simultaneously. Above all he was an actor whose stage was a bed and whose audience consisted of a voyeur's eye.

The first affair with the sisters had a charming vivacity. The three were matched in age and experience, and Casanova recalled their love as being perfectly happy and unselfish. They thanked "eternal providence" for protecting their menage a trois. Nineteen-year-old Jacques was still expecting preferment from the church, and in 1744 he was obliged to tearfully leave Venice and his angel "wives" in search of a patron. On a journey to Rome he was precipitated into his second menage. The affair shows both his quickness of mind and member.

En route Jacques shared a coach with a pompous Neapolitan lawyer, his flirtatious wife, Lucrezia, and her much younger sister. (The names are pseudonyms—Casanova long after the facts had the delicacy not to embarrass either the living or their descendants.) That night the four also shared a room at an inn, the women sleeping in one bed in a kind of closet, and the men in another, typical of an age when privacy was rarely insisted on. During the night, fighting broke out between Spanish and Austrian troops garrisoned nearby, and the lawyer went to view the action. Jacques made a maneuver of a different sort, jumping into bed with the sisters, the elder of whom eagerly received him.

No sooner had Jacques clasped Lucrezia to him than the bed collapsed under the weight of three. Outside, shots and shouts filled the air, and inside the dark closet Casanova lunged again, getting under the nightie of the other sister, Angelica. Prudent Lucrezia insisted her overly ambitious lover leave them. Ten years Jacques's senior, she was quite willing to share her sister with him under more discreet circumstances. The British diplomat and Casanovist, J. Rives Childs, urbanely explains, "The relative frequency of incest, and the facility with which men and women went to bed together in the eighteenth century, are strongly suggestive that . . . sexual intercourse had hardly greater significance than the act of eating or drinking."

The more we read history, provided it is intimate in nature, the less we can accept any theory about an ineluctable genetic programming of sexual behavior. Equally unacceptable is the moral absolutism that has for so long attempted to rule those needs. When choosing to make love, the individual doesn't respond to a social or biological paradigm but rather to his or her mind—that is, to the images and expectations harbored therein—as the true stimulant and governor of passion. Casanova understood this precisely. His great secret of seduction is that he took pains to present himself in the most agreeable light. In England, he would turn aside the advances of a beautiful and famous courtesan because, not sharing a common language, they couldn't fully communicate while making love.

After this adventure, young Casanova found himself in Rome with no limit to his aspirations. He entered the employ of Cardinal Acquaviva, who, as the ambassador of Spain and governor of the Spanish Quarter, was nearly as powerful as the pope. Casanova's duties were light and the future promising; thus he had leisure to court Lucrezia. Unfortunately, Lucrezia could not escape from her husband's supervision long enough to consummate their love. Casanova perceived Lucrezia as already his and felt her husband ought to consider it a compliment. "I was amazed at the advocate," he reflected, "for he could not fail to know he owed me his wife." The lovers managed several quickies in arbors and carriages. Casanova seized any chance, insisting that "the lover who is not ready to take love by the forelock is lost." Rapid thrusts were easy since women in the eighteenth century wore no underwear.

Casanova made the most of an invitation to visit Tivoli in the company of Lucrezia's family. With her husband away on business, she shared a bed with the virginal Angelica. Her lover peered through the keyhole to observe the sisters undress. Lucrezia arranged for seventeen-year-old Angelica, nude but unwitting, to pass before her lover's view. She knew this would incite the young man to prodigious deeds. Once admitted, he tore off his clothes and rushed into her arms. They became "a single being at the same instant. . . . The raging fire which urged us on was scorching us; it would have burned us had we tried to restrain it." Casanova calls the act a "sacred service" done "devoutly and in the most religious silence."

Voyeurism and the transformation of sacred imagery to sensual are two keys to Casanova's lovemaking and writing, and again these could be shared, at least in theory, with the Marquis de Sade. But for the son of Venetian actors, who had taken all Europe as his stage, performance was paramount. He needed a witness to his proficiency, a third. Casanova's show was one in which the audience eventually participated. However, Angelica would have to be content to watch, since the pair continued their embraces till dawn.

With the early light, Lucrezia invited her curled-up sister into the act: "Turn and see what awaits you when love makes you his slave." The girl, who hadn't slept a wink, happily embraced first her sister and then Casanova. Lucrezia enjoyed the spectacle of her sister in her lover's arms. But Casanova once again entered Lucrezia while Angelica looked on—and he reveled in watching her watch him! Next Lucrezia transferred her vigorous lover to her sister. Angelica threw her arms round him in orgasmic delight. He pressed on, deflowering the girl. While Lucrezia wiped the sweat from his brow, he brought Angelica to several climaxes.

Concerning the great lover's performance—numerous orgasms on his and the women's parts as well as a seven-hour stint with Lucrezia—we have only his account. But he had discovered one of the advantages of a menage: it encourages the ardor of the participants and, in the man's case, keeps him hard and coming much longer. Casanova milked the voyeuristic element for all it was worth. In his impotent old age, he sighed over the "happy moments for which I hope no longer, but whose precious memory death alone can take from me!" Even death has been transcended by the immortality of the *Memoirs*.

Casanova was often his own worst enemy, particularly in his need to act the gentleman to compensate for his questionable birth. In Rome, with everything in his favor, he befriended a lady in distress (not a lover) and ruined his chances at advancement in the church, the only respectable career open to him. The details are unimportant, save that here he first ran afoul of the police. Cardinal Acquaviva, an old rake, admired his protégé's chivalry but needed a sacrifice to mollify the papal authority. Casanova, in his twenties, was banished from Rome; after a sojourn at Constantinople he returned to Venice in 1746. There he earned a meager living as a violin player (and teacher) at the theater owned by the Grimanis, his refuge of last resort. Interestingly, his contemporary and fellow Venetian, Vivaldi, had taught the violin at the only orphanage where young women studied music. Their virtuosity had become the talk of Europe, while the composer's menage a trois with a pupil and her sister had caused a scandal that forced him to leave for Rome.

Casanova's luck again flip-flopped when he happened to save the life of an elderly gentleman who turned out to be the rich and powerful Senator Bragadin, a supposedly reformed man about town who adopted him. Casanova had found an understanding patron willing to indulge most of his whims. The young man dressed and spent extravagantly, gambled foolishly, and liked lots of highly spiced food, which made no dent in his iron digestion. He preferred his women pungent too: "I have always found that the one I was in love with smelled good, and the more copious her sweat, the sweeter I found it."

Novelist John Masters has elucidated a pattern whereby Casanova "sees a girl, A, in some sort of difficulty, often with her lover, B. He gets her out of the difficulty and in the process falls madly in love. . . . After a period of violent sexual athletics Casanova discovers that he is unworthy of her, and arranges for her to marry, or be taken over by a more suitable man." Casanova rarely left a woman in the lurch, less out of a sense of honor than professionalism. By passing on an old favorite to another man, he asserted both his camaraderie and superiority in the game of lovemaking.

In certain company, he was content to fill the role of the agreeable third, offering what the other man lacked. The keen observer noticed that many well-placed men didn't know how to entertain their mistresses. Casanova thus joined couples for supper; he talked, joked, and ate heartily to become the center of attention. In a more gruesome scene, Casanova once became a voyeur as the British ambassador, Sir John Murray, pleasured his dying mistress, an aging courtesan. Casanova watched the woman, her face half-devoured by cancer, moan in delight. The amorous Italian dispassionately recorded the event.

But according to Masters, Casanova went beyond being an agreeable third party employed by aristocrats. He had a direct involvement with men: "he, the universal bull, was also, and perhaps by preference, a fairy." Masters cites notes found among Casanova's papers indicating homosexual affairs omitted from his autobiography. These cast a different light on such matters as the patrician Bragadin's "adoption" of the young scamp; probably he was keeping him for his favors. The senator's warning to his protégé to seduce only women of the upper class and thus avoid venereal disease assumes a more urgent tone. Masters sums up, "The revelation, or acknowledgment of sexual bipolarity makes Casanova a difficult, complex and constantly varying figure, [who] changed from situation to situation, from person to person." An appropriate term for the chevalier would be polyamorous: he took what came along, never mind the gender, age, or condition. Violating sexual taboos excited him.

In 1753 the prodigal returned to Venice, to the joy of his adopted father, Bragadin. Soon he was entangled in a serious love affair with a fifteen-year-old virgin—known to the *Memoirs* as CC—whom he wished to marry. While Bragadin negotiated with CC's father, Casanova took her maidenhead. He was stunned when the father refused his offer and placed his daughter in a convent at Murano. Casanova's reputation had already grown unsavory. Still, he demonstrated his honorable intentions by visiting CC once a week for some months. They plotted her escape, complicated by her having become pregnant.

The convents of Venice, like its other institutions, were run for the convenience of the wealthy, and often the women living there had no religious vocation. However, Casanova was surprised when one day he received a mysterious letter from a nun, known only as MM. He guessed that she was CC's roommate, high-born, twenty-two years of age but sufficiently capable that she'd managed to conceal CC's miscarriage from the abbess. They met and conversed with the customary railing in between. He was delighted by MM's tall, pale, blue-eyed beauty and her keen intelligence. Brainy women stimulated his libido. He agreed to meet her at a private casino nearby belonging to her allegedly broad-minded lover.

Casanova decided he was dying for lack of love. CC would want him to live, he rationalized. Besides, he delighted in tasting forbidden fruit. By the elegant furnishings of the casino and the food and champagne provided, he deduced that MM's lover was French. Because an intrigue with a nun required constant bribes, this lover must possess a limitless source of income. In fact, Casanova soon realized that he was rival to the French ambassador, Pierre de Bernis. The evening took a strange turn. MM, though stripped, held him off, always shifting her position. It became clear that someone was watching them from a concealed place.

Casanova became intrigued by the idea of a threesome. Fortunately he'd hit a winning streak at faro. He rented and furnished his own luxurious casino. All the rooms held erotic touches, such as tiles showing the postures described by the poet Aretino in an infamous Renaissance book of pornography. The pièce de résistance was the octagonal trysting room covered by mirrors so that one might view oneself and partner from various angles simultaneously.

MM's charms overwhelmed him. He described her as "the most beautiful of all the sultanas of the Master of the Universe." He arrived early at the meeting place. Her gondola arrived an hour later. When she'd finally entered the casino and was examining its details, the impatient seducer admired "in her clothing what kind of man the lover who possessed her must be." The third was never far from his mind.

Casanova rummaged through MM's pockets and lingered over her jewelry, admiring even her makeup. He was always vigorous yet sensitive to what was subtly conveyed by items of fashion. Casanova's androgyny went beyond "bisexuality" as commonly understood: his male and female sides worked in tandem rather than alternately or in conflict. When he learned that MM's lover actually brought her to the tryst, he was speechless with joy. By coupling with the mistresses of men of power and wealth, he shared their attributes—indeed, outperformed them. Herein lay a vital source of the pleasure the great lover derived from his conquests.

The evening began with a discussion of Bernis's many merits. However, though the ambassador had a ready wit, he inspired MM with gratitude rather than love. When, after supper, Casanova and his nun adjourned to the room of mirrors, passion swept them away for seven hours. They also indulged in the "most feeling talk." More than athletics, Casanova was turned on by his beloved's ecstasy, by the dissolution of all constraint. Once intimacy had been established, MM nervously confessed that their initial encounter had been witnessed by Bernis, hidden in a closet. It had been arranged as a test, which Casanova had passed with flying colors. MM described their more recent encounter to her lover, and he again wished to man the peephole.

Casanova was flattered. "I consider him [Bernis] my friend too, and I love him," he assured MM. He then explained his views on voyeurism. A third, rather than distract him, would permit him to share his pleasure. His only concern was that Bernis, driven frantic, might abandon the role of voyeur and claim MM. Here he was betraying his own need to take center stage. Bernis valued the stimulation provided by watching two beautiful young people copulate, but as a man of wealth and power he had nothing to prove. For Casanova, a threesome with Bernis slacked the pain, if temporarily, of being forever on the outside looking in.

For a week, until the next meeting, Casanova remained celibate. On the appointed evening he consumed six egg whites and took great care with his toilette. At supper, he and MM played at one of his favorite games, sucking oysters from each other's mouth, the sauce being saliva. At midnight MM showed him to a sofa placed in full view of the concealed voyeur. Knowing he was observed made Casanova more conscious of his form. He wrapped a bandanna about his head, which he fancied gave him the look of a sultan in his seraglio. He stripped himself and his "sultana" naked, carefully posing her: "A pillow which I had fitted under her buttocks and one of her knees bent away from the back of the sofa must have afforded a most voluptuous vision for our hidden friend."

Inspired by Aretino's erotica, the lovers entwined in a variety of sexual postures: "the classic," standing, sitting, prone on the Persian carpet, but always within view of the witness. After the fourth bout, MM lay with her eyes closed, looking like a corpse except for the visible beating of her heart. Casanova showed no mercy, but, putting her in the position known as "the straight tree," he "lifted her up to devour her chamber of love." Next they reversed the tree, MM sucking on Casanova's "weapon." But when he came the last time, after making love for seven hours, it was with drops of blood, which terrified her. He made a jest of it, explaining it was "the yolk of the last egg, which is often red."

In 1754 Casanova appeared to be at the top of his form. Two stunning nuns were begging him to violate them, and the ambassador of France, who soon fully revealed himself, encouraged and protected this blasphemy. Bernis was willing, should MM become pregnant, to regard the child as his own. Nor was the youthful CC put out, since MM had initiated her into lesbian love. "I am often her wife or her fond husband,"

CC confessed, and added that she disdained jealousy and was glad he loved them both. Casanova, the focus of two intersecting menages—one involving CC, MM, and himself, the other with MM and Bernis—made the most of the feast. "I have always held that there is no merit in being faithful to a person one truly loves," he wrote in all sincerity.

Another wild moment in the menage occurred when Casanova joined MM and CC in a bed built for three. He watched the "two tigresses" caress each other's bare breasts and demonstrate postures for his benefit, but when he tried to join in, MM threw him onto CC. After taking her, he turned back to MM while CC acted as witness. Finally, he recalled, "all three of us, intoxicated by desire, played havoc with everything visible and palpable which Nature had bestowed on us, freely devouring whatever we saw and finding that we had all become of the same sex in the trios which we performed." Thus the menage culminated in an androgynous cohesion likened to animals in the wild. It was at once decadent and savage, a complex state that the Marquis de Sade could achieve only in fantasy.

Casanova proved his sophistication when he allowed Bernis to make love to CC. Although beholden to the ambassador, he genuinely admired Bernis. The men were united by intimate "mysteries." Both MM and CC wrote to Casanova about their joint night with Bernis, but they made clear that the older man in no way approached him in fortitude or technique. All participants regretted that he had not been on hand to observe them.

One night the menage did become a quadrille. Casanova, CC, MM, and Bernis shared a sumptuous dinner before adjourning as couples to separate beds—but this evening was a sort of summing up. Bernis had been called to Vienna. Although he assured MM that he left her in Casanova's hands, he warned his friend to end his dangerous, costly affair with the nuns. Indeed, Casanova had gambled away a small fortune. With the casinos a memory, his affair with MM dwindled into the next year. Casanova, turned thirty, found his youth and hopes behind him. He was shortly to become a fugitive and at last a pariah.

Joseph LeGras, a French biographer, states, "Far above all, the beautiful nun of Murano, the incomparable MM . . . takes first place in the long list of Casanova's amours. . . . None of his conquests gave him as much satisfaction as this one." From here on the great lover's affairs grew sleazy and his business dealings more crooked. He stopped practicing safe sex—yes, there were condoms in Casanova's day—and consequently he became prey to syphilis and gonorrhea. Doctors treated both conditions with ingestions of mercury, which did little other than destroying the intestines and kidneys. Wisely, by treating himself with herbs, fasting, and abstinence, Casanova came through several bouts of venereal disease.

In 1755 the state inquisitors of Venice, regarding Casanova as generally undesirable, arrested and incarcerated him in the Leads, a prison under the roof of the Doge's Palace from which no one had ever escaped. Just before, Abbe Chiari, an important playwright who was after Casanova's scalp, satirized him in a roman à clef:

> Personally his appearance is as meticulous in every detail as that of Narcissus. He cocks himself up, he puffs himself out like a balloon, he is forever on the go like a wind-mill. His desire is to show himself everywhere, to flirt with all the women ... to discover new ways of acquiring money or hearts. He is everything to everybody, while in the eyes of intelligent people he only manages to make a fool of himself. In one single day he may be your greatest friend and your most mortal enemy. [But] he is really no one's friend.

Casanova came to agree with his critics that he had wasted his life. To verify his existence, he kept hold of the gushing letters he'd received from his lovers. One day these would enable him to write a history of his life, the first true confession.

Casanova's break from the Leads prison was a masterpiece of daring and tenacity. Despite close surveillance, he and another prisoner, using a primitive tool, escaped not only from the prison but from the ensuing manhunt. However, the fugitive Casanova would find himself under suspicion wherever he went, and so difficult was the exile's life that his companion gave himself up. Our hero went on to investigate the mysteries of anatomy for another four decades.

However, Casanova had lost the measure of grace that made an art form of philandering. From Paris to Madrid to London to Moscow, he played out a similar hand. It was as though he always attended the same play with a new title. Ostensibly, the chevalier's business was the promotion of a state lottery to cash-starved monarchs. This philosopher's stone of finance was supposed to produce the magical result of more revenue and less taxes. It's a sucker's game currently being embraced by many American states. Casanova, despite his old-world frills, had a cold, modern eye for politics. Of course, the chevalier's real purpose was seduction—of practically anything that moved. Yet his old readiness was disappearing, and he came to rely on the menage with ever kinkier twists.

In 1758 Casanova found himself in a coach near Paris with a beautiful young woman and her aristocratic lover. The girl, whom he fancied, perched on both men's thighs. Casanova claimed the jostling coach deluded him into supposing he caressed the female, while his hand actually fondled the male's organ. Coming, the grateful recipient thanked Casanova, saying, "I am obliged to you, my dear friend, for a piece of your country's politeness." Casanova passed off the incident as a blunder.

In 1761 he visited Naples to enjoy the hospitality of the impotent duke of Matalona, who kept a beautiful young mistress for the sake of appearances. The duke, to prove his relations with Leonilda were platonic, dared Casanova to a contest. Both perused Chinese pornographic scenes that decorated a salon, while the girl looked on. The elderly duke showed his flaccid member and checked whether his guest's stood erect. Finding Casanova equally dormant, he gloated.

Casanova, challenged, stared into Leonilda's eyes while pressing her hand to his lips. As she blushed, Matalona masturbated him until he soaked the ducal hand. "It was one of those delicious little games which so effectually stimulate Love," Casanova reflected. There are a sufficient number of such incidents in his *Memoirs* to send the message that the great lover of women was also a male hustler. *Gigolo* is a more polite term, but basically he made his living by selling his favors.

Casanova became almost an adopted son to the duke, who encouraged him to marry Leonilda. An interview with her widowed mother seemed a formality. But when the mother saw Casanova, she fainted. Speechless, he looked on his early flame Donna Lucrezia—she of the collapsing bed—whose deceased husband had regarded Casanova's offspring as his own. Tears and breast-beatings ended once the duke suggested that although Casanova couldn't marry his own daughter Leonilda, he might renew his former affair with her still-beautiful mother. This compromise Italian-style suited him. Here was an excuse for the family to sleep three in a bed.

Reviving an old love was a specialty of the chevalier, which he would carry to its logical conclusion in his *Memoirs*. In Naples, always favorable to him, mutual recollection led to boundless desire, especially when the present encompassed both the past (Lucrezia) and the future (Leonilda). Casanova spent the night of his dreams with both mother and daughter, all three naked. He admired his daughter's body as his handiwork. Leonilda, a virgin, observed her parents in the act of love, commenting that was how she herself had been made eighteen years earlier. As

Casanova withdrew to avoid Donna Lucrezia's becoming pregnant, Leonilda "sends her mother's little soul on its flight with one hand and with the other puts a white handkerchief under her gushing father."

The lovemaking continued till dawn and beyond. Casanova was spurred to repeated endeavors by the sight of his daughter's beauty and by kissing her all over, though at the last moment she slipped away and turned him over to her mother, who ordered him to make another Leonilda. The duke arrived afterward to hear from his pro forma mistress a blow-by-blow account of the night's work. After agreeing to provide Leonilda with a handsome dowry, Matalona gave Casanova a grand farewell dinner at which he was admired by all the Neapolitan nobility.

Why did Casanova leave this city where he was happy and could have lived in comfort? Perhaps he was more fearful of transgressing with his daughter than he admitted even to himself.

Casanova had farther to descend: from promoter to con man, from hanger-on at court to paid spy. In 1763, after swindling twenty thousand pounds out of a dotty old lady, the marquise d'Urfe, he arrived in London and gambled away all the money. He did just as badly with romance. Self-doubt and self-loathing, absent in the past, caused him to attempt suicide—circumvented because a friend caught him about to jump off Westminster Bridge. Next year Casanova fled England; he was ill, poor, and discouraged.

At forty, the great lover felt old. "There were times I found the pleasures of love less intense, less seductive. . . . I no longer interested the fair sex at first sight, I had to talk, rivals were preferred to me, I was made to feel that it was already a favor if I was secretly allowed to share with another man." He wore outrageous outfits of rose velvet embroidered with gold spangles, many rings, his skin artificially whitened, his hair stinking of pomade. Increasingly he turned to pubescent girls in a kind of incestuous withdrawal from the world.

In Salerno he again found Donna Lucrezia and Leonilda, the latter married to an impotent seventy-year-old nobleman. If she failed to have children, her husband's family estate would be forfeit to mercenary relatives. Donna Lucrezia, needing expert assistance, arranged matters so that father and daughter were left alone in a romantic setting. "My daughter called me 'husband,'" reflected Casanova, "even as I called her 'wife.'" He couldn't help but shudder when he heard that a son had been born from this illicit passion. Years later he met the young man, but although he was delighted by the lad's looks and charm, he turned down Leonilda's hospitality and continued his lonely wanderings.

Like the Marquis de Sade, Casanova was finally compelled to drink the dregs. In 1771 in Frascati he encountered another former mistress, now the mother of Guglielmina, a precocious ten-year-old, also his handiwork. Her mother and adoptive father welcomed Casanova into the family, introducing him to thirteen-year-old Giacomina, the natural daughter of his brother. Casanova developed an obsession for his niece. His former mistress, though aware that he had designs on the girls, let the big bad wolf view them. Asleep, they touched their private parts. Casanova rhapsodized, "It was the only moment in my life when I knew for a certainty the true temper of my soul, and I was satisfied with it. I felt a delicious horror."

We will leave Casanova at this archetypal moment. He will carry his diary forward only a few more years until 1775, even though he will live until 1798. In his last lonely years he acted as librarian to Count Waldstein at his castle in Dux, Bohemia, ridiculed by those he considered barbarians. He had long since substituted the pen for the prick, and he spent his waning hours in a final massive act of voyeurism, the vicarious reliving of those many nights of love. While his imitators were and are legion, they cannot compare in deeds and still less in the wit necessary to make of these the greatest of confessions.

THE ORIGINAL SADIST

At the library of a prestigious New England college near where we summer, the twelve-volume English translation of Casanova's *Memoirs* gathers dust. We were the first to check out the volumes since 1974, the year before the student aide who stamped them was born. In contrast, the grotesque daydreams of the Marquis de Sade do a brisk business among the student body. A recent biography of Sade sold to a Hollywood producer for a seven-figure sum, while the last full-length film treatment of Casanova's life, by Federico Fellini in 1976, was a triumph of image over content. When Donald Sutherland, who played Casanova, asked the director how he viewed the man Italians are supposed to emulate, Fellini replied, "He's a piece of shit."

We have entered a period favorable to Sade, an alleged connoisseur of pain, and critical of Casanova, who sought pleasure. Despite the raw wish-fulfillment quality of the marquis's writings and despite his reveling in the gratuitous torture and dismemberment of women, certain of his apologists are women. The trend was begun by Simone de Beauvoir's *Must We Burn Sade?*, which claimed the marquis wasn't a run-of-the-mill sadist but a literary one who "chose the imaginary." Feminist scholars point out that in works such as *L'Histoire de Juliette*, the female protagonist wreaks as much havoc as her male mentor. In any case, this line continues, Sade's "unorthodox sexual practices" stemmed from a "patriotic intention" triggered by his concern over France's excess population. Presumably he wished to remedy the situation by tossing a few more infants onto the fire.

Edmund Wilson, writing in the 1960s, remarked that his subject had become so popular he was referred to in Paris as the marquis de Fade. Wilson aptly characterizes Sade's works as "unique and most uncomfortable productions, which alternate between descriptions of orgies on an impossible multiple scale, which may horrify the reader at first but which soon become routine and ridiculous, and vehement disquisitions ... intended to justify them." The critic admits Sade's writings are simultaneously repulsive and dull, and his "impulse to cruelty ... was a lifelong obsession that gets in the way of his success as both a literary artist and a thinker." The marquis's importance, he thinks, is that he expresses human malignancy at a time when murder, rape, and torture have achieved official sanction in much of the world. Wilson's judgment is reinforced by the subsequent horrors of Cambodia, Bosnia, and Central Africa, which lend to Sade the mantle of prophet.

However, we are concerned with the sex life of the "divine marquis" and in particular with his liking for the menage. Sade, a slight, foppish, blue-eyed young man neither handsome nor brave, generally had to pay for sex. Since what he wanted was out of the ordinary, he could rarely afford more than one or two prostitutes. Before the madams barred him from their houses, his favorite demand was to combine active and passive sodomy: he would bugger a whore while his valet, Latour, buggered him. There is no sex act of which he speaks so often and with so much satisfaction and even vehemence. He liked to watch while his valet, called "the marquis," buggered a prostitute, or he would settle for fondling or even whipping her while his valet buggered him. Sade, who married and fathered three children (or did he?), felt "a deep disgust for women's 'fronts.'"

Sade is bisexual in the crudest sense. He wants to get between a man and a woman in a position that must resemble the fetal. Like Casanova, Sade had callous parents who had no interest in him, indeed who denigrated him. He was an emotional orphan, and his feelings never matured beyond seeking the primitive gratification of giving and receiving pain. Even the corrupt ancien régime forbade his pleasures. The police, spurred on by his domineering mother-in-law, locked him in prison for ten years. The revolution, though it freed Sade from the Bastille, treated him no better, and before he died in the madhouse of Charenton he had spent half of his adult life behind bars. The deeds we associate with the marquis were performed mainly in his mind—he had no ability to carry them out. His favorite fantasy involved being penetrated and beaten while he himself was penetrating and beating a submissive victim.

Sade is the meat in the sandwich. He apparently idolized his father and detested his mother, but to a worshiper of power that was a safe stance. He abused his name and wasted his estates until even the prostitutes spat on him. Sade couldn't kidnap and torture a beggar without her escaping and putting the police onto him. The cataclysmic events of his time—revolution, the Terror, the Napoleonic empire—ground the demented marquis into hamburger. Confinement came to be his natural habitat. When he was temporarily free in 1800, he wrote a pamphlet attacking First Consul Napoleon Bonaparte and even Josephine. Predictably, Sade spent the rest of his days confined at Charenton where he ate himself into grotesque corpulence and masturbated anally with specially fashioned wooden "boxes."

Sade's writings present the triangulator who manipulates others around himself, but these manipulations are described in a manner that resembles a black mass. The writer hates the church but is possessed by its definition of evil. He will go to his grave, which he wished effaced, a lapsed Catholic. Strangely, he demonstrated a husband's conventional jealousy over his wife, yet he understood that jealousy both "subordinates" and "unites" all other passions. Sade's fictional characters subvert jealousy by merging it into a greater unit, the ritualistic orgy. There is, as Camille Paglia points out, a Busby Berkeley quality to Sade's depiction of a conga line of "a hundred nuns linked by dildos"! The reader instinctively understands that Sade would rather fantasize than act, view than do. In life, rather like his admirers, he was a paper fascist.

Sade involved himself in one actual menage a trois with his wife, Renée, and her younger, prettier sister, Anne. In 1771, after Renée gave birth to their third child, he installed Anne, a canoness on leave from her convent, in a wing of his château in the south where he was on probation. Anne, her mother's favorite, was more inquisitive than her dutiful sister, but she knew nothing of sex other than what Sade taught her. Here he committed incest with the complicity of both sisters, who combined against their fearsome mother to deceive her. They performed together in the marquis's lost plays, playing his heroines who acquiesce in the acts perpetrated against them.

Predictably, Sade grew bored. An episode in Marseilles with Latour and several prostitutes in which he poisoned the girls caused the issuance of an order for his arrest. He fled back to Renée. She helped him get away to Savoy with Anne. A trio makes a good gang, but it must be based on relations more durable than tyrant and victim. Sade's mother-in-law found him out, had him arrested, and sent Anne back to the convent. From then on, with occasional time out, the marquis would be locked up with pen, paper, and dildos.

The problem with Sade is his failure to understand the appropriate use of pain, which is to contrast with pleasure. Casanova put it expertly: "Happy moments have always made up to me for unhappy ones, and to such a degree that they made me love their cause. It is impossible to relish to the full a pleasure which has not been preceded by pain, and pleasure is great in proportion to the pain suffered."

Both these figures, who gave their names to their predilections, practiced amour as they saw it toward the end of the eighteenth century. Yet the gulf between them is as wide as the distinction between a menage and a triangle. Casanova was caught in the dream of ever new and abundant love, while the Marquis de Sade perished in the nightmare of cruelty that never ends short of self-destruction.

chapter 7

THAT HAMILTON WOMAN

{Admiral Horatio Nelson, Emma Hamilton, and Sir William Hamilton}

My love is no common love . . . it is a Crime worth going to Hell for.
LADY EMMA HAMILTON

*Y*OU MAY HAVE SEEN, ON LATE-NIGHT cable channels, the movie *That Hamilton Woman*, which was shot in 1941 during the early days of World War II. Alexander Korda produced and directed it; he was a refugee from Hungary who had first fled to England, where he was naturalized, then to Hollywood. The parallels between Britain's courageous resistance to Hitler's Luftwaffe and Admiral Lord Nelson's defeat of Napoleon's navy are striking, and Korda never did his adopted country a better service than by recounting Nelson's love affair with Lady Emma Hamilton and the sacrifice of his life in the fight against tyranny. Curiously, Winston Churchill's favorite movie, which helped put America in a warlike mood, focused on the betrayal of Emma by the country that Nelson had saved.

The movie opens on a foggy night near the docks of Calais after the Napoleonic Wars. An aging, besotted Emma (Vivien Leigh) is caught stealing a bottle of wine. When the gendarmes arrest her, the harlots come to her rescue, and after a tussle they are all thrown into jail. Emma tells how she was once beautiful and beloved of heroic Nelson (Laurence Olivier), who as he lay dying at the Battle of Trafalgar implored his coun-

86

try to care for her. Instead, an embarrassment, she was sent into poverty-stricken exile. The whores, who think she is one of their own, smile knowingly as she talks on.

The scenario strays from the facts but captures their spirit. The neglect of Emma Hamilton and of Horatia, her daughter by Nelson, was even more shameful than the movie portrayed. The hero was snubbed by King George III while he lived. After the admiral's death, Emma fell victim to the venality of his relatives, who were rewarded handsomely, and to the hypocrisy of the ruling class. They took their cue from "Farmer George," a heavy-handed monarch whose portrait was painted indelibly by Thomas Jefferson in the Declaration of Independence. This dour, unimaginative ruler, more dangerous during his fits of sanity than when mad, was a devoted family man who cost Britain her American empire. Meanwhile, the foundation of Britain's Second Empire, in Africa and the Middle and Far East, was laid by a parson's son, a blacksmith's daughter, and an aristocratic connoisseur who formed a notorious menage a trois.

Recently we have seen the publication of a biography of Emma by Flora Fraser, one of Nelson by Christopher Hibbert, and, most interesting, Susan Sontag's *The Volcano Lover*, a novel written from the point of view of Emma's husband, Sir William Hamilton. Each of these attempts is meticulous both in research and craft but slanted toward the evocation of a single subject. Even Sontag's sally into imaginative history remains "a kind of triptych, divided among Hamilton, his wife and Lord Nelson." The *New York Times*'s reviewer could find nothing more intimate to unite the three lovers than a patriotic devotion to England.

However, without an understanding of the very non-English tradition of the *cavaliere servente*, the escort of a married woman, there is a vital piece in the puzzle missing. This institutionalizing of the menage a trois, which looks back toward courtly love and the paeans of Petrarch to his lady, as well as forward to the place of the bodyguard in modern pop culture, permitted the alliance of the Hamiltons with Nelson to take root and bloom at the court of Naples, which ruled southern Italy. It provided cover for behavior that Nelson's peers thought indiscreet and ruinous to his career.

Alas, this peculiar custom traveled no better than the ancient vases that arrived smashed when Sir William attempted to ship them home. Contemporary attempts by the British to comprehend the functions of the *cavaliere servente* foundered in half-truths. Lady Knight, a member of Dr. Samuel Johnson's circle, declared, "Some of these connections were undoubtedly innocent, but all are indelicate." James Boswell, Johnson's biographer, who was carrying on with a certain Signora B., needed to get round her two *cavalieri*. He described the species as "a lover without love . . . a being who is more a drudge than is a *valet de chambre*, who does continual duty, and enjoys only appearances!" The British, by contrast, liked to keep their affairs actual but secret.

A *cavaliere servente* appeared on the scene after a married woman had given her husband a male heir. He might or might not become her lover, but he must in any case execute her every desire and whim. He accompanied his lady to the opera, balls, gambling dens, handed her a fan, folded her scarf, produced any dainty her heart might desire. In the morning he assisted at his lady's toilette, provided the latest gossip, and helped her dress. In the absence of her husband, the *cavaliere* must protect his lady from insults or robbery. Nor could he neglect the husband but rather must court his favor through his amiability. The threesome was a unit as familiar to Italian society as the married couple (and the closet lover) was to the English.

EMMA'S ATTITUDES

In 1793 the Hamiltons first met Nelson briefly. He was thirty-five, married, and a captain already known for his bravery. He was not quite as tall as Emma and a good deal shorter than the elongated, beak-nosed Sir William. His figure was compact, his complexion fresh, his features strongly marked but regular. Nelson had already adopted a pensive if not melancholy air, and some thought him homely. Not the perceptive Sir William, to whom Sontag gives the line: "Mark him. . . . He will be the bravest hero England has ever produced."

In 1758 Horatio Nelson was born into an East Anglian family partial to clergymen. The boy, on the sober side, early envisioned a career at sea. Frail but determined, Nelson did duty in the West Indies during the American Revolution, and the president of Nevis described the captain as "that great little man of whom everybody is so afraid." In 1787 Nelson married Frances Nisbet, a demure widow with one unlikable son, Josiah. In the way of sailors, he had romances in foreign ports, all the while dutifully writing to his stay-at-home wife. Nelson had a sense of destiny that caused him to seem vain, as though he were posing for a statue on a pedestal atop a column in a public square. He was a martinet to the extent of hanging sailors who demanded improvements in their conditions. Ironically, he didn't hesitate to disregard his own orders in the heat of battle. Truly, before he met the Hamiltons, Nelson's mistress was Bellona, the Roman goddess of war.

The connoisseur Sir William was a fine judge of art, music, men, and women. It was his earlier collecting of Emma Hart that led to his close association with Nelson. She was a blacksmith's daughter from an impoverished village in Cheshire who, at sixteen, had fallen into prostitution in London and was rescued by Charles Greville, the disinherited son of an earl and favorite nephew to Sir William. From 1782 Greville kept Emma and began the illiterate young lady's education. In August 1783 his uncle, fifty-three, arrived in London on leave from his post as ambassador to the kingdom of Naples. The first Lady Hamilton had just died, and the loneliness of Sir William, distinguished but aloof, was mitigated by the charm of his nephew's mistress.

What was so special about Emma? First, she was by classical standards beautiful. The painter George Romney accomplished dozens of portraits of her, including Emma as Nature, a bacchante, a saint, and Circe. In Flora Fraser's description, the young woman's "huge, violet eyes were dominant under long, heavily marked eyebrows in a short oval face. Her nose was long ... but sat delicately enough above an exquisitely indented upper lip." Meanwhile, aside from her kissable mouth, "her flawless complexion induced thoughts of marble in those who preferred statuary to life."

Emma's beauty was voluptuous. Her body in those early years was statuesque yet round, very attractive as a subject to Romney, whose god was Raphael. Indeed, Emma married the litheness of figures on the Greek vases that Sir William collected to a warm, motherly quality that attracted the boyish heart of Nelson. In 1785, nephew Charles, sunk in debt and desperate to please his uncle whose fortune he hoped to inherit, offered to make Sir William a gift of Emma. He didn't wish to part with her, he wrote, but he'd noticed his uncle's attraction. He assured the older man that Emma was good-natured, not a flirt, and had "good natural sense and quick observation." To close the deal, he added that "a cleaner, sweeter bedfellow does not exist."

Sir William, from his ambassador's post at Naples, hesitated. He was twenty-five years older than Emma, and since his first wife's death he had shunned earthy pleasures. But he was foremost a lover—no, a connoisseur—of beauty. Hamilton's vases would form the basis of the British Museum's department of Greek and Roman antiquities. Yet underneath his polished exterior stirred a libido easily excited by women—and perhaps men. He was fascinated by Mount Vesuvius, to which he gave "the profound, exploratory attention of a true eighteenth-century dilettante." Sontag describes him as "analytic, solitary and detached," but the Italians, in dubbing him "the Cavaliere," not only complimented his manners but hinted at a romantic nature.

Sir William admitted to his nephew that he loved Emma but feared he would be cuckolded. "I should like better to live with you both here and see you happy than to have her all to myself, for I am sensible that I am not a match for so much youth and beauty." This proposal for a menage a trois fell flat on Charles, who had his eye on an heiress. Emma's nature was passionate; if she loved, she did so wholeheartedly. Little else explains her attachment to the dyspeptic nephew, who now tricked her into believing she was going to visit his uncle at Naples while he went to Scotland. She perked up at the thought of studying music and Italian. So in the spring of 1786 the smith's daughter, chaperoned by her valiant mother, was delivered into the hands of an elderly sophisticate at an entirely corrupt court.

After Paris, Naples was the most populous city on the Continent; it was the capital of a realm that stretched from the Papal States to Sicily and was ruled by a Bourbon monarch, Ferdinand IV, and his formidable Austrian wife, Maria Carolina, daughter of the Empress Maria Teresa and sister to Marie Antoinette. The city swarmed with life, most of it ragged and dirty, yet it remained provincial. The king was occupied with hunting or adultering, and the queen was laid up half the time birthing one of her eighteen children or recovering from the effects. The large landowners were both selfish and myopic, keeping the peasants on a short leash and thus earning little themselves. Sixty thousand *lazzaroni* (loafers) caused mischief, bathed naked, and cheered the monarchy that provided them with bread and spectacles. Meanwhile *cavalieri serventi* and their ladies gathered nightly to gossip at card parties called *conversazioni*.

Under Sir William's tutelage Emma was transformed into a proper lady. She studied music and foreign languages and acquired poise and the art of entertaining guests. The ambassador lived on an operatic scale, putting up or feeding a stream of curious Britons, including the royal princes and their entourages. At the elegant and spacious Palazzo Sessa, furnished to English neoclassical taste, Sir William held a court to rival that of the monarchs. Here he installed Emma as centerpiece. By 1787 she had adjusted to being bartered, and the uncle wrote reassuringly to his nephew, "She is wonderful. . . . I see my every wish fulfilled."

Hamilton commissioned outstanding painters and sculptors from several countries to make likenesses of his goddess, and she became central, as subject, to the neoclassical movement. Out of all this posing and from the observation of ancient statues, her famous "attitudes" evolved.

In 1787 the wandering poet Goethe described her performance at the palazzo:

> Dressed in [a Greek costume], she lets down her hair and, with a few shawls, gives so much variety to her poses, gestures, [and] expressions that the spectator can hardly believe his eyes. He sees what thousands of artists would have liked to express realized before him in movements and surprising transformations: standing, kneeling, sitting, reclining, serious, sad, playful, ecstatic, contrite, alluring, threatening, anxious, one pose follows another without a break. . . . The old knight idolizes her and is quite enthusiastic about everything she does.

Emma, with the help of Sir William, probably invented these attitudes and the classical poses that she performed for select guests; an imitation of Medea, for example, was said to heighten the viewers' emotions. Attitudes, which are a form of mime, were to be greatly in vogue during the nineteenth century. In the 1860s the American actress Adah Isaacs Menken became wildly popular with her attitudinal poses in the play *Mazeppa*. Like those of Emma, they featured a degree of disrobing or striptease. Menken, briefly the world's highest paid performer, influenced the posing of silent screen stars, a line that leads erratically to the slinky stances taken in a Madonna video. Interestingly, Sir William was close to David Garrick, the actor who first broke from oratory to use body language to express the feelings behind the words. Emma's attitudes point in the direction of modern acting technique.

Emma's dramatic sense could be erotic, captivating her audience. She boasted of a performance at Sorrento of song and dance with a tambourine: "I left some dying, some crying and some in despair." Loyal, she turned down munificent offers from opera impresarios. Emma's favorite role remained that of consort. Sir William was grooming her to be the ambassador's wife. Once he became convinced of her steadiness, Hamilton decided to marry her. He needed only to gain permission from King George, but they were practically brothers: Sir William's mother had been the king's father's mistress for years. The couple wed September 6, 1791.

Emma, usually dressed in white, swept London. Talk of her vulgarity was drowned in the appreciation of her talents. Whenever she merely appeared in a drawing room, she became the center of attention. She had what today we call star quality. Sir William basked in the admiration shown his wife. The newlyweds returned to Naples where Emma became his perfect helpmate. She became a defender of the Neapolitan royal family and so close a confidante to Queen Maria Carolina that gossip circulated about a lesbian affair. The queen, who ruled the king, feared the French Revolution's influence on the lesser nobility and the commercial class. The energetic Emma dealt with problems before her aging husband woke up to them. When, in 1798, she heard that the British fleet had decimated the French at the Battle of the Nile, stranding Napoleon's expeditionary force in Egypt, Emma was so struck she fainted dead away. For that matter, so did Earl Spencer, first lord of the admiralty.

Nelson had won a complete and characteristic victory. He attacked the bottled-up enemy as soon as he sighted their ships and pounded them the night through until the bay east of Alexandria was littered with debris and corpses. He knew that the prize wasn't merely control of the eastern Mediterranean but the land and sea lanes to India, and he dispatched news of the rout to the governor of Bombay. Then, before writing to his wife, he sent a letter to Lady Hamilton: "I may now be able to shew your ladyship the remains of Horatio Nelson, and I trust my mutilations will not cause me to be less welcome. They are the marks of honour."

THE HUMAN VESUVIUS

In the Bay of Naples on September 22, Emma met a man covered with medals but, in Sontag's words, "haggard, coughing, his hair powdered but too long, his empty right sleeve pinned to the breast of his dress uniform, a red gash above his blind eye where he had been struck by a fragment of grapeshot." The matron of thirty-three, larger but still lovely, "fell into [his] arm more dead than alive." Thus began the extravagant, romantic, and recklessly public love affair between her ladyship and the admiral, which some writers have suggested Sir William, by nature a voyeur, both enjoyed and directed. In Nelson, Sir William, who would found the study of volcanoes, had acquired a human Vesuvius.

Emma nursed Nelson's wounded, shattered frame, which suffered from malaria and exhaustion. She kept him sequestered in bed and fed him on ass's milk. The city, festooned with "Viva Nelson" banners, celebrated from king and queen down to the *lazzaroni*. By week's end he was well enough to attend a massive fete for his fortieth birthday: "80 people dined at Sir William's, 1,740 came to a ball, 800 supped, conducted in such a style of elegance as I never saw," Nelson informed his wife. He and Emma scarcely bothered to hide their budding romance.

In England everyone celebrated the defeat of "Boney," firing cannon, ringing church bells, and drinking bumpers to Admiral Nelson. The king of England, however, when told of the victory, had nothing to say. He may already have detected a whiff of scandal, for he awarded the victor the title of baron, small potatoes for such a smashing victory. Nelson, sensitive to any perceived slight, grumped. Nor was he complimentary to Naples, which he called "a country of fiddlers and poets, whores and scoundrels." Longing for action, he and Sir William conspired with Queen Maria Carolina, whose sister queen had been beheaded in France, to get Ferdinand to launch an invasion of Rome. Nelson had correctly estimated the martial ardor of the Neapolitan army, however, and after a defeat by the French, it dissolved. Naples was open to the enemy and a homegrown rebellion of the thinking class.

The British fleet evacuated king and court to Palermo, where they continued their petty pursuits. Emma gambled, and Nelson sat beside her, sipping champagne while she lost as much as five hundred pounds a night. He was her *cavaliere*, loudly applauding her attitudes, although she had grown so large as to be almost ungainly. British consular officials reported the hero of the Nile had turned into "the laughing stock of the whole fleet." Flora Fraser supposes that Emma and Nelson didn't have "sex on a regular basis" until early 1800, but she is too late by a year. While in exile in Palermo, when they were separated, Nelson dreamed that he and Emma "enjoy'd the height of love." Here a Spartan warrior had become an emotive lover, the frugal parson's son morphed into a sensualist. Emma, too, fell madly in love.

But Emma didn't neglect her husband. Nelson, while he came to loathe his own wife, grew close to Sir William, who stood godfather to this illicit union. "Sir W. and Lord N. live like brothers," Emma insisted in the face of gossip that had them quarreling. Through her large, motherly nature, she succeeded in pleasing both men, and they all chose *Tria Juncta in Uno* for their motto. Each contributed uniquely to this threesome that so dramatically shaped history.

In June 1799 Nelson, at the request of the queen, returned with a fleet of warships to the Bay of Naples. The republic that had functioned there for several months with the backing of the French crumbled before royalist Calabrians, cutthroats from the south. Nelson disregarded a negotiated armistice that would have saved the best and brightest Neapolitans from the marauding of the vengeful irregulars bent on establishing a republic. The result was days and nights of murder and plunder. Afterward Nelson made prisoners of thousands of republicans and clapped both men and women in irons, a sight that distressed even his own seamen.

Once King Ferdinand arrived from Sicily, he set up in the admiral's cabin. From the fleet, prisoners were sent ashore daily to be judged by a kangaroo court that either hanged or beheaded them—or, worse, sent them to dungeons to be tortured. The victims included nobility, distinguished scholars, and even a bishop. The executions were carried out in the market square before a drunken, raucous mob. The commotion carried out to the ships in the harbor. Among the many victims of the weeklong slaughter was Eleonora Pimental, a poet and journalist who had been a guest of the Hamiltons. With Eleonora's "testament" Sontag closes her novel: "I cannot forgive those who did not care about more than their own glory or well-being. They thought they were civilized. They were despicable."

Apologists for Nelson have failed to explain his double-dealing, not to mention his sanction of reactionary excess that equaled the Terror in cruelty. Sir William advocated a milder course. Emma begged for mercy for particular individuals, so that Nelson became annoyed with her for bothering him with "excuses from Rebels, Jacobins and Fools." Judged politically, the admiral's conduct was brutal and unwise, and it was dishonorable. Nelson was a military man, not a philosopher. He assured Emma, "We are restoring happiness to the kingdom of Naples." Though he read books on naval strategy, this force of nature exploded in battle. From their first association, the Hamiltons gave Nelson the emotional support and steadying influence he needed in order to destroy Napoleon's navy.

The canard that Emma ruined Nelson's life was believed in their time. In ours, as late as 1984, the National Maritime Museum issued a poster for the London Underground bearing a portrait of Lady Hamilton and the legend "England's No. 1 Enemy." This misreading entirely neglects Emma's patriotic service to her country. Nelson won battles by making the fleet—officers and men as well as ships—instruments of his will. Stories abound of Captain Nelson climbing the rigging to reassure a queasy recruit, of milord's concern for midshipmen before an engagement, of the admiral's chatting with common sailors onshore. The fighting men who worshiped Nelson admired Emma for her larger-than-life beauty, but they loved her because he did. As her biographer, Mollie Hardwick, expresses it, "on the ship of state in Naples she had long been admiral. Now of Nelson's fleet she was the living figurehead."

Susan Sontag sensed the three-way synergy that occurred:

Then the three stroll out on the terrace to look at Vesuvius, which has been unusually calm of late. Sometimes the Cavaliere [Sir William] is in the middle and they are on either side, like his two aging children, which they could well be. . . . The trio seemed so natural. The Cavaliere had a new young man in his life, more son than nephew. His wife had someone she could admire as she never admired anyone before. The hero had friends such as he had never had. . . . And beyond the exaltation of ever more intense friendship, they were united in feeling themselves actors in a great historical drama; saving England and Europe from French conquest.

Sontag is understandably disappointed in the drift of her drama—reaction—and in its dénouement: empire. In a review of *The Volcano Lover* John Banville of the *Irish Times* felt that her taking a side in the historical struggle was the one flaw in an otherwise brilliant resurrection of the past: "Art is amoral, whether we accept this or not." This threesome did not have a progressive political viewpoint. For all their engagement in the world, they were an inward-looking triad who succeeded through very rough times in bolstering each other to an amazing degree. When in 1800 Nelson the narcissist, Emma the exhibitionist, and Sir William the connoisseur set out overland for England, their entourage dazzled and befuddled the courts of Europe.

TRIA JUNCTA IN UNO

When the Hamiltons were recalled from Naples, Nelson realized he would be useless without them. However, he was deprived of his flagship. Lord Keith, sent by the Admiralty, declared that "Lady Hamilton has had command of the fleet long enough." Almost in spite, the trio determined to return home by land, crossing a continent where Napoleon's armies were every day advancing. In July 1800 they went by carriage to Florence, skirting enemy outposts, and finally to Trieste. Here as elsewhere on the journey to Vienna, Nelson was acclaimed as the conquering hero: lights flickered, crowds cheered, symphonies were performed in his honor. Only the British consuls and their wives were cool, one complaining that Nelson spoke of Emma as an angel, while she "leads him about like a keeper with a bear."

Nelson, bedecked in medals, was received with trumpets and the firing of cannon at the Austrian court. At the Esterhazys' country estate Emma sang a cantata accompanied by Joseph Haydn. The British ambassador's wife ground her teeth, and a Swedish diplomat described Lady Hamilton as "the fattest woman I've ever set eyes on, but with the most beautiful head." At table Emma cut Nelson's meat for him, while in company she talked, sang, or laughed while he admired. He was called her shadow, a willing captive, and Sir William, faring badly from the loss of his beloved Naples, was very little in evidence.

The wives of British diplomats were jealous and fearful of Emma. She had two men who adored her, despite the fact that she came from the lower class. In England, which the party finally reached in November, a different fear emerged: the establishment was wary of Nelson's popularity with the people. King George, offended by his admiral's wearing of decorations from other monarchs, gave him the cold shoulder, but Londoners mobbed him on the street with an intensity that would later be shown to movie and rock stars. The merchant class, from the lord mayor to the East India Company, honored the hero with banquets and gifts, and while he spoke confidentially with Prime Minister Pitt, that notorious rake the prince of Wales ogled Lady Hamilton.

For a time Nelson lived with his wife in Dover Street, and the Hamiltons lived together in Grosvenor Square. One night Nelson stormed out and walked the streets, arriving at the Hamiltons' door at four in the morning. He went upstairs and, sitting on the edge of their bed, asked them to take him in. Lady Hamilton was concerned about what society would think, but Sir William declared he didn't care "a fig for the world"! Emma's reticence was due to her being pregnant (with Horatia) and concealing it. The newborn's chances in life would hinge on the appearance that she was legitimate. Unfortunately, Sir William at seventy, distressed by the loss of part of his collection, wouldn't do for the father. The fiction finally hit upon—that Nelson was Horatia's father but Lady Hamilton not her mother—was clung to by the poor girl during her whole long life.

What was the offense of this menage, one that still rankles in some quarters? As one Nelson biographer, Jack Russell, has pointed out, "He never sinned against propriety, which he would have done by taking Emma out of Sir William's house." Society was willing to turn a blind eye to the carryings-on of Hamilton's cousin William Beckford, romantically entangled with both a young boy and his married female cousin. But he was *so* rich. Georgiana, fifth duchess of Devonshire, kept up an unabashed menage with her husband and best friend, Lady Elizabeth Foster. But she was *so* well born, a forebear of Princess Diana. To the ruling class, Nelson was an affront because he was middling born, and the Hamiltons, because they didn't have enough money. There was something subversive about such people becoming a hero, a goddess, and the finest art collector of his age; the situation bore a whiff of democracy from abroad.

By Christmas Nelson had left his wife and was unofficially living with the Hamiltons. Early in 1801 Emma, then thirty-five, gave birth to Horatia in secret. The infant was given out to nurse and not christened for two years. Meanwhile the admiral was obliged to put to sea, and in April he achieved a costly victory at Copenhagen, securing the Baltic for the British fleet and helping pry Russia loose from Napoleon's grasp. By mail from his flagship, Nelson became a doting father and a jealous lover. He was constantly warning Emma against the prince of Wales; Nelson was sure the prince intended to seduce her. Sir William wrote to reassure him. Nelson worried more about this phantom than anything the enemy might do.

In the fall Britain and France agreed to an armistice, and Nelson purchased a little farm in Surrey. "You are to be lady paramount of Paradise Merton, all its territories and waters," he wrote to Emma, who'd chosen it. By the time he arrived home, the Hamiltons were in residence, and Emma was busy fitting up pigsties and chicken coops. Nelson's niece was there to help nurse the exhausted admiral, and eventually Horatia would be brought to gladden his heart. For the first time in his life he knew peace.

Sir William wrote his nephew Charles, "I love Nelson more and more . . . and he loves us sincerely." The Hamiltons never dissolved the bond between them, and they became surrogate parents to a hero who had lost his mother when young and remained emotionally adolescent. Lord Pinto, dear to Nelson, remarked on how he was a combination of great man and baby. Sontag, in portraying Sir William's motivations, writes, "Collecting is a species of insatiable desire, a Don Juanism of objects," suggesting that Hamilton collected Emma and Nelson as the ultimate objets d'art. But we think this gentleman of both sense and sensibility chaperoned their epic romance out of love, both for his "wards" and his country. Jack Russell describes their joint life at Merton: "In all respects it was the happiest place on earth, and the third could always escape for a quiet day at the British Museum." When in 1802 the three sent out cards, "Sir William Hamilton, Lady Hamilton and Mr. Nelson desire to wish you a merry Christmas," they had become a family.

There was some friction between the Hamiltons. She drank and spent too much, and Sir William in his last years had to sell off his vases and paintings to pay his debts. He foresaw her penury when he was gone. Emma entertained on a large scale. A musical evening at their London townhouse in February 1803, at which she played and sang before one hundred guests, very much tired Sir William. He took ill, and after Emma nursed him for six days, Nelson keeping a bedside vigil, he died in both their arms. In his will Hamilton referred to Nelson as "my dearest friend . . . the most virtuous, loyal and truly brave man I ever met with." He left his wife a modest income but the bulk of his property to his nephew Charles, as he'd promised.

Soon Britain and France again made war, and Nelson resumed his command in the Mediterranean. He spent the better part of two years trying to engage the French fleet, chasing it across the Atlantic to the West Indies and back to Spain. Since Nelson's wife refused to grant him a divorce, he and Emma were forced to keep up the fiction that Horatia wasn't their daughter. In August 1805 the couple held a long-awaited reunion at Merton. They strolled arm in arm in their paradise, their love child with them. When the call to battle came, Emma tearfully encouraged her reluctant hero to do his duty. Nelson responded, "Brave Emma! Good Emma! If there were more Emmas, there would be more Nelsons." Emma, pregnant with a child she would lose, never let on. Before Nelson left, he solemnly placed a gold wedding band on her finger.

Emma sensed, as did the people who nearly mobbed him at his departure, that Nelson meant to obtain victory at all costs. In the style of great romances, hers was fated to be cut off prematurely. Lord Nelson and Lady Hamilton never grew familiar with each other's faults. Russell understood: "Their moments together were always stolen moments. In that way they were fiercely in love and they had Sir William to thank for it." We wonder also whether the romance would have flourished if the initial setting hadn't been lush, decadent Naples. There, the admiral stooped to conquer in the time-honored guise of *cavaliere servente*. Sir William played the role not of outraged husband but of the bemused Italian nobleman he'd practically become. All Naples applauded.

On October 21, 1805, off Trafalgar, Nelson employed his armada to destroy the combined fleets of France and Spain for the duration of the war. Napoleon (like Hitler after him) would abandon plans to invade England and eventually turn east to Russia and defeat. The admiral, military decorations on his chest marking him as a target, resisted all efforts to get him out of harm's way. A French sharpshooter put a bullet through his spine and killed him. His last written and witnessed testament stated: "I leave Emma Lady Hamilton a Legacy to my King and Country, that they will allow her an ample provision to maintain her rank in life."

King George would have none of it. So Emma struggled on for another decade, generous and spendthrift, pleading for a pension, selling her jewelry, drinking far too much, and eventually confined to a debtor's prison. In 1814 she fled with Horatia to Calais, where they lived meagerly.

She guarded the sum Nelson had left their daughter, spending the interest entirely on the girl's education. After Emma died the following year of alcohol poisoning, Horatia returned to England where she married a clergyman, bore him nine children, and denied any relation to her mother.

In evaluating the significance of a menage a trois that outraged society in its time, connoisseurship has the last word. Sir William and Emma Hamilton's seminal role in the neoclassical movement is now recognized—he as collector of the antique, she as subject for innumerable paintings. In the mid-nineteenth century, old Sir Moses Montefiore, the Anglo-Jewish philanthropist, was asked for his recollection of Nelson, whom he'd met as a youth. He replied, "Ah, my boy, I only had eyes for Lady Hamilton." Sir William and Nelson himself would have agreed.

part three

THE MOTHER AND THE WHORE

The nineteenth century as a cultural boundary may be said to extend from Napoleon's exile to Elba in 1814 to the outbreak of World War I one hundred years later. The Napoleonic Code embodied the eighteenth century's search for the rational governance of matters both social and familial. In between, the nineteenth century saw the application of such pervasive material processes—from the factory system to national railroad and telegraph networks, not to mention the daily newspaper—that the impersonal workings of progress were substituted for the neoclassical ideal of justice. But was there *sexual* progress during this century?

On the surface and for some, yes. The legal position of women and children improved, while the absolute authority of the father became curtailed. In Britain until midcentury a divorce had to be obtained through an act of Parliament; in America until the 1880s, by a private bill passed in a state legislature. In practice only men could obtain such a bill and then rarely. The establishment of divorce courts led to the enumeration of the grounds of divorce, though a chief cause, adultery, was interpreted differently for male and female.

On the Continent where French law prevailed, a father had to apportion his estate between his children, but his heirs were forbidden to marry without his consent. In Verdi's *La Traviata*, the operatic version of Dumas's *Camille*, Alfredo Germont defies his father to live with the courtesan Violetta. Because the "bad woman" knows her place, the pleas of the elder Germont that she is ruining his son's life separate the lovers more effectively than threats. In Britain or America, by contrast, permission to marry wasn't required, and sons or daughters more often disobeyed their parents. However, a father could disinherit an offspring who wed for love.

During this whole era of "progress," people continued to marry based mainly on social or financial advantage where there was any to be had. In the American West the benefit might be the promise of a woman's labor rather than her material dowry. The ancient moral divide between wives who nurtured men at home and the women who solaced them outside—the mother and the whore—narrowed only slightly from start to finish of the nineteenth century. Bertrand Russell summed up the Victorian double standard: "The possibility of this system has depended upon prostitution."

Friedrich Engels caustically remarked that the major difference between a wife and a whore was that the former didn't peddle her body by the hour but "sells it into slavery for once and all." Toward the end of the century, he ridiculed the legal advances made by women, which they could seldom enforce. Engels, who influenced Russell and later Simone de Beauvoir, understood that monogamy was intended to bind only the wife. The man wasn't expected to be a virgin when wed or to refrain from relations outside the home.

Curiously, none of these urbane writers deals with the "other woman"—neither wife nor prostitute but mistress. This third might be a professional who through well-chosen liaisons, could amass a tidy nest egg. Sarah Bernhardt's mother, for example, was a glamorous courtesan who expected her daughter to follow in her footsteps. Or the mistress might be a junior wife who lived secluded in a *maison secondaire* and reared a man's bastards, as did Émile Zola's Jeanne Rozerot, a former seamstress. The reaction of the legal wife to the other woman, once she found out, was often strained toleration. Occasionally the threesome evolved into a menage a trois.

The overlooked aspect of the century-long struggle between sexual reform and reaction is the stealthy triumph of this other woman. The mistress is the unsung hero of the nineteenth century. Not only did she bridge the chasm between mother and whore but she profited from her role. The "other woman" is the forerunner of the independent woman of modern times. Toward this she evolved slowly and with the help of sympathetic men. By century's end, Lou Andreas-Salomé could become the focus of two menages a trois, involving the great men Nietzsche and Rilke, and afterward she took up with the coworker of Sigmund Freud. But it wasn't until the age of bohemianism, which took hold around the Great War, that woman was promoted as man's moral equal and his superior in the intimate politics of sex.

chapter 8

ROMANTIC REBELS

{Percy and Mary Shelley and Frankenstein;
Lord Byron and the Count and Countess Guiccioli}

*All of Byron's love affairs can be summed up in a few words:
a driving need for women and a distrust of Woman.*

FELIX RABBE

MARY, PERCY, AND THE MONSTER

*T*HE BRITISH ROMANTIC MOVEMENT
evolved from the sea change in perception brought on by the French Revolution. Bertrand Russell calls Percy Shelley its "chief apostle." A rebel
against convention, he opposed the reactionary tide that swamped Europe
after Napoleon's defeat. Shelley's brief, tragic life set in motion the romantic love we all recognize and desire to experience. Russell writes, "Shelley
when he fell in love was filled with exquisite emotions and imaginative
thoughts of a kind lending themselves to expression in poetry." He didn't
wish to spend these feelings in the emission of seed. He needed barriers to
physical fulfillment, a damming of sensation so that its frustration would
cause him to write the poems that thrilled his circle and, after his death,
the world. Therefore, the poet created complications in the form of
aborted threesomes. He chose possessive women who kept him on a leash,
so that his menages remained largely in the realm of fantasy.

In 1792 Percy Bysshe Shelley, the eldest of seven children, was born
to a country squire. His mother was highly cultivated, and he early showed
her influence. While in his teens at Eton, he wrote a pair of gothic novels.
At Oxford Shelley delved into reincarnation, occultism, and the radical

ideas of William Godwin. But it was a personal rebuff—his cousin Harriet's breaking their engagement—that caused the young man in 1811 to write *The Necessity of Atheism*. Her parents had called his love letters "anti-Christian," and he developed a raging hatred for the religion. The pamphlet was a joint production with his chum Thomas Jefferson Hogg, and it caused Oxford to expel them both.

Typically, Shelley turned his romantic ardor into composition. He wrote heedless of consequences and strove to express the evanescent, the sudden. Hogg, earthbound and craggy in appearance, was the first of the men with whom the ethereal poet tried to bond in a platonic sense, mixing them with his women to produce muddled menages. Big, burly Hogg with his cynical manner failed to share his friend's interests, yet he invariably pursued the women close to him. This began with Percy's sister Elizabeth. The infatuated Hogg declared himself her romantic suitor. Shelley instinctively believed in sexual emancipation, but to his penny-pinching friend, "free" love simply promised something for nothing. The repressed Hogg needed a menage to vent unacceptable erotic feelings for Shelley. Basking in his romantic-looking friend's aura, Hogg could forget his own cloddishness.

William Hazlitt described the look that made women swoon for the poet: "His complexion, fair, golden, freckled, seemed transparent, with an inward light, and within him so divinely wrought that you might almost say his body thought. . . . His form, graceful and slender, drooped like a flower in the breeze." A comparison to John Lennon, also a mix of energy and delicacy, is intriguing, because it brings up the relationship between martyrdom and sexuality.

In London the nineteen-year-old Percy met sixteen-year-old Harriet Westbrook, who was being tormented almost to suicide by her stodgy family. On her suggestion the pair eloped and married. Harriet remained enraptured by Shelley long after he lost interest in her. Economic hardship dogged the young couple. In 1813 his poem *Queen Mab*, an attack on monarchy and marriage, was suppressed, causing a sensation. It expressed an iconoclasm the still immature poet hoped to put into practice.

At York, the visiting Hogg tested Shelley's talk of free love by attempting to seduce Harriet in his host's absence. She told her husband on his return. However, Shelley had intentionally thrown his friend and wife together. The poet intended that Harriet, Hogg, and he should live together. He endorsed the reformer William Godwin's idea that a husband had no property rights over his wife's body. Shelley wrote Hogg that Harriet was "prejudiced" against a threesome, but he hoped she wouldn't remain so. "If *she* was convinced of its innocence," he concluded, "would I be so sottish a slave to opinion as to endeavor to monopolize what if participated would give my friend pleasure without diminishing my own?"

Jean Fuller, while an insightful biographer, interprets the aborted affair in the unsophisticated fashion of those who fail to understand the menage a trois. Fuller writes, "The wish to share a woman, rather than to compete over her, so strange to those who are completely heterosexual, will often betray a repressed or unrecognized homosexual desire which finds no outlet save by using the woman as a bridge."

We will beg the questions of who might be *completely* heterosexual and why sharing is so much stranger than competing. Camille Paglia is closer to the mark when she writes that in Romanticism, "femininity is never repressed. If the Romantics repress anything, it is masculinity." Shelley at times pursued the ideal of male companionship and at others the Romantic fantasy of "an incestuous twin," a woman who would be the bride to his spirit. There is a pool of narcissistic reflection on which Shelley floats the paper barques of his poetry. Seeking the harmony of his own sundered nature through an encompassing love, the poet's fantasy drifts toward the wholeness of a menage.

Percy could still write, "When I come home to Harriet, I am the happiest of the happy." But he blamed her for the cooling of his friendship with Hogg. Her incomprehension of poetry or philosophy irritated him. In London, in Godwin's daughter by the feminist Mary Wollstonecraft, who'd died giving birth, Shelley found the soul to be his mate. According to a Shelley biographer, Joan Rees, Mary Godwin was "fair and pretty, quiet yet spirited, with fire and intensity, a considerable intellect, and like Harriet had been when he first met her, aged sixteen." She took the initiative, declaring her love to Percy over Wollstonecraft's grave. He responded by proposing that all three live together, Harriet as his sister, Mary as his wife. Mary agreed, but Harriet, twice a mother, was too distraught to accept a menage.

In 1814, after Godwin refused his consent to an irregular liaison, Shelley attempted suicide by overdosing on laudanum (an opium tincture). A doctor pulled him through. Called to his bedside, a friend found him torn between compassion for Harriet and his new passion for Mary. Soon the lovers fled to France and took along dark-eyed, curly-haired Claire Claremont, daughter of Godwin's second wife. The impulsive girl was in sharp contrast to the cool, blond Mary, who was less eager to become an outlaw. Mary kept an eye on the evident attraction between Percy and her affectionate half-sister, but the three would remain bound together. Claire became Percy's disciple and, if we may judge by the intimacy of their correspondence, his lover early on. After adventures on the Continent, the impoverished trio returned to London.

With the death of Shelley's grandfather in 1815, he came into an independent income. But he was overly generous to friends, and the freeloading Godwin pressed him for loans, so that although Mary was pregnant, she had to make do. Again Hogg showed up to pay court to his friend's woman. Perhaps as a ploy to win back her lover's wandering attention, Mary encouraged Hogg, who'd become a barrister and grown more imposing. Manuscript letters between the two suggest a brief but serious flirtation. One included a lock of Mary's hair as requested.

While Mary was carrying her first child, she intimated to "dear Hogg" that her affection for him was also growing. She wrote that she desired an affair, but it must be put off until the pregnancy was over. Shelley, too, would have to wait to sleep with her. Mary seemed certain he would approve of the threesome. However, Harriet, pregnant for a third time, possibly by Shelley, threw herself into the Serpentine and drowned. Shelley was declared an unfit father for the children he'd had with Harriet, but now he and Mary were free to marry. Hogg, converted to Christian morality, disappeared for a time, and in later years Mary liked to make fun of him as "queer."

Mary, despite her upbringing and looming fame as an author, claimed she was "afraid of men," and therefore, "I was apt to get *tousy-mousy* for women." She typically grew attached to whatever woman fascinated Percy. A mutual friend reminisced that he was "a thorough Mormon. . . . He should have had his fifty wives." If the poet's loves were fleeting, Mary's involvements tended toward the compulsive. In her novel *Frankenstein*, published in 1818, we believe she modeled the relationship between the doctor and his monster on the particular symbiosis between Shelley and his alter ego Hogg. Mary's would-be lover lumbered about with the same bewildered clumsiness as Boris Karloff in the 1930s movie. (The director James Whale was homosexual and blackballed for admitting it, and the movie—even more the sequel *Bride of Frankenstein*—has its three-way kicks.) Shelley once wrote of Hogg, "He is a pearl within an oyster shell." But only he or his woman could pry the hard shell open.

While a student Shelley was inclined toward chemistry, filling his room with experiments. With his frayed cuffs and tousled hair, living on bread and raisins, there was a hint of the mad scientist about him. And to the world of convention, Shelley seemed a moral monster. The cumbersome Hogg, who lived under the domination of his friend's superior mind, resented his fluency both of feeling and expression. After Shelley's death, Hogg wrote, in the guise of a biography, two volumes of sneering caricature devoted to proving that Shelley was a conceited lady's man. In life no less than literature, the monster inevitably turns on his creator.

In March 1818 Percy and Mary and their two small children left for Italy, this time for good. However, as Fuller points out, "Shelley seemed fated to live in a threesome." Claire Claremont came along, and she brought Allegra, her adorable daughter by Lord Byron, whom she'd seduced into an affair before he went into exile. Despite Byron's own scandalous reputation, he was displeased by Claire's wildness and wanted nothing more to do with her. But at the insistence of Mary, he accepted charge of his daughter. From here the story of the British Don Juan, the incarnation of Romantic sexuality, mingles with the Shelleys' until the tragic death of Percy—which Byron may have inadvertently caused.

Shelley now entered his most productive period, encouraged by his Pisan circle of friends. An early fruit of his Mediterranean surroundings was his translation of Plato's *Symposium* and an essay in defense of "Greek love," or the man-boy sex that previous translators had censored out of the dialogue. It is, however, a long jump from Shelley's approval of the same-sex love found in the classics and his wish that there be only one sex in the future to tagging him a closet gay or even bisexual in a contemporary sense. Shelley's famous line, "We are all Greeks," is a statement of pantheism. The poet's title *The Banquet of Plato* indicates his embrace of the totality of life. The Romantics rediscovered and eroticized the whole natural world.

Thus Shelley praises to Thomas Love Peacock the "soft yet piercing splendor" of Venus, which the planet owed to its "divine and female nature." In the same letter he relates that in the afternoon he bathes "in a pool or fountain, formed in the middle of the forests by a torrent. It is surrounded on all sides by precipitous rocks, and the waterfall of the stream which forms it falls into it on one side with perpetual dashing. . . . My custom is to undress and sit on the rocks, reading Herodotus . . . and then to leap from the edge of the rock into this fountain." Here is the nineteenth-century Narcissus who wants no still reflection of his image to contemplate because he is fascinated by the torrent within, the rush of sense impressions. Naked in nature, book in hand—there is the Romantic pose!

Shelley was a narcissist who found his match in a female twin, Mary. But their love became frayed by the irritations of daily living. The Shelleys' marriage was further tried by the loss of the two young children. Fuller maintains that Percy "was sick of the whole apparatus of sex, and wished the intermingling of beings transferred to a higher plane." Yet the search for the twin must be resumed—in another's eyes if not her arms. Percy's infatuation with Emilia Viviani, imprisoned by her father in a convent, is a typically poetic affair. He visited Emilia in the company of Mary, who sarcastically referred to his feelings as "Shelley's Italian Platonics." Emilia, who called herself a caged bird, was hoping Shelley would free her, but the poet was no Casanova to relish such an intrigue.

Instead he wrote "Epipsychidion" to his girlish "Metaphor of spring and Youth and Morning." Actually the poem is a history of his love life and contains metaphoric descriptions of the several women who'd occupied it, including Mary as the moon and Emilia as the sun, "twin spheres of light [who would] reign together, neither one disdaining or eclipsing the other." Claire is a "comet, beautiful and fierce." Shelley had almost wholly imagined Emilia, for whom he felt the "desire of the moth for the star." Her star would dim when she agreed to her father's choice of husband and asked Shelley for a dowry.

"Epipsychidion" has a discarded preface describing a threesome that epitomizes Shelley's fantasy sex life:

> The following poem was found in the P.F. of a young Englishman, who died on his passage from Leghorn to the Levant. . . . He was accompanied by a lady supposed to be his wife, and an effeminate-looking youth, to whom he showed so excessive an attachment as to give rise to the suspicion that she was a woman.

Camille Paglia, reveling in the cross-dressing, terms the preface "Byronic," meaning perverse, and raises the ante by labeling it "a *ménage à trois* as exotic as a Shakespearean acting company on tour." She then implies the wife is also erotically interested in the girl-boy. Here she is onto a barely suppressed aspect of *Mary* Shelley's libido. But for all the attempts to link an openly polysexual Byron with a supposedly bisexual Shelley, their temperaments were far enough apart for the poets to become wary friends and their fates to intertwine otherwise.

Shelley once wrote his printer in London that Italians didn't interest him. For Byron, an Italian by adoption, the situation was reversed. To the astonishment of his English correspondents, he quit a dissolute life to play the *cavaliere servente* with fidelity. Without any stake in the matter, he involved himself in a conspiracy to overthrow the reactionary government of the Papal States, and he courted assassination by both personal and political enemies. Luigi Barzini cleverly observed, "The 'Italianate Englishman' has been a 'devil incarnate' from the earliest days of the Renaissance, for the synthetic reproduction of the qualities that seem most obviously Italian in someone educated in another climate and another religion has really devilish results." Unfortunately, as we shall see, it may have been Shelley who paid for Byron's intrigues.

"MY WIFE—FORMERLY THE MISTRESS OF LORD BYRON"

In January 1788 George Gordon Byron was born in London to an eccentric, aristocratic family. As an adult, his looks and engaging personality would win him admirers. Coleridge remarked, "So beautiful a countenance I scarcely ever saw . . . his eyes the open portals of the sun—things of light, and for light." Stendhal rhapsodized on Byron's "magnificent head," and Sir Walter Scott claimed no portrait did justice to his dreamlike beauty. Byron's deformed left foot alone detracted from his classic proportions. He was well schooled and in 1809 took his hereditary seat in the House of Lords. Wanderlust eventually drew him to Mediterranean lands, where he felt more at home than amid the reserve and hypocrisy of the British upper class.

In 1812 the publication of *Childe Harold's Pilgrimage*, a tribute to his youthful wanderings, catapulted Byron into the first rank of poets. "I awoke one morning and found myself famous," he remarked. At twenty-four, Byron was lionized by London literary circles as both a genius and a man of action. But Byron had already reached the disillusionment with Romantic ideals that Shelley wouldn't approach until his death. He evoked a mood of melancholy congenial to "lost generations" from post-Napoleonic Europe to the expatriates of the 1920s and the Beats of the 1950s. Byron had experienced life too quickly and "felt the fullness of satiety."

The randy lord's love affairs became notorious. From the fast Lady Caroline Lamb, who called him "mad, bad and dangerous to know," Byron escaped into the maternal arms of the slightly faded Lady Oxford. He became erotically entangled with his half-sister Augusta and led a dissipated life. He was bullied into marrying a high-born bluestocking by that young woman's parents. A year later, with scandals building, his wife insisted on a separation that included their infant daughter. In April 1816 at Lady Jersey's party the literary lion was "cut"—that is, ignored with a vengeance—by his former admirers. This form of censure was used to enforce moral standards throughout the century. The peer of the realm had little choice but to go into exile for the rest of his life.

Byron's sin, even during the lax Regency, was to combine the immorality of an eighteenth-century gentleman with the ostentation of a twentieth-century celebrity. During the old regime a man of quality might be thoroughly dissolute so long as he behaved well enough. James Boswell's whoremongering, which included having two bawds at once in a tavern's back room, didn't prevent him from writing the biography of Dr. Johnson, the high priest of orthodoxy. Boswell's descendants merely suppressed his intimate diary, tamping down the dirt for a century and a half. Byron, the world's best-selling poet at a time when poetry was in the mainstream, lived the duality of a modern star: a high-flown image combined with private lechery. Landing at Ostend, Belgium, his party adjourned to an inn. As soon as he reached his room, Byron fell like a thunderbolt on the chambermaid. Next day he set out in his enormous horse-drawn traveling carriage, which like an extra-stretch limo contained elaborate facilities for sleeping and dining as well as a toilet.

Byron's sexual appetites were extravagant, yet he protested he'd done nothing to warrant his wife's separating from him. During the seven years he lived in Italy he was treated with respect by British officials and adoration by Italians high and low. However, far more than Shelley, Byron was a public figure: on his journey into exile his publisher John Murray sent along a reporter to write an exact account. Byron's sex life was news.

In Byron we find the genuine Casanova type to whom sex is performance art. He settled in the master's native city, Venice, where between 1817 and 1819 he lived in a palazzo with a retinue of cutthroat servants and surrounded himself with harlots, pimps, and gondoliers. It was rumored he had two hundred mistresses, many of whom, especially during Carnival, fought among each other. According to a horrified Shelley, Byron's *gondolieri* scouted for boys to perform "practices, which are not only not named, but I believe even conceived in England." However, if someone offered milord a slight insult, such as making fun of his riding style, he would slap his face and fight a duel. He took care to keep John Murray, and thus the world, current on his escapades.

Byron was the ultimate narcissistic personality who saw the world as a reflection of himself. Insecure, he craved the admiration of others. He needed polysexual adventures, the first step toward which is a menage a trois. For this totally self-absorbed type, every moment is an erotic contest. Robert Redford, a sex symbol himself, could have been describing Byron when he explained the polysexual nature of his role in the 1965 film *Inside Daisy Clover:* "I wanted to play him as a guy who bats ten ways—men, women, children, dogs, cats, anything that salves his ego."

Redford understood that to keep things moving, the triangulator can't discriminate.

It's the more remarkable that Byron, who met the Countess Teresa Guiccioli at a *conversazione* (card party) that neither wished to attend, comfortably settled in as her *cavaliere servente* from 1818 until he left for Greece in 1823. The demands of being an official paramour included numerous obligations to the loved one and her household. Ethel Mayne observed, "The code of *serventismo* was even stricter than that of marriage. The improper conduct of a *dama* and her *amino* was more likely to shock polite society than the mere cuckolding of a husband." In choosing Teresa, nineteen and recently wed, Byron took her husband in the bargain. Since Count Guiccioli was suspected of several assassinations, his complicity was advisable. The danger excited Byron, who boasted to his English friends of how the Italians were "liberal with the knife."

Count Gamba, the father of convent-educated Teresa, was so impressed by Guiccioli's wealth that he gave his daughter to a man forty years her senior. Worse, Guiccioli was a regular seducer of his serving girls and had six bastard children by one. He may have poisoned a previous wife. Yet Teresa didn't object to the match and seemed to admire her cold, businesslike husband. She had waived her right to a *cavaliere servente* until she fell in love with Lord Byron. But what about her fascinated him?

Some contemporaries called the thick-waisted Teresa "chumpy." Shelley thought her "very pretty," and Lady Blessington admired "her complexion delicately fair, her hair of rich golden tint, her bust and arms exquisitely beautiful." These parts of a woman's anatomy were crucial because they were on view. Byron himself found Teresa "fair as sunrise—warm as noon." She was vivacious and amusing, and while in her company he forgot his past and became the accomplished *cavaliere*. At first, Count Guiccioli approved of his wife's liaison. Engaged in endless acquisitions of land, the count remained oblivious to the flurry of letters, transmitted by servants and a priest, in which the lovers declared themselves. "I have been your *first* real love," wrote Byron to the countess, "and I assure you that you shall be my last passion."

And so Don Juan announced his retirement from seduction. While Byron attended to his amorous duties, including the writing of billets-doux, he kept up a parallel correspondence in an ironic vein with friends in London. "I have been an intriguer, a husband, a whoremonger," he admitted, "and now I am a Cavaliere Servente—by the holy! it is a strange sensation." Though he claimed to respect the count, he at first urged Teresa to elope with him. Only later did he realize that the purpose of *serventismo* was for the lady to *stay* with her husband.

Guiccioli, beginning to worry about the relationship, moved his household to Ravenna, where Teresa had a miscarriage. Although the child was probably the count's, he invited Byron to come "distract the Countess from her illness." Her family, the Gambas, also dropped their opposition to the liaison, and from this point on Byron became entangled in Italian politics. With his "in-laws" he joined the Carboneria, a secret society dedicated to unifying Italy by overthrowing Austrian rule in the north and the government of the Papal States, in which Ravenna was located. Meanwhile Count Guiccioli, who played a double game, asked Byron to arrange for his appointment as honorary British consul so that he would have diplomatic immunity no matter which side won.

Italian society approved of the affable relationship between the two men. A tolerant husband and a lover who understood his precise duties were both held in esteem. Privately the Englishman complained that the count was "a very polite personage, but I wish he would not carry me out in his Coach and Six, like [mayor of London] Dick Whittington and his Cat." The Italian next demanded the "loan" of a large sum of money. When Byron hesitated, Guiccioli moved the household to Bologna. Milord followed in a train that included his servants, saddle horses, and a menagerie of dogs, monkeys, cats, and caged birds. After a warning from his banker, Byron refused to ante up, and a stormy scene ensued. Teresa spurned the count's demand to give up her "Bairon," and the husband came to the lover to complain about his wife's intransigence! "It is awful work, this love," summed up the poet.

In 1820 Byron moved into the Palazzo Guiccioli, occupying the floor below the count and countess and enjoying the idea that he had acquired a home and a family. The count was pleased to get a good rent for his rooms and wife. Unfortunately, the Guicciolis fell out, and Teresa, obtaining a separation by papal decree, moved back to her father's house. Byron continued to live in the palazzo, although he was warned to beware of an ambush by a hired assassin when he went out riding. The plot to overthrow Austrian rule had become transparent, and the authorities were planning a "stilletation" for milord. A pitched battle between the Austrian army and the patriots intervened; the liberals were defeated and scattered. The Gambas and Teresa and Byron joined the Shelleys and their friends at Pisa in 1821.

Reunited in Pisa, Byron and Claire Claremont disagreed over how their precocious daughter was to be cared for. Byron feared that in the Shelley household, which was vegetarian, Allegra would "perish of starvation and green fruit." He favored the Catholic religion and so deposited the five-year-old in a convent located on marshy ground near Ravenna. In April 1822 little Allegra died of a fever, and Byron, though shocked, accepted it with his usual fatalism. The high-strung Claire was dispatched to Russia as a governess, and the Pisan circle drew closer together. Byron and Shelley got on well, with the former referring to the latter as "the Serpent," presumably for his atheist views. Teresa was liked by the women but patronized for her limited English.

Also in the household were Jane and Edward (Ned) Williams, an Anglo-Indian couple with two children; Jane and Ned couldn't legally marry because Jane's husband, a forger and blackmailer, was alive and menacing. They had linked up with the Shelleys in Pisa shortly before the arrival of Byron, and while he took no notice of the pretty, mild-mannered Jane, Percy fell in love with her in his poetic way. Since his relations with Mary were strained, he was attracted by the "aura of love, joy, and untroubled communion" in which the pair lived. Jane and Ned pitied Shelley's unfulfilling domestic life, and the three grew close enough for Shelley to write his last love lyrics to her and act as literary mentor to him.

Every writer on the Romantics questions whether Percy and Jane became lovers. Byron's biographer Quennell declares that "there is no doubt of the quality of [Percy's] feeling for Jane Williams and almost as little doubt that the heavenly love-affair reached an earthly conclusion." He is certain this caused Mary to grow "restive and miserable." Rees precisely cites "the actual fulfillment of passion one evening, after an Italian *festa*, which [Jane and Percy] together had attended." The assumption that either Mary or Ned would have been conventionally jealous is unwarranted. The circle at Pisa was a community on the Godwin plan where husbands and wives weren't supposed to own each other.

Both Percy and Mary Shelley imbued Jane with the ideal qualities they sought. Mary said she developed an obsessive crush on Jane. Reasonably intelligent, Jane had a gift for homemaking and for singing. Her calm English temperament was the rough equivalent of Teresa's Latin vivacity in terms of charming great men. Percy in his last months turned to her for comfort and inspiration. Ned, who worshiped Shelley, was gratified—an example of the sexual symbiosis between master and disciple typically found in an art colony. But what of Jane? The attention flattered and excited her but instilled fear. She was to receive letters from both her husband and admirer, their final recorded words.

Shelley had named his sailboat, built by a Captain Roberts at Leghorn, the *Don Juan* in honor of Byron, who was presently sailing his own yacht out of that port; the name was emblazoned on both the hull and the sails. Leaving the women and children at Lerici, Percy and Ned at the end of June 1822 set sail for Leghorn, about eight hours away. On July 8 they embarked on the return trip. Shelley had experienced dreams and portents that the sea would claim him. A storm blew up, and the *Don Juan* wasn't heard from for days. Then the bodies of both men washed up on the Tuscany coast, Shelley's with a copy of Keats's poems doubled in his back pocket. There followed the famous last rites in which the bodies were cremated on the beach, Byron in despair swam the lengthy distance to his yacht, and Mary recovered Percy's heart from the pyre, intact.

After the heartbroken Jane left for England and while Mary hesitated, the *Don Juan* was recovered. Captain Roberts believed the vessel hadn't capsized but that it was run down by another boat, under the mistaken impression that the *Don Juan* belonged to the wealthy Byron. Piracy came to be accepted as the motive. However, at this time the papal authorities, fearful of insurrection, were particularly vexed with Byron. Had milord's enemies murdered Shelley in his stead? We shall never have a certain answer. But each of the metaphysical threesome of Byron, Shelly, and Keats was aware of what the other two meant to his art and to the evolution of poetic feeling.

Before he died, Shelley had come to believe in reincarnation, so it is fitting that he became the center of a ghost menage. T. J. Hogg, the emotional hyena, pounced on Jane shortly after her return to London. In letters to Mary she played down their growing attachment. "With him I get a little rational talk," she wrote, "and our constant theme is Shelley and my own Edward." A married woman without means, the mother of two children not by her husband, could scarcely refuse the advances of an up-and-coming barrister. Jane was admittedly "the slave of appearances." Hogg, once he'd grasped the depth of his late friend's involvement with Jane, had to have her.

Only after Shelley's death did Hogg achieve a menage a trois with the man he'd so admired and envied. A complication was Mary's ardent flame for Jane, which was not returned. "I love Jane better than any other human being," Mary wrote in her journal, "but I am pressed upon by the knowledge that she slightly returns this affection." Mary moved to a London suburb to be near the woman to whom she declared herself "wedded." Jane, however, would soon be openly living with Hogg and bearing his child. That he never actually married her, despite the opportunity, is another kink in the barrister's unattractive character. Mary was left with the painful task of editing her husband's posthumous poems and bringing out an edition in 1824. Shelley's father promptly had this suppressed, but

Mary triumphed with the publication of a complete edition in 1839. Her admirers, at least in a platonic sense, were numerous.

While Shelley's work found little public acceptance at his death, Byron was the most famous poet in the world when he perished in 1824 while fighting for Greek independence. That he was refused burial in Westminster Abbey is a sign that the hypocrisy associated with the Victorian age had already taken hold. Byron escaped to Greece as a means of declaring his own independence from *serventismo*. He was tired of a life devoted to serving a woman's every need. His publishing prospects in England were dim. As he told Lord and Lady Blessington, with whom he formed a platonic menage in the spring of that fateful year, "though only thirty-six, I feel sixty in mind." He departed with death in view, fated to join his fellow poets in the Romantic Trinity.

What of Teresa? She went back to the count until he died, and then she married an elderly, enormously wealthy French nobleman, the marquis de Boissy. In the best society he always introduced her as "my wife—formerly the mistress of Lord Byron."

chapter 9

THE GREAT MAN, HIS WIFE, AND HIS MISTRESS

{Friedrich Engels and the Burns Sisters;
Alexandre and Ida Dumas and Roger de Beauvoir;
Victor and Adèle Hugo and Juliette Drouet;
Ivan Turgenev and Pauline and Louis Viardot}

The eternal companions of monogamy are hetaerism and adultery.
FRIEDRICH ENGELS

TWO IRISH GIRLS

$\mathcal{T}$HE AMIABLE FRIEDRICH ENGELS WAS no Karl Marx. He was born in 1820 into a wealthy German fundamentalist family. His father, proprietor of a cotton mill in the Rhineland, forbade him to attend the university, demanding instead that he prepare for a business career. In Berlin, Friedrich sided with student radicals and bohemians, the alternative camps to the bourgeois hegemony. Although in 1842 he dutifully went to work in the Manchester branch of his father's firm, he also wrote *The Condition of the Working Class in England*, which impressed the better-educated but naive Marx. Friedrich was guided into the miserable slums of the city and the domestic lives of the proletariat by the formidable Mary Burns, a nineteen-year-old Irish patriot. She, and later her sister Lizzie, shared his bed but continued to work in a factory.

Engels's writing on social questions, unlike his theoretical economics, was influenced by his having a uniquely dual view of love among the classes. From his experience, he observed, "Sexual love in man's relation to woman becomes and can become the rule among the oppressed classes alone, among the proletarians of our day—no matter whether this relation is officially sanctioned or not." Engels dared to voice the common practice of the Victorian era: the rich married for advantage, the middle class to beget heirs, but men sought their pleasure with a mistress or more casually among whores. Industrial workers could afford neither, and to them children meant more mouths to feed. By necessity they formed alliances that were rarely monogamous or lasting.

When Friedrich left for the Continent, where in 1848 he and Marx wrote *The Communist Manifesto*, Mary Burns followed. After the liberal revolutions of that decade failed, Engels returned to Manchester and became a partner in the family firm until he resigned in 1869. Living the life of a well-to-do man, he kept Mary in a *maison secondaire* in the suburbs, entirely separate from his business, clubs, and cultural activities. Blithely, he assured Marx that "the poor girl loved me with her whole heart." Her younger sister Lizzie, who lived with the pair in the sham guise of a housekeeper, loved Friedrich as well. Information on the particulars of this threesome are vague, but this was probably a sexual menage a trois.

Marx's wife, Jenny, a snob, refused to acknowledge the Burns sisters in public. Her husband, who depended on Engels for daily support of his family, had to be diplomatic. Engels's liaisons became an item of discord in Communist circles. He was regarded as a rich mill owner who exploited working-class girls. It is certainly true that Engels was a womanizer. In the late 1840s he cheated on Mary to have an affair with the wife of a former mentor, and he kept various other mistresses, including a "Flemish giantess."

As late as the 1850s Friedrich described himself to Marx as a "BACHELOR" and bored. By the 1860s he was living full time with both Burns sisters in a household he considered communistic.

When Mary died of heart disease in 1863, Friedrich took it hard. He quarreled with Marx over a letter expressing lukewarm condolences—Marx wished it had been his own mother who died! Engels began to live openly with the fiercely Irish Lizzie. He praised her "passionate feeling," which was "worth more to me than any of the blue-stockinged elegances of 'educated' and 'sensitive' bourgeois girls could have been." Marx's daughters called her "Auntie Lizzie," and they all went to the seaside together. Now that the Engels household had turned monogamous, Jenny Marx befriended the woman who guided Engels among the rebels in Ireland. He married Lizzie on her deathbed in 1878.

Engels's menage with Mary and Lizzie Burns rings Victorian chords we will hear again. The dread of eros felt by most wives and the sexual contempt in which their husbands held them cannot be erased by historical revisionism. It was an age in which a virile man demanded a third, an "other woman" who wasn't repressed. She might be a radical, a courtesan, or a bohemian—even the sister of a man's wife. The Freudian scholar Stevan Marcus reminds us that the Burns sisters had the same names as Engels's favorite sister Marie (Mary) and his mother Elizabeth (Lizzie). In Marcus's words, a threesome may have "depths of meaning."

THREE IN A BED

Alexandre Dumas *père*, famous as a man about town, exemplified bohemianism. He flourished in Paris during the late stages of the monarchy and into the Second Empire, the period of the opera *La Bohème*. Dumas's father, a mulatto from Santo Domingo, had been a general under Napoleon, and from him Dumas inherited something of the African. Lucas Dubreton, a biographer, describes him as "a man of fantastic clothes, dazzling waistcoats, golden chains, [who] kills horses and loves women." The dashing author of *The Three Musketeers* was fond of romancing other men's wives. However, Dubreton tells an anecdote, occurring sometime in the 1840s, in which the tables were turned.

Dumas's reigning mistress was Ida Ferrier, a young but rotund actress whom the author foisted on the Comédie Française, which was eager to put on his historical dramas. After seven years, Dumas made the classic mistake and in 1840 married his mistress. His enemies chuckled that her father, to whom Dumas owed money, had blackmailed him: Ida or debtor's prison. The boulevardier acquiesced but kept up his old habits. The couple shared an apartment on the Rue de Rivoli, where Ida occupied sumptuous rooms on the first floor and her husband had quarters above.

One rainy night Dumas, drenched to the skin, arrived home early from a ball. He sought comfort in his wife's heated rooms. Ida, snug under the cover, repelled his advances. Dumas warmed his feet, then sat down to write the night away. (The popular Romantic novelist hired others to do his research and first drafts, which he would then improve before calling his own.) Tonight, as though on cue in a domestic comedy, the dressing room door opened to reveal Roger de Beauvoir, Alexandre's best friend, clad only in his shirt. Dumas, a deadly duelist, was briefly enraged while Beauvoir shook. But then, staring at the pouring rain, he changed his tone. How could he put out his dearest friend in such weather? Instead, he offered him an armchair and then climbed into bed with Ida.

As the fire died down, Dumas unhappily watched his friend shiver. He invited Beauvoir to join him and Ida. Dubreton's assertion, "There they lay, the three of them, sleeping the sleep of innocence," is only a surmise. We don't know what the threesome did in bed. Regardless, Dumas behaved with considerable savoir faire. We are reminded of his son's description of him as "a grown-up child I had when I was very small."

The next morning Dumas, plucking Beauvoir's sleeve, demanded, "Shall we two old friends quarrel about a woman, even when she is a lawful wife? That would be stupid." They clasped arms like old Romans, their bond strengthened by sharing the love of the same woman. This might not have flattered Ida!

"WOMEN FIND ME IRRESISTIBLE"

André Gide, asked who was the greatest French writer, replied, "Victor Hugo, alas." Since the great Romantic's exuberance contrasts so markedly with Gide's classical restraint, the response has been taken as a literary one. However, Gide, gay and guilty over it, may have been reacting to the unabashed self-confidence that caused Hugo to remark to his mistress, "Women find me irresistible." In nineteenth-century literature, Hugo looms as monumental as the Cathedral of Notre Dame whose bells were rung by his creation, the hunchback Quasimodo. As a model great man of his time, Hugo seems impeccable: he enjoyed a lifelong wife who bore him four children, a lifelong mistress whose devotion went unquestioned, and dozens of quickies on the side. Beneath the surface we find a man whose need for the mother and the whore, the classic male-centered menage, best explains his artistic and amorous lives.

Victor, born in 1802, was a puny infant "no longer than a case knife," according to his mother Sophie. He was so ugly that his young brother called him "a beast," but he quickly showed that he was a prodigy: gifted with a photographic memory, he taught himself to read. His father Leopold Hugo, a crude man, was a successful general in Napoleon Bonaparte's army. He and his wife were entirely incompatible. Well before Victor was born, Sophie had become the mistress of General Victor Lahorie, of Republican principles, after whom her son was named. She harbored her fugitive lover when he conspired against Bonaparte. In 1812 Lahorie was executed, and Sophie went into perpetual mourning. General Hugo, who found consolation in the arms of a Corsican woman, left his boy with the example of sacrificing all for liberty—a prize that had been provided by the man who may have been the boy's unacknowledged father.

Young Victor, a mama's boy, was delicately built. He was handsome with beautiful auburn hair; his tiger yellow eyes were steady and keen. His most striking feature was his pronounced forehead, compared by the writer Théophile Gautier to a tower. Fortunately, Sophie insisted her son become a writer. In 1822 he attracted notice with his first book of poems, which won him a pension from Louis XVIII, the restored monarch.

Shortly after his mother died, Victor married his childhood sweetheart Adèle Foucher. The pretty Adèle had a mass of dark hair, a moonlike forehead, and large, brilliant black eyes. Victor, though poor, was domestic by nature and determined to avoid the difficulties that beset his parents' marriage. Yet the wedding ceremony was marred by an ominous event: Victor's brother Eugène, in love with Adèle, went mad and had to be institutionalized. It was the first of the romantic triangles that shadowed Victor's glittering public life as author and statesman. The young couple's love appeared to be blessed by angels. But Victor had a devil in him.

By 1831 Adèle, having weathered five pregnancies and four surviving children, ceased to sleep with her husband. Instead, she took a lover, Charles-Augustin Sainte-Beuve, a perceptive critic who was Victor's most fervent admirer. The slight, sandy-haired Sainte-Beuve seemed to have been born old. Yet his air of melancholy and suave conversation attracted women. Sainte-Beuve candidly admitted, "I have always lived in other people's houses. I have always sought my nest in their souls." To Victor he attached himself like a leech, telling him, "What little talent I have has come to me through your example. . . . I am inspired only beside you, and by what is around you. . . . I am only happy and at home when I am on your sofa or beside your fire." Sainte-Beuve might have added, "Or in your wife's arms," for his affair with Adèle flourished for five years.

On learning of his wife's infidelity with his best friend, Victor found it hard to dismiss the man who'd organized the *cénacle* (literary circle) that defended his works against the old guard. Eugène Ionesco mockingly writes, "When Sainte-Beuve openly admits that he loves Adèle, that the situation has become intolerable, . . . Victor Hugo replies that it doesn't matter and asks him to keep up the publicity efforts." Sainte-Beuve, who had a taste for "private understandings," preferred a discreet menage a trois. As for Adèle, the biographer André Maurois has written, "What she would have liked would have been to keep husband and lover in a joint relationship of chastity." But chastity had flown the coop with fidelity, and the great man felt obliged to send "this flea" Sainte-Beuve packing.

The reaction of the most influential critic of his day was to turn against his former idol, deprecating his work and spying on his personal life. Yet Sainte-Beuve suffered "horrible torments of the soul. . . . My ailment and crime is not to be loved." We are reminded of Shelley's intimate, Hogg, in whom desire could only be roused in a triangular relationship with the poet and his loved one. In these rare instances the communion (or rivalry) between the two men enhances, for the parasitic one, his relationship with the woman. However, both Hogg and Sainte-Beuve give off the odor of scavengers, those who feed on leavings. Without Shelley, Hogg settled into mediocrity; without the Hugos, Sainte-Beuve became impotent.

After Victor Hugo's death, relatives found in the library of his home on Guernsey an envelope with three black seals and "Pudenda" inscribed in his handwriting. The word, meaning genitals, stems from the Latin, "something to be ashamed of." The envelope contained compromising letters from Adèle to Sainte-Beuve that the scoundrel had sent to his mentor "to make him understand the extent of 'his Adèle's' betrayal." Although Victor had preserved this evidence, his relatives destroyed it. Later, by order of a government official, hundreds of additional love letters were consigned to a roaring fire. The nineteenth century didn't tolerate confessions from major figures, and even the sins of their wives were swept under the rug.

Victor, having lost faith in the mother, turned to the whore—or more precisely the courtesan. Juliette Drouet (her stage name) was born in 1806, was orphaned, and then educated in a strict Benedictine convent. At sixteen she fled to Paris's Latin Quarter and became a sculptor's model and mistress. In 1826 she bore the sculptor a daughter, whom he cared for while abandoning the mother to her fate. Since Juliette was beautiful, with dark hair, brown eyes, and a doleful gaze, she quickly attracted new lovers. One, a director, put her onstage, where she was graceful but delivered her lines poorly. By 1832 she had become the mistress of a wealthy Russian nobleman and had learned to charge jewels and clothes to his account.

When Juliette heard that Hugo was casting a new drama, *Lucrezia Borgia*, she showed up. He was captivated, called her a "bird of flame," and assigned her a minor part. The rehearsals became an extended courtship. On a February night in 1833, when Victor and Juliette were expected at an artists' ball, they consummated their love. "Outside we heard Paris singing and laughing, and the masked revelers passing by, shouting. Amid the general festival we had, set apart and concealed in the shade, our own sweet festival. Paris had the false, we had the true blissfulness." So the great man wrote in his mistress's diary, the record of a liaison that would last for the next fifty years.

The mechanics of Victor and Juliette's situation were dictated by his hope of patronage from the court of Louis Philippe, the Bourgeois King. Neither Juliette nor Victor entertained any thought of his leaving Adèle and the children. Juliette, while not worldly, was practical. Théophile Gautier recorded her appeal: "Mme Juliette's head is of a regular and delicate beauty. . . . Her eyes are limpid and sparkling; her mouth is lively, moist and red." Juliette spruced up Victor's musty wardrobe, and he strutted around Paris with a newfound confidence. Of course, she didn't tell him where she'd acquired this sense for men's fashion.

The Hugos moved to a mansion on an elegant square, presently the Place des Vosges. Over Adèle's protests, Victor moved his Juliette close by, seeing to the transfer of her goods. The honeymoon ended abruptly when Victor's *Marie Tudor* flopped. Juliette gave such a poor performance she was yanked after the first night. This disaster ended her theatrical career. Juliette, like Camille, had been a courtesan without a head for finance. She was fifty thousand francs in debt, and her creditors descended on her, seizing her fancy furniture. Victor, made aware of her extravagance, broke with her, driving her to thoughts of suicide.

The lovers were reconciled but on the great man's terms. Juliette sold everything she had left and moved to a two-room apartment. Victor agreed to supply her with a meager allowance, half of which went to pay debts. She had to live on the rest, giving up former friends, shops, and cafés. Since Victor was jealous, Juliette rarely went out, and she shivered through the winter to save on fuel. She became the subject of an experiment that to modern eyes appears cruel and absurd—the redemption of a fallen woman. Victor set his mistress to work making fair copies of his writing, acting as a clipping service, and memorizing his unpublished texts. Her "adored tyrant" ordered Juliette to write him letters that he collected when he dropped in to spend the night. Eventually, these amounted to two thousand worshipful missives, almost prayers to a god.

Only during the summer, on their annual holiday, did Juliette have Victor to herself. In 1835, lounging beside his mistress, he wrote home to Adèle, "I love you. Till we meet again write to me often and at length. You are the joy and honor of my life. I kiss your lovely brow and your lovely eyes." Victor loved his wife according to his own lights; he deluded himself that he'd achieved a synchronicity between her and his mistress. Adèle, concerned about her social position, left off demands in order to work the levers of guilt. "Do not deny yourself anything," she replied to her husband. "I have only one desire . . . that those I love should be happy; happiness in life is gone for me." Likening herself to an "old woman," she assured Victor he needn't trouble himself: "Be happy, very happy!" Her spite is evident.

Victor insisted that his fallen angel do penance, and for a dozen years Juliette lived as a nunnish concubine, lacking even female companionship. "This life of isolation is really killing me," she wrote him. "I wear out my life pacing up and down in a chamber twelve foot by twelve. What I long for is not the world and its stupid pleasures—but *freedom*." When Juliette convinced Victor to let her appear in his drama *Ruy Blas,* Adèle refused to let him flaunt her rival in public. Over time Juliette accepted her seclusion, harsher than that of the convent from which she'd fled. After five years she wrote her master, "I would not exchange the role you have given me for any riches in the world." When at thirty-five she turned prematurely gray, Victor slightly relaxed his rule over her.

The great man saw no need to be faithful to his mistress. He scandalized Paris by dedicating poems in books to her, yet the verses did double or triple duty, for Victor privately presented them to would-be conquests. His philandering was only temporarily halted by the drowning death of his daughter Leopoldine, who'd been kind to Juliette.

In April 1845 Victor Hugo became a peer of France. In July he and Leonie d'Aunet Biard, a blond society woman, were caught in the act by her husband. Suspicious of his wife, Biard had hidden a magistrate underneath the sofa at the apartment where she met her lover. He was astounded when the culprit turned out to be the much-admired Hugo. The infuriated husband demanded that the pair be jailed for adultery, a very serious charge. Victor invoked parliamentary immunity and was set free, which left Leonie to languish behind bars. Adèle, who implored the king to intervene for France's honor, smoothed over the affair. Her looks had become grotesque, and after Sainte-Beuve she never took another lover. Instead, she took Leonie into her own home in order to promote her as a superior mistress to Juliette. In the cafés, Victor's rivals traded barbed jokes. Lamartine quipped that in France a man could rise again—even from a sofa.

Until the scandal died down, Victor hid out with Juliette; she was the sole Parisian ignorant of what had happened. At the age of forty-five, he had become the financial mainstay of three households. His sexual, or more likely psychological, needs drove him to bed down other courtesans. Victor was a true triangulator, demanding the faithful love of several women at once. "The day that no one loves me," he confided to his diary, "I trust that I shall die." But his mistresses must also be *seen* to love him. The exhibitionist plays out his life on a public stage. Victor understood voyeurism or the eroticism of vision, and that is why the deformed hunchback of Notre Dame, Quasimodo, gazing on the flirtation of his love Esmeralda with a handsome soldier, is so sympathetic.

In 1848 Louis Philippe was ousted from power and the Second Republic born. Riots broke out and Victor championed the party of order. He founded the daily paper *L'Événement,* in which he defended liberty. In 1851 Louis Napoleon's nephew, who'd failed at two coups d'état, ran for president. Hugo, his supporter, felt betrayed after the treacherous Bonaparte abolished parliament and declared himself dictator of France. Victor had kept from Juliette his attachment to Leonie. She was still meditating and praying as the Benedictine sisters had taught her. But in June Leonie sent her a packet of Hugo's love letters. The younger mistress, with whom Victor was spending most of his time, expected the elder to give him up, but she was steadfast. When confronted, Victor refused to make a choice. And after Louis Bonaparte defeated the Republicans, Hugo was forced to leave France. Politics had solved his romantic dilemma. Now the cloistered Juliette smuggled Victor, disguised as a working man, out of Paris to Brussels. He gave her full credit:

> The fact that I was not captured and shot, and that I am alive at this hour, I owe to Juliette Drouet who, at great peril to herself, saved me from every trap, watched over me unceasingly, found me shelter and rescued me. . . . She was awake day and night, wandering alone through the murky streets of Paris, avoiding guards, throwing off spies, boldly crossing the boulevards under gunfire, sensing always where I was and when my life was in danger, always finding me.

Adèle remained in Paris to liquidate the Hugo property. When she visited her husband in Brussels, Juliette, despite her new importance, acceded the place of honor to the legal wife. But the Belgians, fearful of Bonaparte, sent the entire Hugo clan into exile on the isle of Jersey in the English Channel.

The Hugos settled into Marine Terrace, a spacious house facing the coast of France. Juliette was set up down the road in a small apartment, from which she could watch her lover pacing his sundeck. Mornings, Hugo wrote furiously, both out of hurt pride and to support his extended family. His first production, *Napoleon le Petit*, was a signal call for liberty that stung the usurping regime. In the afternoons, Victor visited Juliette, then spent the evenings with Adèle and family.

Really, there was but one household. Adèle kept up a pretense of not recognizing the other woman, but she permitted her to solve the problems of adjustment to a beautiful but boring island. In their own ways, wife and mistress learned to cope with exile. When in 1855 the Jersey government expelled the Hugos, Juliette took charge of the details of resettling them all on nearby Guernsey. Victor was disappointed that the people of

France appeared fooled by Napoleon's "bustle of public works, bright lights, Te Deums, parades, [the] whole glittering imperial spectacle." He resigned himself to an indefinite stay and bought a house.

The four-storied Hauteville House was a Romantic fantasy, complete with carved oak walls, oriental draperies, and gothic candelabra. True to form, Juliette was established in a nearby cottage that Victor deeded to her. Her terrace overlooked his, and she could watch his morning hydrotherapy routine while they signaled back and forth. Working in a glass-enclosed belvedere perched on the roof, gazing over the Channel isles, Victor wrote his masterpiece, *Les Misérables,* which was banned in France. Visitors, such as Alexandre Dumas *père,* testified to Victor's youthful vitality. He hosted an occasional dinner party at Juliette's, and his two sons dined there often. On Guernsey Victor attained the peak of his creative power. Wife, children, and mistress formed a family that permitted the great man to concentrate his efforts on the overthrow of the tyrant. The pen proved mightier than the sword.

In 1859 Napoleon III issued an amnesty to the exiles. Victor, contrary to Adèle's wishes, remained in Guernsey until full liberty was restored in France. That year he fell ill, which caused the two women to attend his bedside together. Bending over his prostrate form, their shared concern united them. Victor recovered, but once the window of compassion had opened it would never close. Adèle effectively ceded to Juliette wifely duties and prerogatives. She returned to Paris and was often absent from Hauteville House, which in any case Juliette managed. By now the "other woman" was gratefully accepted by Adèle and admired by the two Hugo sons and remaining daughter.

In 1864, at a dinner in Brussels, Victor's wife and mistress were seated on each side of him. Adèle offered a toast to Juliette: "I drink to you, madame!" In 1867, when Adèle was ill, she presented Juliette with a cameo brooch that Victor had given her during their engagement. When tragedy struck, Juliette sustained the family. They leaned on her after young Adèle went mad from a failed love affair and had to be committed to an asylum. She made herself useful in countless ways and read to the older Adèle, whose eyes were growing weak. In a tender letter to Victor, his faithful mistress wrote, "My heart can find no words in which to express what I feel for all of you. I am overflowing with gratitude for all the happiness which has come to me."

Adèle died in 1868 in her husband's arms. Victor missed her and made no move to marry Juliette, who now lived openly with him. This saint-mistress established what Maurois calls "a cult to Adèle," writing to

Victor, "I love you now with the great heart of your dear departed as well as my own." She understood that her happiness would end once the great man returned to Paris and its temptations. This occurred in September 1870 after Napoleon's defeat by the Prussians and his abdication. Parisians unharnessed the horses of Hugo's carriage and led him down boulevards lined with cheering crowds. He immediately plunged into affairs amorous and political. As Joanna Rich, one of Hugo's biographers, quipped, "The satyr remained a patriot." He held to his Republican principles during Bismarck's siege of Paris and the upheavals of the Commune. The sixty-eight-year-old, living on rat stew, emerged lusty as ever. "Now it is your turn to be happy," sighed the aging Juliette.

Victor, looking like "an old socialist carpenter," was ever ready to bed adoring fans ranging from the actress Sarah Bernhardt to a communarde of eighteen. Juliette worried only over his more serious affairs, such as one commencing in 1872 with Judith Mendes, daughter of his good friend Théophile Gautier. "May I be his forever and useful and beloved by him," Juliette prayed in 1873.

In February 1883, on the golden anniversary of their liaison, Victor sent Juliette a picture of himself inscribed with the line, "Fifty years of love, that is the most beautiful marriage." She passed away that year. Victor, though he continued to enjoy his grandchildren, went into decline and died in 1885 at eighty-three. For over sixty years he had captivated the imagination of readers, including Queen Victoria; he was interred with every honor in the Pantheon. To the end he remained a voracious eater and lover of several women at a time.

A DESPOTIC DIVA

Ivan Turgenev, Victor Hugo's contemporary, was born in 1818 in the Ukrainian countryside. His father was also a military officer who triumphed in battle and knew many women; like the elder Hugo, the colonel, indifferent to his son, died young. Ivan's mother, like Sophie Hugo, erected a shrine to her dead lover, though in her case lover and husband were one. Both writers as boys admired and were supposed to emulate distant heroic figures. Each son became the center of his mother's existence, erotic and otherwise. But how different were these two women!

Sophie Hugo, the attractive, cultivated Parisian, spoiled Victor and insisted he become a writer. She was certain no girl was good enough for her son. Varvara Petrovana Turgenev, by contrast, was a homely girl from a common but rich family; the aristocratic Sergei had married her for her fortune in land and the five thousand serfs she owned body and soul. Varvara

Petrovana was certain that writing was no occupation for a gentleman and that her son was good for nothing. A sadist, she punished the boy on a whim. Thus Ivan's lengthy involvement in a single menage a trois in which he was sometimes odd man out (the mirror image of Hugo's) was an expression of his longing for the benevolent family he never had. Unfortunately, he carried into adulthood a well-developed taste for pain.

In 1918, twenty-five years after Turgenev's death, the Soviet authorities opened a museum to him in Orel, where he was born. This action taken in the midst of civil war shows their concern to honor a writer whose values, unlike those of Dostoyevsky or Tolstoy, were progressive and European. Turgenev was friendly to the Russian revolutionaries of the nineteenth century and a hater of the xenophobic Slavophiles. He was undoubtedly reacting to the tyranny his mother exercised over her vast estate, Spasskoe. She invented a despotic queendom, sat on a throne, appointed domestics to fancy-sounding titles, and authorized them to flog the serfs for imaginary transgressions. Ivan, her favorite, had the worst of it. According to a childhood friend, "no one could equal her in the art of insulting, of humiliating or of causing unhappiness, while at the same time preserving decency, calm, and her own dignity."

Nonetheless Turgenev received a broad education that induced travel abroad and studies in Berlin, where he fell under the influence of German Romanticism. He sat at the feet of Lettina Van Arnim, who'd been a lover of Goethe when she was very young. "In love one is the slave, the other the master," was the wisdom she imparted to Ivan. In his midtwenties, Turgenev was described by Dostoyevsky after a first meeting as "a poet, a talent, an aristocrat, superbly handsome, rich, clever, educated. . . . I can't think what nature has denied him." That something was self-confidence, which he never achieved. He had recently met the renowned soprano Pauline Garcia Viardot, who at twenty-two had come to Saint Petersburg to sing Rossini at the Imperial Opera. Leonard Schapiro, Turgenev's major English biographer, claims Ivan fell in love with Pauline at first sight and "loved her until the last conscious hour of his life, with unquestioning, submissive, undemanding devotion." In brief, he became the slave of a despotic diva.

Pauline, the daughter of a Spanish gypsy, came from a famous family of singers. The possessor of a superb voice, at eighteen she married Louis Viardot, twice her age and director of the Italian Opera in Paris. It was a brilliant career move, for with Pauline's dramatic flair allied to Viardot's business acumen, she would become one of the great stars of her time. A description of the diva by Heinrich Heine is instructive:

She is ugly but with a kind of ugliness which is noble, I should almost like to say beautiful. . . . At times when she opens wide her large mouth with its blinding white teeth and smiles her cruel sweet smile, which at once charms and frightens us, we begin to feel as if the most monstrous vegetation and species of beasts from India and Africa are about to appear before us.

When Ivan met Pauline she had one child by Viardot and she would have more. Her menage, too, would be for life.

It is curious that otherwise excellent critics have failed to comprehend how the Turgenev-Viardot triad was crucial to the art of both Ivan and Pauline and to the peace of mind of Louis Viardot. At first Ivan, despite his impressive stature, dark blue eyes, and long chestnut hair, and his constant praising of Pauline, was treated by her as one of a pack of admirers. Sopranos were the sex symbols of the Victorian era, and men went bankrupt or fought duels over them. In 1845 Turgenev quit his government post and left Russia for France, where he lived with the Viardots at their estate outside Paris. Varvara Petrovana was furious at having lost her son to another woman, but she had to admit, "That damned gypsy sings well."

On his own, Ivan was awkward with women. He had occasionally taken a serf girl and had even fathered a daughter by one, but this hardly called for finesse. In 1846 Ivan broke with his mother over her terrible treatment of her peasants. This left him free to write against serfdom, and his *Sketches from a Sportsman's Notebook*, which portrayed serfs as human, helped pave the way for their emancipation. Ivan had also freed himself, for he could spend the years until 1850 as an appendage of the Viardots. This may have led him into emotional bondage, but it formed the taste of the young writer. He attended Pauline's performances and scouted new operas for her. To exiled radicals such as Herzen he seemed a dilettante, but Turgenev was becoming the most sophisticated of Russian writers.

The influence of Louis Viardot was crucial. He was an impresario but also a writer, translator, and left-wing politician, a true man of 1848. George Sand, another of Pauline's admirers, had introduced her to Viardot, whom she considered "a fine fellow, and altogether worthy of the charming young woman." Viardot played the good shepherd for Ivan much as he did for his wife. He accepted him as a third in his household, encouraged him as a writer, worked with him on joint translations of Russian writers into French, and lent him considerable sums of money when his mother cut off his allowance. Viardot became the accepting father that Ivan so desperately needed.

Did Ivan repay his host with treachery by making love to his wife? He and Pauline first grew romantic toward the end of 1845, but according to Schapiro the pair didn't consummate their love until the summer of 1849. In May Ivan came down with cholera while staying with Herzen in Paris. He recovered, but her lover's close brush with death showed Pauline what he meant to her, and she yielded. Turgenev's journal records: "26 June I was for the first time with P."

Since Pauline traveled all over Europe for engagements, the pair carried on their amour by correspondence, Ivan writing in French but slipping in passages of endearment in German. "I think of you every minute, of the pleasure, of the future," he gushed in the early transports of their love. Then he was compelled to wonder, "What is the matter with Viardot? Does he perhaps dislike the fact that I am living here?" Viardot soon made it clear that he chose Turgenev over Pauline's other would-be lovers. Still, the devotion among the three would take time to build.

In 1850 Pauline became infatuated with handsome Charles Gounod, who was composing his opera *Sappho* for her. The miserable Turgenev forced himself to return to Russia where an implacable Czar Nicholas I was imprisoning all opponents. He had pressing practical reasons for visiting his native land, but Pauline's coolness was the decisive factor. He put his feelings into the play he was writing at this time, *A Month in the Country*, the most enduring expression of his idée fixe: love leads to loss. The scenario resembles Ivan's dilemma. The lead, Rakitin, is in love with Natalia Petrovna, whose name resembles Ivan's mother's but whose self-centered character is a version of Pauline. Her husband Arkady is friendly toward Rakitin, who has for years devoted himself to Natalia. As David Garnett, the chronicler of Bloomsbury, observed, Rakitin plays the *cavaliere servente* in the same way Turgenev did in the household of the Viardots.

A tutor for Natalia Petrovna's small son, Alexey, arrives, and Natalia falls in love with him, leaving Rakitin in the cold. Yet the latter's subjection to Natalia knows no bounds. "I belong to her absolutely," he admits in act two. "To part with her would be, without any exaggeration, like parting with life." When Rakitin confesses his love for Natalia to Arkady, the husband takes his side and is concerned that he suffer no emotional damage. "I am not as good a man as you are," Arkady tells him. He even promotes the *cavaliere* to his wife!

It is no use. In act five, the defeated Rakitin bears his anguish and resentment of Natalia to his rival, the tutor. "You will find out how these pretty hands can attack, with what kind of devotion they can tear your heart to pieces." When we recall that Pauline's two best features were her black eyes and lovely hands, it becomes certain that Turgenev expressed his own deep feelings in this masterpiece. Indeed, years later, he admitted to an actress, "Rakitin is myself. I always portray myself as the unsuccessful lover." In reality the bumbler Ivan won the heart of Pauline and her husband Viardot, who sided with him to oust Gounod. He had, in Schapiro's words, "interwoven his life with theirs, that of the whole family."

In Russia, Turgenev's work was either censored or ignored. For the crime of praising Gogol, author of *Dead Souls,* he was arrested and jailed, then exiled to Spasskoe, of which he was now master. He arranged for his serfs to buy their freedom, passed the time by writing and shooting, and took a serf girl as sexual companion. But he wrote a friend, "Even immorality is no cure for boredom." Ivan corresponded frantically with Pauline, still couching his true feelings in German. Two lines, a carnal couplet, describe the sexual acts with Pauline about which he fantasized: "I kiss your feet for hours on end. A thousand thanks for the dear fingernails." Viardot, understanding the needs of his wife, was pleased to have a steady, submissive third in the family.

During the 1850s Turgenev was in and out of Paris, sometimes returning to Russia, depending on where Pauline had an engagement. If they were lovers, it was only intermittently, and meanwhile she bore two more children by her husband—or was Turgenev the father? We may never know. He hated living in France and disliked French poetry, music, and scenery. When, in rebellion, he became attracted to his youthful cousin Olga, Pauline called him back to the Viardot hearth. In 1857 he wrote a Russian friend, "I love this woman so much that I am prepared to dance on the roof, stark naked and painted yellow all over, if she orders me to."

If Pauline was away on tour or acting cool, Turgenev and Viardot went shooting or together translated Russian authors. Schapiro makes clear, "There is no evidence of any kind of friction or strain between the two men." When in 1863 the Viardots took a villa outside Baden-Baden, a fashionable watering place in the Black Forest, Turgenev moved nearby, living with his natural daughter Paulinette, whom the Viardots helped raise. At forty, Pauline's voice cracked on the high notes, and she was obliged to sing in smaller German theaters. Her house became a center for concert artists, and she constructed a theater there for performances. The king and queen of Prussia, Bismarck, and the French empress Eugénie, not to mention Richard Wagner, were among the Viardots' guests.

Pauline's romantic feelings revived, which led to a resumption of her sexual relations with Turgenev. The years at Baden-Baden were his most blissful. He set Russian poems to music, collaborated on operettas with

Pauline, and promoted her singing, though he realized her voice was gone. She forbade him to use snuff and molded him to her standards. Turgenev was in love with the whole family. He doted on their daughter Claudie, to the neglect of his own, and included Claudie in his will. At the conclusion of the Franco-Prussian war he returned with the Viardots to Paris. The famous author continued to devote himself to the fading star, while her husband accepted Turgenev's presence as part of daily life. The surviving correspondence between the two men testifies to the genuine friendship between them.

Surprisingly, in 1872 Turgenev published *The Torrents of Spring*, a partly autobiographical novella that indicates a suppressed hatred of Pauline. The story deals with "an obsession leading to a man's ruin" when he falls in love with a seductive woman who though rich, stems from the peasantry. The narrator must give up his young true love for this nymphomaniacal sadist, and in the end he has become a shell left with only regrets. The author appears to say loneliness is the inevitable fate of those who would perch "on the edge of a strange nest." The seductress is clearly modeled on Pauline, and *Torrents* was one of the few works Turgenev didn't submit for her approval before publication. Yet in 1879 we find him extolling the beauty of Pauline, "whom I love so deeply and tenderly!"

Turgenev spent his last years as a semi-invalid in the home of his old friends. Many distinguished guests came to call, among them Henry James. In 1883, dying of cancer and delirious with pain, Turgenev recognized Pauline. "Here comes the queen of queens," he whispered in Russian, "and how much good she has done." The subconscious reference to his mother is unmistakable. All in all, the menage disappointed the man but made the artist. Indeed, Turgenev wrote his autobiography and called it *Life for Art*. Pauline took charge of the manuscript, destroyed a portion, and requested that the remainder be published ten years after her death, which occurred in 1910. Her heirs have refused to make it public.

OURS IS SO MUCH BETTER

Let the Italians have the last word on the mistress. Luigi Barzini, writer and politician, retells a famous joke about the Italian sense of propriety where the "other woman" is concerned: The wife of a wealthy Milanese manufacturer discovered her husband was keeping a young woman half her age. On a gala evening at La Scala the wife spotted her rival in a box, splendidly dressed and glowing with diamonds. Afraid of a scene, the husband pleaded, "Don't be stuffy, darling. Everybody in my position has a mistress. Even my partner. Do you want to see his girl? She is sitting two boxes beyond mine." The wife pointed her mother-of-pearl binoculars at this other woman and looked at her for one long minute. Then she turned to her husband: "What a choice! Vulgar, dressed in bad taste, loaded with cheap jewelry and not pretty at all." And she added with pride, "*Ours* is so much better."

Barzini, who died in 1984 but whose fond recollections of mistresses extended back to the turn of the century, stressed both their institutional place in the scheme of things and their "otherness." He reminisces, "European children took for granted, years ago, that there were two kinds of women: women like one's mother, aunts, grandmothers, sisters, cousins, family friends; and the others. The others were habitually called 'them.'" Even as a boy Luigi realized the others were more beautiful and better turned out than their domestic sisters. They were mysterious and lived out of sight. They adored children but never had their own. They often appeared bored.

Family women never acknowledged mistresses in public, but in private they were the leading subject of gossip. Ladies recorded the habits, caprices, and love affairs of "them," and some mistresses became as casually talked about as today's movie stars. Because Luigi's grandmother was liberal minded, she took him and his siblings to visit "one of them." It was Christmas and the woman became nearly hysterical over the children, piled on expensive gifts and cried when they left. The mother and the whore, both loving the same man and each secretly desiring the place of the other—until recently, this was the arrangement that ruled the boudoirs of much of Europe.

Barzini claims that although the "other woman" has become more scarce, she can never be abolished. "A good mistress," he points out, "very often keeps a leaky legal household afloat." He adds that "such *ménages à trois* are seldom broken up by a *crime passionel.*" The bloody triangle remains rare on the Continent. Yet Barzini admits most mistresses have become modern. "They live exciting lives, ski, play golf in the best clubs, drive their own Lamborghini, have open love affairs, . . . are received everywhere, and can be distinguished from the certified ladies [only] by a diminishing number of qualified experts."

While this sounds American, it is merely that the mistress has evolved over time into the unmarried woman whose life, as well as her car, is her own. In a sense she was always the independent one, the guidepost in the morass of the industrial era. "What would many of us do without *them?*" concludes Barzini. He needn't have worried—the menage will reform on more solid and equal ground.

chapter 10

THE QUEEN AND
HER CUCKOLDS

{Catherine the Great; Queen Victoria;
Harriet and John Taylor and John Stuart Mill;
George Eliot and the Leweses;
John and Effie Ruskin and John Millais;
Jane and William Morris and Dante Gabriel Rossetti}

Most fair and fearful, feminine, a god!
ALGERNON SWINBURNE

*C*uckold IS DEFINED BY THE *Oxford English
Dictionary* as "a derisive name for the husband of an unfaithful wife." The
word is a corruption of *cuckoo,* and the sense stems from that bird's habit
of laying its eggs in another bird's nest. Originally, the term applied
equally to the adulterer, though never the adulteress, thus leaving the dubi-
ous honor to the male sex. Chaucer asserts that he who has no wife cannot
be a cuckold, but male psychology has changed since his day. Women, as
well, feel a sense of outrage at being cheated on. Essentially the cuckold is
a ridiculous figure, and the notion of his wearing horns probably stems
from the hornlike projections of the cuckold fish, also known as the cow-
fish, an unhandsome aquatic specimen.

Society has scorned the cuckold who wears his horns lightly. This is
not because, as some scholars via Engels have alleged, the husband is
being cheated out of his property by his wife's lover. Rather, adultery has

been taken as a breach of both holy writ and the social code. The Spaniards in the sixteenth century would mount a cheerful cuckold on an ass and parade him for the populace to jeer at. Othello is thought wrong to have murdered Desdemona largely because he is mistaken about her cuckolding him. In the O. J. Simpson criminal trial, one issue we feel sure influenced the jurors to acquit him was Nicole Brown's alleged free and easy sex life, which was bound to enrage her ex-husband. By contrast, living in a menage a trois can involve being cuckolded and accepting, if not liking, it. There have always been women who inspired devotion in their cuckolds.

Queens excelled at this game, at least before the present royals gave their profession a bad name. Catherine the Great, born into the minor German aristocracy, was a beautiful, proud, and shapely young woman who was married off to Duke Peter of Holstein, selected as her successor by the reigning monarch of Russia, Elizabeth. The feeble-minded Peter was unable to consummate his marriage. While her husband played with toy soldiers, Catherine, goaded by Elizabeth, took a lover and bore a son and heir. Isolated, she tried new lovers, read the French Encyclopedists, and became a talented horsewoman. In 1761, within months of Elizabeth's death, Catherine, in a gorgeous uniform and mounted on her stallion Brilliant, led troops against her husband, Peter III, deposing and murdering him.

As empress of Russia, Catherine continued the modernization begun by Peter the Great; she liberalized the economy and promoted education and the arts. She replaced torture with a genuine code of laws. In time Catherine grew fat and notoriously sexually voracious, but she weathered wars and revolts without much difficulty. However, the menage a trois she established with Gregory Poterakin, her trusted chief deputy, and Peter Zavadofsky, her young Polish secretary, caused an avalanche of censure and gossip. The Russian nobles on whom she depended had winked at promiscuity, but the open making of devoted cuckolds troubled them. Toward the end of her reign, Catherine was obliged to reinstitute the hated secret police to watch her enemies.

After the empress's death in 1796, her son, Paul I, had the remains of his murdered "father" exhumed and buried next to his mother at the main cathedral of Saint Petersburg. After all, Catherine had ruled at the sufferance of the men around her, through her choice of lovers and cuckolds. Elizabeth I of England, the so-called Virgin Queen, was equally careful to balance one suitor against another, notably Raleigh and Essex. Whatever the state of her hymen, Elizabeth learned from the fate of her mother,

Anne Boleyn, never to grow dependent on a husband and always to appear, if not be, chaste.

Queen Victoria, ruler of Britain, empress of India, and the ultimate Victorian, may have taken a lover even before her beloved Albert died. Her bodyguard John Brown, a redoubtable Highlander, had risked his life to save hers. He was constantly at Victoria's side and took amazing liberties. The public believed the rumor but saw a discreet menage as their dumpy queen's prerogative.

The "queen" on which we focus here was empress only of her own home. Despite her image as a passive couch-bound woman, the wife in a solidly middle-class family of the nineteenth century had quite a domain to rule. As mother she received obedience from her children, of whom there might be a good many. She supervised their education, music lessons, and social life. Of course she ordered the servants about, received and haggled with the tradesmen, not to mention the seamstress and milliner who made her elaborate wardrobe to order. At the center of the Victorian household was no angel but a shrewd monarch in miniature.

In a democratization of the title, any bourgeois wife was now entitled to be called a "lady," provided she grasped the hypocrisy demanded by the system. And a lady was permitted to manage a lover. Scholars, notably Peter Gay, have brought to light the lubricity of the Victorians. Theirs was an age rampant in prostitution and pornography, yet people seldom admitted to what they were hiding, not even when it became obvious. Virginity before marriage was crucial, and thus the sexuality of women, not to mention children, was rigorously denied. Yet female bohemians and artists were known to collect men. Turgenev, with surprising candor, remarked, "I have never understood passion felt for a young girl; I prefer the married woman who is experienced and free and is better able to manage herself and her passions." Terming the married woman "free" reverses our present-day standards, which we suppose to be sophisticated.

In Louisa May Alcott's rediscovered *A Long Fatal Love Chase*, Rosamond is swept away by the man of her dreams, Phillip Tempest, but while honeymooning at Nice she becomes suspicious of his fidelity. To distract her from his clandestine rendezvous at the opera, he tells her that a young Italian has been hanging round: "The boy is in love with you and thinks you an iceberg like most English women because you don't see the necessity of having a lover as well as a husband." The novel's reference to a *cavaliere servente* was partly why it was thought too sensational to be published in the 1860s. The Victorians didn't foresee the sexual liberty to come;

rather, they longed to go back to the Romantics or still farther to the pagans. Their schizophrenia about sex—never owning by day what they sneaked at night—stems not from a new era imagined only by utopians but from the nostalgic memories of an earlier, more permissive time.

TWO HIGH-MINDED MENAGES

There were a few who did look forward, who both acted and spoke in a daring manner. During the summer of 1830 the eminent Unitarian clergyman W. J. Fox brought the promising young philosopher John Stuart Mill to a London dinner party given by a rich merchant and his wife. John and Harriet Taylor, married four years and the parents of two sons, were Fox's parishioners. Harriet had confessed to him that despite being at the center of a group of intellectuals, she felt smothered. Fox intended the bachelor Mill as a gift to the lonely young wife, whose older husband was absorbed in business and reform politics.

Fox, though portly and married, was carrying on a practically open affair with his beautiful ward, Lizzie. When his wife complained, he moved her upstairs while he entertained Lizzie down below. Fox was no hypocrite, and when his wife went public with her accusation of adultery, he denied it was any business of his parishioners. He split the congregation but kept his ministry and his mistress! Yet even Fox must have been surprised by the result of his matchmaking.

Mill, of Scottish ancestry, was a victim of the educational theories of the Utilitarian philosopher Jeremy Bentham, as applied by his father. The elder Mill had attempted to turn the "gifted and amiable youth . . . with rich auburn hair and gentle pathetic expression," as Thomas Carlyle described him, into a rational thinking machine, permitting neither frivolity nor friends. Every moment of the boy's time conformed to a rigid schedule. At four years old he read Greek, and after training in logic and exposition, he became a formidable debater. However, Mill in his *Autobiography* admitted, "I grew up in the absence of love and in the presence of fear." In his early twenties, on the threshold of a brilliant parliamentary career, he broke down. Though reading the Romantic poets solaced him, he wouldn't fully recover until he met his soul mate.

Harriet, married to John Taylor at age nineteen, was described by a contemporary as "possessed of a beauty and grace quite unique of their kind. Tall and slight, with a slightly drooping figure, the movements of undulating grace. . . . Large dark eyes . . . with the look of quiet command in them." Actually, Harriet was only five feet tall, much shorter than Mill, and soft-spoken, but her bearing had a regal quality.

Carlyle, who hoped to make Mill his protégé, wrote ironically of the results of Mill's meeting Harriet: "That man, who up to that time had never looked at a female creature, even a cow, in the face, found himself opposite those great dark eyes that were flashing unutterable things." Mill was thrust into an impossible situation. John Taylor was his colleague in the Reform Club, a group that would help found the Liberal party. Taylor was broad-minded and accepted his wife as his intellectual superior, deferring to her opinions. Mill described him as "upright, brave and honorable" but insisted he lacked the sensitivity to be a suitable mate for such a paragon. Phyllis Rose in *Parallel Lives* makes the unlikely claim that Taylor's "aggressive and brutal" sexual demands disgusted his wife. But Harriet continued to sleep with him and would bear another child, a daughter. Instead, it was Mill himself who motivated Harriet to involve herself in a stimulating relationship with another man.

Michael Packe, Mill's biographer, summed up the dynamics of the three-way connection that would span nineteen years: "All revolved around Harriet.... Two men were devoted to her; both were distinguished, and one was rich. She managed the household of one and the philosophy of the other. Both were perfectly content that the extraordinary equipoise should last indefinitely." This claims too much for the menage, which would encounter some rocky stretches.

Mill and Harriet saw each other daily or exchanged impassioned letters. He compared her to Shelley in thought and feeling and wanted to spend every moment in her company. Together they read poetry, while Harriet introduced him to the beauty of art distinct from its utilitarian value. Her enthusiasm swept away years of arid study. Mill, a child in the instinctual realm, let Harriet lead him toward emotional maturity. By mid-1832 John Taylor became disturbed by malicious gossip and asked his wife to break off an involvement that was leading her into danger. Mill, whose own career was threatened, agreed on the surface.

At first letters and then secret meetings kept the pair in touch. Taylor went to his club when he supposed Mill was going to visit his home. "I have been well and happy since that delicious evening," wrote Harriet to Mill. In 1833 she left for Paris for six weeks to sort out her future. Mill joined her and wrote to the Reverend Fox that Harriet was "convinced that we are perfectly suited to pass our lives together." Meanwhile her letters to her ever-generous husband grew warmer, almost romantic. "Harriet Taylor was not unusual in finding deep satisfaction in being the apex between two men," writes Rose.

The Parisian interlude sealed Harriet and Mill's resolve to be together. However, neither wanted to cast off Taylor, who couldn't imagine existence without his wife and family. Harriet's solution was to invoke the Utilitarian credo of the greatest happiness for the greatest number. The most amenable solution was for her to continue to live with her husband while she entertained her lover. After repenting of his possessiveness, Taylor rented a house in Kent where Harriet could receive Mill most weekends. When not in London, she and her infant daughter occupied this place, which her husband and sons visited on occasion. Amazingly, both men accepted the arrangement as a sacrifice on Harriet's part.

Taylor's toleration encouraged the pair to appear arm in arm at an evening party. In *John Stuart Mill and Harriet Taylor,* F. A. Hayek reports that "the manner of the lady, the evident devotion of the gentleman, soon attracted universal attention, and a suppressed titter went round the room." Everyone was shocked at a married woman being escorted by an eligible bachelor assumed to be her lover. The men were cold to Mill, the women cut Harriet. Their bold attempt to appear together in London drawing rooms redounded against them. The lovebirds had violated the unspoken Victorian code: sin in private. The pair were obliged to sever their social ties and withdraw to a little fortress. All three remained politically active, however, and their partnership brought forth such seminal books as *Principles of Political Economy.* When the Italian patriot Mazzini arrived in London, the Taylors opened their home to him.

Whether Mill and Harriet became lovers in the usual sense has been as hotly debated as whether Mrs. Taylor was the coauthor of Mill's works, especially *On the Subjection of Women,* a demand for equal rights that influenced Earl Russell, Bertrand's grandfather, when he was prime minister. Mill insisted the pair had remained chaste; he also credited Harriet with an equal or superior part in his productions. On both subjects he probably exaggerated. Mill and Harriet both suffered from bad health due to what was then termed "consumption." But Mill rallied whenever he and his love traveled unchaperoned on the Continent. Did Harriet have a masochistic streak? Or did she detest physical love because she felt it exploited women? She did conceive three children, and John Taylor was not the type of man to force himself on her.

The fragmentary evidence we have of her love affair makes her sound quite normal. During 1836, the pair spent two months on a lark in Italy. On another vacation, word filtered back to Carlyle, jealous that Harriet had absconded with his protégé, that they had been seen "somewhere in France . . . eatin' grapes together off o' one bunch, like two lovebirds." She and Mill hated to be apart, and in London they would rendezvous at the zoo, safe from interruption. In the country, Harriet waited breathlessly for Mill's love letters. He sent these poste restante (general delivery), which is how most interesting Victorian mail arrived. Wendell Johnson, author of the perceptive *Living in Sin*, points out, "If there was nothing illicit about their relations . . . there was certainly an air of intrigue and even, sometimes, of secrecy."

During one trip in 1839, the pair proceeded alone from Rome to Naples, where they spent three weeks. They behaved as though they were lovers. "They had covered their traces well—so well that they could risk unusual intimacy. They stayed in the same hotel . . . in beautiful, discreet Sorrento [where] they took rooms on the same floor at an inn called La Sirena." Mill called Harriet "Beauty," she dubbed him *"caro mio."* Although their intimacy was obvious to all, Mill, as a gentleman, continued to deny it. The Victorians (Matthew Arnold for one) thought it worse to condone adultery than to commit it.

That Harriet was able to remain Mrs. Taylor, a mother whose children doted on her, was due in part to the severity of the law that would have taken away her children (and property) if she had left her husband, no matter the reason. Divorce—freedom of self—was the essential right women finally obtained during the nineteenth century. Harriet's education of her lover and husband on the evils of marriage as it stood helped bring about gradual reform. This menage, which couldn't have existed without the cooperation of John Taylor, ended well enough. Harriet, returning from a stay abroad in 1849 with Mill, found her husband stoically suffering from cancer. She nursed him round the clock, and he died in her arms. A decent period of mourning intervened before Harriet became Mill's wife. Their collaboration in the few years they had left, writing the seminal *On Liberty*, helped loosen the legal and social bonds in which humans are forever entangling themselves.

George Eliot was no lady. Born Mary Ann Evans, she came of respectable if commonplace forebears and attended school in the industrial Midlands where she learned little more than piety and manners. She educated herself through her aptitude for languages; plain looking and earnest, she seemed cut out to be a schoolmarm. Yet she fascinated men of an intellectual bent, and in 1851 she was invited by John Chapman to stay with his family in London. Chapman published the reformist *Westminster Review*, edited by John Stuart Mill. Evans gladly fled the "grim satanic mills" for what she supposed were the greener pastures of the mind.

Chapman regarded Evans as a prodigy whose literary ambitions he wished to further. He neglected to inform her that his household was a menage a trois, since the governess of his children was his mistress. Wendell Johnson comments, "John Chapman must have been an extraordinary man. His diary's frank account of his affairs suggests as much." We have seen that husband, wife, and mistress comprised a common Victorian triad, and the personal diary was the discreet place in which to confess it. As the wife grew tired of birthing children, the arrangement suited all concerned.

However, Evans, the nascent novelist, brought to the Chapmans a prying eye and inquisitive mind. There was about her the purity of a woman who refused to play in the garden of love. Chapman's clandestine but functional threesome was transformed into a bickering quadrangle. The two other women turned on Evans, and within a few weeks she fled. Several months later she returned more cautiously to London and became the subeditor of the *Westminster Review*, launching her career. She and Chapman worked together, but he had learned better than to bring her home.

After a failed adventure with the social Darwinist Herbert Spencer, who found her too homely to marry, Evans met George Henry Lewes, a liberal critic and biographer of Goethe. They first became intellectual companions and then lovers, sealing their bond in 1854 with a "honeymoon" in Germany. Lewes was already married, and because he had long been part of a menage a trois with his wife Agnes and another man, and Agnes had borne children by both men, a divorce was unlikely. Indeed, Lewes continued to support Agnes and all her children. Meanwhile he and Evans, who published her novels under the pseudonym George Eliot, lived openly, almost proudly, "in sin" for twenty-five years until Lewes's death in 1878. Their home became a center for writers and artists happy to be entertained by the so-called adulterous couple. Yet they could not dine out together, and Eliot wryly remarked that truly loose women took their lovers on the sly and were "still invited to dinner."

The fortress of Victoriana, defended by the impenetrable walls of hypocrisy, was sniped at from the camps of political liberalism and artistic bohemia. But not until the twentieth century would this stronghold be undermined by the sappers of the Freudian unconscious. Till then the souls fettered by "propriety" and tortured by sins of their own devising, raised a lament to the steely idols of "progress," "survival of the fittest," and the "white man's burden." With temptation everywhere, shop girls a dime a dozen, prostitutes underfoot, and drugs as unregulated as sharp business dealing, our supposedly upright forefathers held to one surety: *appearances mattered.*

BEATA BEATRIX

On his wedding night in 1848, John Ruskin, who dominated art criticism in the latter half of the nineteenth century, informed his childlike bride Effie Gray that he would never defile her purity. Effie, who wanted children, was not pleased, but Ruskin preoccupied himself with defending that small band of idealistic artists who formed the Pre-Raphaelite Brotherhood. Their idea was to return to the simplicity and feeling of devotional painting before the Renaissance. Ruskin supported this principle, and while the weight of his opinion made the Pre-Raphaelites respectable, their own talents and savvy helped some of them to become rich and famous.

John Millais, the obvious prodigy in the lot, gravitated to the Ruskin home. He pleased the critic by flattery and Effie by noting her beauty and asking her to pose for him. As Wendell Johnson writes, "the emotional triangle developed rapidly in that strange household of neurotic husband, virgin wife, and eager young guest." In the summer of 1853, the trio went to Scotland on a working vacation. Ruskin ignored the pair, who were falling in love, and examined rocks instead. Effie had bit of the apple and found out what she was missing; that year she demanded and got an annulment. By failing to deflower his wife, Ruskin had neglected the husband's sacred duty.

Johnson supposes Ruskin wasn't impotent or homosexual, just too sensitive for the task. At any rate, the "triangle" he describes here was typical of a menage centered on a dissatisfied wife. Usually the disgrace of a formal separation was avoided. But Millais's career had been launched, and he and Effie were unusually well matched: they married and had eight children. Ruskin would fall in love with a ten-year-old, court her until she was sixteen, and then be rejected by her parents. He ended by losing his mind. But before this came to pass, he attached himself to one of the more intriguing Pre-Raphaelite couples: Dante Gabriel Rossetti and his model Elizabeth Siddal, called Lizzie.

The young men of the brotherhood came from the professional middle class. They were gentlemen, and as artists they were strongly attracted to beauty. Images of the models they painted, loved, and married created a corresponding desire in other men on the rise, as well as emulation in their women. A higher sort of erotic interaction among model, artist, and viewer was the special province of these rebels who would become highly successful but would fail to accomplish an artistic revolution. That was left to the outcasts such as Van Gogh, Gauguin, and Modigliani.

The Pre-Raphaelite Brothers were always on the lookout for working-class girls to pose cheap. Lizzie, from a respectable but desperately poor family, worked in a milliner's shop near Leicester Square. In 1850 one of the artists, a rake, spotted her languorous form and flowing red-gold hair. He persuaded her to pose for him. She was taking a bold step because artist's models, at that time, were lumped in with prostitutes in the eyes of society. Lizzie's discoverer realized that she was different. "By Jove! she's like a queen," he boasted, "magnificently tall, with a lovely figure, a stately neck, and a face of the most delicate and finished modeling." He compared Lizzie to a goddess, and she must have felt like one when the Brothers fought over her for a model.

The most famous portrait of Lizzie is Millais's *Ophelia*, in which she is portrayed as a corpse floating on a river, a purely innocent victim. More indicative of the woman is her self-portrait. Where the artists saw Lizzie as, in Ruskin's words, "a noble, glorious creature," she painted herself as troubled, aware that she was just a step away from immortality in more ways than one. Dante Gabriel Rossetti pictured Lizzie in the guise of saint or Madonna, the better for having been raised up from a shop girl. Lizzie had an air of purity that bowled over poets. Ruskin's place in the metaphysical menage was soon taken by the effete but caustic Algernon Swinburne.

Rossetti, the son of an Italian patriot, exuded a brooding sensuality that charmed both sexes. His olive skin, shadowed eyes, and melancholic temperament qualified him to be a leading man. He went clean shaven, had flowing locks, and dressed in a casually elegant fashion. Gabriel was one of four gifted Rossettis, including his brother William (the critic) and sister Christina (the poet). However, a thread of lunacy ran through the family, and Gabriel from the start showed a paranoid fear of exhibiting his paintings. Extreme narcissism drove this conflicted bohemian.

Rossetti's early studies of Lizzie and his 1860 portrait of her, *Queen of Hearts*, which eliminates perspective in favor of color and design, are some of the finest Pre-Raphaelite work. Both before and after their wedding, long postponed due to Lizzie's failing health, Gabriel was openly unfaithful to her. He had a penchant for his fellow artists' mistresses as well as for buxom Fanny Cornforth, a prostitute whom he painted in sensual poses. Lizzie, on her doctor's advice, became addicted to the easily available laudanum. Ever faithful, she distilled her sorrow into a handful of delicate poems. This mating of a brilliant artist with his ideal model—Rossetti, according to his sister Christina, viewed her "not as she is, but as she fills his dream"—foreshadowed tragedy.

One night after the pair had dined with Swinburne, Gabriel and Lizzie quarreled. According to Oscar Wilde, he thrust a bottle of laudanum in her hand, shrieking, "Take the lot." Then he slammed out to see his cheerful Fanny. On return he found Lizzie comatose, the bottle drained. Gabriel spent the rest of his life trying to exorcise the guilt of her suicide. He made the supremely romantic gesture of tucking a notebook of his unpublished poetry in her golden hair to be buried with her. Gabriel painted one last picture of Lizzie, *Beata Beatrix*, in which she is portrayed as Dante's pure love on the point of dying—or rather, rapt in a vision of heaven. She is the martyred fair one, in communion with the unknowable.

Gabriel next made Fanny his main mistress. She inspired him to paint erotic yet refined images. Swinburne, who now shared a house with Gabriel and Fanny, called her "a bitch." To forget his guilt over Lizzie, the most imaginative painter of his time plunged into "an 'alternative,' quasi-bohemian lifestyle [that] was developing, mainly among artists and in Chelsea." Here the menage a trois was as common as later in Bloomsbury, though its practitioners were more forgettable. Two of Gabriel's friends and associates do stand out: Edward (Ned) Burne-Jones and William Morris. Each had married his model and would be involved in a menage in a manner suitable to his character.

PROSERPINE

In 1857 Gabriel and his protégé Ned, while at an Oxford theater, spotted "a stunner"—eighteen-year-old Jane Burden. They discovered that their goddess was the daughter of a poor horse groom and lived off a stinking alley, yet within a few years Henry James was speaking of her as an apparition, the synthesis of all Pre-Raphaelite paintings: "Imagine a tall lean woman . . . with a mass of crisp black hair heaped into great wavy projections on each side of her temples, a thin pale face, a pair of strange, sad, deep dark Swinburnian eyes, with great thick black oblique brows, joined in the middle and tucking themselves away under her hair." When Lizzie's poor health caused Gabriel to return to London, he handed over his discovery to another disciple, William Morris, a dreamer.

Morris, who'd grown up rich, refused to shave or visit a barber. Nicknamed "Topsy," his long, shaggy beard and mane of hair became a trademark. He had an aversion to washing. Morris reveled in resembling the honest laborer, the craftsman of medieval times, whose great defender he would become. He idolized Woman in his monumental verse cycle, *The Earthly Paradise*, but of women in the flesh he knew nothing. It is telling that

Morris's earliest poems were fantasies around the romantic triangle in which a woman must choose between two men. He always identified with the rejected lover. Menage or triangle, the expectation usually exists in our minds before we play it out in life.

At Oxford, Morris, misguided by Rossetti, was trying to become an easel painter, and he asked Jane to model for him. He posed her as *La Belle Iseult* mourning for her absent Sir Tristan. Morris identified himself with dutiful King Mark and Rossetti with the unfaithful knight. During the tedious sittings, he correctly scrawled on the back of his canvas, "I can't paint you, but I love you." Jane agreed to marry the shy young man with the large income. She later admitted to an intimate that she'd never loved Morris. More important to Jane was that she be adored. Swinburne, who understood abasement, exclaimed, "The idea of marrying her is insane. To kiss her feet is the utmost men should dream of doing."

For Jane, Morris created Red House in Kent, a home that would become a landmark in domestic architecture. It was a Pre-Raphaelite dream house with individually designed glass, carpets, wallpaper, and furniture. George Bernard Shaw, a frequent visitor, marveled, "Everything that was necessary was clean and handsome; everything else was beautiful and beautifully presented." The family grew vegetables, kept cows, brewed beer, and churned butter. Indeed, the Morrises appeared to be king and queen of their own earthly paradise, parents of two princesses. However, during their courtship, Morris had written "Praise of My Lady," a poem depicting Jane as King Arthur's adulterous queen, Guinevere. What he foresaw came to pass.

In the mid-1860s Jane rebelled against being an ornament in her husband's collection. Her health declined—the Victorian wife's typical means of avoiding marital relations. A move to the Bloomsbury area of London gave Jane the opportunity to reach beyond her home. This coincided with the renewed availability and interest of Gabriel Rossetti. Morris, who had an explosive temper, was a difficult man to live with. Worse, his sense of romance was confined to medieval legends and Norse tales. As Shaw remarked, "he never discussed his family affairs with me; and I am not sure that he ever discussed them with his family." Jane, who hadn't posed for years, now became Gabriel's model. She badly needed his adoration and could be sure of it.

Jan Marsh, in *The Pre-Raphaelite Sisterhood*, recognizes that Jane, "the chief actor in the drama," made the first move. In 1865 she sat at Gabriel's home in Chelsea for five portrait drawings and posed for a series of photographs that the artist exhibited in a tent in his garden. Marsh observes,

"These construct an image rather than a portrait of Jane. . . . The general effect is decidedly glamorous . . . the pose and gaze expressing the same intriguing melancholy as *La Belle Iseult*, married to one man and in love with another." From this renewal of Jane and Gabriel's passion stem the paintings of Rossetti's dark lady that are among his best; they virtually define the Pre-Raphaelite aesthetic.

Marsh understands that such paintings as 1868's *The Blue Silk Dress* are collaborations between artist and model. Across the top Gabriel wrote, "Jane Morris . . . famous for her poet husband and surpassingly famous for her beauty, now may she be famous for my painting." Jane spent more and more time posing at Gabriel's, and at first Morris accompanied her. It was a threesome of husband, wife, and lover within the headily artistic context of the brotherhood. Then Morris, fatalistic about sexual attraction, withdrew to the background, leaving his wife and former mentor to play out their attraction. Believing that a husband couldn't hold his wife as property, he allowed Jane to come and go and always return. He acted not out of masochism but for the same reason that Hugh Guiler later tolerated his wife Anaïs Nin's far more widespread infidelities: in order that she stay.

By spring 1869 both Jane and Gabriel were paying a price for their love. She suffered from crippling back pain that made her a semi-invalid. Her doctors ordered Jane to a spa in Germany, and Morris accompanied her to Bad Ems. Gay Daly, insightful on the Pre-Raphaelite women, decided that Jane broke down from indecision. She couldn't face the consequences of leaving Morris and realized that Gabriel's own psychic and physical health were shaky. "It is possible that Jane engineered this private interlude with her husband, hundreds of miles away from Gabriel, as a means of renewing the marriage," Daly hazards. If so, she failed. Morris hated the inactivity, and Gabriel continued to pursue Jane via letters, some of which, when she felt poorly, were answered by Morris.

Gabriel, always shy of showing his art, now made a stab at obtaining recognition. He employed another to dig up Lizzie's remains and remove his early poems. The ghoulish incident is well known; the story goes that Gabriel found his notebook partly eaten by worms but was assured that Lizzie's body remained beautiful. Rossetti published his tribute to lost love in order to proclaim aloud that he'd found a *new* beloved. He was willing to transfer his artistic soul from Lizzie to Jane. His brother William called Jane "an ideal more entirely responsive than any other to his aspiration in art." Morris, unwilling to stand between an artist and his muse, had to acquiesce.

With Jane's return to England, the menage resumed. In April 1870 Morris delivered her to Gabriel for a month's stay at a cottage near Hastings. Jane was strong enough to walk with him in the fields and make love alfresco. A sonnet of Gabriel's written at this time exhorts Jane to let him lie on the "sweet bank" of her head while her luxurious hair is spread out. He begs her to shut her eyes and accept his kiss on her warm throat and lips.

Rossetti's *Poems* appeared this same month. Morris effusively praised the cycle of sonnets, "The House of Life," which celebrates Jane, as the finest in the language since Shakespeare. Morris acted according to his communist principles; he derided the notion of women as property and even the nuclear family. He looked forward to a sexual revolution after which mates would choose one another purely out of love. Yet he must have been hurt by the lovers' indelicacy when they returned to London. Edmund Gosse, the critic, described them at an artists' party, "Jane sitting on the model's throne like a queen in a long ivory velvet dress and Rossetti, too stout for elegance, perched on a hassock at her feet." While the *cavaliere* delicately fed his lady berries, tongues wagged.

For the summer of 1871, partly to avoid scandal, Morris and Rossetti jointly rented Kelmscott Manor, an Elizabethan house in deepest Oxfordshire to which the former delivered his wife and daughters. Here the artist and his muse walked in the fields, read and wrote poetry, and painted. Theirs was an idyllic love. Morris meanwhile took off for Iceland where he ranged about, soaking up the atmosphere of the Icelandic sagas. In the fall, despite Gabriel's offer to adopt the girls, Jane returned to Morris in London.

While Gabriel continued to court Jane in paint and verse, an article in the *Contemporary Review* that damned his sonnets as immoral dealt him a blow. He had disguised his verbal lovemaking to Jane by putting the words into the mouth of a husband caressing his wife. "Animalism is animalism," thundered the *Review*. "One might tolerate the language of lust more readily on the lips of a lover addressing a mistress than on the lips of a husband virtually wheeling his nuptial couch out into the public streets."

Though the article was written by a hack, it reveals the seamier side of the Victorian social code. Sex, being dirty and brutal, was what a man did with his mistress or a whore. Wives were for getting children as expeditiously as possible. Above all, love must never see the light of day. Small wonder this moral milieu gave birth to the sadomasochistic sublimation of Bram Stoker's *Dracula!*

From this time forward Gabriel's paranoia had free rein. Tortured by guilt over Lizzie's death as well as his equivocal position with Jane, he was wracked by terrible dreams during sleep. He drank to excess, and worse, he mixed whiskey with chloral hydrate, a depressant that induces physical dependence and mood swings. When Gabriel's friends, worried about his addiction, deprived him of the chloral, he became delirious. Finally he attempted suicide by drinking a bottle of laudanum, but he miraculously survived. He recovered slowly, and in September 1872 Gabriel was reunited with Jane at Kelmscott.

Morris, meanwhile, found consolation with Ned Burne-Jones's wife, Georgie. An affectionate woman, she provided the affection and approval withheld by Jane. It has been theorized that Morris, because he failed to make love to the abandoned Georgie, was impotent. However, as Daly recognizes, "guilt tied him up in knots as his love for [Georgie] conflicted with his love for Ned. He needed them both but worried that he would have to choose." It seems he made a clumsy try, but she repulsed him. Instead, Morris and Georgie studied Karl Marx together, she mastering his theory of surplus value.

At Kelmscott, the half-mad Gabriel painted his masterpiece: *Proserpine*. This mythical figure was carried off by Pluto while gathering flowers and became empress of Hades. Jupiter wished to release her, but since she'd already tasted of the pomegranate she could only ascend to the world of light for half of each year. The picture is composed of a gradation of grays, except for the shocking red of the fruit and Jane's mouth. She is Eve the sensual, one hand restraining the other. Gabriel painted this picture several times over, but his addiction caused him to lose both his ideal subject and artistic touch. He descended into a chloral stupor, and Jane, afraid for her daughters, could no longer visit him. Long before Gabriel died in 1882, still avowing his love for Jane, their relationship consisted only of letters from one semi-invalid to another.

Jane's care of her daughter Jenny, an epileptic, occupied much of her time, and visitors to the Morris household saw a harmonious family. George Bernard Shaw remarked that Jane was the "silentest woman I have ever met. She did not take much notice of anybody, and none whatever of Morris, who talked all the time." But to one man, the minor poet Wilfred Scawen Blunt, she opened herself as never before. Their affair began in 1883, a year after Rossetti's death, and continued for a decade, during which Shaw noticed nothing of it.

Blunt was a Byronic figure, widely traveled in the Middle East, a seducer of other men's wives. His sympathy with women won the forty-year-old Jane as it had his younger conquests. Blunt immediately made love to the woman, who, far from being a statue, was starved for affection.

Blunt was the sort of narcissist Shaw identified as the eternal amateur in art. Yet, Daly writes, "he drew Jane out on the subject of Rossetti, who was in fact more interesting to him than she was." Blunt, a habitual menager, used Jane in a ghost menage to commune with the spirit of the one modern poet he admired.

When Blunt admitted flat out to Jane, "I think I loved you for Rossetti's sake," she wasn't disappointed. "If you had known him you would have loved him," she responded, "and he would have loved you." Blunt continually compared his relationship with Jane to Rossetti's and was pleased when she confided she hadn't become as physically passionate with the dead poet. He compared the live woman with Gabriel's portraits of her, commenting, "In her prime she must have been the most beautiful woman conceivable." But he realized that at heart she was a commonplace, if intelligent, woman who had been in thrall to her appearance.

Jane invited Blunt out to Kelmscott Manor where he found Rossetti's ghost a "constant presence." Morris was there, and the admiring Blunt cultivated him, knowing that an affair with a married woman hinged on "the pleasant relations one may establish with her husband." So a second menage a trois was born round this enigmatic woman. A charade ensued in which Morris, while pretending not to notice, carefully announced his arrival by loud, clumping footsteps. Blunt slept in the next room to Morris, and in the evening, if Jane wanted him, she left a pansy on his bureau. Blunt, once he heard the husband's snores, tiptoed down the creaking hallway to the wife's room and their nightly gymnastics. Certainly there is an Oedipal air about Blunt's needing Morris's tacit approval. But what delighted his second-rate soul were the initials on the dinner napkins: DGR. So desperate was Blunt to acquire Rossetti's talent, as though by osmosis, that he badgered Jane into entrusting him with Gabriel's love letters to her.

During Morris's last illness in 1896, Jane spent hundreds of hours embroidering a coverlet for the bed she had studiously avoided. As did all who knew him, Jane respected the authentic great man who had raised her up from poverty. Her mysterious looks had doomed her to become an icon of the Pre-Raphaelite movement. Only Rossetti, the tortured genius, could perceive and thus mythologize Jane's classic beauty. He couldn't successfully love her, but he did paint her as a queen, a mystic maiden, a sex goddess. In any time or place, such a woman is likely to make her husband a cuckold. If wise, he knows that sooner or later she will leave the other to return home.

chapter 11

FEMME FATALE

{Lou Andreas-Salomé, Friedrich Nietzsche, Paul Rée,
Rainer Maria Rilke, and Sigmund Freud}

Assuredly, a friend thus loves his friend as I love you, O Life, mysterious life.
LOU ANDREAS-SALOMÉ

WHEN IN 1912 LOU ANDREAS-SALOMÉ
arrived in Vienna to study psychoanalysis with Sigmund Freud, her reputation as a femme fatale had preceded her. Earlier, the philosophers Friedrich
Nietzsche and Paul Rée had both found her irresistible. Her second menage a
trois involved the poet Rainer Maria Rilke and Lou's husband, F. C. Andreas,
an orientalist; while Rilke enjoyed her physically and spiritually, Andreas settled for a celibate marriage. Writer and playwright Frank Wedekind caricatured Lou as the bisexual tramp Lulu. Freud, an admirer, called her
intelligence "dangerous," but he later admitted that "we all felt it as an honor
when she joined the ranks of our collaborators and comrades in arms, and at
the same time as a fresh guarantee of the truth of the theories of analysis."

This femme fatale started as Daddy's little princess. Lou was born
Louise von Salomé to an aristocratic German-speaking family in Saint
Petersburg, Russia, in 1861. Her father was a general, and she grew up in luxury near the czar's Winter Palace and at a country dacha. The youngest child
and only girl in a family of five brothers, she was spoiled silly by the men.
Lou shared "a secret bond of affection" with her father. She liked her
mother less; once while watching her swim, the girl cried out, "Dear mother,
please drown!"

Lou had a Russian nurse and a French governess, and was well educated in German. The ignorance in the countryside and the poverty of the capital's back streets were distant to the princess. When Lou grew older, she attended the magnificent balls depicted by Tolstoy in his novels, and since she was pretty, rising young men courted her. But the debutante idolized liberated women, even those with the courage to be terrorists. She felt alienated and longed for a god. Her first adventure was with Pastor Hendrik Gillot, the most brilliant Protestant preacher in Russia, with whom Lou instantly knew she must study.

Lou had chosen her first father-lover. Gillot was rigorous as a teacher but a little too warm. He gave the seventeen-year-old hugs and kisses along with his lessons, which took place while she sat on his lap. On one occasion, with the pastor petting her hair, she fainted. We can imagine which part of the mature man's anatomy she *felt*. Gillot, though married, had plans for Lou to become his mistress. She demurred—not because she wasn't attracted but on the contrary, because her new father figure (the general had died) did stir her bodily. Lou was already certain that "the stronger the desire the stronger the subordination." At eighteen she demanded her mother remove her to Zurich, where she could attend the university.

Lou had discovered one leg of the triad she was to construct for the rest of her long life. She would be strongly attracted to an older mentor, feeling a pull that she claimed was due to her precognition of their intertwined fates. Next she would seek a brother or companion with whom she was more likely to surrender erotically. Salomé learned that her independence from any one man came from positioning herself between two men who loved her equally.

The psychoanalyst Irvin Yalom, in his novel *When Nietzsche Wept*, describes Lou at twenty-one as "a woman of uncommon beauty; powerful forehead, strong sculpted chin, bright blue eyes, full and sensuous lips and carelessly brushed silver blonde hair." Angela Livingstone, a biographer, adds, based on a photo: "She looks resolute and unsmilingly opposed to her own beauty. . . . Not a bluestocking perhaps, but proud and taking pleasure in the fortress of herself." Lou was attractive and highly intelligent but sexually complex, bordering on kinky. Louise Brooks, who played the lead in the silent German film *Lulu* based on Wedekind's novel, captured the flamboyant sexuality that bloomed in Lou Salomé.

In Rome during the winter of 1882, Lou visited the grand relic of the revolutions of 1848, feminist Malwida von Meysenberg. Here Lou met Malwida's protégé Paul Rée, a philosopher in his thirties. This son of a West Prussian landowner had gambled away all his money and come round to Malwida's for a loan. To Lou, this gave him more of an air of romance than his pudgy figure and soft, round face warranted. The two strolled all the moonlit night past the ancient ruins. Rée had never before met a woman with whom he could share his ideas, which, to give them a twentieth-century tag, were existential. After other such excursions, Rée declared his love to Lou.

While flattered by this promising man's attentions, Lou was physically repulsed by him. This trait she thought useful in a comrade or a husband. Lou sensed the morbidity under Rée's affable surface. Tormented by his Jewish origins, he once fainted when they were revealed. Lou tried to win Rée over to her ideal of brotherhood sans sex. She told him of a recurrent dream in which she and two "brothers" were sharing a large apartment filled with books and flowers, each with their own bedroom. According to H. F. Peters, "They were all three living and working together in perfect harmony and it made no difference at all that they were men and she was a woman."

Rée knew the perfect third: his brilliant friend Friedrich Nietzsche. Some years before he and Nietzsche had shared a villa in Sorrento, overlooking the Bay of Naples, with Malwida. This had been a true and glorious metaphysical menage, and Rée hoped the new threesome could create just such an atmosphere. He didn't bother to tell Lou about the peasant girl he and Friedrich had smuggled in at night. Nor did he inform her about the relationship, recently strained, that Nietzsche had with Richard and Cosima Wagner.

In the realm of love Nietzsche was destined to experience little, yet his losses shattered him. The philosopher who would open the Pandora's box of modern thought was born in 1844 in Saxony to a Lutheran pastor and the daughter of a Lutheran pastor. His father died from so-called softening of the brain when Friedrich was still a boy; the cataleptic symptoms of this disease would strike down Nietzsche himself forty years later. The lad grew up surrounded by women. One of them, his sister Lisbeth, would take control of him when he became incapacitated and appoint herself guardian of his legacy. The thinker who became famous for the Superman and the Will to Power was, during his life and afterward, at the mercy of others.

Nietzsche served briefly in a Prussian artillery regiment, but he was so nearsighted that his military career ended when he suffered a serious injury while trying to mount a horse. Absurdly, he would refer to himself as an "old cannoneer." Teaching classical philology at Basel, his poor health caused him to leave on a small pension. During the few years of sanity left, migraines—with accompanying pain, vertigo, and nausea—tortured him unbearably. Nietzsche lived in boardinghouses in Switzerland and Italy, a recluse addicted to a suitcase of drugs used to sustain him by day and quiet his raging brain at night.

The lights of this seedy ex-professor's life were Richard and Cosima Wagner, Liszt's daughter. Exiled from Mad King Ludwig's Bavaria, living with their children (though Cosima was still legally married to the composer Hans von Bülow), the operatic couple presided over a court of adherents in Lucerne. Until 1872, when they left for Bayreuth, Nietzsche visited the Wagners numerous times—a suite in their mansion was reserved for him—and he became both disciple and confidant. It was the most flattering attention he'd ever received, and Nietzsche conceived of the three as the reincarnation of a mythical triangle: Wagner as Theseus, slayer of the Minotaur with the help of Ariadne, whom he deserts; Cosima as the deceived Ariadne; and himself as Dionysus, who rescues and weds Ariadne. He even began a drama along these lines, which thankfully he never completed.

Nietzsche had some justification for his fantasies, since Cosima, twenty-four years younger than the composer and seven years older than the philosopher, mothered him unmercifully. Further, Wagner, a noted philanderer, was tempted to stray from Cosima. Ironically, Wagner was convinced that *he* was the reborn Dionysus, wreaker of havoc on the bourgeoisie. Wagner and Nietzsche were on a collision course, but for a period of several years the threesome, facilitated by the woman Nietzsche called "my beloved, Princess Ariadne," worked mightily to spread the gospel of the "music of the future."

Cosima was tall, spare, and severe. She was talented, but Nietzsche sensed self-doubt in her. The philosopher eventually came to view Cosima as a drain on Wagner. Disillusioned with the woman he once idolized, Nietzsche wrote, "In many cases . . . love is merely a more refined parasitism, a creeping into the being of a strange soul, sometimes even of a strange body, and ah! at what expense always to the host!" Cosima saw Nietzsche as useful to the Meister, but she alternately flattered and cajoled him. A French speaker, she took to correcting the German of the greatest stylist since Heine. While Nietzsche reverently courted both Wagners in long walks and conversations and letters, he held some special fascination for Cosima. Her diary mentions him over 250 times.

The break came in 1878 when Nietzsche fled from the festival at Bayreuth, claiming Wagner's music gave him a splitting headache. That year he published *Human, All Too Human*, an attack on Wagner's (and even more Cosima's) neurotic anti-Semitism and the Meister's final masterpiece *Parsifal*, which he characterized as "employing hysterical heroines and actors with contorted throats." The Wagners were furious, attributing Nietzsche's apostasy to the influence of his friend Rée, "a smooth, very cool Israelite." This turnabout plunged Nietzsche from a seat at the Meister's right hand into the darkness of tawdry rooms, illness, and drugs. No wonder he put so much stock in the offer that reached him in Sicily of another metaphysical threesome.

"THE HOLY TRINITY"

When Nietzsche first met Rée and Lou at Saint Peter's in Rome in April 1882, he bowed gallantly before her, demanding, "From which stars have we been brought together here?" Lou saw a man of middle height, carefully groomed including his bushy mustache, yet one who seemed to stand alone. His half-blind eyes stared at her: "[They] appeared like guardians and protectors of his treasures—silent secrets—not to be glimpsed by the uninvited." Nietzsche promptly fell in love with the free-spirited Lou and, via Rée, proposed marriage. While they were climbing a mountain in the Italian lake district, Lou even kissed him, though how she got past his mustache remains a mystery.

Romantic matters were postponed until May, when the pair met in front of the lion's statue in Lucerne Park. Nietzsche, sure he'd found his "twin brain," nonetheless agreed when Lou insisted she wanted to live and study with both him and Rée in an aptly termed metaphysical menage. The three called it their "holy trinity." H. F. Peters, an astute biographer of both Salomé and Rilke, refers to the three as a "mélange à trois." But due to the two men competing for Lou's attention, a harmonious menage never came about. The experiment does represent a break with the fatuous mores of the nineteenth century. Not even the greats—Wagner, Hugo, Dickens, or Mark Twain—dared to deviate from the reigning doctrine of hypocrisy, or "sex under the covers." Here a broken-down classics professor, a cynical Jewish philosopher, and a czarist general's daughter thought to administer, as Malwida put it, "a slap in the face to the whole world."

Speculation about the three has been abundant. The feminist scholar Biddy Martin suggests Nietzsche and Rée were lovers who wished to include Lou as protection from rumors circulated by the Wagnerians that they were gay. The evidence is sketchy, but even at his craziest, Nietzsche's fantasies conjured up women. At Bayreuth, Lou, incensed by Lisbeth Nietzsche's hectoring, announced that her brother had made indecent advances but that both philosophers had agreed to learn from her.

The photo usually captioned "The Holy Trinity" tells much of the story. In Lucerne the three went to a well-known photographer to seal their pact with a portrait. For a prop they chose a small farm cart, and Rée and Nietzsche were yoked to it in place of draught animals; round each one's arm was tied a piece of rope held by Lou as reins. In the cart, she wields a makeshift whip, and her expression is sly. Rée seems uncomfortable, Nietzsche ecstatic. In view of Lou's excursions into the psychology of sadomasochism, she was probably the one who instigated this unforgettable snapshot of a menage at play.

The vicissitudes of the threesome over the next several months were predictable. For some weeks Lou stayed with Rée on his family estate, then joined Nietzsche, chaperoned by the hated Lisbeth, for an idyll in the mountains. Lou wanted camaraderie from Rée, instruction and inspiration from Nietzsche. Yet she encouraged the men's fantasies, until Nietzsche observed, "I must not live too long near you." In October the three reunited in Leipzig, planning to establish their menage in Paris. However, Lou, concerned by the intensity of Nietzsche's feelings toward her, began to lean toward the calm, brotherly Rée. When Nietzsche finally accepted that he must lose both his beloved and his best friend, he bid them a sad good-bye.

A vicious interchange of letters followed. In one, Nietzsche pinpointed Lou's weakness, a narcissism that oddly reflected her inner strength: "This cattish selfishness of yours that is incapable of love, this feeling for nothing, are to me the most repugnant traits ... worse than evil." Influenced by Lisbeth, he raged against "this dry, dirty, nasty-smelling monkey with her false breasts." Threatening suicide, he boasted of surviving an overdose of opium. Then he admitted he was "nothing but a semi-lunatic, tortured by headaches, who has been completely unhinged by his long solitude." From being significant in a daring menage, he'd become again the loner.

Nietzsche may have recognized the necessity of his amorous failure. In ten days the next February (1883), he blasted off from the launchpad of depression to write half of his masterpiece *Thus Spake Zarathustra*. In the spring he completed the prophetic statement in another burst of creative passion. As Lou's biographer, Angela Livingstone, points out, "there is pain in the book, and some of it is a direct reflection of his disappointment in Lou von Salomé." *Zarathustra* exhibits a misogyny directed against Lou: "You go to women?" the sage asks. "Don't forget the whip." Here Nietzsche's Superman is a lovesick puppy pretending to growl, but he notes that "this year the solace of more cheerful and airy colours was essential to my life." The brief hope of a haven given to the tormented philosopher, who would sing and dance if he could, had made itself felt.

For the next five years Lou Salomé and Paul Rée lived amid a group of intellectuals in Berlin, sharing an apartment but not a bed. Social gatherings were centered on Lou, who was addressed as "Excellency," while Rée was called her "Maid of Honour." She continued to torment her "brother" by permitting brilliant mentors to court her. Expert at playing off rivals, she didn't hesitate to display Nietzsche's picture or mention intimate details about him. Indeed, while writing the first of her semiautobiographical novels, Lou made clear that she favored Nietzsche's passionate quest over Rée's pragmatism. She took the admirable step of introducing Nietzsche's works to the influential critic Georg Brandes, who then began to spread the word. In a real sense Lou discovered the most important philosopher of the nineteenth century.

"I am at home in happiness," she once summed up her life, then added, "Why is it that my most spontaneous actions have caused so much unhappiness?" Nietzsche did forgive Lou for toying with him. But he became unhinged in 1889, presumably from the effects of tertiary syphilis, and while in an asylum he drew two shadowy figures embracing under the heraldic cross at the lion memorial of Lucerne Park—where Lou had refused his proposal of marriage.

Paul Rée was even more affected by Lou. When in 1887 she agreed to marry one of the father figures who relentlessly pursued her, Rée left for good. She didn't wish this, wanting her "brother" to stay as a balance to a man she feared. But Rée refused all communication, and eventually he was found in a Swiss river at the base of a cliff from which he had fallen or jumped to his death. It was near the spot where years before he and Lou had spent many happy hours.

"MY SISTER, MY SPOUSE"

Lou's choice for a husband, F. C. Andreas, was of mixed German and Malayan stock and was a scholar of Persian who was fifteen years older than Lou. He was a short, powerful man who with his thick black beard and hair, resembled an Eastern monk. He turned up on Lou's doorstep one day, and the moment they met he was determined to win her. Although she admired his command of language and culture, he unnerved her. She resisted him until one evening, exasperated, he picked up a knife and plunged it into his chest. Lou rushed into the street, found a doctor, and Andreas was saved. But he'd nearly killed himself, a deed for which the blame might have fallen on her.

A rational woman would have fled. But to Lou the bloody moment confirmed that she was fated to marry Andreas. Or it may be that she realized his ardor gave her leeway to name her terms. Lou would marry Andreas if she could have her freedom and, most important, not make love with him. Reluctantly, he agreed, but in the middle of one night Lou awoke to find him on top of her, trying to force her, her hands grasping his throat so tightly that he was choking to death. From then on Andreas behaved as Lou wished him to.

Lou got a great deal from a man whom, in her memoir *Looking Back*, she relegates almost to an endnote. She adopted from this father figure vegetarianism and an ease in nature that included communing with plants and animals. He became her official husband based in Berlin (later Göttingen) while she spent much of the year first in Paris, then Vienna. Lou wisely hired as housekeeper a certain Marie who played the part of "wife substitute" to Andreas. The three lived comfortably together when Lou was in residence. Marie had two children by Andreas, and the survivor Mariechen cared for Lou even after her father had passed on. Of the several menages a trois in which Lou became involved, this was the most successful.

Salomé continued to break men's hearts and to defeat their expectations. But once in her thirties, sustaining her virginity as a married woman and an author known for steamy novels seemed absurd. Lou launched an affair with Friedrich Pineles, a young but intense Austrian physician who was as popular with women as she was with men. Pineles became Lou's unofficial husband, and they even wed, though the ceremony lacked legal validity. Lou enjoyed this cool, comradely liaison for a few years until again she was swept off her feet by a truly great man, though he was still just a boy.

Andreas was growing accustomed to his wife's extended travels when in the spring of 1897 a mutual friend in Munich introduced her to Rainer Maria Rilke, then twenty-two. The unknown youth was slender and gentle but had the bearing of an Austrian man about town. His deep-set, anxious eyes peered out at the world from a pale face framed by a scraggly beard and drooping mustache. Lou was about to repeat her pattern of playing with the fire of genius while keeping open a path of retreat to a more malleable man. She described going home to Andreas as "a reunion of two planets who have returned from a great distance." But her collision with Rilke was that of two comets and would in time shed its glow over all Europe. Rilke the poet and Salomé the analyst were created by one another.

Rilke sought her out with the same single-minded intent Andreas had shown, only he didn't offer his blood: "With a few roses in my hand I have been walking about the town. . . . I have been carrying them around, trembling with eagerness to meet you somewhere." Lou found it hard to resist Rilke's lyrical assault and his pose of a child seeking his mother. He was more experienced than he let on. Lou, a poet herself, told him that he was her "spring wind," that he reminded her of "summer rain" in June. She found him along a "thousand pathways." Erotically, she sighed, "I am in you."

Rilke gushed a vein of poems and letters, many of which were destroyed at Lou's insistence. She edited the sentimental from his work and generally tried to make a man of him. The incestuous element in their relations was obvious even to them, and Rainer liked to read to her from the Song of Songs: "Thou hast ravished my heart, my sister, my spouse." Something has been made of their frequenting a decidedly homosexual photography salon in Munich, but as an illicit couple they naturally gravitated toward other outlaws. In a small farmhouse built over cow stalls, their love bloomed with the verdancy of summer; in the moonlight they took barefoot walks over dewy grass until the poet and the woman of the world had touched deep inner chords. That fall Andreas announced his arrival; if the honeymoon was ended, the menage had begun.

The husband and his Newfoundland dog moved in with his wife and her lover. They lived happily together, sharing meals and excursions and critiquing Rilke's poetry. Lou was inexorably drawn to the outstanding men of her age—Nietzsche, Rilke, and Freud—yet with the exception of the last she failed to gauge their real worth. While she helped Rainer to combat his phobias and periodic depression, she also planed down his poetry much as Cosima had corrected Nietzsche's prose. Nietzsche, sure of himself, had laughed it off, but Rainer was still so unformed that Lou could influence his style, perhaps for the better, just as she had improved his handwriting.

Andreas liked the young poet and encouraged his return to Berlin with Lou and him. Their month in the country caused Andreas to adopt a strategy reminiscent of Monsieur Viardot's with Turgenev and Pauline: he chose from among his wife's suitors the man with whom he got along best. According to Lou, the three led "a private life in which we held everything in common. Rainer shared our modest existence on the edge of the forest . . . near Berlin." The triad grew still closer when in April 1899 they embarked on a lengthy journey to Russia. Peters calls this a "strange trio" in view of Andreas's "suicidal tendencies" and Rainer's exuberant love.

But the Persian scholar was actually a gentle man, and all three became immersed in the common outpouring of piety and warmth exhibited by the people during Orthodox Easter.

Rilke was thrilled to hear illiterate peasants recite Pushkin's poems by heart. Andreas was pleased when on a visit to Count Leo Tolstoy, the famous novelist ignored his traveling companions and grilled him closely about Persia. But for Lou, so confident in her rational approach to life, the embrace of Mother Russia was overwhelming. This elemental state, she decided, was the wellspring that must water the intellect if it is to create. In the toll of bells sounding through solemn, packed churches or among chanting Volga peasants, Lou sensed a unity that preceded division, and she began to formulate her theory of a primal narcissism or sense of self that was connected to all life.

For Lou, neither a threesome nor a coupling was possible for long. She needed to explore her own psyche, about which she had rationalized but knew very little. She couldn't be wife to either Andreas or Rilke, each possessive in his own way and the latter given to the sudden panic and doubt that seize the most creative of beings. Andreas returned to Berlin, and Lou abandoned Rainer in a garret in Saint Petersburg to flee to her family's summer home in Finland. From here she wrote a last appeal to her poet lover to find himself in his work. Strange as it sounded, she felt she was "growing . . . into my youth." In a tattered diary from her adolescence she had found a prophetic remark: "I am faithful to memories forever. I shall never be faithful to men." In fact, there would be one exception: Sigmund Freud.

THE ID AND I

The symbiosis between Freud and Salomé, which lasted for twenty-five years until her death, is the most surprising of her involvements with great men and proved the most fruitful. Her theory of narcissism, which is inseparable from her view of women and her artistic style, tended to modify the thick, male, Germanic world of the Freudian brotherhood. Briefly, Salomé insisted that at birth a primal, undifferentiated state (the world as oneself) preceded any other, including the ego or the Oedipus complex, and that the experience left a memory in the form of a longing for reunion with the All. Woman, the giver of life, was as close to the All as one could be, as potentially complete as a sleeping cat rolled into a sphere, tail tucked up. Significantly, Freud told Lou about the cat that had paraded through his collection of antiques, aware of but indifferent to his admiration, and his rather pathetic attempt to woo her with a bowl of milk, which got him nowhere.

Salomé believed that for woman, receptivity is creative; she needn't share man's need for external results. Yet her communion with the original narcissism is the wellspring of artistic creativity. This is the "enlightened" narcissism that leads to the universal. Woman has the superior biology, and in conceiving a child, "her union is with God, not with the mere man who helps her to the union." Here Salomé approvingly echoes the doctrine of the Virgin birth, as well as the worldview of South Sea islanders who believe it takes three to conceive. In *Eroticism,* Salomé attempted to reconcile the roles of the two Marys—Madonna and Magdalene. She didn't shy away from her own propensity to wear alternately the mask of mother and of whore, to live beyond good and evil.

By the time Lou at fifty attended the Psychoanalytic Congress in Weimar in 1911, accompanied by her younger lover, Dr. Paul Bjerre, she had written ten novels, a famous study of Nietzsche, and dozens of articles on a variety of subjects. She had finessed the unstable Rilke from lover to confidant (almost analysand) and conceived a child by the physician Pineles. When the father-to-be demanded she divorce Andreas and marry him, she forced him to perform an abortion. Pineles, successful and popular, never married, while Rilke, from his deathbed in 1926, would call for Lou in vain. From Bjerre, a Swedish analyst who introduced her to Freud and whom she then discarded, we have a close-up view of Lou as femme fatale:

> There was something terrifying about her embrace, elemental, archaic. Looking at you with her radiantly blue eyes she would say, "The reception of the semen is for me the height of ecstasy." And she had an insatiable appetite for it. When she was in love she was completely ruthless ... a vampire and a child. As far as men were concerned who wanted to love her she trusted her instincts entirely.

Bjerre went on to describe how Lou, frustrated because of a lover's absence, chewed and swallowed his recent letter to her.

Nietzsche was the ghost at the banquet of the Weimar Congress. His sister Lisbeth, living there, headed the Nietzsche Archives, which she used to distort her brother's thinking to make him appear a proto-Nazi. She was jealous of and furious at Lou, who offered an entirely different view of the philosopher and who soon became "the living link between Nietzsche and Freud." With Nietzsche's emphasis on dream content and the force of subconscious drives, the "old cannoneer" had so uncannily anticipated psychoanalysis that Freud, who distrusted intuition, admitted he was afraid to read him closely. For this conference of Jewish, Viennese doctors, who—what was worse—claimed her brother's legacy, Lisbeth had nothing but contempt.

The complex relationship that developed between Salomé and Freud followed her pattern of discovering a father-god, finding he was mortal, and then undercutting his authority by seducing a disciple. Freud famously ruled as a patriarch who discarded or destroyed his sons, yet when Lou returned to Vienna in 1912, a number of younger analysts applied to be her lover. Was it accidental that she chose the Croatian doctor Victor Tausk, at thirty-five a tall, handsome, independent man who greatly annoyed Freud? A "beast of prey" the patriarch termed his wayward son, but the man attracted Lou, who saw in him a masculine reflection of herself: "Brother-animal," she addressed Victor.

In the end Salomé remained true to Freud. It helped that there was nothing sexual between them, but more was due to Lou's ability to successfully play the roles, one and the same to Freud, of daughter and interpreter. For a time Lou defended her lover from the patriarch, but he proved, as had all her younger ones, too demanding of her allegiance. Victor made the interesting remark that Lou's multifarious intellectual relations with men were "sublimated polyandry." In fact she usually contained her intimacy to a triangle, attempting to convert male rivalry into cooperation. But in learning from and flirting with the father and sleeping with the brother-son, Lou intended to have it all. She was an incurably optimistic narcissist.

The men often felt let down or, worse, betrayed. In 1913, on the cusp of the Great War, Lou terminated her affair with Victor Tausk. He served during the war as head of a field hospital. Afterward he returned to Vienna, and when he was about to marry, he first castrated himself, then committed suicide with a pistol. Lou admitted she had loved him but was helpless to end his suffering. She began to accept the universality of guilt.

Lou took up the practice of psychoanalysis. Freud remained devoted to her and referred patients, and she wrote many technical papers as well as a biography of Rilke and her memoirs. She lived peacefully in Göttingen with Andreas until he died in 1930. The rise of the Nazis was particularly difficult for her, since her old enemy Lisbeth Nietzsche, visited by Hitler himself, started the rumor that she was a Finnish Jew. It may be that her well-known association with Nietzsche saved her. Immediately after her death in 1937 the Gestapo confiscated her papers and library. But her priceless correspondence with Nietzsche, Rilke, and Freud was in safe hands. Besides, what the woman believed she had expressed in novels, essays, and in person. As her admirer Anaïs Nin wrote, "Lou Andreas-Salomé symbolizes the struggle to transcend conventions and traditions in ideas and in living."

If there is one aspect of her unconventionality that comes close to home, that is especially relevant now, it is her dogged attempt to reconcile the conflict between marriage and love, which to the nineteenth century was inevitably the stuff of tragedy. "We all need a life's partner, a husband or a wife, who is our refuge, our support, our helpmate, our brother and the guardian of our solitude," admitted Lou. "But we also need the rejuvenating power of love." Her answer to the dilemma was to construct a menage a trois, with herself at the apex.

part four

THE
AMERICANS

Did the Victorian-era experience for threes differ markedly from the Old World to the New? If the frontier shaped American culture, did it also define our sexuality, especially regarding liaisons out of wedlock? For some groups—blacks, Hispanics, Native Americans—their own communal ways governed erotic behavior. The great middle class *claimed* to be wedded to one partner for life, period. This was an untruth clung to blindly—or consciously by a moral cynic such as Mark Twain. The American threesome hasn't been as ubiquitous as the French or even the British, but under the covers there has often lurked a third.

The Old West as a region wrote its own rules. Its records of amorous doings have been so mythologized by the motion picture that we know of no hard line between fact and fiction. A friend in the industry tells us that you could hear ecstatic noises while *The Last of the Mohicans* was being filmed on location in the North Carolina woods; the actors playing the scantily clad Indians were rollicking with the makeup girls sent out to daub them with greasepaint. The frontier spirit was alive and well!

After the Civil War, New York began its meteoric climb to the heights of wealth and hypocrisy. The Reverend Henry Ward Beecher was its representative man, and Victoria Woodhull, dubbed Mrs. Satan, its woman of protest. If their minds never met, their bodies communed in bed, where they also shared a handsome young poet lover. When Woodhull accused Beecher of adultery, he went on trial and denied the undeniable evidence. He won. Fast-forward to the O. J. Simpson frenzy.

The quaint New England town of Amherst had its balls. Gossip was its great avocation. The reclusive Emily Dickinson peeked through the keyhole at others' loves to make out of voyeurism the truest American art. The squire, a nutty professor, and the professor's musical wife communed in the back bedroom. Today, thousands visit the Dickinson home. Can they hear the echoes of those old strokes?

Anaïs Nin and the two Millers constitute our final all-American menage, characteristically set in Paris. In the days before Europeans on vacation flocked to Greenwich Village searching for depravity, Americans would escape to the Left Bank where they could hang out in cafés and get into late-night discussions and entanglements. Henry Miller epitomized the scene, and Nin in her diaries embroidered on every stitch of their time in bed. Many and much are in the American vein.

chapter 12

THE WILD WEST

{Sir Richard Burton and the Mormons;
Butch Cassidy, the Sundance Kid, and Etta Place;
Tom Mix; Bonnie and Clyde's Three-Way Capers}

*Man is by nature polygamic whereas woman as a rule
is monogamic and polyandrous only when tired of her lover.*
SIR RICHARD BURTON

$\mathcal{F}$ROM BIBLE THUMPERS TO *banditos,* THE
three of hearts was a trump card in the old Wild West. The American frontier was long a place of sexual adaptation. Eighteenth-century fur traders, imi-
tating tribal chiefs, took multiple Indian wives. The early nineteenth-century
Midwest attracted numerous visionaries who founded secular and religious
communities. In the 1820s, Welsh industrialist Robert Owen gathered hundreds of people at New Harmony in Illinois to establish a commune on
utopian principles. Frances Wright, a crusader for so-called Free Love and
interracial love matches, was his sometime associate. She was a riveting speaker
damned by the press as "a bold blasphemer and a voluptuous preacher of
licentiousness." Owen favored masturbation as a means of birth control and a
way to lighten the burden on women. After New Harmony wrangled itself
apart, Owen, Wright, and Robert Jennings lived in a menage in New York
and published an influential newspaper. This "harmonious" experiment
lasted only a few years until Wright married and Owen returned to England.

For the most part, idealistic communes, such as John Noyes's
Oneida, which practiced group marriage and frowned on male but encour-

aged female orgasm, glimmered briefly in the wilderness. Then the founders' inspiration dimmed, leaving behind dashed hopes and disoriented children. Religious communes showed more resilience. When in 1843 the Mormon prophet Joseph Smith introduced plural marriage among his followers, he so infuriated the good citizens of Illinois that they burned down the temple city of Nauvoo and martyred him. The Mormons fled west and settled in the inhospitable great American desert. Within a few years they had built Salt Lake City and dominated an immense territory from the Rockies west to the Sierra Nevada and from Oregon south to the Colorado River. Not until 1890, with Utah set to become a state, did the church forbid men to take more than one wife. By looking backward to the patriarchy of the Old Testament, Smith and his successor Brigham Young instituted the largest sexual experiment to take place in Victorian America.

THE MORMON MENAGE

In 1860 the British explorer Richard Burton arrived in Salt Lake after an arduous stagecoach ride from Missouri. He'd come to investigate what he termed "*ménage à trois*, in the Mormon sense of the phrase." Burton was able to interview Brigham Young, said to possess more than forty wives, and the Mormon leader was candid with him. Burton's biographer Fawn Brody calls him "one of the least credulous observers of the Mormon scene. He looked at it with immense curiosity and absolutely without reproach." Burton, because of his travels in Arabia, could compare the Mormon version to Moslem polygamy. Both respected taboos on intercourse with a woman during pregnancy and lactation, a period of three consecutive years. This prohibition made it likely that a man would take either a second wife or a concubine. All in all, Burton found Salt Lake City orderly and moral—indeed, glum.

Under Mormon law adultery was a capital offense. The system had "abolished prostitution, concubinage, celibacy and infanticide," not to mention old maids. Burton found the women, American or British converts, handsome and healthy. The first wife had to give permission for her husband to take a second or third, which she would do in order to increase Mormon progeny (Burton came to believe that polygamy was the best way to populate the empty Great Basin). Certain women assured him they preferred to marry "a man who has abundance of means" and was worthy to sire "his own warriors, born in his own house." Even today, polygamy is practiced by about two thousand families of Mormon background in and around Utah. There is an argument made by them, cited recently in the *Washington Post*, that has a rather postfeminist spin: "A woman who wants a career might even find a menage a trois or cinq more convenient. . . . She would have two or more partners to help share the chores of child care. . . . Who would not rather be Jack Kennedy's second wife than Bozo the Clown's first?"

Burton's one telling criticism of plural marriage was that it prevented "the choice egotism of the heart called Love." The large family with its wives and children provided "affection, circumspect friendship and domestic discipline" but was fatal to romance. Ardor was transferred from the individual to the group, in this case the church. The ever-curious Burton asked to become a Mormon, but Brigham Young, with a twinkle in his eye, reminded him he'd falsely converted once before to gain admission to the holy sites of Mecca. Burton returned to England to court and marry the Catholic Isabel Arundell, who after his death searched through his papers and, in a ruthless holocaust, burned his erotic writings and translations.

SAINT JEAN AND HER MEN

The romantic triangle is essential to the facts and fictions of the West. The Mormons subsumed sex to the cause, as did the various secular communes. But a different skein runs through our national libido: the confusion of lust for nooky with lust for gain. The latter has been accorded more respect, but perhaps it, too, masks a Nietzschean Will to Power over the flesh. Certainly in the Wild West, when it came to land, cattle, gold, or women, more was deemed better.

Paint Your Wagon, the 1969 movie musical about a wife who lives with two husbands in a California boomtown, is a turned-on-its-head allegory of the American drive to acquire. Based on Lerner and Loewe's 1950s stage hit, the twenty-million-dollar movie laid an egg. Reviews went from scathing to, at best, mixed. But the locale, No Name City, and the three roles are symbolic and aptly illustrate our take on the Old West. Paddy Chayefsky wrote a first-draft script that chronicles the rise and fall of a mining town in the Sierras. It's a story of hope verified by the accidental discovery of gold, its exploitation by men from every corner of the globe, their building a town of saloons and gambling hells, and the inevitable crash of the whole kit and caboodle. *Paint Your Wagon* remains a tale of sullied innocence that ends in destruction. It's the Jean Seberg story told with prescience.

Briefly, Lee Marvin, a grizzled prospector, stumbles onto gold while burying Clint Eastwood's brother. He takes the injured Clint as his partner and declares to the sober, untrusting farm boy: "I gamble, I whore, I cheat at cards. But there is one thing I don't do. I ain't never gulled a partner. In this lawless, godless, womanless wilderness, the one sacred thing . . . is a man's partner." In a few sentences Chayefsky has summed up the code of the buddy, adhered to by both lawman and desperado. The partners are going to share the gold they find fifty-fifty. The one catch in Lee's offer is that when he gets falling-down drunk, Clint must pick him up out of the mud and carry him home. The partners hit pay dirt, and a thriving boomtown mushrooms around them. When a disgruntled Mormon with two feuding wives arrives and decides to auction one off, Lee accidentally makes the winning bid for Jean before he collapses into a drunken stupor.

Pauline Kael describes Jean Seberg as "a pale, lovely, dimpled movie queen" who looks "somewhat used." Discovered by Otto Preminger in Marshalltown, Iowa, as the result of a search for an unknown to play Joan of Arc, the corn-fed blond bombed in the movie about the French heroine. Preminger, treating her as an article of merchandise, sold her contract. But beginner's luck held, and she escaped from Hollywood to Paris to play Jean-Paul Belmondo's treacherous lover in Jean-Luc Godard's *Breathless.* Seberg became a sixties icon, the all-American girl ready for anything. She married French novelist Romain Gary and became a political activist espousing typical sixties causes. Not until Jean's return to America to make movies did her life begin to imitate art.

In *Paint Your Wagon,* sodden Lee takes the sheltered Jean as his wife, only to discover she is "a full-grown tiger." In order to distract the other miners from his prize, he hijacks a wagonload of hookers and brings them to town. The town now boasts a street preacher who dubs it the "Sodom of the Sierras." Meanwhile, hardworking Clint becomes "wretched with love" for Jean. She finds a beautiful and practical solution by proposing a switch on the Mormons: if a man can have two wives, why can't a woman have two husbands? Since Lee and Clint share and share alike, they agree. The pact is sealed by Jean's casual remark that they will be three for dinner.

Jean is pleased because Lee has been prevented from leaving for the Siskiyou Mountains by his affection for his partner. "You don't see his kind much anymore," she explains to Clint, "trappers, bordertown men, drifting from one wilderness to another, exulting in their independence like savages. . . . They westered this country for the rest of us." Jean, determined to become a woman of property, takes over the laundry business from the Chinese, adds another room to her cabin, and enjoys both men. The partners get caught up in a scheme to tunnel under the floorboards of the saloons and gambling dens, where over the years miners have let spill a fortune in gold dust. A cabal of "bummers"—old-timers—digs a maze of tunnels under No Name to capture the yellow dust.

Judgment Day comes when a bull is let loose in the underground network, and the entire town, building by building, collapses in a heap in a comic-horrific scene. With the claims played out and the homesteaders advancing, Bibles in hand, Lee decides to move on. Singing "Wandrin' Star" with a chorus of bummers, Marvin, a caricature of Daniel Boone, leaves the good guy, Clint, to settle in with his industrious wife, who is pregnant by one of them. The glory days are gone, with laundry, kids, and churchgoing in the offing.

Off the set, Clint and Jean were rumored to be having an affair. When Romain Gary, the French consul in Los Angeles, heard of it, he flew to Oregon and challenged the future Dirty Harry to a duel. Clint demurred, and Jean's menage remained on screen only. But her life was already headed toward the extremes. Next year while filming in Mexico, she revived her romance with her estranged husband, Gary; meanwhile, she had an affair with a revolutionary known only as El Gato. Simultaneously, she became involved with the Mexican novelist Carlos Fuentes, who recently told all in his roman à clef *Diana: The Goddess Who Hunts Alone.* The image he presents is far different from Saint Jean of the sixties, victim of an FBI attempt to smear her.

The affair with Fuentes was brief. However, in *Diana,* the novelist describes an unforgettable moment when he was on top of Jean and glimpsed Clint Eastwood's picture on the bedside table. Neither Fuentes nor Paul Theroux, reviewing *Diana* in the *New York Times,* quite understands that this is a ghost menage: Clint, since he is in both of the others' minds creating the excitement, is the third in bed. To Jean, who later tells Fuentes she gets no pleasure from him, Clint is her movie-star lover who proves that she is a star. For Fuentes, Clint's having been her previous conquest adds to his potency, putting him in the star league.

Seberg, like those other narcissists Lou Salomé and Henry Miller, needed a picture of her former lover to spice up her present affair. When the classical Narcissus saw his image, he believed it to be a water spirit who was looking back at him. The illusion was reinforced by the nymph Echo, who gave the image a voice. The narcissist adoring a reflection sees the reflection adore him or her back. So it may be that Seberg imagined Eastwood's picture watching her make love to another. The narcissist who needs to be continually adored gives rise to a Casanova type—or an actress who creates triangles. Fuentes, who invokes Diana, the goddess who punished Narcissus for spurning her nymphs, is aware that Seberg is playing an involved game.

Jean's alleged low self-esteem appears to have been a mask behind which she indulged in ample helpings of sex and drugs. Her triangles grew more dangerous, until finally, in September 1979, she was found dead in a car parked on a quiet Parisian street. Her body had gone unnoticed for days. She left a note that blamed a harsh world for her suicide, but the circumstances remain murky. At the end, Jean found herself as alone and outdated as Lee Marvin in *Paint Your Wagon*. She had lost her narcissistic double, Saint Jean, her better self, somewhere on the never-ending sexual frontier.

BUTCH AND SUNDANCE AND ETTA

A good woman and two bad men are a classic Western theme. Take Butch Cassidy and the Sundance Kid—the way Etta Place did. Sundance was born Harry Longabaugh in the East in 1866, but while still in his teens he served eighteen months in jail at Sundance, Wyoming, for horse thieving. When he was released he thrashed three cowboys and committed armed robbery, and the name of the place stuck to him. No good from the start, he grew into a lean, handsome man who sported a trim mustache and didn't hesitate to use his gun.

Butch, born Robert Parker in 1866, grew up a stocky, towheaded innocent in a hardworking Mormon family. He came under the influence of a cowboy named Cassidy, who taught him to ride and rope and rustle and whose name he adopted. In the mining town of Telluride, Colorado (now known for its film festival), Parker got into worse company and robbed a bank. Though he kept his youthful square-jawed look, Cassidy became a criminal genius. He perfected the three-man heist: "One man to hold the horses, one man to hold the gun, one man to grab the money." Sometimes the third was a woman.

It's said that beautiful Etta Place, five-five, green-eyed, and chestnut-haired, was a young music teacher whom Sundance found in Denver. Well mannered, she was rumored to be the granddaughter of the earl of Essex or, perhaps on better authority, a girl from a sporting house in San Antonio's Hell's Half Acre. We know she was graceful and preferred to dress in black, but not much else. What is certain is that these three made outlaw history.

Historians unduly belittle movie research. In fact, a good script takes as long to research as to write. In the case of the 1969 *Butch Cassidy and the Sundance Kid*, the director, George Roy Hill, respected screenwriter William Goldman's meticulous work. Writing in the shadowland where fact and legend overlap, Goldman got the story straight and the characters properly tangled. The attraction between the laconic Sundance (Robert Redford) and clever Butch (Paul Newman) may be thought of as outlaw partnering or as a kind of man-to-man love affair. That the partners needed a menage for reasons more intimate than robbing banks, and shared Etta (Katharine Ross), is the script's surmise.

Butch and Sundance began operations in the 1890s during the Johnson County (Wyoming) War, fighting on the side of small ranchers against the cattle barons. They met each other and the members of the Wild Bunch while hiding out in the Hole in the Wall, an almost impregnable valley that could be entered by only one horseman at a time. Here Sundance brought his mistress Etta, and there were a few other women who shared the hell-raising drives of their men. A community of log cabins sprang up in the even more remote hideout of Robber's Roost in southeast Utah.

Butch and the gang robbed banks and payrolls, including the Pleasant Valley Coal Company before the eyes of dozens of miners lined up waiting to be paid. They escaped by riding fast horses in a relay system stretching hundreds of miles back to Robber's Roost. Well-planned train robberies were their trademark. Train crew and passengers went unharmed, but the use of tremendous quantities of dynamite usually turned baggage cars into piles of debris. The railroad companies responded by bringing in the Pinkerton detectives, who relentlessly hunted down the outlaws. The movie hardly strays from this line of fact.

Butch, writing to the mother of a jailed gang member in 1902 from his ranch in the southern Andes of Argentina, mentions "our little family of three." Goldman had only such scraps of evidence on which to base his three-way romance. Early in the movie, Etta is shown in a schoolhouse grading papers. At night, she locks up and goes to her small house next door. Sundance is secretly waiting, gun in his lap. He orders her to undress, and since she is silent, a mimic rape is played out. But Etta's last line before they tumble into bed is a wish: "That you'd once get here on time."

The first shot next morning is of Butch's head as it glides past the bedroom window, intimating that if only as voyeur, he is part of the action. "You're mine, Etta Place," he calls theatrically; "mine, do you hear me?" She climbs out of bed to find Butch on a newfangled bicycle; seated on the crossbar, she goes for a ride with him. Like Superman's flying with Lois Lane, their careening downhill and almost tumbling is a metaphor for sex. Goldman's instructions on the background music are emphatic: "What we hear will *not* be a song like 'Bicycle Built for Two.' The song will be poignant and pretty as hell." Once Butch gets the hang of it, the pair glide past bucolic scenery, chased suggestively by a young boy and girl who can't keep up. Butch playfully kisses Etta, and she says, "Do you ever wonder if I'd met you first if *we'd* been the ones to get involved?" Butch replies, "We are involved, Etta." She hugs him tight in a tender scene.

The Pinkertons hire the best tracker in the West and, after a long chase, nearly capture Butch and Sundance, but the bandits finally get away to Etta's place. The action reads, "Without a word she moves to meet them and her arms go around them both. They stand that way a moment, Etta and her men." This is as explicit a menage moment as Goldman could have written into a major motion picture in the sixties. Movie threes have murdered each other all along and even slept together, but they have seldom been allowed to show love.

In the movie, the threesome, with the rest of their gang behind bars, journeys to New York and has a high old time shopping and dining. Then, abruptly, they find themselves in poverty-stricken Bolivia. Etta saves the day by teaching the boys Spanish so they can properly rob banks. In real life the three lived as a peaceful menage for years on their Argentine ranch. Running out of money in 1906, they resumed their outlaw career. They were still swift and sure, and Etta held the horses and kept watch. Then, pregnant and wanting an abortion, she returned to Denver and entered a hospital. There her trail disappears.

Butch and Sundance continued to hold up banks and mule trains in Bolivia, where the mines were rich and police scarce. But one day in 1911 in San Vicente they were spotted, then surrounded by the Bolivian cavalry. There are three versions of the final shoot-out. In one, adopted by Goldman, the holed-up outlaws, though wounded and absurdly outgunned, make a last stand and charge into the plaza. As a fusillade of shots rings out, the frame freezes. Another version claims the pair somehow got away, returned to the United States, changed their names, and died peacefully. Butch's sister stated he visited the family home in 1925.

Finally, in 1994, a team of American forensic experts examined two bodies in a cemetery in San Vicente and pronounced that they were Butch and Sundance. Evidence from their skeletons indicates that at last, hopelessly outnumbered, Sundance shot Butch in the forehead, then killed himself with a bullet in the temple. Each man saved his partner from being captured and executed as a criminal. That's love.

TOM MIXES IT UP

In 1982 the *New York Times* called Clifford Irving's historical fantasy *Tom Mix and Pancho Villa* "a gully washer of a novel . . . a stump mover, a real frog strangler." Set against the panorama of the Mexican Revolution and featuring a rogue's gallery of bandits—including Villa's sidekick Rodolfo Fierro, who once shot a stranger to settle a bet on whether a dying man falls forward or backward—the novel centers on the greenhorn's sexual initiation and culminates in a sizzling menage a trois among Tom, a young senorita, and a somewhat older German woman. It provides an interesting fictional background for the man who would become the greatest of the silent-movie cowboys, the prototypical white hat.

In the novel, Mix, at fifty, is well off but a has-been; he narrates the tale of his youth, which is set in Chihuahua across the border from his home in El Paso, Texas. The time is 1913 to 1917, and the idea that Mix fought with Villa is historically accurate. Many of Irving's bloody tales of the revolution are factual, but the author admitted that Tom's women were mainly his own invention. In the novel, the virgin Tom, soon after being inducted into Villa's irregulars, succumbs to two sisters from New Orleans, Yvette and Therese. This one-night stand foreshadows the more serious menage on which the plot turns.

Once Tom meets fair-haired Hannah Sommerfeld, his fiancée who represents prestige and wealth, he resolves to halt all sexual high jinks. The daughter of a Jewish Texas businessman who backs Villa, Hannah inspires the young man to be her knight in battle. Tom's good intentions hold until he meets Rosa, a teenage widow. Cocoa-colored, more Indian than white, Rosa symbolizes the true Mexican spirit. Although Tom's intimacy with Rosa deepens, he fights against breaking his vows. After the battle of Zacatecas, the good scout bids Rosa good-bye and presents himself, in body if not in soul, to his hometown sweetheart.

When Villa summons Tom back to Mexico, Hannah demands that Tom choose between her and the revolution. Secretly delighted to escape the noose of respectability, Tom heads for the border and Rosa. But like Ulysses, he meets a Circe who diverts him. In Parral, the tall, blond Elisa Griensen, a German widow who knows how to use a rifle, entertains Tom in her four-poster bed. Again torn between dark and light women, Tom finds it simpler to rejoin Villa and the fighting. In Torreón he accidentally finds Rosa, now seventeen. They resolve to remain together, but Tom is ordered across the dangerous Sierras. Elisa offers to house Rosa in his absence. Tom heads back to win the revolution.

By the time the wounded man returns to Elisa's home, the women have become fast friends. Recuperating, he suspects a budding lesbian relationship. When questioned, Rosa answers, "That never happened, although it could have. But she loves me. And I may love her." Tom gives himself permission to enjoy having two women. "Last night, Rosa," he sighs. "Tonight, Elisa. No qualms, no bad feeling in the bones." It does worry him that Rosa in particular shows no jealousy. "I would be a foolish girl to be angry," Rosa assures him, "if the man I love and my best friend in the world gave each other pleasure." Evenings Tom wonders which woman to bed down. One night he joins the women in a passionate menage a trois.

The three sleep together for a week both at night and during daytime siestas, mingling so completely "that you didn't know who was where or who was doing what to the other." Tom is forced to admit he'd always wanted a menage but hadn't dared plan it. "But I was ready. No guilt impeded me. . . . We were innocent partners in our desire. We were happy." The cowboy acts out his Garden of Eden fantasy.

Rosa likes to watch the older, more experienced Elisa perform with Tom in the bedroom. Mix waxes poetic over the memory of how, one afternoon,

> I took Elisa from behind, while Rosa straddled me to rub her fur against my thigh, hands cupping the weight of her own breasts. Elisa flattened out and rolled over on her back, mouth red from the bite of her own teeth, breath coming quickly. I moved behind Rosa who lay on her side . . . and then Elisa pressed against her and kissed her and bit one swollen brown nipple. . . . It roused me powerfully and I fired into Rosa like a cannon, while she gasped into Elisa's mouth, threw her buttocks back at me and thrust her hand between Elisa's thighs. . . . They [had] loved each other as sisters, as kindred souls, as beautiful women, and now all that could find expression and voice. Elisa cried Rosa's name and mine in a way I knew too well.

Afterward Mix reflects that the women felt no jealousy. He felt apart from them, almost a stranger, but blessed. Irving has captured the magic of a completed menage a trois. There is free communication, and even gender has dissolved in love. The author may well have described a treasured experience of his own. Irving ultimately dooms the menage by killing off Rosa in childbirth, but this frees his hero to ride into the sunset—in the direction of Hollywood.

Briefly, the real Tom Mix fought in several fin-de-siècle wars from China to South Africa, punched cows and broke broncs, and became a champion rodeo performer. He was a sheriff and a Texas Ranger. He got into the movies as a stuntman and learned to write, direct, and star in one-reel Westerns. Mix joined the Fox studio in 1917 and became the leading Western star of the twenties. His screen character dressed all in white and never drank, swore, or used violence without cause. On-screen Tom Mix was a precursor of Gene Autry, Roy Rogers, and John Wayne, the cowboy who loves his horse but can't be besmirched by a kiss from a woman.

Mix was married and divorced five times. He drank so heavily that when sound came in, he couldn't help slurring his lines. He did love the West and made a point of filming on location in national parks. In 1940 Mix's car, after failing to make a curve near Florence, Arizona, plowed through a detour sign and rolled over, breaking his neck. The state has erected a statue of a riderless pony to mark the spot.

BONNIE AND CLYDE'S THIRD

The brief, bloody careers of the Texans Bonnie Parker and Clyde Barrow, both born around 1909, mark the transition from the old to the new West. The pair became hot copy during the depths of the depression, but in a departure from its favorable treatment of earlier desperadoes, the press portrayed them as homicidal maniacs and sexual deviants. In our time, Warren Beatty's 1967 movie, *Bonnie and Clyde*, reversed the pair's fortunes. The posters trumpeted, "They're young. They're in love. They kill people." The members of the Barrow gang were presented as folksy, fun-loving, sympathetic heroes, robbing banks that foreclosed on poor farmers; the officers of the law once again became the villains. Beatty chose a sympathetic sexual role with a respectable Freudian resonance.

Screenwriter David Newman admitted:

The first draft had a menage a trois between Bonnie, Clyde and a third male character who was a different version of the C. W. Moss character. He was more of a dumb stud type, a conglomeration of three or four different drivers the real Barrows had used. In our research we came across references which suggested that several of these guys had been in a sexual thrall with Bonnie and Clyde. . . . In fact, in the original draft, there was a shot of the three of them lying in bed together after having sex.

Ironically, Beatty, a famed Hollywood Casanova, feared what Newman termed "sexual ambiguity." So he ordered Clyde's character rewritten to be impotent. This was supposed to win over the audience and explain the man's fascination with the gun as a substitute penis that actually worked. While Faye Dunaway played an inviting, if edgy, Bonnie, Michael J. Pollard acted the sanitized third. This was some improvement on the thirties myth that Clyde was a "snake-eyed" homosexual and Bonnie a nymphomaniac and "steely, imperturbable killer." The authorities who couldn't catch the Barrow gang defamed them, but Warren Beatty and director Arthur Penn also created a myth to suit their time—of star-crossed lovers who might have settled down if the breaks had gone right.

The real Clyde grew up dirt poor on a farm before the family moved to the half-rural, garbage-strewn slum of West Dallas, a breeding ground for criminals. The boy was bright but quick-tempered and dropped out of school at sixteen. His passions were the saxophone and hot rods, and he had a couple of steamy romances with girls. From stealing cars he graduated to safecracking. He was caught and sent to prison but paroled by Governor "Ma" Ferguson to help make room for a new crop of convicts.

Bonnie was five feet tall and weighed less than one hundred pounds. The pet of a working-class family in Dallas, she was blond, blue-eyed, and cheerful. She was a good student who liked to write poetry and act, but she married young. The newlyweds didn't get along, and her husband was sent to prison. In 1930 on a Dallas street corner Bonnie, now a waitress, met Clyde Barrow, a quiet man on the effeminate side. He was a slight twenty-three-year-old with slick, dark hair parted in the middle, pixie ears, a weak chin, and soft hazel eyes. Like Bonnie, Clyde adored his mother and hated cops.

In a few weeks the couple picked up a boyfriend of Bonnie's, Raymond Hamilton, and embarked on a series of petty holdups in a dozen states. They stole fast cars and loaded them down with submachine guns, rifles, and pistols. Bonnie helped Clyde learn to quick draw with a sawed-off shotgun. They were able to terrorize victims at stores and gas stations in small southern and midwestern towns. In Sherman, Texas, they held up a butcher shop, and when the elderly proprietor objected, Bonnie gunned him down. According to John Roland, a chronicler of early gangsters, when Hamilton was caught, the Barrow gang went looking for another driver, "not only to assist in the robberies but to help satisfy Bonnie's sexual aberrations. Clyde, who had homosexual tendencies ... enjoyed sharing her pleasures."

William Jones, a seventeen-year-old car thief, idolized what he considered to be a romantic gang. A few days later, with Jones at the wheel of a stolen car, the owner jumped on the running board; Clyde blew him away. Now the kid grew frightened, but it was too late. Clyde's brother Buck, recently released from prison, and his wife joined them, and they hid out in a house in a respectable neighborhood in Joplin, Missouri. Clyde and Bonnie both dressed well, and the gang entertained themselves by reading their press clippings and posing for innumerable snapshots with their weapons, including one in which Bonnie smokes a cigar.

The Barrow gang, lacking political connections, were outcasts among outlaws. They ran, hid, and shot their way out of scrapes. As the law, complete with armored cars, closed in, and Buck was killed, young Jones grew desperate. He tried to quit but Clyde chained him to a tree when he wasn't wanted for endeavors sexual or otherwise. Jones got away, turned himself in to the police, and made a twenty-eight-page confession that described him as the pair's sex slave. Its reliability is doubtful.

Bonnie wrote one last ballad—"Suicide Sal"—to explain her defiance. She recalled Clyde when he was "honest and upright and clean." She claimed he'd been hounded into a criminal life, and she damned cops and stool pigeons. "I will meet a few of them in hell," she proclaimed. She insisted the gang wouldn't give up until they died.

By now the FBI was on their trail, and on May 23, 1934, an ambush was arranged on a farm road near Arcadia, Texas. Lurking in the woods were six crack shots armed with rapid-fire shotguns and Browning automatics. The outlaws' car pulled up and stopped on schedule. Clyde was speaking with the father of a gang member when the trap was sprung; a broadside killed him and Bonnie as they went for their guns. Fifty bullets riddled their bodies. The movie scene that depicts this was shot in slow motion, a ballet of love and death. The bodies, a heap of wet red rags, were taken to Arcadia; even in this tiny town a large, unruly crowd of souvenir hunters formed around the funeral parlor and invaded it. They tore apart the corpses' clothes, snipped Bonnie's blond hair, and pulled their car to pieces. Folks knew something big had happened the day Bonnie and Clyde went down. The Wild West died—and an American legend, kinky and bloody, was born.

chapter 13

THE GREAT AMERICAN SEX SCANDAL

{Victoria Woodhull, Theodore Tilton, and Henry Ward Beecher}

Marriage is the grave of Love.
HENRY WARD BEECHER

*T*HIS IS THE STORY OF A MAN AND A woman who each projected their image mightily on the Gilded Stage—to pun on Mark Twain's description of post–Civil War America. Both were publicity hounds who are half-forgotten today. They came from disparate backgrounds and sported contrasting reputations—he for purity and virtue, she for loose morals and blackmail—yet the two converged on a third, a man of charm, good looks, and too much ambition. The scandal caused by the intercourse among these three, along with a retinue of their sisters and spouses, would result in the first—but far from last—grand national sex scandal. Though the trial that followed lacked gore, it lasted six months and drew an eager crowd and ever more eager reporters until the end. Based on a charge of adultery, the trial focused media attention to a degree unmatched until the O. J. Simpson extravaganza. It, too, would be resolved by moral issues extraneous to the undeniable bedroom doings.

THE GOSPEL OF LOVE
Henry Ward Beecher was America's most popular preacher at a time when the ministry still wielded considerable influence. He was equally admired

by nonbelievers because of his progressive views, and his sermons were syndicated in the press from coast to coast. Henry was born in 1813 into an evangelical New England family. After his mother died early, his preacher father remarried. Lyman Beecher was stingy and domineering; he related to his offspring by quizzing them on knotty points of theology. Although Henry's sister Harriet, later to write *Uncle Tom's Cabin*, helped to raise her brother, she admitted the Puritanical community had no place for children. Henry, called stupid by his father and deceitful by his stepmother, recalled a youth of "wrongdoing" in which he felt "shame and terror."

Henry was a stocky, well-set-up lad with straight blond hair and a round, malleable face. Because he stuttered and was slow, he made a mediocre student at Amherst College. He dreamed of his lost mother and recreated her as the one person who had understood him. He grew to idealize Woman and even women, provided they were all love and tenderness. When Henry had a conversion experience, he envisioned not a God of wrath but one of forgiveness, especially for sinners such as he. Indeed, Henry's God was his mother writ large. At the same time, he was able to cultivate what Harriet called his "genius for friendship." He formed a homoerotic attachment to a fellow student that he termed "a marriage of man to man."

Henry married, early and wrong, Eunice Bullard, a rather plain schoolteacher, and they moved to Indiana where he ministered to several rural parishes. Gone was any hesitation in his speech, replaced by a style that was fluid, friendly, and dramatic. Young Reverend Beecher was an instant success, and he knew why. "Preach little doctrine," he advised his neophyte brother. "Take hold of the most practical subjects; popularize your sermons." Eunice, typically burdened with children and housework, aged rapidly. By 1846, when Henry was called to Plymouth Church in fashionable Brooklyn Heights, Eunice's features had hardened and her hair turned gray. Behind her back, parishioners dubbed her "the raven."

With the improvement of ferry service, the rapid growth of antebellum New York spilled over into Brooklyn. Walt Whitman in his poem "Brooklyn Ferry" describes the "living crowd" of commuters who crossed to work in Manhattan's offices and then returned in the evening to "Brooklyn of ample hills," homes, and churches. Plymouth Church was founded by successful merchants to take advantage of newcomers and the prosperity they engendered. Its building, completed in 1850, resembled a theater. Within, the effect increased, because Beecher preached from a platform (not a pulpit) surrounded by the church's three thousand pews in two tiers. He acted out his sermons, which resembled current melodramas, to the largest, most responsive congregation in the city.

Henry C. Bowen, a silk merchant, was the leading founder of Plymouth and the official who had recruited Beecher. He was evidently pleased with the minister's propounding the gospel of love, which did away with the old Puritan fear of hell. This was Christianity Lite, and it emphasized freedom for its adherents—from dogma, guilt, and even family ties. Freedom of choice and association with new friends and allies—to be met at church socials—were the lures that drew so many up-and-coming couples, yesterday's yuppies, who packed into Plymouth's pews on Sundays and listened spellbound to the reverend's performance.

Beecher lived well and grew more portly. He liked expensive, flowing suits (an Armani look) without a clerical collar, and he liked to carry uncut gems in his pockets, rolling them about in his hand. Plymouth auctioned its pews to the highest bidder and caused local real estate prices to soar. Bowen founded an abolitionist newspaper, the *Independent*, as a vehicle for Beecher, and it grew to be the nation's leading religious weekly. Beecher became *the* voice of liberal Christian morality. However, Puritanism lingered in his psyche. When he seduced his benefactor's wife, Lucy, and she responded passionately, he felt tormented by "a sense of sinfulness and inefficiency."

Lucy eventually made a dying confession to her husband, but Bowen agreed to forgive the errant pastor in order to "work on for God and humanity." This echoes the menage of conscience, in which personal differences are submerged in an overriding cause. Actually, Bowen's silk business had failed, and he was dependent on Beecher's name to sell his newspapers. The minister gave the paper no more than that, since he hated to write and couldn't meet a deadline. While Beecher was the official editor of the *Independent*, a young journalist named Theodore Tilton was assigned to ghostwrite his articles. Since Tilton and his wife were avid followers of the minister, Theodore could easily slip into Beecher's style.

Thus evolved the so-called Trinity of Plymouth Church—the three men who shared the secret of its minister's transgression. Bowen needed both Tilton and Beecher, but he was also driven to complain about being cuckolded, and he did so privately to Tilton. Tilton, a tall, handsome man who wore his auburn hair poetically long, had rejected the strict Calvinism in which he had been raised. A scribbler of verse and a literary jack-of-all-trades, he hoped to make a name for himself even if he had to stand in for someone else. But when he and Beecher were thrown together in the early 1860s, an intense father-son relationship developed. The pair "spent hours in intimate conversation, on long walks and in visits to shops and galleries." Tilton claimed that not the older man's fame but "just your affection has been the bond between us." He recalled "lov[ing] that man as well as I ever loved a woman."

Tilton had married his childhood sweetheart, Elizabeth, whose mother kept a boardinghouse where the couple lived for the first several years. Elizabeth was petite and pretty, dark-haired and gentle, the opposite of fashionable. This grated on her upwardly mobile husband, who complained that Elizabeth lacked both presence and cultivation. "My life has been marred by social influences coming from your mother," he chided her. In 1861 Tilton took over the editorship of the *Independent,* and he began to lecture widely for a few months each year. Admired, he dressed and spoke in imitation of his patron Beecher, but he was troubled in mind.

Tilton now had to bear the cost of a handsome residence in the Heights. Though he mixed with a circle of well-known reformers and suffragists, Elizabeth was too withdrawn to take the lead in entertaining them. Complaints turned to abuse, and Tilton locked up and berated his wife for hours on end or embarrassed her in front of guests. Her apologies only infuriated him. On tour, he became unfaithful to her, probably employing prostitutes. True to the upbringing he hadn't escaped, he felt "spotted, miserable and unworthy," and he confessed his sins to his "espoused saint." Then he blamed his wife for not being sexually responsive.

Tilton's solution to his domestic problems was to encourage Beecher to take up Elizabeth in order to give her confidence. Away much of the time, Tilton urged the reverend to make his home his own. "There is a little woman down at my house who loves you more than you have any idea of," he teased. The preacher, in his fifties, had turned gray and grown portly, but he remained a magnetic figure, and he understood intimacy. Tilton knew he was a philanderer, and he had heard the quip that on any Sunday Beecher was preaching to at least twenty mistresses. But Tilton had grown tired of his wife, with whom he had conceived four children, and he must have wanted Beecher to take her over. The woman, though flattered, was being treated as an intermediary between the two men, who shared both the love and rivalry of father and son.

It took two years and the death of an infant for Elizabeth to succumb to Beecher's blandishments. Rejected by her husband, she turned to her minister for comfort, which he provided in bed. Beecher assured Elizabeth, who considered him "a great and holy man," that they shared a "high religious love." Beecher honestly believed sex to be the natural expression of love, but he would never dare say so in public. He cautioned

Elizabeth to maintain secrecy, which he termed "nest hiding," a concept he adopted from watching birds camouflage their nests.

The neglected wife's self-esteem soared, only to shudder under the mounting weight of guilt. On July 3, 1870, after nearly two years of infidelity, Elizabeth told her husband all. Tilton, hardly surprised, was tender and loving and promised to keep her secret. He urged her to continue seeing Beecher, and later that summer when she shied away from her lover, Tilton "playfully reproached her." But he gradually grew obsessive and soon began to swear that Elizabeth was trying to seduce every man who paid a social call on the house. He berated her for "having her bosom and legs fondled by many men." She was by nature "sensual"—that is, evil. Certainly the man's jealousy suggests suppressed homoerotic yearnings.

In late 1870, Tilton found himself fired from the *Independent*. He badgered Elizabeth to put in writing her confession of adultery. She had no sooner given in than Beecher, learning of it, rushed to her bedside and demanded she write a retraction. Elizabeth, "white as marble," lacked the strength to resist. She wrote what he dictated, revoking her first letter. When Tilton returned home after midnight, Elizabeth again confessed. Furious, he insisted she write a nullifying explanation of her retraction. She did this, too, but she was so distracted she would have signed her death warrant. This night's work destroyed Elizabeth Tilton as a functioning wife and mother.

Ironically, the men were able to make it up. Through the good offices of a parishioner they met, and Beecher performed his apology act complete with tears and threats of suicide should the affair become public. He offered to back a new weekly for Tilton to edit if he kept silent. But like Bowen, Tilton had to tell someone about his cuckolding. He chose to talk to his new mistress, a suffragist named Laura Bullard. Via her, gossip of the Beecher-Tilton imbroglio reached the ear of the editor of another weekly, whose masthead proclaimed its mission: "Breaking the Way for Future Generations." Finally, in May 1871 the woman soon to be dubbed "Mrs. Satan" broke the salacious news to the public. The chosen method, then as now, was a letter to the *New York Times*.

MRS. SATAN

Victoria Claflin was born in 1838 and named after the reigning queen of England. Her family of ten children and hanger-on relations were the social outcasts of Homer, Ohio. Her father, Buck, was a horse trader, cardsharp, and counterfeiter who rivaled Beecher's in abuse. He liked to use a braided switch to enforce his orders. Victoria, a beauty with blue eyes, brown hair, and a delicate profile, escaped grim childhood reality through leaps of the imagination. From a tree stump, she told her playmates stories of Indian captives and of sinners consigned to hellfire.

Victoria's mother, Annie, happily illiterate, discouraged her daughter from attending the local school, instead giving her chores at home. Allegedly she passed on her clairvoyant powers, such as predicting events or finding lost objects, to two of her daughters, Victoria and the slightly younger Tennessee. In 1850 the Claflins were run out of Homer after Buck burned down his grist mill to collect the insurance. He soon set up Tennie as a fortune-teller, a surefire occupation among midwestern farmers dependent on the weather. Tennie may have communed with spirits and tipped tables, but her personality was that of a spitfire. Flashier than her elder sister, she cared nothing for what others thought of her.

Meanwhile the Claflins married off Victoria at fifteen to Dr. Canning Woodhull, whose gallantry quickly wore thin. He gave Victoria two children—one retarded—between binges of drinking and whoring. To earn the family living, Victoria became alternately a cigar girl, a seamstress, and an actress. A spirit guide summoned her back to the Claflin clan, whose caravan rambled round the Midwest in a medicine show. Tennie, "the Pioneer Child who can cure the most obstinate diseases," was the star. An infirmary set up by the Claflins in Ottawa, Illinois, was found to be filthy, the patients neglected. The clan left town just ahead of the law.

In 1864 Colonel James Blood, city auditor of Saint Louis, went to Victoria Woodhull for a spiritual healing. Tall, broad-shouldered, and well-mustachioed, he looked the part of a Civil War hero. Victoria, who had matured into a handsome woman, immediately fell into a trance. "I see our futures linked," she whispered. "Our destinies will be bound together by ties of marriage." Then she invited him to make love to her. After more of the same, the colonel abandoned his position and wife and daughter and went with Victoria to Illinois to obtain her divorce from Canning Woodhull. The pair moved to Dayton, Ohio, where they were married. Unfortunately, Blood neglected to get a divorce, so their marriage had no legal validity. This didn't worry the woman who would become the staunch defender of Free Love. "There stands my lover," she would cry at political rallies, pointing to Blood, "but when I cease to love him, I shall leave him."

The Claflin sisters had grown weary of selling snake oil to rubes. They decided to peddle it in the most gullible market of all—the New York Stock Exchange. Settling in 1868 on Jones Street in the Village, they stalked the crusty railroad tycoon Commodore Vanderbilt. The richest man in America recognized the sisters as "ladies of resource." Tennie's obvious charms snared him. She was soon seen perched on the commodore's lap, reading the papers to him—he was almost illiterate—and pulling his whiskers if he dozed off. Tennie was also spotted "rosy and tousled in the commodore's bed in the morning." Vanderbilt wanted to marry her, but his family interfered. Victoria let her sister do the work she was good at.

In 1869 Jay Gould, with connections to the White House, tried to corner the gold market. Vanderbilt set up against him and bought stocks to calm the market. Woodhull was posted in a carriage outside the exchange on Broad Street. The mania to buy gold spread, and police could barely control the mob of speculators. Woodhull, having inside information, sold short, and when President Grant ordered the government to sell gold from its reserves, the speculators were ruined. Woodhull became a wealthy woman. Vanderbilt called her "a bold operator," and he backed the sisters as Wall Street's first female brokers. Their firm became so successful that Gould himself placed orders through them.

Money wasn't an end in itself to Woodhull. She was germinating the notion of becoming the first woman president of the United States. Of course she would need to court the press. She moved into an opulent home in Murray Hill and gave elegant soirées on Saturday evenings to which she invited men who were powerful or interesting. Educated Colonel Blood wrote the invitations. He conspired with Tennie to involve the editor of the *Tribune*, Whitelaw Reid, in an affair; as far as his own wife was concerned, he knew when to get lost. Woodhull became involved with Stephen Pearl Andrews, a philosophical anarchist twice her age. His long, flowing beard had gone out of fashion and so had the ideas she adopted from him.

"The sisters used men rather than being used by them," writes Woodhull's recent biographer, Lois Beachy Underhill. In fact, the men used them back—Blood lived off his wife, and Andrews found his outworn communalism given new currency. Perhaps Woodhull's most useful alliance was with General Benjamin Butler, a short, chubby man known as "Beast" when he had ruled over occupied New Orleans, but at the time an influential member of Congress. According to Underhill, "in Butler, Woodhull had found Washington's strongest power behind the scenes, and she entered into a brief, intense connection that brought her something more than sex." It does seem that Woodhull's erotic life became intertwined with her reach for power. We have dubbed such persons triangulators, and though they are usually found with two or more in tow, they often end up empty-handed.

Woodhull's reception by the suffragists, especially Susan B. Anthony, a dour Quaker, was distrustful from the start. They supported a sixteenth amendment to the Constitution to enfranchise women, but Woodhull, after founding her own weekly paper, declared it unnecessary. In January 1870 she argued before the House Judiciary Committee that the Constitution didn't distinguish between male and female citizens and that all citizens who were taxed had the right to vote. Her personality, if not her reasoning, captured the House. She was given an audience with President Grant, who predicted she would one day occupy his chair. But a wily Judiciary Committee turned the question over to the courts. In the meantime Woodhull's effective ploy, claiming that women *already* had the right to vote, had antagonized the antisuffrage women, in particular Henry's older sister, Harriet Beecher Stowe.

For a time, a groundswell of acclaim swept Woodhull to the forefront of the women's movement. But Woodhull's campaigning for public housing and abortion rights alienated conservatives. Privately, Beecher Stowe called Woodhull "a snake who should be given a good swat with a shovel." However, it was her own mother, Annie Claflin, who opened wide the door for her daughter's enemies. She brought a complaint against Colonel Blood for threatening her life. During the trial it was shown that Blood was a bigamist. Woodhull was castigated for again taking her ex-husband, Canning, into her household. Vanderbilt's name was dragged in, and he cooled toward the sisters.

Harriet Beecher Stowe attacked Woodhull through a satiric novel that appeared in installments in the *Christian Union* newspaper. She portrayed Woodhull as Audacia Dangyereyes, a so-called New Woman who frequented men's laps and asked them up to her room for a smoke. Woodhull fought back with what would later become the Gary Hart defense: her private life was her own business. When that failed to quiet the moralists, she launched her secret weapon, designed to sink "that infamous, hypocritical scoundrel, Beecher" and his sister, too. But Woodhull's initial letter to the *Times* about Beecher's infidelity was veiled, a shot across the bow. Beecher's response came in the person of Theodore Tilton, dispatched to put Woodhull under "social obligation."

The Woodhull-Tilton liaison began at once. Tilton invited Woodhull home for dinner and a discussion with his wife, "a wretched wreck of a woman," about her affair with Beecher. Elizabeth was soon left behind while for the next six months Tilton became a love slave. Woodhull would confide to the press that "he slept every night in my arms." Come spring, the handsome pair was seen about town rowing on the Harlem River or bathing at Coney Island. Their favorite haunt was the rooftop of Wood-hull's home on East Thirty-eighth Street, from which they watched day-light dim over the East River and the glow of a million gaslights rise to meet the stars in the sky.

There was a third in the menage, Colonel Blood. "He made no com-plaint, absented himself whenever possible and greeted Theodore [Tilton] pleasantly at the breakfast table or any other unlikely place that he might appear." The two men cooperated on a biography—or hagiography—of Woodhull that Blood had begun and that appeared in September 1871, published by Tilton's weekly, the *Golden Age*. Woodhull was thrilled by its fulsome praise, but reviewers found it ridiculous. An important rift devel-oped between Tilton and Woodhull because of his evasiveness on her run for the presidency. In any case, she had squeezed him dry, and she turned to the one man whose endorsement would make her a serious candidate: Henry Ward Beecher.

Tilton arranged a late-night tête-à-tête at his house between the man and woman who meant most to him. Beecher was overweight and jowly, but Woodhull took him on as a lover. Writes Underhill, "The two leaders shared a brief but mutually exciting and satisfying sexual encounter." Once again Tilton and his mentor were involved with the same woman—except this time, she was the one in charge. She would write openly in her weekly of "the immense physical potency of Mr. Beecher" and insist that he had "the right to the loving manifestations of many women," herself included. Despite Woodhull's talk of love as guided by nothing but itself, we find it hard to disentangle her bedroom adventures from her platform ambitions.

In the summer of 1871, Woodhull on the one hand entertained politicians, including members of President Grant's own family, and on the other founded the Equal Rights party. Under this banner she courted reformers, suffragists, and labor leaders. Next both Blood and Tilton pro-moted her at a convention of Spiritualists, who were plentiful and open to the leadership of women. That fall Woodhull and other women attempted to vote in municipal elections and nearly succeeded. Universal suffrage seemed to be on the horizon. Woodhull, needing money, took to the lecture circuit, where the big draw was Free Love.

Woodhull advocated the sexual equality of women with men and free and easy divorce—stands not very different from those that John Stuart and Harriet Mill had proposed. But her methods of manipulating men amounted to blackmail. Before a major speech at Steinway Hall in New York, she demanded that Beecher introduce her and identify himself publicly with the gospel of Free Love, which he privately practiced. Beecher refused, and when Woodhull threatened to expose him, she recalled that "he got upon the sofa on his knees beside me [and], while the tears streamed down his cheeks, begged me to let him off." Tilton had to introduce Woodhull to a packed house of over three thousand. To their delight she gave a speech beginning, "Yes, I am a free lover," in which she claimed the right to complete sexual freedom.

Woodhull was still flying high. In January 1872 a suffragist convention, over the objections of its leaders, endorsed her for president. But the next month, in a New York speech titled "The Impending Revolution," Woodhull attacked the leading financiers of her time, Vanderbilt and Astor, as well as capitalism itself. In her weekly she took a Marxist line, claiming that Jesus Christ, if alive, would be a Communist. Now the press would show her no mercy. The *Times* set an abusive tone, which Woodhull called "wife beating." The famous Thomas Nast cartoon appeared, depicting her as Mrs. Satan, and other papers and magazines followed suit.

In May 1872 Woodhull's Equal Rights party held a convention in New York to nominate her for president. But the labor reformers held a parallel convention of their own, and so did the suffragists. Susan B. Anthony managed to keep the latter from endorsing Woodhull. Amid the presence of a myriad cranks and much hoopla, the Equal Rights convention did nominate Woodhull, but it represented the fringes of society. An editorial in the *Brooklyn Sun* summed up the attitude of most Americans: "The reasonings of a Tilton or of a Victoria Woodhull carried into practice would bohemianize mankind." From then on, Woodhull would no longer be taken seriously.

The stock market crash of 1873 finished Woodhull financially. She lost her home, and no landlord dared rent her another. She was not only notorious but poor. Desperate and abandoned, she appealed to Tilton and Beecher, who ignored her. Reformers backed Horace Greeley for president, and Woodhull was forgotten. Newsmen would no longer carry her *Weekly* on their stands. Woodhull reached for the last weapon left her: she printed a thorough version of "The Beecher-Tilton Scandal Case." Not for his adulteries did Woodhull damn Beecher but because he refused to stand by her in support of Free Love.

Woodhull admitted that she timed her exposé to coincide with the twenty-fifth anniversary of Beecher's coming to Plymouth Church. Her attack smoldered like a time bomb. Woodhull herself was so discredited that Beecher could stonewall her charges, answering none of them. Her announced intent to reveal the private lives of figures prominent in finance and politics led, as she should have guessed, to the U.S. Post Office confiscating her *Weekly* and charging her with sending obscene material through the mail. Anthony Comstock, head of the YMCA's Committee for the Suppression of Vice, spearheaded a campaign of raids, arrests, and punitive bail for Woodhull, Tennie Claflin, and Colonel Blood.

The hounding of Victoria Woodhull is reminiscent of latter-day witch hunts aimed at women who seem to be growing too powerful. While she did receive support from suffragists such as Elizabeth Cady Stanton, the Spiritualist communities were Woodhull's last and true resort. Interestingly, when she again lectured on the sexual emancipation of women, her popularity revived. She traveled around accompanied by her sister and Blood, claiming, "Ours is a trinity. . . . We are three in one in spirit and purpose, and [therein] lies all the strength we have." The threesome, like the triangular bastion of a fort, makes for an effective defensive unit.

Meanwhile, Woodhull continued her amorous adventures. She claimed not to be ashamed of any desire she had gratified, and in a speech before a Spiritualist convention in Chicago she gave a flowing description of a female orgasm, ending, "The whole being thrills with ecstasy as it recognizes and embraces the companion." Woodhull's actual sex life tended to be more complex. An MIT student named Benjamin Tucker related, fifty years later, how Colonel Blood had recruited him in Boston to help out with publicity tasks. Victoria dismissed her husband and kissed the lad, placing herself on his knee. Benjamin conquered his timidity to return to the hotel the next day. Victoria announced, "I should dearly love to sleep with you." He stammered that he was a virgin, which pleased her.

Significantly, Victoria waited until Blood was present to continue her seduction of Benjamin. The colonel joked, "There's altogether too much magnetism about here for me." He left, and with Victoria showing the way, Benjamin within the hour had become "a proud and happy youth." When he inquired if the colonel would be jealous, Victoria replied that Blood had said, "I know very well what I would do were he a girl." The element of voyeurism in sparking Blood's libido was perfectly paired with Woodhull's sexual showmanship. However, Tucker insisted she was "by no means insatiable in her lovemaking, but enraptured and happy." He felt that Woodhull loved Blood and that he approved of the menage, which went on for some time. According to Underhill, it was "an additional satisfaction [to Blood] to have Tucker on the scene."

The menage a trois suited breakaway Victorians. It was private and manageable, yet its practitioners gained the added satisfaction of slipping the intolerable straitjacket of a loveless marriage. Victoria Woodhull was a pioneer in speaking out *publicly* for women's sexual rights. She refused to let up on Beecher, hammering at him while her *Weekly* scraped along. The reverend, who had accepted a lucrative contract to write a life of Jesus, countered by convening a church council to judge his alleged crimes. In October 1873, Plymouth's elders turned on the messenger of ill tidings and expelled Theodore Tilton—for slandering Beecher! On August 20, 1874, Tilton finally swore out a complaint against Beecher in city court. He demanded $100,000 in damages "for his having wholly lost the comfort, society, aid and assistance of [his] wife."

Beecher's philandering was discussed in Brooklyn's shops and saloons, on streetcars, and in parlors and kitchens. During the second half of 1874, the *New York Times* fanned the flames by running 105 stories and thirty-seven editorials on the scandal. The diarist George Templeton Strong remarked, "A capital low comedian was lost to mankind when [Beecher] professed religion." The trial, begun on January 11, 1875, may best be described as a farce. Tickets were sold on the black market, and thousands of people were turned away, a boon for nearby saloons. High and low alike missed lunch in order to hold seats and train their opera glasses on the witness of the moment. Eunice Beecher sat stiffly in a black dress beside her husband, who sniffed violets as though unconcerned.

Elizabeth Tilton, when put on the stand and quizzed about adultery with her minister, denied everything. Her sacrifice of truth to expediency transformed her husband, from whom she'd separated, into the villain of the piece. Beecher's corps of expensive lawyers portrayed Tilton as a godless conniver and bohemian. As one midwestern minister put it, why should Beecher have resorted to a drab, married woman when "there were plenty of young girls that he could have had, plenty of them."

Tilton vs. Beecher resembles the Simpson case not only because it exposed the innards of a love triangle but also because each trial spent many months hearing testimony that would not matter to the jurors. Early on a Beecher lawyer advised the jury, "Upon the result of your verdict to a very large extent shall depend the integrity of the Christian religion." Beecher had sent damning love letters to Elizabeth; servants testified they had seen her sitting on his lap and in other compromising positions; he had even confessed the affair to reliable witnesses. All of this was reduced to nothing by the chief attorney for the defense, William Evarts, who warned the jurors that in admitting the possibility of his client's guilt, "You have struck a blow not at Mr. Beecher, not at Mrs. Tilton, but at your own wives and your own daughters."

Windy summations rife with biblical and literary quotes took five weeks during the steaming summer. Afterward the jury was sequestered. The Brooklyn courthouse was mobbed by curiosity seekers, many of whom camped out. After fifty-two ballots, a jury emerged that was hung but leaned nine to three in favor of Beecher. Bedlam broke loose. The jurors were besieged by reporters while jubilant supporters of the minister carried him home in imperial style. In the last years of his life Henry Ward Beecher retained his prominence. It was rumored that someday he might be a Republican candidate for president. He died in 1887 beloved and honored. Thousands of distraught women filed past his coffin—a preview of the funeral, decades hence, of Valentino.

Theodore Tilton was never forgiven for having sullied Beecher's reputation. He moved to the Left Bank of Paris, where he frequented cafés and wrote poetry and romantic fiction. He had nothing to do with his former wife, who in 1878 made a public admission of her adultery, which the Beecherites dismissed as deranged raving. Elizabeth became a blind, impoverished recluse who enjoyed having her ex-husband's novels read to her by their daughter. Victoria Woodhull moved to London, married a respectable banker, and went to great lengths to erase her past. She engaged in charities, ran a little magazine, and eventually acquired a motorcar.

When Henry James published his novel *The Siege of London,* about an American adventuress who attempts to marry into British society, reviewers took his protagonist to be a portrait of the one-time Mrs. Satan. She went to James, and he gave her a written statement that he had no intention of "representing or suggesting Mrs. Victoria Woodhull." Then he portrayed her again as Verena Tarrant in *The Bostonians.* Woodhull, who died in 1927, might or might not object to the movie that Richard Gere's production company plans to make about her life. Her story, along with Beecher's and Tilton's, has not been laid to rest.

chapter 14

THE BALLS OF AMHERST

A New England *Peyton Place*

Darling, darling, *DARLING!*
MABEL LOOMIS TODD

*I*DYLLIC AMHERST, MASSACHUSETTS, WAS
a nineteenth-century Peyton Place. The surrounding area was still mainly
rural and rife with adultery, polygamy, child abuse, alcoholism, opium
addiction, idiocy, and an occasional killing—but these things were swept
under the Turkish rugs that covered proper parlor floors. Amherst is
located in the Connecticut River Valley where Jonathan Edwards's hellfire
preaching had terrified the sinful populace of an earlier century. But in the
later decades of the 1800s, perhaps because the Civil War had killed off
its idealists, a lenient hypocrisy became the town's ruling virtue. It would
take the charged air of the courtroom to expose the dirty linen of the
leading family for the delectation of all those beholden to them.

Edward Dickinson, the old squire, was an unsmiling man who once
represented his district in Congress. He was serving in the state legislature
when he died of apoplexy in 1874. Business ceased when the railroad
brought the body home. The funeral services were as severe as the man had
been. The feelings of his younger daughter, Lavinia (called Vinny), were
mixed; her father's intolerance of suitors had caused her to become a maiden
of forty. His son, Austin, the new squire, kissed his dead father's forehead,
an act he'd never dared in life. And his elder daughter, Emily, forty-four and
given to writing poetry furtively, watched from her upstairs room "with the
door open just a crack, where she could hear without being seen."

Austin, while a student, was tall and handsome with wavy auburn hair. He lost the hair after a bout with malaria and thereafter wore a bushy red wig. Edward had already turned over his position as treasurer of Amherst College. Austin, a better attorney, presided over meetings in lavender trousers and a Prince Albert coat. He was a big man in a small compass. His lover later marveled how, in one way or another, he helped every citizen in Amherst. By 1890 a photo of Austin shows that his youthful dash is gone. His spouse, Susan Dickinson, known to her neighbors as "The Power," by all evidence was a manipulative wife and mother, a show-off hostess, and a fickle friend—a woman who didn't hesitate to threaten murder to get her way. Because Sue always wore black, she came to be known as The Black Mogul. Sue had what the Victorians termed "presence," but her talents were circumscribed by her parochial time and place.

Austin, secure in his social position, had courted the poverty-stricken Susan Gilbert for years. She was Emily's age and her great friend. Sue's mother died young, and her tavern-keeping father drank himself into disgrace. Sue was sturdy, dark-haired, and good-looking, with a defiant wit. But underneath she was fearful and calculating, the opposite of Austin, whose aloof bearing hid a romantic nature. The pair had misjudged each other even before their 1856 marriage, which elevated Sue to mistress of the Dickinson household and eventually all Amherst.

After his father's death, Austin's sisters, Emily and Lavinia, fell under his stewardship. They continued to live in the Homestead, the family's Federal-style home on Main Street, while Austin, Sue, and their elder son, Ned, as well as young Martha and baby Gilbert, lived across a wide lawn in the Evergreens, a tan-colored structure of the black-walnut mid-Victorian era. The two maiden sisters coped well enough with everyday details but counted on Austin to take charge of weightier matters. Their house remained his home in some significant ways.

In a preface to *Austin and Mabel*, Polly Longsworth's account of the menage a trois that rocked Amherst, the scholar Richard Sewall writes, "Veteran novel readers will rub their eyes to remind themselves that this really happened. And since it happened close to Emily Dickinson, it is important." But we need to be wary of hindsight. To the citizens of Amherst, Emily was a kook, about on a par with her sister, Vinnie, who doted on "her pussies and her posies." In contrast, the squire's affair with a sophisticated, married woman from the big city, her husband's complicity, and The Power's grim attempts to get even with the lovers—that was news! The passionate drama of three-way adultery provided a thrill to onlookers for the fourteen years that it ran nonstop.

Since Emily played a supporting role as accomplice and voyeur, we will treat her here as an active witness in the Amherst of her day rather than as a monument to literature. Emily, born in 1830, was a very good child. She attended the Mount Holyoke Female Seminary, where a daguerreotype taken in her eighteenth year shows a serious young woman, a bow round her neck, who is attractive in a plain way. Her gingerbread was highly prized. If she had flirtations with young men, they didn't amount to much; her strongest attachment was to her elder brother Austin. Then, in her early twenties, Emily appears to have fallen in love with the woman Austin was laboriously courting, Sue Gilbert.

For Emily, voyeurism—in particular, enjoying women through friendships with their male suitors—surfaces at about this time, though it vies with a more direct admiration. Emily's feelings for Sue were those of lesbian love but probably not in the sense of lovemaking, for she was never intended for carnal knowledge. During the 1850s Sue was the recipient of scores of letters from Emily, charged with images of kissing and clinging, in which the writer assumes the role of wounded lover. If the poet's seclusion was caused by a romantic disappointment—as some biographers have claimed—then Sue was the one who spurned her, ironically by choosing her beloved brother.

Emily Dickinson's withdrawal from normal life was described by her sister, Vinnie, as "only a happen." Sue herself, for her own reasons, several times put off the wedding. When the event finally occurred on July 1, 1856, Emily understood she had lost out to *maleness*. "I am keen but you are keener," she chided her brother, "I am *something* of a fox, but you are more of a hound!" Emily failed to congratulate her new sister-in-law, and for the next two years she corresponded with no one. She began to write again in 1858, her first serious poetry.

Emily's sister, Vinnie, could be caricatured as a typical New England spinster. Emily depended on Vinnie: "Without her life were fear," she informed a friend, "and Paradise a cowardice, except for her inciting voice." In turn, Vinnie had a fanatic devotion to her sister's poetic genius. As a young woman Vinnie was pert and popular. After an early romance soured, Vinnie too withdrew into her domestic fortress. Thereafter, she protected the fragile Emily.

Both Austin's notion that by marrying a tavern keeper's daughter he would introduce "bodily vigor" into the Dickinson line and Sue's conviction that she had elevated her social status by capturing a docile mate would be exploded, his promptly and hers when Austin all but left her for Mabel Loomis Todd. Sue, who dreaded having children, tried to keep

Austin from her bed. But she couldn't remain Mrs. Dickinson without giving in to her husband's desire. Mabel confided to her daughter that "Sue had several abortions . . . as she thought it disgusting to have children." Sue attempted to abort Ned, the Dickinsons' elder son, but instead he was born an epileptic, given to frightful fits in his sleep. Mabel believed Austin's life had been "in all home things a terrible failure."

Austin solaced himself with his deep love for nature. Sue, meanwhile, gave elaborate dinners and hosted dances that would have been termed balls if held in the South. Austin complained to his diary about Sue's "sprees" and "riots," especially "a wild tear and revel" on Ned's twenty-first birthday. While he worked tirelessly to help his neighbors and beautify Amherst, Sue instructed her children in snobbery. Socially, she ruled the town with an iron hand, ashamed of her two old-maid sisters-in-law, whom she treated as poor relations. Emily summed up in 1877, "Austin is overcharged with care, and Sue with scintillation."

This was the atmosphere into which Amherst College's new astronomer, David Todd, and his wife, Mabel, were precipitated in August 1881; the most exciting couple to arrive in decades, they were immediately taken up by its leading hostess. But if the polished Dickinson exterior hid a loveless marriage, the Todds' freshness masked a sensuality unusual for a professor and his proper wife. To some, Mabel would appear an arch flirt and David a college Casanova.

THE TRANSCENDENTAL MENAGE

Mabel Loomis was born in 1856 of New England stock. Although raised in Boston boardinghouses, she exuded gentility. She idolized her father, Eben, whom she praised for his heavenly nature. As a clerk drudging away in Washington's Nautical Almanac Office, Eben's head was in the clouds literally and figuratively. His pride was having walked in the woods with Thoreau and later round Washington with Whitman. Mabel inherited her father's love of nature and poetry and a disposition so airy that her husband would compare her to a perpetually blue sky.

Mabel's mother, Molly, scrimped along on a meager salary to present a refined image. She inculcated in her daughter the idea that the Loomises were superior to their straitened circumstances. Mabel's adolescence was punctuated by annual summer reunions in New England with a clan whose ancestors dated back to the Mayflower. Molly sent Mabel to study at the costly Boston Conservatory of Music where Mabel learned to play the piano and sing in public; she later would become an accomplished artist and book illustrator. The young woman, certain she had unique abilities, confided to her diary, "It is not that I have a genius for painting, or for piano, or for writing—but it is a great, independent genius I know which would give its sacred touch to a lifetime devoted exclusively to anything." Mabel's self-confidence—and later her husband's devotion—gave her the strength to transcend tragedy.

Mabel, "coming out" socially, presented an odd mixture of naïveté and conceit. As the critic Peter Gay describes her, "she was handsome without being beautiful. . . . But she radiated vivacity and good health." Living in boardinghouses and always looking on the bright side had taught her how to attract male admirers. However, husband hunting in Washington, populated by on-the-take politicians and profiteers, was a disappointing proposition. Mabel's hourglass figure and ingratiating ways failed to compensate for her lack of a dowry, and the suitors dwindled away.

In 1877, Mabel met David Todd one wet day at the Nautical Almanac office, where he'd come to borrow a telescope. She thought the young blond astronomer very handsome; she described his teeth as "magnificent." Although he came from a modest farm background, he was a direct descendant of Jonathan Edwards, and Mabel approved of his manners. It appeared that her only rival would be David's passion for the planet Jupiter.

David's courtship of Mabel progressed in true Victorian style: larks leading to high-minded talk about aspirations, followed by letters that grew more introspective and candid. Marriage, expected to last until death, was taken seriously, and one's choice of a spouse often determined success or failure in life. David, rather than wishing to keep Mabel at home, immediately encouraged her to achieve her heart's desire. Occasional heavy petting helped seal the engagement in November 1878—a step taken against parental wishes.

Then came David's confession of a "dreadful thing" that upset Mabel terribly. The biographer Longsworth surmises that the young astronomer, who was lodging with his supervisor, had been carrying on an affair with the man's wife. This is especially interesting because the house was directly across the street from the Loomis lodging, and earnest David, while declaring his undying love for his virgin bride-to-be, was continuing an "animal" affair almost within earshot.

Mabel reacted in a forgiving and high-minded manner. Thereafter, she devoted herself to uplifting and purifying David, whose sweet nature enchanted her. The couple married, and their first years together were one long honeymoon. Mabel knew little of love, but she was eager to learn. Gay tells us, "David Todd, adoring and avid at the same time, doubtless stimulated by his wife's delighted discoveries, generated a steamy domestic atmosphere that Mabel Todd enjoyed and fostered." At night he would undress her before the fire, take her in his arms, and tuck her in bed, kiss her over and over—then go to his desk to study for an hour or two!

Mabel's diary is chockablock with entries about her happiness being too much for this world. She wrote about the night "we retired at seven and had a magnificent evening, David and I." We know that on this occasion they had intercourse twice, because Mabel was using marginal symbols to denote frequency of sex and her orgasms. These she had in plenty, and she somehow related them to the couple's primitive method of birth control: a combination of rhythm and withdrawal. On the morning of May 15, 1879, "a very happy few minutes of love" resulted nine months later in the birth of daughter Millicent.

Mabel loved being a wife, but at first found motherhood difficult. Once the newborn began attracting compliments, she changed her mind. The Todds and Loomises moved into a new home, and Mabel turned the care of the infant over to her mother. She returned to entertaining rooms filled with people, singing and flirting with men in a manner she herself termed outrageous. David showed pride in his wife's conquests.

We have already noted the man as a sexual adventurer. Now he enjoyed this taste of voyeurism, a wine of which he would drink deeply later. It differed only in degree from the pride any man takes when others admire his wife. After David accepted a position at Amherst and the Todds moved there in 1881, David took a similar pleasure in watching Mabel fascinate the students at their balls, dancing and flirting with the young men as though she were one of their dates. In private he continued to spoil Mabel like a child, on cold mornings warming her clothes by the fire and dressing her in bed, goo-gooing all the while. If away, he pined for her, signing his letters, *"Lover/Husband/David."* How many women, then or now, would wish for such a mate!

This aura of perfection encouraged Sue Dickinson to take up the young couple. Her own marriage had worn to a frazzle after twenty-six loveless years. In turn, Mabel was impressed by her hostess's elegant house, Austin's collection of fine books and paintings, and his horses and carriages. Mabel found Sue sincere and charming, captivating in every respect. Mabel felt that they understood each other. Indeed, Sue's magnetism had won the plaudits of Emerson and attracted the roving eye of Henry Ward Beecher. One college dean suggested awarding her an honorary degree in social skills.

Mabel wasn't instantly drawn to Austin. She admired his dignity and strength but sensed something a little odd. The Evergreens became a refuge for her, a retreat from the suspicious, stern-visaged townsfolk. What could they make of a professor's wife who hand-painted flowers on her dresses? Mabel, who had to flirt, chose to captivate twenty-year-old Ned. This sickly scion of the Dickinsons, though he tried to act older than his years, was a neophyte in love. He began to court Mabel so openly that the next spring she fled to Washington, hoping to give her "intense lover" time to cool off.

Mabel's clumsiness in permitting Ned to fall in love with her while she was becoming attracted to Austin created two triangles. First, she turned father and son into rivals for her affection; then, once she explained to Ned he had no hope, the jilted young man became her enemy and was estranged from his father. In January 1883 he informed his mother that her husband was straying. For a while the two women talked about Austin calmly, but relations between the Todds and Dickinsons became strained. Sue cooled off toward Mabel, then cut her.

On September 11, 1882, Austin fetched Mabel to come to a whist party, but they strolled past the gate of the Evergreens. Eyes met, hands clasped, hearts swelled with emotion. That evening Austin wrote the portentous word "Rubicon" in his diary. Later, he wrote it in the margin of Mabel's diary, which shows that each had access to the other's inmost thoughts.

On the path to passion neither looked back. If Romeo and Juliet had lived into middle age and been transported by time machine to nineteenth-century New England, they couldn't have been more ardent lovers than Austin and Mabel. Defying the shadow of Jonathan Edwards and the harsh stares of his Puritanical descendants, not to mention the warfare waged against them by Sue, the fiftysomething pillar of the community and the midtwenties faculty wife embraced their romantic destiny. They carried on at home and abroad, under trees and dining room tables, aided and abetted by the old maids Emily and Vinnie and with the participation of David Todd. A heart-rending tale of love and devotion, this is a full-fledged menage a trois.

As often happens when a menage begins, the acquiescence of the third was not achieved at once. Austin, a savvy lawyer, took the measure of his rival one night on the piazza: "After a while the little man [David] appeared in the darkness. Littleness is not preferred." David was no better pleased. Shortly after Austin and Mabel had reached an understanding, the astronomer departed for California's new Lick Observatory to photograph a transit of Venus. Mabel stayed behind. David succeeded in his work admirably and fell in love with southern California, which suited his outgoing temperament far better than chilly New England. But when he returned to his wife in January 1883, he moaned about having left her.

In order to evade the legion of gossips that made up Amherst society, as well as Sue's wrath, the adulterers needed allies and a safe house. They found these next door at the Dickinson Homestead. Austin's time was taken up with town business, but he could always pay an extended call on his sisters. Preparing the way, he'd already taken Mabel to play and sing for Vinnie, while Emily listened outside—that is, from the corridor between the parlor and dining room. Afterward, she sent in a glass of wine and a poem to signify her appreciation.

Next morning Emily sent Mabel flowers and a note, and over the following three and a half years dozens of notes and favors were exchanged between the two. Although these never mentioned Austin, their mutual affection for him initiated a ghostly, symbiotic relationship. The Homestead became a house of assignation, and according to Longsworth, "Emily, fully aware of what was occurring in her home, rejoiced in Austin's renewed happiness and his more frequent presence, and enjoyed indirectly the gaiety and spontaneity Mabel brought to the quiet mansion."

From the first, Vinnie acted as go-between, receiving letters from the cautious pair and readdressing them in her own handwriting, or simply allowing them the use of her mailbox. These early missives are blissful in tone, filled with a shared appreciation of nature, from moss on an old stone wall to a brilliant sunset. Two souls were soaring in transcendental rapture. Optimistic Mabel predicted a great future for them. She insisted that Austin love her every minute.

However, the Great Black Mogul had begun to issue threats. As a precaution, Austin, after copying Mabel's early letters and entrusting copies to Vinnie, burned the originals. He warned his sister that if anything happened to him she must burn the file without opening it. At this time it is possible the affair hadn't been entirely consummated.

The death of the Dickinson's young son Gilbert in 1883, one year after the crossing of the Rubicon, precipitated Austin's final flight into Mabel's arms. The bright boy had been the apple of his father's eye and a great favorite with everyone. His demise almost killed Austin and severely weakened Emily. But when Austin turned to Mabel it was with new fervor: lovemaking, after all, is the most powerful denial of death. Austin's symbol (=) and Mabel's (-) indicating sexual union are first found in their respective diaries on December 13, 1883, and a slip with that date and the invented word AMUASBTEILN were found in Austin's wallet when he died. The word is formed by alternately combining the letters of their two names.

The tryst took place in the dining room of the Homestead—more specifically on the rug and, to muffle their cries, under the mahogany table. Emily, in her room one floor above and across the narrow hall but no more than twenty-five feet away on a direct line, must have heard this pair—desperate and elated—expend their dammed-up passion. Remember, Emily is the poet who wrote, "I heard a fly buzz—when I died." Emily's hearing was so acute that to her a breeze sounded "like a Bugle" as it "quivered through the Grass." Remember, also, that Emily kept up her connection to the world by listening with the door cracked to what went on downstairs.

In *Sexual Personae* Camille Paglia presents Emily Dickinson as a sado-masochistic exhibitionist, indeed "Amherst's Madame de Sade." Her claim is that Emily's reclusiveness was a device to gain attention, an inverted sort of self-promotion. Unfortunately for this theory, it wasn't Emily who promoted her poetry, it was Mabel. Emily was an auditor par excellence, able to take in life at close or far range through hearing as fine-tuned as a cat's. But we are indebted to Paglia for insisting that the poet had a catty side. When Emily writes to a friend, "My Brother is with us so often each day, we almost forget he ever passed to a wedded home," she is getting in a dig at Sue.

Certainly Emily's wearing white in face of the funerals that marked Victorian life was almost showy. And sometimes when there were guests in the parlor she frequented the shadowy corridor, listening while keeping out of sight. Did this sometimes mordant observer of life, creeping downstairs, ever peek through the keyhole while Austin and Mabel consummated their yearnings—again and again during the winter of 1884? Dickinson's biographer Sewall writes how Emily measured people with her "narrow probing eyes." She became a ghostly fourth—the poet as inevitable voyeur—to what had become a transcendental menage a trois.

The fleshly meal in the dining room took place with David's concurrence. Mabel and David had talked it out beforehand, and with her certainty of a special fate, she turned the profane into the spiritual. "My life has a sort of consecration now," she informed her husband. "[Austin's] love for me is something sacred; it dignifies me and elevates me. I thank God daily for it." The preachers at nearby churches who thundered of eternal damnation wasted their breath on Mabel. She was a nature worshiper, verging on the pagan. Her God wouldn't be so vulgar as to hold a lady to petty morality. Moreover, she was confident that history would exonerate her. In 1888 she wrote to Austin, "We should have been born later. . . . One or two hundred years from now the world would rejoice with us." Touchingly, Mabel trusted to the future.

"SO DIVINE A LOVE"

The wife who didn't flinch at adultery with another woman's husband was determined to keep her own. The ardent young couple had evolved into tender and devoted companions, who continued to have sexual intercourse several times a month. Mabel found her married life sweet and peaceful. She loved and appreciated David all the more, and she remained determined to make him happy.

This contrasts to the rapture Mabel felt when she was in Austin's presence or even thinking of him. "Oh! beloved!" she wrote—three years after their first declaration of love. "Are not our loves inextricably interwoven? And is it not bliss unutterable? I *love* you, dear. . . . Oh! darling! my soul is yours—forever and ever. Keep me in your innermost heart, which you told me is your home for me, and never let me get out."

Austin returned her ardor, showering Mabel with romantic prose: "Every day I love you more, more sweetly, more thrillingly, with larger power. Every day I am filled with profounder gratitude and joy for you. . . . No other heaven could ever compare with you." On occasion, Austin's Puritan heritage would come back to haunt him, and he wondered rhetorically who could blame such star-crossed lovers. Austin, after all, had to adjust not only to his wife's rancor but to becoming intimate with his beloved's husband!

Mabel, a naive narcissist, felt no guilt, only occasional self-pity that she couldn't have both men entirely to herself. During Christmas 1885, when Austin was consumed by family obligations, she reflected, "I have a strange sort of life . . . not a bit like anybody else's. . . . It is sometimes infinitely happier." But Sue's growing hostility and the need to keep up appearances would try even her sunny nature.

David, whom Mabel felt to be a remarkable man, was her solace. She still thought of herself as David's happy little wife. Mabel and David tried to see Austin every day, usually at the Homestead. Sometimes all three went for a walk in the beautiful New England countryside. They roamed the woods, picked wildflowers on hillsides, went for sleigh rides. Austin commended Mabel's loyalty and affection for David, admiring the constancy of a woman once known for her flirting.

David took a tack more suited to his overactive libido. Years later, Mabel found herself unable to criticize her husband's amours, commenting in her journal, "David is innocently unmoral." She listed ten pages of examples but ripped them out. David had begun his conquests of the women of Amherst and vicinity before Austin and Mabel crossed their Rubicon. He was a Casanova type, drawn to the new, shunning nothing in a petticoat. As his daughter Millicent wrote, "he had most of the women guests who came to our house, even beginning on my friends when I grew up." David was devoted to being "animal," and love had nothing to do with it.

In spring 1884 David began a lengthy affair with Caro Andrews, Mabel's cousin, who was married to a wealthy Bostonian. She was plump and pretty, expensively dressed, and bored with her husband. Caro and David's love letters were transmitted roundabout, and Mabel read them and complained about their lustful language. But she remained on such friendly terms with Caro that in the summer of 1885 she accompanied the Andrews on a three-month tour of Europe. Austin and David were left alone in Amherst.

The two men grew close. Austin suffered but David comforted him. The first to get a letter from abroad ran and shared it with the other. When David fell ill, Austin nursed him back to health. The younger man had been in awe of his aristocratic elder, but now he grew fond of him. Mabel claimed to suffer greatly while making a hit among the ship's passengers and touring the monuments of England. Austin insisted Emily read her letters, or parts of them, so she could travel vicariously. She sent Mabel a letter with the memorable line: "Touch Shakespeare for me." By this time the poet's health was failing and she no longer ventured from her room.

That summer Austin hit on an idea guaranteed to horrify the burghers of Amherst. He wrote to Mabel, "I think we three would have no trouble in a house together in living as you and I should wish." Whether he meant to leave Sue isn't clear, but The Black Mogul showed her claws. Generally Sue and Austin waged wars of attrition; sometimes they didn't speak, at others Sue begged Austin on her knees to quit Mabel. But now she threatened him with a carving knife. Austin was made to understand that Sue had nothing left but her social position; if he threatened that, it might result in murder.

Mabel returned in the fall; Emily died the next spring. Curiously, Sue, not Vinny, saw to the laying out of her sister-in-law's body. Of late Sue had disparaged Emily, claiming she had once found her in the drawing room "reclining in the arms of a man." This would be Judge Otis Lord, who was a close friend and perhaps a suitor of Emily's. Sue took charge of her voluminous and scattered poems, scrawled on every sort of paper, with a view to sorting and publishing them.

Work had begun on the so-called third house, the Dell. Austin owned this Queen Anne cottage situated in a meadow adjoining the Homestead. David supervised the construction while he also oversaw the building of an observatory at nearby Smith College. The Dell had an unusual feature: a back staircase provided private access from outside to the second floor. There, in her bedroom with a fire glowing, Mabel would spend nights waiting for her lover while David was at the observatory, stargazing.

At times, a tall figure would arrive and climb directly to the bedroom. Then the door was locked. Elsewhere in the house young Millicent Todd, old enough to suspect but too uneasy to inquire, cowered. After a time, the figure would exit, accompanied downstairs by Mabel, who threw her arms round him for a parting kiss, crying, "My king!" Later, as Millicent lay restless in her room, a whistle floated through the night. It was David signaling that he had come home. Finally, she could sleep.

If Emily had been a willing voyeur, the new onlooker, Millicent, was trapped into observing things she didn't wish to know. Mabel had taken to wearing two sets of rings: a diamond engagement ring and wedding band from David on her right hand and a nearly identical set from Austin on her left. She considered herself both men's wife. The sight of those rings made Millicent feel "degraded . . . and in a way disinherited." The child worried about the town's disapproval.

What the trio did with Millicent on Sunday evenings isn't clear. But at the Dell the three made love. Austin's symbol (=) in his diary is on numerous occasions accompanied by the notation "with a witness," and there is corroborative evidence from Mabel's diary that David watched his wife and best friend couple. Peter Gay, after noting David's vicarious pleasure in Mabel's sexual adventures, adds a note of homoeroticism: "On the most obscure, most tenaciously defended levels of his unconscious, [David] must have taken considerable erotic pleasure in the emotional intimacy that Austin Dickinson's affair with his wife permitted him with her lover." We also believe that David was free enough to enjoy the homoerotic element consciously and likely to join them in bed to make love to Mabel.

The threesome did more than engage in erotic games. Each continued to play a role in the life of Amherst. Certainly, the gossips noted Austin and Mabel's long buggy rides, during which the lovers would pause for hours beneath a clump of trees. The townsfolk saw the grim look on Sue's face as, rain or shine, she showed her august presence on Main Street, and they felt the lash of her tongue. They couldn't have missed David's carrying on with women high and low. But their suspicions were never voiced out loud.

Austin remained treasurer of the college and was elected head of the parish committee. He worked hard to give the town a public park, landscape the college grounds, and build an idyllic new cemetery. Who would challenge the squire as he held forth, gold-headed cane in hand in front of the hotel, solving everyone's petty problems on the spot? He worked tirelessly for the benefit of his neighbors.

David fought on for his first-class observatory, mounting two solar-eclipse expeditions, one in 1887 to Japan and the second in 1889–90 to West Africa. He wasn't fortunate—cloud cover both times ruined his observations—but the Japan expedition, on which Mabel accompanied him, laid the basis for her career as a magazine writer. She became the first woman to climb volcanic Mount Fuji. An account of her experience was published in the *Century,* and additional articles followed. Mabel took to lecturing before women's clubs and attending conferences on women's rights. But it was her involvement with Emily Dickinson's poetry that would reserve her a significant niche in literary history.

In the late 1880s, after two years of Sue's stalling and finally deciding Emily's poems were a hopeless case, Vinnie brought them to Mabel. At times no more than scrawls, the poems had to be collected, transcribed— according to Sewall, "a task often of cryptographic proportions"—and edited with sensitivity, then published. Austin could help Mabel with the first tasks, from presenting her with a handsome oak desk to giving her insights on Emily's character, but Mabel still had to persuade reluctant editors that the poems were worth publishing.

The story of Mabel's courage and faith in Emily Dickinson's poetry has been told elsewhere. Suffice it to say that the first volume appeared in autumn 1890—soon followed by a second. William Dean Howell, in *Harper's,* was effusive in his praise; American poetry had found a new, distinctive voice. Mabel went on to collect and edit Emily's letters, an arduous project not completed until late 1894. For a time, she was the foremost expert on Dickinson and was kept busy lecturing on her life and work.

Mabel was enjoying this newfound freedom when in the spring of 1894, Austin's health began to fail and she hurried back to Amherst. Sue, furious over her rival's success, now had her husband firmly in her clutches. Simultaneously, Mabel had to read proof for the *Letters* and contend with Vinnie's reluctance to give up control over what she thought would be immense profits from Emily's work. Mabel now realized that Vinnie could be "an awful snake."

Throughout the year Austin was afflicted with lung trouble that by winter turned into pneumonia. Sue kept him a prisoner and Mabel was forbidden to see him. She managed to get letters to him via Ned. She had never been so unhappy and wrote, "I *want* you so! . . . I want to see you out and about, and running in with the dear fresh roses in your cheeks, and your old ulster on. . . . I cannot bear it rightly." Austin wrote hardly at all because the nurse who watched him forbade it.

On August 12, Mabel wrote a short, desperate note saying she was certain she could kiss and love him back to health. "And yet China is nearer in possibility." Her last letter concluded simply, "I love you." No answer was forthcoming. Austin Dickinson died on August 16, 1895, at age sixty-six. The whole of Amherst wept for her departed lover, Mabel noted in her journal. Yet she supposed she was the only true mourner. In fact the squire meant much to many people. Among them was David, who wrote, "My best friend died tonight, & I seem stranded." A bewildered Millicent watched both parents cry for hours. David swore he had never loved any man so.

At noon on the day of the funeral Mabel went to the Evergreens, where Ned secretly let her in a side door. "The dear body, every inch of which I know and love so utterly, was there, and I said goodbye to it," she wrote that night. She had kissed Austin's cold cheek and held his hand, while in the dining room Sue was entertaining guests. Mabel didn't attend the funeral; The Power, who had lost her husband's love, had possession of his corpse.

Sue would make certain that the bequest of land and stocks left by Austin to Mabel, via Vinnie, remained in Dickinson hands. She engineered a lawsuit between Vinnie and Mabel, which in 1897 resulted in a trial. All the dirty linen that Amherst had spoken of in whispers was aired. Vinnie did as Sue ordered, and the testimony of a peeping maid at the Homestead was especially damaging. Mabel lost what Austin wished her to have because the judge disapproved of her character. On appeal, no less a personage than Justice Oliver Wendell Holmes, Jr., upheld the trial judge's right to come to a subjective decision. Sinners were not going to have their day in a Massachusetts court!

Amherst supposed the Todds would leave, but they braved the storm of gossip. They moved into a new house, and David supervised the construction of a properly equipped observatory. Mabel continued to lecture, mainly about her travels, and she joined David on astronomical junkets to North Africa and the Andes. She had warned him she would never be the same, and her gaiety and impetuosity were gone forever. Until she had a slight stroke at fifty-six, she liked to ride about Amherst on a blazing red bicycle, Austin's last gift to her. She had one or two affairs of little consequence.

David Todd, who as he matured grew handsomer, with a trim beard and sophisticated air, kept up his womanizing. Mabel didn't object in general, but in 1911 when he took up with a mere typist, she lost her temper. David also became fixated on the idea of intelligent life on Mars. In the early 1900s he went up in a balloon with a newly invented radio, hoping to communicate with Martians. By 1920 he'd been placed in an insane asylum, and Mabel retired to Florida. When Millicent, grown and married, visited her father, he affirmed his affection for Austin. Then, confusing her with Mabel, he tried to make love to her.

In 1886 Mabel confided to her journal, "I have read a great many stories, & I have had a good many love letters, and I have heard a good many lovers talk, but I never heard or read or imagined . . . so Divine a love. . . . No love story approaches it." Indeed, the love between Austin and Mabel and David exhibited the magic found in the best menages a trois.

chapter 15

THE ROLLER-COASTER

{Anaïs Nin and Henry and June Miller}

Writers do tend to devour people, themselves included.

ERICA JONG

"THE MOST BEAUTIFUL
WOMAN ON EARTH"

*M*ONTPARNASSE, HOME TO ARTISTS AND
exiles since the early twentieth century, was compared by one of its chron-
iclers to a handkerchief. At first, the Parisian *quartier* was a pretty spot of
color, then an artist's rag used by the likes of Modigliani and Picasso, then
the overused rag of their imitators. Finally, the rag became filthy, fit for
the garbage can—except that the American expatriates had arrived and
demanded to buy it as a souvenir.

The story of the menage a trois among Henry Miller, his actress
wife, June (née Mansfield), and Anaïs Nin is coming to resemble this
"glad rag": the secrets are spilled while tourist buses cruise the trio's boulevard of dreams. The pulse of events has become muffled under the weight
of later speculation. More is the pity because the tale of Henry, June,
Anaïs, and Anaïs's voyeur husband, Hugo Guiler, presents a paradigm of
three (or four) in love, an attempt on their parts to soar that only spun
them into a black hole. The relationship rode an emotional roller-coaster,
plunging from the-sky's-the-limit to the depths of recrimination.

In the early 1930s the crashed American economy was dragging down
the other industrial countries. Russia and Eastern and Southern Europe
had fallen under the heel of dictatorship. Germany, despite the red-lit

glimmer of Berlin, was supine before the Nazi Black Shirts. Only the Left Bank of Paris remained open and creative, a refuge for painters, writers, filmmakers, and remittance men, the place where the Jazz Age would blare its last obbligato before Hitler and Stalin turned out the lights.

Sex was on everyone's mind. Toward the close of 1931, Anaïs Nin, then twenty-eight, was going over galley proofs with Lawrence Drake, an editor for the publisher that was to bring out her appreciation of D. H. Lawrence. Between the wars Paris hosted a cottage industry of English-language publishers that specialized in the avant-garde—meaning racy. Drake, a Russian émigré, made a pass at the budding author.

After a few kisses on a divan, which Anaïs enjoyed, she said she had her period. Drake dropped his pants, exposing his sex. "He makes me get down on my knees," the ingenue complained to her diary that evening. "He offers it to my mouth. I get up as if struck by a whip." Out of pity, Anaïs let him come without penetration. She ran home to tell her husband, and the couple made seamless love.

This *décoratif* banker's wife was the daughter of Joaquin Nin, a well-known Catalan pianist. He was a sadist who liked to whip her and her brothers. A Don Juan, he told his daughter she was ugly, then photographed her in the nude. Anaïs was only ten when Joaquin deserted the family by running off with a young heiress. Her convent-reared mother, Rosa, swept the girl off to New York, where they lived among Spanish-speaking expatriates. Anaïs began to write to her errant father but never sent the letters. Instead, the material evolved into her "Journal of Love." Growing day by day, it eventually amounted to 35,000 handwritten pages, 150 volumes. Anaïs regarded the diary as her confessor and used it to absolve her of whatever sins she'd committed.

The shapely adolescent dropped out of school to help support her family as an artist's model. She was well connected in Havana, where in 1923 she married Hugh Guiler, called Hugo, an educated American of Scottish descent. The fragile bride of twenty began the honeymoon a virgin. Hugo, eight years her senior, had little more sexual experience and less talent in bed. Anaïs's first hint of what she was missing came from reading Lawrence's novels.

In 1925 Guiler was made vice president in the Paris office of First National Bank (ancestor of Citibank), where his dollar-denominated salary allowed the young marrieds to live in high style. The crash of 1929 caused the Guilers to move to the middle-class suburb of Louveciennes, where they appropriated a rambling old house once the property of Madame du Barry. Hugo could afford servants, and he delighted in indulging his wife in such hobbies as decorating and astrology.

Anaïs had stillborn affairs, including one with an American author, Hugo's mentor at college. She was pleased when a confession of her would-be infidelity fired up Hugo's performance. She continued to entertain her husband's clients in their unique Spanish-Moorish home. At this stage, Anaïs and Hugo retained the image of a "golden couple" in the style of expatriates Gerald and Sara Murphy.

In December 1931 a lawyer, Richard Osborn, off whom Henry Miller was living, brought him to Louveciennes for a free lunch. Henry was born in the German section of Manhattan in 1891. His father ran a tailor shop, and the family moved to Williamsburg and then deeper into Brooklyn to escape the new immigration of Jews and Italians. The elder Miller drank, and his wife cursed him. Henry thought of his mother as "a first-class bitch."

Henry was a reader, not a tough guy. He engaged in a youthful homosexual relationship with two friends and, when he attended City College, quit school after he was assigned Spencer's *The Faerie Queene*. All his life Henry was edgy about homosexuality. He became involved in an affair with an older widow, then enmeshed in a triangle with the younger Beatrice, whom he married in 1917 to avoid the draft. The unhappy marriage, to be quickly terminated, was leavened by her mother, Catherine, who came to live with the couple. Henry found Catherine sexy and later claimed he'd gone to bed "first with the daughter, then with the mother."

Miller could be a spiffy dresser, a regular dance-hall Dan. Yet his biographer Robert Ferguson recognized a streak of the Puritan, not to mention a note of misogyny, beneath his belabored talk of "pussy." The man Anaïs met was past forty, a café philosopher unknown outside Montparnasse. Despair had made him contemplate jumping in the Seine, but now he sponged off friends to survive. One, the oddly named Wambly Bald, was gossip columnist for the *Paris Tribune;* he pictured Henry as a carefree tramp: "The only thing that bothered him, he said, was that he didn't have a toothbrush. 'Being on the bum is all right if you can clean your teeth occasionally—say, every third day. Otherwise you feel bad.'"

Miller's second wife, June, who'd encouraged him to leave New York for Paris but neglected to wire money, assured him he was Dostoyevsky's rightful heir. However, his first three novels, which he failed to publish, were clumsy and laced with gratuitous anti-Semitism. Erica Jong has observed that Miller at that time was "writing in a pastiche of Victorian romance and Dreiserian realism," searching for his voice. He began to find it at lunch at Anaïs's enchanted castle, where he was attracted to his seductive hostess. Anaïs had huge, almond-shaped dark eyes, a long, thin nose, a red cupid's-bow mouth, and an oval, chalk-white face. Jet-black hair and her original way of dressing made heads turn—even in Paris.

Henry relied on a familiar ploy and talked up June, who had unexpectedly arrived from New York—penniless with a wardrobe of slit-up-the-side gowns. By parading his wife's vamplike appeal, he could advertise his sexual prowess and still present himself as the victim of her wiles. This was a combination potent to Anaïs, who, insecure about her worth, liked to play lady bountiful to the less fortunate.

Intrigued by the brutality in Henry's writing, Anaïs was surprised to find him "warm, joyous, relaxed, natural." Partly bald, he reminded her of a sensuous monk. She noted his cool blue eyes and vulnerable mouth. The opposite of sober Hugo, Henry drank the wine of life and made her laugh. Enthralled, she invited the author and his wife to dinner on New Year's Eve. Anaïs recorded her first impressions of "the most beautiful woman on earth" (she was referring to a portrait of June that won an amateur photography prize sponsored by Kodak under that rubric). June was compared by contemporaries to Greta Garbo. Anaïs felt overwhelmed by her, a magnificent blond, pale with plucked eyebrows and a devilish, disarming smile. June wore a black cape and a fluttering dress; a cat's-eye earring dangled from one ear. Anaïs desperately wanted to be her.

Standing in the elegant parlor, Henry and June spat like alley cats. They rehashed old quarrels against each other. Hugo tried to joke, which made Anaïs furious with him. She'd heard that June used drugs, knew the lingo of gangsters, and had a female lover. Yet Anaïs sensed that June's Baudelairean beauty, which caused such dramatic reactions in others, left her unsatisfied.

At dinner in the apricot-colored dining room, Henry picked at a soufflé and failed to recognize the filet mignon as steak. Afterward the foursome went to the theater where the two women, arm in arm, created a stir. At a café the women held hands. Anaïs, across the table, heart pounding, was fascinated by June's haunted eyes, her aura of the oldest profession. She invited her to lunch.

Henry and June, longtime confederates, had already swindled johns attracted to June. They considered pulling a scam on the well-heeled couple. June analyzed the situation: "Anaïs was just bored with her life, so she took us up." Nin craved sacrifice. She admitted to her journal that she could surrender everything to June. Ironically, Nin would be the taker in this menage a trois of three married lovers.

In 1907, when June was a small child, her parents emigrated to Brooklyn from a district in the Carpathian Mountains of the Austro-Hungarian

Empire. They came from Galicia (now southern Poland); among Jewish immigrants, the women of Galicia were famous for their sensuality. An aspiring actress, June dropped the family name of Smerth and adopted that of Mansfield (after the writer Katherine). She dissolved any trace of accent and hung out in Greenwich Village dives, which were booming because of Prohibition. In 1923, the year Anaïs married Hugo, June, seventeen, was helping to support her family by taxi dancing at a Broadway hall. She became attracted to a short, nearsighted, balding customer because he talked about literature.

Henry, unhappy with his wife and job, found in June a "sex goddess who had climbed down from the magic world of the stage" into his humdrum life. He laid siege to June, divorced Beatrice, and the next year he and June married. Within a few years the marriage went on the rocks. In New York, while Henry tried to write, June earned a spotty living by what the 1920s termed gold digging. A kindly old man she bled for money, Pop Roland, killed himself over her. It was this femme-fatale aura that excited Anaïs and inspired her to take the other woman as a model for a tougher self.

The woman Anaïs admired was far less gifted and complicated than herself. Yet Anaïs also realized that Henry ignored his wife's talent as an actress. When June had pursued her career, directors cast her; she played roles written by Ibsen and Shaw. Anaïs reminded Henry how he'd kept June from the Broadway stage because he disapproved of it. But June's interests soon get lost in Nin's retelling of events in her diary. And because Henry promised not to compromise Anaïs until after her husband's death, he was unusually reticent about the Paris menage in his own writings. Then, since Miller's death in 1980 preceded Hugh Guiler's, Nin's diary, one participant's point of view, has become by default the major source of information on this seminal threesome.

June's surprise at the outcome of the three-way affair was intense. To the end of her life she claimed, "Henry and I were molded into one being." More important, the way it was *then* has become obscured by Miller's and Nin's reputations. To contemporaries June seemed the star, the one worth reporting on, which is not the least reason why her character, played by Uma Thurman with a gauche Brooklyn accent, steals Philip Kaufman's movie, *Henry and June.*

Wambly Bald wrote of June on her arrival at Paris, "She wears the mask of death and her ghastly beauty makes them stare. She crosses the street and walks into the Select. . . . Montparnasse is just a stage for June Mansfield."

Orgiastic scene of a menage a trois in a sylvan setting, from an engraving by J. Elluin, 1781.

Adam, Eve, and the Serpent.
The original threesome.
Engraving by Albrecht Dürer, 1504.

A satiric, diminutive engraving, from circa 1800, depicting Casanova with a big nose and carrying a cane. The engraving makes fun of his habit of posturing and showing off.

Jane Morris as drawn by her lover, Dante Gabriel Rossetti. Jane was the wife of William Morris and the mother of two daughters; her beauty inspired the work of both her husband and Rossetti.

William Morris, the renowned socialist and author who spearheaded the British arts and crafts movement. Morris, a complaisant husband, encouraged his wife's love affair with his friend Rossetti.

Dante Gabriel Rossetti, the flamboyant Pre-Raphaelite painter-poet who notoriously buried his poems in his first wife Lizzie's grave, then dug them up later.

The "Holy Trinity"—Lou Andreas-Salomé, Friedrich Nietzsche, and Paul Rée. Salomé, the center of this metaphysical menage, holds the whip hand over two brilliant philosophers ready to play by her rules.

Motion-picture still photograph from *Butch Cassidy and the Sundance Kid* (1969), which starred Paul Newman, Katharine Ross, and Robert Redford.

Motion-picture still from *Paint Your Wagon* (1969), starring Clint Eastwood, Jean Seberg, and Lee Marvin.

Henry Ward Beecher's female parishioners swooned over their golden-tongued minister, who though married, spread his favors among them. Beecher's trial for adultery with Elizabeth Tilton, the wife of Beecher's protégé, caused a public furor of O. J. Simpson proportions.

Theodore Tilton, an ambitious journalist, worked for Beecher and encouraged his wife to accept Beecher's attentions. Tilton also formed a menage a trois with Victoria Woodhull and her husband. This photograph is by Napoleon Sarony, New York's leading portrait photographer of the era.

A satiric cartoon of Victoria Woodhull from *Harper's Weekly*, 1872. Woodhull, branded as "Mrs. Satan" by her detractors, ran for president—with Free Love as part of her platform. Both Beecher and Tilton were involved with this persuasive campaigner.

Noël Coward entwined with actors Alfred Lunt and Lynn Fontanne.
This photograph captures the final scene in the New York production of *Design for Living* (1933).
Coward wrote this menage romp for himself and the Lunts, his devoted friends.

Henri-Pierre Roché, a journalist and art dealer. His autobiographical novel *Jules et Jim,* filmed by François Truffaut, has become a classic; Roché was the model for Jim.

Franz Hessel, the real-life Jules of *Jules et Jim,* was a German writer who shared many women with Roché. He and his wife, Helen, lived in a menage with Roché for a dozen years.

Helen (née Grund) Hessel, here shown as a nude bacchante, was the model for Catherine in *Jules et Jim.* Helen divorced and remarried Franz, then divorced him again during World War II because he was Jewish.

A rare photograph from Vanessa Bell's family album provides a dark, psychologically complex view of a woman who appears placid and Madonna-like in most photographs. One of Bloomsbury's founding members, Vanessa became the center of a menage with Duncan Grant and David (Bunny) Garnett.

Bunny Garnett and Duncan Grant. During World War I, Bunny and Duncan were pacifists and lovers who retreated to the country with Vanessa Bell. Bunny—who went his own way after the war—eventually married Duncan's and Vanessa's daughter, Angelica.

Dora Carrington and Ralph Partridge at their country home. Her true love, the homosexual biographer Lytton Strachey, lived with them in a menage that worked well until Ralph fell in love with Frances Marshall.

A jovial photograph of Lytton Strachey, the biographer known for his searing wit. Lytton developed a consuming passion for the heterosexual Ralph Partridge, who, on a platonic level, returned his feelings.

Salvador Dalí and Gala on the beach in Northern Spain. This photograph shows the young couple in an early romantic phase during which Gala inspired the Catalonian artist to come out of his shell and express himself. Gala, who became both Dalí's muse and his nemesis, was previously married to Paul Eluard, the surrealist writer.

Paul Eluard. The menage-prone Eluard participated in one with his first wife Gala and the artist Max Ernst. Eluard expected that Dalí would follow Ernst's example and join him and Gala in a menage. Instead, Gala divorced Eluard to marry Dalí.

Menage a quatre at Juan-les-Pins in southern France, 1937. Picasso in back view; Eluard with a hat on; Nusch, Paul Eluard's second wife, in the center smoking a cigarette; Picasso's mistress, Dora Maar, on the far left. The sweet-natured Nusch had a weekend menage with Picasso and Eluard while Dora Maar sulked in the wings.

Pablo Picasso and his chauffeur at Juan-les-Pins. Women were Picasso's models, muses, and obsession. Picasso admired Paul Eluard; to cement their friendship, they sometimes shared women.

The young Eugene O'Neill during his early playwriting days. His friendship with John Reed led to a menage with Reed and Louise Bryant. O'Neill's and Bryant's intense romance took place in Greenwich Village and Provincetown.

John Reed and Louise Bryant at their country retreat in Croton-on-Hudson, circa 1917. These radicals, who subsequently married, put their left-wing philosophy into action. Both journalists, they fascinated Eugene O'Neill, whose conservative bent clashed with their activism.

Louise Bryant. A beauty whose dramatic style prefigured "radical chic," she thrived in menages. Her leftist political philosophy allowed her to have a guilt-free menage with Reed and the possessive O'Neill.

Lord Louis Mountbatten, Prime Minister Pandit Nehru of India, and Edwina Mountbatten. While Lord Mountbatten served as the last British viceroy to India, his wife and Nehru found a love that intoxicated and nurtured them both.

Ottoline Morrell at Garsington, her country house. The imposing Lady Ott, a "hostess with the mostest," aided the Bloomsbury war resisters. She engineered a menage of her own involving herself, her husband, and Bertrand Russell.

D. H. Lawrence and his wife, Frieda. Typical of their relationship, the couple gaze in opposite directions. Frieda had many lovers; before Lawrence's death from TB, the weakened novelist accepted Angelo Ravagli as the third in his marriage.

Frieda and her third husband, Angelo Ravagli, at Kiowa Ranch in Taos, New Mexico. Frieda married the Casanova-like Angelo after Lawrence's death. She bore with his infidelities, and both remained friendly with Ravagli's ex-wife and children back in Italy.

Motion-picture still from *Casablanca* (1942).
In this classic film, Paul Henreid, Ingrid Bergman, and Humphrey Bogart's altruistic menage
provides a powerful subtext to a story about winning the war.

Not June *Miller!* Expatriates were abuzz about this ravishing American. Her mysterious actions, on top of her extraordinary appearance, made her into a legend: hair flying in the wind, "a gold-kissed rust," lashes midnight blue and lipstick black, and her eyes, "a pair of tawny pits." June, a punk fifty years before the fashion, was sufficiently striking to draw Cocteau and Picasso to her and naive enough to brush them off as impostors. To Henry, June seemed the one valuable thing he had acquired. To Anaïs, this mirror image of a wished-for self was both rival and prize, one whose very being she cannibalized.

"I FEEL YOU IN ME"

At a tête-à-tête in her home, Anaïs asked June, "Are you a lesbian?" The latter dodged, then complimented her host on her lovely rose dress. Anaïs became excited by June's surprising timidity. She admired her full body and wanted to see her naked. She ached to kiss June's breasts. Anaïs played the seducer's role.

Nin, like Casanova, depended on the introspection her diary permitted. She confessed to having a "masculine element," to loving weak men. She envied June her freedom and spontaneity. When they met again, Anaïs, to heighten her Mediterranean look, wore a coat with a Medici collar and a black turban. Yet June, in shabby shoes, a worn cape, and old violet hat, dazzled. Anaïs heaped stockings, sandals, coral earrings, and a turquoise ring on her. She felt that by clothing June, she possessed her. She was thrilled when June wanted to smoke opium with her.

Henry felt frozen out. Meanwhile Hugo shied away from June. Anaïs's normally complacent husband tried to tear off her wrist June's present of a bracelet with a cat's-eye stone. Hugo would not enter the erotic triangle she was constructing. A male rival excited his homoeroticism, but he had difficulty accepting a woman as his wife's lover. Hugo was puzzled by the lines Anaïs wrote about June in *House of Incest:* "Your beauty drowns me, drowns the core of me. When your beauty burns me I dissolve as I never dissolved before man. . . . I feel you in me; I feel my own voice becoming heavier, as if I were drinking you in."

Anaïs desired June's big-breasted body, but she could only hold it for a moment before the evasive June slipped away. They had a last rendezvous before June sailed for New York. Russian gypsies sang while the two nibbled caviar. "However bad things are for me I always find someone who will buy me champagne," confided June. A third who completed the party was Count Bruga, a purple-haired marionette in a sombrero. His maker, Jean Kronski, one of June's former lovers, had been institutionalized, but June carried the count as a substitute child.

The women put their affair on hold. Saying adieu in a taxi, Anaïs kissed June for a long time. "The love between women is a refuge and an escape into harmony," she told Henry when afterward they walked in her garden, puzzling over his wife like two Cabalists with an obscure text. Anaïs realized Henry saw June as other men did: on the surface. Wambly Bald had called her "the girl with the golden face," meaning she was a hooker. To create herself both as woman and artist, Nin needed to adopt some of June's ruthless narcissism, to take on her persona. This is the meaning of that kinky moment in the Kaufmans' movie when Anaïs, in bed with Hugo, demands, "Make love to June's beautiful body." Hugo, who disliked June's forwardness, doesn't get it that his wife, playing June, is imaginatively making love with Henry. Anaïs, in turn, doesn't understand Hugo's function as the fourth in the menage a trois. He is the audience who views the action, just as later he will make arty films around his wife.

From Henry, Anaïs wanted the physical and the thrilling, even if it hurt. She reveled in his homeliness, his "bestial nose." Anaïs assumed the author and the whoremongering protagonist of *Tropic of Cancer* were one and the same. Following their initial bout on March 8, 1932, at the Hôtel Central, she looked disappointed. "You expected—more brutality?" Henry asked in his Brooklyn rumble. In the semidarkness on the mantel a portrait of June presided.

The Miller-Nin relationship had begun, and it would prove crucial to the writing of twentieth-century autobiographical fiction and to the current merging of these two previously distinct genres. But we are concerned here with the need that demands a third in the affair. Anaïs found herself ensorcelled (a favorite word) between Henry's genius and June's temptation. Talking with him about June while the other was at a distance heightened the thrill of their coupling.

The lovers felt overwhelmed by a Lawrencian passion. Henry, habitué of whores, was abashed by Anaïs's ferocity. "Came away with pieces of you sticking to me," he wrote her. "I am walking about, swimming in an ocean of blood, your Andalusian blood, distilled and poisonous." Anaïs contrasted the small, shabby room they rented with Henry's rich voice and mouth. She felt herself "sinking into warm blood." Miller used slow undulations, pauses, and twists to thrill her.

She had climaxed, which she later admitted to her analyst she found difficult. She concluded that her incompatibility with Hugo was physical: his sex was so large and his thrusts so direct that he gave her discomfort rather than pleasure. She began to push her husband away from her emotional core, and he never regained that place.

Anaïs's fascination with June carried into every moment with Henry. In her diary, she pictured the other woman as a vampire who destroyed the boundary between day and night. She praised June's courage in inflicting pain on others and, on a more mundane level, her refusal to perform a housewife's chores. Anaïs began to read to Henry from her diary, revealing her desire for June, claiming it would make him love her more.

In March 1932, in order to rendezvous more easily, Anaïs paid for Henry's move to a flat in the working-class suburb of Clichy. Finally, he had a roof over his head and she had a lover who was dependent on her. Reams of indiscreet letters flew back and forth between them, and Anaïs read them in bed and tucked them, crackling, beneath her pillow. She had a delicious terror of Hugo reading them once she fell asleep. Instead, he grew excited and possessed her night after night. Anaïs adopted the passivity of a prostitute who takes pleasure with only one man, her pimp; imagining that Hugo was Henry, she confounded the roles of wife and whore.

Anaïs began to dream of martyrdom, of sacrificing her beautiful home and hardworking husband. She fantasized about Henry's murdering her. She wrote, ensconced in the safe haven that Hugo provided, then dashed off to Clichy for yet another erotic triangle. She liked to flirt with Fred Perles, Henry's sycophantic Austrian roommate, a delicate sort of man with poetic eyes. Her diary records scenes in their crash pad: "In the small kitchen, we three almost touch each other. Henry moved . . . to kiss me, and Fred would not look at the kiss. . . . There were Fred's feelings for me, touching a more delicate region, so that while Henry kissed me I wanted to extend my hand to Fred and hold both loves."

When Anaïs and Henry made love, complete with bites, convulsions, and groans, she knew Fred was listening. In the future, she would mine an autovoyeurism by rehashing her passions in her journal in order to exploit the voyeurism of her readers. It was by giving herself imaginatively that she overcame her inhibitions. When Anaïs as a young woman had taken communion, sexual desire had caused her to choke up. Now taking Henry in her mouth as he came brought her to orgasm. He'd become the Father whom she ate.

Anaïs balked at the four-letter words Henry urged on her. But she reveled in his cannibalism, which left marks on her delicate skin. Once, after she'd sneaked off to Henry in the guest room at Louveciennes, Anaïs paraded before Hugo in underclothes stained from their lovemaking. Her husband, who liked to sniff her underwear, surely noticed. Anaïs continued to torture him in order to arouse a savage passion, the only way she could enjoy him. Nin was a natural triangulator, setting out the lure of jealousy to ensnare.

The liaison of Henry and Anaïs displayed an amusing monstrousness. Henry bit flesh with an avidity that would have pleased sadomasochist Algernon Swinburne. "You are food and drink to me, the whole bloody machinery," he wrote. She would have been pleased that he was repeating an earlier time with June when he bit her shoulder, causing a dull red stain. But Nin's own bent was more psychological. She brought Henry to her enchanted den, where he described her as a princess who deigned to give herself to a nobody. While her lord was working at the bank, milady invited Henry to screw her in the marital bed, draped with a red coverlet. She cuckolded her husband in time-honored fashion. The sleeper leaves something of himself, if only dreams, in his bed; thus Hugo was present at the infidelity, a ghost.

In the spring, Anaïs began psychoanalysis with Dr. René Allendy, one of its pioneers in France. She quickly added him to a growing list of admirers. The doctor recognized Anaïs's tyrannical need to be loved, but she sought the cure elsewhere. "That Henry and I can sit and talk about our love of June, about her grandiose moments, is to me the greatest of victories," confided the diarist.

Indeed, the absent one was the cause of an unusual rift between the writers. As Henry was beginning *Tropic of Capricorn* and Anaïs *House of Incest*, she realized that he'd borrowed *her* vision of June. It was a gift she had no intention of giving. Her literary solution was to fashion a character that was a twin of her own darker side, including subterfuges and evasions. Nin's subterranean style followed Jung's advice to proceed from the dream outward in an effort to capture June's evanescence.

Meanwhile, the lovers grew still more indiscreet, making it on the dining room table, then the carpet. Henry fantasized about becoming the new lord of the manor. In August 1932 he wrote Anaïs, "It was a marriage at Louveciennes. . . . It is this dream I want to realize. Life and Literature combined, love the dynamo . . . home wherever we are." Henry put pressure on Anaïs to leave Hugo and run off with him to Spain. She paid his rent, bought him eyeglasses and clothes, and when she left briefly to have plastic surgery on her nose, she even sent him money for whores. She called him her "eternal husband."

When June began to wire Henry from America, it distressed him but excited Anaïs. She imagined June as a beautiful moth in a cocoon of silk who compelled strangers to do her bidding. She anticipated her arrival with a moist dream: "She awoke me with a kiss. . . . She asked me to masturbate her. I did so very skillfully and experienced the sensation as if I were doing it to myself. She was grateful for the pleasure and left thanking me. 'Now I am going to see Henry,' she said."

What Anaïs searched for in the other woman ran deeper than sex. June had abandoned social and gender restraints, while Anaïs herself was kept by Hugo for his pleasure. Thus she felt compelled to act out fantasies of degradation with Henry. In October June swept in with the panache of a silent movie star. All Montparnasse knew at which hotel she was staying. Henry intimated he was his wife's captive and only Anaïs could save him. The diarist was tempted "to face June with Henry, to let her torture us both, to love her, to win her love and Henry's."

For all three, the contest between jealousy and compassion went into high gear. The emotional roller-coaster swooped through a darkening night. June, fragile as an Scott Fitzgerald heroine, embodied the fading Jazz Age. "People hate me because I destroy them," she boasted while sipping absinthe. "I awaken their slumbering vices." However, the pretensions of a June Mansfield would be lost in the coming world drama, to be set in trenches and prison camps. Americans living it up in Paris would go home to write their memoirs.

Paris, ever on the edge of fashion, was entering the Age of Cannibalism. Café society went wild for the pseudo-African. Josephine Baker reigned onstage in her banana skirt, parading the boulevards with a leashed leopard, and the author most quoted was the American adventurer William Seabrook, famed for dining on human flesh in the Congo. Meanwhile the true cannibals were sharpening their teeth in the heart of Europe. In the fall of 1933 for the menage a trois of Henry, June, and Anaïs, the pot was boiling.

"A COLOSSAL TALE OF GREAT LOVE AND GREAT BETRAYAL"

Third persons in a menage are often shadowy to our view. No matter their importance at the time, if they don't leave records of continuing interest— letters, books, paintings—their memory will be effaced. While June Miller wasn't a writer, she became the subject of a large body of fiction and nonfiction. Henry Miller dedicated *Tropic of Capricorn* to "Her," and she was the main character (besides the author) of his autobiographical trilogy, *The Rosy Crucifixion*. From his first dance with her at the Orpheum Palace, June pervaded Henry's life and letters. She was his Molly Bloom. But like Boris Pasternak's Lara, she was an actual woman as well as an imagined lover. Anaïs Nin also portrayed June—in her novellas and more openly in her diary. We even have a third view in the oversexed character played by Uma Thurman in the most vivid moments of the movie *Henry and June*. After all this exposure, why does the historical June Miller remain so undefined?

Here was a menage ruthlessly devoted to art. Those two monster authors, Nin and Miller, devoured June down to her last gesture. While they disgorged their creations, the woman, left to fend for herself in the real world, became a shadow. This was a cannibal menage, not uncommon among artists, that ate its third. That June eventually reconstituted herself is heartening.

In October 1932 June, preceded by a blizzard of cables, arrived broke in Paris. She checked into a hotel, asked the desk clerk to pay the cab fare, and began to run up a tab she had no intention of paying. After cabling friends for money, she went to the Dôme to greet her admirers. "The curtain goes up," marveled Wambly Bald. "June loves her audiences." One week later she visited Henry, and after scanning his *Capricorn*, she hurried to Louveciennes to defend herself.

Anaïs reported that a calm, eloquent June begged for protection from her own husband. June complained bitterly that Miller made her "complex," that he "devitalized" her and "killed" her. "He has introduced a fictitious personage who could make him suffer torments, whom he could hate: he has to whip himself by hatred in order to create." Anaïs agreed Henry had distorted and wounded June, and a feeling welled up that she would do anything for her. But she was wary of June's discovering that she had been betrayed in the most common way. At the train station, Anaïs embraced the trembling woman and kissed the pale, beautiful face she wished were hers.

The diarist had landed in the midst of Henry and June's One Hundred Years' War. Back in the 1920s, supposedly to give Henry time to write, June had become a professional hostess, first in a Greenwich Village dive, then in a "bohemian hellhole" speakeasy they ran. She knew how to snake-charm a man, and Henry figured she was peddling more than her allure. Relations between the couple grew dramatic once June invited a lesbian girlfriend to live with them in a basement flat on Henry Street in Brooklyn.

According to June, Jean Kronski was an orphaned Romanoff princess, a sculptress, painter, and poet. June treated her pickup as a goddess not subject to normal limits. Henry saw a confused twenty-year-old, handsome with long, black hair, high cheekbones, and violet eyes but a mannish body—"a da Vinci head stuck on the torso of a dragoon." Her habits were paranoid, especially efforts to keep the walls of her room from collapsing on her at night. When Jean festooned the apartment with surreal frescoes and painted the ceiling purple, Henry was both fascinated and repelled.

Life at the Henry Street flat, which had no heat besides a choked-up fireplace, quickly deteriorated. Miller later described how the bed stayed unmade, soiled shirts doubled for towels, and dishes were washed in a greasy black-rimmed bathtub. The shades were always down, the windows were never washed. In this sepulchral atmosphere, the floor was strewn with plaster of paris, tools, paints, books, cigarette butts, garbage, soiled dishes, and pots. Jean ran around all day in overalls. June, always half-naked, complained of the cold.

Nonchalance about dirt, coupled with the women's indifference to money, grated on Henry's Teutonic craving for order. He claimed to be mystified by the relationship between the women, though they often embraced, kissed, and slept together in his bed. When he confronted June in third-degree style, she told him he had a dirty mind and was demeaning "something rare and beautiful." She admitted she loved both Henry and Jean but in different ways. And when he and June slept together, she gave herself "body and soul . . . all her heart on fire and her passions burning to cinder." By contrast, his affair with Anaïs would be a more conscious excursion into eroticism.

For a while Henry plotted to drive Jean back to the Bellevue psychiatric ward from which June had rescued her. But he was drawn to this weird waif, bewitched by her strangeness. He would applaud her latest poem, comb out her mane of hair, trim her talonlike toenails. Even if he embedded a knife in the door of Jean's room, he knew she was right, that suffering would make a writer of him.

The threesome was breeding art in him through a process of refined voyeurism. From Jean, Henry absorbed the desire to paint, and it was she who introduced him to Eastern art. From June, he acquired a torrent of words. High on cocaine, she wanted "to gush, to rhapsodize . . . to sparkle, not car[ing] what she said." Her influence ignited the Miller verbosity, and though his style would be dismissed by Genet as "chatter," his desire was to write with the immediacy of events. This particularly American approach was adopted by Jack Kerouac, who also depended on a wild one, Neal Cassady, for inspiration.

One day in 1927 the women embarked for Paris without telling Henry. After a howling fit, he began to make notes on the story of his life with June and Jean: "a colossal tale of great love and great betrayal." He racked his brain for details, showing the meticulous eye of a novelist. His manuscript would become the basis first of the unsuccessful *Crazy Cock* and later of his major fiction. Miller had found his central theme: the perfidy of women.

THE SECOND COMING

Before the second coming of June to Paris, Henry and Anaïs had treated her as a sublime mystery incapable of solution. They theorized that she was a "child of nature" and tussled over who would record her anarchic doings. Even when they were making love, June's presence hovered ghostlike near them. In Harold Pinter's *Old Times* a husband and wife talk about a woman they knew in the past. Pinter recalled, "I became aware that the third character was somewhere in the room, not in the present, shall we say." In his play the third exists in the subconscious of each protagonist, and the struggle between them will be decided by the one who remembers best.

Now the corporeal June manifested in the small flat shared by Miller and Perles in Clichy, throwing careful arrangements into disarray. "I love June and I love you," Henry wrote to Anaïs. He swore to keep both women, but Anaïs could do what she liked with June. Nin's analyst and would-be lover, René Allendy, urged her to give up his rival. In response, Anaïs confided to her diary, "June is my adventure and my passion, but Henry is my love." The pleasure she took in June was complex and narcissistic. She wanted to see herself in the other woman, to preempt her life, which included her husband. At the same time she congratulated herself for revealing Henry and June to each other.

For a time Anaïs saw each of them separately, and while the intensity with the man abated, that with the woman flared up. June and she frequented cafés and, knees interlocked, talked about Henry. They danced cheek to cheek at a jazz club or petted while zipping about in taxis. This flirting panicked Henry, and he wrote a hasty letter to Anaïs swearing he thought about her while making love to June—an ironic reversal. He wailed about being lost if she deserted him. She realized she had to save this big baby, for she knew how to make him into a Dostoyevsky.

Anaïs decided that June destroyed instead of loving, even though June had made herself small in Anaïs's arms and revealed her fears. Anaïs herself wasn't averse to a little destruction. When Hugo, inflamed by jealousy, flung her down and bit her shoulder, she pretended to be pleased. She confessed that she had always wanted her dress torn! Unfortunately, Hugo had violated his role as the onlooking fourth. Anaïs preferred to concentrate on the "superb game the three of us are playing. Who is the demon? Who the liar? Who the human being?"

The answers were for the future to determine. In the meantime whatever one told the other was twisted before being passed on to the third and then savored or resented. One evening in mid-November Anaïs ventured to Clichy and got into a mock argument with Henry over literary matters. June, intimidated, got drunk on chartreuse and vomited, collapsing on the floor. Since Henry was nearly as drunk, Anaïs, acting as femme de menage, cleaned up both Millers and put them to bed. She slept clothed in between the soused pair. Before she left in the morning Perles slipped her a note: "You are the only woman I love."

A few nights later when the threesome gathered, sparks flew. First Anaïs dissected Henry's faults, applauded by June, then the women found themselves alone on Henry's bed. June launched into an insightful confession of what she had become and of the harm she and Henry had caused each other. Anaïs wondered if she was abdicating her place. Finally at dawn, the women embraced, kissing passionately, entering into an aborted sex scene that climaxed their relationship, the force of which carries over into the movie *Henry and June.* June, summing up both her desire and ambivalence toward Anaïs, hissed, "How little you are—I want to become like you. . . . I could break you in two."

Love and jealousy were balanced as each walked a tightrope over the depths of emotion. June, although admiring Anaïs's beauty, pulled back. The moment that had been voluptuous passed into regret. Later that morning, June confronted Henry with his love for Anaïs, telling him she had "pulled a lesbian act" to smoke out the truth. Henry's denials went for nothing, and June stormed out. He ran to Louveciennes for comfort. Two days later, returning to Clichy, he discovered that June had been there, leaving Anaïs's gifts and a love letter from her. On a piece of toilet paper she'd scrawled that she wanted a divorce. The menage had descended into a love triangle.

The triumphant Anaïs waxed philosophic: June possessed her memories of Henry, while she had the genius who could turn experience into art. She believed both women were bowing to destiny. But blaming an external compulsion is a sure symptom of a love triangle, with its usual consequences. In this case, June again descended on Henry, harangued him with threats and recriminations, and seized the money Anaïs had given him to flee to England. Before leaving for good, she spat, "Now you have the last chapter for your book!"

After June's departure, Henry occasionally felt he'd acted badly toward her. He and Anaïs continued their intimacy, sometimes under Hugo's nose. In May 1933 while he was polishing *Tropic of Cancer,* he received a letter from his old friend Richard Osborn, who'd returned to New York. Osborn's news that June was seen in the Village with an escort "considerably your junior" devastated Henry. He began to drink, writing an all-night letter to an old school chum, which in its naïveté mixed with self-awareness is unalloyed Miller.

"I love her still but do not want her," he insisted about June. Turning bitter, he cursed "this damned Jewish vulture gnawing into my vitals . . . first with her possessivity, her jealousy, her overwhelming sex and clawing beak, and now with hatred and malice and vindictiveness." After proclaiming his hatred for the woman he called "June-Smith-Smerth-Mansfield-

Miller-Cunt-Balls-Whore," Henry, suddenly weeping, offered to kill himself for her, then fumed against her "five and ten cent store athlete with his 'considerably my junior,' etc."

In the letter's mordant incoherence, grim and funny at once, Henry Miller has achieved his unique style. It is surely akin to June's "coketalk," about which Wambly Bald wrote, "when she talks to you, the ground slips from under your feet." This charged yet hallucinatory flow distinguishes Miller's best writing. Style in a different sense—a sexually promising allure—set off Anaïs's coming femme-fatale stage. Wearing June's pencil-thin eyebrows, her nose surgically altered to resemble June's, she modeled her conduct on June's boldness with strangers. Becoming a scientist of libido, keeping a husband on each of America's coasts, Anaïs would split the Adam.

Henry in his novels, Anaïs in her candid multivolume diary, the Kaufmans in their controversial film all digested and regurgitated the original menage for their readers and viewers. But how did the real June fare? In New York she married the young man she was spotted with, Stratford Corbett, an insurance executive who at the outbreak of World War II entered the navy. Sometime during or after the war the marriage ended. In 1946 Irving Stettner, at Miller's request, visited June in the Park Slope section of Brooklyn. Stettner, the streetwise bard of the East Village, found "a woman in her early forties, with dark flashing eyes . . . a thin, frail figure." She spoke fluently but intelligently, claiming, "Henry, I made him find himself. I made him reach for the stars."

In 1965 Kenneth Dick, an eccentric who wrote and published a biography of Miller in a limited, rare edition, interviewed June in Queens about Henry. He learned that at some point June had been picked up by the police and incarcerated in Pilgrim State Hospital, a brutal excuse for an insane asylum. When she told the doctors her favorite reading was Dostoyevsky, they responded with electroshock treatment. Unattended, the patient slipped from the table. Dick recorded, "She was left with broken bones, one leg permanently shortened, the muscles of her heart and back distorted." She was forced to sign a release and then was discharged.

By the time of Dick's interview, June had became a case worker for the Welfare Department. She struck him as lively, curious, and forgiving of Henry, if not Anaïs, and she had a man friend. However, she was nearly unrecognizable, with "a slightly hunched back, gnarled hands, [and] a withered face." The single time Henry Miller visited his ex-wife—the second in what would be a total of five wives—he was horrified by the contrast with his imagined June, "the most beautiful woman in the world."

part five

THE
BOHEMIANS

Hollywood, they say, is a state of mind. It's sure hard to pinpoint in hazy springtime Los Angeles, and what you do find is often rundown and seedy. Maybe it's made of images, the ultimate material of art. But the Academy of Motion Picture Arts and Sciences is an actual, pleasant place. A modest Spanish-style building on the fringe of Beverly Hills houses offices and a library devoted to movie lore. After picking up our credentials in the Bob Hope lobby, the three of us mounted the Kirk Douglas Grand Staircase to the Cecil B. DeMille Reading Room. No trumpets blared; we saw no hints of imperial splendor, only a long, bookcase-lined room dotted with preoccupied people in faded denims.

We'd come from different directions, both now and earlier. On occasion Michael had flown over the West Coast, but he hadn't landed there since 1969 when he was at Berkeley during the demonstrations in People's Park. That same summer, Barbara, who'd misspent her youth hanging out at an arty coffeehouse in Philly, was playing hippie at New Mexico's Pig Farm. Coincidentally, Letha was then entering the University of New Mexico. Her strict Hungarian father wouldn't let her date any boy she wasn't willing to marry, so naturally she married her first date. That we three would touch in the seventies and merge in the eighties, then settle down to the trench warfare called life in New York, couldn't have been foreseen by any of us.

At the academy, under the aegis of Mr. DeMille, we went to work. Barbara had been trolling the ultra-modern Humanities Research Center at the University of Texas for information on the inhabitants of Bohemia. Since this place, too, is a state of mind, it hardly mattered whether they were fictional personae, such as Noël Coward's threesome in *Design for Living,* or actual persons, such as the French and German models for *Jules and Jim* (and Catherine) who would become immortalized in a novel (and movie) that François Truffaut called "a perfect hymn to life."

Now Barbara struggled along with an old-fashioned card catalog. Letha looked for threes among the wonderful, nostalgic collection of still photos. Michael tracked down an obscure film by Liliana Cavani, *Beyond Good and Evil,* in which the director makes overtly sexual the metaphysical menage among Friedrich Nietzsche, Lou Andreas-Salomé, and Paul Rée. He immersed himself in gossip aged to the point of becoming history. At the academy, where Hedda Hopper counts as a primary source, glamour can wash the dirt clean.

By day's end we'd had our fill, and it was time to fill up on Mexican food at the nearby Farmer's Market. Seated outdoors in the balmy evening while imagining the north wind whistling back home, we made up for lost time. Michael had been in San Francisco seeing an old friend; Letha had been visiting her septuagenarian mother who paints murals in Albuquerque. What does a threesome talk about when reunited? Not the kids or the house. R. D. Lang once wrote, "The family's function is to repress Eros." He didn't live to see the shell of the nuclear family crack and all the congressmen try vainly to put Humpty Dumpty together again. Instead, what if we applied creativity to the family, made it up as we went along? We would have to seek, in the words of Jeanne Moreau, "joy rather than happiness."

That Friday evening we took a suite for three at the Beverly Hills Hotel. Tales of this Mission Revival palace on Sunset Boulevard awakened a sybaritic strain we seldom indulged. Normally writing and being together enriched our lives sufficiently. But in Hollywood, we were shooting for the stars. Formerly at the Beverly Hills, the illicit coupling of Marilyn and Yves had made columnists' tongues wag, and JFK, installed in a bungalow, had run through Peter Lawford's date list. Did a hardworking menage belong in such company? The opulent, pink lobby was filled with gardenias. A glass flower-petal chandelier hung over our heads. The looming cost made our credit cards cry ouch.

We checked in without a murmur from the desk clerk, then ascended to our beautifully appointed suite; with an ottoman big enough for three, it looked like a set from a Coward comedy. Later Nino, the manager, introduced us to the mysteries of the Polo Lounge, which got its name because polo enthusiasts such as Daryl Zanuck and Will Rogers used to show up in their sporting outfits. Michael and Letha relaxed in plush green elegance at a table near to Charlie Chaplin's, but Barbara demanded to sit on Marlene's favorite stool at the bar.

Next day we did the town *à trois,* nibbling at the City of Angels the way Casanova sucked oysters off a pretty breast. Decked out in our finery, we invaded chic eateries until, for a change of pace, we visited Grauman's Chinese Theater on Hollywood Boulevard. Letha got keen over the footprints of her teenage idols. Afterward Barbara, known to shop till she drops, insisted on a Rodeo Drive spree. Once it became clear that the prices were meant for oil sheiks and microchip billionaires, we adjourned to the West Hollywood thrift shops. We combed the racks for vintage boudoir attire:

Letha selected a salmon-colored negligee, Barbara a frilly bed jacket, and Michael a satin smoking jacket bordered with velvet.

On our last night in L.A. we sprang for room service. *Grand Hotel* had nothing on us. Champagne and the camaraderie of many years' duration permitted us to feel at home together. Menages a trois monopolized the conversation. Letha commented that bohemian menages had the most flair, and she brought up the ambient sexuality of Bloomsbury. Michael wished he could have lived in Paris when Sartre, Beauvoir, and Giacometti met for all-night chats. Barbara, suddenly sentimental, harked back to her own first Parisian trip. She'd walked all round Saint-Germain-des-Près clutching one of Anaïs Nin's diaries, wondering if she would have similar adventures.

We started to role-play. Michael took the male parts, Letha various mistresses, and Barbara the wives down through the generations. The bubbly fueled our improvisations and helped us decide that we were brilliant. Finally, we interpreted Coward's *Design for Living.* Michael played both Leo and Otto, nearly interchangeable anyway, Barbara got Gilda's devil-may-care lines, and Letha was stuck with Ernest, the voyeur. After plenty of present laughter, woozy and intertwined like pretzels, we fell asleep on the divan.

The morning's alarm reminded us that nobody had packed for our return flight to New York.

chapter 16

MENAGE AS
GAY METAPHOR

{Noël Coward and *Design for Living;*
Christopher Isherwood (and Bob Fosse) and *Cabaret;*
W. H. Auden}

A duo is dull-o.
KEN CORDAY

BLITHE SPIRITS

*D*URING THE AUTUMN OF 1933 HENRY
Miller was pounding away at a project he would never complete, the
lugubrious-sounding *Palace of Entrails.* Needing a break, he went looking for
a bad movie at which to relax, maybe snooze. Since he hated the director
Ernst Lubitch, he chose his *Design for Living.* Henry was surprised to find
himself entranced by the female lead, Miriam Hopkins. In a letter to Emil
Schnellock, a school chum from Brooklyn, he described the actress as a
"truly charming female" and the spitting image of Anaïs Nin, especially
in her expressions and grace of movement. That afternoon a member of a
threesome gone to pieces watched while on-screen a menage a trois triumphed over respectability.

Design for Living is one of the most provocative comedies to come out
of a decade that abounded in memorable comedy. The film was an adaptation by Ben Hecht from the play that became Noël Coward's signature
piece. Despite the ensuing sexual revolution and reaction, Coward remains
topical, and his work has been revived by actors ranging from George C.

Scott to Joan Collins; in fact, *Design* was the surprise hit of the 1995 London season. In the 1930s the playwright was at the height of his powers. He'd been born in a drab London suburb in 1899, eight years after Miller and to parents poorer than Miller's. Noël was precocious, didn't get on well at school, and, at ten, went onstage to help support his family. Coward has this in common with Miller: each fobbed off on the public a created, mythical self, and the public bought that persona as genuine.

Coward was self-educated and multitalented; he wrote dramas, farces, revues, composed hit songs, and acted with brilliance. He was anxious to please. "Consider the public," he warned the Angry Young Men of the 1950s, "treat it with tact and courtesy." Actually, Coward cultivated an insolent charm to go with his studied appearance. "I take ruthless stock of myself in the mirror before going out," he claimed, "for even an unfortunate tie exposes one to danger." Onstage he often played the cad, while in public he acted the debonair single man. Friends knew he was homosexual, but he set up a screen of "cocktails, countesses, [and] caviar."

Within this swirl of sophistication lies Coward's fascination with the menage a trois, which he used as a metaphor for being gay. In his day a menage, though officially frowned on, could be made the subject of a successful play. Depicting a gay or bisexual relationship was forbidden. Nonetheless *Design for Living* (1932), conceived of as a triangular tangle, rests squarely on a gay subtext. In the 1980s John Osborne, irascible as ever, ranked it one of the three best comedies in the English language. In today's revivals the play's triad continues to jest toward a new morality in a society grown more brash but no less hypocritical. The play's two men, Otto and Leo, may seem interchangeable, but Gilda, pillar of the menage (though one who prefers to rest on her fanny), remains a memorable creation of the comic stage.

In 1921 Coward, an unknown, had lived in a New York boardinghouse with a struggling, unmarried couple of actors, Alfred Lunt and Lynn Fontanne. The three became inseparable and remained close all their lives. They made up a metaphysical menage, pooling their hopes and dreams. Since the trio apparently read one another's minds, spontaneously switching roles onstage, we'll call them a psychic menage. Coward remembered, "From these shabby, congenial rooms, we projected ourselves into future eminence. We discussed, the three of us, over delicatessen potato salad and dill pickles, our most secret dreams of success. Lynn and Alfred were to be married. . . . When all three of us had become stars of sufficient magnitude . . . we would meet and act triumphantly together."

Eleven years later, the Lunts, who'd become the leading couple of the theater, cabled Coward, who was cruising on a freighter off South

America: "What about it?" By the time the playwright arrived in New York, he'd composed what Brooks Atkinson of the *New York Times* would declare "an actors' lark [for] an incomparable trio of high comedians." But good gray Brooks had missed the play's point. *Design* assumes the rightness of its protagonists' struggle to set themselves against the world, to take shelter in what we would term an alternative family. At first, in inverted fashion, the trio declares itself to be the problem. Their menage curdles into a love triangle, and Gilda even runs off with the voyeuristic fourth, Ernest. But at the dénouement, the three, together again, mercilessly turn on the solid citizen, who is an art dealer. They laugh him out of his penthouse, where he displays a collection of paintings that represent his identity.

Britain's Lord Chamberlain took *Design* seriously enough to ban it, and the play couldn't open in London until 1939. Then, with the war on, bad manners had become secondary. Although Broadway theatergoers greeted the comedy warmly in 1933, its daring caused reviewers to modify their praise by damning the subject as "unpleasant," "immoral," and "decadent." *Design's* real achievement is to dismiss the decorum of the straight world and to opt for a radical gay aesthetic. Its attitude matches the theme Coward wrote into the song "Let's Live Dangerously," in which he endorsed a spectacular rowdiness, ending, "Let's lead moralists the devil of a dance."

Curiously, this banner of the outlandish, bringing to mind gay bars and gay parades, was borne aloft by an actress whose private life appeared devoid of interest except as a model stage wife. Lynn Fontanne was born near London, date vague. At sixteen she fled from an unhappy home to the stage. She became the protégée of the popular American actress Laurette Taylor, whom Coward would satirize in *Hay Fever.* Laurette was a flirt who had open liaisons with lovers under the gaze of her husband. Lynn, though timid, carefully studied those women who attracted men. It helped when the 1920s brought in the slender look with a dropped waistline that suited her figure. Recalled Ruth Gordon, "Lynn was the envy of every young actress. There wasn't one of us who didn't want to look like her . . . and be as wonderful."

Lynn acquired a star quality independent of Alfred Lunt, an American actor whom she married in 1922 and acted with her entire career. Critics have failed to realize, however, that *Design for Living's* Gilda is more Laurette than Lynn. She has the narcissism of the triangulator—the one who acquires two or more—a proclivity that at its best carries over from life into art.

When the curtain rises on act one, Gilda is sharing a bohemian lifestyle in Paris with Otto (Lunt), a handsome painter. Ernest, a mature connoisseur, drops by their shabby studio, eager to show an acquired Matisse to the artist. Gilda claims he is asleep, and Ernest, an old friend, demands to know why Gilda won't marry Otto. She replies she doesn't like children or want a home, and besides, she respects Otto too much.

Coward draws Gilda as sincere and likable as well as pretty and frivolous. She refuses to be a predatory tease. Ernest the voyeur, an archetypal fourth, takes note when Otto bounds in from *outside* the studio. Gilda informs him that their playwright friend Leo (Coward) has returned from America, a success. She begs the elated Otto to go visit him at his hotel. As one critic commented, "It is not clear in the play that Otto and Leo are lovers, but it is clear that they were friends before Gilda entered their lives, and . . . they project an intimacy with each other more intense than their intimacy with her."

Actually the gay, or bisexual, subtext is crystal clear. Gilda feels apologetic for having "spoilt" the two men's relationship, she refers to the menage as "the Three Famous Hermaphrodites," and Otto calls himself "the Gypsy Queen." Act one continues as Otto and Ernest leave and a nervous Leo emerges from the bedroom. He and Gilda have spent the night there in Otto's absence—and in his bed. Leo tries to reassure her, "I love you. You love me. You love Otto. I love Otto. Otto loves you. Otto loves me. There now!"

The critic John Lahr realized that Coward's comedies were written with a gay or "camp" sensibility: "The homosexual sense of the capriciousness of life is matched by a capricious style." The playwright's ironic sense of detachment, of sexual nonchalance, never falters, and he refuses to place wit at the service of morality. In *Design*, Coward uses laughter with surgical precision to expose hypocrisy. His subject is the wry sort of love about which both he and Cole Porter wrote songs.

Gilda, while worried about Otto, happily recalls last night with Leo—a violently romantic surprise she anoints "Gala." When Leo reminds her that they'd been eyeing each other for years, she replies, "There seemed to be something new about you: Perhaps it's having money." This last Otto can't match. When Otto returns to berate his friends, Leo insists on the inevitability of their completing the menage. Otto responds that he feels more alone than ever in his life. Accusing the pair of laughing at him, he storms out. He has left Gilda and Leo to face what they dread: monogamous coupledom.

Act two takes place in a fancy flat in London. Leo's superficial plays are the talk of the town, and to Gilda's annoyance, he has become infatuated with himself. When she warns him about the perils of success, Leo counters with an offer to make an honest woman of her. As bait, he dangles an elaborate marriage ceremony and afterward a magnificent "do" at

Claridge's. Gilda remains the bohemian, claiming marriage would upset her "moral principles." Leo demands to know if she isn't concerned about the eye of heaven. "Only when it winks!" she answers.

Gilda, who has the wittiest lines, is Coward's spokeswoman. She is the advocate of what Lahr terms "the daydream of sexual abundance." This fantasy is a reality for some; a plenitude of sex is the meeting ground for many gays, bisexuals, and threesomes. But Coward's wit is "gay" because it remains relevant to a distinctive lifestyle, if not one shared by all homosexuals. Gilda's witty disdain of marriage would not necessarily hold for the menage a trois, though the menage often arises out of marriage.

In act two, scene two, Leo is off at a fashionable house party when Otto shows up. This reverses the symmetry of the first act, and indeed the play's overall structure is that of an equilateral triangle: the characters and audience exit just about where they entered, hopefully wiser for the tour. In addition, Otto is returning from New York, which to Coward meant success, and as Gilda says, "Your whole personality reeks of it." Ecstatic, she admits that she and Leo are unhappy by themselves.

Gilda and Otto consume a sumptuous brunch while they reminisce about their early, bohemian days in Paris. He recalls how he and Leo struggled to paint and write and Gilda kept them going. She sighs at the memory of love among the artists, then adds, "Perhaps not love, exactly. Something a little below it and a little above it, but something terribly strong." Even Coward is uncertain how to characterize three-way affection.

It *is* an outlaw kind of mating, the memory of which leads Gilda to distrust respectability, which has changed the things she loved best. She was content in Paris where both men adored her. Still, she hesitates to resume her intimacy with Otto, who now paints portraits of the so-called best people. He reminds her that society won't accept them but will look on the three as "loose-living, irreligious, unmoral degenerates"—society's view of homosexuals during much of Coward's lifetime.

Coward, as a writer, values talent and wit over respectability. He sees the menage a trois as a private world responding to hidden imperatives that resemble those of his own clandestine liaisons. Otto, to persuade Gilda back into bed, argues, "A gay, ironic chance threw the three of us together and tied our lives into a tight knot at the outset. To deny it would be ridiculous. . . . The only thing left is to enjoy it thoroughly, every rich moment of it, every thrilling second." From early adolescence Coward was attracted to other men, but as late as 1969 he fought this being revealed in a biography. What he dared not speak plainly he could hint at by presenting a menage a trois onstage.

Otto and Gilda make love on the sofa while the curtain falls on act two. Coward knows that Gilda can't help but be affected by society's absolute demand that she choose one of her two suitors. She opts out of the dilemma by escaping into the safe, secure arms of Ernest. He is to Gilda what Hugo was to Anaïs Nin: a backstop. A fourth in a menage occurs frequently but is usually inconsequential to its dynamics, and Ernest's function here is to provide a pause in the action. Act three commences in Ernest and Gilda's New York penthouse after they have been married for two years.

A more self-confident Gilda is entertaining guests while Ernest is away. An air of commerce pervades the place; every piece of furniture or painting on the walls is for sale. Gilda, who has become an interior decorator, refers to the apartment as her "shop." She is having cocktails with a society woman and a rich young couple, clients she doesn't care for. Enter Otto and Leo in evening dress, and the stage is set for what in lesser hands might turn into slapstick.

Screenwriter Ben Hecht, who boasted how little he kept from the original script, accomplished just such a desecration. The movie that Henry Miller liked, starring Fredric March and Gary Cooper, is funny but not genuine Coward. Absent are the camp humor and the strong female lead that Miriam Hopkins's intelligence partly restores. Coward's Gilda is a strong woman who returns to the menage only after she succeeds in her own right. The stage Gilda is careful of Ernest's reputation and leaves the penthouse for the night. When in the morning Ernest discovers Leo and Otto, he bursts out, "God bless my soul!" Otto counters, "He couldn't fail to!" To Coward, Ernest typifies the straight world: righteous, conventional, and boring. Gilda has been longing for the two scapegraces to show up so that she could leave with them. Ernest pronounces her "stark staring mad!" The instincts of this husband and wife are too opposed for them to communicate.

John Lahr observed that for Gilda "the menage is not a vocation but a destiny." Still, she *chooses* to have a pair of lovers over monogamy. "From now on we shall have to live and die our own way," she insists. "No one else's way is any good, we don't fit." She is speaking for sexual misfits in general. Otto tells Ernest, "We have our own ethics. Our lives are a different shape from yours." When we recall that "bent" used to be a common term for gay, it's obvious Coward was speaking for those whom Christopher Isherwood later dubbed "his kind."

At the finale, after Ernest has properly denounced "this disgusting three-sided erotic hotch-potch," he trips on his canvases on the way out. Gilda, Otto, and Leo flop onto the couch, roaring and weeping with laughter. The photo of Lunt, Fontanne, and Coward wrapped around one another like a pretzel is one of the most famous in theater annals. Gilda gets to keep both men, and they are all delighted.

CABARET

Noël Coward understood that laughter is the solvent, the *aqua regia*, of jealousy. But when war broke out in central Europe, the playwright asked Winston Churchill how he could aid the defense effort. Churchill replied, "Go and sing to them when the guns are firing—that's your job." (The prime minister was especially fond of the wacky song "Mad Dogs and Englishmen.") However, the royal family never forgave Coward's youthful affair with Prince George, the youngest son of King George V. That liaison had ended when he met Jack Wilson, the handsome ne'er-do-well who remained his lover for many years.

Coward did travel widely as an unofficial government agent. He was appalled by the British exile community in Hollywood, where with the blessing of the Foreign Office, many English writers and actors lived and worked. Coward finally took Churchill's advice and served his country by diverting it. He wrote *Blithe Spirit*, a comedy about death that features a menage among a man, his wife, and the ghost of his former wife. *Spirit* proved so successful that it ran for the duration of the war. Unfortunately, its misogynist tone mars the relations of the three protagonists and makes for an evening more cutting but less clever than *Design*.

Christopher Isherwood was another British expatriate who rode out the war in Los Angeles. He shared with Coward being gay and needing to disguise it in his early work. Of patrician background, Christopher often referred to himself in the third person. A left-leaning pacifist, he hoped to break with both the motherland and his own domineering mother. At first he chose Germany to be his homeland, because it was there he confirmed his homosexual identity and found a companion whom he loved. But when the Nazi storm troopers took over, they drove out Christopher and his kind. During the 1930s, Isherwood, something of a vagabond, wrote *The Berlin Stories*, sections of an epic novel intended to chart the rise of Nazism. The work turned out more personal, and its central section—"Sally Bowles"—was initially published by Leonard and Virginia Woolf's Hogarth Press. Despite the narrator's asexual pose, the stories are charged with an ambiguous sexuality as uneasy as the times. If the material gave to Prussian prewar Berlin the image of a kinky paradise, that's due more to Hollywood than Isherwood.

What had originated as a diary Christopher made into a kind of fictional autobiography, which in the 1940s was transformed by John van Druten (with Isherwood's cooperation) into the play *I Am a Camera*. The "eye" character is called Christopher Isherwood, as he is in the film of the same name; there, the main character, played by Lawrence Harvey, gets drunk and tries to rape Sally. This film version disregards the original narrator's passivity and Sally's go-for-it sexuality. In 1972 the material was transmogrified by director Bob Fosse into *Cabaret*, which Vincente Minnelli called "the perfect movie." It starred Minnelli's daughter Liza as the free-wheeling Sally and Joel Grey as the sardonic café emcee.

When Isherwood finally wrote a factual account of his life in Berlin, *Christopher and His Kind*, he complained that he himself confused the original of Sally—the nineteen-year-old Brit, Jean Ross—with the actresses who'd played the part. In the course of their friendship, Jean and he grew as close and scrappy as brother and sister. They occasionally shared a bed in their boardinghouse, but nothing happened.

Once, recalled Christopher, Jean, who, like Sally, boasted of her affairs, halfheartedly tried to seduce him. "I remember a rainy, depressing afternoon when she remarked, 'What a pity we can't make love, there's nothing else to do.'" Christopher evaded her. He added that Jean knew his lover, Otto, and other working-class tricks, "but [she] showed no desire to share them, although he wouldn't have really minded." Christopher's laissez-faire attitude was typically gay for his time and class. However, the uncommitted narrator of *Berlin Stories* is not just a troubling feature; it reflects the early sexual confusion of the author.

When in 1929 Isherwood first visited Berlin, he had an affair with a bisexual hustler who threw away the money he gave him on whores. The hustler had to skip town, and the police questioned Christopher, which gave him the not-unpleasant sense of being a criminal. Back in England, he had his first affair with a woman. He grew hard and they both climaxed; he wondered if he could become heterosexual. "Why the hell should I?" he argued with himself. "Well, it would be a lot more convenient for you.... You wouldn't have all these problems. You wouldn't be out of step with nearly everybody else."

Girls were what the state and church ordered him to prefer and what his battle-ax of a mother had in mind so he could produce an heir to the family name and estate. He identified his mother with "nearly everybody"— all those whose dictates would annihilate his persona. Christopher ultimately rejected being heterosexual in the same principled way he declared himself first a leftist, next a pacifist, then outspokenly gay and the follower of a Vedantist swami. He was searching for a truthful identity in all spheres.

The makings of a menage a trois are inherent in Isherwood's life and art. He and his two comrades, the poets W. H. Auden and Stephen

Spender, made up a metaphysical menage that has profoundly influenced literature, not to mention current sexual politics. While Christopher once quipped, "Berlin meant Boys," even this pursuit depended on the tolerance of a crazed world. Auden termed him "our great ambassador to the mad." Luckily, Isherwood's stories fell into the hands of Bob Fosse, a man whose self was intensely woven into his work.

Fosse, at a midlife crisis, plunged into the reading of *Berlin Stories* "until that book was falling apart." In the film version of *Cabaret*, Christopher, called Brian Roberts, is played by Michael York as a blond, fresh-faced, slightly effete English teacher who is uncertain of his sexual identity. When Sally (Liza) grills Brian on his preference, he replies, "The word for my sex life now is nil." While not true of Isherwood, the line echoes his alienation from society. The love affair Brian enters into with Sally brings him into bed and into contact with the demimonde of the cabaret, decadent but vulnerable. Burlesque numbers on the tiny stage (Fosse had been a vaudeville hoofer) are intercut with scenes of Nazi violence outside.

Cabaret, with its invention of the German Baron Maximillian, puts the menage front and center and allows a fully initiated Brian to make his choices. Max the triangulator is Fosse himself, who during the filming in Munich was cheating on his wife, dancer Gwen Verdon, by sleeping with any pretty woman available to him, often two at a time. Like the slick Baron Max, Fosse's extravagant sex life was an escape from his inner fears.

In *Cabaret* it's 1932, Germany is in financial turmoil, and the Nazis are showing their muscle. Battles rage in the streets, but Max in his limo whisks away the young lovers to his country mansion. "It's my duty to corrupt you," grins the Serpent, his cashmered arms around them both. Sally loves the adoration of two men, who have an understanding between them that she hasn't grasped. The budding threesome is intercut with Joel Grey's ludicrous song-and-dance routine, "Two Ladies." Strutting a pair of buxom chorines, slapping their rears, he guffaws, "They like it—two for one!" Stripped of pose, the lowest dive and the opulent mansion are moral equivalents.

Fosse has co-opted Isherwood's parallel structure, but rather than counterposing hetero- against homosexual outlaws, the movie's alternatives are decadence versus violence, or action as opposed to acquiescence. Reflecting his own disintegrating marriage, Fosse's view of personal relations is bleaker than Christopher's, but his movie is politically more engaged. After the weekend, the lovers quarrel over the baron. "Screw Max!" shouts Brian. "I do," Sally bursts out. "So do I," he smiles, savoring the upper hand.

Soon after the menage has surfaced, Max, wary of the political climate, departs for Argentina, leaving the pair a sum of money. As they realize they are no better than whores, laughter defuses the tension between them. When Sally becomes pregnant, Brian offers to marry her. Instead, she has an abortion. Isherwood complained, "Brian's homosexual tendency is treated as an indecent but comic weakness to be snickered at, like bed-wetting." He missed Fosse's take on the menage as rite of passage. At the start, Brian has failed with women. Loving Sally, he becomes straight and, in the ensuing menage, bisexual. By the end it's clear that he is gay, but he has deliberately chosen his sexuality. At the same time, Brian identifies him-self as anti-Fascist and gets trounced by Nazi goons. He has come of age.

Despite Isherwood's ultimately finding his philosophy in Vedanta and his allegiance in the gay rights movement, we are left with the notion that he never fully explored his feelings toward women. At least compared to those two showmen, Coward and Fosse, Christopher's understanding of triangular relations remained literary. To a young man of his connections, which included E. M. Forster, it may have seemed advantageous to be gay, secretly at first and then finally coming out. By now, due to the gay rights movement, being trisexual is a more difficult identity to affirm than gay because it's scarcely recognized as an identity at all.

An example of the invisibility of troilism (a sexologist's term) occurs in the acclaimed 1994 movie *Four Weddings and a Funeral*. In this comedy of serial monogamy, a moment occurs when the leader of the pranksters, Gareth, played by Simon Callow, drops dead from dancing too vigorous a Highland fling. At the funeral in an old church, Gareth's longtime com-panion, Matthew, delivers a eulogy, which as reviewer Janet Maslin noted, "provides a sobering contrast, jarring the principals to see past their idle wedding going and get serious about falling in love." Matthew finishes by reciting a memorial poem written by Isherwood's pal Auden to his lover and collaborator, Chester Kalman; the congregation is moved to tears by this triumph of gay fidelity and normalcy.

The bittersweet truth is that Kalman, though the love of Auden's life, was a hell-raiser, a promiscuous bisexual who was persistently self-destructive. Auden, who kept the madcap at arm's length, was jealous of Chester's involvement in a menage a trois with a woman who ultimately married Chester's father and wrote a book about the experience. Kalman, like Fosse, grasped the serpentine possibilities of a threesome only too well. In *Four Weddings* the tears that flow on-screen, and among some in the audience, are being triggered by an ode to an inconstant, unrepentant bohemian menager.

chapter 17

THE ROMEO AND JULIET OF THREES

{Henri-Pierre Roché and Franz and Helen Hessel}

Sleeping with people must be one of the best ways of getting to know them.
JEANNE MOREAU

IN 1955 FRANÇOIS TRUFFAUT, A TWENTY-four-year-old film critic, found a copy of *Jules et Jim* while browsing through a pile of books in a stall at the Place du Palais-Royal. What caught his attention was "the resonance of the two Js" and that the author, Henri-Pierre Roché, had published this, his first novel, at age seventy-four. It had passed unnoticed. Truffaut, who liked "tales actually lived," guessed that it was based on a true story. He calls it "a false novel," more of a memoir. Later he would discover that the novel was written at white heat in Vichy France in 1943, solely from memory, about a menage a trois that had taken place before and after the Great War. To the grief-stricken author, the words flowed freely, "like blood from a good cut."

Truffaut was impressed, and while writing a review of a mediocre Western, he praised *Jules et Jim* for presenting what the cinema hadn't to date: a love story of two comrades and their one woman so tender that the audience couldn't take sides. Here at last was "a new and esthetic moral ethic which is constantly under review"—which is to say, it represented a series of existential choices. Roché anticipated Sartre and Beauvoir by decades, and they never achieved in life or art his "triangle of pure love."

Truffaut was surprised to receive a letter from Roché, who invited him to visit his house in a Parisian suburb. Over the next few years they corresponded and occasionally visited.

Truffaut would make the film *Jules and Jim*, his third, in 1961, and according to the *Chicago Tribune* it has become "the single best loved and most influential picture of the entire French New Wave." James Paris, author of *The Great French Films*, has deemed it his "personal favorite," and it may well be the most influential film of all time. It continues to inspire not only screenplays and novels but actions taken in real life. We confess it put some big ideas in our heads.

Jules et Jim is unique in that Roché was able to recreate painful, intimate memories in a novel, which became scrupulously translated by Truffaut into his memorable film and to which he added his own autobiographical elements. It starred the one woman who could make the role of Catherine come alive, Jeanne Moreau. She was already a famous stage actress and had worked in films that had mostly been forgettable, except for Louis Malle's *The Lovers*. Moaning "*mon amour*" in her gravelly voice, she was the first woman to enjoy cunnilingus on screen. The act wasn't shown, but the play of an orgasm across Moreau's expressive face certainly was. Truffaut was sufficiently impressed to court her for years, though he had no money to put her in his own film. Eventually Moreau would coproduce *Jules and Jim*, investing her own funds in the film and cooking lunches for the cast and crew. She made Catherine "plausible, crazy, abusive, passionate," admitted Truffaut, "but above all worthy of admiration." Jean Gruault, the screenwriter, quipped that women all over the world could thank Moreau for giving them permission to two-time their husbands.

Moreau ushered in a new era of female role models. A small woman without classic features and with shadows under her eyes, she was at first considered plain and chubby. Yet among the trio of French sex icons—herself, Bridgitte Bardot (kittenish), and Catherine Deneuve (glacial)—she alone seems to improve with age, artistically and aesthetically. Early on she passed on several major roles, including that of Mrs. Robinson in *The Graduate*. She was compared, a little condescendingly, to Bette Davis, an actress she doesn't care for. The role of Catherine permitted Moreau to be beautiful, feminine, and tough all at once. She avoided the "bad woman" stereotype (Lana Turner), the woman wronged (Joan Crawford), and most important, the bitch (Davis). Her more-than-sexual allure could plausibly attract and keep together a menage. "From the late 1950s on, she was the woman at the center of the story," writes critic Caryn James. If later movies that show one woman captivating two men—or, as in *Three of Hearts*, entrancing a man and a woman—have generally been less successful than *Jules and Jim*, blame the imitators, not the inspiration.

Moreau, who nostalgically reflects on that youthful period "when we are in love with love," has led a fascinating amorous life, even a wise one. She has so far married and divorced twice and lived for a five-year stretch with the famous couturier Pierre Cardin. "I was aware of the reputation he had in Paris," she remarked. "I knew all about it and I didn't care." To Moreau, whose roles often feature a hard-boiled attitude, Cardin's elusiveness made him more attractive. Her list of conquests includes Louis Malle and Marcello Mastroianni, but she is far more than a femme fatale, having served on government commissions and the jury at the Cannes film festival. Moreau's fantasy of a menage of many is to have "a really big house where she could live with all the men she had ever loved," a vision that would have pleased Catherine and perhaps Roché himself.

Henri-Pierre Roché, the man whom Jean Cocteau called "the most delicate and noble of souls," died in 1959, after he'd written Truffaut about Jeanne Moreau: "I absolutely must meet her: bring her to me." He saw neither of his novels made into films nor anything else of Truffaut's. Roché, who remains too little known, once stated he wished to write his autobiography "like Casanova but in a different spirit." He left 346 notebooks containing erotic comments on his lovers, whom he numbered at about one hundred women, single and married, virgins and sophisticates. Gertrude Stein said of him, "He knew everybody, he really knew them." Since Roché disguised the names of his lovers, his diaries went unpublished until recently when his code was cracked and editing could begin. Fortunately, Roché's fiction is close enough to his life that we may understand this man who was willing to share his lovers with his comrades.

Roché was born in 1879 and, after his father died, was brought up by his mother, whom he idolized. He studied to be a diplomat but lacked the fortune needed to succeed. Instead, he made a profession out of his taste in art. He introduced Picasso to the collector Leo Stein (Gertrude's brother), and he championed and then purchased the art of Duchamp, Picabia, Braque, Paul Klee, and Max Ernst for American millionaires and Indian maharajas. He lived with his mother until her death but also kept three regular mistresses, as well as having passing affairs. Truffaut's intriguing *The Man Who Loved Women* is based on Roché's unpublished diaries, transposed in time and place. But what turned this tall, thin, mild-mannered aesthete into a modern Don Juan?

LES DEUX ANGLAISES ET LE CONTINENT

This was the title of the Roché novel that covers his first love affair, turned by Truffaut into *Two English Girls* in 1971. The film's subtext, rooted in actuality, explains Roché's hesitancy toward intense love affairs, especially the one-on-one sort. Starring Jean-Pierre Léaud, Truffaut's alter ego in the Antoine Doinel series, the film has autobiographical relevance for the director as well. The youthful Truffaut was torn between marrying the daughter of his idol Alfred Hitchcock and the niece of his other idol Jean Renoir. In the end he chose a third, the daughter of a producer who brought with her a dowry that financed his early directorial efforts. Under Truffaut's romantic sweetness lies a cynic who is convinced that "the couple is not really satisfactory, but there is no alternative." Yet it is the alternative, the menage, that fascinated him.

In *Two English Girls* the center of gravity is Claude Roc (Roché's pen name), a young French art dealer and the "Continent" of the title. The narration is by Truffaut himself, reciting passages from Roché that he'd memorized. His screenwriter, Gruault, wasn't allowed to alter these. Both men had read the gothic novels of the Brontë sisters, using them as models for the young women Anne and Muriel Brown, and the remembrances of Proust for the character of the hesitant aesthete. (Imagine pitching to a Hollywood executive the concept of Proust meets the Brontës in Wales!)

Roché's romantic career did begin with two English sisters barely twenty, Violet and Nuk (a nickname for Margaret) Hart. In the early 1950s when he was writing the novel, he had not only his own diaries to work from but also Nuk's journal and her letters from 1902 through 1909. Roché masterfully evokes deep feelings from long ago, though without nostalgia. In the film, Claude meets Anne (Violet), the daughter of his mother's English friend, in Paris. She is an apparently liberated student of sculpture and the elder sister to Muriel (Nuk). Anne invites Claude home to Wales for a summer vacation at her family's cottage by the ocean, with the intention of matching him up with the serious Muriel.

In life, Violet the artist worshiped Nuk, who was religious, high-minded, and a beautiful redhead. Despite Violet's matchmaking, what resulted was an "incomparable trio," platonic and innocent. In London and in the country, the trio spent two years "like a fairy tale." It is interesting that in the film whenever Claude is obliged to go off with one of the sisters, a quarrel breaks out. Claude feels like a pawn, and his mother, Madame Roc, insists he must love *both* women. After all, he is her "monument," which she has raised "stone by stone," and while he is permitted to break hearts, he can belong to no one but Mama.

In life as in the film, Roché finally proposed to Nuk (Muriel). His mother forced him to return to Paris and wait for one year without corresponding with his fiancée. Madame's strategy succeeded when her son, after reading Nietzsche, embarked on his "lifelong career—the study of women." He slept around with married women and bohemian types. He wrote to Nuk to break off the engagement, but she had fallen in love with him, or his image. She wrote back to say they should never see each other again. Several years passed during which Nuk masturbated furiously and—shades of the old wives' tale—went nearly blind! When Violet visited Roché to tell him of her sister's distress, these two became lovers.

In Truffaut's film version of Nuk, Muriel writes Claude, "Whether you want it or not I am your wife." Her passion stems from her Puritanism and only excites her sister and Claude to indulge their appetites the more. Their lovemaking gives Anne a roving eye and a sexual aura. "I always have success just after I leave your arms," she tells Claude, apropos of taking a new lover, a rugged Pole named Diurka. To Truffaut, the treacherous love of couples is contrasted to the purity of the three-way bond among Proust and his Brontës.

Truffaut said his film dealt with "loves hindered and thwarted, but the obstacles are moral, inward, I would even say mental." The difficulties encountered by the real triad were more concrete: an English mother afraid of scandal, a French mother who was overly possessive. While Roché accepted maternal domination, marrying when he was fifty, Truffaut paid back his own uncaring mother by showing her as a slut in his *400 Blows*. Roché understood the sexual dynamic that causes two to become three, and thus he preferred the menage, but Truffaut remained skeptical about love in any form, certain it was dangerous, even fatal.

In *Two English Girls*, Anne eventually confesses her liaison with Claude to Muriel, which nearly kills her sister. In life, Nuk renounced her love for Roché in deference to Violet, who earlier had done the same for her. However, comparison to the Brontë sisters breaks down in reality: Violet, who'd two-timed her sister, married and settled down. Truffaut, the romantic filmmaker, has her character waste away from tuberculosis. Years pass. Diurka has published Claude's novel, *Jerome and Julien*, a little joke that reminds us how tightly intertwined are the movie and novel with Roché's life. Muriel at thirty, despite her masturbatory fantasies (these would be interesting!) remains technically a virgin. She arranges to meet Claude at Calais and inveigles him into bed. The next morning the sheets are stained redder than the hair on Muriel's head. Yet she will leave Claude forever, explaining that for her love must be absolute, while for him it was "a relative concept." We can't help wonder if she was simply getting even.

The film ends on a melancholy note when middle-aged Claude, walking in the Trocadero garden, sees a young girl he has reason to believe is Muriel's daughter (she has married) but finds himself tongue-tied. The actual ending was similar. Roché wrote in his journal in June 1939 that the girl he'd seen "had the same hair, walk, legs, mouth, smile" as his lover Nuk (Muriel). The wind had blown off the girl's hat, and it landed at his feet. Yet when he handed the hat to "Nuk's daughter," he was unable to speak. "Why did I not ask her?" lamented Roché.

The aging dilettante would never have an answer, and that would drive him to write his novel.

TROIS

Trois was Roché's original title for *Jules et Jim*. Certainly it's no worse than Truffaut's notion to title his film "Jules and Jim and Juliette." American newspapers in a fit of monogamy sometimes listed the film as "June and Jim." In the novel, the two buddies share a number of women before Catherine. The first woman with whom Roché formed a satisfactory menage was Marie Laurencin, who before the Great War was a disciple of the new painting. Roché was her first lover and collector, and he shared her with the young German-Jewish writer Franz Hessel, who eventually became the fictional Jules. Roché in his diary describes her as "direct, frank, plays the tomboy, talks tough, a mixture of boldness and naïveté . . . very much the virgin." Not for long. Laurencin and Roché didn't shrink from attending an occasional orgy spiced by opium.

For five years Laurencin was the lover of the poet Guillaume Apollinaire, but she remained more faithful to Roché than to him. Notoriously contrary, Laurencin married a German painter on the eve of World War I, with Roché acting as witness. Their friendship and correspondence lasted until her death in the 1950s. Another virgin, whom he met in 1915, was Beatrice Wood, the legendary potter. Called the "Mama of Dada," Wood was then a would-be actress in New York. During the war, Roché was attached to an American mission studying French industry. Marcel Duchamp, the acknowledged Daddy of Dada, whose famous *Nude Descending a Staircase* caused a commotion at the 1913 Armory Show, was also in town. Three-quarters of a century later, Wood reminisced to a *Los Angles Times* reporter, "I was having an affair with Roché while being in love with his best friend, Marcel Duchamp. I dreamed of Marcel while in Roché's arms."

When she told her lover, he was delighted, "for Roché loved Marcel too.... The two of them agreed about everything concerning me and conspired to see that my education took the course they approved. The three of us were something like an *amour à trois;* it was a divine friendship." In 1917 the trio collaborated on *The Blindman,* a journal of tongue-in-cheek provocative writing and images that influenced the development of our contemporary "cool" aesthetic. After the war, when Roché had returned to France, Wood consummated her affair with Duchamp, the man with "penetrating blue eyes that saw all." She had committed herself to becoming an artist, and she is now the last living relic of the formative period of modern art.

An "aesthetic morality constantly reconsidered" aptly describes the spirit of the bohemian art scene that was centered in Paris from the turn of the century until the crash of 1929, thinned out in the thirties and then fled fascism to relocate in New York, and finally was revived after the war in the abstract expressionist painters and the Beat poets. For the bohemians, what was aesthetic was moral, so long as that aesthetic could claim to be "modern."

Absent a church or aristocracy to support them, the shifting group of artists and freethinkers who made up Bohemia required an outside source of income, which was provided by art dealers and collectors. Roché acted as scout for some of the great collectors, such as Walter and Louise Arensberg. Gertrude Stein called him "a general introducer," and his acquaintances included such diverse figures as the photographer Man Ray, the composer Erik Satie, and the writer Jean Cocteau. The notes he made in the process of satisfying his insatiable curiosity produced a wealth of material, which, once published, will describe the birth of the entire modern art movement.

Still, Henri-Pierre Roché will ultimately be known for *Jules et Jim,* a poignant tale of the friendship of two men and the woman they couldn't live with or without. Beatrice Wood has been credited as the model for Catherine, but she denies it. She even claims the Truffaut movie bored her! Franz Hessel was the model for Jules, the short, plump introvert played by Oskar Werner; Roché himself is the slender bon vivant Jim played by Henri Serre; and Helen Grund, an art student, becomes their shared lover Catherine, acted by Jeanne Moreau, her nationality changed from German to French. Roché's novel attains a tragicomic dignity because with an inevitability reminiscent of *Romeo and Juliet,* its lovers are sundered by forces beyond their control. When Jules insists that Catherine is their teacher, Jim asks what she teaches; Jules replies, "Shakespeare!"

In Paris in 1906 Henri-Pierre took Franz, a newcomer fleeing a broken heart, to the Bal des Quat-z'Arts. Franz chose the costume of a slave.

After that they saw each other every day, talking endlessly and translating each other's poems. They shared women but desired different things from them and were not rivals. They compiled a growing list of *amours à trois*. While they were traveling in Greece they fell in love with the marble bust of a goddess, and they swore to follow the smile of such a woman if ever she appeared.

In 1912 Franz met Helen, who while she may have duplicated the enigmatic smile, was a determined character. Her handwriting in her 250 letters to Henri-Pierre crowds the page just as she took center stage with the men. While Roché might have better suited Helen, Franz claimed her with the line, "Not that one? Eh, Pierre?" Helen agreed that Franz's innocence and her sophistication balanced out, so they would make a good couple. The pair of Germans married the following year and moved back to Berlin. They had two children. Roché was pursuing his career and seeing Germaine Bonnard, the ever-faithful Gilberte in the film. However, he understood that camaraderie was the fortress against the world's troubles.

In 1914 the war further separated the three. Roché, unlike Jim, didn't worry about encountering his friend across the trenches, because he was safely in America. With this change to the original story, Truffaut was commenting on the artificial hostility between France and Germany. These changes from either Roché's life or the novel are small but enhancing. After the war Henri-Pierre joined Franz and Helen and their children in a small town in Bavaria where the Hessels had built a house. On meeting, the men "kissed each other, on the mouth, quickly and naturally." They immediately resumed "their great conversation."

Franz, who had fought on the Russian front, had changed. He couldn't satisfy Helen, and she and Henri-Pierre fell in love. Franz gave his consent. The three, working and playing together, knew real happiness. The Hessels translated into German Roché's collection of stories, *Don Juan*. It's worth noting that his was a Gallic Don Juan, not a killer at all. In turn, Henri-Pierre helped Franz with his new novel. Roché and Helen decided to have a child, but relationships within and without the menage became complicated. Helen, who said she believed in "running risks and paying for them," was unfaithful to both men. A goddess demands worship; she cannot be neglected for a moment.

Helen Hessel was an odd combination of bravado and paranoia. Whatever she saw as betrayal, even neglect, demanded retribution. Her motto was "If there is to be war, strike first, unexpectedly and hard." Truffaut turned Helen into an admirer of Napoleon. Yet Henri-Pierre, in spite of his innate caution, became as obsessed with her as Franz remained. He held to the notion that the birth of a child would wipe away bitter memories and renew love. When he and Helen failed to conceive a child, he returned to Paris and Germaine. Helen first divorced Franz and then, because she needed his unquestioning acceptance, remarried him.

In 1925 the Hessels moved to Paris where Helen worked as a fashion correspondent for German newspapers. She and Franz and their three children, as well as Uncle Roché, set up housekeeping in the suburb of Fontenay. Truffaut wisely reduced the children to one daughter, Sabine, but in life as in the film the adults were happiest when playing with a child—indeed, when playing at being children. Helen was unpredictable and sometimes rash. Henri-Pierre, thinking to escape from his feelings for her, secretly married Germaine. But he couldn't break with Helen. The catalog *Henri-Pierre Roché: An Introduction,* which is the first step toward a biography, states that "periods of calm [were] interspersed with periods of turbulence filled with recriminations, betrayals, . . . and threats from Helen with her revolver. Through it all, Hessel is compassionate and supportive, trying to be friend and confidant to both his wife and to Roché."

Life seldom aspires to tragedy. The Hessels quietly returned to their house in Bavaria. In 1930 Franz, hoping to entice Roché, wrote his friend that "we three can live together very well in my house, you would sleep with Helen in the big double bed in the small bedroom." Although he painted a cozy picture of them working together before a roaring fire, he ominously referred to Helen as "the general."

In any case it was too late to reconstitute the triad. Henri-Pierre and Germaine already had a son. In 1936, to conform to laws enacted under the Nazi regime, Helen divorced her Jewish husband for the second time. In 1938 Franz left for France, but after the German victory, the Vichy authorities incarcerated him in a camp. He died in January 1941, though Roché didn't get the details until a year later. He was shocked and saddened, but by early 1943 he was ready, in the form of a novel, to resume his dialogue on wisdom with his old friend.

"LE TOURBILLON"

This is the song, "The Whirlpool," that Catherine sings to the guitar accompaniment of Albert, a friend of Jules and Jim and also her lover. Albert is a fourth trying to become a third, and the actor who played the role actually wrote the song. It is key to the meaning of Truffaut's *Jules and Jim* and incidentally began Jeanne Moreau's successful recording career. Roché supposed Franz would be the central character of the novel that he wrote in homage to their friendship. Therefore at its end, after Jules witnesses Catherine and Jim's joint suicide, he goes on living with his daughter, the fruit of the menage. In the film Oskar Werner, who played Jules, couldn't compete with Jeanne Moreau, whose wild mood swings commanded the camera's attention. Her theme song is a translation into music of Roché's tragic ending, the one aspect of his novel that he invented out of thin air.

It is curious that one of the founders of auteur theory, which holds that a director is the true author of his movie, should have adhered scrupulously to the language of another author. A second irony is that he was able to inject aspects of his own life into Roché's autobiography. Truffaut's biographer Don Allen declares, "The failure of the heterosexual couple is the major theme of the film, together with the corollary that all other solutions, including the *ménage à trois*, are equally doomed." On a deeper level Truffaut is making the statement that only art is worth living for, and that unlike sexual conquest, a form of war, art keeps its practitioners alive. In the film, over a period of twenty years, 1912 to 1933 (when the Nazis rise to power), Jules and Jim seem perpetually young, even wearing the same old clothes. Meanwhile the countenance of Catherine, who wields power and worries about aging, alters from that of a romantic goddess to military severity.

Roché as man and memorialist was as fascinated by three in love as Casanova. In the novel he accurately relates his mother's last illness and a visit to her by two of his women, Michelle, a new love, and the ever faithful Gilberte. Roché, most in love with his mother, imagines she communicates something mystical to Michelle, and he decides that she, not Gilberte or Catherine, should be the mother of his son. Roché did in fact marry twice, and he had children, but the ghost of his mother no doubt joined the wedding parties. Again in the novel, Catherine wishes to meet and accept Gilberte, but Jim keeps them apart. He is afraid they will join forces to overwhelm him. Jim, while he engaged in multiple love affairs, preferred a menage a trois composed of himself, one woman, and his best friend.

Jules, because he has less ego, is more easily suited than Jim to a menage. He asks the question of Jim, "Why is it that Catherine, who's so much in demand, nevertheless makes a gift of her presence to us two? . . . Because we paid complete attention to her, as if she was a queen; because, between the two of us, we've been better than anyone else at giving her what people call love." Jules realizes that the two men together make up her ideal. Jim, in contrast, pulls back to Paris, and so Catherine brings in a fourth. "Albert," she says, "equals Gilberte." But she only succeeds in destroying the harmony of the menage, which is an emotional and not a logical construct. It is no more equal than a friendship or a marriage, where one is always giving more than the other.

The entire story of *Jules and Jim* and the film's many excellencies are too well known to bear repeating. But what of that ending where Catherine, her smile inscrutable, drives the car with Jim in it over a ruined bridge into the Seine? Jules, as does the audience, watches, sick at heart. Roché had dedicated his novel to "those who try to jump from bridges," but he removed this just before it went to press. Truffaut has "The Whirlpool," a light, airy tune, playing in the background as the car sinks beneath the turbulent water. Earlier, Catherine's thoughts are described as being in a whirlwind (*tourbillon* means both). It is the whirlwind of life that has splintered the menage, which can only be reunited in death. All three have permitted the forces of dissolution to pry them apart. They failed to maintain an ideal triad. Jules's futile attempt to stop the slaughter—a yell—"sketched a fiery triangle in the air over their heads."

There is a postscript when Jules, at the crematorium, watches his loved ones' coffins go up in flame. He decides that Jim had taken nothing from him; rather, he'd given Catherine, "the best he had to give," to his friend. He wants to mingle their ashes and scatter them in the wind. But the law prevents this last coming together, which would also be an emancipation for Jules. The menage, though profoundly social, goes against the grain of a society that prefers a jackbooted march to a jaunty little tune.

chapter 18

THE BELLS OF BLOOMSBURY

{Vanessa and Clive Bell, Duncan Grant, and David Garnett}

If I had to choose between betraying my country and betraying my friend,
I hope I should have the guts to betray my country.
E. M. FORSTER

*B*LOOMSBURY WAS AN EXTENDED FAMILY of like-minded artists, writers, war resisters, and progressive thinkers who initially lived in the Bloomsbury section of London. While the date of Bloomsbury's actual inception varies from 1905 on, there is no doubt that the members of the Bloomsbury circle cross-pollinated each other socially and artistically. Their legacy of books and paintings presents unquestionably one of the richest creative periods in British history. The work of several Bloomsbury stars—including writers Virginia Woolf, Lytton Strachey, Bertrand Russell, and Aldous Huxley; painters Dora Carrington, Duncan Grant, and Vanessa Bell; and economist Maynard Keynes—was profoundly innovative.

To be a Bloomsberry was courageous in the Britain of that time because pacifism and homosexuality were crimes punishable by imprisonment at hard labor, as Oscar Wilde learned to his sorrow. These politically concerned intellectuals banded together for mutual protection. Although some biographers feel that Bloomsbury's enduring fame comes from the lively journals, letters, and biographies written by its members, it was actually their radical sexual behavior, especially their menages a trois, that kept them together and ignited their work. Although trading lovers and sometimes switching sexual identities to fit the occasion hardly raised an eyebrow among them, Bloomsbury could be an emotion-packed can of worms.

The essential family unit for the Bloomsberrys consisted of *three*, a sensible living arrangement for creative polysexual people. Opinions vary as to the identity of Bloomsbury's queen bee. Some credit the famous historian, wit, and "Bloomsbugger" Lytton Strachey, described by Harold Nicolson as "a bearded and bitchy old woman, rude rather than witty in society, injecting with his unnaturally treble voice jets of stinging poison into otherwise convivial gatherings." Lytton's collective biography *Eminent Victorians*, written in 1918, summarized Bloomsbury's quarrel with their elders, especially with the Victorian "breed for your country, die for your country" ethic.

Lady Ottoline Morrell's Garsington Manor, a Cotswold stone Tudor house located on two hundred acres of gardens and farmland in Oxfordshire, provided a lush country refuge for the war resisters and their friends. At Garsington intellectuals mingled with sympathetic government figures. Lady Ott delighted in Lytton's stinging repartee at her dinner parties. A flamboyant queen, he courted and sometimes burlesqued her in her own clothes. Ott's husband, Philip Morrell, a member of Parliament, defended the war resisters in court. Maynard Keynes provided financial help and political advice.

Bloomsbury's founding members inform us that their group first coalesced at the Gordon Square home of sisters Virginia (who later married Leonard Woolf) and Vanessa Stephen. Vanessa, a classic beauty, married Clive Bell, a wealthy, influential art collector. His income, government connections, and tolerance allowed Vanessa to develop her artistic talent. Clive also facilitated Vanessa's two menages: the first involving her mentor, the Quaker Roger Fry, a major art critic, and the second including the dashing painter Duncan Grant.

Bloomsbury biographers all suffer from a myopia that fails to recognize threes. An image evocative of Bloomsbury is a turning carousel, with lovers hopping on and off. The esprit that made it go was that of the menage a trois. If a couple formed, sooner or later a third joined them, though the woman remained central. Vanessa Bell and Dora Carrington (with Lytton Strachey and Ralph Partridge) provided the focal point for their menages, which supplied the bed, board, and intellectual stimulation that made Bloomsbury's high-toned lifestyle possible.

Bloomsbury flowered in the British countryside where great houses, like stage sets, provided the backdrop for writing, painting, conversation, parties, and three-way lovemaking. Carrington and Vanessa, both significant painters, rebelled against the restraints of conventional family life. Each married a traditionally masculine man but loved another who was quite different. Their long-term involvements were with gay men who nourished their creative side. Carrington and Vanessa enlarged upon couple-love and in so doing they gained a world.

The intellectual groundwork for Bloomsbury was laid in the early 1900s at Trinity College, Cambridge, by a nucleus of inquiring undergraduates. The Apostles, a select society whose past members included Tennyson and Thackeray, discussed moral and philosophical issues. Certain of its members became Bloomsbury's avant-garde: Maynard Keynes, publisher-to-be Leonard Woolf, and Lytton Strachey, the father of the modern psychological biography.

When Thoby Stephen introduced his Apostle friends to his sisters, the Bloomsbury group was born. Leonard Woolf described meeting Vanessa when she was twenty-one and when Virginia, his future wife, was eighteen: "In white dresses and large hats, with parasols in their hands, their beauty literally took one's breath away." Woolf said the experience was like suddenly coming face to face with a Rembrandt. Thoby Stephen's death from typhoid in 1906, at age twenty-six, devastated Vanessa. She wrote to a friend that nothing she did really mattered: "I should be happy living with anyone whom I didn't dislike . . . if I could paint and lead the kind of life I like." In 1907, after refusing him several times, Vanessa married Clive Bell.

Early on, the Bloomsbury contingent held Thursday evening gatherings at the Bells' home on Gordon Square, near the British Museum. Clive, a rugged sportsman on the one hand, a bon vivant on the other, had an open-door policy. He never allowed his wealth to distance him from his poorer comrades. David Garnett remembered his exhilaration on visiting the Bells. "When the door was opened," he wrote, "a warm stream of Clive's hospitality poured out, as ravishing as the smell of roasting coffee on a cold morning."

In her *Notes on Bloomsbury* Vanessa recorded how they talked "till the wee hours of the night . . . sometimes about books or painting or anything that occurred to one. . . . We seemed to be a company of the young, all free, all beginning life in new surroundings, without elders to whom we had to account in any way for our doings or behavior." One spring evening in 1908, Lytton introduced a bawdy element. Clive and Vanessa were quietly seated in their drawing room. Lytton, pointing his finger at a stain on Vanessa's white dress, asked coyly, "Semen?" Everyone roared. Thereafter, sex permeated Bloomsbury conversation. Vanessa particularly enjoyed and loved to tell dirty jokes.

In 1908 Vanessa glowed with a refined sexuality. Henry James described her as "articulate and entirely handsome." David Garnett described her face as "a perfect oval like that of a gothic madonna sculpted at Chartres or Reims. Her mind and manners were not in the least masculine yet she was the only woman that any of us knew who could join in the talk of a group of men and allow them to forget that she was a woman." Vanessa was tall and striking yet sensitive, with gray-blue eyes and straight brown hair parted in the middle and worn in a bun.

By 1914 Vanessa could write to Maynard Keynes, who later married a Russian ballerina, "Did you have a pleasant afternoon buggering one or more of the young men we left for you? . . . It must have been delicious. . . . I imagine you [in] the ecstatic preliminaries of Sucking Sodomy." Something of a voyeur, Vanessa later gained vitality by living with two gay lovers. As Clive Bell's wife, she became the focus of several menages a trois. There was a brief interlude during which Virginia became involved with Clive. Passionately bonded to Vanessa, Virginia suffered from her sister's marriage and felt compelled to join the newlyweds on their honeymoon. Virginia wrote that Clive was "the first person who ever thought I'd write well." Their flirtation revived on and off for several years.

Whatever Vanessa felt about Virginia and Clive's romance, outwardly her attitude was stoical, and she carried this reserve into other relationships. In 1909 Clive also took up with a former mistress. Vanessa's first pregnancy, which clashed with her devotion to painting, drove a wedge between the Bells. Gradually, the couple drifted into separate emotional spheres, which made room for third parties.

In 1911 Roger Fry fell in love with Vanessa, and she responded. He had been an art critic for *Athenaeum* magazine, writing what he called "weekly snippets that ruined [my] mental digestion." Vanessa thrived as Roger encouraged and directed her painting. Bloomsbury biographer Leon Edel has said that "Roger Fry gave Bloomsbury a center and a focus in art between 1910 and the outbreak of the war." But it is clear that his influence actually reached far beyond that. In 1912 he started the Omega Workshop as a cooperative enterprise to employ artists on practical projects.

Interestingly, this art critic, who had a Quaker background, was the one to bring an appreciation for French Post-Impressionism to Britain. Fry had worked as a curator at New York's Metropolitan Museum, which had sent him on buying expeditions with the Met's president, J. Pierpont

Morgan, in search of Renoirs and Italian Renaissance masters. By the time he returned home, the focus of his aesthetic had shifted in reaction to celebrating ordinary objects such as a display of bottles on a sign. Carrington, Vanessa, and other English artists were put to work painting such signs. Fry's Omega Workshop celebrated the inherent beauty of household objects and innovation in interior design. Its members also made pottery, carpets, textiles, and furniture. Commissions from the Omega Workshop provided both a focus and a partial living to Duncan, Vanessa, and others. Omega fulfilled its aesthetic mission—to make fine art domestic.

Omega, aside from leading to Bloomsbury's preoccupation with interior design, forged the intimate relationships of several of its members. Clive accepted Roger as part of his extended family. His sexual credo was polyamorous: "It seems very absurd that people who are fond of each other shouldn't all live together always. What's this modern notion of pairing off instead of living in rookeries?" No one thought it unusual that Vanessa and Clive continued marital relations despite his mistresses and her romance with Roger. Their contemporaries were impressed with their skill at juggling relationships.

In 1912 Virginia married Leonard Woolf. With civility typical of Bloomsbury, Clive wrote a short, pained letter to Virginia, declaring his love for both her and her husband. Nearby Roger sat painting Vanessa. That same year Vanessa and her clan rented Asheham, a country house in Suffolk. Husband, lover, children, relatives, maids, and long- and short-term guests coexisted in a tolerant atmosphere verging on anarchy. Now in her early thirties, Vanessa was in command of herself and her art. Her biographer Frances Spalding describes her life as an "accord with which all her faculties—maternal, mental, sexual and artistic—flowed together."

It seemed that Vanessa and Roger, who shared artistic theories and worked together to prepare her works for exhibition, would achieve prominence together. However, in 1913 Vanessa was struck by the astounding development in Duncan Grant's painting. Both were founding Bloomsberrys who had observed each other carrying on other romances. Duncan had a classical education in art—he had studied painting in France and had met Picasso and Matisse—but his style was idiosyncratic and decorative. In time, she realized that neither Clive nor Roger had the originality she craved.

A HAPPY DOMESTIC IMPROVISATION

Duncan was considered the most promising artist of his generation, expected to trump the French in Post-Impressionism. He had a genius for creating a melodious, rhythmic line, and his paintings were fresh and imaginative. Two decades younger than Roger and six years younger than Vanessa, Duncan had an abundance of charm. A child of nature, Duncan made no excuses for his voracious homosexuality. His willingness to sacrifice everything for art disarmed everyone he met.

Duncan came from a modest Scottish military family. His sex appeal stemmed from his indifference to social norms: he wore mismatched clothes and looked as though he needed a hot meal. His luxury resided in the rich colors and fluid lines of his paintings. Vanessa flirted with Duncan, once even taking a bath in front of him in her casual style. She eased out the devoted Roger gradually, with Bloomsbury finesse. Vanessa's letters to Roger in 1912 show her absorbing new skills from working with Duncan.

Duncan and Vanessa were unconventional, deeply sensuous, and basically shameless. She did not question his affairs with men—he'd had involvements with Lytton Strachey, Maynard Keynes, Vanessa's brother Adrian, and many others. Duncan thrived on being adored. The new menage players became Vanessa, Duncan, and his male partners. Nevertheless, Clive remained crucial to her extended family. During the first year of Vanessa and Duncan's affair, she found herself facing a bisexual rival eleven years her junior, David (Bunny) Garnett.

In January 1915 at a dinner party, Maynard Keynes seated the two young men together. Their ensuing romance temporarily changed Bunny's sexual preference from straight to bisexual and permanently altered his career. Duncan's influence turned him from a scientist into a literary man. Bunny wrote that Duncan was "the most original man I have ever known. If any slender talent has expressed itself with originality and success I owe it to . . . the formative years I spent in Duncan's company." Bunny went on to write a three-volume memoir that includes much intimate Bloomsbury material, though not the details of his affair with Duncan. He also wrote several novels, one of which, the semiautobiographical *Aspects of Love*, became a Broadway musical.

Clive and Roger, now the odd men out romantically, continued to socialize with Duncan, a master of Scottish reels, sword dances, and outlandish costume designs. His new lover Bunny was fair-haired and muscular, and his blue eyes readily attracted women. But all Bunny's attempts to sleep with Vanessa failed. She viewed Bunny as a means to keep Duncan home at his easel. There were nasty scenes when Bunny came home to find perfect strangers in his and Duncan's bed, but on the whole peace was kept with Vanessa's marmalade and supervision.

At times she bared her soul to Clive: "I am now alone with the two young men. So you see we're three and I suppose I ought to feel *de trop*. But I can't say I bother about it much. After all if you have your nights together [with Duncan] it seems to me your days can be spent *à trois*." Vanessa wrote Roger a less flippant version about sharing her partner: "I see that Bunny really does care a good deal for him; I had been afraid he didn't and that would mean unhappiness for Duncan." She sometimes felt resentful about the menage, but she was determined to keep the threesome together at all costs. Paradoxically, Vanessa had become dependent on Bunny for that.

Her stiff upper lip froze in place when confronted with Bunny's affairs with women. She tried writing teasing notes: "Do you make love to all the young women in the way I've so often had to blow you up for?" Bunny's escapades caused Duncan to explode, with Vanessa acting as referee. In 1917, while visiting his mother, Duncan wrote to Bunny about the ambiguities of their situation: "I am so fond of Nessa. I am ashamed she should be so fond of me and you are fonder of me than I deserve and I must abjectly love both of you and hope not to be too much noticed for it."

When Britain went to war, Duncan and Bunny were prepared to accept prison sentences rather than be drafted. The authorities in rare cases offered conscientious-objector status to those engaged in work of "national importance," such as farming. Vanessa moved her menage to Wisset Grange in rural Suffolk. Raising chickens and plowing fields flew in the face of Bloomsbury elegance, but the pacifists risked getting into trouble if they stayed in London.

Wartime brought out Vanessa's nobility. She became the head of the family, as well as a practicing artist. Other than occasional luxuries brought by Clive or Maynard Keynes, now a high official in the Treasury Department, the menage lived on their own harvest. In 1916 the triad moved to remote Charleston, situated at the end of a farm road, a hike from Berwick and Glynde, the closest villages. This outpost, where they raised rabbits to supplement their meager food ration, became Vanessa's base for the rest of her life.

Vanessa's paintings from this time reflect her physical and emotional isolation. *The Tub* from 1917 adopted the motif of three flowers, one of which is separated by distance and color from the other two. Instead of enjoying her bath, a woman stands next to the tub, fingering her braided hair while looking downward, lost in thought. Vanessa's letters to Clive written during this period also reveal irritation at the wartime hardships that took a toll on her family.

Bunny, subjected to backbreaking farmwork, nearly cracked from the strain. Meanwhile, after jealous clashes over Bunny's other lovers, a furious Duncan banged his head on a barn wall. He threatened suicide and plotted revenge. In 1918 Duncan made a diary entry that he hoped Bunny would read: "I copulated on Saturday with her [Vanessa] with great satisfaction to myself physically. Also the pleasure it gives is reassuring. . . . That's one for you Bunny."

The result of this "letting off spunk" was Duncan and Vanessa's daughter Angelica. Clive Bell gave her his name and his love. Never without a mistress, he accepted legal fatherhood of his wife's third child as amiably as he had the two that were his own. Angelica was born on Christmas Day 1918. Bunny was transfixed by the infant's beauty and wrote a portentous note to Lytton: "Its beauty is the most remarkable thing about it. I think of marrying it; when she is twenty I shall be forty-six—will it be scandalous?" Since Angelica's birth coincided with the armistice, Bunny regarded the event as a harbinger of hope for humankind. He exclaimed in his diary, "The thought of a child filled me with delight, an affirmation of belief in life at the time of blackest despair."

Once the war no longer posed a threat, the Charleston menage splintered. Duncan stopped sleeping with Bunny and Vanessa. He claimed that he ended sexual relations with Vanessa because "the psychological strain was too great." But their emotional connection remained intact. Vanessa protected Duncan, then in his early thirties, from scandal. Her tact had strengthened her position as enthroned matriarch.

Leon Edel, in *Bloomsbury: A House of Lions*, admired Vanessa's skill in coordinating disparate relationships. "It was Vanessa's fate to live with shared love; she had none she could call her own." Edel continues in a breast-beating manner to describe how Vanessa felt the rage of Medea or Clytemnestra, but he fails to mention that her menage a trois had provided her and her loved ones with protection and artistic plenty. Unfortunately, most biographers like to report the score of wins and losses in the great coupling game. They would be gratified if Vanessa had vanquished Bunny once and for all and lived with either Duncan or Clive. That was not to be the case.

A "PERFECT DARLING"

Duncan and Vanessa continued to produce an outpouring of work. Clive, the official head of the family, provided comfort and stability and got on quite well with Duncan. Both men stood by Vanessa after she lost her son Julian during the Spanish Civil War. Quentin, her other son, said that the letters that Vanessa and Julian had shared during their separation were like love letters and that Julian was more like a lover than a son to her.

Angelica, a lively, impish child, delighted everyone. But she was not happy. In her book *Deceived with Kindness,* Angelica expressed her anger at not having had a more normal upbringing. She felt that her mother's image and personality always overwhelmed her own. Angelica imitated Vanessa but resented her dominance.

Mother and daughter competed for Duncan's admiration. His daughter adored him. She wrote, "In my eyes he could do no wrong." But Duncan and Vanessa presented a united front that shut out others. Their shared devotion to art and scorn for bourgeois values made them indifferent to Angelica's desire for normalcy. The daughter complained that her family spent more time and care arranging paintings in their home than preparing her for the outside world.

In the 1930s Duncan and Vanessa's art was widely acclaimed. Roger Fry marveled that Charleston's undisciplined inhabitants had produced such fine work among the disorder. There was a touch of "camping out," he wrote, "a happy domestic improvisation which completely clashed with sturdy middle class comfort and fastidious culture." Carrington, not so kind, complained about Vanessa's sloppy housekeeping—that a dead mouse might be found in a corner.

Oddly, Vanessa maintained that Clive was Angelica's father. The act was so convincing that Clive once asked whether Angelica looked more like a Bell or a Stephen. Vanessa waited until Angelica was seventeen to confirm the girl's suspicion about Duncan. To stifle her guilt, Vanessa spoiled her daughter with suffocating affection. She insisted that Angelica not mention the confession to Clive, thus manipulating her love of both fathers.

Duncan was occupied with his art and love affairs, so Clive superintended Angelica's sex education. He suggested a range of literary works in English and French as guides, including a Bloomsbury favorite, *Les Liaisons Dangereuses.* Despite Clive's countless affairs, he remained loyal to the mother of his children. Angelica wrote, "He never tired of [Vanessa's] beauty and he appreciated her love for her children. . . . Neither had he, in spite of his knowledge and love of painting, any understanding of what it meant to be an artist: to him it was a mystery which he both loved and feared, because in Vanessa it was indissolubly linked to her femininity, her almost goddess-like capacity to love and to crush."

Bunny remained on the scene, if peripherally. In 1921 he married a woman named Ray Marshall. Duncan became depressed but eventually capitulated and as a wedding present painted Ray's portrait.

Observers noted the bond between Duncan and Vanessa. Bunny described how Duncan and Vanessa "painted together in harmony, perfectly happy while they were at work, and rarely resting from it." In 1930 Virginia Woolf added, "I am persuaded that nothing now can be destructive of that easy relationship because it is based on bohemianism." Whether at Charleston or traveling to Italy or France, Duncan made room for Vanessa.

Throughout her fifties Vanessa accepted Duncan's philandering and behaved, in his words, like a "perfect darling." He would spend the night with a juvenile delinquent he picked up on a train, and she would quip, "Duncan's gone criminal again." His portrait of Vanessa from 1934 shows her thoughtful, her hands folded under a hat. In another, done in 1942, she assumes a cold regal quality.

In 1930 Duncan became seriously involved with an American painter whom Vanessa resented. Pressured on both sides, he wrote to Bunny expressing anguish over the conflict that was tearing him apart. "Why does she not realize that my love for George gives me more power to love her instead of less? And when she is not here I feel too that something is wanting in my life. The truth is I want them both. Sometimes I find the tears rolling down my cheeks simply because I love both so much . . . but at the same time I cannot help thinking that if Nessa could see into my soul at such moments she would see that everything is all right."

Meanwhile the beautiful Angelica, in her early twenties, found herself being courted by the ubiquitous Bunny, twenty-six years older than herself. That Bunny's wife Ray was dying of cancer didn't prevent him from conducting a lively courtship. Angelica knew that Bunny was a father surrogate, but she fell for him nonetheless. "Duncan was simply not there," she wrote, "and as a result my sexuality, nourished on romanticism, was of an unbelievable fragility, hardly calculated to attract young men of my age." She decided that the platonic nature of Duncan and Vanessa's liaison left her starved for warmth. Bunny's worldly experience, plus his reputation gained as a novelist, impressed her. Besides, in what more Bloomsbury manner could a girl trump her "negligent" mother and "absent" father than to marry the man who had been her mother's suitor and her father's lover?

Initially, in 1936, Vanessa took a wait-and-see attitude toward Bunny's flirtation with Angelica. But Duncan assumed a fatherly role and demanded to know Bunny's intentions. He realized that his objections to Bunny and Angelica's marriage were convoluted when he wrote, "I was very much agitated by the whole affair. . . . It may be of course jealousy on my part, mixed up with some curious complex/taboo about sex."

By 1941 Ray had died; Bunny first made love to Angelica in H. G. Wells's spare bedroom, and they married soon afterward. Vanessa, saddened by Virginia's suicide and the loss of her eldest son, was in no mood for a confrontation. She wrote Bunny a placating note: "I'm simply very grateful to you for giving her so much." But Angelica soon realized that her marriage was doomed. In her memoir she complained that "Duncan, Bunny and Vanessa were too closely bound together for there to be any room for me. The last thing they wanted was an illumination of the past, of the obscure corners they hoped to forget." She grew to be troubled by the incestuous overtones. But with the Angelica-Bunny marriage a fait accompli, Bloomsbury tact again prevailed. Duncan and Vanessa's productive lives in London and at Charleston discouraged brooding.

In later years Vanessa preferred Charleston, while Duncan kept a London studio as his trysting spot. In 1948 he wrote Vanessa, "I suppose I have made several unhappy long ago, [but] I think you do not understand at all how much I love you and Angelica. I never say so. It is quite out of my power. I try to show it sometimes by what I do."

Vanessa remained the center of her intimate circle and the delight of her grandchildren. Frances Marshall, Ralph Partridge's second wife, observed, "As she got old and moved more slowly, it was as if one of the statues from the Acropolis had stepped down from her pedestal and was taking a stately walk." Vanessa died in 1961 at the age of eighty-one, after she had achieved substantial renown as a colorist. Leon Edel summed up her powers admiringly: "Vanessa had in effect surmounted and kept intact husband, lovers and family, as long before she had taken hold of the disorganized Stephens in Kensington and kept them unified. Small wonder that Bloomsbury called her monolithic."

Duncan mourned his longtime companion, who had exalted his paintings above her own. Angelica found a note that expressed Duncan's grief: "After lunch I suddenly became aware that I am on my own for better or worse. . . . Now henceforth I think I shall always defer to her opinions, I know or can guess at often what they would be." Most descriptions of Vanessa's association with Duncan and his lovers stress her patient, almost martyred diplomacy and acquiescence. Biographers have missed how she must have experienced pleasure being in the presence of such vital sexual energy. Duncan and his lovers provided a fountain of youth, a well of vicarious gratification.

Duncan's later paintings develop themes of Matisse or Picasso but evidence swirls of vivid color uniquely his own. Many critics value the male nudes he did in the 1950s as his best work. Vanessa, taking off on

Duncan's theme, did a series of female nudes at the same time. Their cross-fertilization produced a body of work that epitomizes Bloomsbury's bold yet ordered aesthetic.

Leon Edel pointed out that all the members of Bloomsbury "were connected by love, a linked chain. . . . Bloomsbury broke barriers and redefined androgyny, the blending of two sexes and the blending of life and art. The Victorians had tried to bury sex as if it didn't exist. But Bloomsbury freed sex of guilt and shame."

Charleston has recently been opened to visitors. The atmosphere at this Sussex farmhouse is so creatively charged that one expects Duncan and Vanessa to emerge from their huge studio waving paintbrushes. Their touch is everywhere: in the whimsical colors and textures, in the sophisticated decorative scheme that suggests villas in the south of France. A trust operates this monument to them, painters in the vanguard of British modernism who worked side by side for decades.

Charleston blends the fanciful and the practical with playful painted designs on door panels, fireplaces, windows, walls, furniture, and curtains. Its joyful aura recalls parties when Duncan dressed as a woman, Roger wore a baboon mask, and Virginia came as Sappho. Restored gardens add to the fauve effects.

The Bloomsbury industry—published memoirs, art books, and biographies—is in full swing. As we approach the end of a fragmented century, naturally we yearn for the sense of community that was Bloomsbury. Beyond being teacup revolutionaries, they took risky political stands. They were civilized in a way the world may never see again.

chapter 19

CARRINGTON'S LOVERS

{Dora Carrington, Mark Gertler,
Lytton Strachey, Ralph Partridge, and Gerald Brenan}

*It seems so good when we're all three together
that I grudge every minute that keeps us apart.*
LYTTON STRACHEY

*C*HRISTOPHER HAMPTON'S MOVIE *Car-
rington* is rich in sensitive details and colors, like a fine painting one must
view from several angles to appreciate fully. It opens in 1915 with Lytton
Strachey taking the train to visit Vanessa and Clive Bell in the country.
Jonathan Pryce gives a nuanced portrayal of Strachey, Bloomsbury's
Queen Father. He arrives at the station, allows his bags to be carried by a
young porter, and ogles a handsome carriage driver whom he impresses
with his animated conversation. At Vanessa's, he admires a "ravishing boy"
playing ball with Vanessa's son: Dora Carrington, played by Emma
Thompson in knickers and a bowl-shaped haircut, is introduced.

When Lytton meets Carrington, he inquires, "Mark Gertler's
friend?" The girl shrugs, realizing that the man with a bushy red beard is
not really interested in her. Tellingly, he turns his back on her. Later on,
Carrington provided Lytton with a collection of beautiful, talented, and
exciting young men; she seduced, married, or entrapped them as offerings
to her bearded idol. She has remained misunderstood by Bloomsbury
biographers, inclined to view her as a victim because she has not been considered the center of a quirky but productive menage a trois.

In 1913 London's Slade School of Fine Art awarded Dora Carrington the coveted Melville Nettleship Prize for figure composition. A distinguished career in painting was predicted for her, but Dora rarely exhibited her art publicly. She kept it domestic, decorating walls and cupboards. Her award-winning oil painting was of a woman nude with a distorted right foot. Carrington, like the figure in the painting, had an awkwardness about her, which partially explains why she fixated on Lytton Strachey, master of the quick barb.

If Carrington could have looked into a mirror and seen the incarnation of intellect and upbringing she most desired for herself, she would have seen Lytton. She adored him with what she described as "a most self-effacing love." According to Virginia Woolf, she was "not really pretty, having a broken nose, moonlike face, uneven teeth. . . . Her voice was flat, somewhat mincing and precise, and from time to time she would give an affected little gasp." Subject to swift changes of mood, she was impulsive, self-conscious, restless, and eager to please.

Yet her childlike round cheeks, large blue eyes, and bobbed golden hair attracted quite a lot of attention at Slade, where she dropped her first name, Dora, and thereafter called herself Carrington. Born in Hereford in March of 1893, she hated her prudish, ex-governess mother, who made her dislike being female and confused her about sex. She desperately loved her father, a railway engineer, who became paralyzed and deaf after suffering a stroke. Perhaps her father fixation partly explains Carrington's worship of the crotchety older man she selected as her mentor.

When we view Carrington as the center of a dynamic menage, it becomes clear that the usual assessment of her as a mousy failure is flawed. Carrington did her best work living in a threesome. After suffering what she called "an awful childhood," she craved the approval and protection, not to mention an unorthodox sexual outlet, that a triad provided—with the addition of an occasional fourth. A family of her own construction healed her and gave her power over a miniworld she devised to her own specifications.

Sophisticated Lytton Strachey bowled Carrington over with his distinction and wit. Bloomsbury dinner parties often revolved around him. Frances Marshall, of the younger crowd, described Lytton in her memoir, *Love in Bloomsbury*, as "tall and willowy and with very long and beautiful hands . . . [and] a peculiar elegance in the way he used to walk, or rather stalk across the lawn into a deck chair. His velvety brown eyes were full of expression." The peculiar Strachey voice was a family trait. According to Frances, "it had a life of its own, starting low and soft, rising to a faint scream, stopping altogether, swallowing itself, and then sinking to the depths again." In contrast, Cecil Beaton, the well-known fashion photographer, observing Lytton at the opera, compared him to "a sloppy asparagus."

Born in 1880, the eleventh of thirteen children, Lytton was very precocious. Not the typical Victorian, his mother Jane wrote children's poetry and essays, smoked, and read John Stuart Mill's feminist philosophy. Richard Strachey, alternately a soldier, engineer, and civil administrator, hoped that his son would enter public service. Lytton, a gangly teenager, felt isolated from his clan and lost in their home at Lancaster Gate, "a portentous establishment, dark, rambling, badly planned, ugly both within and without. It was size gone wrong," he wrote, "size pathological; it was a house afflicted with elephantiasis."

At Cambridge in 1902, Lytton, like many of his Bloomsbury contemporaries, was elected to the Apostles Society. Michael Holroyd, Lytton's biographer, compared Lytton's bohemianism at Cambridge to that of Oscar Wilde's at Oxford thirty years before. Both adored the stage, won poetry prizes, abominated organized religion, and insulted boors. Like Wilde, Lytton chose clothes for their shock value: green gloves, a purple scarf with an intaglio pin, and an Italian cape. He wore earrings and long hair. By the time he met Carrington, his clothes were a more conservative tweed.

Another bond between Strachey and Wilde was their masochism. While Wilde found his Lord Alfred Douglas, Lytton made a fetish out of pining over unavailable men. The cycle began at Cambridge, repeating itself with regularity as Lytton grew older. The Apostles provided Lytton and Maynard Keynes with a hunting ground for ripe undergraduates. Maynard's glibness usually won out, and jealous Lytton called Keynes a "decayed and amorous spider." It irked him when his favorite nephew Duncan Grant and Keynes moved in together. Early on Lytton became accustomed to accepting an auxiliary role in a triangle. He squeezed what juice he could from a good sexual story. And Carrington would provide both men and stories.

Carrington rapidly developed a taste for triangulation. She could be certain she was desirable if two men wanted her. She played one against the other, not committing to either while benefiting from both. She transformed her admirers into her teachers. One example, Mark Gertler, a poor Jewish student from London's East End, became a star at the Slade Art School. Mark soon gained recognition as a painter in the style of the Old Masters and was launched on an impressive career.

Carrington, who had met Mark earlier at the Slade, envisioned a relationship in which both he and Lytton would each critique her painting. But Mark demanded exclusive rights to her. He fervently pursued Carrington from 1912 to 1918, while she refused to give up her virginity. Mark considered her to be the "purest and holiest" girl he knew, yet he alternately berated and entreated her to give in. Gertler introduced her to society patrons such as Lady Ottoline Morrell and the Bloomsbury crowd. Lady Ott, since she wanted Mark for herself, encouraged Carrington to yield to him—a ritual offering of the virgin.

In August 1915 Carrington formally entered the Bloomsbury circle. Lytton and she found themselves guests, along with Vanessa Bell and Duncan Grant, at Virginia and Leonard Woolf's house near Lewes. An incident happened there that changed Carrington's life: to be naughty, or in a flash of desire, the thirty-five-year-old Lytton kissed the twenty-two-year-old flirt. At the time, Carrington had no idea that Lytton was homosexual—nor even what the term meant.

After the kiss, an indignant Carrington swore to take revenge on Lytton by snipping off his beard while he slept. At night she sneaked into his room, scissors in hand, ready to perform the vengeful surgery. Suddenly, he awoke and looked into her eyes. Carrington was holding a phallic weapon in her hand. Their sex roles were reversed; she had overpowered him. That is how she fell in love with Lytton—on her own terms. She had control. Carrington's sexual relationship to Strachey was indeed ambiguous. She was a girl who looked and acted like a boy. He was a "bugger" to whom virile men usually condescended. Was he attracted to Carrington because of her androgyny?

Mark Gertler was not included in this house party, but he had met Lytton earlier when the biographer had rented a cottage near Marlborough to finish his subsequently acclaimed *Eminent Victorians*. The two men had gotten along well, taking long walks in the country and discussing fine art. The connection among Mark, Carrington, and Lytton evolved because each person needed the other, either for emotional or aesthetic validation. Mark wanted Lytton to convince Carrington that he was an important artist, one from whom she could derive practical benefits. He felt that Lytton's intercession would make Carrington into his complaisant bed partner.

Carrington craved an education in arts and letters, but Lytton wanted Mark for his own sexual needs. This lopsided association, which in Hampton's film Lytton describes as "girls loving buggers and buggers loving young men," lasted several years, roughly from 1915 through 1918.

Gertler produced some of his finest antiwar paintings during this period but nearly cracked from the strain of loving the quixotic Carrington. Lytton finished his *Eminent Victorians* in 1918, and Carrington, having learned a great deal about painting from Gertler, sold her first drawing.

Later Carrington gave Lytton all the details of her cat-and-mouse game with Mark. If Lytton could not have Mark for himself, he at least enjoyed hearing about him. When Carrington finally yielded to Mark's demands in 1918, she complained that the sexual act made her feel dirty. But she was no prude: she had tried sex with Lytton two years earlier. Although their encounter had not been successful in the conventional sense, it made them decide to live together, and it opened her up to other affairs. But the driving force of her relationship with Lytton was not having sex but winning his approval.

By eventually making love with Mark, Carrington acted as proxy for Strachey. Put another way, through Carrington, Lytton could vicariously associate with the handsome young men he desired. Carrington allowed him to indulge his refined voyeurism. Though he was feeble in body and always ailing, Lytton found that the sexual titillation Carrington provided was invaluable to his sense of well-being. She continued to offer details about her burgeoning bisexuality for Lytton's pleasure. In letters to him, she described several conquests dating from 1916. In one she described sleeping with a young woman wearing a "crepe de chine nightgown with pink rosebuds round the neck."

In another letter to Lytton, Carrington referred to ravishing "votre petit [Geoffrey] Nelson for you." Here Carrington was standing in for Lytton, who also became the indulgent parental authority she'd always strived to please. Under his approving eye she expanded her sexual as well as artistic horizons. A few years later, she described her conquest of an American girl with "the face of a Giotto Madonna." She made such "wonderful cocktails," wrote Carrington, "that I became completely drunk and almost made love to her in public." Carrington leaves no doubt about their affair when she blames herself for having been "such a blasted fool in the past, to stifle so many lusts . . . for various females."

Carrington, a great tease, was riddled with self-doubt. But her association with the leading wit of Bloomsbury elevated her importance in the eyes of the men of that circle. David Garnett wrote, "Tens of thousands of young women have china-blue eyes, talk in little gasps and have sex trouble, but . . . Carrington would have always been attractive to her friends; what makes her interesting and fascinating to subsequent generations is her relationship with Lytton Strachey." To keep Lytton in her orbit at all costs, she structured menages a trois; otherwise, she feared that her emotionally stingy partner might wander off.

Frances Marshall observed that it was no accident that Carrington concentrated her most intense love on someone who was unattainable. For Carrington was in awe of Lytton. He dared to say things she could not. He was an idealized alter ego, and this translated into romantic ardor. "I think you are the most eminent, graceful person," she wrote. "The most worthy, learned and withal charming character. And I shall always love you in your entirety."

In December 1917 Carrington and Lytton moved into the Mill House at Tidmarsh in Berkshire. Carrington waited on Lytton day and night, providing hot milk, herbal tonics, hairbrushes, and sympathy. In turn, Lytton taught her French, exposed her to great literature, bore the expenses, and provided protection from philistines. More than this, Lytton's growing literary distinction caused high society to court him. He gave Carrington a valuable identity as his helpmate. At Tidmarsh Lytton set aside generous studio space, gave Carrington expense money, and when she sent paintings to galleries, helped her select and price them. He was more excited by praise of her work than she was. But the sexually incompatible couple needed a third—a big, strong, take-charge, practical chap to keep them together.

"TRIANGULAR TRINITY OF HAPPINESS"

The man who would provide the third in the principal menage of Carrington's life was Ralph Partridge, an athletic war hero. A friend of her brother, Ralph was tall and handsome with striking blue eyes. He was the opposite of the effete Lytton. The commander of a battalion in World War I who had been awarded the military cross, he attracted acquiescent, beautiful women. However, Carrington's slapdash bohemianism drew him. When first invited to tea, Ralph treated Lytton to a macho prowar diatribe. Lytton, admiring Ralph's ardor, not to mention his muscles, was fascinated.

Ralph, the son of a civil servant, had earned a scholarship to Oxford, where he became a brilliant debater. School came easy for him, as did most things. A friend described his complex personality by saying, "He combined immense vitality and energy with an almost equal capacity for doing nothing. He was an athlete, a top-notch rower, but had refused to play games. He was extremely observant and intensely curious about his fellow human beings and this combined with a sharp and delightful sense of fun."

Ralph's indifference to the arts should have made him the last person to fit in at Tidmarsh, but his blatant, robust sexuality made up for other shortcomings. Ralph initially regarded Lytton as a freak standing between himself and Carrington. Carrington, whom he described as "a painting damsel and a great Bolshevik," knew her housemate was salivating over the muscular specimen seeking refuge from the bloody hell of war. The ever-confident Ralph expected Carrington to be a pushover. Instead, she teased her "Norwegian dentist," encouraging him one moment, discouraging him the next.

Ralph became a regular at Tidmarsh. He ran errands, weeded the potato patch, and posed nude for Carrington. She, as usual, gave Lytton a full report, especially when Ralph proved stellar between the sheets. The more Lytton lusted after Ralph, the more attractive he became to Carring-ton. Bloomsbury biographer Holroyd noted that "beneath the clash of opinions and the contrast of personalities, at a more elemental level, the three of them had already begun to form that summer the basis of an odd triangular union, which despite strains and crises, would persist over the next thirteen years, until the death of two of them."

Although homosexual Lytton and "ambidextrous" Carrington needed a third, Ralph provided the ideal candidate, one they both desired. Carrington and Lytton, though they were equally close, could not work together as did Duncan Grant and Vanessa Bell. Ralph, curious and eager to learn, even cemented the pair's intellectual and creative bond. Initially, he acted as Lytton's disciple and secretary and later he worked at Leonard and Virginia Woolf's Hogarth Press, a key Bloomsbury institution.

Both Carrington and Lytton loved and considered themselves mar-ried to Ralph. While Ralph carried out household chores beyond the ail-ing Lytton's ability, the mature man enjoyed a voyeur's paradise. Lytton, a hypochondriac who complained of being "a martyr to the piles," needed to be cared for. In return, his housemates acquired the education and sophistication they lacked.

The traditional male in Ralph wanted to own Carrington, but she resisted his marriage proposals. By January 1920 Ralph practically lived at Tidmarsh. Lytton's readings of Campion, Marlowe, and Shakespeare opened up a previously undiscovered, sensitive side of Ralph. The war had made old values hollow, and he needed a new direction and a philosophy to suit his shattered world. Lytton provided a refuge as well as a renewing force.

When Carrington and Ralph visited Oxford, Lytton wrote Ralph, "It seems so good when we're all three together that I grudge every minute that keeps us apart." Carrington greatly enjoyed the men's "long discus-sions on Einstein's theory whilst I darn the socks." Once Virginia and

Leonard Woolf hired Ralph, he found a source of income that made marriage feasible. Lytton began to pressure Carrington on Ralph's behalf, informing her, "If Ralph wants marriage it is best for you and for him. . . . But I hope that apart from his happiness, it won't make much difference to anybody."

Carrington feared Lytton might abandon her. He let slip once that without Ralph, their life at Tidmarsh could not continue. Lytton had also told Virginia Woolf that he feared Carrington would make a claim on him if they lived together for a long time. Carrington wrote a heartfelt letter on the eve of her marriage assuring Lytton that he was the only person for whom she had "an all absorbing passion." She pleaded for his sympathy: "I cried to think of a savage and cynical fate which had made it impossible for my love to ever be used by you. You never knew . . . the very big and devastating love I had for you." She said she adored every curl in his beard, the smell of his face in his sponge. But after all, it was Lytton, taking his own needs into account, who had chosen Ralph to be Carrington's husband.

On May 21, 1921, Ralph and Carrington, with Virginia Woolf as a witness, were married in a civil ceremony. Carrington promptly lost her wedding ring. Lytton paid for their honeymoon, which they spent in Paris before joining him in Italy. Carrington wrote to reassure Lytton that he must not worry about "his children," that each of them in his or her own way loved him more than he knew. That year Lytton wrote, "The curious menage works . . . quite well. Ralph is really a charming creature and seems quite content, and Carrington appears to be happy."

A fourth was introduced into the idyllic menage when Ralph's best friend, Gerald Brenan, visited Tidmarsh. Carrington had flirted with Gerald in London and Spain before she'd married Ralph. She wrote him in 1919 offering to visit him in Spain to share intimate romantic secrets and to make "marmalade." When Gerald arrived at Tidmarsh in July 1921, he had a shattering experience, similar to the one Carrington had had on viewing the recumbent Lytton. Afterward, Brenan wrote a friend, "I was sitting in an armchair in the sitting room when Carrington passed across the front of the window with the evening light behind her, and I knew I was in love. It was like the first attack of flu to a Pacific Islander—I was completely, totally under from the first moment. I had fallen for her in the same way in which she had fallen for Lytton, and just as violently. And she was in love with me."

Gerald was a bold adventurer and writer. At eighteen, to escape family pressures, he set out with a friend to see the world with no source of income and nothing but a few good books. He traveled throughout the near East and Asia and in 1913 ended up freezing and penniless in Siberia. He had walked 1,500 miles and was ready to go home. After World War I, he spent four years alone in a remote part of Spain, south of Granada. There he embarked on a self-education program with the aid of two thousand books he had transported on the backs of donkeys to his shack. He later wrote several of the best books in English on Spanish literature and culture.

Gerald was more than Ralph's best friend and war buddy. He looked up to Ralph and competed with him sexually. He had actually fallen in love with Carrington even before he'd met her, thanks to Ralph's description of her daring. His biographer, Jonathan Gathorne-Hardy, described Gerald's first impressions after hearing about Carrington: "She sounded exactly the sort of 'modern' girl he longed to meet. And 'modern' in this context meant not just unconventional, bohemian, emancipated, but also that she might, perhaps, let him make love to her. He spent the war years dreaming about her."

There is a strong element of voyeurism in Brenan's relationship with Ralph. When they'd met as young soldiers, Gerald's sexual experiences had been nil, while Ralph was a hero in every sense. Making love to Ralph's wife would have boosted Gerald's wobbly self-esteem. Carrington, aware of Ralph's possessive nature, defined the parameters of the now four-way interaction. Gerald accepted a closet arrangement and lied to Ralph to protect the smooth-running menage that his lover counted on.

Carrington arranged what she called "embrascades"—stolen hugs and kisses—with Gerald, convinced that this form of wooing posed no threat to her marriage. In visits to London, Ralph had casual affairs that he supposed he kept secret from Carrington. A traditional male, he expected his wife to be faithful to him. From Spain Gerald wrote letters to Carrington in code. She warned him not to pressure her to divorce Ralph or expect to oust Lytton. Gerald thus accepted an auxiliary role that didn't influence the main action. Fourth fiddle suited his gypsy temperament. Gerald's home was where his tent was, preferably in some exotic spot. At this point, he was in neither a financial nor an emotional position to become a responsible husband to any woman—let alone the conflicted Carrington.

In October 1921 Carrington, burrowed in for the winter—canning vegetables, making jams, baking steak-and-kidney pies—wrote to Lytton, "Bless you my dear one. Do you know how much you are loved by some people?" Everything seemed idyllic, though never boring, until Carrington's college friend Valentine Dobree and her husband came to visit. They upset Tidmarsh's delicate balance. Valentine and Ralph, who became involved, used Tidmarsh as a trysting spot on weekends. To complicate matters, Carrington also became attracted to Valentine.

Then Valentine told Ralph about Carrington and Brenan; chase scenes, ultimatums, furious arguments, and all-night third-degree sessions unleashed emotional mayhem. Lytton, caught between warring factions, reassured Carrington, "You and Ralph and our life at Tidmarsh are what I care for most in the world, the only things I care for. It would be horrible if that were to vanish." To keep Ralph happy, Lytton invited fascinating guests, such as E. M. Forster. He interceded with Virginia Woolf to raise Ralph's salary, and finally he bought a car for Ralph to drive on excursions à trois. He cautioned Gerald to remain in Spain, out of direct touch with Carrington.

Gerald, once hostile to Bloomsbury, came to admire Lytton, its embodiment. Lytton told him, "Never forget that, whatever happens, and in spite of all estrangements, you are loved by those you love best." Lytton had patched up Carrington's and Ralph's marriage temporarily. In June 1922 Carrington wrote, "Thank you Lytton for all you have done for me, and for him, trying to make us both happy. You alone prevented me many days from committing acts of madness." These lines eerily foreshadow what was to come.

The rupture in Ralph's and Carrington's marriage was predictable. He couldn't cope with her convoluted sexuality, and she refused to bear his children. Tidmarsh's inhabitants held their breaths. Carrington, hopeful their menage might endure, sighed with relief in November 1922 that "Ralph agreed yesterday that nothing mattered compared to our Triangular Trinity of Happiness." In 1924 drafts in the house were causing Lytton respiratory problems, so the menage moved to Ham Spray house, between Newbury and Hungerford, where proper heating was installed. Carrington decorated the interior with popular Bloomsbury shades of wallpaper and fabric— mauve, olive, and cloudy yellows. Outside she created a tulip garden.

Because of Lytton's influence, Ralph became a book reviewer for the New Statesman and subsequently an author; his militarism had changed to ardent pacifism. He also viewed Carrington from a more detached perspective, suggesting that they visit Gerald in Spain. But Ralph's generosity owed something to his new love affair with Frances Marshall.

Frances, a recent graduate of Cambridge, was in her early twenties. Dark-haired and attractive, Frances had a sensible disposition that contrasted with Carrington's flights of fancy. At first Carrington welcomed the new addition, partly because she felt very attracted to Frances physically. Ralph courted Frances in a whirlwind fashion. His desire to be with her full time altered his priorities. In order to square the triangle, he invited Gerald back to England. But Carrington could not cope with Gerald as a demanding, full-time suitor.

Carrington admitted to Frances, "The bare truth from my point of view is that if Ralph leaves me . . . it really means an end to this life." Meanwhile Lytton, doubting his physical capacity, threatened to abandon Ham Spray. But during the spring of 1926 an important compromise was reached. Lytton was not in the habit of meeting with young girls, even if they were Ralph's lovers. But he met with Frances in order to arrange the menage's living schedule: Ralph would stay with Frances during the week in London and they would visit Ham Spray on weekends, allowing the Triangular Trinity of Happiness to continue.

Weekends blazed with sexual crosscurrents—one being Carrington's desire for Frances. Above all, Carrington's love for Lytton remained primary. Now in her midthirties, Carrington became obsessed with her age, calling herself "a lonely middle-aged haggis." She had a fling with a seaman that left her pregnant. Ralph, who would have been the legal father, in consultation with Frances and Lytton, arranged and paid for an abortion.

In the early 1930s, Lytton became seriously ill. Certain he was going to die, Carrington went into the garage and turned her car engine on. Ralph found her there and dragged her out, which she sorely resented. Then in January 1932 Lytton died at age fifty-two. A week before, delirious, he whispered an emotional tribute to his devoted companion: "Carrington, why isn't she here? I want her. Darling Carrington. I love her. I always wanted to marry Carrington and I never did."

Carrington was left with nothing. Brenan was in Spain. Her menage with Lytton and Ralph was over. No new menage was possible with Ralph and Frances, an exclusive couple, as good as married. Lytton, the man who had made her, restoring the self-image that had been shattered in childhood, had left her definitively. The mirror image that she desired for herself, the idealized reflection, was broken. On the day before her marriage to Ralph she had written to Lytton, "I cried last night, Lytton . . . at realising I never could have my moon." Carrington was the moon's shadow. There was now no place for her.

On March 11, 1932, a couple of months after Lytton's agonizing death from stomach cancer, Carrington put on Lytton's yellow silk dressing gown and shot herself in the stomach with a shotgun she'd borrowed. It was two weeks before her thirty-ninth birthday. Years earlier she'd written, "I often hope I shall die at forty. I could not bear the ignominy of becoming a stout boring elderly lady with a hobby of sketching in water colours." There was no funeral. Carrington left instructions that her body was to be buried in the garden at Ham Spray next to Lytton's.

Gerald Brenan made a comment on human relationships that serves as a proper epitaph for Carrington: "I hate the stupid geometrical figures by which people try to render the emotions of others, imposing hard, straight lines on tender curvaceous human beings who have none." Frances and Ralph married a year after Carrington's death and moved to Ham Spray, where they lived happily for thirty years and raised a son. Neither Lytton nor Carrington lived to witness the 1957 act of Parliament that legalized homosexual acts between consenting adults.

chapter 20

PORTRAITS REAL
AND SURREAL

{Augustus and Ida John and Dorelia McNeill;
Paul and Gala Eluard and Salvador Dalí;
Pablo Picasso; Alberto Giacometti; Stanley Spencer; Leonor Fini}

My development as an artist depends on having both of you.
STANLEY SPENCER

LOVE AND THE FLAME

*A*T TIMES, WHEN GREAT ARTISTS HAVE blazed with the passion of creation, their spouses have been singed by jealousy. It is hard to love someone drawn to a model's beauty like a moth to a flame. Artists' wives have found themselves in a sensitive spot: should they be expected to give up their beds in the service of their husbands' work? As we shall see, some have joined in threesomes and become champions of art at whatever personal cost. Sometimes the model has gained the upper hand. Often the friction has augmented the creative process.

Augustus John, one of the most successful British artists of the twentieth century, was called "the most notorious nonconformist England has known." He formed a five-year rollicking menage a trois in Paris with two women and their combined total of eight children. Although his wife Ida died young in childbirth, his lover Dorelia (Dodo), whom he called his "missus," and he lived together for nearly sixty more years. By 1912 their tribe was growing at Alderney Manor, located on sixty acres of woodlands in Dorset, as John added an occasional child from his countless affairs.

John was born in Wales in 1878 to a proper, umbrella-toting solicitor and a lovely, frail mother. By the time Augustus was eighteen he'd already grown into the imposing figure his biographer, Michael Holroyd, described as "nearly six feet tall, with a Christ-like beard, roving eyes and beautiful hands with long nervous fingers that gave a look of extreme intelligence to everything he did." His father had warned the family that gypsies kidnapped children; through much of the century it was a serious crime to "associate" with roving gypsy bands. But gypsies became Augustus's favorite subject for painting, and a little later he would copy them by wearing one earring, an open sailor shirt, and a floppy hat.

In the 1890s as a student at the Slade School in London, Augustus showed remarkable talent. John Singer Sargent exclaimed that his drawings were beyond anything seen since the Italian Renaissance. In 1901 Augustus married Ida Nettleship, eloping to foil her parents, who regarded him as uncouth. Ida's father was a well-known Pre-Raphaelite painter, and she'd been pampered as a child. Though a fellow student at Slade, her baby-talk letters to girlfriends reveal that she continued to live in the make-believe world of romance assigned to women before the Great War.

Ida conceived five children within the first six years but Augustus was never faithful to her. He needed amorous attention from someone not pregnant. In 1903 he met Dorelia McNeill, and though they never married, she would bear him three additional children and share his life until the end. Both women modeled for him. In 1902 his portrait of Ida, called *Merekli*, which accented her slanted oriental eyes, sensuous mouth, curly hair, and dark complexion, proved a prototype for a series of vivacious portraits of brunette women draped in provocative colors. But portraits of Dorelia had something more—her mysterious smile that some likened to the Mona Lisa's. Dorelia was classically beautiful in an earth-mother, fecund style, and she was actually a wonderful gardener.

Off-canvas, Augustus's "Smiling Woman," as he tagged Dorelia's portraits, was unhappy in the role of mistress. His passionate letters didn't make up for her living alone. She soon left for Italy with Augustus's sister Gwen, also a painter, who was getting over an affair with Rodin. When Augustus heard that Dorelia was posing nude in Paris, which she had refused to do for him, he grew frantic. Ida dispatched her husband to bring Dorelia back into the family fold.

It seemed too late—the errant mistress had already taken up with a young Belgian artist. But while Augustus fell apart, Ida plotted a campaign to win Dorelia once again. Gwen was instructed to reason with her, warning that she would destroy a great genius. Augustus was ordered to pull himself together and write her love poems. But Ida took the crucial step by admitting that she too desired Dorelia: "O my honey," she wrote, "let me say it—I crave for you to come here. . . . You are a mystery but you are ours. I don't know if I love you for your own sake or for his." Michael Holroyd admits that Ida was passionately attracted to Dorelia but supposes it was largely vicarious.

Dorelia moved into the John household. She helped Ida, usually pregnant, and Augustus's work flourished. Although Ida's love for Augustus had given rise to her affection for Dorelia, a three-way desire was fanned. In another letter to Dorelia, Ida implies that the women were lovers: "I was bitter cold in bed without your burning hot, not to say scalding body next to me," writes Ida. A great fan of Kipling's *Jungle Book*, she described Dorelia as "a lovely forest animal." Her love with "Darling Dorel" may have been the consummation of desires that began in girlhood.

In 1906 the gypsy menage set up camp in Paris. The three were very poor, living in one room on the Left Bank. According to Holroyd, "There was only one bed between them—the children sleeping in boxes on rollers, the babies in baskets." Yet Ida could write to her mother, "It is a beautiful life we live now and I have never been so happy." The menage flourished away from England and its Victorian morality. The women sewed, cooked, hung wallpaper, went to the Louvre, and posed for Augustus. However, his roving eye was still on the lookout for new models, allegedly for inspiration.

In 1907 Ida, after bearing her fifth child, died of complications. A few days later her mother descended on Augustus, scooped up the three eldest sons, and laid plans to acquire the rest. The constant struggle over the children helped to keep Ida's ghost alive. "Ida keeps teaching me things," Augustus confided to a friend. He had thought of the children as obstacles to his art but now realized they were "the real material and soul of it." He got back his sons, gypsy fashion, by kidnapping them on an outing to the monkey house at the London zoo.

John's next years with Dorelia were very productive. W. B. Yeats described Augustus as "a delight, the most innocent, wicked man I have ever met. He wears earrings, his hair down to his shoulders, a green velvet collar and had two wives who lived together in perfect harmony and nursed each other's children." Even before the Great War John had became the darling of English society, pursuing lucrative commissions and notable affairs. His most important patron was the regally homely Lady Ottoline Morrell. She'd fallen head over heels for the painter, whom she compared to "a Macedonian king or a Renaissance poet." But Augustus steered their liaison toward platonic shores, and Dorelia provided Lady Ott with a substitute amour in the person of her own lover, Augustus's protégé Henry Lamb.

"I love no one living more than Dorelia," declared John, despite his many affairs, "and in loving her I am loyal to my wife." In 1961, after painting colorful likenesses of the great, talented, and merely rich, he died in Dorelia's arms.

THE GREATEST TREASURE

By the 1920s the literary, artistic, and political movement known as Surrealism—a term coined by Appollinaire—had succeeded Dada among the avant-garde. Drawing on the Freudian subconscious, Surrealism presented European artists with a distorting mirror that melted the clear delineation of self and other, of logical mind and personal vision. The lid was off the id: writing and painting became cryptic confession, aided or obscured by symbols. We find many menages when we turn to this loose-knit group of creators who lived, worked, and loved in Paris.

Three is the key number in art. Involved are the artist, the model, and the image their relationship produces. Throughout history the artist has painted his, and lately her, beloved, often with a spouse looking on. The canvas elicits its confession, and secret love surfaces as restraint melts like a Dalí watch into the landscape.

There was a spark that ignited the passion of the Surrealists. Her name was Gala, née Elena Dmitrievna Diakonova. Delicate, raven-haired, mysterious, she married poet Paul Eluard and later Salvador Dalí. She inspired poems, paintings, and thirty years of devoted love letters. Eluard always felt that her loving him was an honor.

Paul and Gala were seventeen when they met in 1912 as patients in a tuberculosis sanatorium in Switzerland. Five years later they married in Paris and soon had a daughter, but they rejected any concept of mutual possession, which they considered sentimental and common. Gala had affairs with several of their artistic friends, including Pablo Picasso. Her career as artistic catalyst had begun. By 1929, with lovers on both sides, the couple parted company geographically, though not emotionally or amorously.

Paul wrote from Paris to Gala wherever she happened to be; this continued after their divorce and his marriage in 1934 to Maria Benz, whom he called Nusch. Gala and Dalí married that same year and lived in Spain, but she continued to enjoy an occasional rendezvous with Paul, during which they made love. His romantic letters always included a salute to her anatomy: "I adore your sex, your eyes, your breasts, your hands, your feet, your mouth and your throat, all of my Gala. Freedom makes me faithful." A letter from 1931 reveals the poet's highly charged voyeurism:

Last night there was a broad strip of moonlight in the room and I saw you, really saw you, completely naked and your legs spread and possessed by two men, in the mouth and in the sex. And you were tan and very beautiful. And even now, at the memory of it, I can't help thinking that you are the embodiment of love to me, the most acute embodiment of desire and erotic pleasure. . . .

Why haven't you printed those nude photos of yourself? And I'd like some in which you're making love. And I'd make love with you in front of Nusch, who could only play with herself. . . . You are a marvelous wellspring of imagination and freedom.

Paul's sickly childhood had left him weak and moody. In his letters to Gala, the imagined voyeurism transfers to him some modicum of her sexual energy. He imagines Gala undressed, in love play with himself or other men. In one actual instance the pair would make love as Dalí watched. The Eluards created opportunities for voyeurism. An earlier menage with the expressionist painter Max Ernst began in 1920 and lasted for most of the decade—despite the enmity of Max's wife, who described Gala as "that slithering, glittering creature with dark falling hair [who] reminds me of a panther." The Ernsts and Eluards spent the summer of 1922 together in the Tyrol. Max frequently bedded with the Eluards in their room and romped with Gala in the lake, watched over by a benevolent Paul.

The other man's presence rekindled Paul's poetic flame. In the 1920s Max occasionally lived with the couple in Paris; he painted frescoes on their walls that gave their daughter nightmares. The menage broke up in 1927 after Max, his new second wife, and Paul became embroiled in a three-way row over Gala, who was in Leningrad at the time. Max told his wife that she couldn't hold a candle to Gala. Insults were flung and finally Max made "a boxer's argument." Paul wrote to Gala, "My best friend has hit me, disfigured me. . . . I shall not see Max again. EVER." The friends were later reconciled but the menage wasn't revived.

Paul spent most of the next two years in a TB sanatorium, during which time the entire Surrealist movement was courting Salvador Dalí as a possible recruit. Born in Catalonia, Spain, in 1904, Dalí was ten years younger than the Eluards, suavely handsome, and thoroughly eccentric. It's hard for today's reader to imagine Dalí doing anything unmotivated by his genius for publicity. In the twenties, he was a fashion forecast for the sixties, wearing pearl necklaces, gaudy colors, a huge flower behind his ear. But in 1929 a Surrealist delegation under the Marxist André Breton went to Catalonia to win over the young painter. Unfortunately, Dalí couldn't stop laughing, and only Gala could communicate with him. As the art historian Fiona Bradley writes, "He claimed her for his saviour, his inspiration, and eventually his wife."

To Paul Eluard's surprise, Dalí and Gala instantly became inseparable. She read his tarot cards daily. He couldn't maneuver travel of any kind or make practical decisions without her. If forced to change locations, he attached his paintings to himself by strings. This glorious nutcase had a matching sex life, which may have been driven by his fascination with death.

Dalí's elder brother (also named Salvador) died when the younger boy was little, and despite his father (also Salvador!) being an atheist, the Catholic family mourned incessantly. The brother's photo—he could have been Dalí's twin—was enshrined in the child's bedroom. Young Salvador's earliest sexual involvement was with García Lorca. Years later, on hearing that the great writer had been murdered, Dalí shouted, "Olé!"

Gala was the only woman he ever allowed to touch his body. He dreaded venereal disease and claimed to hate breasts and vulvas; he preferred masturbation to sex. Dalí was a voyeur with a strong exhibitionist bent. Gala, who appreciated her consort's crowd of handsome admirers, offered the painter many opportunities to watch. There was also her dark side, which matched his own.

One real-life scene Dalí biographers are fond of recounting took place on a high cliff. On the brink of sexual contact, Dalí and Gala faced each other on the precipice. He grabbed her hair and demanded she tell him—"in ferociously erotic language that would make them both feel ashamed"—what she wanted him to do to her. "I want you to kill me," she replied. Dalí had found the living link between love and death, which is his major artistic theme.

Dalí and Gala were together for fifty-three years. She built his fame and raised the price of his art. She bragged she could make any of his young friends who became her lovers equally famous. The Surrealists quipped that when a painter had achieved something special, "He must have been in love with Gala." Paul Eluard never stopped loving her. An idealist who remained in Paris through the Nazi occupation, he praised his ex-wife even when she and Dalí fled to Beverly Hills and went the way of glitz, money, and fame.

During their years together, Dalí had an important love affair with his patron, Edward James, godson of Edward VII. Gala grew jealous but James bought her off with expensive gems and Schiaparelli gowns. A brief, most unusual threesome took place during the painting of *Venus Awaiting a Phone Call*, whose model was Ultra Violet, an actress from Andy Warhol's Factory. The third was a lobster, and Dalí is supposed to have tickled Ultra Violet's private parts with the lobster's tail. When she reached to embrace him, he screamed, "Not yet, my little Catholic girl!"

In 1958, at age fifty-four, Dalí embraced his mother's Catholicism. It didn't change his kinky sex life. Gala came to represent an objectification of the artist's vision as well as the means of fulfilling his desires. This he expressed in the absurdly Dalínian, "Good evening Gala. . . . You are me, you are the pupils of my eyes and of your eyes," which could serve as a text for one of the "autoportraits" in which Gala appears in the corner of the artist's eye. He also liked to paint her staring into a mirror that has been removed, so that you see her doubled front and back. As one art critic notes, "The Surrealist mirror is the conjunction of and potential transition between reality and possibility." More down to earth, we are reminded of Woody Allen's producer friend in *Annie Hall*, who describes his time in bed with two young women by exclaiming, "Think of the possibilities!"

Dalí once painted an enchanting portrait of Gala on a cheap paper doily. In his model for so many varied paintings he saw what used to be called a man's "better half." Dalí used his wife to enjoy by proxy the erotic life that his paranoia forbade him. Perhaps such a three-way eroticism is more understandable in the case of a man's physical, rather than psychological, incapacity. This is the theme of the prize-winning 1996 film *Breaking the Waves*, in which the paralyzed victim of an oil-rigging accident hopes for a vicarious sex life. But as employed by Dalí, voyeurism led to a striking creativity rather than the ritual destruction of the woman in which the film indulges.

The bad boy of Surrealism, whose world takes place on the other side of Alice's looking glass, is a more profound painter than the critics have rated him. What he wrote in 1970 applies particularly to his own work: "Let us beware of the contemporary art mess! Perhaps we are throwing away the best of it because the best is always hidden." Gala, Dalí's "greatest treasure," made no attempt to hide her charms. At eighty, after death had overtaken the artist, she pursued the young lead singer of the hit musical *Jesus Christ Superstar!*

THE MAN OF MANY FACES

Picasso and Portraiture, the Museum of Modern Art's comprehensive 1996 show, made clear that portraits were crucial to Picasso's oeuvre and that his approach had revolutionized the genre. His portraits are not likenesses in the conventional sense but depict his own emotions toward the subject—usually one of the women whom he loved and who at times hated him. But when it comes to the women, there is no clear, matching delineation of artistic period: Blue, Rose, Cubist, Surreal. Picasso's "autobiographical portraits," as William Rubin, the show's curator, calls them, overlap not only in style but in substance; the triangles he paints aren't mere geometry. Here is the artist's love life on canvas if we have the wit to see it.

Pablo was born in 1881 in Malaga to a Catalan family. His father was a painter who became a professor of art in Barcelona. Pablo had no normal childhood; like Mozart, he was a prodigy. Early on he did religious paintings and anatomical studies. At the turn of the century his work was influenced by the Post-Impressionists, notably Toulouse-Lautrec. In 1900 Pablo, in the company of his buddy Carlos Casamegas, son of the United States consul in Barcelona, first visited Paris.

The young men shared everything. Carlos paid Pablo's bills, and Pablo introduced his friend to Rosita, his favorite whore. He even did a drawing of the occasion. But the unstable Carlos developed an obsession over Germaine, a model. First he tried to kill her, then he shot himself in front of horrified friends. Shortly thereafter, in 1904, Pablo moved permanently to the City of Light and commenced on the portraits—often of street people—of his Blue period. Their somberness and disillusion directly reflect Pablo's feelings about the loss of Carlos; never again would he grow that close to another man. This period set the precedent for Pablo painting his own state of mind rather than an accurate representation of persons or places.

The handsome but disheveled young Spaniard, with his dark, piercing, almost staring eyes, got to know everybody on the Left Bank: Max Jacob, Modigliani, Cocteau. Henri-Pierre Roché introduced him to Gertrude Stein. Paul Eluard, who recognized his extraordinary genius, grew to idolize him. He offered Pablo his wives and tried to sleep with his mistresses. Eventually Picasso would paint him as a green transsexual, grinning under a straw hat and suckling a cat from one breast. The portrait is comprehensible once we know of Eluard's sickly dependence on the high energy of other creative men and that he tried, in a sense, to get under their skin.

In August Pablo met and made love with Fernande Olivier. The date is visible on a commemorative drawing he did in which her ample hips envelop him, a switch on Dalí's swallowing Gala. They moved in together in Montmartre in a studio in a building they called *"le Bâteau Lavoir"* because it resembled the houseboats on the Seine where women washed clothes. Gertrude Stein wrote that "everything was natural in Fernande." She gave some stability to Picasso's Rose, or Harlequin, period, during which he painted circus people assured of their talent.

However, in Pablo's 1906 portrait of Fernande she looks drawn, tense, with an eyebrow lifted, lips pursed. If Calvin Tomkins is correct that Picasso is "the most autobiographical artist of all time," we can surmise he has been sexually straying, especially from the evidence of his most famous painting, begun this year. *Les Demoiselles d'Avignon* is a collective portrait of five nude and fierce prostitutes who seem real enough. But more important was the portrait of Gertrude Stein, which was abandoned after ninety sittings, until Pablo bought from a thief an ancient Iberian head stolen from the Louvre and his aesthetic underwent a transformation. He was able to finish the Stein portrait without a sitting, producing a masklike result that only she appreciated.

In 1912 Picasso fell for Eva Gouel and parted from Fernande, painting his first Cubist masterpiece, *J'Aime Eva.* But from this point on he would never entirely relinquish a painting style or a woman. He was not the monster the Merchant-Ivory movie *Surviving Picasso* makes him out to be but an artist in need of polarity in order to strike sparks. The tender, placid Eva, Picasso's model for *Ma Jolie,* a term inscribed in several Cubist paintings, died in 1915 of TB. The artist, bereft of emotional support, fell into the clutches of the tempestuous Olga Kokhlova, a Russian ballerina. He married her, thereby combining wife and model in a surrender to orthodoxy that he would come to regret.

Picasso, becoming famous and rich, led the haut-bourgeois life Olga desired. They lived in a fashionable Parisian neighborhood and wintered on the Riviera. In 1921 they had a son. But Picasso was growing bored; he needed a new woman and a new style. William Rubin suggests that he found love with Sara Murphy, the wife of Gerald Murphy, then a painter himself. The Murphys, Americans of sufficient means, became famous for their image as the ideal expatriate couple and for their friends, who included Ernest Hemingway. Gerald was stylish, elegant, and, according to Hemingway, bisexual; Sara was beautiful, sympathetic, and, according to Rubin, she engaged in an affair with Picasso in the summer of 1923 at Antibes.

Pablo painted Sara with great tenderness in a variety of styles. The painter stepped back to a classical realism and beauty of line. All in all he would do some two hundred drawings and forty oil paintings during this entire period, using Sara as a model far more often than his wife. Pablo portrayed Sara and his own son Paolo in the adoring *Mother and Child*, which he purposely misdated to throw Olga off the scent. Sara was the famous *Woman in White*, the monument of Picasso's neoclassic period. Whatever Olga suspected, Picasso would have kept her in the dark. This didn't prevent him from dressing Sara in Olga's clothes—in a painting and perhaps in life, a favorite turn-on for some husbands.

Rubin suggests that Gerald knew and approved of Sara's liaison with Pablo and was himself engaged in an affair with Cole Porter. Men with a feminine side did fall for Picasso's gargantuan energy, and he was more successful in conducting a menage a trois that included an approving husband than with his wife and a model or mistress. In the early 1930s Picasso found a new mistress, the very young, blond, physically satisfying Marie-Thérèse Walter. Olga's jealousy grew more vehement—she is painted with a pitchfork tongue—and in 1935 they separated. She continued to haunt him on occasion. After Marie-Thérèse bore him a child, thus becoming his de facto wife, Pablo took the more volatile Dora Maar, a Yugoslav photographer, as his mistress. The women tolerated each other, but there was no love lost between them.

Picasso had an acquisitive urge for art and women and rarely gave either away. When questioned on his mania for keeping things, he responded, "Why should I throw away that which was kind enough to reach my hands?" In his fifties, the artist alternated between painting the sunny Marie-Thérèse, the chief model of his Surreal period, and Dora, whose rich black hair and intense eyes made a startling contrast. He found in the latter a perfect inspiration for his Expressionist agonies and a companion in his anti-fascist efforts, indeed a collaborator who photographed and aided in composing the *Guernica*.

Typically, Picasso tucked Marie-Thérèse away at a rural retreat while he held court with Dora in Paris. At first, in 1937, Picasso painted a beautiful, serene Dora. Marie-Thérèse showed up on canvas flabbier and uglier. Gradually each woman accepted the existence of the other. Every Monday and Thursday, Picasso visited Marie-Thérèse and their daughter. He sometimes painted identically posed portraits of the two women, or he mixed their clothing. When he was in residence with one, he wrote passionate love letters to the other.

Françoise Gilot, a later mistress, wrote a memoir entitled *Life with Picasso*. She is made the narrator of *Surviving Picasso*—the shift in the title expresses a very different concept—and not surprisingly she disapproved of the movie. Picasso had enough distance from himself to describe to her the scene that ensued when Marie-Thérèse showed up to demand that he choose between her and Dora. "I decided I had no interest in making a decision," recalled Picasso ten years later. "I was satisfied with things as they were. I told them they'd have to fight it out among themselves. So they began to wrestle. It's one of my choicest memories." Picasso continued to paint and live with both women, and he didn't permit even the Nazis to upset his routine. But he couldn't have been entirely comfortable with both women, and occasionally a third, claiming ownership of him.

Frustration, incompleteness, may have built the desire that fueled the artist's work. This can be seen in the 1932 *Girl Before a Mirror*, which is a mixed Surreal and Cubist portrait allegedly of Marie-Thérèse. Looking more closely, the face before the mirror is split in two halves. One is blond with white skin and an innocent softness, like other paintings of Marie-Thérèse. The other half is of a dark woman with red lips and cheeks and deep, green-black eyes—Dora. The woman in the reflection presents still another face, with dark red and green features, a nose very different from the split-creature who faces the glass. She is a third woman—Olga perhaps, or one yet to come.

In contrast, Picasso more easily formed a menage with another man whom he trusted and admired, Paul Eluard, the writer of passionate Surrealist poetry. In 1936 Picasso illustrated Eluard's poems. Paul, who finally let go of Gala, married a fragile, exotic waif whom he met streetwalking in Paris. He dubbed her "Nusch the perfect," and she became the inspiration for some of Picasso's most tender portraits. Nusch had a delicate, vulnerable beauty that harked back to the painter's Rose period. In the summer of 1936, according to Arianna Huffington, Paul offered "the woman he loved so passionately to the friend he also loved with passion, a form of primitive sharing and ultimate bonding, new neither to Picasso nor to Eluard." There is more to it than that; this is the forming of a threesome in order to multiply creativity. Art is a communal affair replete with artists borrowing not only each other's lovers but, sometimes more importantly, each other's ideas.

Certainly Paul and Pablo's friendship figured into the menage, as well as the dejection shown by Dora, whom Picasso no longer favored. While he painted her with a dog face or as the famous weeping woman, his portraits of Nusch are much lighter but still moving. After she died in 1946, the shattered Eluard moved in with Picasso and his current mistress, Françoise. He proposed marriage to the cast-off Dora. Huffington concludes that "loving someone Picasso had loved . . . becoming a vehicle for Dora to re-enter their circle as Madame Paul Eluard, creating a fascinating new foursome with Dora, Françoise and Pablo—it suddenly seemed the best possible arrangement in his vision of the best of all possible worlds." Dora refused the gentle poet, allegedly replying, "After Picasso, only God."

After the war Picasso—"a mighty ego," as Norman Mailer terms him—moved to the Riviera and entered on a long, productive old age. He acquired many things, including châteaus, but he only had strength left to dominate one woman at a time. Like Oedipus, he'd lived out his fantasies and, better, painted them. We don't yet fully understand him and have to be content with surmising Picasso. A criticism free of moral blame accepts Picasso and his work according to its inherent worth. We give the last word on the painter to Norman Mailer: Picasso was "the embodiment of a mighty ego: That is equal to stating that he was not vain except in the largest manner—he was wholly dedicated to the importance of his work."

THE EXISTENTIAL FIGURE

James Lord, the biographer of Alberto Giacometti, admitted that the sculptor "sometimes liked a third person present at moments of physical intimacy." In fact, he loved and needed a menage. All artists are voyeurs to some degree, and all are exhibitionists because they must at least exhibit their artworks, in which, if they are any good, their soul is revealed. Artists are inspired by models and fantasies about models. The menage of artist, model, and wife domesticates this inherently erotic situation. But Giacometti, in what we may call a French twist, put his wife and his favorite male model together in Paris during the 1950s.

Alberto was born in 1901 in Italian-speaking Switzerland. Thin and bushy-haired, with an overly large head and elongated arms and hands, he resembled one of his own sculptures. Early on he preferred prostitutes, remarking, "They present the bill right away. The others hang on and never let you go." In contrast to Picasso, he was obsessed with living provisionally, with not owning things. While he kept his emotional range narrow, his longest-lasting attachment was to his brother Diego. The pair set up an atelier in Paris in 1925 and, under the banner of Surrealism, soon prospered.

Giacometti couldn't brook the dogma of the Surrealists, either their leftist politics or their insistence that he not sculpt from models. He was expelled from their group in the 1930s, but in wartime Paris he fell in with Jean-Paul Sartre and Simone de Beauvoir. Returning to Switzerland, the sculptor laid low and met Annette Arm, whom he would marry after the war in Paris. For sexual rapport, the pair always depended on thirds. As Lord puts it, Giacometti found in "the repeated proof of others' desire the most satisfying affirmation of his own." Perhaps for some related reason, Giacometti, who attempted likenesses, could only sculpt figures that were at first so small they fit into a matchbox. Later, his figures became severely elongated and distorted. By the 1950s these later sculptures had made him famous, but Giacometti still obliged Annette to continue modeling and to share a poor studio with him.

The sculptor became fascinated by a Japanese professor named Isaku Yanihara, who modeled day and night for him, and he encouraged Isaku to sleep with Annette. Giacometti was so taken by the strong jaw, high forehead, and piercing eyes of this foreign man that he became passionately involved with him. Eventually the sexual rapport of the two men eclipsed the liaison between Isaku and Annette. She would grow jealous, drink, and throw tantrums until Isaku appeased her again. Fortunately the professor was a student of Existentialism and able to postpone his return home.

While it lasted, their menage a trois proved fruitful for all concerned. Giacometti, gratified by his wife's happiness, also enjoyed the stimulus to his own ardor. "See how happy she looks," he remarked. "Since I love her, isn't it natural I should be glad?" Isaku wrote glowing poetry about the couple, describing Annette as a smiling angel alongside her husband. According to Lord, Annette "could love two men without losing her sense of wholeness." More to the point, she accepted the primacy of art to them both. The relations of the three and the work they accomplished are inextricable.

Giacometti's sculpture began to more closely resemble his own body, though in an exaggerated form. By 1960 his artistic (and therefore erotic) focus shifted to a petite, brown-haired prostitute known as Caroline, who had connections to the mob. Annette was enraged when Isaku, returning to Paris for the summer, also fell for Caroline, and this new threesome of the artist and his models would go out clubbing at night. Or Giacometti and Caroline, far more intense as artist and model than as lovers, would go to an obscure hotel. Here, finding a third, "Alberto was able to see what he needed to see"—as Lord delicately phrases it. Meanwhile Diego also despised this "common whore and tawdry chiseler" on whom his brother lavished huge sums. The symbiosis of the Giacometti brothers was sundered.

With Caroline, Alberto became his art. Staring at her for hours, he absorbed her beauty and youth, which gave him new life. Mentally at least, he crossed to the other side of artistic creation, like a movie director who jumps in front of the camera. He regarded Caroline, who had a collection of toads, a pet crow, and a dog named Merlin, as an enchantress. His sculpting and sexual talents only seemed to improve until in 1964, Alberto Giacometti passed away. He had led a modest, unconventional, and artistically fulfilling life, nearly always in a threesome as he chose.

It was Henry Lamb who introduced the shy, quiet Stanley Spencer to the circle of Augustus John, critic Roger Fry, and Lady Ottoline Morrell—the world of important commissioned artists. The trouble was that Spencer came from Cookham, a village in Berkshire. He returned there after graduating from Slade and began to paint huge canvases featuring the villagers in biblical scenes. Our own favorite is a takeoff on Leonardo's *Last Supper* that shows the enormous clodhopper feet of Jesus and his disciples sticking out from under the table. You could take this boy out of the village, but he would always come back to it.

Stanley was born in 1893 into a musical family and said he wanted to paint with the ease of Bach or Beethoven. He came away from Slade with little except the advice of a professor who told him, "Think of the form and the roundness of form . . . expression, not style." Stanley's portraits and landscapes expressed great vitality and a weird joy for living. In his best-known work, an eighteen-foot-high *Resurrection in Cookham Churchyard*, the rustics of his village rise from their graves. In their midst a small, naked Stanley (he was only a bit over five feet tall) looks off in the distance, while his first wife, plump, maternal Hilda, is portrayed three times, smelling flowers or reclining on a tomb. From the center of the painting a group of Africans emerge from the soil. Life throbs in the graveyard.

Stanley had grown up listening to the Bible and considered himself a Christian. He believed that free, fully expressed love, including sexual freedom and involving all races and religions, could lead to salvation and high artistic achievement. He'd married Hilda Carline, the sweetheart of his student days, and they had two daughters. She grew bored with Cookham and took long trips with the girls and long naps when her husband expounded on his views of sexuality. In the 1930s he wrote, "During the war, when I contemplated the horror of my life and the lives of those with me, I felt the only way to end the ghastly experience would be if everyone suddenly decided to indulge in every degree and form of sexual love, carnal love, bestiality, anything you like to call it. These are the joyful inheritances of mankind."

During one of Hilda's absences Stanley took up with Patricia Preece, who lived on the moor with her girlfriend Dorothy. They were both painters, quite poor, and they were probably lesbians. Patricia was tall and elegant, upper class and sophisticated, the opposite of Hilda. She posed in the buff for Stanley. The village peeked and gossiped, but at first Hilda and the new model got on well. "Patricia supplies what I miss in you," Stanley wrote his wife. "You supply what I miss in her. You each make the other supportable and enjoyable." Hilda also enjoyed Patricia and even painted her. But she was shocked when in 1936 Stanley asked her for a divorce in order to remarry.

Stanley had been conned into this move, signing over his property to Patricia. He began to spend lavishly on her wardrobe, asking her to parade before him in tony London shops in fancy underwear and very high heels. Patricia would later call Stanley's taste "execrable . . . flashy blouses, gaudy hats, hideously embroidered underclothes," and she hinted that he was a foot fetishist. Obviously, he was dressing her like the prostitute he fantasized about having. Once the new couple got married, Patricia took off on a honeymoon—with Dorothy but minus Stanley, who was left to paint in Cookham. He responded by inviting Hilda to return, bedding her, and demanding that she become his unofficial second wife. "My development as an artist depends on having both of you," he informed the women.

By the time of his death in 1959, Stanley Spencer had been knighted, honored, and grown rich, but neither Patricia nor Hilda would have anything to do with him. He implored the one and wrote hundred-page love letters to the other, even after her death. Patricia, now Lady Spencer, was heard to remark, "There was something appalling about Stanley."

The artist's paintings became his sex life. He portrayed himself as beyond gender—an adoring girl, a leering old man, or a passionate sunflower. Stanley Spencer became a one-person menage a trois.

"EROTIC DREAMS IN PARIS"
In contrast with Spencer, Leonore Fini, whose January 1996 obituary in *The Guardian* was entitled "Erotic Dreams in Paris," constructed a successful lifelong menage with two men who were each the sort to have a wife and mistress. Termed the last of the Surrealists, Fini defied category. She wanted to be known not as a female painter but simply as a painter. Born of Italian and Slav parents, she grew up in Trieste in the circle of James Joyce and Rainer Maria Rilke.

Her large outpouring of work beginning in 1936 includes automatic drawings, book illustrations, clothes design, and paintings in oil, gouache, and watercolor. One show of her "fantastic art" at New York's Museum of Modern Art was introduced by Paul Eluard. From the 1940s on, she designed for musicians, playwrights, and choreographers, including Jacques Ibert, Benjamin Britten, Jean Cocteau, and Balanchine. Fini was in great demand for her gorgeous style as well as her art. Elsa Schiaparelli lent her gowns for the publicity value. At one opening she wore a Siberian wolf fur coat with nothing underneath. On another occasion she was photographed wearing only black feathers. In the late 1930s, she took up with Max Ernst and boarded the merry-go-round of the Eluards, Picasso, and Dalí.

Fini's surreal paintings express an inner reality with female forms floating in the air, gliding on swings, and traveling through landscapes that subvert logic with a dreamlike ambiguity. A number of her paintings show groups of three, expressing an underlying relationship among the subjects. *Prima Ballerina* shows two women dressing a third, whose gossamer wings envelop them all. *Capital Punishment* also shows three women: one, a judge naked except for high heels, contemplates a goose, whose long phallic neck is stretched and drooping. The goose is held up by a second girl who kneels before the judge, while a third woman, eyes covered to represent justice, grasps a long knife. Fini was fond of painting herself with dark, catlike eyes and a sensuous mouth.

She didn't believe in marriage or motherhood. "I belong with the idea of Lilith," she wrote; "my universe is that of the spirit." Nonetheless, like certain other women painters—Carrington, Frida Kahlo, Georgia O'Keeffe—she needed two fleshly lovers at once to inspire her. Before World War II she pried loose from the service of fascism the Italian Count Stanislav Lepri. She also attracted Polish writer Constantin Jelenski. All three lived together harmoniously in Paris for forty years producing art. Little is known of their private lives, and we lack portraits of these two formidable gentlemen. But we know that until the end, they remained enamored of the woman who called herself "the anti-Eve."

The men and women influenced by the Surrealist movement explored the fertile soil of the female psyche either as artists, spouses, or models, lovers all. Often they shared meager lodgings, crusts of bread, and lumpy beds, suffering society's neglect or the pains of jealousy. The poverty and irregularity of *la vie de Bohème* don't necessarily lead to art. But creativity often requires a group effort, involving the artist, his/her inspiration or model, and the artist's family, who act as support. This spirit of generosity, an opening of consciousness beyond the self, makes both the menage a trois and fine art possible. Love and compassion are the fruits, just as much as art, of this shared spirit.

part six

THE SEX OF POLITICS

chapter 21

STATE SECRETS

{François and Danielle Mitterrand and Anne Pingeot;
Émile and Alexandrine Zola and Jeanne Rozerot;
Charles Parnell and Katie and Willy O'Shea;
Franklin and Eleanor Roosevelt and
Missy LeHand and Earl Miller; the Kennedys}

I would rather have a president who does it to women
than a president who does it to his country.
ATTRIBUTED TO SHIRLEY MacLAINE

$\mathcal{F}$ORMER PRESIDENT FRANÇOIS MITTERRAND,
the longest-serving French leader since Napoleon III, passed away on January 8, 1996, in Paris. In accordance with his will, he was buried in his hometown, Jarnac, and shortly thereafter his most carefully guarded secret was revealed. Mitterrand's will stipulated that his wife Danielle and their two sons, as well as his longtime mistress Anne Pingeot and their daughter Mazarine, accompany his casket to the grave. The *New York Times* wrote that they all did so "with such grace that they evoked sympathy and admiration" for a man whose chameleon-like career had made him a sort of French Richard Nixon. However, the existence of Mitterrand's second family, which he had supported at state expense in a government-owned apartment in the shadow of the Eiffel Tower, did not destroy his reputation. On the contrary, Mitterrand's menage a trois appears to have secured his place in history!

In 1994 the magazine *Paris Match* broke the story of how the president doted on his twenty-year-old daughter by Pingeot, an art historian. The cover photo of father and daughter was taken as they exited a trendy restaurant, showing that this was truly an open secret. Nonetheless the magazine was attacked for invading Mitterrand's privacy—to which its editor replied that a decade earlier, during a breakfast with journalists, the president had already admitted to having a second family.

Suppose President Bill Clinton casually remarked that he had a daughter by Gennifer Flowers and that she was lodged at Blair House? Fancy the American press sitting on that for ten years! The French expect figures of power to be sexually potent and to have discreet outside interests, while the British national pastime has become voyeuristically pursuing copulating royals. This starkly contrasts with the American demand that our politicians live monogamously with their sometimes alcoholic, drug-taking spouses. *Vive la différence!*

Though Mitterrand generally kept his two families apart, they weren't strangers to each other. French political insiders had known him to vacation with his wife, Danielle, with whom he remained close, and his adored Mazarine. True, his sons refused to officially recognize their half-sister until their father did, but the watershed occurred in 1994, when Mitterrand underwent a second operation for cancer. Wife, mistress, and children closely cooperated to manage the president's last year. After the funeral they jointly protested against photos of his corpse, which again *Paris Match* splashed on its cover.

However, all along both families had kept a far more important secret than that of their domestic arrangements: Mitterrand, since 1981 when he was first elected, suffered from terminal prostate cancer. The only other person to know was his doctor, Claude Gubler, whose book *Le Grand Secret* claims that the president was sometimes too ill to carry out his duties. Gubler disguised the nature of the illness for fourteen years, and because he told all after Mitterrand's death, he may be subject to discipline by the French medical association.

For a political figure, what is secret and damning in one culture boosts his poll ratings in another. "French politicians can sleep in peace," quipped the editor of *Paris Match*. "And with whomever they please." Although no French politician has had to resign over an extramarital relationship, it's not that anything goes. A menage a trois is designed to regulate and even to provide cover for a sexual liaison. Frenchmen, to their credit, have been able to strike the right balance between their public lives and private desires.

ÉMILE ZOLA'S TWO AFFAIRS

François Mitterrand was famous for his way with women. But earlier, in the 1890s, the more reserved Émile Zola achieved an amity between his wife and mistress that became crucial in his fight for justice, particularly to free Captain Alfred Dreyfus from prison on Devil's Island.

Zola was a respected novelist who unlike the elder Dumas or Victor Hugo, was monogamous at heart. But his childless marriage had grown stale when in 1888 he took Jeanne Rozerot, his wife Alexandrine's maid, as his lover. The author, fat and middle-aged, though fearful of his possessive spouse, set Jeanne up in an apartment near his Parisian dwelling. The situation grew complicated when Jeanne gave birth to a daughter, Denise, and afterward a son, Jacques. Alexandrine knew nothing until she was informed in 1893 by an anonymous letter. That evening the servants scurried for safety while she threw plates and furniture at her husband. Alexandrine charged over to Jeanne's and destroyed Émile's letters to her— foolish behavior if she was interested in a divorce. However, Alexandrine remained the wife of the famous author, and he would have to bear years of her recriminations.

After the initial crisis, Zola split his time between the two households. He slept most nights by his wife's side, slipping over to his *maison sécondaire* every afternoon. He suffered that he could not acknowledge his mistress and children publicly. He wrote to Jeanne, "I had hoped to bring some happiness to your youth and not to make it necessary for you to live like a recluse. I should have been so happy to be young with you . . . to have carried my darling little girl in my arms, and to have shown Jacques how to make a sand castle." That Zola never considered a divorce has outraged at least one contemporary American biographer, who posthumously berates the author for not thinking of his children.

In fact, Zola showered them with affection. Later in life, Denise, writing of her indulgent father, recalled, "How many treats there were!" Jeanne accepted a sheltered life, and eventually Alexandrine accepted the children. A more insightful biographer, Frederick Brown, has written, "In the course of time, [Zola's] shuttling between his two lives had made the boundary that separated them indistinct enough for Alexandrine herself to cross over." By 1895 she began to accompany him regularly on strolls with Denise and Jacques, bringing gifts for the children, watching them play "with a benevolent smile." The two households, though separated, had become united. As Denise reminisced, "we loved one another dearly, parents and children, nothing seemed capable of diminishing this happiness."

The menage a trois was, on the whole, a blessing to Alexandrine. While she remained on polite terms with Jeanne, she embraced the children with "grandmotherly solicitude." Both women realized that a divorce would have finished Zola's career, not as a novelist, perhaps, but as a moral force. In the corrupt and rapacious Third Republic, he was one of the few spokesmen for the poor and disadvantaged. When in 1898 he wrote his famous editorial "J'accuse," which accused the military command of framing Dreyfus because he was a Jew, Zola became the subject of continual abuse in the press. The right wing hunted for any weapon to use against him, yet so fixed was his reputation for domesticity that his second family went undiscovered. Zola saved Dreyfus, and he helped to save France from the disgrace of *l'affaire Dreyfus* by exposing the most reactionary elements in the government and army.

His enemies may have retaliated by murdering him. After Émile Zola died in 1902 under mysterious circumstances and his body was laid to rest in the Pantheon, Alexandrine and Jeanne grew to be close friends. Frederick Brown wrote in *Zola* that the two widows formed "a pious sisterhood, cherishing in Denise and Jacques the man they had divided between themselves." Alexandrine became the children's second mother, saw to their education, and ensured that they could legally adopt their father's name. Zola's two families now blended smoothly into one menage.

ACROSS THE CHANNEL
Some years ago there was a perennial hit show in the West End called *No Sex, Please, We're British*. The activities of Britain's politicians have belied the title: they have had numerous extramarital affairs, gay and straight. When their bed partner's spouse connived in the affair, they got away unscathed. Lord Palmerston, Queen Victoria's prime minister, was linked with a number of ladies of the court, including Lady Jersey. Her husband, when asked why he refused to duel in defense of her honor, replied that he would have had to fight every gentleman in town. David Lloyd George, the World War I leader, fathered a child by his doctor's wife. He wiggled out of the divorce case by pinning the blame on another of her lovers.

Ireland, however, is a different story, having held its heroes to stricter standards. The publicizing of a discreet menage, for example, brought down the greatest of Irishmen, Charles Stewart Parnell.

When in 1937 Hollywood filmed the life of Parnell, he was a figure so esteemed that only Clark Gable could play him—except that Gable gave a weak imitation of Parnell's inner fire and exterior ice. Despite a literate script by John Van Druten, *Parnell* was a clunker. It accurately depicted the romantic liaison between Ireland's uncrowned king and Katherine O'Shea and how Parnell's love for the woman he called "little wifie," though she was married to Member of Parliament William O'Shea, cost him his career and delayed his country's independence. What the movie lacked—a concept that still eludes the major studios—was the menage a trois, which the treacherous O'Shea breached.

Charles Stewart Parnell was born in County Wicklow in 1846 to a Protestant landowning family. Charles's mother, daughter of an American admiral, spoke out against English rule in Ireland. Parnell left Cambridge before graduation, seeking his destiny. He was tall and athletic, and his dark brown beard and mustache added distinction to his looks. Late in life, Katherine O'Shea wrote a biography of Parnell that recalled how his brown eyes had "an odd compulsion and insistence in their direct gaze. . . . A thousand little fires seemed to burn and flicker in their somber depths." Katie, as she became universally known, revealed that the iron-willed patriot was "subject to night terrors, very much as a highly strung child is." Parnell suffered from a congenital weak heart, and only Katie's incessant care kept him alive into middle age.

In 1875 this proponent of home rule for Ireland was elected to the British House of Commons. Not yet thirty, Parnell had a talent for bringing Irishmen of different persuasions together. After the election of 1880, he was the acknowledged head of the Home Rule party in Parliament and the Land League in Ireland, which fought against landlords who evicted their tenants. Among his most enthusiastic supporters were the ex-lieutenant William Henry O'Shea, elected to represent County Clare, and his attractive, lively wife.

Willie, then thirty-five, was a handsome Irish Catholic who sat his horse superbly and affected a clipped English accent. A dandy, he involved himself in mining ventures in Spain that drained his capital. Neither he nor Katie had enough money to support their lifestyle or Willie's political ambition. Their only hope lay with Katie's Aunt Ben, a widow of eighty-seven who provided a house for them near her at Eltham. She had promised to leave her fortune (worth ten million dollars in today's money) to her favorite niece. Katie was the daughter of an Anglican clergyman who'd been chaplain to the queen. She was literate, musical, and spirited, alluring rather than beautiful. The mother of three, she remained fond of her husband, but after thirteen years that included separations and quarrels, their marriage had cooled.

Willie soon urged Katie, a gifted hostess, to invite Parnell to one of the dinners they gave at their townhouse in London. Her repeated invitations brought no reply. Finally, on the June day of her husband's maiden speech, Katie went to the House of Commons, where she put herself in the way of her quarry. She recalled that a rose fell from her bodice and Parnell picked it up, brushed it with his lips, and placed it in his button-hole. In a style more romantic than a Hollywood movie, love bloomed at first sight.

Katie O'Shea brought warmth and comfort into Parnell's drudging existence. She made certain her "king" wore wool socks, rubbed his shoulders with firwood oil, and cheered on his cause from the sidelines. By autumn Parnell was already writing to "my own love." Katie always insisted that her husband knew of and encouraged her in the affair. Willie was witty but cruel, a raconteur who was often away at dinner parties. He was an opportunist, while Parnell, considered aloof, never varied from his heartfelt goal of freeing Ireland. Opposite types, these two men were to share not only one woman but a common destiny.

Conditions in Ireland grew desperate just as Parnell and Katie were falling in love. Famine racked the country, and the tenant farmers couldn't afford to pay their rents. Landlords employed soldiers to evict them, but their neighbors would boycott (the term originated at this juncture) any new tenants, refusing to sell them necessities. An English witness wrote that as Parnell toured the countryside and cheered the folk, "his journey-ings can be compared only to the progress of Caesar." Then he would disappear for a week at a time, sequestered with Katie at Eltham while Willie luxuriated in Paris on so-called business.

Suddenly in July 1881, Willie, returning to England, challenged the leader of his party to a duel. Willie had learned of Parnell's staying at Eltham without his permission. This created more of an appearance of impropriety than when he was present, off in a different wing of the large country house. Ten years later, Katie's attorney replied to a divorce action by Willie, "The Petitioner constantly connived at and was accessory to the said alleged adultery from the autumn of 1880." But though Willie was currying Parnell's favor, he wanted to keep control of the goings-on, and he was terrified that Katie's Aunt Ben would hear talk of an affair.

Political rather than amorous jealousy caused Willie to play the aggrieved husband. He was a rake who gave his reserved seats in the Ladies' Gallery of the House of Commons to his mistresses, while his wife had to sit in Parnell's seats. Willie wrote the challenge to Parnell dur-ing the wee hours of the morning from the London home of his current mistress: Anna Steele, Katie's sister! Willie knew that to most men adul-tery meant your wife's affair with her lover, not yours with another woman. He didn't wish to be thought of as a cuckold. But he made it clear he could be bought off, provided the lovers paid more attention to appearances and to his importance.

While Ireland drifted into rebellion, Parnell's popularity soared. Pitched battles were followed by the suspension of the Home Rulers from Parliament. Willie, the temporizer, was every day more unpopular in Clare. Although the government readied coercive measures, Prime Minister William Gladstone was sympathetic to a form of Irish home rule. Willie became the confidential link between Parnell and Gladstone, and it indeed took a man deluded about his own importance to run errands between these giants. Ironically, Katie similarly acted as the hinge between her two men. Thus on her familial diplomacy rested the fate of Ireland.

Parnell called Katie his "queen" and signed his many intimate letters to her, "Your Own King," but she still called Willie her "boysie." In Parnell's absence, she continued to sleep with Willie at least until 1882 and probably longer. Was this out of habit or merely to pacify him? Probably Katie retained a good deal of affection for the man she had married so young and hopefully. Willie never became as infamous to her as he did to history. When Katie became pregnant in the summer of 1881, with a child who would die in infancy, each man supposed it was his.

The government, grown desperate, arrested Parnell, and from October 1881 to May 1882 he was a prisoner in Dublin's Kilmainham jail. Well treated, his main concern was that Katie not be at risk. He wrote ordinary letters to her but used invisible ink between the lines to conduct business. She passed on his proposals to Willie, and he forwarded them to Gladstone. In this way, the menage of convenience did its sub-rosa political work. In the mid-1990s, we have seen the British government negotiate with Sinn Fein, the political wing of the Irish Republican Army, which it had branded as terrorist. In the early rounds of such talks secrecy is essential and depends on the reliability of the go-between. Willie performed well, and even the infamous murders at Phoenix Park, Dublin, when the English chief secretary for Ireland was hacked to death by extremists, failed to extinguish the negotiations. A concerned Willie went to the authorities to secure police protection for Parnell, once again living at Eltham with Katie and himself.

After 1882 Katie gave birth to two more daughters, Clare and Katherine. Willie claimed they were his, but he eventually admitted they were Parnell's. Until 1886 the menage ran smoothly. Parnell visited Eltham with or without his host present, and Willie sometimes stayed with Parnell at his estate in Ireland. In 1883 they all three took the children to the beach at Brighton. Willie could afford no scandal while Aunt Ben lived, and she stubbornly kept on living. Besides, he was playing a duplicitous game with Gladstone by secretly attaching himself to another wing of the Liberal party, which was less accommodating to the Irish. In sum, Willie was a traitor. The reward he expected was to become chief secretary for Ireland.

In the movie *Parnell*, Katie O'Shea was played by Myrna Loy, an actress known for her intelligence. The real Katie took over from her husband, whom Parnell did not entirely trust, as his personal emissary to Gladstone. The prime minister was known to intimates for his "night walks," on which he consorted with prostitutes for the alleged purpose of reforming them. Now he had a private interview with Katie (unbeknownst to Willie) in which they discussed Parnell and, according to her autobiography, Gladstone's "wonderful eagle's eyes showed just sufficient admiration in them to savour of homage without offense." On this metaphysical menage—Gladstone, Katie O'Shea, and Parnell—was founded the alliance between the Liberals and Home Rulers that should have resulted in an independent Ireland—a step that taken in time, would have immeasurably improved Anglo-Irish relations.

In the general election of 1885 the Home Rulers elected a sufficient number of delegates to hold the balance of power in Parliament between the Liberals and Conservatives. Katie began to visit Gladstone at Downing Street, taking him drafts of Parnell's proposals. Since her husband had become anathema to the Irish voters, she attempted to secure a government post for him. Willie, to squelch gossip, assured the *Pall Mall Gazette* that he had no objections to the friendship between his wife and Parnell. No one really cared. In 1886 Gladstone introduced a historic home-rule bill, but it was narrowly defeated. The Conservatives were voted into office, which they held for most of the next twenty years. Willie, who resigned from Parliament, kept up the facade of the menage, which had conceived and was parenting a total of five children. Once Aunt Ben died in 1889, Willie sued Katie for divorce, naming Parnell as corespondent.

Aunt Ben had left her fortune to her niece but in a manner that prevented Willie from getting hold of it. Furious, he joined other relatives in contesting the will. If it could be shown in court that Katie had deceived both her husband and aunt, she would lose not only her inheritance but the children. Contemporaries believed that behind Willie were British politicians intent on keeping hold of Ireland. Indeed, this was no replay of the heroic Nelson-Hamilton menage that saved England but rather the disintegration of a productive triad into a vicious love triangle. Willie, on the threat that he would "send a blackguard's reputation with his deluded countrymen into smithereens," savaged his native land.

Parnell refused to contest the divorce. He wanted Katie free of Willie at any cost. He may have supposed that his reputation would see him through. However, the judge's damning him as a man "who takes advantage of the hospitality offered him by the husband to debauch the wife" foreshadowed his troubles with the Catholic church. James Joyce wrote, "The priests and priests' pawns broke Parnell's heart and hounded him into his grave." But it was Parnell's choice of Katie over Ireland that turned the Irish people against him. He and she were married and lived together lovingly until he died in her arms in 1891. "Kiss me, sweet wifie," the exhausted patriot whispered, "and I will try to sleep a little."

As Parnell's biographer, Robert Kee, writes, "in Catholic Ireland and in Nonconformist Britain, adultery itself was the only moral issue." It was inconceivable to the folk that Willie had connived at the affair in order to make his reputation. Later times would make him a despised figure. Ironically, though Willie O'Shea won the divorce case, legal fees ate up his gains. He learned the meaning of the Spanish gypsy curse: "May you have lawsuits—and win them."

UP FROM HYDE PARK

It is a feminist maxim that the personal is political. For office seekers or holders, politics gets personal. But is there a relationship between a figure's political stance and the manner in which he or she beds down? Do we find the menage a trois, which can seem either adventurous or conservative, on the left or the right? Whether or not a person's party defines his or her partying, it is class, in the larger sense, that sets the tone of a threesome. President Franklin Delano and First Lady Eleanor Roosevelt, certainly members of the American aristocracy if we ever had one, were participants in the menage of civility. During their lifetimes, the Roosevelts succeeded in keeping their liaisons, which the historian David M. Kennedy describes as having "the air of a Borgia court," shielded from public view. Even today, their carryings-on at the family estate of Hyde Park or the White House are hard to decipher.

In September 1918, the tall, bony, bucktoothed wife of the assistant secretary of the navy, as much a wallflower as he was a handsome, debonair "sport," discovered a packet of incriminating letters from her husband's mistress, Lucy. During a thirteen-year marriage Eleanor had borne Franklin six children, five of whom were still living. For much of that time she had been indisposed. In wartime Washington, where temporarily detached men and women from all over the country were thrown together, it was common for affairs to bloom and then fade. But to this wife, her husband's cheating was aggravated by his mistress's being her social secretary, a woman who was beautiful and pleasing to men, everything Eleanor supposed she was not. Still, the dalliance might have been consigned to the dustbin of local gossip if both her maiden and married name hadn't been Roosevelt.

Eleanor never forgave her husband (and distant cousin) for falling in love with Lucy Mercer. Feeling abused and humiliated, she offered Franklin his freedom. Since Lucy was of a sufficiently patrician background, he might have married her. His monster of a mother, Sara Delano, who'd tyrannized over her son's single and wedded life, found Lucy "*so* sweet and attractive." This time, however, she took Eleanor's side. She thought her son "deserved a good time," but as the father of five, he had better stay married to Eleanor. He was never again to see that Mercer woman. Otherwise Sara was prepared to cut him off without a cent. Personal adviser Louis Howe, dedicated to making a president out of unlikely material, warned Franklin that scandal would mean the end of his political career. The future FDR kept that in mind ever afterward.

The love triangle and its dissolution went a long way toward defining the Roosevelts' relationship. They began to lead independent personal lives, and the gulf widened when Franklin was stricken with polio in August 1921 and during the grueling years of his recovery. Paralyzed from the waist down, he spent much time at Warm Springs, Georgia, where young and pretty Missy LeHand became not only his private secretary but "the junior wife." Eleanor was no nurse, but she was excellent at filling in for Franklin, and she became a force in the Democratic party on her own. She wrote popular articles and campaigned for world peace. Eventually, with the aid of steel braces, Franklin managed to walk. When in 1928 he was elected governor of New York, Eleanor, forty-five, began a long career as the great man's wife. Remarkably, her private life also flowered.

Eleanor insisted on driving her own car, and Franklin assigned state trooper Earl Miller to be her bodyguard. They had first met during World War I when Miller, an amateur boxing champ, had provided security for him. Franklin was impressed by the man's hearty good looks and charm. Miller, once a circus acrobat, was a superb swimmer and marksman and knew judo. Warm, affectionate, and loyal, he provided a physical element for Eleanor that Franklin lacked. Did the governor suppose his friend Earl would become his wife's lover?

Eleanor Roosevelt stemmed, as did Franklin, from an old, landed New York Dutch family. Her uncle Teddy, then president, gave her away at the wedding. But all of Teddy's brothers, including Eleanor's father, were abusive alcoholics. In her teens, Eleanor had to sleep behind a triple-locked door. After her handsome father drank himself to death, her beautiful mother died of grief. Her crotchety grandmother, with whom she lived, refused to fix Eleanor's buck teeth. It is no wonder that Eleanor had empathy for the downtrodden, whether immigrants or poor blacks, but especially for orphans—and her intimate friend Earl was an orphan.

This thirty-two-year-old *cavaliere servente* taught his "Lady," as he called her, to swim, dive, and shoot. He built her a tennis court and played the piano, filling her cottage Val Kill (on the Hyde Park estate but separate from the main house) with music and laughter. They shared a progressive worldview, both were in earnest about issues such as prison reform, and they frequently traveled together on state business. They enjoyed weekends in rustic cabins perched high in the Adirondack Mountains. Eleanor's chronic migraine headaches disappeared. Squired by Earl, she assumed the relaxed look, as Erica Jong says, of a woman who has been "well fucked."

After Franklin was elected president in 1930, he appointed Miller personnel director of the New York Department of Corrections, leaving him behind in Albany. Blanche Cook, who has resurrected the living Eleanor, speculates that "ER's initial panic and reluctance to become First Lady involved, in some part, her impending geographic separation from Earl Miller." It is unnecessary to ascribe Machiavellian intentions to the president-elect. Since the Secret Service would guard Eleanor, the Roosevelts could no longer explain Earl on that basis. But he remained welcome at the White House or for a weekend in the Greenwich Village apartment that Eleanor took in the 1940s. Franklin trusted him with family and political secrets. Earl repaid his confidence with a cavalier's loyalty and willingness to do almost anything for his patron. As he remarked, "I got married in 1932 with plenty of publicity. I got married with someone I wasn't in love with. Same with the second marriage. But I was never successful in killing the gossip."

Part of the problem was the freedom Earl took with his Lady. While both were in bathing suits, he would slip his arm round her waist. She, too, would place her hand suggestively on his knee. This was a physical affair, which even the Roosevelt children couldn't help but notice. James remarked, "I believe there may have been one real romance in Mother's life outside of marriage. Mother may have had an affair with Earl Miller. . . . He became part of the family, too, and gave her a great deal of what her husband and we, her sons, failed to give her. Above all, he made her feel that she was a woman. . . . Their relationship deepened after Father's death and ended only with Mother's death."

Earl and Eleanor's love affair, under the benevolent eye of Franklin, generated a meaty correspondence, which was meticulously destroyed. This is an unfailing sign of carnal goings-on. And contrary to our confessional era, Earl refused to talk about the private lives of the Roosevelts. "I don't cash in on my friends," said the cavalier to reporters. The sentiment is admirable but death to biographers. Fortunately, there is a trove of photos and home movies that Earl and Eleanor took to document their love, and this pictorial record has survived. "You don't sleep with someone you call Mrs. Roosevelt," Earl once remarked. Clearly, there were plenty of times when he called Eleanor something more intimate.

Franklin Delano Roosevelt once referred to himself as a juggler who never let his right hand know what his left was doing. Born to privilege, Franklin grew up pampered by his strong-willed mother and indulged in snobbery by his father, known as the Squire. Whether at Groton or Harvard or serving in the state senate, Franklin was not taken very seriously. He married young against his mother's wishes, quickly produced five young ones, and then began to sow his wild oats. Polio put an end to his carousing and threatened to derail a career running at only half speed. Somewhere in his despair, the man found ways to move a spirit, as well as a body, that had become paralyzed.

Franklin's interest in women was an adjunct to his political life. Aside from his wife and Lucy Mercer, he was most seriously involved with Marguerite (Missy) LeHand. In 1920 Franklin was defeated as Democratic candidate for vice president. In the words of his biographer Joseph Lash, Eleanor hired a "young, pretty, highly competent" campaign worker to assist him with his correspondence. She couldn't have missed that Missy, like Lucy, was tall and blue-eyed. But Missy came from a Massachusetts factory town where she had grown up in her mother's boardinghouse and then gone to secretarial school. She was naturally perceptive and at Hyde Park proved herself indispensable when Franklin came down with polio and Eleanor began to travel for him, Missy's duties expanded to surrogate wife: supervising the house, paying bills, giving the children their allowances.

But there was more. At Warm Springs, where Franklin recuperated, Missy was a kind of psychic nurse, cheerful, attentive, encouraging. "In terms of companionship," economist Eliot Janeway observed, "Missy was the real wife. She understood [Franklin's] nature perfectly." Moving with the Roosevelts to Albany, Missy acted as hostess, played poker with the pals, laughed at Franklin's well-worn salty stories, and in quieter moments, shared his passion for stamp collecting. She was surrogate mother to the children, who adored her. She did the domestic things that Eleanor, caught up in her mission to save the world, would have found dull and taxing.

First when FDR was governor and later when he became president, Missy would organize his day, inviting guests and presiding over the dinner table. If Eleanor arrived, whether at the White House or Hyde Park, Missy smoothly receded into the background. Curtis Roosevelt, a grandson, opined that because Missy came from a lower social class, Eleanor was not threatened by her the way she had been by Lucy Mercer. She was thankful for the freedom Missy's tending to Franklin permitted her. Eleanor was intuitive, and she trusted that Missy's love was for Franklin and not his position. Only when it was suggested, as happened in a *Saturday Evening Post* story in the mid 1930s, that Missy played a central role in presidential politics did Eleanor take offense. Missy always made up to her, writing one Christmas, "Dear ER: I have had such a happy year and I hope you know how very much I appreciate being with you. . . . I love you so much. I never can tell you how very much."

Were relations between Franklin and Missy sexual? Son Eliot wrote, "Everyone in the closely knit circle of father's friends accepted it as a matter of course." Polio had partially paralyzed the president's legs, not his sex. From time to time Missy could be found on his lap, in his arms, or entering his bedroom in her nightclothes. Franklin took a healthy interest in sex generally. On the eve of World War II, with Nazi armies marching over Europe, Roosevelt made a crucial speech, then, in his study, he spoke by phone to Britain's new prime minister, Winston Churchill. Afterward, he turned to Helen Gahagan Douglas, actress and ardent New Dealer: "Now, I want you to tell me exactly what happened under the table at Ciro's between Paulette Goddard and Anatole Litvak." It was the current gossip of Hollywood that the vivacious actress and the Russian-born director, while having dinner at the elegant club where dress was formal, had dived under the table to have a quickie. As moans were heard across the room, waiters rushed to cover up the pair with extra tablecloths. "I love it, I love it!" roared Franklin.

Missy's delicate physique finally buckled under the strain of White House business, however. In 1941 overwork and insomnia culminated in a major stroke that left her partially paralyzed and unable to speak coherently. Franklin responded by ordering round-the-clock nursing care, and he changed his will to leave her half his personal fortune. But he couldn't bear to see her, not even when she was well enough to leave the hospital and walk with the aid of braces.

Eliot Roosevelt felt that his mother was more upset about Missy's illness than Franklin's. Five years earlier, on Christmas, Missy had written to the Roosevelts, "Please let me do things for you—you are the ones who have my love and only real devotion—without that I would have little excuse for taking up space." Now, realizing she could be of little use at the White House, she went to live with her sister where she died at age forty-six. Eleanor, who was writing a syndicated newspaper column, "My Day," stated that Missy's loss would be felt deeply by all who knew her. "She was a member of our family for a good many years," concluded the First Lady.

Although Franklin showed little emotion, Missy's death took its toll, and he soon suffered a minor heart attack. On April 12, 1945, the president was cut down at Warm Springs by a massive stroke. At his side was Lucy Mercer. He had recently given her a photo of them taken in Washington when they'd first met, and there had been a "new blossoming of those old memories." Once the doctor arrived and it was clear the love of her life was dying, Lucy left silently.

Eleanor, who Franklin had confided to Eliot was "the most extraordinarily interesting woman," was shocked to learn that her rival had been present at her husband's death. Once again he had cheated on her. She couldn't forgive Lucy or, to an extent, the man she had married. But she realized that over the course of their life together the self-centered son of Hyde Park had become the international statesman FDR. Eleanor Roosevelt spent the next two decades, until her death in 1962, founding the United Nations and relentlessly pursuing world peace.

DOWN FROM CAMELOT

The thousand days of John F. Kennedy's presidency, with the gracious Jacqueline as First Lady, were sprinkled with recreational menages a trois. Jack's formidable father, Joseph, a Boston-Irish banker, founder of RKO, and later ambassador to England, provided a role model. In December 1927 Joe Kennedy, who according to Gloria Swanson "looked like any average working-class person's uncle," visited her and her husband, a French marquis, at their Palm Beach hotel. After he'd sent the marquis off fishing, Joe attacked Gloria with the energy of "a roped horse, rough, arduous," and she scarcely resisted. After it was quickly over and they lay quietly side by side, she knew she would be his mistress.

Joe was a minor player in the movie business, but he took over Swanson's production company on the promise of making her the greatest star in the world. The petite, slinky Swanson was a silent-film stunner, a sex goddess in a Hollywood just acquiring the knack for creating them. Unfortunately Joe, though a good moneymaker, would fail at both movies and menages.

Joe put the marquis on the payroll, at a distance, and told Rose Kennedy that squiring Swanson around was strictly business. Rose, a mother of eight, looked the other way while Joe humored her with diamond bracelets and a twelve-room colonial house in a posh Westchester neighborhood. He delighted in bringing Gloria's two kids, including little Gloria, age eight, to play with the Kennedy brood. Little Gloria got stuck on Jack, age eleven, but the childhood romance was stillborn. Joe wanted to have a child by the elder Gloria, and though she refused, he coaxed her in 1929 to summer in Hyannis Port with the clan. Rose kept up the pretense of trusting her husband, which led Gloria to wonder, "Was she a fool . . . or a saint? Or just a better actress than I was?"

The height of the menagerie was reached during an ocean crossing by Joe, Gloria, and Rose in which he conspicuously spent more time in the actress's stateroom than his own. So far Joe had lost a bundle on Gloria, but he had backed a talkie and the trip was for the purpose of publicizing it. Once they docked at Le Havre, Rose treated Gloria as a good friend with whom she went shopping for clothes in Paris. Crowds mobbed the tiny star, but Rose was more impressed by Gloria's knowledge of haute couture. When Gloria discovered that her husband the marquis was playing around with a younger actress, she blew up. Rose felt sorry for her, and Joe begged the married couple to keep up their public image. With the menage cracking, Joe, after merging his movie company into RKO, took a five-million-dollar profit and bowed out. He was too late to deter his wife from acquiring jewelry and a wardrobe that would become legendary. The acquiescence of Rose, the first great Kennedy shopper, would cost Joe plenty.

Gloria Swanson's career slid downhill. Her great role wouldn't come until 1950 when as the faded star Norma Desmond in *Sunset Boulevard*, she famously replied to William Holden's put-down, "I *am* big. It's the pictures that got small." Joe and Gloria were still seeing each other into the 1940s. During the late twenties when the affair flourished, Jack Kennedy was entering his adolescence. That his sexual identity was ultimately polyamorous may stem from what he observed at the time. Years later, Joe would brag to son Jack and daughter-in-law Jacqueline about his sexual prowess with Swanson, who he claimed was "insatiable, having orgasms not once but five times a night." Not until Jack became president and was bedding gorgeous but unstable Marilyn Monroe did he have a sex goddess as hot as Dad's.

However, Joe, who liked to hedge his bets, would have been shocked by his son's tolerance for risk. Because of the jiving effects of a mix of steroids and amphetamines, prescribed by a doctor feel-good for a degenerative spinal condition that was kept hushed up, the president demanded his extramarital morsels regularly and often *à trois*. As a lover, Jack Kennedy was no Clark Gable. He was both indiscreet and undiscriminating. Judith Exner, an ex-Mafia moll, reported that he tried to persuade her to join in a threesome with "a tall thin secretarial type in her late twenties with brownish hair and rather sharp features." Jack pressured her, "I know you. I know you'll enjoy it."

Kennedy's presidency began with a shocking debauch on the night of his inauguration. According to David Heymann, a Pulitzer-nominated biographer, Peter Lawford lined up six women as possible bed partners. "Jack chose two of them. This menage a trois brought his first day in office to a resounding close." But the White House *la ronde* had just begun to whirl. Jack Kennedy mixed and matched the sorts of women generally available to politicians in power: call girls were sneaked into the Lincoln bedroom while at times naked secretaries rode the elevator. Whether in the bedroom of Air Force One or hotel rooms on the hustings, Jack took what was handy. As Heymann bluntly writes, "naturally, every local beauty wanted to fuck the president. . . . The parties often involved two or three women."

How much Jacqueline knew remains conjecture. Secret Service agents joined the parties and kept a weather eye out for the First Lady. A few simple precautions were taken; for example, frosted glass was installed around the White House pool. Heymann tells how Ken O'Donnell, a trusted aide, was warned not to disturb his boss, supposedly doing his laps. O'Donnell "barged past the agent into the swimming pool area and found the President relaxing in the pool with two young ladies." Kennedy, unembarrassed, called out, "You dumb prick . . . get lost." Hubris, backed by money and power, goes a long way in obtaining silence.

One recreational menage eerily foreshadows Kennedy's tragic end. In 1960 he met a young Russian woman, later to be implicated in the Profumo sex scandals in London, at a party hosted by singer Vic Damone. According to Heymann, the pair went to bed that night. At their return engagement, Jack requested a spicier scenario. It "involved two other prostitutes dressed as doctor and nurse: in the ensuing sex game, Kennedy played the role of the patient." Which brings to mind that JFK's quickie menages were a sign not of potency but of his need for the ultimate aphrodisiac: three at a time.

Meanwhile Jackie kept her own counsel. But it's worth pointing out that from her father, Black Jack Bouvier, to her second husband, Aristotle Onassis, her karmic involvement was with dangerous, unfaithful men. Among them, if not from them, she got what she wanted.

Politics in the English-speaking world is the last secular profession to demand that its practitioners lead hypocritical sex lives. If the politicians are men, they will be expected to exude a degree of macho sexiness. Those who appear to have been faithful to their wives may occasionally win an election but rarely the public's heart. Roosevelt, Eisenhower, and Kennedy all screwed around, and the electorate sensed it—and rewarded them. But to paraphrase a remark Sam Goldwyn made about Danny Kaye, "nobody wants to fuck Richard Nixon." On the left, those faithful husband types George McGovern and Michael Dukakis stirred little enthusiasm. And we shall see whether true-blue Al Gore does as well as scandal-tarred Bill Clinton.

In pseudo-Victorian style, the life between the sheets of today's president or prime minister must stay undercover. In the eighties, Senator Gary Hart was known to have an unzipped habit, but when the *National Enquirer* published a photo of the presidential candidate with swimsuited model Donna Rice seated on his bare knee, Hart's race was run. Wife Lee's declaration that as long as she didn't mind, why should anyone else, infuriated the voters. Hart had crossed the line not of morality but of secrecy. He had violated the discretion essential to a political menage a trois.

chapter 22

ON THE LEFT

{George Bernard Shaw, May Morris, and Henry Sparling;
Jack Reed, Louise Bryant, and Eugene O'Neill;
Comrades Lenin, Nadezhda Krupskaya, and Inessa Armand}

I am not faithful, but I am attached.
GÜNTER GRASS

*T*HE POLITICS OF SEX—GENDER INEQUAL-
ity and such—is a well-traversed if recently staked-out field. But what
about the sex of politics? Do liberals love longer? Do leftists agree to
mutual arrangements while rightists gun down their cheating spouses? Are
Tories likely to get cozy *à trois?* We have found that the menage is a family
affair that cuts across social and political boundaries. Yet the beliefs of
individuals drawn into a threesome help determine its outcome. The seesaw of the triangle will respond to the weight of convictions held. On the
left there has been the rhetoric, and sometimes the reality, of camaraderie—of sharing for the cause.

BERNARD SHAW
Frank Harris—journalist and author of *My Life and Loves,* an erotic confession that scandalized his era—in January 1930 put to his fellow Irishman
Bernard Shaw several leading questions. Shaw guessed that he intended to
use the answers as the basis for a biography. The playwright, rich and
famous, turned down his old friend, who was only a few steps ahead of
his own creditors. Harris persisted, and Shaw finally plied him with mater-

ial, the better to influence the result. Harris, shortly after finishing the work, died. Shaw stepped in to "correct" his own life. This world figure in his seventies was much concerned to put forward his own version of growing up "in a *menage à trois* . . . an innocent and beneficial arrangement."

George Bernard Shaw was born in Dublin in 1856, apparently of an alcoholic father, George, of proud but penurious stock and a mother, Elizabeth Lucinda (Bessie) Gurly, whose expectations were defeated by her well-off uncle leaving his money in trust to her son. Well before young George was conceived, another George, a Catholic, intruded in the Protestant household, assuming the duties that George Shaw was too soused to perform. George Vandeleur Lee, though handicapped by a limp and no social connections, had made himself the most talked-about voice teacher in Dublin. He taught singing using an experimental method. Bessie, a gifted mezzo-soprano, became his protégée, and when young George was eight, Lee and the Shaws openly set up a menage in a large house on a respectable street. Here were the headquarters of Lee's musical society, administered by Bessie, and here George Shaw stumbled in on drunken evenings, and from here young George was sent to school in order to get him out of the way.

All his life, Bernard Shaw remained touchy on the subject of which George had sired him. Lee, not George Shaw, paid the menage's rent. Bernard Shaw told Harris and anyone who would listen that he clearly resembled his legal father. But his socialist comrade Beatrice Webb wrote in her diary, "The photograph published in the Henderson biography makes it quite clear to me that [Shaw] was the child of G. J. V. Lee—that vain, witty and distinguished musical genius that lived with them. The expression on Lee's face is quite amazingly like G.B.S. when I first knew him."

Physical resemblance aside, Shaw's genius was not likely to stem from his milquetoast father or chilly mother. All his life Shaw defended Bessie's honor as though she were a virgin. Yet he adopted Lee's strongly held beliefs, from sleeping with the window open in winter to vegetarianism. Shaw recognized the advantages of plural paternity. He was a member of an elite club—the sons of a mother who had both husband and heroic lover, either of whom could have been their natural father and both of whom acted the paternal role. In addition to Shaw, Victor Hugo, Richard Wagner, and Orson Welles were raised by a similar menage a trois. In each case the hero became the boy's role model, and in each case, grown to adulthood, the man sought out a threesome to recast his youth. This is a twist to the Oedipal story that Freud didn't anticipate.

Young George respected Lee while he pitied his father. Bessie, involved in singing, ignored her son. When in 1871 Lee moved to London, his mother abandoned her family to follow him. Father and son moved to cheap lodgings, and the elder Shaw became a teetotaler while the younger clerked for a while. In 1876 the twenty-year-old said good-bye to Dublin and joined his mother, whom he hadn't heard from in years. The tall, gangly, red-haired fellow with projecting ears and a prominent nose, who dressed abominably, spent most of his time in the reading room of the British Museum. Here he discovered Karl Marx. Shy but with an impudent air, he forced himself to join the discussion groups that abounded in London.

Shortly, Shaw attached himself to a like-minded Irish couple, Pakenham and Ida Beatty. He sparred with the husband and flirted with the wife. Biographer Michael Holroyd comments, "This was the first of numerous triangular relationships where he recreated his mesmeric but chaste version of Vandeleur Lee with Lucinda (Bessie) and George Carr Shaw." In 1885 his father died and left him a little money. Now *Bernard*— at this point, he dropped his first name— Shaw purchased a Jaeger suit— knit of wool and guaranteed to improve the wearer's health and make him attractive—and the awkward virgin turned into Don Juan!

Shaw became entangled in several menages in the mid-1880s, but one of the longer lasting ones involved Hubert Bland, a founder of the moderate Fabian Society, and his wife Edith Nesbit, who would become a popular children's author. The aristocratic Hubert, frock-coated and monocled, was Shaw's sparring partner. In contrast to Shaw, who was skinny and swift, he was a handsome, muscle-bound womanizer. The Bland household was already a menage a trois, since Hubert's mistress Alice and her daughter lived there, and Edith was bringing up the child as her own. The attractive Edith fell for the red-bearded Irishman, whom she found completely irresistible. She claimed he was a great flatterer. In the style of the New Woman—who occupies the historical space between the suffragette and the feminist—Edith pursued her reluctant swain nonstop, finally cornering him in his mother's house while Bessie was out. Shaw sent her home.

"You had no right to write the Preface if you were not going to write the book," Edith complained. But it was the *adoration* of married women that Shaw desired, not their bodies. Their husbands, he supposed, blessed him for it, since he harmlessly fed their wives' imagination and relieved the men of "the strain of being the family idol." Shaw needed to reenact the fateful threesome of his youth and to prove by his remaining chaste that Bessie had done so and that he was the son of his legal father.

By showing his loyalty to a comrade husband, he reassured himself of the innocent nature of a menage. A virgin, he could insert himself between a more experienced man and woman and become the center of attention. Shaw's voyeurism gave way to exhibitionism, compensating for a childhood in which he'd gone practically unnoticed.

In 1885 Bernard Shaw's fifth unsuccessful novel caught the eye of the famous socialist William Morris, who invited him to address his Sunday group and then come to supper. His visits to Kelmscott House on the Thames transported the former clerk into an enchanted world furnished with gorgeous carpets, massive solid-oak furniture, and pomegranate wall-paper, all manufactured by the Morris workshop. Morris soon became a surrogate father who combined the qualities of both of Shaw's earlier fathers. His wife Jane, celebrated in the paintings hanging on the walls, took even less notice of Shaw than his mother had. But this "magical house" held a fair maiden, May Morris, who adored her father. Despite Shaw's hideous suit, May flirted with the crowd-pleasing orator whose theories on socialist politics fascinated her.

Shaw, under Morris's tutelage, left off Irish nationalism for an ideal-ized socialism, which became his creed for life. His romance with May blossomed. She had also grown up with two fathers, her own and Dante Gabriel Rossetti, her mother's lover until he died in 1882. During the time Shaw courted May, Jane was having an affair with Wilfred Scawen Blunt, the triangulator who was fascinated by Rossetti and did his best to get close to Morris. Did Shaw remain entirely unaware of the erotic undercur-rents in the Morris household?

Morris had informed Shaw, "I do not consider a man a socialist at all who is not prepared to admit the equality of women." May, handsome, artistic, and politically aware, was Shaw's equal, and he praised her extrava-gantly to other women. One Sunday evening after supper he was admiring May when she made a deliberate gesture of assent with her eyes. Shaw understood that "a Mystic Betrothal was registered in heaven, to be ful-filled when all the material obstacles should melt away." During the next four years Shaw assumed they were engaged, but he said nothing on the subject to her. He claims to have been shocked when in June 1890 May married Henry Sparling, an unprepossessing socialist, part of the same circle.

Actually, Sparling had confided in Shaw as early as 1886. And as we will see, by 1890 Shaw, the socialist Launcelot, was already deep into other flirtations. In November 1892, complaining that he couldn't stand Bessie's house being painted, he moved in with May and Henry at Hammersmith

Terrace, a few doors down from Kelmscott House. "Everything went well for a time in that menage a trois," recalled the famous playwright decades later. "She was glad to have me in the house; and he was glad to have me because I kept her in good humor and produced a cuisine that no mere husband could elicit. It was probably the happiest passage in our three lives." However, the attraction between May and Shaw became so flagrant that Henry complained to all the other socialists. Although Shaw describes him as "brave, kind, sincere and intellectual," Henry couldn't compare to his guest in gallantry.

To the distress of Jane Morris, concerned for her daughter, Henry Sparling broke off his marriage and fled to Paris. May was pleased, but the playwright, confronting a dénouement where he would win the girl, backed down. Faced with a New Woman who made clear she wanted him, his uncertain manhood shriveled. "As I had enough sexual satisfaction available elsewhere I was perfectly content to . . . go on platonically; but May was not." By June 1894 May Morris and Bernard Shaw, once close fellows in the cause, had grown uncomfortable together. "I mount my bike and fly," Shaw noted in his diary. He was pedaling into the tempest of a classic triangle.

Candida: A Mystery, produced in 1897, is Shaw's play most reminiscent of the menage with May and Henry. The critic Sally Peters suggests that "the subtitle . . . reflects the mystic, medieval and maternal aura surrounding Shaw's relationship to May." Candida represents a pure mother to both Marchbanks, her young would-be lover (Shaw's alter ego), and her husband, Morrell. She condescends to them and comforts and pets them as though they were children. Morrell, a high-minded socialist clergyman, resembles William Morris. Actually, the significant Oedipal triangle that had formed was among Shaw, Morris, and his daughter, who substituted for Jane in many wifely functions. Indeed, May would devote her life to chronicling her father's accomplishments in two massive volumes.

In April 1885 the socialist flirt had lost his virginity to Jenny Paterson, his mother's best friend and musical pupil, fifteen years his senior. They had begun by singing duets and, after Jenny made the initial advance, had progressed to the bedchamber. Shaw would visit the voluptuous brunette often, usually after attending some socialist event. Their lovemaking was ardent and repeated, but from the first Shaw was both obsessed and repelled by guilt. As Holroyd puts it, "his embraces with Jenny became part of a furious wrestling match between her possessiveness and his independence." Typically, he turned to a third.

Florence Farr, a sophisticated actress, was both amiable and determined. She was slightly younger than Shaw, delicately built and pretty, a perfect heroine out of those novels of his that hadn't been published. Their liaison began in 1890, and soon he was calling her "the very inmost of all my loves." The pair shared a witty, detached outlook, including regarding sex as a "hygienic gymnastic." But since Shaw was the older Jenny's all, she took any excuse to spy on him. Quarrels and reconciliations increased in intensity, until late one evening in February 1893 Jenny burst into Florence's lodgings (near May Morris's). "There was a most shocking scene," Shaw confided to his diary, "JP being violent and using atrocious language." He had to restrain Jenny physically from mauling her rival before he could coax her home.

These years saw Shaw ceaselessly invading others' nests, and some of the women he involved—including Eleanor Marx (Karl's daughter) and feminist orator Annie Besant—were considerable personages. The accumulated experiences went into Bernard Shaw's plays, beginning with the delightful *The Philanderer*, in which Shaw caricatures himself and which opens with a reprise of the unruly scene that closed his affair with Jenny. The threesome theme permeates his 1914 *Pygmalion*, which ends on the suggestion of a chaste menage among Henry Higgins, Colonel Pickering, and Eliza Doolittle. Much later, in 1934 at age seventy-eight, Shaw wrote *The Simpleton*, a comedy that advocates the marriage of one man to two sisters on eugenic principles.

In 1898, his philandering days done, Shaw wed the well-to-do Charlotte Payne-Townshend. By all accounts the marriage was high-minded and sexless. The playwright, however, continued to create a gallery of New Women who were brazen, bright, and sexy, and he wove through his work more triangular complications than we have space to enumerate. Shaw, despite his high principles, had no compunction about helping himself to the wives of his comrades. Yet he never wavered from socialism, and he consecrated his political life and art to bettering the human condition.

STRANGE INTERLUDE

While Bernard Shaw lived to be a curmudgeon without taking any life-threatening risks, John Reed and Louise Bryant threw themselves into the thick of radical politics—a choice that ultimately caused Reed to perish in the frozen wastes of Russia. Warren Beatty's landmark 1981 film *Reds* depicts a romance punctuated by high drama; it includes a third who adds a menage component to this tale of doomed lovers. *Reds* opens in the summer of 1914 at a Portland gallery show that has attracted the city's smart set. Louise Bryant, married to respectable Paul Trullinger, is doubly present: a nude photo of her hangs on the wall. Paul, with all eyes on his naked wife, is scandalized. The scene makes clear that their marriage, for all the liberty it permits a dentist's wife, won't last. Louise, the first coed at her college to wear lipstick, is a bohemian destined for the challenge of a big city.

After her Louisiana mother was abandoned by her Irish father, Louise Bryant enjoyed an odd upbringing by her grandfather, a rancher in Nevada. She got to know animals, gamblers, and prostitutes rather than other children. By the time she attended the University of Nevada, she was a first-class flirt. Her eyes were a deep violet blue, her hair a soft black, her features pretty, her figure lean and graceful.

The restless dentist's wife met up with journalist John (Jack) Reed when he visited his wealthy family in Portland. Reed was a celebrity for his daring coverage of the Mexican Revolution. In his midtwenties, large-boned, lanky, and rugged-looking, Jack was a big, breezy boy who'd been a cheerleader at Harvard and became the cheerleader of the revolution that was to come. Louise, a left-winger herself, sold subscriptions to Max Eastman's *The Masses*. But it was Jack's status as "the wonder boy of Greenwich Village" that really appealed to her. She approved of his bohemian lifestyle that scorned schedules. After a few tête-à-têtes, Jack left to cover the war in Europe, telling Louise he would send for her within a year. When in January 1916 Louise boarded a train to join him, she was thirty and eager to make up for lost time.

The Village was a true Bohemia of unlocked doors, quaint cafés, utopian notions, and all-night parties attended by poets, painters, schemers, and hangers-on. Here the men, often longhaired, admired Louise's pure beauty, which needed no makeup to enhance it. Women of a serious bent, often shorthaired—Emma Goldman for one—noted Louise's taste for extravagant clothes and dramatic effects, and they wondered if she was a fit companion for Jack Reed. Dorothy Day, who would later found the Catholic Worker movement, complained, "She had no right to have brains and be so pretty." But Jack and Louise entered into what the critic Max Eastman described as "a gypsy compact that would allow each to live life, which meant to live in freedom and stark reality and immense honesty." They called this arrangement "Free Love," and to Louise it was a sacred tenet.

In the early nineteenth century, when we first hear of Free Love from the Romantics, it meant the right to marry for love rather than to be sold by one's parents for their own advantage. To John Stuart Mill it included the right to divorce and remarry. To Victoria Woodhull Free Love meant having sexual relations outside of wedlock according to her desire. But to the radicals of the early twentieth century, Free Love meant doing away with marriage and all social restraints on love. Jack and Louise moved in together, worked in adjoining rooms, and pooled their money. Mabel Dodge, Jack's previous lover, took Louise to a group called Heterodoxy, for "women who did things openly." Louise wrote articles and poetry for *The Masses,* and she thrived on the expansion New York afforded her.

Expectations would cause problems. Louise thought of Jack as "so free and so exquisite and so strong," while he talked of Louise as "wild and brave and straight." The reality was that Jack's small apartment on Washington Square was often crowded by drinking, smoking, and arguing radicals whom he seemed powerless to get rid of. Louise couldn't work and felt she was tolerated only because she was Jack's woman. He was often away covering stories, and she grew lonely. That spring Louise turned to Andrew Dasburg, a handsome painter. In Dasburg's open marriage, husband and wife kept separate apartments, and he would become one of the other two men in Louise's life.

Jack had never entirely recovered from his war experiences. In late spring his weak kidney began troubling him. He and Louise, hoping for a quiet, productive summer, rented a white clapboard cottage on the seashore at Provincetown. But the Village had already begun its warm-weather hegira to the tip of Cape Cod. That summer saw the birth of modern American drama in the persons of the Provincetown Players, who began in a converted fish house on the bay giving one-act plays by Reed and Bryant. They soon drew into their orbit the troubled genius Eugene O'Neill.

It's ironic that Gene's first play, *A Wife for a Life,* written in 1913 but thankfully not produced in his lifetime, was a brief melodrama about two miners who are partners in a claim and who share the same woman, at first unwittingly but then on purpose. The piece ends with the older miner proclaiming a modified version of the well-known verse from John 15: "Greater love hath no man than this, that he giveth his wife for his friend."

Son of a gregarious actor and withdrawn mother, Gene was born in 1888 literally on the stage of a Broadway theater. A graduate of Catholic schools and a dropout from Princeton, he was by turns a seafarer, prospector, and salesman in South America, a drinker in dives, and a victim of tuberculosis. Gene met Jack Reed in the Village in 1910, and Jack invited him along to Mexico. He was attracted to Gene's dark side and proximity to the working stiff. In the summer of 1916 Jack was delighted to find the reclusive playwright at nearby Truro. The Players put him to work on a production of his *Bound East for Cardiff*, which was performed to a back-drop of real fog and ship's bells. This production made the old wharf vibrate with applause.

Gene smoldered with an intensity that attracted women. Gaunt, slender, and poetic, with a cruel mouth but vulnerable eyes, he could be at once brutal and tender—a paradox captured by Jack Nicholson's portrayal of him in *Reds*. Even his destructive drinking appealed to Louise's maternal streak. He needed her the way a heroic Jack Reed seemingly didn't. Gene, along with a buddy, moved into a sailmaker's loft across from Jack and Louise's house, which was usually crowded with visiting Villagers. While Jack went to Chicago to cover the Progressive party convention—where he claimed Teddy Roosevelt sold out the party—Louise and Gene rehearsed for another one-act drama in which they played lovers. Since Gene greatly admired Jack and was afraid to betray him, it was Louise, tanned as a sun goddess, who did the pursuing. She assuaged his guilt by telling him that because of Jack's health, they lived like brother and sister. Louise and Gene's affair soon became the talk of Provincetown, and Jack couldn't fail to hear of it on his return.

Louise's recent biographer, Mary Dearborn, insists that "the situation was amicable all around . . . with the three of them living and working so closely together. Jack respected Louise's freedom and genuinely believed in their vows of free love." Nevertheless Provincetown gossip grew intense. One hanger-on threatened to kill O'Neill as a favor to Reed. Jack reassured Gene and invited him to take all his meals with Louise and himself. The triad, though it centered on Louise, thus received its official approval from Jack. Dearborn writes, "Her relationship with Jack endured, even thrived. O'Neill was always secondary, despite the heat of their relationship." The radical set, to whom Jack was a demigod, held what they considered to be Louise's infidelity against her. Their attitude was encapsulated by Emma Goldman's remark: "Louise was never a communist, she only slept with a communist." But it's doubtful that the ailing Jack was up to much sexually. He gave her and the lovesick playwright every chance to be together. Louise needed Gene's brooding dependence, his "dark eyes," to which she wrote a poem. But his demand for exclusive devotion would eventually frighten her away.

During the summer of 1916, this was a true three-way relationship. Dorothy Day, who at nineteen became fascinated by Gene, observed, "Bryant without Reed would not have affected him so strongly." The man was jealous and wildly in love, confiding to a friend, "When Louise touches me with her fingernail, it's like a prairie fire." But to the writer, romantic suffering was the stuff of which plays are made. "All Gene's experiences were 'copy' to him," decided Dorothy Day, forgoing an affair.

In the fall the Provincetown Players moved bag and baggage to Greenwich Village. Gene took to drinking at his favorite dive, the Hell Hole. Louise and Jack lingered at Croton-on-Hudson and got married. Jack was going into Johns Hopkins to have one kidney removed and feared he wouldn't survive the operation. Louise, as his wife, would be his legal heir. Once Jack left for Baltimore, Gene moved into their flat on Washington Square. He and Louise worked together at the theater, though where they got together alone is a mystery since a number of hangers-on were also living at Jack's. Then Louise's unexplained illness—likely an infection caused by a botched abortion—caused her to hide out at a friend's West Side apartment and to seek treatment.

Louise kept Jack, who was undergoing tests and an operation, only partially aware of her emotional ties to Gene. Agnes Boulton, who later married the playwright, charted Louise's position: "On and on this had gone," Agnes recalled, "that summer, that winter, another summer— Louise sharing herself, never willing to give up one for the other, confused herself perhaps, but always the pivotal person, beautiful, passionate, strange." There was also the issue, made much of in *Reds*, of Louise's heated reaction to Jack's casual sex with young women who vamped him while he was on assignments. Louise claimed that her liaison with Gene was entirely different. The threesome was vital for Gene, who needed both a mother's breast to wean him from the bottle and an understanding male figure. He "admired Jack . . . almost loved him," he later told Agnes.

The menage crumbled on August 17, 1917, when Louise informed Gene she was leaving with Jack as a foreign correspondent to Russia. The unexpected news sent him on a long binge, complaining about his misery to anyone who would listen. Then one evening at the Hell Hole he stared at a young woman, eventually introduced to him, who remarkably resembled Louise. In Dorothy Day's opinion, Agnes was better looking, though she lacked Louise's intelligence and daring. Soon the determined Agnes, knowing Gene was still in love with "that girl," disentangled him from his cronies, and together they left for Provincetown. Later they would marry and, after having two children, divorce. But that winter Gene O'Neill, drawing on his life among seamen and laborers, attempting to verbalize unconscious drives rather than thought, began to revolutionize the American theater.

Strange Interlude, a nine-act drama that runs for six hours, was O'Neill's first great Broadway success, and it has been considered by knowledgeable critics as his most important work. It was written in 1926–27, when his marriage to Agnes was souring and he was thrown back in memory to his heartbreak in the relationship with Louise and Jack. John Howard Lawson, the father of modern screenplay technique, writes that the play "is the [old] story of a married woman who has a child by a man who is not her husband." The woman, Nina Leeds, "regards love as a right with which nothing can interfere." She is certainly based on Louise Bryant, and O'Neill represents her as taking obvious pleasure in her hold over three men. "I feel their desires converge in . . . one complete male desire which I absorb." Nina, as O'Neill saw her, "gets away with everything." In life, Louise eventually would be tripped up by her love for another woman!

It is Marx—not Karl but Groucho—who succinctly summed up the theme of O'Neill's convoluted play. In *Animal Crackers*, Groucho, leering, propositions a pair of curvy starlets, "We three would make an ideal couple." Then, to the audience, "Pardon me while I have a strange interlude!" For Louise, who came back from Russia before Jack, Gene was more than an interlude; in 1918 she tried to spin him again into her orbit. Agnes understood Gene had never really made a break with Louise. "They both expected that when she returned from Russia there would be a renewal of their relationship." Louise even promised that she and Gene would live together with Jack consigned to the role of visitor. But somehow Agnes kept her man in Provincetown, and a defeated Louise turned to the mild-mannered Andrew Dasburg for consolation.

Their relationship, as Dasburg recalled it, involved no secrecy. "We loved each other very much, [but] our lives were dictated by circumstances." These would inevitably force Louise and Jack into opposition to their government and into exile. For a time Louise, her hair cut short to resemble George Sand, galvanized the Village in her Cossack outfits, which included knee-high boots, silver belts, and furs. Somebody quipped, "That's what the revolution is for—so everyone can have a fur coat." Ironically this points to Louise Bryant's most enduring contribution: radical chic. She instinctively understood that a political revolution unaccompanied by a revolution in morals and even dress would fail—or worse, turn repressive.

In New York Louise was publishing the articles that made up her book *Six Red Months in Russia*—journalism that was at once personal and expert. When Jack finally returned from the revolution, and customs confiscated all his notes and interviews with Lenin and Trotsky, Louise anchored their chaotic existence by finding a small townhouse on quaint Patchin Place in the Village. From here they both launched speaking tours to combat the hysteria of the Red Scare, which was instigated by Attorney General Mitchell Palmer, running for president on a Red-baiting platform, and his henchman at the Federal Bureau of Investigation, J. Edgar Hoover. In 1919 Louise appeared before a congressional committee investigating the Bolshevik menace. Her factual testimony about Russia was gaveled down as the committee demanded "yes" or "no" answers and probed for personal dirt. Louise's confidence about her actions and her ties to Jack enabled her to stand up to the witch-hunting senators.

In 1920 Jack Reed—though denied a passport—again left for Russia, which was now besieged by invading armies. He was first imprisoned in Finland and then released. As a member of the Comintern executive committee, he addressed the Oriental Congress at Baku. Louise Bryant underwent a perilous underground journey to join her husband in Moscow. They lived one glorious week of love before Jack was struck down by typhus and died on October 17 after much pain. Louise was at his side day and night, the medicine that might have saved him denied by the Allied blockade. This scene from the tale of the revolutionary Romeo and Juliet has been immortalized in *Reds:* Warren Beatty expires nobly while Diane Keaton wails her heart out.

Actually, Louise had hated to leave Dasburg. Just before she sailed for Sweden they spent a few idyllic days together in Woodstock. They made love intensely, about which she felt no more guilt than he did toward his wife. Andrew, fearful of the danger she was undertaking, tried to dissuade her from going. Louise grew angry, sputtering, "You have to help me believe. . . . You love Jack too, you once said so. . . . We're in it all together." Andrew accompanied Louise to the Hudson River pier and helped bring her luggage on board the tramp steamer. Louise kissed him passionately and was gone into the legends of the Left.

Lenin heaped praise on Jack Reed's *Ten Days That Shook the World,* and he admired Louise Bryant as well. But while Reed lies entombed in the Kremlin, Louise lived on to marry a rich, fatuous American diplomat. She become an alcoholic and had an affair in Paris with a woman, which led to divorce and destitution. By 1936, suffering from a rare crippling disease, Louise was left with nothing but Reed's papers, which a committee from Harvard wheedled out of her. She couldn't write his story or theirs, and perhaps it is yet to be written.

THE RED MENACE

"Lenin is always with us" ran a frequent headline in the Soviet press. Vladimir Ilyich Ulyanov, better known by his nom de guerre, Lenin, was born in 1870 in Simbirsk, Russia. His well-off family could boast of noble lineage. Nevertheless in 1887 Czar Alexander III hanged Lenin's elder brother, a university student, on trumped-up charges. Lenin turned to reading Marx, and by the early 1890s he was leading a small socialist movement in Saint Petersburg. Lenin traveled abroad to build ties with exiles, and on his return the czarist secret police arrested him. Lenin's three-year sentence to Siberia was alleviated when Nadezhda Krupskaya joined him as his bride. He'd met the tall, pale teacher over blini at a party. A revolutionary who dressed in dark, shapeless clothes, she disdained cosmetics and wore her luxuriant hair parted in the middle and drawn back. To Lenin's unexpected proposal of marriage, supposedly based on her organizing ability, Krupskaya replied, "Your wife? Why not."

In Siberia men found the young wife attractive. However, the couple would spend the next twenty years in exile in Paris, and there the standards of beauty were higher. Here Lenin met Inessa Armand, a beautiful Russian woman inspired by the ideals of Tolstoy. Part French, Inessa came from a theatrical background. Her face oval, hair curly, brows finely arched over wide eyes, charming and fluent in several languages, at eighteen she had married the son of a Moscow industrialist. In five years she gave birth to five children. But she had already become a feminist and devotee of Free Love, and one of the children was by her husband's brother.

Inessa, after reading Lenin's call to arms, *What Is To Be Done*, plunged into the uprising of 1905. She was arrested and sent into exile in the far north. Her husband and his brother supported Inessa in and out of jail, then helped her to escape and flee with her children to Paris. There in 1910 she met the forty-year-old Lenin, already balding and termed "the old man." Normally the Bolshevik leader scorned sentimentality, singlemindedly pursuing the goal of revolution. All his life he'd been surrounded by adoring women, from his sisters to secretaries—yet it is no great surprise that comrade Lenin fell in love with comrade Armand, whom a contemporary called "a hot bonfire of revolution."

Inessa was welcomed into Krupskaya's Paris home. The latter went on vacation by the sea, leaving her husband to fall more deeply in love. Soon Lenin, uniquely for him, was addressing Inessa in the intimate familiar tense. He arranged for her to live next door. Krupskaya regarded Inessa as a comrade rather than a rival. Robert Payne, a biographer of Lenin, writes, "Krupskaya not only did not disapprove of [Lenin's] new attachment, but she seems to have welcomed it. She was genuinely fond of Inessa, enjoyed being with her and was delighted with the children."

Lenin's mistress worked as tirelessly for the cause as he and his wife did. Inessa wrote and translated articles for the Bolshevik press, organized conferences, and acted as a courier of secret instructions. When the Lenins moved to Kraków and Switzerland, Inessa followed. On one issue alone did she and Lenin disagree: Free Love. When she wrote a pamphlet on women's rights, he branded the concept "a bourgeois demand" rather than a proletarian goal. In matters sexual Lenin was a typical nineteenth-century Victorian. The so-called family values espoused by some Americans today became the dogma of his Soviet state.

Krupskaya, whose appearance was marred by thyroid trouble, occasionally made noises about leaving, but Lenin wouldn't hear of it. He valued his comrade-wife too much. In 1917, after the czarist government collapsed, the Germans sent back Lenin, Krupskaya, and Inessa in the famous sealed train to the Russia they'd left many years before. At Finland Station in Saint Petersburg, when the crowd acclaimed their leader-to-be, both women stood by Lenin on the platform. There was no hint of jealousy, and the two women helped to make the revolution as surely as the man they shared.

Friends of Inessa insisted that she had a sixth child, fathered by Lenin, but it lived only briefly. Certainly this dour, morally orthodox man gave his heart to a woman whose spirit remained free. The Bolshevik Alexandra Kolontai stated, "[Lenin] could not survive Inessa Armand. The death of Inessa precipitated the illness which was fatal. . . . [In] 1921 when they brought her corpse from the Caucasus [where she died of typhus] and we marched in the funeral cortege, Lenin was unrecognizable. He walked with his eyes closed and every moment we thought he might fall to the ground." Krupskaya propped him up, but to others he seemed lifeless, wanting only to get nearer to the corpse.

In 1924 Lenin died, paving the way for Stalin and the Terror, which ended only with the dictator's death in 1953. There were plenty of menages a trois among Russians, from politicians to artists, during and after the revolution and not only because housing was scarce. The defensive aspects of the menage came into play. In an extreme example, Boris Pasternak's lover Olga Ivinskaya was sentenced to four years in Siberia as a proxy for the poet who was both feared and admired by Stalin. Olga, the model for Lara in Doctor Zhivago, entered late into Pasternak's life, but she was his great love and inspiration. Nonetheless he refused to divorce his wife, Zinaida Nickolayvna, a coarse card player, and continued to live peacefully with her at his country dacha. After Olga's release, she took a "little house" within strolling distance. Oddly, the women's attachment to this truth-speaker both endangered and sheltered them. The traditional arrangement—the great man, his wife, and his mistress—may well have soothed the KGB, whose bugs told them more about this relationship than we'll ever know.

The facts of intimate life under Stalinism are still murky. But the tawdry reality has been captured by what Vincent Canby in the *New York Times* called a "silent movie opera," *Bed and Sofa*. Originally made as a movie in 1927, it ignored the sweeping conventions of Soviet film. Provided with minimalist music and lyrics, the show was the surprise hit of New York's long dreary winter of 1996. The cast of three consists of construction worker Kolya, his wife Ludmilla, and Kolya's old army buddy Volodya, who moves into their one-room flat in Moscow because he can't find anyplace else. He sleeps on the sofa. Kolya leaves town on a job, but when it's over he finds wife and buddy in bed together. He storms out but soon returns to sleep on the vacated sofa.

"Man is a sensuous being," crackles a radio with a mind of its own. At least woman is, and Ludmilla decides to keep both men. But then their friendship resumes, and it's anyone's guess who'll end up in bed and who on the sofa. Finally, Ludmilla gets pregnant by one or the other, but both men insist that she get an abortion. She decides to keep her baby, and Kolya and Volodya, who are playing chess, scarcely notice as she leaves. They know she'll be back to have the kid, who is going to have two fathers. Which is where we came into this show.

TORIES À TROIS

{Radclyffe Hall, Mabel Batten, and Una Troubridge;
Admiral and Edwina Mountbatten and Pandit Nehru;
Harold and Dorothy Macmillan and Bob Boothby}

To be faithful very often is to chain up the other person.
SASCHA GUITRY

*I*N BRITISH POLITICS *Tory* MEANS A MEMBER of the Conservative party. We also use *tory* to refer to a well-born member of the Establishment. Tories, upper- or lowercase, have rather favored the menage a trois, showing in equal measure civility and kinkiness. Here are a favorite few.

"OUR THREE SELVES"
There's a story that movie mogul Sam Goldwyn, on hearing of Radclyffe Hall's novel *The Well of Loneliness*, wanted to film it. One of his lieutenants objected that the leading character was a lesbian. "So what?" replied Goldwyn. "We'll make her an American." Born during the reign of Victoria in 1880, Hall, who demanded that she be called "John," was—in ways other than sexual—a proper British tory. She was conservative in politics, a devout Catholic who haunted the old churches of Italy, and a home-owner who complained about her servants. She looked on being a lesbian, which she felt was inborn, as a handicap that often caused problems for her. Yet her 1928 novel, suppressed at the time, proved a milestone in writing sympathetically about love between women. Hall's dedication of her

work to "Our Three Selves" tended to be forgotten in the outraged reaction and court battle following publication.

Although Radclyffe Hall's father left the household early, she inherited from him her name, talents, temper, and roving eye. The asthmatic child was raised by an Italian stepfather and a mother whom her companion, Una Troubridge, considered "brainless, vain, [and] selfish"; John was subjected by them to emotional and physical abuse. Her education was sporadic. Still, she developed strong interests in nature, music, and the arts. Later she would become an excellent horsewoman and raise show dogs. Tall, thin, and fair, masculine in manner, with a chiseled profile that hinted of Native American blood, John had the air of a hunting squire in a Jane Austen novel. At eighteen she inherited a trust fund from her natural father. She was already composing songs, but around 1907 she began to turn the lyrics into poems. In this she was encouraged by her first serious lover, Mabel Batten (called Ladye), whose male admirers included the renegade Tory and connoisseur of threes, Wilfred Scawen Blunt.

At fifty Ladye, a grandmother, was a beautiful woman who had been much painted and photographed. A noted amateur singer who sponsored the music of Percy Grainger, Ladye traveled in the best society and was accustomed to the homage of both sexes. She took the brash Hall, fond of smoking and swearing, under her cultured wing. She converted her disciple to Catholicism, a faith adhered to by both menages that were to develop. The two women traveled abroad together, but in England they carefully kept up appearances. Ladye's elderly husband grew very fond of "Johnnie," demanded her presence during his last illness, and died relieved to know that his wife had found love and protection. Though younger than she, John was the pragmatic husband to Ladye's bohemian, self-indulgent wife.

In 1913 Ladye was badly hurt in an auto accident that left her a semi-invalid. John, whose eye roved now and then, devoted herself to caring for her companion. The war forced material stringencies on both of them. In 1915 Lady Una Troubridge, a pretty young mother and wife to an admiral, came on the scene. Feeling "deeply depressed and intensely lonely," she went to a tea where she met John with Ladye, who was her cousin. John, who looked like "a very handsome young man," reminded Una of a caged eagle. She became engrossed in the life of this stranger. Since John was devoted to caring for Ladye, a menage a trois was the only possible arrangement.

John's demands were extraordinary, such as insisting that her pet goldfish be permitted to exercise daily in the bathroom tub. After the death of Ladye in May 1916, John's eccentricities began to evolve into productive work habits. The menage, rather than ending, was strengthened by John's following Ladye's expressed desire "that they would meet again beyond the grave." She went full tilt in seeking out Ladye's spirit, investigating psychic phenomena, and contributing papers to the Society for Psychical Research. The war and its slaughter of millions caused Spiritualism to thrive, but no ghost was called up more often or was more carefully consulted than Ladye's.

One medium reassured John that Ladye "thinks Una's influence was and is good and she likes to think that Una is with you." Still, Ladye was possessive about John, calling her "my Jonathan" as late as 1936 and referring to "our house" in which she insisted on arranging the furniture. During sittings, she conversed about everyday matters. Una had to ask permission of Ladye's spirit before John could cut her long hair, which she had doted on. At another sitting, when Una asked Ladye if she should take care of Johnnie, the medium responded, "She says yes, she wants that, she puts her in your charge." Ladye assured the two survivors that they were "both good children."

The deepening of Troubridge and Hall's relationship, aided by Ladye's hovering presence, resulted in a bounty of literary achievement. In the 1920s the sometime poet became a prolific and successful novelist. Hall's *Adam's Breed* won a pair of prestigious prizes. The book's dedication, which was repeated in each of Hall's novels, aroused curiosity, but the author refused comment. Una Troubridge finally explained, "The Three Selves referred to in the dedication were Ladye, who had encouraged her first efforts in prose, . . . myself whose glad and humble service to her talent she chose thus to acknowledge, and . . . Radclyffe Hall."

Troubridge, a talented sculptor, made her companion the center of her world. She rewrote John's letters and read aloud draft after draft of her novels, meanwhile correcting spelling errors. She bolstered an ego given to lacerating self-criticism. Before Hall wrote *The Well of Loneliness*, she came to Troubridge, who advised her to consult her own heart and publish the truth. The autobiographical novel, which deals with the love affair between an older and younger woman, is far from graphic, but it became the subject of an obscenity trial. Despite support from the likes of Virginia Woolf, George Bernard Shaw, and H. G. Wells, it was banned in Britain.

Reaction in the press was damning. Typically, the *Sunday Express* editorialized, "I would rather give a healthy boy or a healthy girl a phial of prussic acid than this novel." *The Well of Loneliness*, though a classic, is less remembered for its literary qualities than because it helped change attitudes toward lesbianism and sexual variance in general. Like D. H. Lawrence, Radclyffe Hall wrote from a private well of feeling while leaning on a stronger, more practical partner. Hall, again like Lawrence, was hopelessly romantic, and it is not surprising that she became involved in a last grand passion, which she managed to encompass within her menage.

In 1934 a thirty-year-old Russian émigrée, Evguenia Souline, acting as a nurse to John, who'd taken ill in southern France, sent the author into an amorous paroxysm that lasted for most of the nine years left her. Una, who'd felt that she and John were a unit unto themselves, was shocked. She had lived with Ladye's ghost for a long time, but Ladye was another upper-class Englishwoman. This odd-looking refugee daughter of a deceased Cossack general was "a creature of impulses and violent surface emotions . . . a savage." She was also more reactionary than the menage, indifferent to John's writing, and a heavy drinker apt to follow any crazy whim. Yet a new trinity evolved, albeit with some change in who was sleeping with whom. That Evguenia was or claimed to be a virgin excited John. Where one partner couldn't have held John for long, the combined attentions of the two women kept her occupied.

John reassured Evguenia that she and Una loved her and, when she was away in Paris, missed her. But the final word came from beyond. At a séance, the medium conveyed Ladye's message: "Tell Una I have been helping her. I've helped them both . . . and I have been helping our third one."

John, at fifty-four, nursed Evguenia through lung trouble that was aggravated by cold weather. John enlisted Una's support, or as the latter expressed it, "I rallied whole-heartedly to her determination that we should devote our combined energies to that end [Evguenia's health]." From 1936 on the menage wintered in Italy, where they were granted an audience with Gabriele D'Annunzio, the hermetic father of fascism. Sometimes they journeyed in a blue bus big enough for fifteen people. As they passed, inhabitants came out to cheer for the three women and their large dog, mountains of luggage piled in the boot.

In the true noblesse-oblige style, Una cared for the "joint lives" entrusted to her. In 1939, after World War II broke out, the menage had to winter in England. Although Evguenia "resent[ed] the war as a personal insult," it was now John who fell ill with cancer. Una gave Evguenia, who had fled to younger friends, regular reports of her progress and insisted that she send letters and telegrams that she could read to bolster the patient's morale. After John's death in 1943, Una remarked that their twenty-eight years together hadn't been easy, but "John's variety was infinite and it was always interesting."

Evguenia Souline married. Una Troubridge, who died in 1963, ordered carved into her headstone beneath her name: "The friend of Radclyffe Hall."

THE SETTING SUN

Edwina Mountbatten, née Ashley, born in 1901 at the end of Victoria's long reign, was sole heir to the immense fortune of her German-Jewish grandfather, Sir Ernest Cassel, an international financier. Edwina's mother died young, and her weak-willed father permitted his headstrong daughter to do as she pleased. How, from a reckless society girl addicted to fast cars and flings, Edwina became an effective politician and humanitarian is a story that begins with her marriage to Lord Louis (Dickie) Mountbatten, who became the last British viceroy to India, and from her two lengthy menages a trois, one involving Jawaharlal Nehru. Edwina's love life became literally inseparable from the birth of India as an independent nation.

Ernest Cassel arrived in London in 1870, about the time Friedrich Engels, having sold his business interests, moved there to assist Karl Marx. Almost as an illustration out of *Das Kapital*, Cassel devoted himself to making money and doing favors for his upper-class clientele. He became a close friend of the rakish prince of Wales (despised by Victoria) and paid off his debts. The prince, on becoming Edward VII, returned the favor by supplying Cassel with inside information that made both of them richer. The financier, who helped modernize the armaments industry, became an intimate adviser to the throne and a go-between to the German kaiser. If he wasn't entirely accepted in the highest circles, his granddaughter was to the manor born.

Sir Ernest sensed that Edwina's childhood, peopled by governesses and a cruel stepmother, lacked love. He took over her upbringing and doted on her, and she grew into a classic English beauty, slender, fair-haired, with large blue eyes. She debuted at eighteen; the press dubbed Edwina "Richest Heiress," and she was never out of public view for long. In 1921 the heiress met Louis Mountbatten, a twenty-one-year-old naval lieutenant with bleak financial prospects. However, he was a great-grandson of Victoria and was related to nearly all the European nobility; most notably, he was cousin to the succeeding prince of Wales (who as Edward VIII would abdicate to marry the divorced Wallis Simpson) and his brother, who would become George VI. Dickie, as everyone called him, was tall, slim, with a strong aquiline nose and wavy hair. His own childhood had been marred by his father's resigning as first sea lord because of his German descent. Garrulous and amiable but bumbling, like Edwina he had something to prove.

Both Edwina's grandfather and Dickie's father died in 1921. Sympathy propelled the young couple into a secret engagement. Dickie supposed he was getting the "perfect ally" that his admirable mother had been to his father. Although Edwina's inheritance gave him pause, because she would hold the purse strings, his status markedly attracted her. Their marriage was delayed while Dickie accompanied the prince of Wales on a fence-mending tour of India, but when the nuptials took place in 1922 police had to contain a crowd of ten thousand, eager to view what the press dubbed the wedding of the century. Dickie presented Edwina with a Russian enameled egg that had belonged to his aunt Alexandra, the executed czarina, while Edwina gave him a Rolls-Royce. The honeymoon couple paid visits to family estates and embarked on a tour of their royal relations in Europe. Janet Morgan, Edwina's biographer, comments, "Already after two days the Mountbattens' private life and public appearances were becoming one and the same."

Both Dickie and Edwina were virgins, but they gamely went about the business of making an heir. They sailed for New York, and on their arrival, an army of reporters met their boat. Douglas Fairbanks and Mary Pickford went with them to the movies, and at the World Series Babe Ruth shook their hands. They departed by private railroad car for California, sightseeing along the way when not being interviewed. At the Pasadena station the newlyweds were met by Charlie Chaplin, and in Hollywood Cecil B. DeMille showed the couple sets for his latest film. For the newlyweds, America became a perpetually whirling carousel of receptions held to the music of Paul Whiteman's band. Edwina's style suited the fast-paced twenties.

Edwina's petted youth and starstruck honeymoon spoiled her. She did produce two daughters on time but then turned them over to nurses and forgot about them. While Dickie pursued his career in the navy by attending technical schools and inventing numerous devices (including one-piece undergarments), Edwina was driven—in speedboats or high-powered cars—by her terror of being bored. Dickie's inexperience made Edwina tense up in bed. But when she did choose other men to sleep with, they were clones of her husband. Morgan describes Edwina's lovers as "good-looking, energetic and well-connected."

Edwina's first significant affair was with Laddie Sanford, an American playboy who was considered a not too bright but very good polo player. She soon included him in the Mountbattens' normal London rounds: lunch, tea, dinner, and the theater, after which Dickie went home. Edwina and Laddie stayed out nightclubbing until the wee hours. When she chose a close female companion, Jeanie Norton, it was a woman who except for short, curly hair, looked like her. Together, to help break the British General Strike of 1926, they manned the telephone switchboard for long hours at Lord Beaverbrook's *Daily Express.* Beaverbrook was Jeanie's lover with the full approval of her film-producer husband. Dickie, certain the strike was a Communist plot, bragged about his wife to anyone who would listen.

Edwina's love life grew more tangled. While Dickie began his service at the naval base on Malta, Edwina carried on in London. She was the proverbial girl who couldn't say no. Several men, each eyeing her fortune, pleaded with her to divorce Dickie and marry them. Thin and drawn, she retreated into headaches and dizzy spells. A friend described how the butler announced he had stashed one caller in the morning room and a second in the library, then inquired, "But where should I put the other gentleman?" Edwina could have been a character in a Noël Coward play.

When Jeanie finally informed Dickie, he blamed himself. Ironically, the prince of Wales, counseling prudence, encouraged him to preserve his marriage and accept his wife's lovers. "I wish I had sown many wild oats in my youth," Dickie confessed to Edwina, "and could excite you more than I fear I do." Edwina, a child of the Jazz Age, refused to slow down or act discreetly. She would be linked romantically with William Paley of CBS, and later Sir Malcolm Sergeant the conductor, and once, by a squib in the press, with Paul Robeson. Concerning the story about this "coloured man," as the Sunday *People* termed the great American singer, the king advised the Mountbattens to sue, and their lawyers obtained a public apology in court.

Edwina took her affairs on the road—to the Caribbean. When she came home to England in 1931, a domestic crisis ensued, but it was got over by an agreement between the Mountbattens to sleep strictly in separate bedrooms and with the right sort. Dickie, reconciled with Laddie, suggested their respective teams meet on the polo field. However, Laddie was replaced by Bunny Phillips, described as "Dickie with the volume turned down." Bunny, tall, slim, and handsome, was an officer in the guards. Soon the children became accustomed to seeing him eat breakfast in Edwina's boudoir, and he fit effortlessly into the Mountbattens' lives. This was a menage a trois that would become, once Dickie found a girlfriend, a menage a quatre.

The chic Yola Letellier, in her midtwenties, was leggy and blue-eyed. She had married a much older and wealthy man, a circumstance elaborated by Colette into a novel, *Gigi,* which became the musical film of that name. Meeting Dickie in 1932, Yola found him exciting, which infuriated

Edwina. But she soon appropriated her. "Your girl is sweet," she wrote her husband, "and I like her and we got on beautifully and are now gummed and I am lunching with her at her house." The pair of women got on so well that there was gossip they were lovers. In any case Dickie slept with Yola for the next thirty-five years. Usually Edwina had Bunny on hand— that is, when he wasn't off with Dickie sailing or playing polo. There was also talk that Dickie and Bunny were bisexual.

Noël Coward was close enough to the Mountbattens to make fun of them in *Hands Across the Sea,* a one-act cocktail party at which the guests of honor are rudely ignored. In his *Private Lives,* perhaps with the Mountbattens in mind, Coward makes a statement about alienation. Amanda and Elyot, once married but now divorced, meet at a swank hotel on the Riviera while on honeymoon with their new spouses. Since each is self-centered, their lives have been private even from each other. Originally played by Coward and Gertrude Lawrence, the characters speak in glib repartee, and although they have traveled, they are disdainful of the outer world, which includes their new mates. They expect their marriages to be dull, well-mannered shams.

In a civilized Noël Coward twist, both Bunny and Yola became part of the extended Mountbatten family. They were ensconced at Broadlands, the country manse, when in England, and the Mountbattens stayed with the Letelliers in Paris. Dickie, based on Malta, enjoyed Edwina's visits, during which they would play the devoted couple for the benefit of the naval officers. She and Yola and Bunny became an item, and they met Dickie when his flotilla steamed in to the Riviera in July 1935. The cheerful foursome celebrated the Mountbattens' thirteenth wedding anniversary. The only discordant note came when Edwina, who'd parked their daughters in Hungary for the summer, forgot where. By November, as the girls' light clothing was becoming impossible, she and Yola found them.

A good deal of what Edwina termed "communal living" went on among the foursome. During the war the men grew closer, and Bunny confided in Dickie that "Edwina found love-making tedious." Janet Morgan supposes Edwina's youthful promiscuity was a rebellion against the passivity expected of women. Once the German blitz of London began and she was given a position of authority with the Red Cross, Edwina accomplished executive wonders. She worked day and night to provide medical care and shelter for the civilian injured and woolen garments for the troops. She drove through the wrecked streets oblivious of bombs and brooked no interference with her mission. In energy and authority, she was a chip off the old Cassel block.

Dickie's war career reads like the adventures of Captain Horatio Hornblower. The destroyer he commanded was sunk by the enemy in the Mediterranean, and many men were lost. When the *Kelly* went down, Dickie called for the survivors who clung to its wreckage to give three cheers! His admiration for Edwina never wavered, and he insisted she was the only wife for him. In 1941 he explained to her, "The fact that I encourage the Rabbit [Bunny] is not that I don't care but that I love you so very much that I want you to be happy and I like him better than all your friends and have no doubt he is *au fond* nicer than me."

By 1943 Mountbatten, a favorite of Churchill, had become supreme Allied commander for Southeast Asia. He would play a major role in liberating that area from Japanese rule. He never failed to include letters from Bunny, who served along with him, to Edwina in his diplomatic pouch. In 1944 Dickie wrote Edwina that he'd parted from her lover, his closest buddy, nearly in tears. He signed the letter, "Your unchanging but devoted old Dickie." When Bunny decided to marry, both Mountbattens took it equally hard. That year Edwina, overseeing a medical unit, found herself in Paris. Neither she nor Dickie had heard from Yola since 1941; now, borrowing General Eisenhower's staff car, Edwina managed to locate her husband's mistress and convey a letter to her. The three remained close while they all lived.

In September 1945 Mountbatten received the Japanese capitulation at Singapore. Edwina's flying rescue mission to the wretched prisoner-of-war camps scattered throughout the South Pacific was daring but effective. By quick action she saved thousands of lives. But the wartime adventures of the Mountbattens were just a prelude to their 1947 appointment as British viceroy and vicereine to India with the purpose of arranging a transfer of power to an Indian government. The prime minister, Labor's Clement Attlee, hoped the process could be accomplished in fourteen months. It was, in Edwina's words, "a horror job" for which their own class would despise them. By agreeing to partition the subcontinent between Muslims and Hindus, the new viceroy, who demanded a free hand, achieved the creation of two nations in five months. However, millions of people were uprooted, and hundreds of thousands died in the massacres and starvation that followed. Had Mountbatten's judgment been unduly influenced by Edwina's falling in love with Pandit Nehru, head of the Congress party and India's first prime minister?

The political situation faced by Dickie on his arrival was explosive. Sectarian rioting had already devastated whole regions, and religious and ethnic groups were at each other's throats. Edwina faced the protocol and rituals of a viceregal court that was byzantine in its splendor and intrigue. She cleaned out the cobwebs and threw open the enormous Viceroy's House to all with business there; caste and influence peddling were abolished. She took lunch by the pool but otherwise kept continually busy, holding receptions and talking with men and women of every stamp. Most important were Edwina's informal chats with Nehru.

A handsome widower in his fifties, fit and trim, he wore a freshly plucked rose in the buttonhole of his mandatory homespun tunic. In May, with the temperature in Delhi soaring past 110 degrees Fahrenheit, he joined the Mountbattens and a few trusted aides at the viceroy's summer residence in Simla. Nonstop conferences and, it is said, Nehru's walks with Edwina in the garden produced agreement on India and Pakistan remaining in the British Commonwealth and receiving independence at once. After the transfer of power in August at a ceremony attended by a crowd of half a million, Mountbatten stayed on as governor general of India for another year, which was marred by civil war, famine, disease, and the assassination of Gandhi. Edwina worked ceaselessly on feeding and clothing the refugees, often with Nehru.

By the time she had to leave, Edwina, initially reluctant to serve in India, had fallen in love with both the country and its leader. A week before her departure, Nehru and Edwina went out at dawn to ride in the mountains above Simla. Both were middle-aged and world weary, but at core they were romantics. Afterward, with an understanding achieved, she wrote to him, "Nothing we did or felt would ever be allowed to come between you and your work or me and mine—because that would spoil everything." At her departure, Edwina gave the man pledged to austerity her personal treasures, including a Saint Christopher medallion her mother had given her father. He had enabled her to open herself, which she had never considered before.

Back in England, Edwina wrote to Nehru daily via diplomatic pouch or telephoned him. Since operators in India listened in on their conversations, gossip spread. But to Edwina, life in England or France (where they visited Yola) seemed unreal and trivial. She disliked dining with the cabinet wives at Downing Street and staying with Dickie's relatives, the royal family, with whom they played games and watched gangster movies. She lived for Nehru's warm but guarded letters in which he indulged in romantic flights, quoted English love poetry, and included his own. He was so distracted that his close friends all guessed the reason. Nor could Dickie, with whom Edwina was curt, fail to notice that this relationship involved his wife's very soul.

Over the years Nehru visited the Mountbattens at Broadlands (eight times during the 1950s) and she returned to India while Dickie attended to his duties as an admiral. The threesome with Yola remained intact: "We are all such friends that it is fun being together," Dickie reminded Edwina. But a new menage had formed, no less potent because it spanned continents. A mutual friend remarked of the Mountbattens and Nehru, "I can't think of any three people who had such a natural and uninhibited affinity with each other." The threesomeness of the Mountbattens thrived because of their unceasing civility and the willingness of each to give the other romantic space.

Nehru became Edwina's "first and only great love." After one trip she found Nehru's woolen handkerchief in her pocket and was cheered up. She clung to such reminders of the country and man she adored. Those close to Nehru believed that he couldn't have withstood the strain of the early years of independence without the safe harbor Edwina provided. Richard Hough, one of Edwina's biographers, insists, "It is impossible to believe that [their relationship] did not extend to the physical level." He adds via a reliable source, "Certainly Mountbatten himself knew that they were lovers. He was proud of the fact." Indeed, Dickie remarked to his eldest daughter about her mother and Nehru, "They really dote on each other in the nicest way. . . . We've been such a happy family." That ability to incorporate others is the key to the Mountbattens' success, both personally and professionally. Philip Zeigler, Dickie's official biographer, comments that "what kept them together was . . . their belief in the family and their conviction that they were a unique partnership and that life could never offer the same possibilities, the same excitement, in other company." Exactly, if we define "family" as including a third and sometimes a fourth.

Zeigler sums up the Mountbatten-Nehru menage: "[Dickie] was happy and proud to open [his marriage] to the man he esteemed so highly. To call it a triangle, or Mountbatten a complaisant husband, would be to belittle a relationship that was enriching to all concerned." After Edwina's death in 1960, Dickie cherished his wife's correspondence with Nehru, referring always to "the love letters." As she wished, her body was put aboard a frigate to be buried at sea. Nehru sent an Indian vessel, and while the archbishop of Canterbury delivered a eulogy, her lover's wreath of marigolds was tossed upon the waves. Nehru was quite inconsolable until he died four years later.

Edwina's romanticism, Dickie's civility, and Nehru's great humanitarianism all contributed to fashion a nearly perfect menage a trois. In 1969

Earl Mountbatten, who had long since retired as admiral of the fleet, was blown up in his yacht off the coast of Ireland. The IRA claimed responsibility, warning the English people, "We will tear out their sentimental, imperialist heart." Love, especially of the nuanced kind, is incomprehensible to zealots.

TORY SLEAZE

Noël Coward depicted the menage a trois as "an elite with its own code of conduct." In his day it broke society's matrimonial rules in a manner similar to today's same-sex marriages. Until the midsixties, for persons in high places, the menage was kept private and protected. Harold Macmillan, the Conservative prime minister of England from 1957 to 1963, overlapping the Eisenhower and Kennedy administrations, lived in a thirty-year triad that included his wife Dorothy Cavendish and her lover, his closest political connection, Bob Boothby. While Macmillan maintained his diplomatic aplomb toward a passionate connection that might have doomed his career, the press kept its counsel. How ironic that his government should be brought down by the exposure of a threesome featuring a (Russian) James Bond–like spy!

Macmillan came from a family of Scottish crofters who founded a business both educational and profitable: the publishing house of that name. His scholarly father married a strong-willed American woman, who became a mother ambitious for her brood. Harold, born in 1894, was sent to exclusive schools culminating in Oxford, where the political bug bit him. Wounded in World War I, left with a slight limp, the future prime minister was no Lord Byron. He smiled weakly and wore gold-rimmed glasses, a Groucho Marx mustache, and unfashionable clothes. In 1919 the stiffly starched Harold met the nineteen-year-old Lady Dorothy Cavendish, daughter of the ninth duke of Devonshire. Harold, swept away, wrote his mother, "I love her so much I can hardly know what to do or say or think." When some of her family objected to Macmillan's common ancestry, the duke, whose older daughter had married into a brewing dynasty, countered, "Books are better than beer."

Dorothy was striking, frank, warm-hearted, and earthy. She referred to the interlude before marriage as one of "unalloyed enjoyment—in many ways the happiest of my life." In 1921 the Macmillans' only son was born, to be followed by three girls. In 1924 Harold, largely because of his wife's charm, won election to Parliament. In the House of Commons he found himself related by marriage to sixteen other members. He became the close ally of the stylish Robert Boothby, considered by higher-ups to be a future candidate for prime minister.

A first triangle consisted of Harold and Dorothy and his domineering mother, who did her best to undermine the marriage. Hot-tempered Dorothy once ripped a phone out of the wall after speaking with her mother-in-law. Bored with Harold and politics, she fell in love with Bob Boothby, with whom she shared a liking for jazz and Hemingway's novels. He was a different man from her glacial husband. Bob drove an open two-seater Bentley and was handsome and excellent company. He was bisexual and liked to pick up young men, especially of the rougher sort. He regarded his liaison with Dorothy as tragic but unavoidable, "on the scale of Wagner, George Sand, if you like, Parnell."

Recollecting, Boothby supposed the menage had cost him high office. In fact he was too devil-may-care to be suitable, and he became instead a leading radio personality. His closeness to the Macmillans was the one fixed point in his life. Dorothy's passion engulfed both men, and though she phoned Bob daily and slept with him nightly for a time, she never let go of Harold. She told Bob that her last child, Sarah, born in 1930, was his and that she no longer slept with Harold. But Bob, who freely admitted to fathering other illegitimate children, denied his paternity of Sarah. The troubled young woman was never certain which man was her father, though Macmillan acted the part.

Dorothy held onto Bob for most of their adult lives. When he became engaged to an American heiress, she pursued him across Europe to break it off. When Bob married her cousin Diana, Dorothy pressured him to divorce his wife, which he soon did. "It is impossible to be happily married when you love someone else," he recalled. Though Bob claimed that Dorothy was both cruel and selfish, she became to Harold a superb political wife, always there for her husband, whether on the campaign trail or during his six years at Downing Street. Her solution was for all three to "settle down ... into a menage a trois." It's not likely that Macmillan, who entirely lacked charisma, would have become prime minister without the strength that living in a menage gave him.

Still, he fought it for a time, especially because it underlined his emotional and sexual incapacity. Lord David Cecil recalled seeing him in despair, "banging his head against the wall of a railway compartment." But Harold could never have held Dorothy otherwise. "In doing what was difficult, I had my reward in the end," he admitted. He remained on good terms with his wife's lover, ennobling him as Baron Boothby. In time husband and wife, sharing a career and children, drew closer together. In 1966 they went on a second honeymoon, during which they achieved a deep amity. Dorothy died unexpectedly a few days after their return.

This caused Harold and Bob to share their grief and bury any differences. The two men cooperated to destroy all of Dorothy's letters, even when there could be no consequences if the menage were revealed. But it was Dorothy Cavendish who turned a rake into a dedicated lover and a political mediocrity into prime minister.

"POPSIES FOR RICH PEOPLE"

A wag once remarked about the Profumo affair, "If only Macmillan had been alive, it wouldn't have happened." Of course he was in office at the time, and John Profumo was his war minister. No one has seen fit to write a biography of this former hero and devoted civil servant. However, *Lord Denning's Report*, presented to Parliament in September 1963, chronicles the spy scandal associated with Profumo, and thanks to its attempt to whitewash everyone concerned except Stephen Ward, the Serpent in Tory paradise, it is more revealing than later books on the whole kinky business. Military secrets were stolen, and someone had to take the blame. Ward, a rural parson's son who courted the rich and famous, was sufficiently déclassé for Lord Denning to vilify.

It began with a weekend party at Cliveden, the great house of Lord Astor, who managed a stud of racehorses. Although he had donated Cliveden to the National Trust, milord held parties there at which he mixed "the most distinguished and respected people" with call girls. These were provided by Ward, who worked as a society osteopath but frequented West Indian clubs in which he procured drugs and recruited young women. A skillful doctor and portrait artist, Ward, according to Lord Denning, was an "utterly immoral" man and, worse, a Communist sympathizer. His real business was as "provider of popsies [girls] for rich people."

Denning had to admit that Lord Astor gave Ward a cottage on his estate and that on weekends he and his girls would come up to the great house to swim in the pool and mix with the guests. Ward, in the summer of 1961, was cultivating Captain Eugene Ivanov, a Soviet naval attaché and known spy. He brought him to Cliveden one Sunday, where the evening before, Christine Keeler, nineteen, had been observed swimming nude by a number of the guests, including Profumo and his wife, the actress Valerie Hobson. Ward would compare Christine to "Venus emerging from the sea." Profumo had flirted openly with her.

It was the dashing Ivanov who boarded the prize the next evening. Ward, however, fixed up Keeler and Profumo, and they began a liaison that included weekends at the minister's house (when his wife was away) and rides in an official limousine, not to mention mushy notes on War Office stationery. Lord Denning suggested Ivanov intended to have Christine pry secrets from her lover in the way of pillow talk, then whisper them back into the Russian's ear. In 1992, after the demise of the Soviet Union, Ivanov wrote a memoir, *The Naked Spy*, telling some of all. He referred to Christine as "a useless bimbo" who was "only good for having sex." He was interested in blackmailing Profumo, for state secrets, but he had to keep his own involvement with Christine secret from his Kremlin bosses.

The early sixties witnessed a repeated testing of wills between Washington and Moscow. The Berlin crisis was followed by the Cuban missile crisis, with Britain caught in the middle. The 1987 study *An Affair of State* claims that Ward was working for MI5 (British Security) in an attempt to recruit Ivanov as a double agent or at least a conduit for disinformation and that the scandal caused Security to sacrifice Ward and blame him for everything. The doctor is indeed the key, since at the time he was living in London with both Christine and the even younger Mandy Rice-Davies. However, Ward insisted to Ivanov that he didn't sleep with the girls: "I want them to get what they can from life: money, love and happiness." This confused a man who, like James Bond, exploited women to gain military secrets. "Was it a menage a trois or simply the charity of a gentleman who had decided to set two young lost sheep on the right track?" puzzled the spy who liked it hot.

Clearly Ward was both a social climber and a voyeur, a man whose low self-esteem caused him to gain the favor of those in high places by being the candy man. Keeler called him "sexually perverted," and her description of great house parties included nudity, masks, whippings, and bondage, as well as sexual orgies with "names who are household words." In 1963 when the scandal broke, exacerbated by the espionage issue, Keeler was hustled out of London to hush her up. But she wouldn't be safe until the dirty linen had been hung out. At first she asked a few hundred pounds from the press, but as the rumors swirled, she was able to sell her story to the *News of the World* for twenty-three thousand pounds. The era of the handsomely rewarded confession had begun. The Profumo affair gave birth to Britain's contemporary tabloid culture, in which the outing of Tory sleaze has become a national pastime.

Unfortunately, Keeler's career as a striptease dancer failed, and today she is living in poor circumstances. Mandy Rice-Davies married an American millionaire. John Profumo resigned and took up charity work. Lord Astor fell into depression. Ivanov was called back to Moscow and given a desk job. Ward, attacked on all sides, shunned by erstwhile friends, was put on trial for pimping. The only one in the affair with a sense of personal honor, he committed suicide. Prime Minister Macmillan, the last to learn of any trouble, resigned, and Labor formed the next government.

The Profumo scandal has spawned books and, so far, one major motion picture. It was well summarized by Britain's *New Leader:* "a Soviet attaché . . . was sharing a prostitute with the Secretary of War in the Conservative government headed by Harold Macmillan, who was himself sharing an earl's daughter with a Tory member of Parliament. A prostitute being a less socially correct bedmate than an earl's daughter, the Secretary of War was disgraced, whereas Macmillan and the MP were promoted to the aristocracy."

There's the real shame of it.

chapter 24

MENAGE AND
THE HOLOCAUST

Sinners and Survivors

{Dorothy and Ezra Pound and Olga Rudge;
Joseph and Magda Goebbels and Lida Baarova;
Oskar and Emilie Schindler and Mistresses;
Marguerite Duras, Robert Antelme, and Dionys Mascolo;
Isaac Bashevis Singer}

Some cook, some do not cook. Some things cannot be altered.
EZRA POUND

*T*HE LEFT IS A LOGICAL PLACE TO FIND
menages, and Tories have their civil threes, but can there be a truly fascist
menage a trois? Fascists make love, but do they love? What of the survivors of the Holocaust: did menages a trois play a special role in their
adapting to life, and eros, after the war? Here we examine a few colorful
specimens from a dim and murky realm.

FASCIST FOLLY
Much ink has been spilled on the question of Ezra Pound's place in modern poetry and nearly as much on the not-unrelated question of whether
he was insane. In 1946 a panel of American psychiatrists determined he
was mentally unfit to stand trial for treason. Instead, Pound was confined

for twelve years to the federal hospital for the mentally ill, Saint Elizabeth's, in Washington, D.C., where he and the director were on chatty terms. An equally relevant question might be whether the two main women in Pound's life, his wife, Dorothy Shakespear, and mistress, Olga Rudge, participants in a contentious menage a trois for some fifty years, were of sound mind. Pound himself told Allen Ginsberg in 1967, "At seventy I realized that instead of being a lunatic, I was a moron."

Pound and Nazi propagandist Joseph Goebbels, the two most intriguing figures on the maniacal right, share an unhappy youth in which, though their parents doted on them, they were denigrated by their peers. Initially, each was the sort of wallflower Woody Allen referred to when he quipped that being bisexual would at least make it easier to get a date. Ezra was born in Idaho in 1885 of forebears from New England. His grandfather Thaddeus became rich from mining and was elected to Congress. He was denied a place in President Garfield's cabinet because he openly kept a mistress. Ezra inherited Thaddeus's predilection for threes, as well as his populist politics, which harped on the conspiracy of international bankers. He even claimed to have inherited his grandfather's writing style.

Ezra was raised on the Main Line outside Philadelphia, where he imbibed a suburban anti-Semitism. His racism stemmed from a class consciousness imparted by the dual matriarchy of his mother and grandmother, who smothered the boy in chintzy good manners. In time he would rebel against snobbery, but he was more or less ruled by the family's values until old age. At the University of Pennsylvania, Ezra was a failure socially and academically; to compensate, he devised an outrageous personal style we may tag "Renaissance bizarre."

In London from 1908 on, Ezra, in his twenties, came into his own. He ingratiated himself with a literary set that included Ford Madox Ford, Wyndham Lewis, William Butler Yeats, and Olivia Shakespear (Yeats's onetime mistress) and her daughter Dorothy, whom Pound would later marry. Ezra became known for helping other writers, going to great lengths for then unknowns T. S. Eliot and Ernest Hemingway. Yet Robert Frost claimed Pound only did it to increase his own influence. He was very obliging to the Shakespears, escorting the mother and daughter to concerts and later across northern Italy. Like the troubadour he fancied himself, Ezra paid court to Olivia, who was pleased to keep daughter Dorothy in the background.

Ezra, who dutifully reported his doings to his own mother, described Olivia as "the most charming woman in London." A classic late-Victorian beauty in her midforties, cultured, married to a wealthy but boring solicitor, Olivia had published several novels in favor of Free Love and "real marriage." Dorothy, who'd been "finished" at Geneva, painted watercolors but mostly accompanied her mother. Reserve made her perfect features resemble those of a shepherdess on a Grecian urn. According to Humphrey Carpenter in his exhaustive biography of Pound, Dorothy, in turn, was taken with Ezra's "wonderful, beautiful face, a high forehead . . . the eyes gray-blue, the hair golden-brown and curling in soft wavy crinkles."

When Ezra wrote love poems to Dorothy, Olivia reacted angrily and forbade them to see each other. But eventually, as Ezra's influence in London reached a peak, she would be won over. Still, why did Ezra switch from the mother to her much less interesting daughter? Our guess is that from Olivia he could hope for an affair but from Dorothy, marriage. Dorothy came with a small independent income and great expectations, and after marrying in 1914, the poet and his wife lived on her money for a long while. Further, by marrying a reticent beauty whom other men admired, Ezra gained a certain leverage. His major concession was to assure Dorothy that she would never have to cook.

In 1920 Ezra Pound moved to Paris and adopted Dada, wearing pants made from the green cloth of a billiard table. He became fascinated by glands and sex and had a number of affairs, which he claimed triggered his creativity, especially if his "ejector" found the "retentive media" of a passive woman. From this time dates the beginning of Pound's involvement with Olga Rudge, an American raised in Europe who was a classical violinist. Becoming discouraged by his lukewarm reception in Paris, he grew excited by visiting Italy, where Mussolini had seized power. Pound's early enthusiasm for the dictator was shared by the likes of Bernard Shaw and Lincoln Steffens, although the others soon repented. In 1924 Pound, Dorothy, and Olga, verging on a triad, moved to Rapallo, on the Italian Riviera. As Steffens wrote in his *Autobiography*, Pound "had been hurt somehow at home, deeply wounded." The menage protected the angry but vulnerable poet, who would go to the lengths of treason to get even with a native land disposed to ignore him.

Olga, whom Carpenter describes as having an "adrenal personality," was young, slightly built, and energetic. Independent, she was the opposite of Dorothy and soon took charge of Ezra. She wanted a child, though he didn't, and in the autumn she conceived one. Mary Rudge, as the child was christened, was no sooner born than her mother delivered her to the care of a wet nurse. To complicate matters, at thirty-nine Dorothy became pregnant. Pound remained secretive about the birth of Omar in 1926; he probably didn't father Dorothy's son. He already thought of her as "a beautiful picture that never came alive." But now his routine was fixed, alternating between wife and mistress, Rapallo and Venice, for set periods. The women struck a tense balance between rivalry and cooperation. In the thirties Ronald Duncan visited the Pound menage in Rapallo. When Dorothy left the room, Ezra proudly pulled out a snapshot of Mary. On her return, he changed the subject, and she began to talk about Omar.

Olga was living in the small town just up the hill from the Pound household. Duncan remarked that Ezra spent the evenings with Olga and days with Dorothy. "He had a deep affection for both, but neither ever referred to the existence of the other. This omission gave the situation an appearance of Jamesian unreality. . . . We lunched with Dorothy and dined with Olga." Still, all three cooperated in a series of concerts designed to revive the music of Vivaldi, and Dorothy praised Olga's playing. Further, as Ezra became more infatuated with Mussolini, bombarding Il Duce with crackbrained money schemes, both women backed him, apparently out of conviction. The menage helped to insulate Pound from the way in which, with his vicious attacks on Jews, America, and democracy, he was destroying his credibility and reputation.

Once Mussolini joined the Axis and World War II commenced, the menage jointly aided the Fascist powers. Dorothy was blindly supportive while Olga made suggestions for Pound's infamous and treasonous broadcasts aimed at undermining the morale of the Allied troops. According to her daughter's memoir, Olga read "through all sorts of books, mostly history, looking for facts that supported Baboo's [Pound's] ideas, supplying new items for his speeches." Ezra himself, after he was taken into custody by the American army, called Hitler "a saint . . . a martyr." As late as 1949, Dorothy, tending to her husband at Saint Elizabeth's, wrote that "Hitler and Mussolini, especially the latter, were certainly trying against awful odds to further civilization." A menage will magnify the traits of its most forceful member, and woe betide them all if he is a moron.

Joseph Goebbels may actually have been the evil genius that Ezra Pound deluded himself he had become. Goebbels introduced the techniques of publicity and "spin" that govern our politics and purchases today. Like Pound, he only imagined the glories of war, which he never saw close up. The Nazi propaganda minister was a great admirer of American movies, his favorites being *Gone with the Wind* and *Snow White and the Seven Dwarfs!* A frustrated filmmaker, he defined propaganda as entertainment, and he gained control over UFA, the leading German studio. Goebbels made frequent use of the casting couch, and actresses who wanted a leading part had to surrender to his clutches. Hypocritically, perhaps even cynically, Goebbels led the purge of "decadent" art in Germany's museums and shut down the cabarets of Berlin and Vienna, but the man's deep desire was to be surrounded by female flesh in a menage a trois.

The youth of Goebbels (born 1897) was frustrating, much like Pound's, although Goebbels's self-image was further complicated by an illness that resulted in a clubfoot. Joseph's petit bourgeois parents, inhabitants of the lower Rhineland, hid his disability from their neighbors. The Goebbelses were a somber, guilt-ridden lot, but they babied the sickly mama's boy who lived at home till he was thirty. Although Joseph made male friends easily, disqualification from the army during World War I reinforced his sense of being unworthy. Again, compensation led to bravado, and Joseph, like Ezra, became so convinced of his genius that he never bothered to hold a job, relying on others to support him. Women— whom both egoists began to attract in a motherly role—paid the bill.

In 1930 Goebbels met Magda Quandt, the divorced wife of an industrialist. Elegant and assertive, she fell, to the dismay of her family, for both Nazism and its propagandist. Goebbels observed financial ruin, poverty, and hopelessness spread throughout Germany. When Magda became pregnant toward the end of 1931, the pair were married quietly on her family's estate. During the thirties, as the Nazis seized and consolidated power, Magda gave birth to six Aryan children, five girls and one boy (who fortunately all resembled their mother!). Each one's name began with an H—in honor of Hitler.

While Magda grew stout and possessive, Goebbels looked elsewhere for the kind of romantic involvement he craved. He fell hard for Lida Baarova, a beautiful, dark-haired Czech actress whom he made into a star. Although his mistress was of a supposedly inferior race, he appeared with her at official Nazi functions. Goebbels flaunted Baarova at the 1936 Olympic Games; shortly thereafter he had the cheek to campaign against the immorality of the clergy. In the summer of 1938, while Hitler was plotting against Czechoslovakia, his propaganda minister was hatching another scheme: he expected Lida to prepare Magda for a menage a trois. In brief, Goebbels wished to move his mistress in with his wife and children. The Aryan for progeny, the Slav (or Jew) for illicit passion—such was the inherent contradiction of the Nazi's erotic world.

Magda, tired of giving birth, agreed. The three of them tried the arrangement by spending the next few weekends together. Goebbels acted so flagrantly—feeling up Lida in front of Magda and their guests, and in the evening showing and raving about her films—that Magda, in a change of heart, ran to Hitler. There had already been other homo- and heterosexual scandals involving leading Nazi figures, and Hitler, though hardly a moralist, put his boot down: Goebbels must drop the actress or resign. Goebbels seriously considered quitting and taking Lida to Japan, and she, it seems, was willing to go. In the end, Goebbels gave up the woman he most desired, and with her went the little humanity left him. He grew crazier and more destructive, taking a major part in the so-called Final Solution, indeed applying a version of it to his own family. As Russian troops approached Berlin in 1945, even after Hitler's suicide, Goebbels had the opportunity to fly Magda and the six children to safety in South America. Instead, husband and wife, united in a heinous nuclear family, murdered their children before they themselves took cyanide.

A fascist menage a trois is no more compassionate than a fascist family. When in 1944 the Germans strengthened their coastal defenses at Rapallo, the Pounds carried their worldly goods in a horsecart up the hill to Olga's house. They all lived together for a year until Italian partisans arrested Ezra and turned him over to the Americans. There are conflicting versions as to how the three got along. Mary Rudge wrote that Ezra was "pent up with two women who loved him, whom he loved, and who coldly hated each other." After the war the women no longer spoke to each other, but they remained devoted to the great man. Dorothy lived in a poor, ill-heated apartment in Washington to tend to his needs, and Olga, from Italy, mobilized the intellectual community to press for his release.

Ezra turned Saint Elizabeth's into his literary salon, where he acted a part before noteworthy visitors and attracted disciples, especially young women who became his bed partners. In 1958, after the government dismissed the indictment against him, Pound sailed for Italy with his wife and latest mistress on board. At Naples, goaded by reporters, he gave the Fascist salute. However, Ezra ended in the hands of Olga, growing dotty and repentant, indeed helpless, in his old age. He became estranged from Dorothy, who lived alone compiling a guide to the characters in his *Cantos*.

In an unpublished passage from the *Pisan Cantos*, Pound pats himself on the back for managing his near-lifetime menage. He quotes an old Chinese emperor: "If you can keep the peace between those two hell-cats you will have no trouble running the empire."

Control, power, self-esteem—these are the rewards and pitfalls of a threesome for the wounded child turned misanthrope.

THE MAN WHO LOVED LIFE

The question is inevitably asked about Oskar Schindler: why did an egotistical bon vivant, a speculator and womanizer, risk his own life to save some 1,100 Polish Jews from the Nazi gas chambers? The question contains the seeds of its answer. Schindler was no saint, no martyr, but a healthy narcissist. If it can be said about anyone, he was normal. Oskar grew up in a small town in German-speaking Czechoslovakia. He was an outgoing, good-looking young man who liked to drive fast cars and to be the center of attention. He met his wife, Emilie, when she was twenty and he was a door-to-door salesman. Their simple wedding was attended by Jewish friends.

Oskar soon had a mistress who bore him a child and lived a block away from the Schindler home. Needing money, he mindlessly joined the Nazi party and acted as their agent until German armies swept over Czechoslovakia and Poland. In 1939 he went to Kraków to make his fortune. He borrowed funds from the Jewish community to buy back a pots-and-pans factory confiscated from its owners, and he put Jews to work, paying them next to nothing. To Schindler war meant opportunity, which is a cynical but sane point of view. He was no hero but in his wife Emilie's words, "a man who loved life . . . a great *bon viveur.*" Girlfriends were part of the abundance he craved.

Oskar quickly acquired expensive tastes. He was a suit-and-tie man who wore distinctive cologne and did what he could about a receding hairline. For a time the black market satisfied his needs, and he dealt in everything from coffee to diamonds and furs. By bribing and flattering Nazi officials, Oskar amassed a small fortune. He learned of planned pogroms and was careful to protect those Jews who worked in his factory, even after they had been forced into a concentration camp. One remarked, "He was [just] a guy who made money." But from 1943 on he turned double agent. Schindler was protected by German Military Intelligence, probably by the same clique that attempted to assassinate Hitler. That year he brought information about atrocities in the Polish camps to the Jewish Agency in Budapest. His reports on the conditions in the camps, which were hidden or denied by the Nazis, could have saved hundreds of thousands of lives if the Allies hadn't ignored them. He acted at great risk to himself and Emilie.

The movie *Schindler's List* underplays Emilie's part during wartime in feeding over a thousand workers, nursing the sick, and hoodwinking the sadistic SS commandant Amon Goeth. "I was like a joker," she recalled at eighty-six, living in Argentina. "When you need it, you play it." Oskar depended on her staying cool, and as she jested, she also protected him from his mistresses. While Emilie remained stoic about her husband's philandering, Thomas Keneally, whose novel led to Steven Spielberg's film, has called Oskar "a sexist brute."

The moment you begin to moralize about sex, you miss the point. The man who is a double agent has in effect two identities, and he will likely demand a doubled sexuality, a wife and mistress—or if the double agent is a woman, a Mata Hari, she may demand both a husband and a lover. Schindler's idealized view of himself as Casanova, as leading man, enabled him to risk imprisonment (the Gestapo jailed him several times), torture, and death to save the despised. After the war, Oskar and Emilie shared an apartment in Munich with Ingrid, Oskar's current mistress. Her Polish was useful to him in the black market, but they were living on scraps. Schindler had lost his knack for making back the fortune he'd spent bribing Nazi officials.

The two women got along well. "From when I first met them we all liked each other," recalled Ingrid to an interviewer. She remembered how charming Oskar could be: "He really cared—he talked to people and he could lift your burden in some way." But the man had spent his own vital force. "He lost the vigor," said Ingrid. Emilie, who was more displeased by her husband's inability to make money than his philandering, compared him to a mushroom. Ingrid would marry a Holocaust survivor and move to New York, where Oskar came to visit them. He lived on the charity of the Jews he had saved—several thousand dollars a month. Oskar hadn't lost the knack of spending, but without the edge of danger, his career as speculator, spy, and lover was over. He couldn't satisfy even one woman.

THE WOMAN WHO DARED

One of the more interesting attempts to deal with the Holocaust on film, from a psychological point of view, is François Truffaut's *The Last Metro*. The movie stars Gérard Départdieu as Bernard, an amorous actor; Catherine Deneuve as Marion Steiner, the manager of a Paris theater; and Heinz Bennent as Lucas, her husband, the former manager who, because he is Jewish, she has hidden for the duration of the German occupation in the theater's cellar. The title refers to the last subway train that theater patrons needed to catch in order to get home before curfew. Wartime for those in occupied France was a contradiction of daily haste and interminable waiting for liberation, of a flourishing theater that was closely monitored so its actors had to communicate between the lines or (metaphorically) from the cellar, where Lucas could hear well enough to direct the action onstage.

The central event of *The Last Metro* is the affair that develops and is at first repressed between Bernard and Marion. She is attracted but despises him as a skirt chaser, and besides, she and Lucas are intimate in the way of an accustomed married couple. She is responsible for his safety, and a collaborator, an influential critic, catches on to this. Truffaut shows that Marion and Lucas have a warm sex life. But these are extraordinary times. Bernard and Marion together hide Lucas from a surprise visit by the tipped-off police. The pressure on Marion, who presents a Deneuvian calm to the world, is too intense to be banished by anything but passion. This she finds briefly with Bernard, who is a Resistance fighter and must leave to fight openly for the liberation of Paris.

Truffaut ends with a flash-forward that is a play within the film: the war is over, Bernard and Marion play lovers, and Lucas, who has directed, takes the curtain call with the others. A beaming Marion, center stage, wears one man on each arm. Typically, the American critics misunderstood the ending. They expected her to choose between the men. But she is Deneuve, the world's most beautiful woman—she can have both.

There is a real-life story that outdoes Truffaut's, and since Marguerite Duras, who lived and wrote it, also directed nineteen films, we wonder why she didn't attempt to bring her own story to the screen. Duras, who was small and doll-like when young and then owlish in later years, was born in French Indochina in 1914 to colonial schoolteachers. An obsessive writer, her major success came in 1984 with the publication of *The Lover*, a prize-winning best-seller that was made into the film of the same name. Duras had worked on the tried-and-true plot for years: the recollections of a young woman deflowered by an older Asian lover, a relationship no more tender than her terse, one-sentence paragraphs. This became the image associated with one of France's most widely read authors. But it wasn't the actual focus of her erotic life, which was defined by her conscious attempt to make a marriage of three.

Duras arrived in Paris in the thirties. She studied law, and just before the war she married a fellow intellectual, Robert Antelme. He was calm and tried to calm her, the spark, who wore the look of a perverse Buddha. She was already the enemy of "the Christian couple, with its fidelity, its unconscious betrayals, its repressed desires." They moved into a large apartment on rue Saint-Benoît in the bohemian quarter of Saint-Germain. Duras died there in 1996. Her life may be read as a series of statements. The first was to have a baby, which died at birth. That year, 1942, Duras met Dionys Mascolo, whom her biographer, Alain Vircondelet, describes as "aggressive and nervous at the same time." He was close to Duras's own excessive bent, and they fell madly in love.

Duras, rather than cheat or make excuses, brought her husband and lover together. Vircondelet writes, "She wants a friendship to develop between Antelme and Mascolo so that the absurd partitions between love and friendship will be abolished, intermingling instead in the drama of love that she would direct. She loves Mascolo in Antelme's love and vice versa, and the two of them love each other in her love." In her late twenties, Duras showed a daring wisdom. She understood that the tedious routine of marriage negates the communion of the couple and results in a renewed isolation. There is opposition in one on one, a polarity that can't be bridged except through an intermediary. Duras, rather than discard marriage, tried to reinvent it. She was careful to leave the men together alone, and their friendship became lifelong.

In her youth, Duras had felt subversive, dissident, on the edge. It followed that in 1943 she and her men would join a Resistance cell organized by François Mitterrand. After all, a menage calls for commitment to something out of the ordinary. Their mission was to support escaped prisoners of war and thus gain information. Duras and Mitterrand, already started on his political career, were attracted to one another, but their rumored affair never happened. "We never met in a house or a café," Duras recalled. "We liked each other so much we could certainly have slept with each other, but it was impossible. You can't do that on bicycles!" In June 1944 the apartment where the cell met, Antelme's sister's home, was raided by the Gestapo, with results that would sear the flesh of the three into one.

Mitterrand, who barely escaped, warned Duras. Although Antelme had disappeared, Duras, with Mascolo's help, was able to determine to which camps he had been sent. While she waited for news—the common experience of a war in which men fought but women waited—Duras kept frantically busy by creating an agency within the Resistance to track the deportees. After the Normandy landings, as the Allies approached Paris, the Nazis took their victims with them in retreat. When Duras gave in to despair, Mascolo would repeat that she must believe Antelme would come back: "Try, we can do anything if we try."

In April 1945, after the German surrender, Mitterrand was sent in an official capacity to Dachau. The concentration camp had been emptied, but there was an encampment of the dead and dying that was quarantined because of typhus. In the morgue, amid the stench, an apprentice corpse gasped, "François." Mitterrand recognized the gap between Antelme's front teeth. Mascolo wrapped the skin and bones in a blanket and smuggled him out, then drove nonstop to Paris, blaring his horn through the checkpoints. All through the ride this scrap of a man kept talking, if only to convince himself he was still alive.

Antelme could not even go to the bathroom by himself. His skin was as thin as cellophane. Duras and Mascolo watched him round the clock, and the pair nursed him back to health in stages. Duras punished her own body to share his emaciation. Antelme's sister, whom he used to call the "cutie-pie," was liberated from a different camp and flown to a hospital in Denmark. She died. Only the shared energy of a combined will to live could save Antelme, who carried on for another forty years. Once he was well, Duras informed him that their marriage was over. She wished to have a child by Mascolo. All three lived in the apartment on rue Saint-Benoît while Antelme wrote his masterpiece, *The Human Race*. He moved out in 1947, and Mascolo and Duras split up ten years later. By then, an alcoholic, she couldn't tolerate a male lover close by.

Duras's story is as complex as her nearly seventy published works. She was both a Communist and a feminist, yet certainly no movement defines her. Although fascinated by the theme of silence, she was always communicative. Duras damned monogamy as "an absolute form of alienation, a metaphor of the many kinds of solitary confinement into which people place themselves." Still, for the last several years of her life she lived *en famille* with a handsome young man who was homosexual. They were in love.

DON JUAN THE SCHLEMIEL

What of the love life of the Holocaust survivors? According to Isaac Bashevis Singer, this became, at least for some, hypercharged. His refugees from the Nazi terror, mainly Polish Jews, congregated on New York's Upper West Side, where they recreated something of Warsaw before the war, complete with the language, foods, deals, and literary activities of the past. Even the affairs begun in the old country were continued. Singer's novels, written in Yiddish and then translated, are laced with autobiographical detail but ultimately depend on the collective memory of an incinerated world. The narrator of the posthumously published *Meshugah* (Crazy), Aaron Greidinger, is the author's alter ego. He speaks more frankly than the Nobel laureate deemed politic while alive. Here Singer means to say that in a world where madmen reign, a unit of three does better than two or one.

The menage a trois is an underlying theme in Singer's earlier work, such as *Enemies: A Love Story*. The protagonist, Herman, is married to a Polish peasant woman who hid him during the war, and he is also involved with a Jewish mistress. His life is further complicated when his first wife, whom he believed dead, reemerges from the netherworld of the refugee camps. As the insightful Dinah Pladott points out in an article titled "Casanova or Schlemiel?," "Herman maintains the delicate balance between these women with the aid of an extensive system of lies and deceptions." A schlemiel, for the benefit of non–New Yorkers, is a well-intentioned but hapless loser. However, in Singer's mind there is not necessarily a contradiction between a loser and a lover, since his Casanovas tend to be schlemiels.

Singer's fondness for sexual pluralism dates back to his boyhood in Poland before and during World War I. His father was a Hasidic rabbi so strict that he disdained the secular world, holding the theater, art, and literature to be idolatrous and forbidden to a good Jew. He wanted nothing to do with either humanism or Zionism and believed that most things were *tref* (unclean). Young Isaac's education was restricted to the Jewish tradition, fortunately including the great Cabalistic books. Isaac, who couldn't fit into the Orthodox mold, never entirely broke from its Puritanism. Rather, he engaged in duplicity, educating himself in matters literary and sexual.

The Warsaw Writers Club of the 1920s introduced the young man to the turmoil and zest of emancipated Jewish life—the new rich, the socialists, Yiddishists, and anti-Yiddishists, among whom was his elder brother I. J. Singer, whose career as a writer influenced Isaac's own choice of profession. He began to explore the mysterious realm of women, finding mistresses willing to overlook his poverty and shabby clothes. "Monogamy," he decided, "was a law established by legislators, not by nature." There was a price to be paid for breaking this law. In the summer of 1926, Maurice Carr, Isaac's nephew, burst in on his uncle Isaac "suffering what looks to be a crucifixion of sorts. His arms are stretched out to their full length and effectively nailed in place by, on the one side, a skinny young woman who has dug her fingernails into the wrist she is clutching and, on the other side, a more buxom one who is doing the same. Each wants him wholly to herself. They wage a desperate tug of war which bids fair to split him down the middle." Here is a snapshot of Singer's loving schlemiel, whose appetite is greater than his ability to satisfy it.

In 1935 Isaac Singer, sponsored by his elder brother, moved to New York, thereby escaping the Holocaust that would consume the rest of his family and the culture in which he was steeped. The guilt of the escapee augmented the guilt of the prodigal son who exists "in a state of perpetual despair." Singer, who wrote serialized novels for the Yiddish *Daily For-ward*, made no attempt to "adjust" to America or to Americanized Jewry. Translations aside, he wrote for an aging group in a language headed for extinction. In *Meshugah*, his protagonist, Aaron Greidinger, is broke, bald-ing, watery-eyed, knock-kneed, and paranoid. Yet the schlemiel is sex-obsessed, fending off a slew of Jezebels who would tumble him into bed just behind their husbands' backs.

The intense *Meshugah* is Singer's final statement on life and love. The personae, congregated on the West Side, are survivors not only of the camps but of the compromises of daily life. One, however, Max Aberdam —a sixty-seven-year-old cigar-chomping speculator—is through with lying. He sweeps into Aaron's office at the *Forward*, demanding, "Come and meet my new girlfriend. If I were not married, she would have been a blessing sent from heaven." She is twenty-seven-year-old Miriam Zalkind, busty and beautiful, from whose "dark-blue eyes shone the joy of a child." She also is married, to a homicidal poet named Stanley. In fact, everyone is married and cheats except for Max, who openly loves and *fresses* (overeats). Even he inadvertently cheats a score of pensioners out of their reparations money from Germany! It is all the fault of a chaotic world, of a crazy human race that is made worse by so-called civilized laws. If there is a God, he has sent us Hitler and Stalin.

Max soon informs Aaron that he wishes him to join in a menage a trois. His health is poor, and he worries about what will become of Miriam. She is an avid reader of Aaron's old-world novels in the *Forward*, is already in love with him, and happily agrees. "When I am with the two of you," sighs Max, "I am young again." Miriam warns Aaron that Max, who has been both father and husband to her, will remain number one, but she still sets out to seduce him. Aaron hears the voice of his father hiss, "Lecher!"—but he doesn't resist for long.

Properly speaking, Aaron is a Don Juan driven by guilt to sin. God, in the image of his father the rabbi, won't let loose the disobedient child, anxious to show how bad he can be. In *Meshugah* and elsewhere, Singer cites precedents to justify the menage a trois, which include Tibetan women who marry several brothers, as well as examples of man, wife, and hand-maiden from the Old Testament. He praises anarchist Emma Goldman, "who regarded free love as the foundation of social justice and the future of mankind." Most interesting, Singer posits a human drive opposed to jealousy: "a will to share, a desire for sexual community." In *Meshugah* and to his biographer Paul Kresh, Singer denounced the hypocrisy of officially sanctioned monogamy and predicted its demise. "Society would be forced to create a sort of sexual cooperation in place of the prevailing sexual deception and adultery," he said. The essence of betrayal lies not in the number of partners but in the cheating each must do in order to be true to his or her nature. Moreover, Singer finds that monogamy does not have its basis in the Hebrew tradition, and he even gives a qualified nod to the sexual revolution of the sixties.

Inspired by Max, Aaron and Miriam neither deceive nor demand sexual fidelity. *Meshugah* traces the narrator's initiation into a new style of relating to both male and female. He learns to be the third without being a third wheel. As Aaron describes making love to Miriam, "the theme of our foreplay, our afterplay and the act itself was Max. We promised never to deceive him and to hold him as a kindred soul." Max, encouraging the pair, is less poetic, declaring, "A man my age should have a stand-in." Singer himself once remarked to Kresh, "Nothing brings two men so much together as sharing the same woman." However, Aaron and Max will have to bear together the weighty burden of Miriam's past.

Aaron shepherds *Meshugah*'s cast of characters to Israel, where Miriam is nursing Max after an operation. He senses that Miriam's devotion to Max is her atonement for accepting favors from the Nazis. He learns she was a *kapo* (collaborator), the mistress of an SS officer, and that she ostentatiously beat Jews in the camps. As the ghosts of Aaron's father and mother rage at him, he feels totally soiled. Max, who in Warsaw was a pimp, insists Miriam can't be judged. Take her as she is, he urges Aaron, marry her. Put in her place, no one would do any better. As Maurice Carr expressed it, "my uncle Isaac was not a believer in the betterment of the human species."

Meshugah ends on an ambiguous note. Max has died, and Aaron and Miriam have returned to New York and quietly married. They will be helpmates, physically and spiritually. Above their bed hangs an enlarged photo of Max: "His eyes gazed upon us, smiling with that Jewish-Polish merriment which death could not extinguish." Yet Aaron insists they won't have children, thus symbolically dooming the tribe to extinction. This is a ghost menage in the deep sense that Aaron and Miriam share the warmth of their apartment and their marital bed with the ghosts of the great crime against humanity.

At one point in *Meshugah*, Aaron discusses with Max and Miriam the idea of writing a novel about the experience of their love. Entitled *Three,* its theme would be "that the emotions heeded no laws, no religious, social or political systems." This is that novel, and Singer made clear to his translator that it had a factual basis in his own life. *Meshugah*, like Roché's

Jules et Jim, presents an idealized menage a trois—centered on a capricious but enchanting Eve—that founders on the rocks of a brutal, indifferent world. Still, the statement is made that one cannot hope to avoid self-division without physical and emotional communion. "To be one is to be none" goes an old Yiddish saying.

Singer's vision, which marks both the virtual termination of Yiddish literature and its apogee and constitutes its most forceful reaction to the Holocaust, departs from traditional monogamy to range back to the polygamy of the earliest books of the Bible and to glance ahead to what may be a New World of sexual freedom. Whether in eating or loving, both of which he presents as social, Singer is fascinated by abundance. He once remarked to his biographer, "If you have one candle, with the flame from that candle you could light fifty others." For this Old World skeptic, the pilgrimage to Eden begins with the sharing of sexual love.

part seven

A CELEBRATION
OF THREES

While there have always been celebrated menages a trois, in modern times the institution presents an altered face: both bolder and more furtive. If you are a menager looking
for recruits or if you wish to join a threesome, search cyberspace and you'll find, in the
blink of an electronic eye, however many you need. During the sexual revolution of the
sixties and seventies, stars sometimes shot off their mouths about their liaisons *à trois*.
During the stalled-out eighties and the uncertain nineties, confessions have come late or
posthumously or third-party in the form of an exposé article or biography. The menage a
trois, though it's legal, moral, and attractive to celebrities, remains the last taboo.

The carryings-on of the British royals illustrate the limits of the old discretion and
the promise of a new day. In 1994 Prince Charles confessed on television to a long-
term liaison with Camilla Parker-Bowles. His wife, Diana, not to be outdone, revealed
her infidelities on camera in November 1995. Her candid confession infuriated the
Herald of Glasgow: "The Princess of Wales is the most dangerous and selfish of the
whole menage a trois."

Diana was denounced in royalist circles. Novelist Fay Weldon in the *New York Times*
claimed that Di had overstepped her role as "a certified virgin to beget a legitimate
heir for all the world to see." The future queen of England could hardly expect a faithful husband, since begetting bastards is part of the king's job description. Weldon
asserted that Di's error was in wanting to be loved, especially by her husband. "A philandering monarch, a tempestuous queen" are in the good old style. Unfortunately, Di
has succumbed to "our therapeutic age." She needs to find herself, to be healed—in
public. Princess Di, a Churchill by birth, is a recovering aristocrat.

Prince Charles (called "Chuck" in the American media) tried his best to form a
proper menage. Even while the couple was engaged, according to *People*, "Di was

taken under wing by Camilla Parker-Bowles." The women attended polo matches together, but Di grew suspicious of Camilla's attempts to befriend her. More important, Di confused marriage with family, as have her supporters and detractors. Marriage is a legal convention defined by the state. A family, however, can be composed of three and can allow each member more space than does a couple. Chuck and Di were a dysfunctional family all by themselves.

Diana, whose lovers were also married, has to date won the press war with the Windsors. She was motivated to step up her media blitz by Charles's escorting the Other Woman about in public. During Di's November 1995 "tell-all," she made the often quoted remark: "There were three of us in this marriage, so it was a bit crowded." *Crowded?* This ex-royal doesn't know what the word means! Since there are rumors that she will move to New York, we'll give her a glimpse of how we natives live.

How would Di like to be crammed into a three-room Greenwich Village apartment—or Letha's two-room Chelsea flat? Her closets are probably bigger than either of our dwellings! These are located a comfortable walk apart. In nice weather you can see the tourists parading by to gape at buildings that were once bohemian pads but are presently occupied by middle-class tenants paying stratospheric rents. Still, John Reed used to live in our building in the days when he was involved with Mabel Dodge; her lower Fifth Avenue salon was the beginning of radical chic. The tiny Edna St. Vincent Millay house is just around the corner. There is a story that the beautiful poet was seeing two men at once, Edmund Wilson and a pal now long forgotten. In the tradition of buddies, they wanted to share her. Vincent assigned each man one-half of her body—Wilson was awarded the top; his cohort, the bottom. Everybody was satisfied.

We wonder whether Di, accustomed to costly coiffures, would be willing to join Barbara on her monthly hegira by subway uptown to "trainee night" at a salon, where she pays twenty dollars to get her hair trimmed. Would she join Letha in Chinatown for an herbal beauty treatment? Letha, a tall blond, sometimes wears cowboy boots and Indian jewelry, a reminder of her Western background. Barbara, a petite, curvy redhead, has curls that halo her face. She's a bit eccentric; we've nicknamed her "the nutty professor." Michael, a huggable bear perpetually worried about stocks that are going the wrong way, sometimes goes with Barbara to be sociable. Occasionally he gets a haircut, an excuse to admire the pretty beauticians. We all converge downtown from our separate ways. No one cares in the Village if you're two or three, straight or gay, or racially mixed. We hope that's what the twenty-first century is going to look like.

On what Di pays daily for dry cleaning we entertain ourselves for a month: either at off-Broadway theaters, poetry readings, and concerts or watching the recent spate of films about threes. We share books, clothes, a philosophy, observations, vacations, and an interest in Eastern thought. Our menage karma—the outward events and choices that have kept us together for over a dozen years—is something we don't often rehash.

But if couples feel "togetherness," so do we. Ours, being outside the norm, has been tougher to come by.

When Di moves to New York she may be noticed but won't be bothered by the hoi polloi. The press is another matter. She has already reversed the ill-fated career move of Grace Kelly, who went from promiscuous Hollywood star to uptight princess. Di has traded royalty for celebrity. She will likely succeed the late Jackie Onassis as *the* society superstar. She has the same understated pizzazz, and like Jackie, she wants to be adored. We predict she'll spawn future triangles and eventually, if her karma is right, a real menage a trois.

chapter 25

FRENCH TWIST

{Jean-Paul Sartre, Simone de Beauvoir, and Bianca Bienenfeld}

We had pioneered our own relationship: its freedom,
intimacy and frankness. We had thought up the idea of the trio.
SIMONE DE BEAUVOIR

THE EXISTENTIAL FAMILY

LET'S IMAGINE SCOTT FITZGERALD, WHO had romantic notions about France, gushing to Hemingway, "The French are different from you and me." Papa, who knows better, replies, "They're just more so." Parisians may not have invented the menage a trois, but in books, art, and movies they fly the tricolor of sexual variety. Is this all fantasy, or do they act on it? A 1995 *Playboy* international sex survey, which included six thousand respondents on four continents, came to no definitive conclusions. Our own educated guess is that California (big enough to be a country) takes the prize for frequency of the quickie threesome and to Britain goes the palm for the serious menage. Still, French writers, from Rousseau to Roché, have given us the classic accounts of three in love. And Existentialism, which influenced high and hip culture so heavily in the second half of this century—its prepunk followers were dubbed "Exis" by John Lennon—was conceived in the midst of a tangle of French menages.

Jean-Paul Sartre and Simone de Beauvoir were global celebrities. From the close of World War II on, they attracted and maintained extensive press coverage. Students who gave up on reading *Being and Nothingness*, written in an odd terminology of its author's devising, were nonetheless inspired by Sartre the political activist. Women to whom the literary and philosophical references in *The Second Sex* meant little were enthralled by Beauvoir the feminist. This Left Bank pair, whose libertarian love lives appeared to mesh suitably with their radical causes, remain newsworthy. Why, then, did these mediagenic characters pussyfoot around their sexual threesomes to the very end?

It was Beauvoir who painted the portrait of the Existentialist couple: unmarried but devoted, true but free, childless but patrons of a family of young achievers. She wove a seamless tapestry with the skeins of her detailed four-volume autobiography, her novels (especially *She Came to Stay*), and the lengthy interviews she granted to the biographers of herself and Sartre. After Sartre's death in 1980, Beauvoir edited and had published his letters to her and others (*Witness to My Life*, 1983), despite the fact that she didn't have the authorization of his literary executor. Sartre's obsessive skirt chasing, revealed in the letters, was a little surprising, but this only enhanced Beauvoir's reputation as a long-suffering feminist. After her death in 1986, her executor found in a cupboard her side of the correspondence, which Beauvoir had declared lost. Published in 1990 as *Letters to Sartre*, these have exploded the myth of the devoted couple, dented Beauvoir's feminism, and made the pair's hoodwinked biographers look like hagiographers.

An entirely new take on the Sartre-Beauvoir relationship, which was part of a larger polygamous arrangement, is called for. Instead, detractors have jumped in with denunciations of the thinkers who violated their own creed of "authenticity" (Exi-speak for "honesty") by exhibiting "bad faith" (that is, lying, especially to oneself). Although *The Second Sex* laid the philosophic foundations of the feminist faith, women have been slow to defend their fallen sister. Even Beauvoir's translator, the urbane Quentin Hoare, writes of the "hint of voyeurism, the whiff at times of Valmont and Mme de Merteuil." Actually both *Witness* and the *Letters*, concentrated in the crucial period leading up to World War II, illumine the genesis of a philosophy inseparable from the characters of Beauvoir and Sartre and their relations with thirds and fourths. The origins of Existentialism are trisexual.

Comparisons of Beauvoir's *Letters* to the 1782 epistolary novel *Dangerous Liaisons* by the military officer Choderlos de Laclos have been made recklessly, and it's useful to remember the differences. Laclos's Marquise de Merteuil and her former lover Valmont, with whom she cooperates to seduce other women, are respectful antagonists. Peter Brooks points out that "the book is structured on a series of erotic encounters which measure the strength of the contestants." The air these two breathe is laced with gunpowder, and their main idea, which belongs to the soldier aristocrat, is simply that a siege well conducted leads to the surrender of the prize. Since the brute power of love (as of war) is to be mastered by intellect, a sort of shady diplomacy rules. Merteuil and Valmont need one another to ratify their conquests; they need to be *seen* to win.

This eighteenth-century pair maintain a certain attachment, but it is no longer eros. Indeed, Valmont finds love only with the innocent Madame Tourvel, and Merteuil becomes jealous of the man who has gone beyond the bounds of the game to a place where she can't follow. Merteuil's interest in men is to use or conquer them. She saves her admiration for younger women, with whom she has sex vicariously via Valmont's descriptions. Of his cousin Cécile, a virgin whom she has persuaded Valmont to seduce in order to take revenge on a lover who abandoned her to marry the wealthy Cécile, Merteuil writes, "She is truly delicious! . . . Everything about her speaks of the most lively sensations. . . . I allowed her to write and say I love you." Christopher Hampton in his adaptation for the theater lets Merteuil admit, "If my morals were less austere, I'd take [Cécile] on myself."

Merteuil's lesbianism is the only hint she gives of a capacity to feel. Valmont despises the cruel society in which he lives, but he comes to realize, through pain, that his seductions, instead of subverting, bolster it. Merteuil, while supposing herself a renegade, lives off the decay of the ancien régime. Her loss of face with the beau monde is brought out cleverly in Christopher Hampton's screenplay for *Dangerous Liaisons,* which ends with a deflated Glenn Close removing her makeup (that is, mask) to the witness of her own mirror, the only confidant left. The story of Narcissus has been reversed, and Merteuil, who has destroyed her alter ego Valmont, sees herself as a hag. Merteuil represents the dying regime.

The story of Sartre and Beauvoir, while it contains surface similarities, is driven by a real rebellion against the binding stereotypes of the Third Republic. The involvements of the pair are subject to the usual human contradictions, but they are not cynical. These two are writers, which is a sacrificial act in itself. Nor can their lives be understood outside the context of the culture of the Left Bank, whose devotees flocked to cafés to consume ideas along with food and drink. We have no space to critique Existentialism, but for our purposes we consider it a style, indeed a mood, rather than a system. As such it inspired brilliant artistic moments rather than a coherent doctrine.

In 1929, after Beauvoir and Sartre passed second and first respectively in their final exams at the Sorbonne, he informed her, "From now on, I'm going to take you under my wing." He was emboldened by the failure of Beauvoir's lover, René Maheu, who'd left Paris in disgrace. The three were close, and the twenty-one-year-old Beauvoir, attracted by Maheu's good looks, had initially approached him. He gave her the name by which she would be known to intimates, "Beaver"; the nickname sprang from her preference for working in a group, as well as from its resemblance to her French name.

Between Beauvoir and Sartre there followed the famous pact on which they would base their fifty-year relationship. By mutual agreement they disdained bourgeois marriage. "What we have," the twenty-four-year-old Sartre told his companion, "is an *essential* love, but it is a good idea for us also to experience contingent love affairs." Their pact included a promise never to lie to one another and for each to tell the other everything. However, they agreed to a "two-year lease" during which they would remain faithful. But the Beaver went on sleeping with Maheu, who eventually grew tired of sharing his mistress. Contrary to his principles, Sartre continued to think about a conventional marriage. He'd already proposed to Beauvoir, who turned him down, and he would offer to marry a number of pretty women, ever younger as he grew older.

Simone de Beauvoir was born in 1908 in an apartment on the Boulevard du Montparnasse whose windows overlooked the cafés where she chose to spend much of her adult life. Her father Bertrand was a civil servant with aristocratic pretensions who did gradually worse in life. Artificial conventions prevailed at home, though Bertrand was dissolute and cheated on his beautiful wife. Beauvoir identified with her rakish father. Sartre, too, was born in Paris (in 1905), and he never distanced himself for long. He remained a devoted city-dweller, and while Beauvoir indulged in a passion for hiking and scrambling over mountains, her companion quipped that he was allergic to chlorophyll.

Sartre came from a distinguished Protestant family (Albert Schweitzer was a cousin), and though his father died young, he was pampered by his mother and remarkable grandfather, who invented the Berlitz system of teaching languages. However, the lad was belittled by a cruel stepfather, and at the age of thirty he wrote to Beauvoir, "Parents lodge like a knife in the skull of their children." He was taunted by his playmates for being wall-eyed, short, and ugly. Once they tricked him into approaching the belle of the class, who in front of the others spat out, "Who is this bum with one eye that says shit to the other?"

Beauvoir's early rejection of the usual domestic role in favor of becoming a philosopher was unheard of. Simone had beautiful eyes and a straight nose set in a patrician face; her harsh voice enhanced her attractiveness to some. She dressed in black, which made her appear even more glamorous. Despite the mismatch in looks between Beauvoir and Sartre, their attraction grew as he explained knotty points in Rousseau to her. She had "the feeling of finding myself: he was the shadow thrown by my future." She would ally herself with "someone more accomplished than myself, yet my equal, my double." This is the wish Narcissus went mad trying to satisfy.

The love of the similar makes for an idyllic courtship but usually goes stale without a third to objectify it. In the subtle psychology of love, an intense pairing calls forth another to act as witness. This is a sort of voyeurism, but in the age of the celebrity we are all steeped in voyeurism. The wide-screen image of movie stars in an erotic clinch exists only in the eye of the camera, which conveys this pseudo-passion to the rest of us observers. As for Sartre, he felt like the Beast who'd won the love of Beauty, and he was inclined to try his luck again. Sartre's heroes—Dumas, Byron, Wagner—were all mighty womanizers. Scruffy and half-blind, the little fellow saw himself as Don Juan. He wanted conquests in order to exhibit his prowess to the admiring Beaver. The Existential pact was in the main carried out but in a manner that sometimes caused pain to those contingent souls taken under the wings of the central pair.

The pair's biographers wrote of their sexual adventures as they understood them. Afterward the publication of their intimate letters came as a shock. Reviewing these in the *New York Times Book Review*, Ronald Hayman wrote, "For a man who said he preferred croissants to sex, Sartre had a remarkable number of affairs." Of Beauvoir he added, "She was almost as promiscuous as he was, carrying on lesbian love affairs with students and other young women who were also involved sexually with Sartre." This ignores the quality of their encounters and, more important, the flavor of their reportage to one another. Sartre's lust was not picky but was located in his head rather than groin. To the Beaver, he admitted he preferred to kiss and masturbate a naked woman without penetrating her, at which he was inept.

Feminists have had the greatest difficulty with Beauvoir's apparent taking advantage of her young partners. Remember that in France, indeed much of Europe, a professor going to bed with his or her students is commonplace. In America we have yet to outgrow the compulsion of the Romeo-and-Juliet image. The age-old tale of a young man who is initiated by an older woman, his mother's friend, when made into a TV movie is still advertised as being "on the edge."

Even so, Beauvoir's lesbian affairs (also no cause for alarm on the Continent) do look a little strained. Hayman writes that "she seems to have got more pleasure from sending [Sartre] bulletins about her lesbian lovemaking than from the sensual experiences themselves." Sartre demanded the details of the Beaver's lovemaking and sent her glowing reports on his, including a "hot off the press" item after he'd deflowered a virgin. In light of the letters, the feminist portrait of a long-suffering Beauvoir, who had no voyeuristic inclinations, needs to be amended. Here we do find a resemblance to Merteuil, who vicariously enjoyed her companion's frolics with young women whom she herself desired. We are a little surprised that Beauvoir and Sartre didn't bed down together with a third; this shows that they kept some distance between them. It would take the flower children of the sixties to put polyamorous theory into practice.

In 1930, with Sartre away doing military service, Beauvoir frequented low Parisian dives, including the infamous Sphinx, where Henry Miller acted as a freelance pimp; then she shifted her attentions to Pierre, a friend of Sartre's who was tutor to the children of a certain married lady. With the encouragement of her invalid husband, this lady had taken Pierre as her lover, and she in turn encouraged him to bring the Beaver to her spacious apartment on the Boulevard Raspail. Here, and later at the woman's country estate, a menage formed between this cultured and fashionable lady in her forties and the much younger Beauvoir and Sartre. She helped to refine the pair of writers and later to shelter them during the war. This menage was the inspiration for Beauvoir and Sartre's adopted Family, which intertwined sexuality, politics, and art.

Beauvoir and Sartre began their careers by teaching in provincial lycées, she in Rouen and he in Le Havre. They made the most of a position for which they weren't exactly suited, talking nonstop throughout the classes but treating the students as social equals. During the midthirties, when the companions held positions in Paris, their attention was seized by two sisters who had been Beauvoir's pupils, Olga and Wanda, aristocratic Russian émigrées. The Beaver was attracted by Olga's "blonde hair straying over a long, triangular face, her pale skin, her large wide-set eyes, her sudden dance steps in the middle of the street, her wild whims, her innate honesty, her spontaneity." Olga had those qualities that Sartre would term "authentic" and that he would raise to an ethic in his tetralogy *Paths to Freedom*.

Like Beauvoir's other students, Olga worshiped her teacher, who gradually seduced her. Beauvoir didn't foresee that Sartre would fall so completely beneath the spell of Olga's "naked, instant consciousness, which seemed only to feel with violence and purity." The menage was at first a dazzling success, and Beauvoir wrote, "Caught by the magic that sparked from our eyes as we met, each of us felt himself playing a double role—enchanter and enchanted at once." However, Olga, whose narcissism could be flattered by either sex, didn't relate to Sartre as a man. Her preference for Beauvoir drove him wild, especially when Olga kissed the Beaver full on the mouth, then merely brushed his cheek. Rather than become the obedient disciple, she had imposed her own whims on her teachers. Beauvoir recalled her as "Rimbaud, Antigone, every enfant terrible that ever lived, a dark angel judging us from her diamond-bright heaven."

Olga remained the Beaver's lover for years, until "the wispy creature's" heavy drinking, tantrums, and pitching herself downstairs soured the woman in her thirties. Still, Olga held off Sartre's persistent advances. His obsessive crush on her can't be disentangled from his frequent hallucination of this time: that he was being followed by a number of giant, menacing lobsters. He had done mescaline, which triggered the mirage, but it doesn't take a Freudian to realize the former mama's boy was externalizing a deep-seated fear of castration. With Olga by his side, he didn't see the lobsters, perhaps because he wasn't sleeping with her and had nothing to prove. Beauvoir admitted that Olga, who'd become more than contingent, endangered the essential pact, but she preferred her presence to Sartre's dementia.

Another young figure who joined the Family, Jacques-Laurent (Little) Bost, Beauvoir described as "quick-witted and droll ... with a dazzling smile and a most princely ease of bearing." He would become a journalist and a lifelong friend of Sartre and his causes, and he eventually took Olga off his mentors' hands by marrying her. Sartre, losing his hair, terrified of age and obscurity, turned to seducing a drama student. He sent Beauvoir detailed bulletins, marveling at how the girl sucked his tongue "with the strength of an electric suction fan" and describing her as "Provençale ... full of odors and curiously hairy, with a little black fur at the small of the back." The girl turned out to be a virgin who wanted deflowering, a task at which this time the underendowed philosopher hesitated.

Enter Maurice Merleau-Ponty, who would become managing editor of Les Temps Modernes, a journal of left-leaning opinion founded by Sartre. He was in love with Mademoiselle Provençale and berated his old school chum for not sleeping with her. Sartre finally managed the act after she performed oral sex on him, intimating to Beauvoir he'd done the girl a favor. This taking of virgins would become a specialty, probably because neither he nor his member posed a threat to the uninitiated. Sartre, in his reports, didn't neglect his long-term partner, calling the Beaver "charmer of my heart and my eyes, bulwark of my life, my consciousness, my reason."

In a society where a woman was, in Beauvoir's famous phrase, "the other"—that is, secondary—she had determined to be a key player but knew better than to let it show. Thus she adopted a Family in which the mother-lover figure could rule. By 1938 Beauvoir lived in a hotel in Montparnasse, Olga, who was engaged to Bost, lived beneath her, and she and Sartre made the nearby Dôme café their general headquarters. Sartre's hot pursuit of Olga's younger sister Wanda, prettier but with "the mental faculties of a dragonfly," was only slightly interrupted by Gallimard's publication of his first novel. *Nausea*, dedicated to the Beaver, brought him instant acclaim. A year later he published a collection of short stories, while a collection written by Beauvoir was rejected and withdrawn. Sartre's early reputation was made as a writer of fiction, a field he would influence less than drama.

The Family enlarged on the original pact of companionship, which Sartre suggested to the Beaver they make permanent: "We must always be together, because no one could understand us as we do each other." But the pair needed always to attach a third, so that even on a vacation to Greece, stolen time, they took along Bost. When Beauvoir recovered from feeling slighted by publishers and continued to write fiction, she chose as subject the trio with Sartre and Olga, with a Bost-like figure hovering nearby. Letting herself be advised by Sartre and his editor at Gallimard, she wrote *She Came to Stay*, which in 1943 became the literary sensation of the Occupation.

Kate and Edward Fullbrook, a British couple, have avoided the fundamental error of trying to disentangle the lives of the two companions and have attempted to capture the complexity of their sexual and creative lives. In their critical biography, *Simone de Beauvoir and Jean-Paul Sartre*, they realize that to these two, voyeurism was indispensable, that each enjoyed both exhibiting sexual feats and hearing of the other's with a third. "De Beauvoir's bisexuality," they write, "which she repeatedly and publicly had a good deal of fun denying during her lifetime . . . was clearly a source of titillation to Sartre." Unfortunately, they tend to ethnologize Sartre's perpetual search for virgin flesh, writing of harem formation and the like. Sartre, addressed by the Beaver in diminutives, such as "most dear little being," never took on two women at once. Virgins are useful to an underwhelming lover because they don't know any better. Sartre's willingness to share his women, not only with the Beaver but with male members of the

Family, is consistent with "common generalized variants of modern bohemianism," as the Fullbrooks put it, but was also clever and productive. It was his brain rather than heart that throbbed.

Beauvoir was more openly sensual yet collected. In July 1938, after noting that she dearly loved him, she informed Sartre, "Something extremely agreeable has happened to me. . . . I slept with Little Bost. . . . It was I who propositioned him, of course." She thought of the affair as "intense, but also light and easy and properly in its place in my life." Bost would prove invaluable to both his mentors, helping to produce Sartre's dramas, doing journeyman work in writing screenplays, and all without demanding credit. However, the next year, with war clouds darkening and both men called into the army, Beauvoir became conflicted. She had to choose which soldier to visit or spend time with on leave, and worse, she had to lie to Olga, who confided in her about her fiancé. Straight-faced, she recounted to Sartre a time when Bost had pulled guard duty and she spent the day in a dreary provincial café reading Heidegger, whom she now felt she understood.

By 1940, Beauvoir's affair with Bost had escalated, and in her letters to him she continually made comparisons between him and Sartre, to the latter's detriment. Bost wrote her at greater length and more amusingly than Sartre did. Beauvoir's ardent interest in the young man was spiced by the opportunity it gave her to take revenge on Sartre for his obsession with Olga. She had redrawn the lines of the menage. As the Fullbrooks note, " 'you and Bost,' and later 'Bost and you,' was to be the leitmotif of Beauvoir's wartime letters to Sartre." That February, Beauvoir, with her new love in Paris, wrote Sartre a long letter, concluding, "Bost forms part of my future in an absolutely certain—even essential—way." She had no intention of giving him back to Olga.

Sartre, stuck in an army camp among men who scorned him the way his adolescent schoolmates had, no doubt felt betrayed. He began to write ardently to Wanda, courting her on leave. Earlier, he'd taken her lightly, telling the Beaver that since her virginity got in the way of her supposed ambition to become a prostitute, she should be grateful to him for deflowering her. But in the winter of 1940, during the uneasy quiet of the phony war, Sartre assured Wanda, "I'd trample on everybody, even the Beaver . . . to be on good terms with you." Still, as the paterfamilias, Sartre blamed himself when his fantasy of a happy menage went awry. He wrote Beauvoir that he felt like "a small-scale bastard . . . a civil-service Don Juan." It was the most sardonic view he had ever taken of himself.

The outbreak of fighting in the spring and the collapse of France in six weeks under the Nazi onslaught, during which Sartre was taken prisoner, would split his and Beauvoir's lives in two. The Occupation that followed put a definitive end to the menage with their most attractive third, Bianca Bienenfeld, the true story of which has only recently surfaced.

A DISGRACEFUL AFFAIR

This is the title of a memoir by Bienenfeld, who is called Louise Vedrine in *Witness to My Life.* Actually the name was invented by Beauvoir in accord with her promise to keep Bianca's identity secret. But the posthumous English edition of the Beaver's "lost" letters has blown the cover. Worse, Beauvoir revealed her sticky affair with the young woman, formerly a student, in cold, Machiavellian prose. Since Bienenfeld is alive and well, she has replied at some length, accusing Sartre and Beauvoir of bad faith and other existential sins and their biographers of being dupes. Actually, the affair, when seen through the eyes of all three participants, is more revealing than shocking.

Bianca, of Polish-Jewish origin, encountered Beauvoir at the Lycée Molière in Paris in 1937 when she was sixteen. Beauvoir was far more forthcoming than any teacher she had known, and Bianca was struck by "her brilliant, piercing, bold intelligence." She seemed to be "a force in motion," headed for fame and glory. But Bianca, who already understood style, thought that Beauvoir's dress and pulled-back hair were plain and even tacky. A photo of the young woman shows that she was pretty, with delicate Semitic features, big bright eyes, and a profusion of carefully curled hair. There is no denying either her innocence or intelligence.

Bianca soon became teacher's pet; because she was dissatisfied with the prospect of becoming a traditional wife and mother, she hoped to acquire what she supposed was her teacher's independence. Bianca, who at first only heard of Sartre, intuited what he meant to Beauvoir, who admitted their relationship invited sexual adventures while demanding "absolute freedom with complete openness." Bianca observed that in fact the companions' obligations to their dependents (they supported Olga and Wanda) caused them to run perpetually short of time and money and to regiment their lives. Beauvoir would sit at a table at the Dôme and meet separately with one person after another.

Bianca is certain Beauvoir and Sartre were no longer having sex with one another by the time she knew them. After her graduation in 1938, the two women, on an arduous backpacking trip, became lovers, "shyly at first." Bianca attended the Sorbonne, where she was platonically involved with three male students of Sartre's, including Bernard Lamblin, whom she would later marry. She quipped that the group consisted of "Sartre and Simone de Beauvoir's offspring!" During the next winter, Daddy, encouraged by Mommy, began to pursue her. Sartre, who knew how to use compliments, was attentive and smooth talking. "No one, and certainly never a novelist, had ever told me I had beautiful eyes," reminisces Bianca. He could be playful or wise, instructing her in the technique used by this or that artist. In Montmartre, at a country-style café, Sartre declared his love for her. Fifty years later, as she read his published letters, she realized the café was his favorite seduction spot.

Bianca, though still involved with the Beaver, was pleased by Sartre's advances. She puts it simply: "We were a *threesome.*" Yet Sartre's behavior toward the young woman was contradictory. He callously took her virginity in a hotel room in daylight, hardly saying a word and making a lasting wound in her psyche. She became frigid throughout their physical relationship. But she was perceptive enough to realize that he was incapable of letting himself go: "His constantly wakeful intelligence broke all ties between his mind and his body." Sartre was at odds with the Freudians, but his vague "existential dread" was really self-loathing dating from an early age.

In contrast, Sartre's letters to Bianca during the summer of 1939, with Europe on the brink of disaster, are thoughtful and romantic. "My dear little Polack," he began in July, ending, "I love you with all my might." He assured Bianca that the Beaver felt likewise, that "our future is your future, there is no difference." Sartre insisted on their mutual closeness: "At some moment during the day when you were thinking of us, we were thinking of you, we were talking about you." On paper the philosopher composed an idyllic menage with all three madly in love and no jealousy. But these letters came from his parents' house in the country, where he admitted boredom was making him sentimental. Sartre was writing a romance novel for three, but since Bianca, after much stalling, had yielded to him, and Bost to the Beaver, he would have to change the plot.

Beauvoir's letters to Sartre about Bianca reveal a sensibility quite different from his. She could be warm and tender but also deceptive. She found herself having to deceive Bianca, Olga, and Wanda; she was usually more honest with the men. To Sartre, depressed in his meteorological unit in the army, she penned a serial chronicle of her sex life, mainly with Bianca. In November Beauvoir wrote, "We had a passionate night—the strength of that girl's passion is incredible. Sensually I was more involved than usual, with the vague, lousy idea that I should at least 'take advantage' of her body." But on another occasion, she compared sex with Bianca to eating "foie gras, and poor quality in the bargain." When she wrote that Bianca wasn't equal to her own passion, it was more true of herself.

Beauvoir now felt the young woman had become too demanding. Bianca's idea that she made an equal third with herself and Sartre angered her, especially because Beauvoir was promoting Bost from contingent to essential. Beauvoir was oriented toward three, but as often happens in a triangular construction, there was a question of who would be at the apex. She had become concerned that Bianca, more intellectual than Olga or Wanda, was gaining too much of Sartre's attention. Or was Beauvoir mainly troubled by Bianca's "passionate embraces," which were causing her to develop "a certain taste for [lesbian] relations?" In February 1940, with the war imminent, Beauvoir ordered Sartre to drop his little Polack. Her leverage over the reluctant soldier was compelling, and he wrote Bianca that everything was over between them. The turnabout in his attitude was so abrupt he couldn't explain it. When Bianca ran to the Beaver, she cushioned the blow a little, but the young woman realized she was to be cut adrift into shark-infested waters. Beauvoir insisted, as Sartre did when he came to Paris in April, that Bianca would get over it.

By June, the thirty-five-year-old philosopher was a prisoner of war, French resistance had collapsed, and the Nazi armies were rolling toward complete victory. Beauvoir could no longer ridicule Bianca's "prophesying doom like a Cassandra." She accepted a ride out of Paris in Bianca's father's car—a man she had ridiculed for his bourgeois ways. It is useless to argue over whether, as Bianca insists, "Sartre and Simone de Beauvoir did me only wrong." They both felt remorseful when she suffered a nervous breakdown, though it was brought on in part by the Occupation. Bianca would marry, fight in the Resistance, have children, and remain lifelong friends with the Beaver. What she considers insults found in the posthumous letters inspired her to write her own confessional book, *A Disgraceful Affair.* We need to remember, as was written of the great actor Henry Irving, "the genius sacrifices parents, spouse, children, friends in the quest for self-fulfillment. It's the nature of the beast."

THE "INNER WEATHER"

The biographer Dierdre Bair wrote that Beauvoir and Sartre "invent[ed] behavior as they went along," followed an "open approach to life," and "confidently welcomed all experience and encounters." Bianca Bienenfeld was certain the two Existentialists were playing a "big voyeuristic game." She faulted their philosophy for being a brand of "individualistic anarchy" that when the war broke out, led only to panic. There were Frenchmen who felt it resulted in collaboration. When the Germans banned the work of eight hundred writers counted unfriendly to the Nazis, Sartre wasn't on the list. During the war, he and Beauvoir published under the censorship, which broke the first rule of the Resistance, and they took advantage of the lack of competition to strengthen their own reputations. In the moral sphere, Existentialism at best resulted in situational ethics, whose vogue has come and gone.

In strictly literary terms, it is a stretch to rate either Beauvoir or Sartre as great. The single most important influence on their fiction was the work of John Dos Passos, and today their novels seem nearly as dated as his. In contrast, Sartre's plays are still performed, and his letters are stunning. Beauvoir's memoirs rank with the best—those of Casanova or Anaïs Nin—even if they are not quite as revealing. *The Second Sex*, regardless of its author's occasional "bad faith," remains a landmark. However, Existentialism as a formal philosophy was stillborn. Sartre supposed he was constructing a successor to Marxism, a system of explaining human behavior. But in the fifties, the ethnologist Claude Lévi-Strauss attacked his pretension by pointing out that his terminology, like his concepts, had failed to pass into general usage even among philosophers or sociologists. Beauvoir and Sartre had engaged in a dialogue only with each other and their tightly knit Family.

Were they successful in providing a living alternative to bourgeois marriage, with its concomitant cheating, hypocrisy, and love triangles? The Family, composed of younger lovers of Beauvoir and Sartre, may be seen as a preserve in which these older companions could poach. Some members eventually married each other, such as Olga and Bost, while others dropped out, and their places were taken by new recruits. Family activities were centered on getting out the magazine *Les Temps Modernes*, but according to Bair, "feuds, gossip, jealousy and spite," not to mention "all varieties of pairings, couplings and uncouplings," amused the two doyens.

Outsiders existed on the fringe, and for a time Jean Genet became the object of Sartre's fascination. But the ex-con didn't take to Beauvoir, whom he called "a tough bitch," while she despised his "silly fairy entourage." The Family welcomed another literary tough guy, Nelson Algren, when he visited Paris as the Beaver's lover. Sartre helped to translate his Chicago-esque prose into French, and the two men got on fine. Algren was puzzled that Sartre, despite being homely and badly dressed, "had no more difficulty finding women to sleep with than Cary Grant." Part of the reason was the highly visible Family itself, which, like Andy Warhol's Factory, attracted insecure young women with outsized artistic ambitions.

The Beaver's romance with Algren, which she chronicled in *The Mandarins*, her finest work in fiction, ended acrimoniously on his part. Like

Sartre's major and sometimes minor flames, Algren expected that he and Beauvoir would marry or at least live together. To Algren, this meant that Beauvoir would come to Chicago. But she never thought seriously of leaving her Paris and Sartre or the Family. In the sixties, toward the end, both elders found amenable younger companions to care for them, their papers, and their reputations. Beauvoir adopted Sylvie Le Bon and Sartre adopted Arlette Elkaim, and at first they formed a foursome for lunch or dinner. But according to Bair, "animosity and competition soon arose between the two young women."

Once again, Beauvoir and Sartre formed a threesome with either one of the women, avoiding bringing the two together. Sartre and Arlette and a male companion for her would vacation together. While this arrangement was easily accepted, Beauvoir's with Sylvie was subjected to continual gossip and surmise. Shortly before Sartre died, Beauvoir replied to a question, "I am fortunate to enjoy a perfect relationship with both a man and a woman." Transcending gender is both a constituent of a menage a trois and one of its rewards.

This freedom to choose one's mate in disregard of conventional or moral sanction was the escape clause in the contract between Sartre and Beauvoir. Their lives exemplified postwar Existentialism, by which we mean a psychological state shared by hip youth throughout Europe and America. The conservative *Spectator* complained because Beauvoir insisted on the supremacy of her moods, as though they were "a sort of inner weather, beyond [her] control." Indeed, Existentialism, exalting the momentary and the contrary, can be as moody as the weather. Sartre, writing to Bianca from the terrace of the Pelican Café in the ratty old port of Marseilles, brilliantly evoked the feel of his and de Beauvoir's accomplishment:

> It grew dark, a mild night without streetlights, darkness falling from the trees, we could hear people going on about their lives but we couldn't see them, it was cool, it was so poetic, and we talked about philosophic reality and we became existential and I looked at an illuminated ad on the opposite sidewalk, and I perceived it as existential. And then we went to bed, completely blissful, heads still full of words.

For Sartre, experience ended in words. For the film directors of the French New Wave—Godard, Vadim, Truffaut, and the others—the way was clear to present a new set of hand-held images, a different sort of antihero and antiheroine, and to begin a transcendence of roles that is very much in progress. It's no accident that the best-remembered Godard female protagonist is Jean Seberg, the *Herald Trib* girl in jeans and a T-shirt, hair clipped short as a boy's, who for no compelling reason turns in her macho lover Belmondo to the Paris police. And more accurately than the earlier wave, the director who consistently depicts the menage a trois in an existential light is Bertrand Blier. Well known for his *Get out Your Handkerchiefs*, which won the Best Foreign Film Oscar in 1978, and the more recent *Too Beautiful for You*, both of which starred Gérard Dépardieu, Blier's 1986 *Ménage* is the film that really pushes the envelope of gender.

Ménage opens in a cheesy late-night café with Monique (Miou-Miou) insulting her adoring, deadbeat husband, Antoine (Michel Blanc). Enter Bob (Dépardieu), big, flashy, and almost godlike. Showing off his roll of dough, he picks up the couple. He turns out to be a kinky burglar, an ex-con who has a thing for mousy Antoine. The trio breaks into several houses in a posh neighborhood, stealing but also getting into an orgy with a bored rich couple. Monique pursues Bob, who keeps after Antoine, who in turn insists he's not gay. The dialogue (even the censored English subtitles) is wonderfully raunchy, and Bob makes it clear just what he wants to do with Antoine.

Monique gets him in bed first, but Antoine eventually succumbs, and he and Bob have a tender affair. The remarkable aspect of Blier's vision, not to mention Blanc's acting, is that Antoine, who is an almost homely man, turns into an attractive woman. Yet even as he becomes more feminine, he grows tougher and takes charge of the menage. To Blier, "love between a man and a woman is always a fight—with the woman always having the overwhelming deep power." Perhaps that's why his women often need two men and why the men are usually buddies who are willing to share.

Ménage ends on an oddly predictive note. Bob, involved with mere mortals, has lost his magical thief's touch. The three have become street-walkers cruising for customers on a cold winter's day. Bob and Antoine are in drag, members of the third sex. Antoine is pretty but tarty, while Bob, dressed in a huge fur coat and a blonde wig, anticipates the hunk as queen, a motif popular on-screen today. The whores, on a coffee break while they prepare to pound the pavement once again, share a moment of bitter camaraderie that would have fascinated Sartre, been well portrayed by Genet, and best understood by Beauvoir, the professional sister.

THE GOLDEN PHALLUS

{D. H. Lawrence; Ernest Hemingway; Georges Simenon}

Every heart has a right to its own secrets.

D. H. LAWRENCE

W<small>ILFRID</small> S<small>CAWEN</small> B<small>LUNT</small>, <small>TO WHOM</small> in Blunt's old age Ezra Pound made a disciple's pilgrimage, was the master of menages a trois, at least of the variety that features a married couple and a third man who is the wife's lover and husband's companion. His memoirs, written toward the close of the Victorian era, declare the menage to be "one of the secrets of the heart which are not known even to our best novelists." Or at least the secret, if known, was rarely expressed.

All this changed in the next generation. Writers as different as D. H. Lawrence and Ernest Hemingway—both born during the reign of Victoria—began to explore, at the instigation of women they'd married, the triad of affections in their lives and work. Georges Simenon, who remains the most popular writer ever published, craved to be always at the center of a menage a trois or quatre. Other distinguished writers of the mid-twentieth century, such as Graham Greene and Jean Rhys, were intimately involved in threesomes but shied away from becoming public figures. Even Beauvoir and Sartre, always in the press, kept their menages quiet during their lifetimes.

Our chosen novelists were exhibitionists who sold themselves along with their work. Each wrote with his phallus—that is, as defined by Norman Mailer, "the sexual force of a man . . . his final moral product."

Partly because their work stays close to their lives, each of the three has contributed mightily to the creation of a modern style. It was Lawrence who made explicit sex the subject of serious fiction. Hemingway gave us economy, brevity, and precision in language—tough-guy talk that seems self-evidently right. Simenon invented the modern detective, and where would airport book racks or prime-time TV be without the gumshoe?

None of the three had much formal education. Each earned a great deal of money: Lawrence after his death, Hemingway much more quickly, and Simenon in movie-star style. For better or worse, each has helped shape the image of masculinity in our time: Lawrence as son and lover; Hemingway as hunter, war correspondent, and all-round celebrity; Simenon as the man who wrote five hundred novels and (perhaps this was a boast) bedded ten thousand women. In theory these men believed in monogamy, but they attracted powerful women so strongly that a menage of some sort became inevitable. More important, each man realized the necessity of androgyny in order for an artist to work at all. It is the third sex—the voice of the Other within—that ensures creation. At their most revealing, the three novelists help to illumine not only what Lawrence called "phallic consciousness" but the secrets of the human heart.

LORENZO'S MEN AND WOMEN

Bold print headlining a *New York Times* review of Brenda Maddox's recent biography of D. H. Lawrence casually referred to the "notoriously carnal-minded novelist." Since the carnal and mental are opposite, "carnal-minded" is a contradiction in terms. Probably the headline writer hadn't read Lawrence. As recently as 1960, attorneys for the British crown, who hadn't read him either, attempted to ban the unexpurgated Penguin edition of *Lady Chatterley's Lover* on the grounds of obscenity, which they defined as "a tendency to deprave and corrupt." Only Penguin's victory rescued the novel from the absurd status of a classic forbidden by law to be read. Compared to James Joyce, say, or current writers, Lawrence seems obsessively romantic but not down and dirty. The master of the four-letter word, Henry Miller, wrote that Lawrence's language is "matchless—reminiscent of the best in the Bible."

However, Lawrence's detractors never give up. The reviewer of Maddox's biography, a professor who studies pornography, complained that the author failed to account for "the bizarreries of Lawrentian sexuality," which he found "a distinctly unappetizing subject." This is a moral judgment thinly disguised as aesthetic. Even Maddox in a sidebar confessed to disliking Lawrence's novels and to finding his Amazonian wife Frieda uninteresting "as a character in her own right." Maddox approached Lawrence's life in the manner of a pathologist viewing a diseased corpse. Her autopsy posed blunt-edged questions: Why didn't Lawrence's marriage to the motherly Frieda dispel his homosexual yearnings? Why should an idealist calmly tolerate being a cuckold? The answers lie in Lawrence's emotional needs, which were poorly matched with a lack of sexual stamina. He demanded, although he was never up to, a menage a trois. Curiously, the headline writer guessed well: Lawrence's carnality could be found where he railed against women for having it—in his head—while Frieda's sexuality was right between her legs.

Writing during World War I to Lady Ottoline Morrell, Lawrence described a young composer friend as a dual person who would need two wives to make "the real blood connection and the real conscious or spiritual connection." Though Lawrence used his own rhetoric, he intuitively grasped the reflected (and thus double) nature of the narcissist. Monogamy, he continued, was for "those who are whole and clear, all in one stroke. But for those whose stroke is broken into two different directions, there should be two fulfillments." He felt that he himself was, if not unified, at least becoming so and that he and Frieda were growing "more and more truly married." Once this was achieved, "we can all three be real friends."

Lawrence wished to evade an affair he'd given Ott cause to believe they would have. Her husband Philip, the MP who worked closely with the Bloomsbury war resisters, already cooperated with his wife's lover Bertrand Russell, and Frieda had no objection to Lawrence going to bed with Ott. Lawrence spoke boldly but was tentative in action, weighing what little he could manage with those women denigrated by Frieda as his "spiritual brides." The man was tubercular all his life. He fled from treatment—long, expensive, and uncertain of outcome—and backed off from expenditures of energy that didn't go into his writing. Harder to explain is Lawrence's vicious satire of Lady Ott's looks, manners, and clothes, portraying her as Hermione in *Women in Love*, where her crush on the author and his disdain are displayed to the world. This caused Ott to hold up publication of the masterpiece for several years.

David Herbert (Bert) Lawrence was born in 1885 in a village in a coal-mining region of Nottinghamshire, a miner's son. His father, a handsome man, wasn't the brute Lawrence portrayed in *Sons and Lovers*, nor was his mother the saint, though she was neurotically devoted to her sickly boy. Bert liked to cook and clean, and to the end he reflected his pious mother's prejudices, such as an aversion to the sight of the naked body of the opposite sex. According to Norman Mailer, his probable fate was "to have the sexual life of a woman"—that is, to become gay. Instead, Mailer believes, he made himself a man "by an act of will." We hold that Lawrence's conscious struggle for the love of both sexes is the mainspring of his work.

The young man got through the local college and taught school in a poor neighborhood south of London. He'd published his first novel and gained some erotic experience when in 1912 he visited Professor Ernest Weekley, his former teacher and a writer of popular books on learning languages. Lawrence desired his help in obtaining a position in Germany. He lunched with Weekley and his German wife Frieda, then thirty-two. She found him tall, thin, intense, already darkly brooding, his needs unmet. The professor went away, and Lawrence and Frieda stayed talking until after nightfall. He was entranced by her "husky and dominant voice." This is an aspect of sexual attraction—the masculinized female voice—that appealed to each of our novelists. Lawrence walked eight miles to his lodging, sat down, and wrote to Frieda, "You are the most wonderful woman in all England."

She was one of three daughters of Baron von Richtofen, a Prussian army officer who was given an administrative post in Alsace-Lorraine, newly ceded from France. He gambled away his money so that his daughters, having no dowry, had to fend for themselves. At nineteen Frieda, "good-looking, fresh-faced, strapping," married her English professor, thought of by Lawrence as an "elegant gentleman." Frieda came to live in Nottingham, bore three children, and out of boredom indulged in pastries and an occasional affair. In 1907 she visited her married sister Else in Munich. While sitting in a café in art-drenched Schwabing, eating Wiener schnitzel, she met Else's lover Otto Gross, an Austrian psychoanalyst whom Freud thought insane. Frieda had begun to live.

Otto was extraordinarily good-looking with tousled red hair, pale, childishly innocent eyes, a hooked nose, and full lips. He was a cocaine addict. Otto's father, a proto-Nazi psychologist, advocated the extermination of "Gypsies, tramps and revolutionaries," while to his rebellious son psychology was a tool of revolution. "The truly healthy state," he told Jung, who reported it to Freud, "is sexual immorality." Otto preached Free Love taken to its extreme. Because the only sickness was inhibition, nothing needed to be repressed. It was a message heeded by bored wives, and Frieda initiated the affair with this "genius at love."

Otto believed in multiple partners. Frieda seems to have had no problem sharing him with Else and with his wife Friedel, Else's best friend, both of whom were pregnant with his children. The pair spent a few weeks together, holed up in Else's husband's pied-à-terre; Frieda wore a blue dressing gown that had been worn by Otto's previous women and would adorn future lovers. Otto immortalized her sexual stamina in the nickname "little Turkish horse," which refers to that most obvious means of birth control, anal intercourse. Indeed, Otto found Frieda a veritable goddess of sex, "free from all the false shame and sham Christianity."

While they were in Amsterdam on her way back to England, Frieda presented Otto with a ring with the heads of three women in relief—herself, Else, and his wife. "You won't find three people like the three of us on every street-corner," she wrote. However, Otto kept adding lovers and drug habits until he overdosed in 1920. Frieda never saw him again, though five years later, when Lawrence walked into her living room, she knew instantly she'd found her second prophet of the phallus.

The pair eloped. Frieda felt no loss at leaving Professor Weekley, who'd grown surly and mocking toward her. But under the law he could refuse her a divorce and keep her from her children. Frieda's breaking into tears at missing them angered Lawrence, who would call her all sorts of names. Their quarrels, which became legendary, sometimes turned physical. Stocky Frieda proved more than a match for frail Lawrence. Their liaison, eventually legalized, coincided with the outbreak of the war. As an enemy alien whose cousin was the flying ace known as the Red Baron, Frieda was watched closely. Lawrence, whose novel *The Rainbow* was declared obscene and banned, was equally anathema to the government. The couple threw themselves on the mercy of admirers, whom Frieda would sleep with, though not Lawrence.

Lawrence was often taken with a particular man, but the attraction was usually intellectual, and he couldn't get on with intellectuals for long. It was Frieda who kept up relations with E. M. Forster and Bertrand Russell after they both became fed up with Lawrence. In Cornwall, where the couple hoped to ride out the war, Lawrence did some work for the wealthy Cecil Gray, a young dilettante who fancied himself a composer. Lawrence courted him, talking much about homosexuality. One day he burst into Gray's cottage to demand, "How long have you been in love with me?" While Lawrence involved himself, perhaps sexually, with a young farmer, Frieda spent her afternoons at Gray's, becoming his lover. The authorities eventually expelled the suspect couple from Cornwall.

In his memoirs, Gray wrote of Lawrence, "His physical personality was puny and insignificant . . . and his sexual potentialities exclusively cerebral." He declared the man to be nearly impotent, which he had heard from Frieda. When Hilda Doolittle, the American poet called H. D., made overtures to Lawrence, they fell flat. H. D., who was sheltering the couple, was certain Frieda and she and Lawrence were eternally wedded, meant to form "a perfect triangle." She asked Frieda to coax her husband to make love to her, but Frieda assured her, "Lawrence does not really care for women." Only in his imagination did the writer achieve gratification, and it was of a polysexual nature.

Lawrence was attracted by the German Romantic tradition of male bonding, and he might have engaged his libido exclusively with young working-class men, as did Christopher Isherwood in 1930s Berlin. Soldiers, athletes, even hustlers were the objects of sexual desire in that milieu, and this is the type whose body viscerally excited Lawrence. But as he looked for an ultimate merging with Woman (his "blood consciousness"), so he wanted from Man a union hardly possible in the literary world in which he moved. Maddox refers to Lawrence's "dream of a triangular marriage, in which his partnership with his wife would be supplemented by the close friendship with a man, a blood brother." Such an archaic comradeship between men, though rare, can still result from the pressures of war or revolution or even the hunt or sport, from all of which Lawrence's poor health disqualified him.

At the very end of *Women in Love*, the Lawrence stand-in tells the Frieda stand-in, "You are all women to me. But I wanted a man friend, as eternal as you and I are eternal." She replies that he's just spouting a theory; he can't have two kinds of love at once. He replies that he doesn't believe her. Actually Lawrence's chance at erotic bonding with another man could only come through Frieda. His novels from the early twenties, such as *The Plumed Serpent*, extol the dominant male for whom blood and sex mix into a magic potion. It is almost a James Bond fantasy, complete with adolescent intrigue, the wish-fulfillment dream of the impotent. One character from *Serpent* stands out: Don Cipriano, the possessor of "an intense maleness," who is modeled on Lieutenant Angelo Ravagli, a follower of Mussolini and Frieda's lover.

The Lawrences met Angelo during the winter of 1925–26, when they rented a villa on the Italian Riviera from his wife Serafina, a teacher of history in Savona. Angelo, a Casanova type, arrived in his dress uniform, which included a blue silk sash across his broad chest and a hat sporting the glossy black feathers of a rooster. Both Lawrences were taken not only with Angelo's dress but with his smart manner. About this short, dark, agile man, Frieda suggestively wrote, "I am thrilled by his cockfeathers. He is almost as nice as the feathers!" According to Janet Byrne, Frieda's biographer, she and Ravagli "began an affair sometime after their first meeting . . . probably with Lawrence's knowledge." Byrne suggests that the couple hoped the addition of the soldier's energy would revive Lawrence's carnal interest. But while he appreciated Angelo's abilities and liked Serafina, he was too far gone with TB to make love.

Frieda, after Lawrence's death, would eventually marry her Angelino, but she didn't entirely take him away from Serafina and his two children. While they lived on a ranch near Taos, New Mexico, she supported his extended family out of the proceeds of Lawrence's royalties, and he visited Italy when possible. Angelo made no attempt at sexual fidelity to his much older second wife, who claimed there were nights when she'd rather read a book. The Taos art community decided Angelo was the model for the gatekeeper Mellors in *Lady Chatterley's Lover*, and he may have been, to the same extent the dying Lawrence was himself the impotent Sir Clifford. After a while, Frieda, Angelo, and Dorothy Horgan, a well-heeled, married New Yorker who liked to dance, settled into a menage a trois. Along with other Lawrence admirers, they perpetuated a cult of Free Love around his name. The collier's son who insisted it was indecent to make love with the lights on would have been horrified!

Back in October 1926 Aldous and Maria Huxley arrived in Italy to visit Lawrence. The bisexual Maria, whose teenage crush on Lady Ott had led her to attempt suicide, now seduced women for her husband. Huxley would become Lawrence's foremost literary disciple, and his *Brave New World* echoes the theme of primitive virtue. Huxley noticed that "Lawrence was in some strange way dependent on [Frieda's] presence physically. . . . I have seen him rise from what I thought was his death bed, when Frieda away came back from a short absence." Indeed, Lawrence on his death bed (he passed away in a French sanatorium in 1930) told Frieda she was all that had mattered to him. What, then, compensated Frieda for the abuse Lawrence heaped on her?

"Always when he was in the middle of a novel or writing I felt happy," she confided in her memoir. "There was a new thing coming into the world." Here was the real triad: Lawrence, Frieda, and a novel. The man wasn't impotent after all.

SINISTER SEX

When the heirs of Ernest Hemingway and Scribner's released the posthumous novel *Garden of Eden* in June 1986, the reviews were mostly enthusiastic. Both E. L. Doctorow in the *New York Times* and John Updike in *The New Yorker* felt that the ailing novelist, who after several attempts killed himself in 1961, had done his best work since *The Sun Also Rises*, his paean to the Lost Generation of the 1920s. Although the published *Eden* was extracted out of an unfinished manuscript of more than twice its size and can't represent its author's final views on bisexuality or menage a trois, subjects that pervade it, Doctorow held that the older Hemingway had shown "the enlargement of a writer's mind toward compassion." Updike realized that the Old Man still regarded Woman as an opponent, a slippery fish to hook, conquer, and display as a prize. However, he wrote that *Eden* "confronts sexual intimacy, marriage, and human androgyny with a wary but searching tenderness that amounts, for a man so wrapped up in masculine values and public gestures, to courage."

Hemingway's holograph manuscripts have only recently become available to scholars. Since he liked to write quickly from his immediate experience, the futile fifteen-year struggle to complete the posthumously published texts, lasting from 1946 to his death, amounts to a failure of will but an equal triumph of content. At last, the inventor of a hard-shelled legendary self—war hero, big-game hunter, and aficionado of the bullring—has delved into ambiguous goings-on under the covers. Hemingway's Eden—his famed "fiesta" way of life—was from the first undermined by a sinister sex: not Woman, though he calls her "Devil," but the Third Sex. That the garden is set on a San Andreas fault of androgyny is one of Papa's final realizations. To understand his pained probing into his own nature, we need to start with his mother Grace, the "all-American bitch."

Ernest was born in 1899 in Oak Park, Illinois, into a family he called "dangerous" but that would now be termed dysfunctional. His father Clarence was negligible, suffered from depression, and in 1928 committed suicide, as would three of his six children. He was a righteous sort who chastised his son on the occasion of his first divorce and consigned him to hell. While Ernest despised his father as a weakling who was "bitched" to death, he both feared and hated his mother. Grace, a former opera singer who never let the family forget it, had a strange fixation: she insisted on being the mother of same-sex twins. Since her daughter Marcelline had been born only a year before Ernest and they looked alike, she created this illusion by dressing them identically.

In preschool years, the siblings were both got up as girls in "fluffy dresses and picture hats." Then Marcelline was kept back a year so she and Ernest could enter first grade together. Grace, wanting the so-called twins to *be* alike, cropped Marcelline's hair in a Buster Brown cut identical to Ernest's. She ignored her daughter's tearful protests and dressed both as boys. When Marcelline tried to fiddle with her hair, Grace forced her to wear a baby bonnet to school. Ernest witnessed the ridicule heaped on her by classmates. The effect of this on the boy's certainty of his gender role is unclear, but according to Rose Marie Burwell he lost the ability to empathize. He once boasted that after eleven he became armored and indifferent to any punishment meted out.

Fast-forward to Horton Bay, Michigan, where in the summer of 1921 in a white clapboard Methodist church twenty-one-year-old Ernest wed Hadley (née Richardson), who was twenty-eight. She came from Saint Louis—as did the first three of Ernest's four wives—solid, handsome, a virgin. Like her man, she was fleeing a tyrannical mother and the crushing moral weight of Middle America. Although Ernest was reluctant to ease off his ties to other girlfriends, he became a loyal husband who taught his wife to shoot and fish. He married a motherly woman with a trust fund and no literary ambitions, who came to seem his buddy.

The newlyweds soon arranged passage to France, where other expatriates, studying how to order wines in French, awaited them in Left Bank cafés and "American bars." On the eve of sailing Ernest urged Hadley to have her waist-length red hair cut off just below her ears. It was the style first worn by radicals such as Louise Bryant; by middecade it would sweep America. Yet Hadley never felt right in short hair. She wore it because Ernest liked the boyish look. For a time her romantic hope that she and her man would be "all and all to each other" was fulfilled. Ernest often contrived to be the center of feminine attention, and Hadley joked he wanted a harem. But Harold Loeb—the model for Robert Cohn in *The Sun Also Rises*—remarked that Hemingway felt guilty if he stared at a streetwalker for too long.

During a magic five years the Hemingways lived *la vie bohème*, hobnobbed with literati, and made a child, Jack, nicknamed Bumby, whose godmother was Gertrude Stein. Ernest worked as a journalist and published short stories in Ford Madox Ford's *Transatlantic Review.* Hadley thought Ernest was a prince, while he wrote to a friend, "So you're in love again. Well, it's the only thing worth a damn to be. No matter how being in love comes out it's sure worth it all while it's going on." One incident marred the couple's bliss: in December 1922, while Hadley was traveling to join Ernest in Switzerland, her suitcase containing the manuscripts of his early fiction was stolen from her train compartment. There were no copies. Ernest never forgave her.

In 1925 in Paris the Hemingways met two couples and one woman who would change their lives: Zelda and Scott Fitzgerald, Sara and Gerald

Murphy, and Pauline Pfeiffer. Ernest and Scott recognized each other as fellow spokesmen for a generation in the way that Byron and Shelley had, not without some jealousy. But the effect of Ernest's watching Zelda and Scott fight was to increase his distrust of the wife of a great man. There is an anecdote about Scott and Zelda dining outdoors with the Murphys on their first visit to the Riviera. Isadora Duncan, already a cultural icon, was seated nearby. Scott introduced himself, chatted, kneeled, and the dancer ran her fingers playfully through his hair. Zelda flung herself across the table and over the terrace. When she reappeared, she was scratched and bleeding. Ernest concluded that Zelda was mad but also that the woman you loved was out to ruin you.

Pauline Pfeiffer, a correspondent for *Vogue*, had dark boyish bangs and shapely legs. This heiress exuded a flapper dash that suited her for the smart set of Americans in Paris. She was Hadley's companion at first, a friendship that gradually included Ernest. That Christmas the Hemingways went skiing in Austria, and Pauline joined them. Biographer James Mellow notes, "Photographs show Hadley and Pauline, each beaming broad smiles, posed with Hemingway; the two women sitting affably together . . . smiling like sorority sisters." Pauline and Ernest became drinking buddies, and he found himself aroused by "the strange wonderful new girl." Back in Paris, Pauline wrote to her adopted buddies, "How I miss you two men!"

Ernest, who left Hadley in Austria while he traveled to New York to speak with Scribner's about publishing *The Sun Also Rises*, wanted an affair with Pauline but not at the cost of his marriage. He had immersed himself in Turgenev, who'd lived so much of his life in a menage, declaring him "the greatest writer there ever was." In Paris on his return, he first slept with Pauline. When (in the memoir *A Moveable Feast*) Ernest wrote about "the unbelievable wrenching, killing happiness" he felt, he may have been describing their contorted sexual experience. Pauline's Catholicism demanded she use no other means of birth control than coitus interruptus, a practice she later admitted Ernest hated. Meanwhile Pauline toyed with the absent Hadley, writing her that "Ernest was a delight to me. I tried to see him as much as he would see me." Hemingway, on returning to his wife and child, indulged himself in a fit of remorse. This led to his feeling closer than ever to Hadley and to the flowing of his creative juices, enabling him to finish *Sun*.

When the Hemingways returned to Paris, Pauline continued to see them as a couple and Ernest on the sly. Hadley ignored the gossip in the American community and, in April, toured the Loire Valley with Pauline and her lesbian sister. But the trip enlightened her, and afterward she and Ernest had a row. He left for Madrid, where he wrote frequently to both women, intending to keep both. In mid-May Hadley took Bumby to stay at the Murphys' Villa America near Antibes, a sleepy seaside town that Gerald had turned into a mecca for expatriates. Bumby came down with whooping cough, and Hadley and he moved over to a villa the Fitzgeralds had vacated. Pauline offered to come and help nurse Bumby, and Hadley accepted. By early June she and Ernest had arrived. The Murphys gave a party, and Scott Fitzgerald, drunk as usual, insulted his hosts for being snobs. Indeed, Hadley felt Sara favored the more sophisticated Pauline. Hadley also resented Pauline's influence on Ernest.

The spring of 1926 was as close as he would come to a threesome in real life. With Pauline in the spare room, "there we were à trois," Hadley recalled. "We were out on the beach a lot, but I couldn't swim." Still, she tanned and looked better than she had in years. The two women sun-bathed nude together, Pauline dark and slim, Hadley fair-skinned and "in bloom." Ernest was sleeping with Hadley and making love to Pauline in secluded coves; the three would eat breakfast in bed together. Ernest, as usual, wrote well when surrounded by women, and in A Moveable Feast he recalled this time: "The husband has two attractive girls around when he has finished work. One is new and strange and if he has bad luck he gets to love them both. . . . All things wicked start from innocence."

In July, along with the Murphys, all three went to Pamplona together for the running of the bulls. But after Pauline returned to Paris, Ernest and Hadley decided to break up. They returned to Antibes, where Gerald advised Ernest to make a clean break with his wife, who he felt only hindered his work. Gerald loaned Ernest money and a studio apartment in Paris and so facilitated a divorce he thought was inevitable. Ernest forever after hated him for his help. And though Pauline became his second wife and the mother of three children, he never forgave her either. After the war, after the brief repetition of a menage in Key West, he left Pauline for journalist Martha Gellhorn, who became his third wife. When he was writing Eden, he made Pauline, in John Updike's words, "both Eve and ser-pent." Reviewers were impressed by the older Hemingway's sexual realism and complexity, but in his garden one woman is called "Devil." His pal Marlene Dietrich made her reputation on the same hoary concept.

Pauline was correct when she said Catholic confession would be good for Hemingway. Eden, though a novel, is a confession: of his playing in bed a passive, feminine role, of his fetishism and incest fantasies. It is a more kinky piece of work than critics have realized. Its protagonist David

Bourne, a flyer in the Great War, is a novelist beginning to have success. He is half of a handsome 1920s couple, on honeymoon in a quiet village on the Riviera. Although the story is told from Bourne's point of view, he is directed by his wife Catherine. In the morning they swim in a private cove. Blond Catherine, to become dark, bakes herself in the sun. Then, in identical fishermen's shirts and shorts, the pair drink their lunch. The townsfolk think they are brother and sister, an illusion heightened by their getting the same short haircut. Much of *Eden* is taken up by descriptions of eating, boozing, and appointments at the coiffeur's.

Catherine's cuts are ever shorter and more bleached. To Catherine short hair means emancipation: "I'm a girl. But now I'm a boy too and I can do anything and anything and anything." In bed with David she likes to do "unspeakable devil things," which translates into climbing on top of him and taking charge sexually: "He lay there and felt . . . her hand holding him and searching lower and he helped with his hands and then lay back in the dark and . . . felt the weight and the strangeness inside and she said, 'Now you can't tell who is who can you?'"

David takes to calling Catherine "Devil," but he also admits he likes the switching of roles, cross-dressing, and blur of gender. He needs the feminine to tap into the well of feeling that his masculine act has shut up. "Don't say that anyone tempted you or that anyone bitched you," he warns his image in the mirror. He is as fascinated as she by their double image when nude: "They looked at each other standing touching in the long mirror on the door." This garden has more mirrors than a New Orleans bordello! *Eden* is essentially about narcissistic twinning, the synthesis of male and female that causes creation to happen. But just as many tribal peoples believe that creation requires a third, Catherine in her shamanistic role of Serpent needs to usher in him-her.

David undergoes an inner change to the feminine to correspond with Catherine's appropriation of the masculine. There is an insubstantial third, a sort of unholy ghost, that inhabits and joins both her and David. But Catherine also introduces a flesh-and-blood third: Marita, little Mary, whose name is no coincidence.

Marita, a small, dark lesbian sporting Catherine's haircut, is breaking up with her girlfriend. Catherine finds her at their coiffeur's and brings her to meet David at their hotel. Marita, whose character is not as well realized as Catherine's, quickly falls in love with both Bournes, and the women drag David into a menage. Marita informs him, "I hope you like having two girls. Because I am yours and I'm going to be Catherine's too." The trio swim naked, drink martinis, kiss, and dress alike. But though the women have a brief hot fling and Catherine flaunts her lesbian love, Marita gravitates toward David, the writer. Now he has a dark and a light girl, but he complains because after a day's work, he misses and loves both.

Catherine begins to make caustic remarks, such as calling Marita "wife of the day." She asks about David's performance—"Was he good today, Marita?"—insinuating that he's too mechanical. It becomes clear that Catherine is jealous of David's creativity; her sexual shenanigans can't substitute for this gift. In the end, the menage will only magnify what's wrong between the couple. The most telling moment comes when David, on what is supposed to be his day with Marita, finds her in bed with Catherine. The latter assures him that Marita was faithful to him but coaxes him to join them in bed, "so we can both be faithful to you." David, whom she calls a puritan, demurs.

Hemingway is closer to David than Catherine is to Pauline. His best-realized female protagonist contains elements of Martha Gellhorn and Zelda Fitzgerald, and Marita has some trace of Valerie Danby-Smith, his final infatuation. In *Eden*, Marita will be left to tend to the writer's needs—including presenting her ass for him to penetrate, underneath him—after Catherine goes off into the sunset. As a parting shot, she burns the manuscript of the African story that he is working on because it represents a world she cannot share: primitive, innocent, and polygamous. This Edenic garden where man conquers beast and the women are under control is David's, and Hemingway's, dreamworld.

Aside from its occasional biological occurrence, twinning is a sort of metaphor. A boy and a girl, though dressed in the same clothes and hair-cut, cannot be identical twins. Ernest's mother created for him an alter ego, one who absorbed the punishments of life. Achieving manhood, he was able to create a kind of Superman image: the novelist as macho hero. But beneath the gun-toting, whiskey-swilling facade beat the heart of a Clark Kent. Ernest was never content with his ideal passive woman, Hadley. He needed to add a more aggressive, dominating type such as Pauline. Ernest, because in bed he was no Hemingway, couldn't get the pair to mix for long. Still, with the nostalgia of Baudelaire, if not the poetry, he could write of his fantasy: Africa, the Garden of Eden.

PULP FICTION

In a 1953 interview for *The New Yorker*, Brendan Gill characterized Georges Simenon, then living with his second wife Denise and their son Johnny in a charming farmhouse in rural Connecticut, as an "addict of domesticity.... He plays the role of beslippered paterfamilias to the hilt."

Simenon boasted that the pregnant Denise acted as his literary and film agent and supervised the burgeoning empire of Simenon, Inc. Later Henry Miller wrote the couple from Big Sur to confess his addiction to Simenon's novels and added, "I shall never achieve the perfection you have arrived at in life. You both inspire me, give me the courage to believe that all is still possible."

Neither the interviewer nor the correspondent realized that this five-year interval in the fifties presented an unusual lull in Simenon's constant migrations accompanied by feverish night-crawling. Even then his first wife Tigy lived a few miles away with their son Marc, along with her devoted servant Boule, Georges's longtime mistress. Biographer Patrick Marnham writes that "for the duration of Marc's childhood at least, Simenon was still trying to keep the ménage à quatre on the road." Simenon was often involved on a casual basis with several women at once, sometimes four in one day. He was an inconsiderate husband, jealous of any male attention paid to his wife or mistress, but a sympathetic father to his children.

The phenomenon of Simenon emphasizes the question raised by the lives of Roché, Byron, Casanova, Hugo, and Sartre: what makes the "man who loves women" continually prowl after the perfect fuck? Denise, who found it interesting to accompany her husband to whorehouses, estimated he'd laid a mere twelve hundred women in his lifetime. To confound his critics, Simenon was an embarrassingly prolific author. He wrote 193 novels under his own name and another 200 using eighteen pseudonyms. His world sales have been estimated at over five hundred million copies in fifty-five languages. This playboy wrote a considerable body of serious fiction. His admirers include fellow writers from Colette to John le Carré and especially André Gide, and film personalities from Jean Renoir to Charlie Chaplin and Dirk Bogarde. Simenon claimed to be "searching for a human truth beyond psychology, which is only an official truth." Might it be that some men (and women) are built differently from the rest of us—that their *minds* are more largely sexual?

In this case we have an answer in the Simenon nose. He was born with an acute sense of smell and a sensory memory that would lead him to create the celebrated "atmospheres" of his fiction. "Big nose," he writes of his adolescence, "for I was inhaling life through my nostrils, through my every pore, the colors, the lights, the odors and noises of the street." In the same passage from his *Intimate Memoirs,* which Simenon wrote in his seventies, he recalls his hunger for "the women I passed whose wiggling hips were enough to give me almost painful erections." Hunger—triggered by any of the senses—best describes Simenon's insatiable sex drive. He loved to eat and make love, so it followed that his most enduring liaisons were with his cooks. He would take Boule, or later Teresa, behind the kitchen door, temporarily interrupting their preparation of dinner, perhaps sausages, "swollen and juicy, served with red cabbage and surrounded by an agreeable hint of garlic."

Two menages a trois bracketed Simenon's womanizing. They provided a domestic structure that kept him on a creative course. Like a citizen of ancient Athens, he kept a wife and a domestic to serve his needs. In addition, he sought adventure with prostitutes. "I wanted to learn the truth," Simenon claimed to a reporter. "I needed women physically and I also had a need for communication. You only know a woman when you have slept with her." To his eternal regret, Simenon would find out how misleading that cliché can be.

In 1903 Georges was born in Liège to a lower-middle-class Catholic family, part of a large Belgian clan. He adored his father, an insurance clerk, one of the models for the character of Inspector Maigret. Early on, Georges found himself at loggerheads with his mother, a stingy woman who reserved her affection for his brother. Georges, a prize pupil at school, thought seriously of becoming a priest. By the end of World War I, the allure of female flesh and his observations of human chicanery in German-occupied Liège had turned the former altar boy into a wise guy.

After his father died in 1918, Georges became a hack journalist to support his family. His writing style evolved out of deadlines on criminal cases that forced him to compress or invent his stories. In looks, Simenon was inconspicuous. Brendan Gill described the famous novelist: "Neither tall nor short, ugly nor handsome, he would pass unnoticed in any crowd save for the extraordinary mobility of his square face." The cub reporter, in a snap-brimmed hat and trench coat, tried to look hard-boiled, and in drinking and whoring he outdid his seniors. His initiation into the Liège underworld formed the basis of his tough view of humanity.

Georges joined a sinister postwar group of bohemians called "La Caque." Several of these nihilists were charged with murder. To Gill he remarked, "The crimes I write about . . . I would have committed if I had not got away. I am one of the lucky ones." Typically, Simenon denied credit to his first wife, who saved him as surely as his second nearly destroyed him.

In 1920 the eighteen-year-old Georges met Régine Renchon, an art student three years his senior. The opposite of the flashy women he usually dated, Régine was plain, small, and mannish. The couple married to satisfy their parents and left for Paris: she to paint, he to write. Georges, out of his need for absolute possession, renamed his women, and so Régine became "Tigy." In his memoirs he mused, "Love? Yes, of course, but mainly an intellectual one."

Georges had no intention of being faithful to Tigy. In Paris to get a job, on the night before he returned to Liège for his wedding, he picked up two Dutch girls and engaged in his first recorded menage a trois. But wanting "a ball and chain," he thrived under Tigy's steadying influence. She gave him the confidence he needed to turn his talent into a career. Aside from a stint working for a right-wing rag, Georges began to write short stories. After Colette, who edited a weekly newspaper, accepted one of these in 1923 and advised him to stop acting literary, Georges pared his prose style to the bone. Writing some five thousand words a day and never revising, the author, under various pseudonyms, churned out a mountain of pulp fiction.

Tigy, devoted to her painting, refused to have children. It is interesting that Georges, after yearning for affection from a cold mother, should have chosen a wife who was both reserved and jealous. He frequented prostitutes, from elegant hookers to Montmartre streetwalkers. In 1925, while on vacation in Normandy, he found part of what he was looking for. The Simenons had rented a big vacant room in a farmhouse, where they slept on bales of hay. The windows had no curtains, and neighboring farm girls would sneak up in the evening to watch them make love. They adopted one (named, as was his mother, Henriette), a creamy-skinned seventeen-year-old with a round face whom Georges christened Boule and made Tigy's servant.

The three of them lived in two rooms on the Place des Vosges in Paris. Georges and Boule petted, but he was held back by her virginity, which he preferred someone else to take. One day she announced, "Now you can!" They began an intimacy that was to last a lifetime. Tigy had warned her husband that if she found him unfaithful she would commit suicide. So he hid his dalliance with Boule for nearly twenty years. Because at first the household was cramped and later the pair copulated all over Simenon's ever larger houses, Tigy must have known. But Boule had taken on the onerous wifely duties, and Tigy chose to look the other way.

In 1929 Simenon took his menage on a one-year tour of the canals of northern Europe, and one sunny morning at a café in Holland, he dreamed up Maigret, the pipe-smoking, nonjudgmental sleuth. The series created a global industry that over the next fifty years resulted in nearly a hundred crime novels and fifty movies based on them. Simenon borrowed people and events he knew firsthand for his stories, and he excused his sexual promiscuity by asking rhetorically, "How could I have created dozens, perhaps hundreds, of female characters in my novels if I had not experienced these adventures which lasted for two hours or ten minutes?" After finally giving up fiction, Simenon wrote his memoirs, in which he reiterates his need to merge with the female. Even less inward looking than Hemingway, he chose the obvious method.

Georges's credo was *"Manger et faire l'amour!"* He was overjoyed when Tigy gave birth to Marc in 1939. With the outbreak of war, he withdrew his family to the rural Vendée where at least there would be food. He continued to publish during the Occupation and permitted Continental, the Nazi-sponsored production company, to turn his novels into films. Simenon was denounced as Jewish by a collaborator and duly investigated. It took three generations of baptismal certificates to satisfy the authorities.

One afternoon during the war, after Boule had awakened him from his usual nap and they were making love, Tigy broke in; Georges would rather have faced the Gestapo than his enraged wife. Yet despite her threats, Tigy saw the necessity of a menage, if only to ensure Marc's safety, so the Simenons struck a deal. They decided to stay together as "good friends." They would remain married but sleep apart. Boule moved into the master bedroom. Until the liberation, they all got on fine. In 1945 Simenon, afraid of reprisals from the powerful French Communists, wrangled visas and left hurriedly for the United States. Tigy refused to let Boule come along, and Georges could do nothing but assure his mistress he would send for her. While Boule remained devoted to her "mountain of a man," he was soon to become hopelessly entangled with another woman. Tigy, in trying to reconstitute the couple, had doomed her marriage.

Because they were having difficulties learning English, the Simenon household settled in a small town outside Montreal. In New York, the fortysomething mystery writer interviewed Denyse Ouimet, a French Canadian, for the position of secretary. He describes her as young, fairly pretty, a brunette with "dark-brown eyes that constantly changed from one expression to the other." She wore too much makeup, and small and wiry, she was the opposite of his usual curvy type. But Georges fell victim to the weakness that had undone Casanova: "a love that was passionate, violent and at the same time very tender." He was captivated by Denyse's "vaginal voice . . . which came from way down in her throat, the kind you hear in nightclubs and cabarets."

Sex commenced in a hotel room where Denyse climaxed so loudly the desk clerk investigated to see if she was being murdered. Though she came from a distinguished Canadian family, she paraded her sexual accomplishments, then informed Simenon that she planned to take her life. Though biographer Marnham calls Denyse a liar, a flirt, and a tease, her suicidal tendencies were real enough. Still, she played Georges's ego with a professional touch, and he jumped at the role of savior. He changed the spelling of Denyse's name to Denise, ordered her to scrub her face clean, and after she'd read him the juicy details of letters from former lovers, he burned them all. The born-again Denise was added to the household in Quebec, where Tigy was amused, and Georges dressed his mistress in his wife's evening gowns before making love with her indoors and out in the snow. Denise in turn taught Tigy to drive and speak English.

From the first, his new mistress encouraged Georges to take other women and tell her about it. In 1946 the menage pulled up stakes and drove to Florida. Staying out the winter, Georges felt he'd found the genuine Denise, unaffected and motherly to Marc, and Tigy joined in the harmony. On a visit to Havana, the lovers attended a sex show in which two young women performed erotic acts. Georges joined in. Although he and Denise would claim a penchant for voyeurism was the other's, they both enjoyed the show so much that they returned several times. Simenon, having met his match, was entranced.

Tigy grew concerned about the depth of Georges's involvement with Denise and sent for Boule. Denise wasn't bothered. While they all lived in a house outside Tucson, Denise would cuddle up to Georges, after he returned from Boule's room, and insist on having her turn. Simenon thrived on his menage a quatre, whether he was playing the fisherman in Florida or the cowboy in Arizona. During this period he wrote perhaps his most memorable fiction. *Three Rooms in Manhattan* and *Act of Passion* both feature a dangerous coquette modeled on Denise, and at the climax of the latter, the Simenon alter ego strangles his mistress while vividly imagining all the men who have made love to her. Jealousy, whether based on an incident of discovery or simply obsessive, feeds on voyeurism still more than does the menage.

Denise's pregnancy at the end of 1948 tilted the arrangement toward her. To avoid complications with American law, Simenon divorced Tigy and made Denise his legal wife. Nevertheless, the menage continued and was transferred to the Connecticut farmhouse. Here the Simenons lived peacefully for five years. Denise, as business manager, negotiated much higher prices for a stream of new, sexually charged Maigrets. While Georges often visited the nearby Tigy and Marc, Denise gave birth to his beloved daughter Marie-Jo. He could afford to smile when André Gide warned him that a "double harness" would dampen his artistic creation. Eventually, Simenon began to feel like an alien and yielded to his wife's longing to live in Europe. The menage, including Boule and the kids, packed up and boarded the liner *Île-de-France*. A pretty blonde countess flirted, and Simenon relates that he invited her to his cabin:

> Pirouetting, she lets her dress slip off and there's nothing under it but her pink, plump body.
>
> In no time I am inside her, and she comes once, and a second time, while D[enise] is undressing. Just as the countess feels that I am about to come in my turn, she pushes me gently away with, "No, that's for her." D is ready and waiting.

Denise, in her counter-memoir, confirms the incident, which represents a high point in their mutuality. While they lived at Cannes, she would accompany her husband to brothels in order to sit and chat with the girls, or she would point out attractive women at cafés. But she had lost interest in Georges and grew more intrigued with the women. This unfolding of Denise—he would call it dissolution—was not to Simenon's liking.

She became bossy and demanded a corps of secretaries and maids. Compulsive about hygiene, she grew fanatic about staying thin. She was thrilled by Simenon's movie friends, such as the comic Fernandel and macho actor Jean Gabin, and she demanded not only to dine and party with the rich and famous but that they pay attention to *her*. Denise and Georges drank and quarreled too often. In an effort to save the marriage, Simenon bought a large house near Lausanne, Switzerland. Upstairs, he wrote in his frenetic style, and Denise would send up one of the serving girls for him to devour in Minotaur fashion. However, in 1961 she mistakenly accepted an Italian maid recommended by the publisher Mondadori; Teresa was plain, good-natured, in her midthirties. Georges responded to her earthy type as he had earlier to Boule.

One morning he caught Teresa bending over a dressing table. "He came up behind me," she recalled, "lifted my skirt, and wow! it was joyful!" For the Latin male, wife and maid have composed a dialectic as traditional as mother and whore. These female figures that bookend desire are not opposed but complementary. Denise, weary of her husband, at first was pleased to see him diverted. Simenon, who wasn't Maigret, had finally found a woman who resembled the inspector's wife: all comfort.

In his sixties and in poor health, Simenon grudgingly accepted limitations. Denise, now growing distraught at being supplanted by a maid, escaped to a psychiatric clinic. She eventually became a psychoanalyst. In 1967 Simenon asked the ever-loyal Boule, who didn't get on with Teresa, to leave his house, and she went to live with his married son Marc to care for his children. Simenon wrote long, romantic letters to both absent women but made no effort to see them. His other love, who for years had been the most important woman in his life, was his lovely, talented, disturbed daughter, Marie-Jo.

When she was eight, she asked her father to buy her a golden wedding band. The teenager wrote love songs to Georges. But she had a close and sympathetic relationship with Denise. Allegedly, when Marie-Jo heard that Teresa had become her father's official bedmate, she asked, "Why not me?" She couldn't accept her mother being replaced by the maid. Over the years, Marie-Jo was in and out of psychiatric clinics. She attempted suicide six times. In 1978 Denise brought out her account of life with Georges, dubbed by the media *"le mariage de Mme Maigret."* Marie-Jo, then in her midtwenties, bought the book that excoriated her father and obsessively annotated it in the margin. She also bought a .22 caliber rifle and got off one shot through her heart. Her last note requested she be cremated still wearing her wedding band. After a brief period of mourning, the Simenons resumed their warfare in the press. He continued to refuse to divorce Denise.

In 1977 Simenon had interviewed Fellini about his upcoming film, *Casanova,* and this became a cover story for the French newspaper *L'Express.* During the interview, with both men claiming to be heir to the film's hero, Fellini revealed that he always made love wearing a bra. Simenon remarked that having added them up, he'd made love to ten thousand women, eight thousand of them prostitutes. "I suffer from no sexual vice," he insisted, "but I have a need to communicate." The film *Casanova* flopped while Simenon became more popular than ever.

In September 1981 Georges published *Intimate Memoirs,* his final statement, in which he denigrated Denise and lavishly praised Teresa. It is an honest work, if self-serving, and shows great concern for his children. The next month Denise brought out *The Golden Phallus,* a roman à clef that features a famous writer who dies and leaves a golden cast of his phallus to his Italian maid. Whatever else may be said of Simenon, no man or woman has employed the age-old institution of menage a trois to write more books or earn more money.

chapter 27

CAROLYN'S BOYS

Rebels Without a Cause

{Jack Kerouac, Neal and Carolyn Cassady, and Allen Ginsberg}

My best pal and my best gal—just don't do anything I wouldn't do.
NEAL CASSADY

I" N THE ARMY IN THE DAYS OF THE DRAFT, from World War II through Korea, each buck private was assigned a buddy. Sometimes you got to choose him. Either way, "you'd be living in a kind of physical intimacy which was unlike any other. . . . And what greater love song in those days than 'My Buddy'?" Vito Russo, author of *The Celluloid Closet*, is quoting Stewart Stern, scriptwriter of *Rebel Without a Cause*, who refers not to the film's covert yet obvious homoerotic relationship between star James Dean (Jim) and Sal Mineo (Plato, the sissy) but to the brief bonding scene between Dean and rival gang chieftain Corey Allen (Buzz). Jim and Buzz are about to run a "chicken" race in two stolen cars to the edge of a cliff; the one who jumps out first loses. Jim, who likes Buzz, tries to call it off, but he succumbs to the logic of the famous line, "We have to do something." We all remember that Buzz catches his black leather jacket sleeve on a door handle and goes off the cliff in the car. The accident, crucial to the story, eerily prefigured the death of James Dean in a senseless car accident one week before *Rebel* was released in 1955.

There was a second writer on the script, Irving Shulman, author of *The Amboy Dukes*, the bible of every self-respecting fifties hood. *Dukes* is a tougher story than *Rebel*, and the protagonist, for betraying his buddies, is clobbered with brass knuckles and tossed off a five-story roof. Before that the gang members share their girls. So it may have been Shulman, the more macho writer, who handed over Buzz's girl, Natalie Wood, to Jim on the theory that to the victor belong the spoils. Shulman understood that women are scarce among outlaws and that outlaw women want the toughest guys, often two at a time. *Rebel* also features a tender menage among Dean, Wood, and Mineo, the adopted child who wants to sleep with Daddy rather than Mommy. Their three-way bonding over the course of one night dominates the second half of the movie.

The real-life James Dean claimed to be bisexual, and his movie persona exuded "a sexuality that seems unresolved, permanently suspended between male and female. Thus we think of him in triangles," writes Molly Haskell. In *Rebel*, the sensitive hood, his moll, and his adoring follower coalesce into a temporary family that contrasts favorably with their screen families, the members of which are shown as absent, frightened, or dim. When Haskell writes that James Dean "gives eloquent expression to our own pre-Oedipal yearnings and confusion, the unwillingness to relinquish one love for the other," she hits on the centrality of narcissism for a threesome. But this narcissistic yearning *not* to divide the world by gender and instead to see others as a reflection of oneself is "*pre*-Oedipal" in the sense of more fundamental, more true than the cock-and-bull tale of Oedipus the innocent malefactor.

The narcissist not only admires his other face but like the Roman god Janus, lord of entrances and exits, he may alternately present his two faces to the crowd. The screen Jimmy Dean could be sensitive, as in *East of Eden*, or vicious, as in *Giant*, or act both together and confused as in *Rebel*, a lover and a loner. It is coincidental but intriguing that the hero of Jack Kerouac's *On the Road*, published in 1957, was named *Dean* Moriarty, and there is no doubt that Neal Cassady, on whom Kerouac based the character, was the Jimmy Dean of the Beat generation.

THE ADONIS OF DENVER

Neal's myth is nearly the equal of Dean's. He came to represent the antidote to the social conventions that threatened to stifle his namesake. He drove the electric Kool-Aid acid bus for the Merry Pranksters and had his public portrait painted in words by Ken Kesey and later Tom Wolfe. Neal, "Cocksman and Adonis of Denver," was the hero of Allen Ginsberg's "Howl," the Beat anthem, and the subject of several other poems and elegies by his sometime lover. Neal was the heart of his buddy Jack Kerouac's

Proustian endeavor to turn flash memories of his personal experience into art. What June meant to Henry Miller—the untrammeled id—Neal accomplished for Jack. More than buddies, each acted as the other's alter ego. In his "spontaneous" works, good Kerouac is heroic Neal.

In *Big Sur*, Kerouac extols the "mighty genius of the mind Cody [Neal] whom I announce as the greatest writer the world will ever know if he ever gets down to writing." But a few lines later he admits that "becoming a writer holds no interest for him because life is so holy for him there's no need to do anything but live it." If Neal had one overriding need it was to drive—on the road or all night in bed. The product of a loveless, motherless home, who struggled into manhood on Denver's skid row, he had to watch out for his alcoholic father. Living in filth, Neal begged for nickels so his father could buy booze. At fourteen Neal stole his first car, and by the time he was twenty-one he'd stolen over five hundred. He didn't sell the cars but drove them around till the police picked him up. He did six stretches in the reformatory.

In New York in 1947 Jack Kerouac, a football player who'd dropped out of college, introduced Neal to convoluted Columbia student Allen Ginsberg. Allen's parents were classic Russian-Jewish Marxist nudists removed to New Jersey. Neal, in contrast, was muscular and athletic, with a broken Roman nose and a wide Western smile. He reminded both Allen and Jack of "a young Gene Autry." Actually Neal looked like Jack's older brother, who'd died as a youth, might have, and he would play that role for him. But this night and for a time afterward, Neal and Allen exercised a fascination on each other that barely included Jack. While sharing a cot in a Harlem pad, Neal apparently made the first overture by stretching out his arm and saying, "Draw near me." Their intense affair, as much mental as physical, began at once. Allen in his poem "Many Loves" concludes his description of the night's activities with "I needed him, cock, for my dreams of insatiety and lone love."

Elsewhere Allen says that Neal transformed sex into "a spiritual social thing as well as a matter of aesthetic prowess." Condemned to poetry, Allen must observe, even if only himself, in order to write what he has seen, while Neal, who like any star needs to *be* loved, must prove himself every time in the sack. Conflict began when Neal returned to Denver and wrote Allen that he "dislike[d] pricks and men" and had forced himself to be homosexual. He suggested the two of them live together with a third, a girl. At this time he may have meant his teenage wife LuAnne, but by July 1947, when Allen took the Greyhound to Denver, Neal was occupied with Carolyn Robinson, a petite Bennington graduate with the beauty and refinement of Grace Kelly, who was studying fine arts at the university. The three lived together in one hotel room with Allen listening to the pair's lovemaking. "Such terrible nights," he recorded in his journal. But what Allen supposed were cries of passion were actually Carolyn's groans of pain.

Carolyn came from a straitlaced academic family—her father was a professor of biochemistry at Vanderbilt in Nashville—and she brought with her what she has called "Victorian, reserved, English values." Her sexual education was nil, and Neal was no Casanova. Caroline has said that Neal didn't know about making love. "He was always rough, no preliminaries." Neal distrusted women because they were his weakness, and he treated them as objects to con. He'd wooed Carolyn by reading to her Allen's lyric poetry, which he passed off as his own. Carolyn's romantic dreams were dimmed by his screwing, which was more like rape. At first she blamed the presence of Allen, but once the poet had found his own apartment, Neal set up a tripartite schedule; high on bennies, he alternated round the clock among Carolyn, LuAnne, and Allen.

At summer's end Carolyn, ready to try her chances at costume design in Hollywood, got a shock when she went to say good-bye to Neal: "There in *our* bed, sleeping nude, were LuAnne, Neal, and Allen, in that order." Of Neal we are told by one Kerouac biographer, Anne Charters, that "it made no difference to him if he loved one person or three." Another, Gerald Nicosia, assures us that "he retained the ideal of monogamy as the most honorable path for a man, even if he never practiced it." The answer to the conundrum of Neal, which Kerouac made his life study, is that he was a Janus—each of his faces as real as the other. According to Carolyn, who married him on April Fool's Day 1948, Neal suffered a "horrible battle inside of being a sex maniac on the one hand, and so spiritual on the other." He claimed to know the devil and that the devil was himself.

Neal, says Carolyn, was immaculate, changed clothes often, and hated to have his hair mussed. He wanted a conventional home—a picket fence and a station wagon—and he was proud of working on the Southern Pacific Railroad to support his wife and children. He also whored, drank, and smoked grass prodigiously, and it was probably a combination of alcohol and Seconal (a depressant) that killed him at the age of forty-two in 1968. Constructive narcissism posits an individual who admires and emulates his better half. But each face of Janus looks out on an entirely different world. Ego and alter ego coexist in one psyche without effectively communicating, and each demands its lovers.

In an amusing 1950s movie, *Captain's Paradise*, Alec Guiness as the captain of a passenger boat has a proper English wife in Gibraltar and a hot flamenco wife in a Spanish enclave in North Africa. In the company of the first he is a fuddy-duddy, with the second a live wire, and he cannot permit his two personalities, or wives, to meet. Eventually the women weary of being half persons and leave him. But the captain is the envy of his crew, suggesting that every man is a would-be Janus.

To Neal and Jack, each was like a long-lost brother, different but complementary. In 1960 Jack wrote an introduction in the form of a résumé to his *Lonesome Traveler*. Born in 1922 in Massachusetts, he describes a "beautiful childhood" in which he was a good student and athlete. He held a variety of laboring jobs, which left his imagination free. He admired his "completely honest" blue-collar father who worshiped Senator Joe McCarthy. After a couple of dissolved marriages, Jack would lead "a kind of monastic life" with his mother. Shy, most of his travels and honky-tonking were done with Neal, whom he thought an American saint. "Jack [was] the dark one, Neal golden," sums up Joyce Johnson.

In late 1951 in San Francisco, Carolyn wrote to Jack, who was ill in New York: "I need your help in making life worth living for Neal. Can you convalesce with us?" He didn't arrive at their house on Russell Place till January 1952. Earlier, Carolyn had tried to free herself of the Denver Adonis, leaving him to go off with an old flame. However, as she writes in *Off the Road*, "Neal's ghost accompanied me, and I inwardly communicated to him all my observations." When they got together again, Carolyn became pregnant. Neal obtained an annulment from LuAnne, and the newlyweds commenced housekeeping in high hopes. However, by the time Jack, responding to Carolyn's plea, arrived at their house in Russell Place, she was a disillusioned wife and the mother of two girls.

The house on Russian Hill still stands in midblock, a brown-shingled cottage with cream shutters and an attic room. Here Jack, fleeing from his second marriage and carrying the fourth draft of *On the Road*, which he'd written in twenty days on one long roll of paper, took refuge. The large attic was only half-finished, but Jack liked it that way, and Carolyn had built him a large desk out of plywood and orange crates. The attic's only access was through the Cassady bedroom, which Jack had to cross to use the bathroom. He was so modest that he kept his needs to himself except when no one else was around. But as Carolyn has mentioned, the three of them "sort of invented the commune."

As Neal spent time alone with Jack, Carolyn at twenty-nine felt like a household drudge. Then, on Neal's twenty-sixth birthday, the smoldering tensions came to a head. Carolyn was suffering from Bell's palsy, which distorted her face, when Neal and Jack stumbled in drunk; they were accompanied by a woman of easy virtue, who wobbled up to the attic with Jack. Carolyn demanded that the trio leave the house. The next day the boys returned, sleepy and penitent. The air cleared, and they began to share confidences and glasses of Tokay at home.

Neal's departure on a railroad assignment upset the household protocol. His parting remark startled the others: "I don't know about leaving you two.... My best pal and my best gal—just don't do anything *I* wouldn't do." Was this one of Neal's devilish jokes? Carolyn claims that neither she nor Jack thought of acting on the obvious hint. Neal, in Beat style, was still the seducer. Earlier, at Allen's New York apartment, Neal had suggested that Jack join him and LuAnne in bed. Unfortunately it was Jack's father's deathbed, which he'd given to Allen. Despite the pleasure of stroking LuAnne, sunk in the sag between the two, he found himself unable to make love under Neal's scrutiny. In *On the Road*, with LuAnne changed to Marylou, Jack reflected that Neal's deprived youth earned him whatever he could grab: "Dean had every right to die the sweet deaths of complete love of his Marylou. I didn't want to interfere, I just wanted to follow." One is the doer, the other the bard of his deeds.

The difference this time was Carolyn, described by Allen as "Ideal Mother Image, Madwoman, chick, and ignu" (by the last word he meant "post-hip intellectual"). Jack and Carolyn's attraction was deep, sincere, and multileveled. Yet she recoiled at being passed from hand to hand, and she was proud of her loyalty to her husband. Jack remained in awe of the sacrament of marriage. But when Neal returned home after two weeks, and Carolyn asked him directly had he wanted them to make love, he answered, "Why not? I thought it would be fine." So the next time Neal left overnight, Carolyn invited Jack to a cozy dinner of wine, pizza, and jazz.

Carolyn, to allay Jack's suspicions, wore jeans and a white shirt. As "My Funny Valentine" played on the radio, he willingly fell into her trap. She experienced a triumph when he whispered, "I wanted to take you away from Neal." The latter had lit the fuse, but it was Carolyn who reassured Jack and permitted him to overcome his moral scruple against sleeping with his best friend's wife. Besides, Jack was a surrogate, an addition rather than a replacement. In *Off the Road* Carolyn writes, "Jack was a tender and considerate lover, but though I could be completely romantically in love with him my heart still ached that it wasn't Neal."

Carolyn's bold stroke thrust her from the periphery to the center of the action. She easily settled into her new role, and Jack embraced her and their relationship more enthusiastically than she'd expected. She continues, "I sincerely hoped that some lasting good would come from this, but for now there was nothing to do but relax and enjoy it." The menage was the happiest time of Carolyn's life, and she basked in the warmth of evenings when the men sat in the kitchen taking parts from Shakespeare or reading Proust aloud while she cooked. "I felt like the sun of their solar system," reflects Carolyn, "all revolved around me. . . . I was functioning as female and my men were supportive. It may have taken two of them to complete the role usually filled by one, but the variety was an extra added attraction. How lucky could a girl get?"

Jay Landsman, who knew everyone concerned, suggests in a review in the *London Times*, "The menage a trois proves to be a marriage builder, for Neal comes back and fights for [Carolyn's] attention. He has to prove he is the best man." But two pals and their gal make up a three-way attraction. It requires sensitivity all around and the kind of decorum the Cassady menage adopted. "Jack, like me," writes Carolyn, "felt Neal's and my marriage came first." When Neal was away she catered to Jack, and he would take her on excursions and to parties in town. "When no big dramatic scenes took place," adds Carolyn, "and Neal saw that Jack and I weren't going to love him any less, everyone relaxed and drew together, and were as discreet and as kind as possible."

Speculation that Neal needed the menage to make his woman interesting to him again, "to renovate her charms," as one biographer puts it, is beside the point. Neal and Carolyn did experience a new tenderness toward each other, a renewed satisfaction within the family unit. With Neal more considerate, Carolyn's ego expanded, and she became the moderator of her men's conversations and arbiter of their disputes. These two buddies, so alike and yet so different, needed a loved third in order to draw closer. Initially the role had been played by Allen Ginsberg, and he continued to function as a metaphysical third. However, frustration between the two buddies would eventually surface. "Each was for the other a visible example of what he would like to do but couldn't," remarks Nicosia. Jack once referred to Neal as an "Irish Proletarian would-be Proust." In fact *he* was the would-be Proust, and Neal offered the seed that could make his ambition bear fruit.

Jack not only sang of Neal's deeds, he used Neal's tempo, his spoken and written language. Yes, Kerouac was influenced by cool jazz, but the flow of the "spontaneous prose" in which he wrote the final drafts of *On the Road* and later works such as *Visions of Cody* was triggered by Neal's lingo and the menage a trois with him and Carolyn. Much as Henry Miller appropriated his wife June's speech, so Jack borrowed Neal's. It is the juvenile delinquent's outside-the-candy-store-window vision that gives backbone to Kerouac's otherwise puzzling celebration of American ugliness. "Dear Jack," begins Neal's letter of July 3, 1949, "I feel like a remembering of things past. So, here's a brief history of arrests. A case history." He delineated the odyssey of a con man, and this went straight into *On the Road.*

"Carolyn is a great woman," wrote Jack. "I never was so happy in my life than in that splendid attic with the eleventh edition of the *Encyclopedia Britannica.*" Predictably, Neal became bored when things went smoothly. Jack was now on Carolyn's side, unavailable for women-hunting expeditions. Neal took pride in his ability to satisfy women. He was so sure of this, he urged his lovers to sleep with his buddies. But Carolyn's continuing romance with Jack, and her clear preference for keeping both, may have troubled him. Jack, restless for the road, departed for Mexico. On the way to see him off in Nogales, Carolyn comforted herself: "It was accepted by all three of us that we would share a home somewhere for at least part of each year."

However, while Carolyn hoped for an ongoing menage with both men in residence, Jack and Neal were growing wary of one another. Plans for a grand reunion in Mexico that would include Allen never came about. In 1952 Jack, at Neal's invitation, rejoined the Cassadys in a spacious house on the outskirts of San Jose where Neal was growing marijuana in the flower beds. Jack and Carolyn spent an ardent first night together. Once more, he became a member of the family, working on the railroad, alternating shifts with Neal. He read to the children, danced to mambos on the phonograph, and played the tiny bongo drums Carolyn gave him. Neal joined them, the three reading aloud or just fooling around.

The tenor of Jack and Carolyn's affair changed one night as they sat drinking wine, both transported by the magic that happened between them. Jack caught Carolyn off guard, whispering, "*God* . . . I love you." As a woman, she drew strength from this moment for years afterward. However, it showed how her marriage to Neal had become devoid of romance. It signaled the end of the menage, since jealousy was now more likely to play a part. Come winter, when Neal and Jack were stuck in the house, they got on each other's nerves. Neal envied Jack's rapport with Carolyn, who was now caught in the middle.

Off the Road fails to mention an incident (denied by Carolyn) cited by Nicosia: "One night [Neal] tried to promote a three-way ball, but Jack guiltily reverted to his old role of observer and was incapable of functioning sexually." His feelings for Carolyn may have gotten out of hand. Neal had the right among buddies to work him over with brass knuckles, at least verbally. But after a little domestic sparring, the boys agreed to make a marijuana run to Mexico, where Jack stayed on. When he sent for Carolyn, she refused to join him. "Tell the old boy to get his own girl," Neal snorted. Carolyn's best of times were over. Her marriage to Neal, though it took her another ten years to accept it, was doomed. Later she reflected, "Funny how Jack always seemed to be the cement that bound our little family together."

"Why did the boys choose me?" asks Carolyn. She lives in London and gives talks on the Beats to a young and curious generation. Jack answered her question in *Desolation Angels*, where he calls her Evelyn and Neal, Cody. He writes glowingly of the domestic woman, the sustenance of her three sweet children. She has "resigned herself to Cody's wildness because it is as it should be." He describes Evelyn as "a very pretty little woman and a topnotch mother. She really has achieved that cold void truth we're all yakking about, and in practice she displays warmth." Evelyn's acceptance of her lot as a Beat wife—able to serve up perfect suppers in the eye of the hurricane—rates her Jack's highest praise: "Super Maw." Carolyn, in turn, avoided the error of leaving Neal, "the do-er, the Yang," for Jack, "dreamer, the be-er, the Yin." As long as the menage lasted, both men served her well.

"HOWL"

In 1954 Jack was succeeded in the San Jose house by Allen Ginsberg. The new Cassady menage was living together happily, according to Carolyn, when one afternoon she found the two boys having sex. While she confronted her convoluted feelings about Neal's bisexuality, Allen recorded his dilemma in a journal entry: "I can sleep with Neal, sleep with Carolyn, sleep with no one and stay. Or sleep with both and no one alternately amid confusions; or I can end this mad triangle." Jack, now Carolyn's long-distance adviser, wrote her, "Poor Neal needs love more than anybody else, try to give it to him. . . . Allen and Neal are old buddies and hit the road together and seen visions together; don't be harsh with our Prophets." Jack never would abandon the Cassadys, though after the 1957 success of *On the Road* he visited less often, and Neal may well have felt neglected.

Allen thought of himself as bisexual, and soon after being banished by the Cassadys to San Francisco, he fell in love with Sheila Boucher, a small pretty blond (like Carolyn?) who'd sung jazz and was working in advertising. She smoked pot, dug his poetry, and on at least one occasion went to bed with him and Neal. Allen made love to her, and afterward, while she slept, Allen and Neal sneaked into the bathroom and started screwing. "That was probably the dirtiest we ever got," Allen recalled. But his choice of lovers whom he considers straight has resulted in a lifetime of involvement in threes.

In San Francisco Allen met Peter Orlovsky and began a thirty-year love affair. According to Barry Miles's perceptive biography, Peter's relationships with women resulted in "more than one menage a trois of unusual complexity, which caused a great deal of tension and strain." Let's accept, as Allen has done in his work, that transcendence of gender is what turns him on. In his 1956 "Many Loves," he praises Neal's "rock buttocks ... rounded in animal fucking and bodily nights over nurses and schoolgirls." It's this aura of the other sex clinging to his lovers that Allen digs so well.

He read "Howl" on October 13, 1955, at the Six Gallery at Union and Fillmore. Present and future stars were there—Rexroth, Snyder, Ferlinghetti, McClure, and Kerouac—among the one hundred Beats crammed into the converted auto-repair shop. Allen, swaying like a Jewish cantor, chanted the lines seemingly torn from the experience they had sought with pot, bennies, and hash. Jack, high on wine, called out, "Go!" at the end of each line, and soon the audience joined in. At the end they cheered wildly, knowing they were part of a legendary moment. Afterward the poets and their girl- and boyfriends went to a Chinese restaurant and then a favorite bar. "And after that there was an orgy," writes Miles. Thus "Howl" epitomized the Beat fifties while pointing toward the sixties, when the menage a trois would look too much like marriage to be hip.

In June 1958 Neal was sentenced to two counts of five years in San Quentin for selling a couple of reefers to narcotics agents. For the first time in their marriage, Carolyn, though on welfare, could be certain of Neal's whereabouts. In 1960 he was released on parole, and in 1963 Carolyn divorced him. During the sixties Jack dropped in only once more and talked about their moving in together in one large house, but Carolyn saw that he was an alcoholic. Neal continued to share at least one more girlfriend with Jack, his old buddy in the hunt for beauties. Typically, Jack ended a letter to Carolyn hopefully, "At least one of these days we'll have one of our old quiet religious arguments by the fireplace as Neal sits there playing self-chess."

The menage a trois made an ideal family unit for the Beats. The *Chicago Tribune* quipped that Carolyn saw herself as "just a Harriet with two Ozzies." Unfortunately the dependence of the men on booze and other substances damaged their relationships. Jack married several times, growing more lonely, while Neal became a communard with the not-so-Merry Pranksters. When in 1968 Carolyn phoned Jack to tell him Neal had dropped dead in Mexico, he insisted, "It's just a trick. He's hiding out someplace, like Tangier." Jack joined Neal in "Tangier" the next year. Carolyn, informed by Allen, reflected, "Other women had tended to the business of their passing, yet in my life I'd been closer to those two than anyone I'd known." The success and failure of this menage, including Allen as the observing fourth, epitomizes the domestic side of the Beats, so closely meshed with their achievements in the arts. Despite the sex, drugs, and profane language—anathema to the country at large—they clung to their version of the American dream of the fifties.

Today, nostalgia for the white picket fences and station wagons of that Blondie-and-Dagwood era runs high. The current affectation of Beat style—smoking pot, drinking espresso, dressing in black, and reciting poetry—is once again handmaiden to so-called family values. Lest we forget how sexually cramped was the time of Neal and Jack and how a rebellion that dared not speak its name was the only sane response, let's look at the 1959 Academy Award–winning script for *Pillow Talk*, with its trisexual subtext that few people caught.

Two years after the publication of *On the Road*, the first of the Doris Day–Rock Hudson–Tony Randall threesome comedies did very well by Universal, its producer Ross Hunter, director Michael Gordon, its scriptwriters, and Doris Day herself. Not only was she nominated for an Oscar but she became the number one box-office favorite, the first woman to head that list since Betty Grable in the middle of the war. Number two was her costar, Rock. *Pillow Talk* perfectly expresses the mores of its time. Reexamined from our perspective, the movie is brilliantly hypocritical. In combining the theme of two buddies who divvy up the girl between them with the motif of doubling—Rock has two personae to which Doris separately relates—it is surprisingly ambitious.

The movie opens with a screen split three ways: Rock, on a party-line phone, is singing to a brunette while Doris, who shares his line, is listening. Visually, triangles abound, and they perfectly express the unadorned geometric lines of the interiors of the period. Rock is a songwriter working on a musical backed by his old college chum Tony Randall, a millionaire sissy who has three ex-wives and an analyst. Rock is a macho philanderer, dubbed by Doris a "sex maniac." She is an interior decorator who is avoiding marriage to make a career, an effort frustrated by Rock's hogging the phone. She insults him, and he tells her, "Don't take your bedroom problems out on me." She replies, "There's nothing in my bedroom that bothers me." In case the audience missed the point, Doris sings in voice-over that she wants "a pillow-talking boy."

So, boy has met girl, they hate each other—often the start of a movie romance—and soon the complications arise. Tony is Doris's persistent suitor, presenting her with trifles such as a Corvette, which she turns down. But he so ardently raves about her to his buddy Rock that this Don Juan can't help being attracted. When he finds out Tony's girl is his partyliner, Rock invents the persona of Rex, a polite Texas rancher, in order to seduce Doris. Like Valmont in *Dangerous Liaisons*, he is looking for the ultimate kick of bedding an honest woman.

Doubling, especially where twins are mistaken for one another, giving rise to confusion and sexual innuendo, can be traced back to ancient Roman comedy. In this update, mirrors abound at the "in" club where Rex (Rock) takes Doris on a date. Here the doubling is brought to an amazing pitch when Rex plays the sissy, talking about his mother, asking for a recipe, and extending his pinkie when drinking. The wolf's ploy is to teach the good girl a lesson. By playing the effeminate gentleman, he is going to make her beg for a pass. And she finds his Emily Post behavior "not very flattering." They kiss, of course, and Doris falls in love with Rex, but it is Rock who falls in love with Doris. Her decorating career and his as a wolf are in jeopardy. The real subtext is that Rock Hudson was gay, and as the documentary film *The Celluloid Closet* points out, we have the absurd scene of a gay man playing a macho wise guy pretending to be gay, which is at least tripling.

At Tony's country house, the scene of consummation, Doris discovers that Rex is her party-line Lothario. She tells him never to darken her doorstep again. Tony comes to the rescue, and when Doris breaks down in a diner, several burly truckers mistake Tony as the cause and sock him. On the advice of his dentist, Tony hands over the problem of Doris to his buddy. The distraught Rock asks, "How do I get her back?" Tony maliciously replies, "You suffer, and I watch." This makes clear that in bed a sissy doesn't even make pillow talk.

The movie ends with wedding bells, and the trio of Doris, Rock, and Tony went on to make two more movies in which gay Rock played the macho straight and straight Tony played the sissy, and Doris needed them both to make up a whole man. Then, come the sixties, Beats turned into hippies while analysts continued to foster an integrated personality in their patients and the United States split down the middle.

chapter 28

THE POP MENAGE

{Superman, Lois Lane, and Clark Kent;
Woody Allen, Mia Farrow, and Soon-Yi Previn;
Count Dracula and Friends}

I am a fan of anybody who can make his living in his underwear.
DAVID MAMET

THE MAN OF STEEL

*I*T'S A BIRD, IT'S A PLANE ... IT'S SUPER-
menage! Who would dispute that the story of Superman is the American
national myth? But who remembers that its hero, the Man of Steel, is an
illegal alien from a distant galaxy? If the star-child Kal-El's rocket landed
in a Kansas cornfield today, the Kents would be obliged to turn him in to
the authorities. No school for the little wog (are they white on Krypton?),
no medical care (not that he needed it)—send him back where he came
from! You say Krypton was destroyed? Let him take his heroics to some
other planet.

Superman, which originated as a strip in a 1938 Action Comics issue,
was drawn and written by two young men from immigrant Jewish families
in Cleveland. The Man of Steel soon became the star of his own comic
book, novel, radio program, TV series, and four major motion pictures to
date. The fantasy offspring of a ninety-pound weakling, Jerry Siegel, and
a half-blind artist, Joe Shuster, both of whom couldn't score in sports or
with girls, Superman became the hero of countless other frustrated lads
and, what may be more surprising, the heartthrob of Lois Lane and a

goodly number of secret female admirers. A few critics have used their X-ray vision to view *Superman*'s subtext and have found this pop myth to be laced with sexual innuendo.

"One of the things that always fascinated us was the love story," said Robert Benton, who jointly wrote the original *Superman* movie. The epic was released by Warner in 1979, broke box-office records, and boasted a premiere attended by President Carter and daughter Amy and a British premiere attended by Queen Elizabeth and Prince Andrew. "[It] could have been like a terrific Lubitch film," continued Benton, "a love triangle in which two people are the same person." *Superman* does resemble *Design for Living*, in which Otto and Leo are really versions of each other, in the sense that the triad (including Gilda) faces off against the world of philistines. Superman, Lois Lane, and Clark Kent are pitted against a set of evildoers, from mad scientist Lex Luthor to the mysterious Mr. Mxyztplk, who defies gravity. But it was Jules Feiffer, one of our great cartoonists, who first realized that here was no ordinary love triangle but "a schizoid and chaste *ménage à trois*. Clark Kent loved but felt abashed with Lois Lane; Superman saved Lois Lane when she was in trouble, found her a pest the rest of the time. . . . This behavior demands explanation."

The basic premise of the Superman myth and its enduring appeal is the interaction of its three different personae: Superman, the handsome, all-powerful hunk who is movie-star material; Lois, the ambitious career reporter on the *Daily Planet* who will do anything for a scoop; and Clark, described by Dennis Dooley in his *Superman at Fifty* as "clumsy, sissified, weak-kneed, yellow-livered, absent-minded," an also-ran who prefers to cover human interest stories for the paper. Feiffer holds that Superman is the basic identity of the Man of Steel and that Clark is a disguise chosen to throw his enemies off the trail. But why would he play-act as an unlikely wimp? Feiffer decides Superman must be a sadomasochist. He enjoys putting down Lois and likes it even better when she brushes off Clark. That women adore Superman while Clark is pussy-whipped only emphasizes the difference between a real man and a sissy. "Our cultural opposite of the man who didn't make out with women has never been the man who did," observes Feiffer, "but rather the man who could if he wanted to, but still didn't."

Feiffer, writing in the midsixties, was accurate about Shuster's and Siegel's comic strip and the Superman of radio and early TV, but Hollywood was going to transmogrify and improve on the story. *Newsweek* observed of the first *Superman*: "One of the charms of [director Richard] Donner's movie is the way in which it de-schizifies and gently unchastes this menage a trois. [Christopher] Reeve's Clark Kent is a bumbling fumbler, but he's no sissy. And his Superman . . . is precisely a super-man. . . . [It is] a pain in the cape to him as he realizes that he loves Lois." Superman and Clark are doubles, variants of one psyche who are distinct personalities. The key conceit is that Lois suspects but dares not acknowledge their joint identity. These two guys are the poles of her dream menage, which she doesn't want to change. Long before the current mildly feminist TV show *Lois and Clark*, the fantasy was hers.

Dooley, relying on psychologists, suggests that we "analyze the Superman–Lois Lane–Clark Kent triangle in terms of an Oedipal theme." The professor argues that Lois loves Superman—"a fantasized father figure of great power and authority"—but mothers Clark, who is "helpless, weak and frightened." Clark is hopelessly in love with her, but Superman cannot return her love because "to do so would be to reveal that he is in reality Clark, whose love relationship with Lois is, in Oedipal terms, forbidden." Which is pseudo-Freudian rubbish.

Clark isn't the son who wishes to supersede his father in order to sleep with his mother. He hardly knows his real parents, and Papa Kent is no competition for superboy. The original Superman stayed chaste because like Jesus Christ, he was seen as the savior of the world. When in *Superman II* he denies his destiny in order to marry Lois and lead a normal life, the result is humiliation and global disaster. In *Superman III*, exposure to Kryptonite causes him to lose his cool and spend his days drinking and wenching. It seems he has allowed the devil to tempt him. But this is no biblical tale or Greek tragedy, because it has neither God nor gods—only Superman, who *chooses* to go straight again.

Jerry Siegel invented Superman as revenge for personal rebuffs in a high school where most of the students were sharper, smoother, and better looking than he. According to Dooley, Jerry had "the soul of a D'Artagnan imprisoned in the body of an undernourished delivery boy." Joe Shuster was even more retiring because his vision was so poor; as a mature man he would become legally blind. They both had a crush on Lois Amster, a bright, pretty, and "nicely-put-together girl" who wouldn't give them the time of day. Instead, she dated self-assured types such as the student council president Clark Schnabel, whose last name was pronounced to rhyme with "Gable." And so our national myth began as the fantasy revenge of a couple of high school nerds.

Superman succeeded because other frustrated kids in the dark days of the depression bought it off the racks and demanded more. World War II, during which Superman joined the war effort and GIs were issued copies of the comic book, solidified this alien's place in the national consciousness. Joseph Goebbels, Nazi minister of propaganda, denounced Superman as a Jew.

Alas for Siegel and Shuster, they had signed away the rights to their creation and received very little of the huge sums it generated. This had the beneficial effect of permitting the story and graphics to evolve with changing times. The writers' main problem in scripting *Superman* was that being invulnerable, he quickly ran out of enemies. Action had to hinge on his dilemma concerning Lois and the conflict between his two identities.

Starring in the first movie, Christopher Reeve emphasized the double persona, playing a passive voyeur for nearsighted Clark and an exhibitionist for Superman. Think of that cape-and-tights getup! It is camp, to say the least, and when worn under a suit, hints at transvestitism. Superman always saves Lois in front of a crowd in downtown Metropolis, then lands daintily on one pointed foot, curl in place on his forehead. The main metaphor for sex between Superman and Lois is when he takes her flying. Freud insisted on the sexuality of flying in dreams, and *Newsweek* raved over the eroticism of the duo's scenes high above the skyscrapers of pseudo–New York. After their maiden flight, Reeve deposits Margot Kidder's Lois on her terrace, says good night, and flies off. "The camera follows Lois as she moves love-drunk into her apartment, and a moment later there's a knock at her door and Reeve as Clark Kent, horn-rimmed glasses, dull business suit and all, comes in to remind her they had a date. . . . The virtuosity of the scene reinforces the sweetness and the humor of the love for Lois felt by two men who are really one man."

More accurately, there's one super-man who is two personae, which has been a qualification for superheroes since the Babylonian epic of *Gilgamesh*. In *Superman II* Lois discovers, or thinks she does, that Clark is Superman, and she convinces him to marry her. But first he must undergo a transformation in "little Krypton" (at the North Pole) and surrender his powers. Afterward Lois finds herself hooked to a schlemiel, and Clark finds that the normal life he wished for means being pushed around. He resumes his heroic mantle, defeats Lex Luthor and his evil cohorts, and erases all memory of the marriage from Lois's mind. Superman stays a virgin, sort of.

By 1983's *Superman III*, sex has become explicit, and Superman and Clark are at war with each other. "If Clark Kent marries Lana Lang and Superman marries Lois Lane, will that be bigamy or menage a trois?" quipped the *Washington Post*. It seems Clark had a crush on Lana, who is prettier than Lois, at Smallville High. At their class reunion they meet again, and Lana, now a single mother and fed up with aging jocks, finally appreciates steady Clark, who lives in the big city. But Superman, who has been exposed to half-baked Kryptonite by the villains (corporate-raider types), puts the make on Clark's new girl! Lana is just a subplot anyway, and Superman goes downhill fast. He drinks and picks fights in bars; he even throws in with the villains to procure the sexual favors of Lorelei Ambrosia, a poor imitation of Marilyn Monroe. Finally, Superman and Clark fight to the death in a scrap-metal yard complete with frightening mashing machines. After the most brutal encounter in all three movies, Clark destroys his corrupt double and emerges as a new Superman, who quickly sets things right. Lois, who is barely present, will reappear with a vengeance in the contemporary TV series, *Lois and Clark*.

In *Lois and Clark*, Superman, having gone through recovery, is a sensitive type who won't change his uniform because Ma Kent sewed it. Lois is complicit in his dual identity, but they aren't going to settle down because neither wants to. Superman's destiny is to be a savior, and Lois is angling for a Pulitzer. Her sex life consists of her two fantasy guys. She likes to dream about those muscular thighs of steel. "How big are you?" she coyly asks Superman. But she needs Clark to nurture and order around. She no longer needs Superman to rescue her, but she lets him do it because a helpless Lois is *his* fantasy! After a sixty-year engagement, in 1996 Lois and Clark married on TV. They tied the knot shortly afterward in the *Superman* comic strip. We wonder whether this power couple will seek out a new third or a fourth? Or will they have super-children? Whatever the future holds, Superman, Lois, and Clark are the archetypal postmodern menage.

DOUBLES AND TRIPLES

Superman led to Batman, Wonder Woman, and other superheroes; Andy Warhol, who early on painted Superman, gave us superstars; and the fashion publicity house of Keeble, Cavaco and Duka made supermodels into household names. In an act of supreme self-knowledge, or commercial cunning, Warhol declined to exhibit the Clark Kent he'd also painted. He had transformed his shy, pasty, pimply self, Andrew Warhola of Pittsburgh, into the slick pop artist of Chelsea. It might tarnish Superman's reputation to remind people of Clark, or Andy's own legend to recall the double left behind in his shadowy youth. More generally, playing off perceived doubles, sometimes identical twins, has been a foundation of comedy since the Roman Plautus. In the eighteenth century, Carlo Goldoni produced the often revived *Venetian Twins* and founded the Italian national theater.

The key conceit of doubling is that the one who is fooled, let's say a woman, never realizes she is being romanced by two people. Thus the figure in the middle keeps making mistakes, kissing the brother who is not her fiancée or berating him for fooling around with another woman, who is *his* fiancé. Since the audience is wise to the joke, we gain the voyeuristic pleasure of knowing more than the players onstage. Sometimes we catch subtle hints that the woman is catching on to the duplicity but that she naturally prefers two lovers to one. A variation on the theme occurs in Edmond Rostand's *Cyrano de Bergerac*, where it takes two men to court one woman because each is half a man, lacking what the other has. The sexual charge in these situations comes not from doubling but tripling—we are actually watching an implied menage a trois. Once the confusion is set right, the play had better end. Lois, when she learns that Clark and Superman are the same guy, has to be made to forget.

The lavish 1990 *Cyrano*, starring Gérard Dépardieu, is the only film that lists a special credit for "nose creation." Depardieu's fake proboscis suits the character's ungainliness and coarse behavior. He bullies an entire theater and mortally wounds a man because he doesn't care for a particular actor. The beautiful Roxanne civilizes him, and in order to win her, he must throw in with Christian, a hunk who is handsome but dumb. In the famous balcony scene, Christian is wooing Roxanne while Cyrano, concealed by the shadows, tells him what to say. When the dolt declares his love, Roxanne asks him to embroider on the sentiment as a courtier should. He is speechless, but Cyrano feeds him elaborate rhyming couplets. The lady's heart is won by this collaboration.

There's a bit of folk wisdom that says the size of a man's member can be judged by the size of his nose. Cyrano is ugly but sexy. He is witty, and while in America that might not endow him with sex appeal, in France it does, especially if he has a rapier wit. In *Cyrano* Roxanne is also being courted by the comte de Guiche, who has the sexiness of power. It takes an alliance of Cyrano and Christian to win Roxanne away from him. In a sense she becomes the wife of both of them. When Christian is killed in battle, the grief-stricken Roxanne retires to the Convent of the Ladies of the Cross. The wounded Cyrano, after an operatic speech, dies content in her arms. The three have been reunited.

The Truth About Cats and Dogs is a mediocre attempt to make Cyrano's story politically correct. Janeane Garofalo is the plain-Jane host of a Santa Monica call-in show about pet care. She has a lovely voice and no social life, and when a charming male caller wants to meet her, she describes her brunette self as looking like her tall, blond neighbor, model Uma Thurman.

The rest is confusion: beautiful Uma poses for dumpy Janeane, and Janeane speaks for ditzy Uma. This isn't, as the press would have it, a bad joke about self-doubt but a play on the disconnection between looks and brains in each of the women. Janeane is homely in relation to her witty air-time persona; Uma is dumb relative to her smart good looks.

Cyrano raged against his fate by acting out, sometimes cruelly. But he was a poetic soul assigned a masquerade face for life. The narcissistic act of admiring his reflection was denied him. So he acquired a handsome alter ego, and by a joint effort they won their mate. In *Cats and Dogs*, despite the willingness of the male in the middle to bed both women, Uma is treated as the complication that has arisen between him and Janeane. In the end, the menage that prevails is boy, girl, and dog.

The Italian *Farinelli* provides a more interesting take on the irony of fate. The story of the eighteenth century's most celebrated castrato, a singer with the power of a man and the vocal range of a woman, this gorgeous film again shows the significance of the voice in erotic attraction. Farinelli, born Carlo Broschi, a peasant, rose to musical and political eminence by delighting noblemen and turning on their ladies. While *New York* magazine's observation that "the castrati were the rock stars" of their day is stretching it, Farinelli became famous, rich, and powerful. He was courted by composers to perform their music and by crowned heads to do so at their courts—and all because of the searing wrong done him as a child: castration.

The story hinges less on this irony than on Carlo's relation to his older brother Riccardo, who in fact managed his career and wrote vapid music for him to sing. Older brother is behind younger in every sense: the women who flock to the famous Farinelli discover that at a certain point in the intercourse, Riccardo takes over. The brothers have made a pact to share the women. Carlo enjoys them as he can—he gets an erection—but Riccardo gets the *"jouissance,"* as one countess puts it, a twinkle in her eye. She means not only pleasure but in argot, "orgasm." The great Farinelli can hold a note seemingly forever, and since he cannot come, his brother must mark "finis" to the act of love.

Does this unique partnership have some general application? The brothers will eventually fall out because Riccardo is greedy and unscrupulous. But where does Carlo go when Riccardo takes over? He watches. The only completion for Carlo is the pleasure of others. That is true for every artist. The performer's enjoyment of his or her art comes as a reflection of the audience's reaction. In each menage, though the roles shift, there are players and an audience, there is an initiator and the one who brings completion.

Woody Allen's *The Purple Rose of Cairo* is a more successful attempt at showing art as life's double, indeed as preferable to so-called real life. *Purple Rose* is a fantasy of plenitude on the part of Cecilia (Mia Farrow), a young woman in small-town depression America who has no love at home. She takes refuge from waitressing at a greasy-spoon restaurant and catering to her dumb, abusive husband by going to the local movie house, the Jewel. She is enchanted by *The Purple Rose of Cairo*, a romantic melodrama set in Egypt and high-society New York. It's the sort of movie Woody calls a "champagne comedy—those comedies from the 1930s and 1940s with all those romantic people who wore tuxedos and went to big nightclubs and lived in penthouses and drank champagne all the time." Cecilia's fantasies echo Woody's own as a poor boy in Brooklyn. Significantly, Woody rates *Purple Rose* as one of only four movies he is satisfied with out of the twenty-plus he has filmed.

At the Jewel, the movie's male lead, intrepid archaeologist Tom Baxter, steps off the screen to declare his love for his most devoted fan. The romance between screen idol and fan pleases them both, but the other characters in *The Purple Rose*, freed from the script, are thrown into confusion. The movie can't continue, and the chaos is spreading like a virus to other movie houses. The studio sends Gil Shepherd, the actor who plays Tom, to break up the romance that is threatening its box office receipts. Gil, too, falls in love with Cecilia, who must choose between the perfect but imaginary Tom and the "real" Gil. She opts for the real man, but since he is an actor, he proves as illusory as his role; he leaves her to return to Hollywood's house of dreams and disappointment. Meanwhile the *Purple Rose* disappears from the screen on schedule.

Woody's message is clear: from one's lover one can expect betrayal. Cecilia's response to her unalterably harsh fate is to return to the Jewel for its next attraction. Woody has crafted a paean to mass voyeurism, to the superiority of watching over doing. "Life is divided up into the horrible and the miserable," remarks Alvy Singer, his alter ego in *Annie Hall*, which is still his signature piece. "You should be thankful if you're miserable."

Annie, like a number of Woody's films, makes reference to a menage a trois, but rarely do we find it actualized. When Alvy and Annie (Diane Keaton) grow bored, he suggests they try something new: a threesome. It is left to his actor pal Max, who has moved to the netherworld of Los Angeles, to investigate the possibilities of sleeping with two sixteen-year-olds. What is shocking, however, is that the naïveté of Woody's movie roles seems real. His performance at the now infamous child custody trial was certain to antagonize the judge, the press, and the public. As *Newsday* columnist Carole Agus put it, "Woody Allen slept with Mia Farrow while he was sleeping with Farrow's daughter. He said she begged him to. . . . He did it to protect the children."

His antagonist, Mia, on the other hand, admitted to wrathful jealousy and claimed she threw him out to protect the children. The highlight of her testimony came when she recounted how Woody had admitted to the affair with her adopted daughter, Soon-Yi: "Allen said the incident might actually strengthen the troubled, eleven-year relationship between Farrow and himself, and could also have therapeutic emotional benefits for [Soon-Yi]." Allegedly he added, "Let's use this as a springboard into a deeper relationship." The great ridiculer of California made a proposal worthy of an Esalen encounter group. He should have known that New York courts will always enforce monogamy, or at least make you pay for violating it. And judges, juries, and the press understand jealousy, even of the murderous kind, and often reward it.

Woody and Mia had never married or lived together, and the adult Soon-Yi was not related to him. Nonetheless it was held that Woody had violated his duties as "a lifetime partner-parent" by romancing mother and adopted daughter more or less simultaneously. The schlemiel Casanova had the book thrown at him. Multiplicity of sexual desire frightens our judicial masters, and they won't hesitate to invent a nonlegal straitjacket with which to tie it down. As for the really juicy stuff at this trial, it was related with the press banished, and the record remains sealed.

NECKING

How frightened our society is of polysexuality—having more than one lover or gender—can be glimpsed in the myth of Dracula and its authentic contemporary rendition, Francis Ford Coppola's 1992 movie, adapted from Bram Stoker's fin de siècle novel. *Dracula* was published a century ago at a time of intense moral hypocrisy. Women were worshiped for a virginity men hoped to deprive them of, wives praised for a fidelity their husbands suspected they lacked. In our time, this tale, which comes down to us from medieval Eastern Europe, is a metaphor for sexual multiplicity. The vampire never dies or wearies and is always on the lookout for fresh new flesh. He or she is the lover who kills, which in Victorian times aroused the fear of syphilis, and today, of AIDS.

There are two sorts of characters in the story: the living and the undead. The live ones, such as Jonathan Harker and Mina Murray, the main love interest, are apparent models of chastity. But they are in imminent danger of becoming undead if they suck the blood of a vampire.

Being sucked on themselves will make them desire to suck another. Count Dracula, played sympathetically by Gary Oldman in Coppola's movie, was, four hundred years earlier, the Hungarian warlord Vlad the Impaler, who was sentenced to eternal undeath. Vlad, on learning of his beautiful young wife's suicide and the priests' refusal to bury her, renounced God and the church. By Stoker's time, let alone Coppola's, Dracula had become more of a panderer to his tribe of vampires than a performer of neck romance, because he is fixed on reuniting with the incarnation of his wife—none other than Mina, played deliciously by Winona Ryder.

Harker, a Victorian yuppie played by Keanu Reeves, has been sent to Transylvania by his firm in order to consummate a real-estate deal: the count is buying up plots of land around London in which to bury himself during the day. At the dreary castle, Dracula warns Harker not to wander around. But the dim recesses call to him, and in the elaborate but musty ladies' quarters he comes upon the count's three exquisite brides, who were once his victims. "All three had brilliant white teeth that shone like pearls against the ruby of their voluptuous lips," wrote Stoker. The brides caress Harker, rip open his shirt, and the youngest bride "works her way up his body, kissing his body, flicking her tongue up his stomach," observes Coppola in writing about his movie. Harker's face shows the ecstatic look movies reserve for a man receiving fellatio.

Soon the three are on him, his blood dripping from their mouths, but the clerk, his passion freed, is exultant. The brides "converge on Harker, their mouths finding each other in a torrid four-way kiss." The count breaks up the party, warning the women that he has reserved the young man for himself. The youngest bride taunts him that he has never loved. Dracula replies, "Yes, I too can love; you yourselves can tell it from the past." Because the count's brides resemble him and may be his daughters, incest is yet another of his perversions.

In his guise as an older gentleman, Dracula takes an erotic interest in his handsome young guest. Francis Coppola noted in his journal, "He's seducing Harker. And that repressed Victorian sexuality becomes a force that works for Dracula with both Harker and Mina. They're depraved on account of being deprived." This works all the more with the aristocrat Lucy Westenra, who eagerly peruses the postures in an illustrated *Kama Sutra* in the count's library. Lucy has three eligible suitors, including a rich Texan, all of whom propose to her on the same day. "Why can't they let a girl marry three men?" she complains. Ironically, she will become another bride in Dracula's harem. With Harker chained up, the king vampire has now moved, coffin, dirt, and all, to England. In the form of a wolf he attacks the sleepwalking Lucy, and though interrupted, he has begun to drain her life's blood.

Arthur Holmwood, Lucy's slightly dim successful suitor, the Texan, and Dr. Jack Seward, who brings in Dr. Van Helsing, vampire expert, all form a brotherhood to protect Lucy. But Dracula, in the guise of a bat, continues to suck the blood out of the bedridden Lucy. The men donate their own blood, each feeling that his fluid in her veins makes Lucy his wife. To the Victorians, blood equated with semen, the medium of the vital life force. There is a sexual undertone to Van Helsing's statement, "A brave man's blood is the best thing on this earth when a woman is in trouble." In a sense, then, Lucy gets her wish and marries the lot of them.

By the time she is ready to join Dracula among the undead, Lucy has become sex crazed; she moans and writhes, demanding in a voluptuous voice that Arthur kiss her so she can suck his blood. The angel has become a whore. Worse, it seems she always had it in her. When the brotherhood confronts Dracula in his townhouse, he boasts, "Your girls that you all love are mine already; and through them you shall yet be mine." This count swings both ways, and a bisexual threesome would be right up his moat. Gary Oldman, in an interview with *Premiere*, remarked that he wanted the young, handsome Dracula to be androgynous, to unnerve people sexually.

In London stalking Mina, his real target, the well-dressed Count Dracula looks like John Lennon with an edge. He romances his bride of yesteryear by taking her to a motion-picture show and to chic restaurants. Mina drinks absinthe and imagines herself a princess. She is dressed in red; they waltz. But Jonathan Harker, who has escaped from Dracula's castle, arrives to rain on the party. Mina, again a good girl, marries him, which is a kind of bigamous union of two would-be vampires, each with a hidden past. Vampirism, the lust for illicit sex, is the secret in the hearts of proper Victorians.

Van Helsing upsets Dracula's resting place, which forces him to return to Transylvania, and the whole crew, carrying the fight to the enemy's country, follows in order to destroy him and his castle. This is convenient for the count, who continues to pursue his original bride, Mina, and her husband, Harker. As David Skall, author of *Hollywood Gothic*, observes, "the vampire's mouth is an ambiguous orifice . . . engulfing yet penetrating, nightmarishly blurring the distinctions of gender." Thus the climactic vampire attack, which occurs when the newlyweds are asleep, is "a thinly veiled menage a trois witnessed by Dr. Seward. Dracula crawls quite literally into the Harkers' marriage bed."

Jonathan, in a stupor, is breathing heavily, face flushed. Mina is kneeling on the edge of the bed next to a tall, thin man clad in black. "His right hand gripped her by the back of the neck, forcing her face down on his bosom. Her white nightdress was smeared with blood, and a thin stream trickled down the man's bare breast." Skall continues, "The true horror of Dracula . . . is his polymorphous perversity." The vampire is the lurking, inner, insatiable craving for unspeakable things. Coppola confided to his journal, "When Mina starts to get sexy, she should top Lucy."

For the ending to the novel or movie, you'll have to read or see the same. But why does Dracula fail to reflect in a mirror? The folkloric (Christian) explanation is that he has no soul. We think it is because he has no ego and thus no alter ego. He is a fallen angel ridden with guilt. Unlike Narcissus, he sees nothing in himself to admire. Dracula, also an illegal alien, is the inverse of Superman, his shadow side. He too can fly, is immortal, and is unfazed by bullets or bombs. But the similarities end where sex is concerned. Superman finds himself locked into a perpetual menage with Lois and Clark. Dracula, ironically, is a covert monogamist, searching for the same wife for several centuries—indeed for as long as the vampire industry endures, which may be forever. No wonder the count wears black!

THE GREATEST PARTY EVER GIVEN

Our Fantasy Bash for Celebrity Threes

I felt like a slice of white bread between two slices of ham.
DOROTHY LAMOUR ON THE
ROAD MOVIES SHE MADE WITH
BING CROSBY AND BOB HOPE

*I*N 1973 MR. BLACKWELL, THE RAZOR-tongued inventor of the Worst-Dressed Women list, gave a party for one of the world's least dressed women, Josephine Baker. At sixty-six, she was performing a one-woman show in Los Angeles. Blackwell, radio personality, fashion designer, and formerly the self-confessed "most prolific boy toy in Hollywood" wanted to honor Baker's talent and courage. Josephine had been born into an impoverished black family in Saint Louis. Discouraged by racial prejudice, she moved to Paris and in the twenties became the rage for her Follies dance routines in a skimpy skirt made of bananas. The French elevated her beyond stardom to the realm of sex goddess. During the war she was active in the Resistance, then returned to an America still torn from the battles over civil rights.

Blackwell was born Richard Selzer into an almost equally poor family in Brooklyn, got into trouble, and reinvented himself as Dick Ellis, aspiring actor and a Hollywood gay hustler. By the late sixties he had made a reputation with his stunning clothing designs and lived in an opulent, period mansion in Beverly Hills. For the party, Blackwell created "an

American version of Versailles." Two hundred celebrity guests arrived in limousines, stepped out under the spotlights in black tie and gown, swept through the foyer and past the grand staircase, which was lined by a dozen violinists, and into the garden to feast under a huge white tent lit by crystal chandeliers from *The Great Ziegfeld*. Everyone waited for Josephine's entrance. Would she have a cheetah or an ocelot on a leash?

Since we can't attend Blackwell's bash, let's give our own fantasy party Tinsel Town–style. We'll invite the living and the dead, the real and the fictional, to celebrate Threedom Day. Imagine a *ranchito* with a large, sprawling house, acres of grounds, and a heart-shaped pool in the hills above Palm Springs. Here, where old movie stars come to retire and play golf into eternity, past and present celebrities mingle, as do all gender and sexual preferences. Blackwell rented peacocks for his affair, but we've got our pet pandas, ostriches, pussy cats—every sort of animal that mates by threes. It's early evening in the desert as one of those Technicolor sunsets lingers and a slight breeze flaps our tricolor flag that bears the motto: "Big Brother out of the Boudoir." Here come the guests in limos real and spectral!

THE GODDESS AND HER DEVOTEES

Blackwell's tent served up "pearl-gray caviar, chilled golden champagne and sizzling French crepes," but like a lot of our guests we're more health-minded. We know what Greta would like—that's Gustafson, daughter of a poor Stockholm family. You know her as glamorous Garbo, but in the 1939 *Ninotchka* she played a Soviet agent dressed in mannish clothes. At a fancy New York restaurant she ordered "bits und carrotz." The trajectory of waif to goddess, like that of urchin to matinee idol, is too compelling to ignore. These women and men are self-made to the point that neither one identity nor one lover is enough. Josephine Baker could never stop looking at her *selves* in the mirror.

Let's mosey out to the barbecue in the cactus garden. Josephine, mother of an adopted Rainbow Tribe of children, is helping out. Instead of an apron she's wearing a G-string of bananas, loads of jewels, a petite live snake around her neck, and nothing more. Georges Simenon is standing by puffing on a pipe, admiring Josephine as she sinks her pearly teeth into an apple. Pepito Abitino, her manager and one of her husbands—she forgot to divorce an earlier one—is hanging around as usual. A Sicilian gigolo, he has style, which he taught to the rough diamond in need of polishing. Jean-Claude Baker, one of her adopted sons and subsequently her biographer, wrote, "Seeing he could not be the only man in her bed, he decided to be her alter ego, make her the most famous entertainer in the world."

Simenon boasts that he could have married Josephine. This pair of sexual tigers is well matched in bed. But Josephine depends on her reliable manager-husband-voyeur Pepito to watch the show and keep score. Marlene Dietrich is made from similar narcissistic stuff. She is seated at our Oasis Bar surrounded by palm fronds and fish tanks filled with glorious multi-colored fish. In top hat and tux, she looks as though she has stepped out of the nightclub scene in *Morocco*, the film in which she teases Gary Cooper and Adolph Menjou, then plants a kiss on a pretty girl's mouth. Husband Rudi Sieber, a handsome man who dates back to her Berlin drama-student days, is on one side and current lover Douglas Fairbanks Jr. is on the other. Marlene dispenses her favors with the amorality of a goddess. She likes to tantalize men, then break their hearts. On any given night she has been known to entertain several lovers, singly or in doubles depending on her whim. Marlene and Rudi live together platonically; he manages her considerable finances.

The affair with Fairbanks dates from 1936, after the death of John Gilbert, Marlene's first Hollywood lover. Marlene met Doug at a London party given by the director Alexander Korda. Fairbanks was younger than she and recently divorced from Joan Crawford. So she comforted him by cuddling him between her well-proportioned breasts. Next to the bed stood a shrine to Gilbert with an ever-burning candle and his photo, as though he was watching his successors.

Marlene calls herself "Mama" and likes to clean and cook for her admirers. She really likes to seduce her directors and leading men—whether Joseph von Sternberg, Gary Cooper, Maurice Chevalier, John Wayne, or Yul Brynner—the better to dominate them while making the movie. Her Prussian background gives her a taste for generals, even George Patton, as romantic as one of his tanks. No matter, Marlene is the active one. She is the headhunter, and a gallery of the photos of her conquests might be titled "The Great Men of Our Time." She could also include female lovers, for this sex pistol fancied women too. "In Europe we make love with anyone we find attractive," she told Budd Shulberg.

In the late thirties, Marlene, in her late thirties, was at the peak of her form. Traveling in a select crowd that included Noël Coward, she performed his wry songs, enjoying—to borrow Ophelia's description of Hamlet—being the observed of all observers. One of the crowd was the French actor Jean Gabin. A street brawler who, like James Cagney, got his start as a hoofer, Gabin was antisocial and a French patriot. Yet the married Gabin wasn't indifferent to Marlene's tender domination. "I loved to mother him day and night," she recalled for the press.

Beginning in 1941, their romance flourished in her bungalow at the Beverly Hills Hotel. She helped the moody actor acclimate to Hollywood, kept house, and acted as "interpreter, sister, friend and more!" Donald Spoto, Dietrich's biographer, theorizes that her self-abasement before her lovers was triggered by her neglect of husband Rudi—and, we might add, of her daughter Maria. But Jean, unlike Rudi, couldn't tolerate Marlene's freewheeling sexual behavior. Under his rugged facade Jean was her "lonely child," while he called her "my Prussian." She told Rudi that Jean was the love of her life.

Yet into this warm, smooching, empathetic romance Marlene felt compelled to introduce a third. She was making *Manpower* with George Raft and Edward G. Robinson, buddies who, in the movie, become rivals for her affections. Meanwhile she was trysting with George in various Warner dressing rooms. Jean was furious and found diversion. Marlene, lunching with George at the studio, telephoned Jean from their table, flirted with him in French, and asked how it went with his girlfriend the night before. For George's benefit, she translated into English this menage à telephone. Gabin left her soon afterward.

Greta Garbo is our guest of honor. The most ethereal of the sex goddesses, vulnerable with a masculine tinge, she was as measured with her favors as her money. While Dietrich bought luxuries on Rodeo Drive, Garbo bought real estate. Here in the cool desert evening, Garbo is wearing her signature trench coat, boots, and dark glasses. We sense that any moment she will run from the crowds. Thus we provide an "icehouse" for her to hide in. Garbo has made the transit from having her larger-than-life face flicker in front of tens of millions worldwide to skulking about New York streets fearful of being seen.

Garbo's heyday came during the 1930s, when she played a succession of heroic yet fallen women: Mata Hari, Queen Christina, Anna Karenina, and Camille. During this time Garbo had affairs with orchestra conductor Leopold Stokowski, health expert Gaylord Hauser, and British fashion photographer Cecil Beaton. Both Garbo and Dietrich also sampled the charms of Mercedes de Acosta: poet, playwright, and film scenarist, she was the most sought-after lesbian in Hollywood.

Originally of Spanish descent, Mercedes married a male painter but took a girlfriend along on the honeymoon. Beautiful women were her lifelong quarry, and her amours encompassed Isadora Duncan and many other artistic beauties. In 1931 Mercedes met Garbo of the incredibly long eyelashes in sunny Santa Monica. The couple enjoyed intimate tête-à-têtes and holidays together. Determined to express their masculine side, the women cross-dressed in men's clothes. As Mercedes' obsession mushroomed, Garbo typically retreated into her shell. Mercedes' complaints to Dietrich about "the Scandinavian child" only added fuel to her grand battles with Garbo, who was apt to fly off to Sweden at any time.

Finally Mercedes elicited the help of Cecil Beaton, who from afar adored the boyish, golden-tanned Garbo. Mercedes enthralled him with intimate details that made him desperate to have her. The foppish Beaton had met Garbo in 1932 and begged her to pose for him. She refused but gave him a yellow rose, saying, "You are like a young Grecian boy. If I were a young boy I would do such things to you." He framed the rose and hung it over his bed until his death fifty years later. Beaton had been a convinced homosexual until Adele Astaire, Fred's sister and dancing partner, exposed him to other possibilities. For now he hung on the sidelines, imploring Garbo to be nicer to Mercedes. It was Garbo's androgyny that swept Cecil and Mercedes off their feet. Mercedes especially admired her legs that had "the shape that can be seen in many Greek statues." Beaton, in his *Scrapbook* of 1937, waxed rhapsodic over the blond boy-goddess.

In 1941 Garbo commenced her long retirement. She had remarked that she wished she could lead two lives: one private and one public. This she accomplished in serial fashion. Gaylord Hauser introduced her to Valentina and Georges Schlee, a married couple who would make up her core menage. Georges came from a wealthy Russian family and fought the Bolsheviks during the revolution. He had to flee and in Sevastopol found young Valentina, an orphaned drama student. She was beautiful, and when she became an exclusive clothes designer, she brought out her own exotic looks and gave the unstylish Garbo fashion guidance. Georges, a lawyer, took over the management of Garbo's finances. According to Hugo Vickers, Beaton's biographer, both Schlees became Garbo's intimates and probably lovers.

Garbo built Valentina's reputation by wearing her fashions. Biographer Barry Paris writes that the two women "dressed identically and made social rounds on Georges's right and left arm." He confessed to his wife that he was in love with Garbo but that she would never marry him. Besides, he and Valentina had "so much in common." For a considerable time the menage arrangement suited everyone concerned. Summers Georges and Garbo went to the Riviera and the Greek isles on Aristotle Onassis's yacht, while Valentina joined her lover in Venice. By 1953 Garbo had moved into an apartment on New York's East Fifty-second Street, four floors below the Schlees.

Truman Capote wrote that "Georges Schlee was an absolute bastard. He was so unattractive, he was grotesque, he was extremely ugly . . . yet he had a hold on Valentina and Garbo." Mercedes and Cecil formed a shadow menage ready to take over if Garbo ever dropped the Schlees. Beaton tracked Georges and Garbo on vacations and pretended to meet them by accident. In 1947 Garbo posed for, and began an affair with, the ecstatic Cecil. He became obsessed with the idea of marrying her. But Garbo would flit between the two competing menages, the Schlees for her domestic side and Beaton or Mercedes for glamour.

Cecil and Mercedes threw in together to win Garbo's company from the detested Russians. On one occasion the threesome spent Christmas Day together. Cecil came to admire Mercedes' tenacity, her devotion to Garbo after nearly twenty years of raw deals. But Garbo's secretive, quixotic behavior left him alternately elated and depressed. He denounced Georges Schlee as an "old Russian sturgeon." He promoted Mercedes to Garbo. But his goddess continued merely to fit him in, sneaking over for brief assignations in order not to antagonize the suspicious Schlee. The latter treated Garbo as callously as she had treated Mercedes. Yet Georges acted as bodyguard, manager, and nurse, standing between Garbo and the public she dreaded.

In October 1964 the carousel ground to a halt when Georges dropped dead of a heart attack in Paris. Garbo disappeared, and Valentina flew in the next day and took charge of the body. Valentina swore she never wanted to see Garbo again and summoned a priest to exorcise her apartment, especially the refrigerator where Garbo had stashed cans of beer. For the next quarter century the two women, living a few floors apart in the same building, did everything possible to avoid meeting. Doormen shuddered at the possibility of their paths crossing.

Garbo can be a real sad sack, but at our party we focus on gaiety. The legendary beauty is moping in the icehouse. We coax her out, take her for a vigorous walk, and she cheers up. She joins other luminaries round the campfire to roast marshmallows. Marlene will sing for us: "Falling in Love Again." It's the theme song of the menage a trois.

THE MATINEE IDOL'S DAY OFF
Other Hollywood menages have been as hidden as the wrinkles on the million-dollar faces that matinee idols show to the world. Past and present, gay lovers who have worked together on films have to acknowledge their sexuality in sly ways. But since the film code of Hollywood's so-called Golden Age barred explicit sexual references, highly charged but

ambiguous scenes could refer either to gay or straight love, and often a three-way situation was constructed for laughs or kicks. In our *ranchito's* screening room we show over and over the older American movies with menage subtexts.

Let's peek into this celluloid closet. We can spot Clark Gable, Ava Gardner, and Grace Kelly, the trio from *Mogambo*, watching Clark Gable, Jean Harlow, and Mary Astor in *Red Dust*, the same story filmed twenty years earlier. "Love flames in the savage heart of the jungle," proclaimed the poster. Both the bad girl (Jean, Ava) and the good girl (Mary, Grace) have the hots for Gable, the big white hunter. So does the proper British husband of each of the good girls, if a bit more discreetly.

Gable's appeal cuts across gender and generation. In *Mogambo* the well-meaning but hapless husband becomes a worshipful protégé, describing Gable as "a prince." The white hunter in turn saves the loyal but clumsy young man's life—heroically becoming indebted to him! This means that Gable, according to a powerful male-bonding code, cannot seduce his protégé's wife. Nevertheless, the proper wife throws herself at Gable's head. The women, though fierce rivals, also bond, but only after the good girl has been defeated and must return to "home and Devonshire" to raise a family.

Gable himself bonded intensely with Spencer Tracy on-screen in *San Francisco*. They play two buddies, a gambler and a priest, almost forcing Jeanette MacDonald to choose between them. She cannot because together they make up her perfect man. The tension is resolved when after the earthquake, the gambler finds faith and becomes more like the priest.

There have been more American movies with a threesome subtext than there are pages in this book. Think of the Rock Hudson–Doris Day–Tony Randall trio, or the everlasting Bing Crosby–Dorothy Lamour–Bob Hope threesome, on the road to somewhere. Nothing decisive could have occurred among these threes, if only because it would have ruled out a sequel. Perhaps the most interesting sort of suppressed menage plays on the bisexuality of the leading man. Cary Grant, the matinee idol personified, quietly exhibited his long-term affair with Randolph Scott in 1940's *My Favorite Wife*, directed by Garson Kanin. Here are the boys now, dressed identically in white satin circus pantaloons, checkered shirts, and large white satin pointed hats—a costume they made famous in the thirties when they were living in a white mansion by the ocean at Santa Monica, "Bachelor's Hall." Despite sham marriages and divorces, the buddies clung to each other for over a decade.

During this time they made *Wife*—the title of which was an "in" joke—costarring Irene Dunne. The premise is that she is Cary's legal wife who is shipwrecked on a South Seas island and presumed dead. She returns in time to find that Cary has remarried. At the honeymoon lodge in Yosemite, he juggles his two wives. "What a man!" exclaims the desk clerk. But the real complication arises when Cary discovers that Irene has spent seven years on the island with macho, athletic Scott, whom she calls "Adam." She is "Eve"; the rest follows. Two triangles form, one with Cary in the middle along with his two wives, another with Irene Dunne and a man on either side. But everyone on the set knew the real lovers were Cary and Scott.

Cary arranges a lunch where he confronts Irene with her paramour. It takes place at a swimming pool. Cary is fascinated by his rival's fine physique. Scott dives off a board into the pool and swims over to the couple. He sprays Cary in the face with pool water as he introduces himself. Cary wipes his hands dry on Scott's terry-cloth robe. These intimate gestures are obvious to the gay audience. Cary also does a stint at cross-dressing, which is found in a surprising number of his movies. In *Bringing Up Baby*, a screwball comedy made in 1938, Cary is caught wearing Kate Hepburn's peignoir. When her mother demands to know why, Cary jumps in the air and blurts out, "I've gone gay!"

Our *ranchito* is even better than the movies. Here you don't have to choose only one gender or one spouse or one identity. You can have them all. Cary Grant certainly tried. Born poor Archie Leach in England, he created an elegant, wealth-exuding persona that became more real than the original. Though he became accustomed to the disguise, he continued to lead the sex life that to him was real. Cary and Scott shared at least one trick—Blackwell when he was still Dick Ellis, aspiring actor. "Neither man was possessive," he wrote, "and I had wonderful relationships with both of them." Blackwell felt that sharing their intense feelings for one another added to the sum total of affection. This is the version of Blackwell we have with us this evening: young, pretty, a high-toned gigolo. Every party needs one or two.

Tyrone Power and Errol Flynn aren't here, but they've been invited out of courtesy. Both were matinee idols to the bone as well as bisexual. But their love lives were too unstable to achieve successful menages a trois or, for that matter, marriages.

The Australian actor Jack Thompson, star of *Breaker Morant*, was at one time heralded as the next Errol Flynn. At our party we notice his potbelly tugs against his flowered shirt. A sign of contentment? For a long time Jack has lived openly as husband and wives with two sisters, Bunkie and Lee, and we find the three by the pool, gazing at fireflies. Jack says he happens to love two women who happen to be sisters and who love him. They live together as though married, with a few more complications. Jack smiles and says the sisters overpower him sometimes, but they all try to be sensitive to each other's needs.

Jack discusses how Bunkie and Lee first bowled him over. The girls' love for each other negated the usual jealousy. They decided to become a menage and, after a week, moved in together. At first their family of three caused an uproar in Australia, but after a dozen years it is accepted. Jack says that "our relationship is filled with generosity, tolerance, and love." How many marriages do you know like that? Especially when you can change partners as easily as T-shirts!

Our pressing question is, what are we to do with our plethora of British guests, especially sophisticated ghosts such as Noël Coward, among all this sage and cacti? We'll call up fountains from under the ground—this is an oasis—and make a proper English garden: grass, lawn chairs, cricket wickets, and all. Elegant Sir Laurence Olivier, who transcends the matinee idol category, is accustomed to top-drawer treatment. He is another example of a poor boy who rose first to stage prominence, then to the aristocracy. His private character was closer to the low comedian he played in *The Entertainer* than to Henry V. Noël Coward became his mentor, and in 1930 Olivier married Jill Esmond, an actor who was a lesbian. In 1936 Alexander Korda brought Olivier together with the polished Vivien Leigh in the aptly titled *Fire over England*. Divorces being frowned on, the pair didn't marry until 1940, the same year *That Hamilton Woman* showed off their love at its height. Not long afterward the two became three.

Danny Kaye, born in Brooklyn, met the Oliviers at a Hollywood party. He attached himself to them, favoring "Lally," as he called his new friend Laurence. The erstwhile star biographer Donald Spoto claimed that "the relationship with Kaye . . . was certainly everything Vivien suspected and far more than Olivier admitted." Kaye and Olivier were lovers, and in the face of Hollywood gossip, Kaye spent weekends with the Oliviers and arranged his commitments around Lally's schedule. Kaye, Olivier, and Leigh appeared as Victorian triplets wearing beribboned hats, short skirts, and patent leather shoes at a London benefit. In 1961 Olivier wrote a letter to Leigh describing as transitory and unimportant the sexual intimacy between the two men.

Here comes Peter Finch, muttering, "Sunday, Bloody Sunday." Olivier guided the young actor's career from obscurity to West End stardom. An erotic attraction existed between the two talented actors. Leigh also appreciated Finch and welcomed him into the crowd that orbited around her at her country home; on weekends, guests included Orson Welles and Tennessee Williams, among other vivid personalities. Leigh started spending more time with Finch, and as a cast member of *Macbeth* remarked, "that seemed to take the pressure off Larry. There were times he seemed happy to have Finch there."

In 1953 the unstable actress departed for Ceylon to star with Finch in *Elephant Walk.* Olivier, wanting a trusted person on the spot, had persuaded the producer to hire Finch. On location Leigh and Finch became lovers. Both were drinking heavily. When she started to behave erratically, Olivier was summoned. One of Leigh's friends claimed that when "she went into one of her mental states, she was no longer able to distinguish between Olivier and Peter Finch ... because Finch was around so much in those days, because he and Larry were so devoted to each other."

At times Leigh appeared over the edge as though she were actually Blanche Dubois, one of her roles. Back in England, she spent the weekends with Finch, while Olivier pursued his own romantic interests. The couple would blithely reunite at midweek. Finch later described his motives as altruistic: "I was just trying to act in Larry's best interests. .... I did what I did to save Larry from embarrassment, Viv too. Shit, she calls me Larry half the time."

In Britain Leigh and Olivier's divorce approached a national tragedy. John Gielgud reported that the once stunning star continued to keep Olivier's photo on her night table, his old love letters in her desk. Olivier went on to marry actress Joan Plowright. Danny Kaye, among his many achievements, starred in one of the most winning menage movies ever made: the 1958 *Me and the Colonel.* Curiously, it has the same theme as Olivier's and Leigh's *That Hamilton Woman:* it takes three to conquer tyranny.

At the threesome party, Viv, Lally, and Danny occupy a table near a flowering cactus. Viv, informally striking "attitudes," wears one of her outfits from *That Hamilton Woman.* Lally, dressed as Lord Nelson, preens. Danny, in a court jester outfit, clinks champagne glasses with the couple—holding hands and rubbing knees.

THE RICH AND FAMOUS

Let's stroll under the night sky choked with stars to the Mill, a former windmill converted into an open-air nightspot. No charge for admission, drinks, or eats—just use your imagination. The specialty of the house is a Threesome Thunder cocktail, the ingredients of which we keep secret, as well as an "erotic endive salad with a menage a trois of Roquefort, pear, and walnuts," the recipe for which we have shamelessly borrowed. There's an actor who likes to play Mafia dons with his two girlfriends; there's a prize fighter who swings both ways; here's a Broadway dancer who thinks she is the female Bob Fosse. Angie Dickinson is having fun with ex-husband Burt Bacharach, and an unidentified male friend. All the revelers munch on heart-shaped ravioli. Roman Polanski has returned, and gossip links him to Jennifer Lee and Warren Beatty. At our splendiferous bash all is forgiven—and all that our lawyers approve is described.

Before the live show, clips from recent movies flash across a screen: *Threesome, Three of Hearts, Wedding Banquet,* and *Boys on the Side* are all three-themed. One additional thing they have in common is the younger generation rebelling against the monogamistic ideas of their parents. Of course the sophisticated, rich, and artistic have always indulged in menages a trois, whether or not they admitted to them. But the movies we mention are about ordinary people. Does this reflect a trend in society? Are the less well-off appropriating to themselves the sexual privileges of the rich?

For the very rich we have reserved a special table with a gold-threaded cloth. Warren Buffett, known as the "oracle of Omaha," wasn't born wealthy but set his mind on becoming so. He is now one of the richest men in the world. Personally frugal, we find him eating his favorite: a Lamourburger, which is a cheeseburger with the bun in the middle. It's a bit slippery but not as hard to handle as two women at once. Yet Warren is as adept at managing his personal life as his investments. According to *Time,* "for nearly two decades [Buffett] has lived with his mistress Astrid Menkes, a former waitress, while maintaining close ties with his wife." In the late seventies, Susie Buffett, her children grown, moved to San Francisco to pursue a singing career in clubs. We've got her onstage now, singing "Send in the Clowns," and Warren is choked up with emotion.

Susie found Warren a substitute wife, Astrid, to cook and keep house. Buffett's biographer Roger Lowenstein wrote, "Susie gave them a push." Astrid insists she is happy with what Lowenstein calls the trio's "rhythm" and that she is living in "the best of all worlds." Susie controls most of the family money, a trust second only to the Ford Foundation. Warren jokes that she is too rich to divorce. People close to him claim he is still madly in love with Susie. Most important, Warren says, "I really like my life. I've arranged my life so that I can do what I want." That's better than wealth.

The two women are friends and associates. When Susie comes to Omaha, wife and mistress lunch together. At a meeting of Berkshire Hathaway, Buffett's holding company, the women were seen sitting "side by side making small talk while their common friend presided onstage." Bill Gates recalled that on a visit to Buffett, lunch on Saturday was attended by Susie and brunch on Sunday by Astrid. A remark by a business associate quoted in the *Wall Street Journal* sums up the Buffett triad: "It's a relationship that never ever had a lie in it to anybody at any time. In some ways that group has created something that is very traditional with all the old values and just has one quirk." But that's no quirk—it's just a successful menage a trois.

We paraphrase an old saying: "Never menage for money, love where the money is." Roxanne Pulitzer followed this advice with initially unfortunate results. But the scandal resulting from her child custody case in Palm Beach made it easier for her to become a best-selling author. Nowadays infamy seems more lasting and lucrative than fame. Ask Dick Morris!

Pamela Harriman (née Digby) was effective in the old style. She juggled her World War II husband Randolph Churchill with American diplomat Averell Harriman—the men knew and appreciated each other—and then Harriman with Jock Whitney. Nearly everyone left Pam a trust fund, and she became still richer when she married her old flame, the widowed Averell, in 1971. She is, of course, the former United States ambassador to France. What could be more appropriate?

The rock-and-roll show at the Mill is about to go on. There are lots of young gatecrashers sitting on blankets out on the sand. The January 1997 "Education Life" section of the *New York Times* declares that college students are avoiding pairing off. "For a good time, call a crowd," crows the headline. The 9,100 students from all over the country interviewed for a study claimed they had never seen a successful adult romantic relationship. They need to stop looking at their parents and read about the great love affairs, which were complex emotionally and involved giving as well as getting.

There at a corner table sits a figure who's on thousands of movie screens this year but can't enjoy a thing: Eva Perón's mummy. After the Argentinean dictator's wife died young of cancer, Juan Perón followed her request and had her permanently embalmed in paraffin. Some say she wanted to enjoy her hundreds of pairs of shoes forever. Perón dressed Evita in her best and kept her in the living room of the presidential mansion. He told his numerous other women that she was a statue. When Perón was overthrown and exiled to Madrid, he transported Evita and kept her in the bedroom where he slept with his third wife. This has been called a "menage of two and a half." Now, due to the magic of Hollywood, the fascist mummy has become Madonna.

What has the menage a trois got to do with rock? It was there at the inception of the most dynamic musical movement of the century. The Beatles got their look, maybe their soul, from a metaphysical menage. Direct from the red-light district of Hamburg circa 1962 we bring you the painfully young John Lennon, Stuart Sutcliffe, an abstract painter dubbed the fifth Beatle, and Astrid Kirchherr, with whom both men were in love.

The boys met at Liverpool Art College in 1959. Stu ignited John's interest in art, politics, and Beat literature. They became intense friends, and John brought Stu, not really a musician, into the band, then called Johnny and the Moondogs. One night the group was attacked by roughs. John defended tiny Stu and broke a wrist, but Stu got a kick in the head. Years later he died of a brain hemorrhage. Until his own death in New York City John kept the scarf Stu wore when they attended art school.

Astrid, who had class, introduced the boys to Existentialist Hamburg. In honor of the Beats, Stu named the group the Beatles. Astrid gave Stu the first bowl-shaped haircut that the group adopted. They were no longer roughs from Liverpool but soulful arty types. These three became nearly inseparable, and their dreams, except for Stu's untimely death, became real. In the 1994 movie *Backbeat* the menage is made sexual. We don't really know, but let's shake our magic gourd and bring back all the Beatles to play for us. Spread out above is Lucy in the Sky with Diamonds.

Mick Jagger is our queen of the desert in white tights, lilac lace cape, high heels, purple eye shadow, and high bouffant blond wig. He is in his twenties and resembles a boyish Marilyn Monroe. Michael Jagger attended the London School of Economics and talked about becoming a lawyer. But in 1961 he and a boyhood chum, Keith Richards, moved into a filthy Chelsea crash pad and shared what little they could scrounge. Brian Jones, a blues devotee, joined them, and all three slept together to keep warm. Rock music and sexual ambiguity—share and share alike—became the house rule. The Rolling Stones were born.

Mick played Keith and Brian off against each other, a trick he would later use to charge up an audience. Yet as biographer Christopher Andersen described them, "all three were inexorably linked emotionally, physically and professionally, infusing them with an energy and creative power they could never have summoned as individuals." The aesthetic menage ignites like the key to an engine, and power is the result.

Into this den tripped Marianne Faithfull, a convent-bred convert to orgies, drugs, and rock. Daughter of an Austro-Hungarian countess and a novelist who had coined the term "masochism," Marianne was already a recording star. She preferred Keith as a lover, having spent with him "the best night I've ever had in my life," but they decided she should shack up with Mick. In her autobiography she describes a night the three made love vicariously. Mick whispered his enticements with Keith listening on the other side of a thin wall. "If Keith were right here now, God, I'd like to lick him all over," he began, loud enough for Keith to hear and going on as though prodding Marianne to ask him to join them. Although she didn't, she took the hint and began to organize menages for Mick—including one with a beautiful dancing girl in Tangier, which she enjoyed more than he.

The Stones were an incestuous lot inclined to stay within their own group. In contrast David Bowie, the most androgynous figure in rock, was for a time the most wide open erotically. In 1968 Bowie, morphing out of a bisexual triangle, had an intense, almost monogamous and ultimately crushing affair with a beautiful English model, Hermione Farthingale. In 1970 he married Angela Barnett, an aspiring American actress expelled from school for a lesbian affair. Angela became den mother to a traveling London–New York–Los Angeles–Berlin crash pad. The night before their wedding, Angela and David had a three-way romp with a new girl-friend, a model they met in Bloomsbury. All three got drunk and passed out during the wee hours; the couple nearly missed their own wedding.

A pattern arose: psychedelic stone age families made up of a lioness who procured and controlled the sexual escapades of her lover-husband. Or was he her servant? Marianne Faithfull found tidbits for Mick while Angela arranged threesomes for herself and David. Angela said, "I wanted what David was getting, so I went and got it." Menages flourished if only for a night or two with pickups from local pubs. Those at Haddon Hall, a Victorian villa in a quiet London neighborhood, had a frenzied, vam-piric quality that David's deathlike pallor emphasized. "We had to lock our bedroom doors because in the middle of the night these people would come looking for fresh blood," recalled a house guest from the early seventies.

Both the Stones and David Bowie eventually ran aground on the reef of drugs. Their habits got out of hand. Brian Jones overdosed and drowned in his pool, and the famous 1968 Redlands bust and trial gave the Stones nasty publicity. Marianne and Mick and David and Angela split up, and through a number of transmogrifications Mick Jagger and David Bowie settled down and may now be considered the senior statesmen of rock music. What did their antics accomplish aside from entertainment?

They broke the gender mold, certainly in terms of fashion. The Ziggy Stardust look—transsexual, freakish, glimmering—ruled punkdom. Bowie once remarked, "Being in love is something that breeds brute anger and jealousy." The menages, orgies, and general acting out of the Woodstock-era rockers was a wild attempt to change the very nature of libido—theirs and that of their fans. "You can't make an omelette without breaking eggs," ran the sixties refrain. But you can't cook well without a recipe, and the rockers lacked savoir faire.

Perhaps they needed a good book to guide them toward compassion. And so, dear readers, it's morning in the desert in the land of desire. Josephine Baker, draped across the piano, is singing "My Way," which for us translates into "Our Way." Even the Mill is deserted. The eastern sky glows golden, palm fronds rustle unheard, every three has gone home. The spiders from Mars are scurrying to their dens. We've spent this long night together, and hopefully we know something more about who we once were and who we may be. Our menage a trois is how we live now but not necessarily who each may become. Of this be assured: we have no sympathy for the devil, and we're satisfied.

Coda: Three in a Tub

SOME TIME AGO, WHEN THE THREE OF US began on our quest for the origins, tradition, and current standing of menage a trois, we were assured by those who claimed to know that the project was a chimera; it couldn't be done. Others, equally expert, warned us that it shouldn't be done. It was a dirty idea. The American public was "too reserved for such a subject." Now, in the year that has seen Larry Flynt elevated to culture hero and Madonna to Saint Evita, we can only accuse ourselves of too much reserve. The American public, like people everywhere, is gossip hungry and insatiably inquisitive about sexual matters.

\ When the movie *Henry and June* appeared out of the blue in 1990, receiving at first an X rating, the critics were even divided on the question of how many persons it was about. Was this the story of two writers coupling or of a love quadrangle? Or was it, as *Newsweek* headlined, "A Triple Play in Bohemian Paris"? Six years later, there are plenty more menage movies, novels, and advertising images out there: What would Calvin or Donna do without their lithe threesomes to sell sophistication? Yet the confusion about menage remains, or perhaps it's simply an unwillingness to see, to move from fantasy to possibility.

Perched on a bleached mountaintop in the midst of New England winter, snug in the bubbling water of a big jacuzzi tub, our three naked selves are taking a respite. We have done our part in tearing down the curtain of obfuscation that has covered this familial, widespread, erotic story. The wood-paneled room is as steamy as *Henry and June* might have been, and we can feel "the tension of complex desire" that director Philip Kaufman hoped to capture.

Since this is no movie but our lives, what are we going to do next? That's partly up to you, dear reader, because you are our witness. What would you like to see? Here's food for thought: While the pronouns *I*, *we*, *he*, *she*, or *they* are defined by number, *you* can refer to one or two or many others. You can say, "I love you" to as many as you wish.

We have given you a long look at the past, including a glimpse of us, in which the menage a trois has fared pretty well. But the future, ours as well as yours, is up for grabs. Come see us again.

Selected Sources

CHAPTER 1. THE MEANING OF MENAGE A TROIS

Three in Love is a work of synthesis that has necessitated our reading hundreds of books and thousands of newspaper and magazine articles, viewing dozens of movies, and continually surveying several electronic databases over the six years we took to accomplish it. We hope to establish a site on the World Wide Web on which we can further discuss menage a trois, its instances and sources. In the meantime we offer this list of selected and readily available sources as a help to the reader.

CHAPTER 2. INTRODUCTION TO TRIOGRAPHY

Foucault, Michel. *The History of Sexuality.* 3 vols. New York: Pantheon, 1978.
Garber, Marjorie. *Vice Versa.* New York: Simon & Schuster, 1995.
Herdt, Gilbert. *Third Sex, Third Gender.* New York: Zone Books, 1994.
Hunt, Morton. *The Natural History of Love.* New York: Barnes & Noble, 1987.
Karlen, Arno. *Threesomes.* New York: Beech Tree Books, 1988.
Paglia, Camille. *Sexual Personae.* New York: Random House, 1990.
Russell, Bertrand. *Marriage and Morals.* New York: Doubleday, 1929.
Russo, Vito. *The Celluloid Closet.* New York: Harper & Row, 1981.
Singer, Irving. *The Nature of Love.* 3 vols. Chicago: University of Chicago Press, 1984.

CHAPTER 3. THE MYTH OF MENAGE

Agonito, Rosemary. *History of Ideas on Women.* New York: Putnam's, 1977.
Appignanesi, Lisa. *Freud's Women.* New York: Basic Books, 1992.
Brabant, Eva. *The Correspondence of Sigmund Freud and Sandor Ferenczi.* Cambridge, MA: Harvard University Press, 1994.
Buber, Martin. *Good and Evil.* New York: Scribner's, 1953.
Campbell, Joseph. *The Mythic Image.* Princeton, NJ: Princeton University Press, 1974.
Moyers, Bill. *Genesis.* New York: Doubleday, 1996.
Mundkur, Balaji. *The Cult of the Serpent.* Albany, NY: State University of New York Press, 1983.
Out of the Garden. New York: Fawcett Colombine, 1994.
Pagels, Elaine. *Adam, Eve, and the Serpent.* New York: Random House, 1988.
Rudnytsky, Peter. *Freud and Oedipus.* New York: Columbia University Press, 1987.
Teubal, Savina. *Hagar the Egyptian.* San Francisco: HarperSanFrancisco, 1990.

CHAPTER 4. THE COURTS OF LOVE

Andrews, Wayne. *Voltaire.* New York: New Directions, 1981.
Barry, Joseph. *French Lovers.* New York: Arbor House, 1987.
Besterman, Joseph. *Voltaire.* New York: Harcourt Brace, 1969.
Chatfield-Taylor, Hobart. *Molière.* New York: Duffield, 1956.
Epton, Nina. *Love and the French.* New York: World, 1959.
Hamel, Frank. *An Eighteenth-Century Marquise.* New York: Pott, 1911.
Henderson, Helen. *The Enchantress.* Boston: Houghton Mifflin, 1928.
Maurel, André. *The Romance of Madame du Chatelet and Voltaire.* London: Hutchison, 1931.
Mitford, Nancy. *Voltaire in Love.* New York: Greenwood, 1957.
Noyes, Alfred. *Voltaire.* New York: Sheed & Ward, 1936.
Strage, Mark. *Women of Power.* New York: Harcourt Brace Jovanovich, 1976.
Wade, Ira. *Voltaire and Madame du Chatelet.* Princeton: Princeton University Press, 1954.
Yourcenar, Marguerite. *The Dark Brain of Piranesi and Other Essays.* New York: Farrar, Straus & Giroux, 1978.

CHAPTER 5. THREE IN MIND

Cranston, Maurice. *Jean-Jacques Rousseau.* New York: Norton, 1982.
Josephson, Matthew. *Jean-Jacques Rousseau.* New York: Harcourt Brace, 1931.
McDowell, Judith. *La Nouvelle Héloïse.* University Park, PA: Penn State University Press, 1968.
Maurois, André. *Seven Faces of Love.* New York: Didier, 1944.
Poirier, Roger. "Le thème du mariage (ou ménage) à trois dans l'oeuvre et la vie de Saint-Lambert." *Studies on Voltaire and the Eighteenth Century* 305 (1992): 1716–18.
Rousseau, Jean-Jacques. *The Confessions of Jean-Jacques Rousseau.* New York: Modern Library, 1950.
Rousseau, Jean-Jacques. *Reveries of a Solitary Walker.* London: George Routledge, 1927.
Schwartz, Joel. *The Sexual Politics of Jean-Jacques Rousseau.* Chicago: University of Chicago Press, 1950.
Spencer, S. *French Women and the Age of Enlightenment.* Bloomington: Indiana University Press, 1984.
Williams, Huntington. *Rousseau and Romantic Autobiography.* Oxford: Oxford University Press, 1983.

CHAPTER 6. IN THE REALM OF THE SENSES

Beauvoir, Simone de. *The Marquis de Sade.* New York: Grove Press, 1954.
Childs, James. *Casanova.* New York: Random House, 1988.
Dobree, Bonamy. *Giacomo Casanova.* New York: Appleton, 1933.
Endore, Guy. *Casanova.* New York: John Day, 1929.
Erskine, John. *Casanova's Women.* New York: Stokes, 1941.
LeGras, Joseph. *Casanova.* London: John Lane, 1928.
Lever, Maurice. *Sade.* New York: Farrar Straus & Giroux, 1993.
Lynch, Lawrence. *The Marquis de Sade.* Boston: Twayne, 1984.
Masters, John. *Casanova.* London: Futura, 1960.
Sabatini, Rafael. *The Fortunes of Casanova.* New York: Paragon House, 1994.
Trask, Willard, ed. *Giacomo Casanova: History of My Life.* 12 vols. New York: Harcourt Brace, 1966.

CHAPTER 7. THAT HAMILTON WOMAN

Fraser, Flora. *Emma: Lady Hamilton.* New York: Knopf, 1987.

Hardwick, Mollie. *Emma: Lady Hamilton.* New York: Holt, Rinehart & Winston, 1969.

Hibbert, Christopher. *Nelson: A Personal History.* Reading, MA: Addison-Wesley, 1994.

Russell, Jack. *Nelson and the Hamiltons.* London: Blond, 1969.

Sontag, Susan. *The Volcano Lover.* New York: Farrar, Straus & Giroux, 1992.

CHAPTER 8. ROMANTIC REBELS

Blunden, Edmund. *Shelley.* New York: Oxford University Press, 1965.

Fuller, Jean Overton. *Shelley: A Biography.* London: Jonathan Cape, 1968.

Gribble, Francis. *The Romantic Life of Shelley.* New York: Putnam's, 1911.

Holmes, Richard. *Shelley: The Pursuit of Truth.* New York: Dutton, 1975.

Marchand, Leslie. *Byron: A Biography.* 3 vols. New York: Knopf, 1957.

Quennell, Peter. *Byron in Italy.* New York: Viking, 1957.

Rees, Joan. *Shelley's Jane Williams.* London: Kimber, 1985.

CHAPTER 9. THE GREAT MAN, HIS WIFE, AND HIS MISTRESS

Barzini, Luigi. *Memories of Mistresses.* New York: Macmillan, 1986.

Carver, Terrell. *Friedrich Engels: His Life and Thought.* New York: Macmillan, 1986.

Edwards, Samuel. *Victor Hugo.* New York: David McKay, 1971.

Engels, Friedrich. *Origin of the Family, Private Property, and the State.* Chicago: C. H. Kerr, 1902.

Fitzlyon, April. *The Price of Genius: A Life of Pauline Viardot.* London: Appleton-Century, 1965.

Grimbaud, Louis. *Juliette Drouet's Love Letters to Victor Hugo.* London: Stanley Paul, 1915.

Hugo, Adèle. *Victor Hugo.* New York: Carleton, 1863.

Josephson, Matthew. *Victor Hugo.* New York: Doubleday, 1942.

Maurois, André. *Olympio.* New York: Harpers, 1956.

Marcus, Stephen. *Engels, Manchester, and the Working Class.* New York: Norton, 1974.

Richardson, Joanna. *Victor Hugo.* New York: St. Martin's, 1976.

Schapiro, Leonard. *Turgenev: His Life and Times.* New York: Random House, 1978.

Turgenev, Ivan. *Three Famous Plays.* New York: Hill & Wang, 1959.

Walk, Henry. *The Romance of Victor Hugo and Juliette Drouet.* New York: Putnam's, 1905.

Wilson, Edmund. *To the Finland Station.* New York: Doubleday, 1953.

CHAPTER 10. THE QUEEN AND HER CUCKOLDS

Bradley, Ian. *William Morris and His World.* New York: Scribner's, 1978.

Daly, Gay. *Pre-Raphaelites in Love.* New York: Ticknor & Fields, 1989.

Hayek, F. A. *John Stuart Mill and Harriet Taylor.* Chicago: University of Chicago Press, 1951.

Johnson, Wendell. *Living in Sin.* Chicago: Nelson-Hale, 1979.

Kamm, Joseph. *John Stuart Mill in Love.* London: Gordon & Cermonesi, 1977.

Marsh, Jan. *The Pre-Raphaelite Sisterhood.* New York: St. Martin's, 1985.

Mill, John Stuart. *Autobiography.* New York: Columbia University Press, 1924.

Morris, May. *William Morris: Artist, Writer, Socialist.* New York: Russell & Russell, 1966.

Packe, Michael. *The Life of John Stuart Mill.* London: Secker & Warburg, 1954.

Pappe, H. O. *John Stuart Mill and Harriet Taylor.* Melbourne, Australia: Australian National University, 1960.

Rose, Phyllis. *Parallel Lives.* New York: Knopf, 1983.
Weintraub, Stanley. *Four Rossettis.* New York: Webright & Talley, 1977.

CHAPTER 11. FEMME FATALE
Andreas-Salomé, Lou. *Looking Back.* New York: Paragon House, 1991.
Livingstone, Angela. *Salomé.* Mt. Kisco, NY: M. Bell, 1984.
Martin, Biddy. *Women and Modernity.* Ithaca, NY: Cornell University Press, 1991.
Nin, Anaïs. *In Favor of the Sensitive Man and Other Essays.* New York: Harcourt Brace,
    1976.
Peters, H. F. *My Sister, My Spouse.* New York: Norton, 1962.
Warner, William Beatty. "Love in Life: The Case of Nietzsche and Lou Salomé."
    The Victorian Newsletter 67 (Spring 1985): 14–17.
Yalom, Irving. *When Nietzsche Wept.* New York: Basic Books, 1992.

CHAPTER 12. THE WILD WEST
Beckstead, James. *Cowboying.* Salt Lake City: University of Utah Press, 1991.
Best American Screenplays. New York: Crown, 1986.
Brodie, Fawn. *The Devil Drives.* New York: Norton, 1966.
Brown, Dee. "Butch Cassidy and the Sundance Kid." *American History Illustrated* 17
    (1982): 57–63.
Burton, Richard. *City of the Saints.* New York: Knopf, 1963.
Deford, Miriam. *The Real Bonnie and Clyde.* New York: Ace Books, 1968.
Fenin, George. *The Western.* New York: Grossman, 1973.
Irving, Clifford. *Tom Mix and Pancho Villa.* New York: St. Martin's, 1982.
Kael, Pauline. "The Current Cinema." *The New Yorker* 65 (Oct. 22, 1995): 176–79.
Toland, John. *The Dillinger Days.* New York: Random House, 1963.
Webber, Everett. *Escape to Utopia.* New York: Hastings House, 1959.

CHAPTER 13. THE GREAT AMERICAN SEX SCANDAL
Carter, Paul. *The Spiritual Crisis of the Gilded Age.* DeKalb: Northern Illinois University
    Press, 1971.
Douglas, Ann. *The Feminization of America.* New York: Knopf, 1978.
Hibben, Paxton. *Henry Ward Beecher.* New York: Readers Club, 1942.
Johnston, Joanna. *Mrs. Satan.* New York: Putnam's, 1967.
Meade, Marion. *Free Woman.* New York: Knopf, 1976.
Sachs, Emanie. *The Terrible Siren.* New York: Harper Brothers, 1928.
Shaplen, Robert. *Free Love and Heavenly Sinners.* New York: Knopf, 1978.
Underhill, Lois. *The Woman Who Ran for President.* Bridgehampton, NY: Bridge Works,
    1995.
Waller, Anita. *Reverend Beecher and Mrs. Tilton.* Amherst: University of Massachusetts
    Press, 1982.

CHAPTER 14. THE BALLS OF AMHERST
Faderman, Lillian. "Emily Dickinson's Letters to Sue Gilbert." *Massachusetts Review* 18,
    no. 2 (Summer 1977): 197–225.
Gay, Peter. *The Bourgeois Experience.* 3 vols. New York: Oxford University Press, 1984.

Hart, Ellen. "The Encoding of Homoerotic Desire." *Tulsa Studies in Women's Literature* 9, no. 2 (1990): 251–72.

Longsworth, Polly. *Austin and Mabel.* New York: Farrar, Straus & Giroux, 1984.

Sewall, Richard. *The Life of Emily Dickinson.* 2 vols. New York: Farrar, Straus & Giroux, 1974.

Walsh, John. *This Brief Tragedy.* New York: Grove Weidenfeld, 1991.

CHAPTER 15. THE ROLLER-COASTER

Bair, Deirdre. *Anaïs Nin.* New York: Putnam, 1995.

Bald, Wambly. *On the Left Bank.* Athens: Ohio University Press, 1987.

Dearborn, Mary. *The Happiest Man Alive: A Biography of Henry Miller.* New York: Simon & Schuster, 1991.

Ferguson, Robert. *Henry Miller: A Life.* New York: Norton, 1991.

Fitch, Noel Riley. *Anaïs.* New York: Little Brown, 1993.

Nin, Anaïs. *The Diary of Anaïs Nin: 1955–1966.* vol. 6. New York: Harcourt Brace Jovanovich, 1985.

Nin, Anaïs. *The Early Diary of Anaïs Nin.* vol. 4. New York: Harcourt Brace Jovanovich, 1985.

Nin, Anaïs. *Henry and June.* New York: Harcourt Brace Jovanovich, 1986.

Nin, Anaïs. *A Literate Passion.* New York: Harcourt Brace Jovanovich, 1986.

Winslow, Kathleen. *Henry Miller.* Los Angeles: Tarcher, 1986.

CHAPTER 16. MENAGE AS GAY METAPHOR

Citron, Stephen. *Noël and Cole.* New York: Oxford University Press, 1993.

Coward, Noël. *Blithe Spirit.* New York: Samuel French, 1968.

Coward, Noël. *Design for Living.* New York: Doubleday, 1933.

Fisher, Clive. *Noël Coward.* London: St. Martin's, 1992.

Gray, Frances. *Noël Coward.* New York: St. Martin's, 1987.

Lahr, John. *Coward: The Playwright.* London: Methuen, 1982.

CHAPTER 17. THE ROMEO AND JULIET OF THREES

Crisp, G. G. *François Truffaut.* New York: Praeger, 1972.

Flaus, John. "Jules and Jim." *Film Journal* 22 (Oct. 1963): 19–26.

Gray, Marianne. *La Moreau.* New York: Donald Fine, 1994.

Henri-Pierre Roché: An Introduction. Austin, TX: Harry Ransom Humanities Research Center, 1991.

Kael, Pauline. "Jules and Jim." *The New Yorker* 48 (Oct. 14, 1972): 147–51.

Modern European Filmmakers and the Art of Adaptation. New York: Ungar, 1981.

Murphy, Kathleen. "La belle dame sans merci." *Film Comment* 4 (Nov.–Dec., 1992): 888–99.

Paris, James. *The Great French Films.* Seacaucus, NJ: Citadel Press, 1983.

Radcliffe-Umstead, Douglas. *Transformations from Literature to Film.* Proceedings of the Fifth Annual Conference on Film, April 7–8, 1988. Kent, OH: Kent State University, 1988.

Wood, Beatrice. *I Shock Myself.* Ojai, CA: Dillingham Press, 1985.

CHAPTER 18. THE BELLS OF BLOOMSBURY

Bell, Clive. *Old Friends.* New York: Harcourt Brace, 1956.

Bell, Quentin. *Bloomsbury.* New York: Basic Books, 1968.

Edel, Leon. *Bloomsbury: A House of Lions.* Philadelphia: Lippincott, 1979.

Garnett, Angelica. *Deceived with Kindness.* New York: Harcourt Brace Jovanovich, 1984.

Garnett, David. *Flowers of the Forest.* New York: Harcourt Brace, 1956.

Garnett, David. *The Golden Echo.* New York: Harcourt Brace, 1954.

Marler, Regina, ed. *Selected Letters of Vanessa Bell.* New York: Pantheon, 1993.

Rosenbaum, S. P. *The Bloomsbury Group.* Toronto: University of Toronto Press, 1975.

Rosenbaum, S. P. *Victorian Bloomsbury.* New York: Basic Books, 1968.

Russell, John. "Clive Bell." *Encounter* 23 (Dec. 1964): 47–49.

Shone, Richard. *Bloomsbury Portraits.* New York: Dutton, 1976.

Spalding, Frances. *Roger Fry: Art and Life.* Berkeley: University of California Press, 1980.

Spalding, Frances. *Vanessa Bell.* New York: Ticknor & Fields, 1983.

Watney, Simon. *The Art of Duncan Grant.* London: John Murray, 1990.

CHAPTER 19. CARRINGTON'S LOVERS

Garnett, David. *Carrington.* London: Jonathan Cape, 1970.

Gathorne-Hardy, Jonathan. *Gerald Brenan.* New York: Norton, 1992.

Gerzina, Gretchen. *Carrington.* New York: Norton, 1989.

Holroyd, Michael. *Lytton Strachey: A Critical Biography.* 2 vols. New York: Holt, Rinehart & Winston, 1967.

Holroyd, Michael. *Lytton Strachey: The New Biography.* New York: Farrar, Straus & Giroux, 1995.

Huxley, Aldous. *Crome Yellow.* New York: Harpers, 1922.

Lawrence, D. H. *Women in Love.* New York: Penguin, 1950.

Partridge, Frances. *Love in Bloomsbury.* New York: Little, Brown, 1981.

Woodeson, John. *Mark Gertler.* London: Sidgwick & Jackson, 1972.

CHAPTER 20. PORTRAITS REAL AND SURREAL

Brion, Marcel. *Leonor Fini.* Paris: Jean-Jacques Pauvert, 1955.

Crespelle, Jean-Paul. *Picasso and His Women.* New York: Coward McCann, 1969.

Dalí, Salvador. *Dalí by Dalí.* New York: Abrams, 1970.

Eluard, Paul. *Letters to Gala.* New York: Paragon House, 1989.

Ernst, Jimmy. *A Not So Still Life.* New York: St. Martin's, 1984.

Etherinton-Smith, Meredith. *The Persistence of Memory.* New York: Random House, 1992.

Freeman, Judi. *Picasso and the Weeping Women.* Los Angeles: County Museum of Art, 1994.

Huffington, Arianna. *Picasso.* New York: Simon & Schuster, 1988.

Lord, James. *Giacometti: A Biography.* New York: Farrar, Straus & Giroux, 1983.

Lucie-Smith, Edward. *Lives of the Great Twentieth-Century Artists.* New York: Rizzoli, 1986.

Okada, Takahiko, ed. *Leonor Fini.* Tokyo: Yomiuri Shimbun, 1972.

Penrose, Roland. *Picasso.* London: Gollanz, 1958.

Pople, Kenneth. *Stanley Spencer: A Biography.* London: William Collins, 1991.

Royal Academy of Arts. *Stanley Spencer.* London: Weidenfeld & Nicholson, 1985.

Richardson, John. *A Life of Picasso.* vol. 1. New York: Random House, 1996.

Rubin, William. "The Pipes of Pan." *Art News* 93 (May 1994): 138–47.

Sabartes, Jaime. *Picasso.* New York: Prentice Hall, 1948.

CHAPTER 21. STATE SECRETS

Abels, Jules. *The Parnell Tragedy.* London: Bodley Head, 1966.

Asbell, Bernard. *The FDR Memoirs.* New York: Doubleday, 1973.

Brady, Margery. *The Love Story of Parnell and Katherine O'Shea.* Dublin: Mercier Press, 1991.

Brown, Frederick. *Zola.* New York: Farrar, Straus & Giroux, 1994.

Cook, Blanche. *Eleanor Roosevelt: 1884–1933.* vol. 1. New York: Viking, 1992.

Goodwin, Doris Kearns. *No Ordinary Time.* New York: Simon & Schuster, 1994.

Kee, Robert. *The Laurel and the Ivy.* London: Hamish Hamilton, 1993.

Kessler, Ronald. *The Sins of the Father: Joseph Kennedy and the Dynasty He Founded.* New York: Warner Books, 1996.

Lash, Joseph. *Eleanor and Franklin.* New York: Norton, 1971.

Lester, David. *Jacqueline Kennedy Onassis.* Secaucus, NJ: Carrol Publishing Group, 1994.

Lyons, F. S. L. *The Fall of Parnell.* Toronto: University of Toronto Press, 1960.

Mosley, Raymond. *The First New Deal.* New York: Harcourt Brace & World, 1966.

O'Shea, Katherine. *Charles Stewart Parnell.* 2 vols. New York: Doran, 1914.

Roosevelt, Eleanor. *This I Remember.* New York: Garden City Publishing, 1937.

CHAPTER 22. ON THE LEFT

Boulton, Agnes. *Part of a Long Story.* New York: Doubleday, 1958.

Clark, Ronald. *Lenin.* New York: Harper & Row, 1988.

Dearborn, Mary. *Queen of Bohemia.* New York: Houghton Mifflin, 1996.

Dervin, Daniel. *Bernard Shaw: A Psychological Study.* Lewisburg, PA: Bucknell University Press, 1975.

Eastman, Max. *Heroes I Have Known.* New York: Books for Libraries, 1942.

Fischer, Louis. *The Life of Lenin.* New York: Harper & Row, 1964.

Gardner, Virginia. *Friend and Lover: The Life of Louise Bryant.* New York: Horizon Press, 1982.

Gelb, Barbara. *So Short a Time.* New York: Norton, 1973.

Holroyd, Michael. *Bernard Shaw.* 2 vols. New York: Random House, 1988.

Krupskaya, Nadezhda. *Memories of Lenin.* 2 vols. New York: International Publishers, 1930.

Lawson, John Howard. *Theory and Technique of Playwriting.* New York: Hill & Wang, 1960.

O'Neill, Eugene. *Strange Interlude.* New York: Boni & Liveright, 1928.

Payne, Robert. *Lenin.* New York: Simon & Schuster, 1964.

Peters, Sally. "From Mystic Betrothal to Menage a Trois: Bernard Shaw and May Morris." *The Independent Shavian* 28, no. 1–2 (1990): 1–16.

Rosenstone, Robert. *Romantic Revolutionary: A Biography of John Reed.* New York: Knopf, 1975.

Shaw, Bernard. *Nine Plays.* New York: Dodd Mead, 1935.

Silver, Arnold. *Bernard Shaw.* Palo Alto, CA: Stanford University Press, 1982.
Vasilieva, Larissa. *Kremlin Wives.* New York: Arcade, 1992.

CHAPTER 23. TORIES À TROIS

Baker, Michael. *Our Three Selves.* New York: Morrow, 1985.
Dickson, Lovatt. *Radclyffe Hall and the Well of Loneliness.* London: Collins, 1975.
Fisher, Nigel. *Harold Macmillan: A Biography.* New York: St. Martin's, 1982.
Glasgow, Joanne. *The Love Letters of Radclyffe Hall.* New York: New York University Press, 1997.
Horne, Alistair. *Harold Macmillan.* 2 vols. New York: Viking, 1989.
Hough, Richard. *Edwina.* New York: Morrow, 1984.
Lord Denning's Report. London: Her Majesty's Stationary Office, 1963.
Morgan, Janet. *Edwina Mountbatten.* New York: Morrow, 1984.
Ormond, Richard. *Una Troubridge: Friend of Radclyffe Hall.* New York: Arno, 1973.
Troubridge, Una. *The Life of Radclyffe Hall.* New York: Carroll & Graf, 1985.
Zeigler, Philip. *Mountbatten.* New York: Knopf, 1985.

CHAPTER 24. MENAGE AND THE HOLOCAUST

Blair, John. *Schindler.* Documentary film for Thames Television, 1983.
Carpenter, Humphrey. *A Serious Character: The Life of Ezra Pound.* Boston: Houghton Mifflin, 1988.
Carr, Maurice. "My Uncle Yitzhak: A Memoir of I. B. Singer." *Commentary* 94 (1992): 25–32.
DeRachewiltz, Mary. *Discretions.* New York: Little, Brown, 1971.
Duras, Marguerite. *The War.* New York: Pantheon, 1986.
Edwards, Alexander. *Isaac Bashevis Singer.* Boston: Twayne, 1980.
French, William. "For Gentle Graceful Dorothy." *Paideuma* 12, no. 1 (Spring 1983): 89–112.
Green, Mary. "Writing War in the Feminine: Beauvoir and Duras." *Journal of European Studies* 23 (1993): 223–37.
Keneally, Thomas. *Schindler's List.* New York: Simon & Schuster, 1993.
Kresh, Paul. *Isaac Bashevis Singer.* New York: Dial, 1979.
Pladott, Dinah. "Casanova or Schlemiel? The Don Juan Archetype in I. B. Singer's Fiction." *Yiddish* 2–3 (1985): 55–71.
"Portrait: Schindler's Wife." *The Guardian* (Feb. 4, 1994), 14, Weekend.
Reuth, Ralf. *Goebbels.* New York: Harcourt Brace, 1993.
Singer, Isaac Bashevis. *Love and Exile.* New York: Doubleday, 1984.
Singer, Isaac Bashevis. *Meshugah.* New York: Farrar, Straus & Giroux, 1994.
Stock, Noel. *The Life of Ezra Pound.* New York: Pantheon, 1970.
Torrey, E. Fuller. *The Roots of Treason.* New York: McGraw Hill, 1984.
Vircondelet, Alain. *Duras: A Biography.* Normal, IL: Dalkey Archive Press, 1994.

CHAPTER 25. FRENCH TWIST

Bair, Deirdre. *Simone de Beauvoir.* New York: Summit Books, 1990.
Beauvoir, Simone de. *Letters to Sartre.* New York: Arcade, 1992.
Beauvoir, Simone de. *Prime of Life.* Cleveland, OH: World, 1962.

Beauvoir, Simone de. *She Came to Stay.* Cleveland, OH: World, 1954.

Beauvoir, Simone de. *Witness to My Life.* New York: Scribner's, 1983.

Cohen-Solal, Annie. *Sartre.* New York: Pantheon, 1987.

Fullbrook, Kate and Edward. *Simone de Beauvoir and Jean-Paul Sartre.* New York: Basic Books, 1994.

Lamblin, Bianca. *A Disgraceful Affair.* Boston: Northeastern University Press, 1996.

Sartre, Jean-Paul. *The Age of Reason.* New York: Modern Library, 1947.

Sartre, Jean-Paul. *The War Diaries of Jean-Paul Sartre.* New York: Pantheon, 1984.

Seaver, Richard. *Sartre by Himself.* New York: Urizen, 1978.

Thompson, Kenneth and Margaret. *Sartre: Life and Works.* New York: Facts on File, 1984.

CHAPTER 26. THE GOLDEN PHALLUS

Baker, Carlos. *Ernest Hemingway.* New York: Scribner's, 1969.

Bresler, Fenton. *The Mystery of Georges Simenon.* New York: Stein & Day, 1983.

Byrne, Janet. *A Genius for Living: The Life of Frieda Lawrence.* London: Heinemann, 1985.

Diliberto, Gioia. *Hadley.* New York: Ticknor & Fields, 1992.

Doctorow, E. L. "Braver Than We Thought." *New York Times Book Review* (May 18, 1986): 1, 4.

Feinstein, Elaine. *Lawrence.* New York: Harper Collins, 1993.

Gill, Brendan. "Out of the Dark." *The New Yorker* 38 (Jan. 26, 1963): 35–53.

Hahn, Emily. *Lorenzo.* Philadelphia: Lippincott, 1975.

Hemingway, Ernest. *The Garden of Eden.* New York: Scribner's, 1986.

Hemingway, Ernest. *A Moveable Feast.* New York: Scribner's, 1964.

Kert, Bernice. *The Hemingway Women.* New York: Norton, 1983.

Lawrence, Frieda. *Not I But the Wind.* New York: Viking, 1934.

Maddox, Brenda. *D. H. Lawrence: The Story of a Marriage.* New York: Simon & Schuster, 1994.

Marnham, Patrick. *The Man Who Wasn't Maigret.* New York: Farrar, Straus & Giroux, 1992.

Miller, Henry. *The World of Lawrence.* Santa Barbara, CA: Capra Press, 1980.

Mellow, James. *A Life Without Consequences.* Boston: Houghton Mifflin, 1992.

Raeburn, John. "Sex and Art in the Garden of Eden." *Michigan Quarterly Review* 29 (Winter 1990): 111–22.

Simenon, Georges. *Intimate Memoirs.* New York: Harcourt Brace Jovanovich, 1984.

Tedlock, E. W. *Frieda Lawrence.* New York: Knopf, 1964.

Updike, John. "The Sinister Sex." *The New Yorker* 62 (June 30, 1986): 85–88.

CHAPTER 27. CAROLYN'S BOYS

Cassady, Carolyn. *Heart Beat.* Berkeley: Creative Arts Books, 1976.

Cassady, Carolyn. *Off the Road.* New York: Morrow, 1990.

Charters, Ann. *Kerouac.* San Francisco: Straight Arrow, 1973.

Charters, Ann, ed. *The Portable Jack Kerouac.* New York: Viking, 1995.

Clark, Tom. *Jack Kerouac.* New York: Harcourt Brace, 1984.

Ginsberg, Allen. *As Ever: The Collected Correspondence of Allen Ginsberg and Neal Cassady.* Berkeley: Creative Arts Books, 1977.

Ginsberg, Allen. *Journals: Early Fifties and Sixties.* New York: Grove, 1977.

Holmes, John Clellon. *Go*. New York: Appel, 1977.

Johnson, Joyce. *Minor Characters*. Boston: Houghton Mifflin, 1982.

Kerouac, Jack. *Big Sur*. New York: McGraw Hill, 1981.

Kerouac, Jack. *Desolation Angels*. New York: Coward McCann, 1965.

Kerouac, Jack. *On the Road*. New York: Viking, 1957.

McNally, Dennis. *Desolate Angel*. New York: Random House, 1979.

Miles, Barry. *Ginsberg: A Biography*. New York: Simon & Schuster, 1989.

Nicosia, Gerald. *Memory Babe: A Critical Biography of Jack Kerouac*. New York: Grove, 1983.

Plummer, William. *Holy Goof*. Englewood Cliffs, NJ: Prentice Hall, 1981.

CHAPTER 28. THE POP MENAGE

Carter, Margaret, ed. *The Vampire and the Critics*. Ann Arbor, MI: UMI Research Press, 1988.

Bjorkman, V. *Woody Allen on Woody Allen*. New York: Grove, 1993.

Coppola, Francis Ford. *Bram Stoker's Dracula*. New York: Newmarket Press, 1992.

Dooley, Dennis, ed. *Superman at Fifty*. Cleveland, OH: Octavia Press, 1987.

Feiffer, Jules. *The Great Comic Book Heroes*. New York: Dial, 1965.

Lax, Eric. *Woody Allen*. New York: Random House, 1991.

Skal, David. *Hollywood Gothic*. New York: Norton, 1990.

CHAPTER 29. THE GREATEST PARTY EVER GIVEN

Andersen, Christopher. *Jagger*. New York: Dell, 1983.

Baker, Jean-Claude. *Josephine*. New York: Random House, 1995.

Blackwell, Richard. *Mr. Blackwell*. Los Angeles: General Publishing Group, 1995.

Bowie, Angela. *Backstage Passes*. New York: Putnam, 1993.

Faithfull, Marianne. *Faithfull*. New York: Little Brown, 1994.

Gronowicz, Antoni. *Garbo*. New York: Simon & Schuster, 1990.

Jones, David. "Just Who Is David Bowie?" *Daily Mail* (Nov. 19, 1996): 32–34.

Kier, Kiernan. *Sir Larry: The Life of Laurence Olivier*. New York: Times Books, 1982.

Lowenstein, Roger. *Buffett*. New York: Random House, 1995.

Norman, Philip. "The Unknown Beatle." *Daily Mail* (Aug. 1993): 38–39.

Olivier, Laurence. *Confessions of an Actor*. New York: Simon & Schuster, 1982.

Paris, Barry. *Garbo*. New York: Knopf, 1991.

Spoto, Donald. *Laurence Olivier*. New York: Harper Collins, 1992.

Spoto, Donald. *Blue Angel: The Life of Marlene Dietrich*. New York: Doubleday, 1990.

Vickers, Hugo. *Loving Garbo*. New York: Random House, 1994.

Wansell, Geoffrey. *Haunted Idol: The Story of Cary Grant*. New York: Morrow, 1984.

Wyman, Bill. *Stone Alone*. New York: Viking, 1990.

Acknowledgments

Conceiving of and accomplishing an unprecedented work on a subject that either has been brushed off with a snicker or has given rise to wild erotic fantasies was a three-headed affair. The research was both exhilarating and grueling, the writing simultaneously liberating and painstaking. First, since authors, like armies, march on their bellies, the concept had to be sold. Our agent, Ellen Geiger at Curtis Brown Ltd., succeeded in the face of skepticism and prudery. Karen Levine and John Loudon at HarperSanFrancisco had the wit and erudition to recognize a good thing when they read it. Karen especially had meticulously edited our brainchild, but we want to thank the entire staff at Harper—editorial, production, and marketing—for being bright, welcoming, and professional.

The types of research demanded by the scope of our subject varied a great deal. Hunter College Library supplied a wealth of material from its own collection, but our special thanks go to Norman Clarius, in charge of interlibrary loans. Other libraries significantly consulted include New York Public's Main Research Collections, Columbia University's Humanities and History Division, New York University, near our Greenwich Village and Chelsea abodes, and Dartmouth College, near our Vermont summer hideout. London's British Library was as gracious and excellent as ever and Harvard's Theatre Collection a pleasure to use. On the West Coast, the motion picture collections of USC and UCLA proved fascinating and invaluable, as did the Margaret Herrick Library of the Academy of Motion Picture Arts and Sciences. We owe a special debt of gratitude to Linda Ashton of the French Collections and Ann Paterra of the Photography Collection of the Harry Ransom Humanities Research Center of the University of Texas at Austin.

In another vein, we were both cheered and informed by Nino Osti, manager, and Steve Palozi, waiter, of the Polo Lounge at the Beverly Hills Hotel, hangout of the stars then and now. Thanks to Sharon Simon for her "tacky tour" of Hollywood. We were afforded those rare ingredients—encouragement and discernment—by fellow writers Ursule Molinaro and Jack Englehard. Thanks also to Arno Karlen, psychoanalyst and investigator of threesomes, and to Marjorie Garber, the latter for breaking ground on the touchy subject of bisexuality. Our appreciation for their talent and understanding goes to Carol Oditz, costume designer *extraordinaire*, and to photographer Yorghos Kontaxis, a regular Zorba. Our publicist, Victor Gulotta, is a real *mensch*.

Finally, each of us wishes to thank the other two—for the help, insights, arguments, despair, and enthusiasm essential to achieve something wonderful.

Illustration Credits

Engraving by J. Elluin, *Le Pot-Pourri de Loth,* 1781, courtesy of the Rijksmuseum-Stichting, Amsterdam.

Albrecht Dürer engraving of *Adam, Eve, and the Serpent* and Dante Gabriel Rossetti drawing of Jane Morris courtesy of the Metropolitan Museum of Art.

Engraving of Casanova, ca. 1800, courtesy of the New York Public Library photo collection.

Photographs of William Morris, Dante Gabriel Rossetti, Henry Ward Beecher, Theodore Tilton, Louise Bryant, and Ottoline Morrell courtesy of the Harry Ransom Humanities Research Center, University of Texas, Austin.

Photograph of Lou Andreas-Salomé, Friedrich Nietzsche, and Paul Rée from authors' private collection.

Motion-picture still photographs from *Butch Cassidy and the Sundance Kid, Paint Your Wagon,* and *Casablanca* courtesy of the Academy of Motion Picture Arts and Sciences, Margaret Herrick Library, Beverly Hills, CA.

Cartoon of Victoria Woodhull courtesy of the New York Historical Society.

Photograph of Noël Coward, Alfred Lunt, and Lynn Fontanne courtesy of the Raymond Mander and Joe Mitchenson Theatre Collection, Ltd.

Photographs of Henri-Pierre Roché, Franz Hessel, and Helen Hessel and drawing of Paul Eluard courtesy of the Carleton Lake Collection, Harry Ransom Humanities Research Center, University of Texas, Austin.

Photographs of Vanessa Bell, Bunny Garnett, and Duncan Grant, Dora Carrington and Ralph Partridge, Lytton Strachey, the menage a quatre on the beach at Juan-les-Pins, and Picasso with his chauffeur courtesy of the Tate Gallery Archive.

Photograph of Salvador Dalí and Gala courtesy of the Salvador Dalí Museum, Saint Petersburg, FL.

Photograph of Eugene O'Neill courtesy of the Yale Collection of American Literature, Beinecke Rare Book and Manuscript Library, Yale University.

Photograph of John Reed and Louise Bryant used by permission of the Houghton Library, Harvard University.

Photograph of Lord Louis Mountbatten, Pandit Nehru, and Edwina Mountbatten courtesy of the Trustees of the Broadlands Archives, University of Southampton.

Photographs of D. H. and Frieda Lawrence and Frieda Lawrence and Angelo Ravagli courtesy of Laurence Pollinger, Ltd.

Index